Public Relations Writing and Media Techniques

FIFTH EDITION

DENNIS L. WILCOX

San Jose State University

PEARSON
and

Boston ■ New York ■ San Francisco
Mexico City ■ Montreal ■ Toronto ■ London ■ Madrid ■ Munich ■ Paris
Hong Kong ■ Singapore ■ Tokyo ■ Cape Town ■ Sydney

**Dedicated to
Marianne and Anne-Marie,
whose love and support
have made this book possible**

Editorial Director: Jason Jordan
Series Editor: Molly Taylor
Series Editorial Assistant: Michael Kish
Senior Marketing Manager: Mandee Eckersley
Composition and Prepress Buyer: Linda Cox
Manufacturing Buyer: JoAnne Sweeney
Manufacturing Manager: Megan Cochran
Cover Coordinator: Linda Knowles
Editorial-Production Coordinator: Mary Beth Finch
Editorial-Production Service: Modern Graphics, Inc.
Electronic Composition: Modern Graphics, Inc.

For related titles and support materials, visit our online catalog at www.ablongman.com/communication

Between the time Web site information is gathered and then published, it is not unusual for some sites to have closed. Also, the transcription of URLs can result in unintended typographical errors. The publisher would appreciate notification where these errors occur so that they may be corrected in subsequent editions.

Library of Congress Cataloging-in-Publication Data
Wilcox, Dennis L.
    Public relations writing and media techniques / Dennis L. Wilcox.
       p.   cm.
    Includes bibliographical references and index.
    ISBN 0-205-41849-X
     1. Public relations—United States. 2. Public relations—United States—Authorship. I.
Title.

HM1221.W55 2004
659.2—dc22

                                     2004044490

Printed in the United States of America.
10 9 8 7 6 5   RRDV   09 08 07

Contents

PART THREE   Writing for Other Media

Chapter 12   Newsletters, E-zines, and Brochures   339

Chapter 13   The World Wide Web   375

Preface

The fifth edition of *Public Relations Writing and Media Techniques* is a comprehensive, up-to-date "how to" manual that will teach you the basic concepts and techniques of effective public relations writing.

It is a user-friendly text written in plain English that contains step-by-step guidelines illustrated by multiple examples from actual public relations programs conducted by many well-known organizations.

Although the emphasis is on the "nuts and bolts" of effective public relations writing and techniques, the text also provides the conceptual framework and broader context of how the techniques of public relations fit into the entire public relations process—research, planning, communication, evaluation. The idea is to ensure that you not only know "how" to write public relations materials, but you also understand "why" they are written in the first place from the standpoint of accomplishing organizational objectives.

This edition has more than 100 major updates, revisions, and additions to reflect today's public relations practice. The changes range from updated and expanded information on the integration of the Internet and the World Wide Web into all public relations activities to step-by-step guidelines on everything from how to write a news feature to introducing a guest speaker at a meeting. The new artwork includes multiple photos, news releases, and other materials taken from actual campaigns.

This text, more than any other one on the market, also strives to give you some continuity by following a single campaign through multiple chapters. One chapter may illustrate the basic news release and fact sheet used while succeeding chapters will follow the campaign by showing other campaign materials such as (1) radio news releases, (2) media kits, (3) publicity photos, (4) pitch letter to editors, (5) media advisories, (6) invitations to product launches, (7) satellite media tour arrangements, (8) news features, and (9) even the budget for the entire campaign. By the end of the book, you will have a good understanding of how an entire public relations campaign is organized.

There are numerous other programs cited, and many of them are about current issues, events, or organizations familiar to you. Some programs cited include Coke's launching of Vanilla Coke, a new book by the cast of *Queer Eye*, New Zealand's tourist promotion based on the movie the *Lord of the Rings*, the Enron/WorldCom financial scandals, the 100th anniversary of Harley-Davidson motorcycles, and even the SARS outbreak in Hong Kong.

Other major strengths of this new edition are:

- New and updated "Professional Tips" in boxed inserts that provide easy-to-read checklists from seasoned professionals in the field
- New "PR Casebooks" in boxed inserts that highlight a particular issue, situation, or actual public relations program
- Expanded material on the ethics of public relations practice and the responsibilities of the public relations writer
- New lists of additional readings and resources at the end of every chapter
- High readability, clear presentation of ideas, and excellent writing style
- Expanded content on how to write and prepare materials for the internet and digital distribution
- Reorganization of topics and chapters to improve thematic development and continuity
- Updated and expanded content on how the Internet and the World Wide Web are used in public relations practice
- The ability to mix and match chapters, depending on the course and the time available
- Summaries of key points and updated additional readings at the end of every chapter

The text, as in previous editions, is divided into four parts. *Part 1, The Basics of Public Relations,* begins to build this contextual framework by discussing the role of the writer in the public relations process—research, planning, communication, and evaluation. The tools and equipment of the writer are discussed before chapters covering the basic concepts of persuasive writing, legal and ethical guidelines, and finding and creating news.

Part 2, Writing for the Mass Media, emphasizes the nuts and bolts of writing news releases, fact sheets, news features, and what you need to know about publicity photos and graphics. It also covers the techniques of writing pitch letters, sending advisories, compiling media kits, and writing op-ed columns. There are also chapters on the distribution of publicity materials and effective media relations.

Part 3, Writing for Other Media, emphasizes writing for a variety of controlled media—newsletters, brochures, online publications, the World Wide Web, e-mail, memos, reports, direct mail, and advertising. The final chapter in this section gives you valuable information about writing and giving speeches and presentations, complete with PowerPoint slides.

Part 4, Managing Programs and Campaigns, puts everything together by explaining the basics of event meeting and event management, how to write a comprehensive program plan, and how to measure your results.

An expanded and completely revised Instructor's Manual with chapter exercises test questions, prepared by the author and Kathleen Smith, is available for this edition. Please contact your local Allyn & Bacon/Longman sales representative for a hard copy or electronic version.

I am grateful to the following reviewers for comments and suggestions. Second edition: William Baxter, Marquette University; E. W. Brody, Memphis State University; Cathy Morton, Texas Tech University; Susan Pendleton, Mansfield University; Bruce Renfro, Southwest Texas State University; Ed Romanoff, University of Pittsburgh; and Susanne A. Roschwalb, American University. Third edition: Janice Barrett, Boston University; Lena Chau, California State University at Los Angeles; Jan Elliott, University of North Carolina; Terry Rentner, Bowling Green State University; Susanne A. Roschwalb, American University; and Joseph Zappala, Utica College. Fourth edition: Douglas P. Starr, Texas A&M University; Shelly A. Wright, SUNY-New Paltz; Leo J. McKenzie, Marist College; Dean Kruckeberg, University of Northern Iowa; David Dollar, Southwest Missouri State University; and Michael E. Bishop, Baylor University.

And a special thanks to the following educators who provided input for the fifth edition: Donn Silvis, California State University, Dominguez Hills; Brenda J. Wrigley, Michigan State University; Claire Badaracco, Marquette University; and Lora J. DeFore, Mississippi State University.

Public Relations Writing and Media Techniques is for students who want to learn how to write, prepare, and distribute public relations materials. It is for professors who want a comprehensive, up-to-date text that accurately reflects contemporary public relations practice in the "real world."

Chapter 1

Preparing for Writing

Public relations writing is an integral part of communication, the third component in the public relations process of research, planning, communication, and evaluation. It is a highly visible product, involving the implementation and execution of tactics in a public relations plan or campaign by expert technicians. It requires writing tools, the use of basic references, the ability to gather information, and knowledge of basic English composition.

From this standpoint, both the public relations writer and the journalist share a common approach to writing. For both, it is an exacting job that does not allow careless, sloppy work. Facts must be assembled and checked before the actual writing is started. The writing itself is an intense process of wrestling with word choice, sentence structure, and thematic development.

This chapter sets the stage and framework for effective public relations writing. It tells you what equipment you need, how to use print and electronic databases, and how to use the Internet for researching information. It also presents the basic elements of composition.

THE FRAMEWORK OF PUBLIC RELATIONS WRITING

This book primarily focuses on one aspect of public relations practice—the writing and distribution of messages in a variety of formats and media channels. To the uninitiated, this activity is the sum and substance of public relations. For them, PR stands for "Press Releases." Because of this, it's necessary to first establish the framework in which public relations writing takes place.

Writing Is Only One Component

First, it is important to realize that the preparation of messages for distribution is only one part of the public relations process. Public relations is actually composed of four core components: **research**, **planning**, **communication**, and **evaluation**. Public relations writing is part of the **communication** component, which only occurs after **research** has been conducted and after extensive **planning** to formulate the goals and objectives of a campaign has taken place. Planning also involves the selection of audiences to be reached, the key messages to be distributed, and the strategies that should be used to ensure the overall success of the program or campaign.

Strategies are statements of direction. A strategy, for example, might be to use multiple media outlets to reach women between the ages of 18 to 30 to make them aware of a new cosmetic on the market. In a public relations campaign, each strategy is made operational through a list of tactics. A tactic, for example, might entail the writing and placement of feature articles and "new product" reviews in appropriate women's magazines. Such a tactic might even be specified to the point of listing how many product news releases and features would be written and what "angle" would be used in each one. Another tactic might be the placement of a celebrity spokesperson on a particular television show that reaches women in the target audience.

Writers as Communication Technicians

Public relations writers and media placement specialists are responsible for implementing the tactics of a campaign or program. They, by definition, fulfill the "technician" roles. They are the "production" staff who write the news releases, formulate the feature stories, and contact the television show producer to make a "pitch" for the company's spokesperson to appear as a guest to talk about the product.

The role of writer and technician is the standard entry-level position in public relations, but some have been writers and media relations experts for most of their careers. This is because most positions in public relations at corporations or public relations firms are at the technician level. A speech writer or an editor of an employee newsletter, for example, may be a skilled technician by definition, but they are also highly prized professionals who receive good salaries because of their expertise.

The concept of public relations roles is the result of research by Professors Glen Broom and David Dozier at San Diego State University. In their research, four roles emerged: (1) the expert prescriber—consultants to top management for strategic planning, (2) the communication facilitator—primarily the liaison between the organization and its public, (3) the problem-solving facilitator—works with management to solve current problems in a process-oriented way, and (4) the communication technician—practitioners who provide technical services such as news release writing, event planning, and graphic design.

Although the concept of four roles is interesting, further research by Dozier determined that it was more useful to simply distinguish between managers and technicians. Dozier says, "Managers make policy decisions and are held accountable for public relations outcomes," whereas "technicians carry out the low-level mechanics of generating communication products that implement policy decisions made by others."

This is not to say that professional practitioners don't fulfill both manager and technician roles. A professional may primarily be a manager but also be deeply involved in preparing a media kit or arranging a special event. By the same token, a public relations writer in an organization with limited staffing may primarily be a technician but also be involved in the planning of an entire campaign.

As you can see, the total framework of public relations is much more than just "press releases." Such materials are important, but they are only one highly visible manifestation of the entire public relations process, which also involves research, planning, communication, and evaluation, in that order. With this framework in mind, we begin our discussion about public relations writing and media techniques. At the end of the book, we will return to the managerial aspects of public relations with chapters on campaign planning and program evaluation.

THE PUBLIC RELATIONS WRITER

Although the public relations writer and the journalist share a number of common characteristics in their approach to writing, the public relations writer differs in objectives, audiences, and channels.

Objectives

A journalist is usually employed by a news organization to gather, process, and synthesize information for the primary purpose of providing news to the organization's subscribers, viewers, or listeners. A hallmark of professional reporting is to present information in an objective manner. A reporter's personal preference may affect the choice of words and the news angle but, in general, the reporter tries to maintain an attitude of strict neutrality.

The public relations writer, in contrast, is usually employed by an organization that wants to communicate with a variety of audiences, either through the news media or through other channels of communication. These organizations may include corporations, government agencies, environmental groups, labor unions, trade associations, or public relations firms that provide information on behalf of clients.

The writer's purpose is advocacy, not objectivity. The goal is not only to accurately inform, but also to persuade and motivate. Edward M. Stanton, former chairman of the Manning, Selvage & Lee public relations firm, once described public relations activity in *Public Relations Quarterly* as "working with clients on strategy and messages, and then delivering these messages to target audiences in order to persuade them to do something that is beneficial to the client."

Harold Burson, chairman of Burson-Marsteller and a longtime leader in the public relations profession, defines public relations activity, including writing, as "advancing information in the public forum for the purpose of contributing to public opinion." To be effective and credible, public relations messages must be based on facts. "Nevertheless," Burson continues,

> We are advocates, and we need to remember that. We are advocates of a particular point of view—our client's or our employer's point of view. And while we recognize that serving the public interest best serves our client's interest, we are not journalists. That's not our job.

Professor Robert Heath, co-author of *Rhetorical and Critical Approaches to Public Relations,* points out that the role of advocate is a time-honored one. It goes back 2,000 years to Aristotle, who conceptualized the term "rhetoric"—the ability to determine what needs to be said and how it should be said to achieve desired outcomes. Heath writes that rhetoric "entails the ability and obligation to demonstrate to an audience facts and arguments available to bring insight into an important issue."

Hence all public relations writing should begin with the question, "How does this help the organization achieve its objectives?" For example, "Does the news release contain the key messages about the product and how it can benefit customers?"

The editor of a company employee newsletter must also consider company objectives when planning various articles. If the company wants to increase employee productivity, the editor may decide to (1) run several features about employees who have achieved high productivity in their jobs, (2) develop a regular column giving tips and advice about how to increase individual productivity, and (3) write some stories explaining how high productivity makes the company competitive and assures job security.

A good example of how an employee publication supports corporate objectives is the strategies developed for the start of a new newsletter, the *Grapevines,* for the employees of Canandaigua Wine Company (CWC) in New York. Lisa

Professional Tips

Writing Is One of Five Skills

Fraser Seitel, a communications consultant and author of *The Practice of Public Relations,* agrees that knowledge of communications, and particularly writing skills, is a basic skill in public relations work. He says, "At best, PR practitioners are professional communicators. Communications is their skill. That means they must be the best writers, speakers, media experts, communication theorists, etc. in the organization."

He also gives four other basic skills that are necessary for success in public relations:

Knowledge of Public Relations: PR people must understand that they must communicate for understanding. He says, "PR is the opposite of confusing or distorting or obfuscating or, worst of all, lying. The essence of PR lies in acting credibly and telling the truth." PR people must "educate" management about the principles that form the foundation of proper PR practice.

Knowledge of Current Events: "PR people are called upon to cover the waterfront. . . ." That means the first thing PR professionals must do is read the papers and be aware of current issues and personalities that are shaping the public agenda. "In the very best sense, the skilled PR person must be a Renaissance man or woman."

Knowledge of Business: Practitioners must have a knowledge of business and how the organization sustains itself. "Unless you can speak the 'language' of the organization, you'll have trouble being accepted as part of the team. . . ."

Knowledge of Management: Public relations, as a management function, must understand and appreciate how organizational policy is shaped and the pressures on management. "An essential part of the PR job is to 'interpret' the philosophy, policies and programs of management."

Source: O'Dwyer's PR Services Report, June 2002, p. 31.

Farrell, director of communications, wanted to accomplish two objectives with the *Grapevine:*

1. Foster two-way communication and share information with employees about the company and key business drivers/goals.
2. Promote "success stories" taking place at Canandaigua Wine and promote a sense of shared values and commitment to CWC core values.

GuideOne, an insurance company, had similar objectives when it established a new magazine, *Going for Great,* designed for employees and agents who sold GuideOne policies. Sarah Bukely, director of corporate communications, wanted to relay consistent messages that incorporated the company's vision, strategic business plan, and corporate culture. Consequently, *Going for Great* provided targeted audiences with in-depth information about current business initiatives, strategic planning, and industry data that contributed to the company's success.

Both of these publications received Bronze Anvil awards from the Public Relations Society of America (PRSA) and will be further discussed in Chapter 12.

Audiences

The journalist writes for one audience—readers, listeners, or viewers of the medium for which he or she works. Newspapers, magazines, radio, and television are usually defined as "mass media" because the audience is numerous and anonymous, and its members have little in common. A suburban daily newspaper, for example, circulates primarily among people who share a common residential area but have a broad range of backgrounds and interests. Such mass media, by definition, usually present material written at the fourth- to sixth-grade level and offer a wide variety of stories and features to satisfy almost any interest, be it sports, local news, or the daily horoscope.

In contrast, the readers of a special-interest magazine share a strong interest in only one subject—a particular hobby, a specific industry, or a highly specialized occupation. Reporters for such magazines write about just one subject for a limited and intensely interested audience.

The public relations writer, however, may write for numerous and radically different audiences—employees, constituents, customers, business people, homemakers, travelers, bankers, stockholders, farmers, and many others. Effective public relations writing is based on carefully defining the audience and its composition so that you can tailor your information to its interests and concerns. A public relations writer does research constantly to determine these audience needs, concerns, and interests. Armed with this information, you can write a more persuasive message. The concepts of public opinion and persuasion are discussed in Chapter 2.

Channels

Journalists, by nature of their employment, primarily reach their audiences through one channel, the medium that publishes or broadcasts their work. The public relations writer, with many specific audiences to reach, will probably use many channels. Indeed, public relations writers must not only determine the message, but must also select the most effective channel of communication. In many cases, the channel may not be any of the traditional mass media. The most effective channel for the tailored message may be direct mail, a pamphlet, an organizational newsletter, a videotape, a poster, a special event, or even the Internet via online newsletters, chat groups, Web sites, and even e-mail. In most cases, a combination of channels is selected to achieve maximum message penetration and understanding. This important concept is illustrated throughout this book by showing various media channels that were used by an organization, such as Korbel Champagne Cellars and Pillsbury, for a single project or campaign.

In this age of cyberspace communications, it is particularly important that today's public relations writer be prepared to write in a variety of media formats. A report on a seminar, sponsored by BusinessWire and West Glen Communications, summarized the beliefs of journalists and public relations professionals attending the meeting. It stated:

It is clear . . . that no single news medium will be able to retain its audience. Media brands that intend to compete will be providing multimedia newscasts to give consumers immediacy, entertainment, interactivity, and choice in how to get their news. For PR practitioners, such news formats will require an in-depth understanding of not only each news brand and its respective audience, but also all of the components of the media mix, as they become more and more diverse in what information they present and how they present it.

PREPARATION FOR WRITING

It is essential for the public relations writer to have a work space that includes a computer and a printer, access to the Internet, and a reference library.

Computer

The most important piece of equipment in a public relations office is a computer. It may be a desktop computer or a more portable notebook (laptop) computer that you can carry with you. Increasingly, notebooks are becoming more popular as prices go down and wireless networks enable users to log on at many locations, including the local Starbucks. See Figure 1.1 for a product publicity photo of a new "tablet" PC.

Public relations people spend most of their working day in front of a computer. Tim McIntyre of Boston University's School of Mass Communications did a survey of public relations practitioners and found that they spent a median of five hours a day on their computers. Word processing is the application that public relations professionals use most. This is followed in descending order by databases, graphic/arts programs, spreadsheets, and Internet access. A survey done today would probably show great amounts of time being spent on reading and responding to e-mail.

Another survey of independent public relations practitioners, many of whom work out of their home, also showed considerable amounts of time spent on the computer. Dr. Vincent Hazelton of Radford University and Dr. Jay Rayburn of Florida State University conducted a study for the PRSA and found that independent practitioners spend 25 percent of their time writing and another 16 percent of their time producing communication tools. Another 6 percent of time is spent on research, and 23 percent is spent dealing with the media. In sum, about 70 percent of their time is directly or indirectly tied to working on a computer.

Indeed, the personal computer allows you to use sophisticated word processing software programs that permit maximum flexibility to write, edit, format, insert artwork, and merge information into a complete document. Word processing packages such as Microsoft Word or MacWrite also have built-in dictionaries for checking spelling and grammar, plus other features such as a thesaurus, page previews, search and replace, word count, pagination, and editing functions. These tools substantially reduce the time needed for revisions and rewrites.

A popular package for public relations writers is Microsoft Office, because the package of programs allows you to do a variety of tasks. Microsoft Office comes in three versions—premium, professional, or small business. Common to all of them, however, are programs that allow you to do (1) word processing, (2) basic

Figure 1.1 Computers for Today's Needs
Notebooks are now popular because of their portability and increased computing power. This photo is an
example of product publicity announcing the introduction of a new Tablet PC that featured a new
Microsoft platform, a 40-GB hard drive, a wireless card, and an integrated DVD-R/RW—all in a 2.6-
pound package. Press coverage reached an estimated 650 million people, and buyer demand caused
Toshiba to increase production by 35 percent.
(Courtesy of Toshiba and its public relations firm, Benjamin/WeberShandwick.)

accounting, (3) e-mail, (4) desktop publishing, and (5) PowerPoint presentations.
You can even easily convert documents and graphics to HTML for use on Web
pages, according to the Microsoft publicity.

The type of computer you use is a matter of personal choice, and both PC and
Apple have their advocates. In addition, some users like desktop models; whereas
others prefer the portability and flexibility of notebooks. A lot depends on your
lifestyle and work environment. College bookstores report that students are buying more notebooks than desktops because they can use notebooks in the classroom and connect to the Internet if the campus is a wireless environment.

McIntyre found that almost 60 percent of his respondents used PCs, compared with 24 percent using Apple machines. Another 12 percent used both systems. In general, experts tend to favor PCs for several reasons:

- New developments in Windows applications (such as Windows XP) have
  made the PC screen more comparable to Apple's traditional user-friendly approach.

- PCs are the industry standard and constitute 95 percent of the market.

- Considerably more software programs run on PCs. In most cases, software publishers first develop programs for the PC because of the potentially larger market.

- PCs tend to be somewhat cheaper than comparable Apple machines. Parts and service are also somewhat less expensive because many standardized components are common to all PC brands.

Apple devotees, however, are undaunted. They cite surveys of *PCWorld* subscribers that show that Apple machines have the highest ratings for overall service and reliability. *Consumer Reports* also ranks Apple highest for overall reliability. In addition, Apple now has the OS-X operating system, which has considerably narrowed the compatibility gap with PCs. In terms of PC reliability, a *PC Magazine* survey of subscribers gave high marks to Hewlett-Packard, IBM, and Toshiba.

Computer manufacturers and software publishers, of course, are continually improving their products, making them even more powerful and versatile. It is now possible to get a basic computer, keyboard, monitor, color printer, and even a scanner for less than $1,000. There are even notebook computers on the market in this price range, although they aren't the extremely lightweight ones you see in the full-page glossy magazine ads. That's the good news. The bad news is that the computer you buy today will be made obsolete by even more powerful and sophisticated hardware in six months.

Working professionals, recognizing the rapid pace at which new computer and software products come to market, often recommend that you buy the most powerful computer and collateral equipment you can possibly afford. A key consideration when buying a computer is whether it can be easily upgraded to add more memory, storage capacity, and processing speed as technology advances.

At the beginning of 2004, experts were recommending that you buy a computer with a minimum 256 MB of memory. But 512 MB was preferred, because new software programs such as the Adobe collection (*InDesign*, *Photoshop*, *Illustrator*, *Acrobat*, and *GoLive*) require a lot of memory to operate at maximum efficiency. In addition, experts recommend a 60 to 120 GB hard drive, a DVD-ROM/CD-RW combo drive, USB ports, and a wireless card as a basic package for a desktop or a notebook. Individuals interested in video editing and sophisticated gaming, of course, should purchase more powerful computer hardware.

Fortunately, printer technology does not change as rapidly as computers and software. You should buy a color inkjet or laser printer that produces high-quality and professional-looking documents. Many public relations writers buy a combination printer, copier, scanner, and fax to conserve work space. Although combination devices are cost-effective, some professionals complain that one machine trying to do multiple functions is more prone to breakdowns and mediocre performance.

In addition to a high-quality printer, most public relations writers also have a scanner. Its value lies in its OCR (Optical Character Recognition) capabilities. According to Kim Komando, computer editor of *Popular Mechanics,* "If you spend any time at all retyping clients' printed materials into your computer, a scanner can quickly pay for itself." She points out, however, that not all scanners are created equal. To get clear reproductions of printed materials with a minimum of garbled letters, you need to invest in a higher-priced scanner with a high-quality OCR program.

References

A reference library is a must for any writer. Basic sources should be part of your book library, but they can also be in the format of a software program, a CD-ROM, a DVD, or online. The key point is to have references that quickly give you instant access to a body of knowledge and enable you to confirm basic factual information.

One popular product is the *Britannica Ultimate Reference Suite*, which is available on DVD and online at www.britannica.com. It is one of the most comprehensive online resources available, having more than 100,000 articles. It also features a dictionary, a thesaurus, an atlas, audio and video clips, and links to thousands of external links. It is available on an annual subscription basis.

Another popular encyclopedia is Microsoft's *Encarta*. It is also available on DVD and online (www.encarta.msn.com), but it has only 68,000 articles. However, *Encarta* features videos from the Discovery Channel, a colorful interface, a storehouse of famous quotations, translation dictionaries for international students, and the ability to download free updates every week. The downside of *Encarta* is that it doesn't offer a full Web-based Mac version and some of the articles aren't accessible unless you have purchased the CD-ROM or DVD version. A reviewer in *Time* magazine chose *Britannica* as the best online program and *Encarta* as the best disc-based encyclopedia.

Dictionary

The most common reference book is an up-to-date dictionary, and many writers keep a paperback version handy for a fast check instead of taking the time to log on to the Internet or bring up a software version.

Most daily newspapers, including *The Wall Street Journal*, use *Webster's New World Dictionary*, college version. Another popular dictionary is Houghton Mifflin's *American Heritage Dictionary of the English Language*, known for its inclusion of up-to-date slang and regional expressions, its lively word histories, and its extensive use of photography.

Dictionaries are readily available as part of Microsoft Word, on CD-ROM and DVD, and even online. For example, one can purchase CD-ROM and DVD versions of *Webster's Electronic Dictionary* and the *American Heritage Electronic Dictionary*. These dictionaries are commonly used for spell-checking, but they are also able to supply writers with words they don't even know. Type "Mexican" and "dog" and the dictionary gives you "Chihuahua."

For an online dictionary, just go to www.dictionary.com. It offers a dictionary and thesaurus as well as translation tools for Spanish, French, German, Italian, and Portuguese. Another good word site is www.yourdictionary.com, which provides links to 60 specialized glossaries in business, computing, law, and medicine.

A good complement to any dictionary, paperback or online, is a thesaurus. A thesaurus is basically a book of synonyms, antonyms, and idiomatic phrases that is often helpful in finding the word that best conveys your intended meaning. *Roget's Thesaurus* is the classic in the field, and it has also reinvented itself in CD and DVD format. Heather Rogers, who is on the staff of the PRSA, makes the best case for constant use of a thesaurus. She says, "My favorite writing tool is a thesaurus. I strive to keep my writing fresh by expanding my vocabulary and not using repetitive words in a piece."

Stylebook

A writer's reference library should contain two kinds of stylebooks, one for general reference and another that deals with the specific styles of various publications.

All writers, on occasion, puzzle over a matter of punctuation, subject–verb agreement, or the use of passive or active voice. Strunk and White's *The Elements of Style,* now in its 4th edition, has saved writers embarrassment over a number of years, but there are a number of other grammar and style texts available. For example, *The Little, Brown Essential Handbook for Writers,* by Jane Aaron, is a spiral-bound, pocket-sized paperback that gives the fundamentals of grammar, punctuation, and sentence structure. It also contains basic information about various style guidelines, such as MLA (Modern Language Association) for term papers and theses.

In terms of journalistic writing, the most widely used stylebook is the *Associated Press Stylebook and Briefing on Media Law.* It is used by most weekly and daily newspapers in the United States, and it is updated and revised on a periodic basis. For example, in the most recent edition, the AP stylebook updated its spellings and capitalization for Internet terms. The following words are AP style, which also are used in this textbook:

CD-ROM: A compact disc acting as a read-only memory device. A CD *disc* is redundant.

cell phone: Two words; an exception to *Webster's Dictionary.*

disc: Use this spelling if you are using a term such as *videodisc.* However, a **hard disk** is located in your computer.

DSL: Acronym for **digital subscriber line.**

DVD: Acronym for **digital video disk** (or **digital versatile disk**).

e-mail: Electronic mail or message. Not capitalized. Also, hyphenate such words as **e-commerce, e-business.** The lowercase prefix is an exception to *Webster's* preference.

FAQ: Acronym for **frequently asked questions,** a format often used to summarize information on the Internet.

Internet: First letter capitalized. **Net** can be used in later references.

intranet: A private network inside a company or an organization. Unlike Internet, it is lowercase.

IT: Acronym for **information technology**; spell it out in a story.

JPEG, JPG: Acronyms for **joint photographic experts group**. Common type of image compression on the Internet.

online: Lowercase and one word.

World Wide Web: The shorter term, **the Web**, is acceptable. Also, **Web site** is two words; the second word is lowercase.

The New York Times Stylebook is also widely used. Writers who cover business or prepare news releases about business topics often use *The Wall Street Journal Stylebook*.

These manuals enable you, as a public relations writer, to prepare materials in the writing style of most newspapers. They cover such topics as capitalization, abbreviations, punctuation, titles, and general word usage. For example, there is a trend in the media to combine words that were once written separately or hyphenated; hence, the proper style is now "software," "database," "lifestyle," "teenager," and "spreadsheet."

Atlas

A current world atlas is an important resource for spelling place names and obtaining vital statistics about various nations. The emphasis here is on the word "current," especially in light of the many changes that have taken place in recent years: Germany has been reunited, the former Soviet Union is now multiple independent nations, Czechoslovakia has divided into two nation-states, and Zaire is now the Congo again. Burma is now called Myanmar, and Bombay is now Mumbai. Even North Tarrytown, New York, has become—thanks to Washington Irving—Sleepy Hollow.

A recent edition of the *National Geographic Atlas of the World*, for example, included 20 new countries and 14,000 name changes. And a good atlas is more than a collection of maps; it is often a comprehensive encyclopedia of geographic and demographic information, illustrated with multicolored maps and comparative graphs. A public relations writer working for a multinational corporation will find a current atlas indispensable.

Media Directory

If you are in the business of sending news releases to the media, it is important to have lists of publications, names of editors, and addresses readily available. Local directories of media outlets are often available from the chamber of commerce, the United Way, or other civic groups. Metropolitan, state, or regional directories also exist. See Figure 1.2 for a sample listing from a media directory.

Media directories are available in paperback, CD-ROM, and online. The most popular are Web-based directories that are updated on a daily basis reflecting daily changes in publications and personnel.

The two major media directory publishers are Burrelle's Information Services (www.burrelles.com) and Bacon's Information, Inc. (www.bacons.com). They sell printed volumes and CD-ROM and DVD versions of their directories, but the trend is toward Web-based media databases that are capable of building customized lists.

A good example of a comprehensive approach to media directories is Bacon's. The firm has 10 different directories: (1) newspapers/magazines, (2) radio/TV/

ESERVER MAGAZINE, ISERIES EDITION (18A-10)   T
3033 41st St NW Dept L6D   **(507) 286-6865**
Rochester, MN 55901-6893   Fax: (507) 253-4799
E-Mail: eservermagazine@mspcommunications.com
Home Page: www.eservercomputing.com

Circ: 50,421; **Audited By:** BPA International; **Freq:** Monthly; Issued: Last Week Preceding; **Pub:** IBM Corporation.
Uses: New Products, Trade Literature, Industry News, Calendar of Events, By-lined Articles, Staff Written Articles, Letters, Color Photos; **Editorial Calendar:** Available; **Publication Available Online.**
Sub Rate: $89.00; **Ad Rate:** $5,230; **Trim Size:** 8.125 x 10.875 Col: 3.
Lead Times: Features - 90 days prior, News - 60 days prior, Advertising - 28 days prior.
Profile: Dedicated to providing education and information for iSeries users programmers and IT managers. Presents new products and services, technological resources, tips and techniques, client access and security issues and other topics that benefit the decision makers in the optimization and management of these systems.
News Executives/Editors:
Publisher . . . . Doug Rock   (507) 286-6865
djrock1@us.ibm.com
Contact Notes: Wed, Between 11am and 5pm, *Preferred order:* E-Mail, Fax, U.S. Mail, Phone. Doug wants all U.S. press releases sent to the attention of the Industry News Editor. Understand the publication and industry prior to pitching a story and keep information relevant to iSeries midrange systems or Heterogeneous computing environments that include an iSeries.
Publisher . . . . Asa Orsino   (Write Only)
orsino@us.ibm.com
Editor In Chief . . . . Doug Rock   (507) 286-6865
djrock1@us.ibm.com
(See above for contact notes)
Managing Editor . . . . Evelyn Hoover   (507) 286-6853
evelynhoover@us.ibm.com
Contact Notes: Tue-Fri, Between 9am and 5pm, *Preferred order:* E-Mail, Phone, Fax, U.S. Mail. As Managing Editor, Evelyn oversees the article contributions so send queries and manuscripts to her attention. She is not interested in press releases. Those should go to the attention of the Industry News Editor. Do not pitch an article that does not tie in to either IBM's iSeries OS/400, pSeries AIX or mainframe platforms. She is interested in any product, service or information relating to IBM eServer machines, including iSeries, pSeries and zSeries. She prefers to be contacted via the general e-mail address.
Associate Editor . . . . Michelle Carlson   (612) 336-9262
mcarlson@mspcommunications.com
Contact Notes: She is not a PR contact.
Mailing Address: 220 S 6th St Ste 500
Minneapolis, MN 55402-4501
SeniorWriter . . . . Jim Utsler   (734) 433-1878
jjutsler@provide.net
Contact Notes: *Preferred order:* E-Mail. Contact him via e-mail only.
Contributing Editor . . . . Neil Tardy   (Write Only)
Contact Notes: Tue-Thu, Between 2pm and 4pm, *Preferred order:* Phone, E-Mail, U.S. Mail, Fax. Understand something about the publication and industry before pitching a story. Keep iSeries users in mind.
Specialty & Title:
Industry News Editor . . . . Ryan Rhodes   (507) 286-6784
rhodesr@us.ibm.com
Contact Notes: Mon-Fri, Between 9am and 5pm, *Preferred order:* Phone, E-Mail, U.S. Mail, Fax. His primary coverage area includes New products. Please e-mail all U.S. press releases regarding new or enhanced products to his attention.
Computers/Hi Tech Editor . . . . Don Rima   (703) 742-3744
dr2@cssas400.com
Contact Notes: He is not a PR contact.

Figure 1.2 Media Directories Provide Contacts

Media directories are important reference tools for building mailing lists and targeting various publications. They provide addresses, names of key editors, phone numbers, Web sites, e-mail, and profiles of various publications. Directories are increasingly Web based, but they are also available on paper, DVD, and CD-ROM. The listing above is from a magazine directory.
(Courtesy of Bacon's Inc., Chicago.)

cable, (3) Internet media, (4) media calendar, (5) New York publicity outlets, (6) California media outlets, (7) international media, (8) business media, (9) computer–hi-tech media, and (10) medical and health media. According to Bacon's, these directories combined constitute more than 80,000 media outlets and 450,000 editorial contacts. The firm also advertises that it makes more than 4,000 updates every business day.

Burrelle's online media database includes contacts for (1) daily newspapers, (2) magazines, (3) radio, (4) television and cable, and (5) nondaily newspapers. The major advantages of online media directories is that they provide the ability to build a media distribution list, print labels, or send a group e-mail.

Other firms, such as Vocus (www.vocus.com) and LexisNexis (www.lexisnexis .com), also offer such services as well as the ability to track media clips generated by your news releases. LexisNexis describes its *PRanywhere* service in the following way: "You can instantly create targeted lists, track recent news coverage to determine your best prospects and pitches, and get your message out to the media with this easy-to-use Web solution." We will discuss media directories at greater length in Chapter 10.

Professional Periodicals

Standard references should be supplemented with subscriptions to professional periodicals. It is important for the professional writer to keep up with developments in the field and to learn about new techniques that can improve the writing, production, and distribution of public relations material.

A number of publications cover the public relations field. Newsletters include *PR Reporter, PR News, Jack O'Dwyer's Newsletter,* the *Ragan Report, Bulldog Reporter,* and *Communication Briefings.* The last one is an excellent source of information about writing techniques. *PRWeek,* started in England and now with a U.S. edition, is a glossy, four-color tabloid that chronicles the public relations business, primarily the campaigns of various public relations firms (see Figure 1.3). The Public Relations Society of America (PRSA) also produces a monthly tabloid newspaper, *Tactics,* filled with many "how to" articles.

In addition, several public relations newsletters are now devoted exclusively to how cyberspace (the Internet and World Wide Web) can be used for public relations. One such newsletter is *Ragan's Interactive PR.* The newsletter has case studies, product reviews, "how to" articles, and lists of new Web sites.

Magazines about the public relations field include the *Public Relations Strategist,* published by the Public Relations Society of America, and *Communication World,* published by the International Association of Business Communicators (IABC). You can subscribe to these publications or receive them as part of your annual membership fees. Other magazines are *Public Relations Quarterly, Reputation Management, Inside PR,* and *O'Dwyer's PR Services Report.* See Figure 1.4 for **O'Dwyer's Daily Report,** available online. The two major scholarly publications in the field are *Public Relations Review* and the *Journal of Public Relations Research.*

In addition to articles about trends and issues in the field, these magazines also carry advertisements for companies that specialize in services such as news release distribution, media monitoring, photography, and video news releases.

Many public relations professionals, especially those who specializie in media relations and placement, also read the journalism trade press. Such publications include *Editor & Publisher, Broadcasting & Cable, Quill, Advertising Age,* and *MediaWeek.* They provide a good overview of trends in the field and changes in executive jobs. For a more critical perspective of media performance and foibles, there are the *Columbia Journalism Review* and the *American Journalism Review.*

Internet Groups

Up-to-date information on public relations and media techniques can also be gained via the Internet. A number of Usenet groups (a global system of discussion areas called *newsgroups*) and listservs (a software program for setting up and maintaining discussion groups through e-mail) are devoted to public relations. You can

Figure 1.3 Publications in Public Relations

A number of publications cover the public relations industry, and they are important sources for events, issues, and trends in the business. This is the cover from *PRWeek*, a tabloid weekly that uses extensive color and an attractive layout.

(Courtesy of PRWeek, *New York.)*

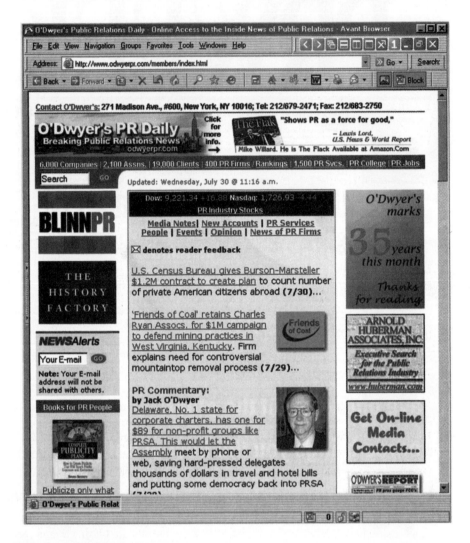

Figure 1.4 Get Your News Online
Newsletters about the public relations industry are also available online. This is the home page of
O'Dwyer's PR Daily (www.odwyerpr.com); it offers links to other public relations sites, an archive of arti-
cles, and directories of public relations services. O'Dwyer also has a weekly newsletter and a monthly
publication, *O'Dwyer's PR Services Report.*
(Courtesy of Jack O'Dwyer, Inc., New York.)

review the possibilities simply by doing a topic search on Google, Yahoo, or AOL
Time Warner. Groups may be sponsored by organizations, public relations firms,
and even individuals.

The International Public Relations Association (IPRA), for example, has a
forum for its global membership at ipra@yahoogroups.com. Members in such diverse nations as India, Australia, Canada, Poland, and the United States make

queries, provide information, and generally give each other tips on how to handle various situations. One IPRA member, for example, asked the group for advice on how to set a strategic communications plan for the Kuwait Institute of Banking Studies and received a number of helpful suggestions from other professionals throughout the world.

Another listserv group, open to anyone, is PRQUORUM (prquorum@ yahoogroups.com). In one message, for example, an individual asked for advice on what should be included in a contract between a public relations counselor and a client. On occasion, students even use PRQUORUM to get information for class assignments and case problems. In general, practitioners are willing to help out if the student makes a specific request instead of asking a broad question that would take an entire book to answer.

As with everything else on the Internet, Usenet groups come and go, so it's a good idea to check with some professionals in the field about current Usenet and listservs for individuals with an interest in public relations. They can also give you some insight into what forums offer the most information and value.

Current Events and Trends

Writing often starts with a creative idea and a good understanding of the world around you. Many public relations employers screen job applicants by administering a current events quiz to ascertain the scope of an individual's interests and intellectual curiosity. Employers require outstanding writing skills, but they are also looking for a second dimension in a public relations writer: knowing what to write about.

Thus aspiring public relations writers should make it a habit to read at least one weekly newsmagazine (*Time, Newsweek, U.S. News & World Report, The Economist*), a local daily newspaper, and a daily newspaper with national circulation such as *The New York Times* or *The Wall Street Journal*. Nationally syndicated public affairs programs on radio and television are also good sources of current event knowledge and interpretative analysis.

Increasingly, alternative magazines such as the *Utne Reader* and *E: The Environmental Magazine* are considered required reading for public relations professionals. Alternative publications often are ahead of the mainstream press in terms of reporting an emerging political issue or social trend. The issue of American garment companies using sweatshop labor in Asia, for example, was first reported by the alternative press. These publications often function as "trend incubators" and help public relations personnel detect early signs of trends that may become major public issues.

Reviewing lists of current nonfiction best sellers should also be part of your reading program. A popular book is an indication of public interest, and often media interest, in a particular topic. Books about diet, health, or wealth are perennial best sellers. *Dr. Atkins' New Diet Revolution,* for example, is the reigning champ on *The New York Times* best seller list. It's been there for more than six years. *Rich Dad, Poor Dad,* a book about teaching one's children to get rich and stay rich, has been going strong for more than three years. Couples expecting their first child have put *What to Expect When You're Expecting* on the list for almost three years. Other books of major public interest include *Fast Food Nation,* an exposé on the fast food industry.

Many people get all their news and entertainment from television. You should know what is being presented to the public for several reasons. First, media coverage sets the agenda for people's thinking. Second, watching the national and local news will show you what kinds of stories are used and how they are handled. Other programs, especially talk shows, will teach you what sorts of stories get on the air and indicate the kind of audience that tends to watch such programs.

In sum, paying attention to current events and the thoughts of opinion leaders pays several dividends. First, it makes you a well-informed person and hence more attractive to employers for public relations writing jobs. Second, knowing the concerns of the public helps you construct more salient messages for your target audience. Third, current events and subjects of popular books often provide a "news hook" for obtaining media acceptance of your material. For example, a company making security locks for computer files was virtually ignored by the media until news stories about computer hackers breaking into national security systems made national headlines. And publicists for food products have long recognized that information about the health benefits of a product will attract more media attention. Using current public and media interests as a "news hook" for generating publicity is discussed further in Chapter 4.

Research: Prelude to Writing

An essential first step to any public relations writing is the gathering of relevant information. The process is called research, and it can take many forms.

In some cases, all the facts will be readily available from a client or employer. All you need to do is pick up some background materials, ask a few questions, and start writing. More often than not, however, the information you need to understand the subject thoroughly and write a well-crafted piece requires some digging.

Let's assume you are given the assignment of writing a news release about a new product. One of your first contacts, no doubt, will be the vice president of marketing, who will give you the general details about the price and availability of the product. In order to understand better the benefits or capabilities of the product, however, you may need to interview someone in the company's Research & Development (R&D) department who was responsible for developing the product.

You may stop there in your inquiries, or you may decide to do some research on the potential market for the product and how you might position the product against the competition. One way to do this is to research competing products on the market to determine why your product is different or better. You may also want to contact some experts in the field to get their assessment. Their comments, if they give permission, could be included in your news release as a form of endorsement for the new product. On another level, perhaps you want to talk with some consumers to find out what would convince them to try the product. Is it price, convenience, brand reputation, or reliability?

With the kind of research outlined above, you are now able to write a comprehensive news release that is factual, persuasive, and interesting. The illustration is perhaps oversimplified, but it does indicate the value of research in any kind of writing. In general, informal research can be divided into two categories:

Inquiries

The telephone and e-mail are your best research tools. Contact experts in the field or people who are knowledgeable about the subject. Although you may think that this is an intrusion, most people will be flattered and pleased to provide information. In addition, they can supply names, places, and examples that will add flavor to your writing.

Interviews

Before the interview, review the information you already have on the topic. This should reveal what is missing and what questions can be posed in the interview. Prepare a list of specific questions, and ask them one at a time. If the answers are not clear, continue to probe until you are satisfied.

If the interviewee goes off on a tangent, that's all right. Tangents often provide information and perspectives that you have missed. Taking notes is a must, and a tape recorder can help you keep an accurate account of what was said. As the interview progresses, it is important to watch the interviewee and to pay attention to tone of voice. Tone, facial expressions, and gestures often reveal more than words alone.

Online Networks

The use of online networks has skyrocketed in recent years. They not only have many of the same services that commercial online databases provide, they also enable you to send e-mail, participate in chat groups on specific subjects, post notes on computer bulletin boards, and fully access millions of documents on the Internet, including the World Wide Web. The Web has millions of "home" pages for various organizations ranging from the world's largest corporations to obscure special-interest advocacy groups.

The largest, and by far the most successful, network is America Online (AOL). It has about 35 million subscribers worldwide, including 26 million in the United States, about 30 percent of the U.S. market. The Microsoft Network, MSN, is a distant second to AOL, with about 9 million subscribers. There are also a number of smaller networks such as United Online, Earthlink, and Yahoo.

The Internet and World Wide Web

Commercial online networks, such as those described above, provide access to the Internet as part of their services. However, you can also access the Internet and the World Wide Web directly by simply subscribing to other commercial services or by getting software that allows you to make a telephone or broadband connection to the vast array of computer networks around the globe.

There are software programs called **browsers** that allow you to view documents created specifically for the Internet's World Wide Web and other Internet services. The most commonly used browser is Internet Explorer.

Professional Tips

Need Information? Use the Library

The library reference section has gone digital. Web-based databases, many of them also available on CD-ROM, make it relatively simple for the public relations writer to research any topic. Here are a few databases that libraries commonly subscribe to that you may find useful:

AccuNet/APMultimediaArchive
Photos and images (700,000) from the Associated Press.

Alt-Press Watch
Full text of newspapers, magazines, and journals of the alternative and independent press.

Associations Unlimited
Basic information on about 455,000 international and U.S. organizations.

Biography Resource Center
Full-text biographies/articles from hundreds of periodicals.

Business and Company Resource Center
Integrated database bringing together comparative information on companies.

CountryWatch
Reports on 190 nations, covering politics, economics, environment, geography, etc.

Dun & Bradstreet Million Dollar Database
A directory of U.S. companies, including location, contact information, total sales, number of employees, executive biographies, etc.

EBSCOhost Magazine Articles
Over 3,000 titles indexed and abstracted. Covers general reference, business, health, social science, education, science, humanities, and current events.

Encyclopaedia Britannica
Full-text of 32-volume set. Includes *Webster's New International Dictionary Unabridged.*

Ethnic NewsWatch
Full-text database of newspapers, magazines, and journals of the ethnic, minority, and Native American press.

Expanded Academic Index
Formerly called Infotrac Web. Over 3,000 periodicals are indexed, and 1,900 include full-text articles.

Factiva
General news as well as company, industry, and other business information.

Gale Business Resources
Data on companies and business groups. Provides company profiles and product lists.

Lexis/Nexis Academic Universe
Complete text of newspapers, magazines, newswires, TV news shows, etc.

Occupational Outlook Handbook
A source of information about jobs and careers. Provides job descriptions and typical salaries.

Opposing Viewpoints Resource Center
A complete one-stop source on social issues.

ProQuest Newsstand

Full text of U.S. and international news sources in newspaper and periodical formats.

Reader's Guide Full Text

Index to popular magazines, covers all subjects.

Simmons Study of Media & Markets

Information on the lifestyles, media behavior, and product purchase/brand preferences of Americans by age, gender, and household income.

Social Sciences Full Text

Indexes and abstracts of a broad array of basic social sciences journals.

StatUSA

Reports and statistics on export and international trade.

Ulrich's Periodical Databases

Comprehensive media directory that lists mail, e-mail, and Web site addresses of periodicals around the world.

World Factbook

Basic information and statistics on the nations of the world.

Browsers work in tandem with powerful online **search engines**, which are essential to finding information about virtually any subject on the Internet and World Wide Web. They are essential because the World Wide Web is somewhat like walking into a vast library without the benefit of a floor plan or even a card catalog. *Time* magazine, for example, reported in mid-1999 that an estimated 800 million pages were stored on the World Wide Web, up from 320 million 15 months earlier. Given this rapid growth, billions of pages are now available.

Search engines make it possible for you to simply type in a key word or two (in the same way as was described for online-retrieval databases) and click "Go." Within a few seconds, the computer screen shows all the links that the search engine has found relating to the topic. The hard part is checking out the promising links, because the search engine may have found several hundred possibilities.

Google, at this writing, is the most widely used online search engine. Of the 4 billion Internet searches conducted in May 2003, for example, Google was used for a third of them. This, according to an Internet research firm, compares with 25 percent for Yahoo and 19 percent for AOL Time Warner. Other popular search engines include MSN, Grokker, Altavista, Hotbot, Ask Jeeves, and Dogpile. A relatively new search engine, www.teoma.com, is receiving favorable reviews from experts because it improves upon Google by displaying prelinked suggestions to narrow your search.

In general, it is a good idea to use several search engines because all of them have different strengths and weaknesses. Peter Meyers, writing in *The Wall Street Journal,* assessed the most popular search engines. He thought Google was best for news, images, and general Web searches. He noted, "Google has the broadest range of solid tools and did the best job of distinguishing between ad-supported results and real ones."

Yahoo, according to Meyers, excels in its Yellow Pages listings, particularly if you live in a major metropolitan market. MSN gets high ratings for its stem-searching tool and its automatic searches for all variations of a word. Yahoo gets good reviews for news searches that also look for audio and visual video clips.

The most important part of your search for information is choosing the right keywords. You should be as specific as possible to make sure you don't get a display listing hundreds of pages. Nouns make the best keywords.

The *Associated Press Stylebook* gives some additional tips for a search:

- Use uncommon words that identify your topic. Unusual proper or technical names are good. Avoid words with dual meanings.
- Use several keywords at a time, or even phrases. You can use two or three different phrases.
- Use synonyms. You might find different information with "attorney" instead of "lawyer."
- Use connecting words such as AND, OR, or NOT. Syntax varies with search engines so check the help page if you are not sure how to structure these queries. Some search engines, for example, want you to put quotes around a phrase.

The editors of the *Associated Press Stylebook* make a final, cautionary point. They say, "Do not mistake the Web for an encyclopedia, and the search engine for a table of contents. The Web is a sprawling databank that's about one quarter wheat and three-quarters chaff. Any information you find should be assessed with the same care that you use for everything else."

WRITING GUIDELINES

The ability to write well is essential for work in public relations. Countless client surveys and interviews with public relations employers confirm that good writing is at the top of their list of expectations. John Beardsley, chairman and CEO of Padilla Speer Beardsley, is quoted in *The Strategist* as saying, "In our business, everything involves language, more so than almost any other activity."

J. Ronald Kelly, senior vice president of Cohn & Wolfe public relations, adds:

> The majority of our entry level work requires good, basic writing skills. I simply do not have the time to teach grammar, spelling, punctuation, subject–verb agreement, use of active verbs, lead writing, inverted pyramid style, etc. And as you know, time is money in an agency setting. Therefore, I seek graduates who can contribute to the bottom line from the first day. I need people who have good mastery of basic writing skills.

Outlining the Purpose

Before beginning any writing assignment, take the time to ask yourself some key questions. Public relations counselors Kerry Tucker and Doris Derelian suggest six basic questions:

1. What is the desired communication outcome? In other words, what do we want our audience to do or not do?

Professional Tips

Surfing the Internet

Public relations writing requires research and facts. Here's a sampling of sites on the Internet where you can find information.

General Information

www.elibrary.com
Provides full-text articles from multiple sources, including newspapers, newswires, magazines, etc.

www.newsindex.com
Access to hundreds of articles.

www.writersdigest.com/101sites/
Best Web sites for writers, sites range from dictionaries to general reference sites and writer's organizations.

www.bartleby.com/people/strunk-w.html
Strunk & White's *The Elements of Style* online.

www.pollingport.com
Compilation of findings from surveys regarding trends in public opinion.

www.thomas.loc.gov
Site for the Library of Congress and the starting point for legislative and congressional information.

www.infoplease.com
Online almanacs on various topics from business to history and sports.

www.biography.com
Backgrounds on current and historical figures.

www.acronymfinder.com
Definitions of acronyms, abbreviations, and initials.

www.howstuffworks.com
Descriptions, diagrams, and photos explaining how devices work.

www.statistics.com
Statistics from government and other sources on a range of subjects.

www.ipl.org
University of Michigan site that gives links to to all kinds of sources from dictionaries to writing guides and newspapers.

www.resourceshelf.freeprint.com
A favorite among reference librarians.

www.salary.com
Salaries in all fields, including public relations.

Public Relations

www.about.com
Lists multiple guide sites. Public relations site offers articles, directories, forums, etc.

www.pr-education.org
Aggregate of PR-related sites and services.

www.prplace.com
Lists Internet addresses and hot links to PR organizations and how-to information in the public relations field.

www.prcentral.com
Good list of case studies and a news release library.

www.businesswire.com
News releases by company and industry.

www.prnewswire.com
News releases by company and industry.

www.workinpr.com
Job announcements, trends in employment, etc.

www.tsnn.com
The Trade Show News Network

Organizations

www.prfirms.org
Council of Public Relations Firms

www.iabc.com
International Association of Business Communicators (IABC)

continued on next page

Surfing the Internet (cont.)

www.prsa.org
 Public Relations Society of America
 (PRSA)

www.ipra.org
 International Public Relations Association
 (IPRA)

www.pac.org
 Public Affairs Council (PAC)

www.niri.org
 National Investor Relations Institute
 (NIRI)

www.instituteforpr.com
 Institute of Public Relations (IPR)

www.ifea.com
 International Festivals and Events
 Association (IFEA)

Publications

www.odwyerpr.com
 Daily update on public relations, plus

archives and links to public relations
articles.

www.prandmarketing.com
 PR News

www.prexec.com
 Ragan's newsletters and public relations
 resources

www.prsa.org/tactics
 Public Relations Tactics

www.prsa.org/strategist
 The Strategist

www.prweekus.com
 PRWeek

www.iabc.com/cw
 Communication World

www.combriefings.com
 Communication Briefings

2. Who is our target audience? (The more specific the segment, the better.)

3. What are our target audience's needs, concerns, and interests?

4. What is our message?

5. What communication channel is most effective?

6. Who is our most believable spokesperson?

Answering these questions goes a long way toward helping you determine the content and structure of your message. Regarding questions 2 and 3, Julie Story Goldsborough, president of a Kansas public relations firm, says, "I try to delve into the minds of the readers. What is the main benefit to them? What do they want to know about the subject?"

The next step is to outline question 4 more fully—what is the message? Usually an outline includes major topics, and minor topics within each major topic. One approach to outlining is to list the major message points as major topics. There may be two or three key messages, for example, that you want to communicate in a news release or a feature story. Under each of these headings, jot down a list of what facts, statistics, and examples you will give to support the major point.

Once the objectives and content of the message are determined, the next challenge is to compose a succinct, well-organized document that uses all of the rules of grammar, punctuation, and spelling correctly. There are entire books devoted to composition, and you should refer to the list of additional resources at the end of the chapter. However, here are a few general guidelines you should keep in mind as you prepare to write public relations materials.

Sentences

Sentences should be clear and concise. Long, compound sentences slow the reader down and are often hard to understand. In general, a sentence containing 25 to 30 words is difficult even for a college-educated audience. This does not mean that all sentences should be 8 to 10 words long; you should strive for a variety of lengths, with the average sentence being about 15 to 17 words.

In many cases, a complex sentence simply contains more words than necessary. Take this bloated sentence, for example: "They have assisted numerous companies in the development of a system that can be used in the monitoring of their customer service operations." Revised, this sentence is more concise and easier to understand: "They have helped many companies develop systems for monitoring their customer services operations."

Communication Briefings has compiled a list of word savers that can help keep sentences concise and on course. You should shorten the common wordy phrases on the left to the single words on the right when writing or editing copy:

a great number of	many
at this point in time	now
come to a realization	realize
despite the fact that	although
due to the fact that	because
for the purpose of	for, to
give approval of	approve
of the opinion that	believe
owing to the fact that	because
since the time when	since
take under consideration	consider
until such time as	until
with the exception of	except for
would appear that	seems

Paragraphs

Short paragraphs are better than long ones. A review of a daily newspaper shows that the journalistic style is short paragraphs averaging about six to eight typeset lines. Lead paragraphs in news stories are even shorter—about two or three lines.

Public relations writing should follow the same guidelines. Short paragraphs give the reader a chance to catch a breath, so to speak, and continue reading. Long paragraphs not only tax the reader's concentration but also encourage the reader to "tune out."

Remember that the paragraph on your computer screen is even longer when set in a newspaper column only 2 inches wide. Your 8 lines become 12 lines in a newspaper or magazine. A typical paragraph contains only one basic idea. When another idea is introduced, it is time for a new paragraph.

Short, punchy paragraphs are particularly important for online news releases and newsletters. According to a study by Sun Microsystems, it takes 50 percent longer for an individual to read material on a computer screen. Consequently, people need key information in short, digestible chunks, says Michael Butzgy, owner of a New York communications firm.

Word Choice

College-educated writers often forget that words common to their vocabulary are not readily understood by large segments of the general public. General-circulation newspapers, aware that a large percentage of their readers have not been to college, strive to write news stories at the fourth- to sixth-grade level. A writer's word choice is further limited by the statistic that an estimated 27 million adults in the United States lack basic reading skills and often cannot comprehend messages written beyond the second-grade level.

If your target audience is the general public, remember that a short word—one with fewer syllables—is more easily understood than a longer one. *Communication Briefings* gives the following list of "stately," multi-syllable words and some shorter, more reader-friendly options:

"Stately" word	Reader-Friendly word
frequently	often
majority	most
regulation	rule
subsequent	future
reiterate	repeat
approximately	about
additional	more
fundamental	basic
individual	person
requirement	need
accomplish	achieve
characteristic	trait
initial	first
additional	more

More complex words, of course, can be used if the target audience is well educated. Most readers of *The Wall Street Journal,* for example, are college graduates, so the writing is more complex than that found in a small-town daily.

Also, if the target audience is professionals in a field such as law, education, science, or engineering, the standard for word choice is different. Educators, for

Professional Tips

Writing Traps to Avoid

Even the most accomplished writers fall into common writing "traps" that slow down and confuse readers. *Communication Briefings* lists the following common "traps" that can be found in sentences:

- Wordy prepositional phrases that begin with *at, on, in, of, with,* or *under.*
- "Very" phrases, such as *very big* instead of *large.*
- Verb-nouns combine a verb and noun where a verb will do. For example, *make a suggestion* instead of *suggest.*
- Buried verbs, such as *beneficial* instead of *benefit.*
- "Doubles," or using two words that mean the same thing. For example, *entirely complete.*

example, seem to like elaborate expressions such as "multiethnic individualized learning" or "continuum."

Scientific writing, too, is loaded with esoteric words. Newspaper editors often complain that they receive news releases from high-technology companies that are so full of jargon that neither they nor their readers can understand them.

If your audience is engineers, of course, you can use specialized words and phrases. Good writing, however, requires that you simplify the message as much as possible. Eric Hatch, writing in *Communication World,* gives an example of the "engineering style" of writing:

> A plan will be implemented to incorporate performance database already available from previous NASA 8 2 6 and BTWT tests on the various UDF® models with the code currently under development to yield more accurate spanwise Cd (drag coefficients) distributions and velocity diagrams between blade-rows for our acoustics prediction use.

In this example, notes Hatch, "the author has jammed everything into one polysyllabic elephant of a sentence." He suggests the following rewrite; though still complex, it is more readable to an educated audience:

> A database compiled during earlier wind tunnel tests on the various UDF® blade models will be incorporated into the new code. This should give us more accurate drag coefficients and velocity diagrams between the blade rows, resulting in better predictions of the engine's acoustical behavior.

Active Verbs/Present Tense

Verbs vitalize your writing. Don't sacrifice verbs by burying the action in nouns or adjectives. You will boost clarity and add vigor to your writing by stripping away excess words around a verb. Active voice is also more direct and usually shorter than a passive sentence. Here are some examples:

original statement: The annual report produced a disappointed reaction among the board of directors.

revised statement: The annual report disappointed the board of directors.

original statement: Our consultants can assist you in answering questions about floor treatments.

revised statement: Our consultants can answer your floor treatment questions.

Use of present tense, as well as active verbs, also improves writing. It is better to write "The copier *delivers* 100 copies per minute" than to write "The copier *will deliver* 100 copies per minute." In most public relations writing, particularly news releases, use present tense as much as possible. In quotations, for example, it is better to write "The copier is being shipped next month," *says* Rowena Jones, sales manager. Doesn't this sound better than "The copier *will be* shipped next month," *said* Rowena Jones, sales manager.

Imagery

Strong visual descriptions are better than generalized statements. Writing that Coca-Cola is sold in many nations or marketed internationally does not have much impact on the reader. A stronger image is created if you write that Coca-Cola is now sold on all continents and is readily available to two-thirds of the earth's population. Or, as Coca-Cola stated in a recent annual report to stockholders, if "all the system's customers lined up along the equator, a thirsty consumer could purchase a Coca-Cola every 16 feet."

Visual descriptions can even be used to portray the wealth of Bill Gates, the world's richest person. One writer came up with the following imagery: "If Mr. Gates' fortune were converted to dollar bills, it would take 296 747s to fly the pile from Microsoft's Redmond, Wash., headquarters to New York. And once there, the loot would cover every square inch of Manhattan, not just once, but six times." Another enterprising writer, commenting about the expensive home of Bill Gates, notes, "he still has enough money left to buy every house in Alaska, Wyoming, and the two Dakotas."

Professional Tips

Devices for Achieving Clear Writing

Example	Say something—then use an example or a statistic to illustrate it.
Definition	Uncommon words call for a dictionary definition or a simple explanation of what you mean.
Comparison	If the reader is unfamiliar with the concept or thing being written about, compare it with something familiar.
Restatement	Say the same thing in different words. This reinforces the concept.

ERRORS TO AVOID

Errors in your writing will brand you as careless, unprofessional, and inconsiderate of your audience. Errors also call into question the credibility of the entire message. Professional writing requires attention to detail and repeated review of your draft to catch all potential errors.

Spelling

Credibility is sacrificed when spelling errors appear in public relations materials. For example, one news release for a company that manufactured a spell-checking program for a word processor included the nonwords "tradmark" and "publishere." Naturally, the company was embarrassed about the "typos"—especially after *The Wall Street Journal* poked fun at the company on page 1. We can only guess at how much these typos cost the company in sales and consumer confidence.

Time magazine does know the actual cost of a spelling error. Some years ago, *Time* ran a cover headline reading "New Plan for Arms Control." More than 200,000 covers were printed without the "r" in the word "control" before the error was discovered. The presses were stopped, and the error was corrected; putting the "r" back in "control" cost the magazine $100,000.

Gobbledygook and Jargon

Every occupation and industry has its own vocabulary. Telephone executives talk about "LATAs" and "attenuation rates." Cable people talk about "pay-to-basic ratios," and even public relations professionals talk about "mug shots," "ANRs," "VNRs," "boilerplate," and "evergreens." All too often, business people slip into a pattern of gobbledygook. Things don't get "finished"; they get "finalized." An event didn't happen "yesterday"; it occurred "at that point in time." In education, we don't have a child "failing"; he's just "motivationally deprived."

All these terms and acronyms may be fine if professionals are talking to each other or sending material to a trade publication, but using such terms in news releases and other messages to the public is a major roadblock to effective communication. Public relations consultant Joan Lowery, writing in *Communication World*, says, "Knowingly or unknowingly, jargon has become the lazy man's way to avoid wrestling with how to communicate clearly, concisely, and with passion to others who may not understand the concepts that some of us live and breathe each day."

The solution, says broadcast news veteran David Snell, is for public relations people to "de-geekify" their superiors. In an article for *The Strategist*, he writes, "To function with maximum efficiency, the public relations person needs to be the 'Outsider's Insider'; the person who understands the jargon, but maintains an active memory of the level of ignorance brought with them to the job." In other words, the public relations writer must always ask the question, "Will someone unfamiliar with this profession or industry be able to easily understand the message?"

Lowery takes another approach. She encourages public relations writers to always ask the question, "so what?" This forces executives, as well as engineers, to understand that the news release to the daily newspaper should skip all the technical details and concentrate on how the new product benefits the consumer. Or, if you like jargon, you can always say "the end-user."

The public relations writer is a wordsmith, not a scribe. He or she has the obligation to educate executives and engineers of the need to provide message context and easy-to-understand analogies to explain technical concepts. Often, the use of jargon comes across almost as a foreign language. Your job is to translate the material into basic English.

Poor Sentence Structure

The subject and the words that modify it often become separated in a sentence, causing some confusion about what exactly is being discussed. Here are some examples from news stories:

> Police will be looking for people driving under the influence of alcohol and distributing pamphlets that spell out the dangers of drunken driving.
>
> The proposed budget provides salary increases for faculty and staff performing at a satisfactory level of two percent.
>
> The student was charged with possession and consumption of an opened beer can, which is against university rules.

Poor sentence structure can also lead to embarrassment. A company newsletter, detailing an employee's illness, once reported: "Jeff was taken to the hospital with what was thought to be thrombus phlebitis. After spending a restless night with a nurse at the hospital, the results were negative."

Wrong Words

A good dictionary user not only checks spelling, but also verifies the meaning of words. An Associated Press (AP) story once told about a man who had inherited a small scenic railroad from his "descendants," who had started it in the nineteenth century. The writer meant "ancestors" but used the wrong word. Another publication also used the wrong word when it reported "Windows 2000 a High-Tech Coupe for Consumers." The actual word is "coup."

More common mistakes involve the usage of "it's" and "its," "effect" and "affect," "there" and "their," and "presume" and "assume." Other frequently confused words are listed in the next section. When in doubt, take the time to use the dictionary. It will save you embarrassment later.

"Sound-alike" Words

Many words sound alike and are similar in spelling but have very different meanings. Although it may be somewhat humorous to read that a survey is "chalk full" of information (instead of "chock-full"), a company's management team is doing some "sole" searching (instead of "soul searching"), or an employee was in a "comma" (instead of a "coma") after a car accident, such mistakes are the mark of a careless writer.

A spell-checking program for your personal computer is extremely efficient at catching misspelled words, but it often does not catch homonyms because they are

Professional Tips

Guidelines for Effective Writing

Suzanne Sparks, a teacher of public relations at New Jersey's Rowan College and author of *The Manager's Guide to Business Writing* (McGraw-Hill) gives the following writing tips:

- **Know your readers.** The more you know, the better you can focus your message. Find out about the audience's age, gender, interests, values, attitudes, and knowledge of the subject. When in doubt, you should write so that a 12-year-old can understand the message.

- **Stress "you" benefits.** Write from the perspective of the readers and what's in it for them.

- **Have a single communication objective.** Do you want to inform or persuade? Determine your purpose and stick to it. With every paragraph you write, ask yourself "so what?" If it doesn't help your objective, don't use it.

- **Use subject lines and short paragraphs.** Announce your focus with a subject line that grabs readers. Make the first few paragraphs relatively short to preserve reader interest.

- **Write strong introductions and conclusions.** The introduction must give the key information; the conclusion should summarize the major points.

- **Write in active voice.** Readers tire easily and find passive writing boring. Emphasize subject-verb-object construction. Avoid such verbs as "to be" and "to have."

Source: Adapted from *PR Tactics*, April 1999, pp. 18, 29.

spelled correctly. Therefore, it is always important to proofread your copy, even after it has been corrected by a spell-checker program.

Here is a list of words that are frequently confused. Do a self-test and write a sentence correctly using the right word.

adapt, adept, adopt	implicit, explicit
callow, callous	lose, loose
canvas, canvass	negligent, negligible
compliment, complement	peak, peek, pique
dominant, dominate	pore, pour
desert, dessert	principle, principal
ensure, insure, assure	stationary, stationery
imply, infer	there, their
foreword, forward	precedent, precedence
who's, whose	adverse, averse

Redundancies

Another major error in writing is redundancy. It is not necessary to use the word "totally" to modify a word such as "destroyed," or "completely" to modify "demolished." Many writers also say that something is "somewhat" or "very" unique. "Unique," by definition, means one of a kind; either something is unique or it isn't. The following redundancy appeared in a news release: "In addition, the company lists $50 million in receivables that it hopes to collect. These are unpaid bills, largely from customers, that have yet to be paid."

Too Many Numbers

People can digest a few figures but not a mass of statistics. Use numbers sparingly in your writing, and don't put too many in a single sentence. Avoid such constructions as "During 2000, the corporation acquired 73 companies in 14 nations on five continents to achieve revenue of $14.65 billion, up $3 billion from the $11.65 billion in 1999." Some other tips:

- Write "$92 million" instead of "92,000,000 dollars."
- Give a readily understood comparison than just an abstract number. Few people will readily grasp the size of a new warehouse that is 583 feet long—but they will immediately form an image if you say that it's about the length of two football fields.
- Check your math. The price of something can go up more than 100 percent, but it can never go down more than 100 percent.

Hype

You can ruin the credibility and believability of your message by using exaggerated words and phrases. When Sharp Electronics Corporation introduced a new hand-held computer, the news release called it "the next true revolution in man's conquest of information." Other companies often describe their products as "first of its kind," "unique," "a major breakthrough," and even "revolutionary," which tends to raise suspicion among journalists.

High-tech companies were once singled out by *The Wall Street Journal* for overusing adjectives. After analyzing 201 news releases, reporter Michael Miller issued a "hype hit parade." In descending order of overuse were the following words: *leading, enhanced, unique, significant, solution, integrated, powerful, innovative, advanced, high-performance,* and *sophisticated.*

Bias and Stereotypes

Stereotypes often creep in as a writer struggles to describe a situation, group, or person. How often have you seen a writer describe a woman with such adjectives as "pert," "petite," "fragile," "feminine," "stunning," "gorgeous," "statuesque," or "full-figured"? How about "blond and blue-eyed"? Would you describe a man as a "muscular, well-built six-footer with sandy hair and blue eyes"?

In general, avoid descriptive terms of beauty or physical attributes and mannerisms whenever possible. In most cases, such descriptions have no bearing on the story and can be considered sexist. For example, here's how one Chicago company described its president in a news release: "A tall, attractive blonde who could easily turn heads on Main Street is instead turning heads on Wall Street." Or consider the news release from a Los Angeles firm about the appointment of a woman to a management position: "Demure, naturally pretty and conservative in her dress and manner, Miho Suda could easily pass as a college student."

You should also avoid any suggestion that all members of any group have the same personal characteristic, be it ambition, laziness, shrewdness, guile, or intelligence. Don't suggest that some characteristic sets an individual apart from a stereotyped norm either. For example, it is inappropriate to write, "John Williams, who is black, was promoted to senior vice president." Nor would you write, "Linda Gonzales, a U.S. citizen, will serve as assistant treasurer." In both cases, you are implying that these individuals are exceptions to some norm for their ethnic group.

Avoid gender bias by using non-gender-related words. Awareness of the irrelevance of an employee's gender is why airlines now have "flight attendants" instead of "stewardesses" and why the Postal Service hires "mail carriers" instead of "mailmen." It also is unnecessary to write that something is "man-made" when a neutral word such as "synthetic" or "artificial" is just as good. "Employees" is better than "manpower," and "chairperson" is more acceptable than "chairman." Some terms may seem difficult to neutralize—"congressperson," "businessperson," and "waitperson" don't exactly trip off the tongue. However, with a little thought, you can come up with appropriate titles, such as "legislator," "executive," and "server."

The problem of avoiding gender bias is particularly difficult because much of our language is geared to the use of the word "man" as a generic term for both males and females. Attempts to avoid this lead to messy constructions such as "he/she" or "his/her" that make for difficult reading. However, another word can be used in most cases. If you make the noun in question plural, the pronoun "their" will serve nicely. In other cases, you can use words such as "personnel," "staff," "employee," "worker," "person," or "practitioner" to describe both men and women in the workplace.

Politically Incorrect Language

Beyond avoidance of stereotypes, there is an ongoing controversy about what constitutes **politically correct** (commonly called "PC") language. In today's world of diversity at all levels of national life, there is increased sensitivity about what words and images are used to describe minorities and other groups of people.

For example, the Alliance for the Mentally Ill of New York State picketed a Daffy's discount clothing store because of a billboard showing an empty straitjacket with the headline, "If you're paying over $100 for a dress shirt, may we suggest a jacket to go with it?"

Such concern has merit, and writers should be sensitive to words and images that may offend individuals or groups. However, critics charge that a flood of euphemisms can cause a loss of clarity and may result in a kind of nonsensical bureaucratic language that impedes effective communication.

For example, some groups think the word "civilization" is politically incorrect because it infers that some people are not civilized. Still others object to the word "disabled" and want to substitute "physically challenged" or "differently abled." In this situation, we no longer have short people, but "vertically challenged" people. Even the old term "Dutch treat" is under attack, because it implies that Dutch people are cheap.

On another level, similar suggestions seem quite logical. For example, in a global economy, American companies now refer to "international" markets because "foreign" sounds too ethnocentric. Today's writers use "Asian American" instead of the now pejorative "Oriental." And the term "Hispanic" is now more acceptable than the politically charged "Spanish-speaking." The term "Latino," however, raises some controversy; some women say it is sexist because the "o" in Spanish is male.

The term "black" seems to be making a comeback, according to the U.S. Department of Labor, which surveyed 60,000 households about the names of race and ethnic categories to use in job statistics. Forty-four percent of the blacks preferred this designation, while another 28 percent preferred "African American" and 12 percent liked "Afro-American." As a matter of policy, many newspapers use African American on first reference and black as the noun of second reference. Headlines almost always use black because it is short.

The University of Missouri School of Journalism has produced the *Dictionary of Cautionary Words and Phrases* to make writers more aware of particular words and phrases in particular contexts. In many cases, it helps make the language more specific. For example, the dictionary suggests that the term "senior citizen" not be applied to anyone under age 65, that "girl" is appropriate only for females under 17, and that "gay" be applied only to men (the term "homosexual" can refer to both men and women).

Language, and its connotations, is constantly changing. The professional public relations writer must be aware of the changes and must make decisions based on such factors as sensitivity to the audience, accuracy, and clarity of communication.

SUMMARY

- Public relations writing and media placements are accomplished within the framework of the complete public relations process—research, planning, communication, and evaluation.
- Public relations personnel who produce news releases, media kits, special events, and so on are considered communication technicians, not managers.
- Public relations writing is similar to journalism in that both strive to provide accurate, credible information. They differ with respect to objectives, selection of audiences, and the variety of media channels that are used.
- A computer, either a desktop or a notebook, is essential for public relations work.
- A reference library is a must for any writer. In addition to books, a person can also do research through search engines, such as Google, and library databases.

- The most widely used stylebook for journalistic writing is the *Associated Press Stylebook and Briefing on Media Law.*
- Media directories are readily available in print, on CD-ROM and DVD, and on the Web.
- Public relations writers should keep current in the field by reading publications such as *PRWeek*, and *Jack O'Dwyer's PR Services Report.* They should also read daily newspapers and weekly newsmagazines.
- Google, Yahoo, AOL Time Warner, and MSN are popular search engines for the Internet.
- All public relations writing starts with the basic steps of determining the purpose and content of the message.
- Word choice, sentence structure, grammar, and spelling are important. Sloppiness loses credibility.
- Public relations writers should work as "translators" of organizational jargon so messages can be understood by the public.
- Hype and exaggerated claims ruin the credibility of a message.
- Writers should be sensitive to words and terms that can be considered sexist or racist.

ADDITIONAL RESOURCES

Calabro, Sara. "How PR Software Is Revolutionizing Workflow." *PRWeek*, February 24, 2003, p. 30.

Gaschen, Dennis J. "Web Sites You Need to Know About." *PR Tactics*, May 2001, p. 21.

Goldsborough, Reid. "Minimizing The Risks of PC Buying For Your Home Office." *PR Tactics*, March 2002, p. 25.

Goldsborough, Reid. "Getting Your Facts Straight With a Little Help From The Web." *PR Tactics*, November 2002, p. 6.

Goldstein, Norm, Editor. *The Associated Press Stylebook and Briefing on Media Law.* Cambridge, MA: Perseus Publishing, 2002.

Grove, Aimee. "Public Records: Extensive and Inexpensive." *PRWeek*, March 25, 2002, p. 26. Government Web sites.

Guernsey, Lisa. "Fishing for Information? Try Better Bait." *The New York Times*, August 21, 2003, p. E8. Web browsers.

Kelleher, Tom. "Public Relations Roles and Media Choice." *Journal of Public Relations Research*, Vol. 13, No. 4, 2001, pp. 303–320.

Kessler, Lauren, and McDonald, Duncan. *When Words Collide: A Media Writer's Guide to Grammar and Style.* Belmont, CA: Wadsworth/Thomson Learning, 2000.

Lowery, Joan. "Cut the Jargon." *Communication World*, October/November 2000, pp. 11–14.

Lunsford, Andrea A. *Easy Writer: A Pocket Guide.* Boston, MA: Bedford/St. Martins, 2002.

Mangalindan, Mylene, Wingfield, Nick, and Guth, Robert. "Rising Clout of Google Prompts Rush by Internet Rivals to Adapt." *The Wall Street Journal*, July 16, 2003, pp. A1, A6.

Snell, David. "De-Geekifying Corporate Speak." *The Strategist*, Summer 1999, pp. 30–33.

Thompson, Terry J. "Whatever Happened to Public Relations Writing." *The Strategist*, Fall 1999, pp. 19–21.

Walford, Lynn. "Getting results from online media databases." *O'Dwyer's PR Services Report*, January 2003, pp. 14–15.

Willey, Susan. "The Pitfalls of Cyberspace and Electronic Database Research." *Journalism & Mass Communication Educator*, Summer 2000, pp. 78–85.

Wylie, Ann. "Cut Through The Clutter. How to Make The Next Piece You Write Easier to Read and Understand." *PR Tactics*, September 2001, p. 12.

Chapter 2

Persuasive Writing

Public relations professionals, for the most part, are engaged in the crafting and dissemination of information that will persuade and motivate people. The International Public Relations Association (IPRA) succinctly makes this point in one of its publications.

> Public relations is the cultivated landscape drawing our attention to concepts, opinions and conclusions. Through sight, sound, and action, professional communicators do much more than deliver messages and impressions. They motivate audiences to participate and to act—both locally and globally. Persuasive communication is an art form with a direct impact upon our willingness to change the way we live, to change the way we work, to change the way we think.

Indeed, messages are designed to change attitudes and opinions, reinforce existing predispositions, and influence people to buy a product, use a service, or support a worthy cause. To be an effective writer, you need to understand the basic elements of communication and the complex process of how individuals respond to different messages. In an age of information overload, writers must constantly analyze public attitudes and shape persuasive, credible messages that cut through the clutter.

You need to keep asking questions. How do you appeal to self-interests? Which spokesperson has the most credibility? What information is most salient to the target audience? What is the most effective communication channel? What are my ethical responsibilities as a writer?

This chapter gives a thumbnail sketch of major communication theories and what social science research tell us about the way people receive, interpret, and act on information. It will also give guidelines about how to make your messages—whether they are for the Sierra Club or General Electric—more persuasive. At the end of the chapter, we will discuss the ethical guidelines and professional standards that should guide the content of your writing.

THE BASICS OF COMMUNICATION

David Therkelsen, CEO of the American Red Cross in St. Paul, Minnesota, conceptualizes the process of effective communication as follows:

> To be successful, a message must be *received* by the intended individual or audience. It must get the audience's *attention*. It must be *understood*. It must be *believed*. It must be *remembered*. And ultimately, in some fashion, it must be *acted upon*. Failure to accomplish any of these tasks means the entire message fails.

To communicate is to make known—to project ideas into the minds of others. This process depends on four elements: a *sender*, a *message*, a *medium,* and a *receiver.* If all these elements are present, there will be communication. If any one is missing or not operating, there will be no communication. Because your purpose is to persuade, you want to communicate your ideas to a particular group of people—those who can help or hinder your organization in attaining its objectives. In describing the process of communication, the four elements usually start with the *sender*, but it may be better to think of the process in reverse order.

Receiver

The receivers are the people you must reach. In public relations, potential or actual audiences are commonly referred to as **publics**. A public can be defined in many ways. For marketing purposes, a public is often defined as a market segment—a group of people who have comparable demographic (income, age, education, etc.) characteristics that will cause them to respond to messages in a similar way. A public also can be defined as natural groupings of elected officials, customers, stockholders, or employees. At times, geography defines a particular public—citizens of a town or registered voters in a district.

You will also hear the word **stakeholder** mentioned in relation to publics. Stakeholders, by definition, are groups of people who can be affected by the actions of an organization. The obvious example is the organization's employees, but the list can become quite long when you consider the fact that many "publics" can be affected—consumers, neighbors, suppliers, environmental groups, investors, just to name a few.

Thus, it is extremely important always to think of publics in the plural instead of as a collective entity called "the general public." By defining publics by income, age, gender, geography, and even psychographic characteristics, you are much better prepared to design message strategies that are more targeted and relevant to each public or audience. In sum, the more you can segment your publics and understand their characteristics, the better you can communicate with them.

As business becomes more global, there is also a growing need to understand the attitudes, customs, and cultures of people in other nations. Poor conceptualization of messages can cause a number of gaffs when one does not understand the language and culture of a nation. A baby formula manufacturer discovered that in its product introductions in one Spanish-speaking country, the term used for "nipple" was a vulgar expression.

Media

The media are the physical channels that carry the message to the receiver. They may include newspapers, magazines, radio, television, letters, speeches, audiovisuals, pictures, newsletters, leaflets, brochures, and even the World Wide Web. Every medium has advantages and disadvantages, as explored in future chapters.

Your job is to determine which medium or combination of media will be most effective in reaching a selected public. If you are trying to reach female college students, it is important to know that there is a vast difference between the readers of *Cosmo, Redbook,* and *Glamour* in terms of readership. This will be discussed further in Chapter 10.

It is also important to know the message format that each media requires. Television, for example, requires highly visual material and short **soundbites**. Home pages on the World Wide Web require strong graphics and interactive mechanisms. A newspaper story requires a strong lead paragraph that attracts the reader.

Message

Planning the message starts with a determination of exactly what key messages you want your receivers to receive, and what you want them to think, believe, or do. Then you must acquire a solid knowledge of what your audience currently knows and believes. If you want to affect attitudes and opinions, you must find out about those that already exist. This calls for research—possibly surveys.

Your message must be applicable, believable, realistic, and convincing. It must be expressed clearly and understandably in familiar words and phrases. Above all, you must convince the receivers that the idea you are presenting is beneficial to them.

Sender

The sender is the organization from which the message comes. Every organization has different publics, divergent interests, dissimilar objectives, unique problems, distinctive beliefs and peculiarities. As a writer, you must know the organization's objectives so that the messages you prepare will advance these objectives.

THEORIES OF COMMUNICATION

A message may move from the sender through the media to the receiver without necessarily conveying ideas and getting them accepted. Yet ideas do get accepted, and there are several theories about how this is accomplished. Space does not allow a full discussion of each theory, but here is a brief summary of the major theories that are most salient to public relations writers. See the list of additional resources at the end of the chapter for books on communication theory.

Two-Step Flow Theory

The flow of communication might be described as a series of expanding contacts. It assumes that opinion leaders first pay attention to messages in the media, analyze them, interpret them, and then pass on the information to their friends and associates.

There are formal opinion leaders, such as an elected official or the president of a company, but there are also informal opinion leaders. All of us rely on various people for information and guidance because we believe they are knowledgeable about a particular subject, whether it be baseball or how to get a file transferred on a PC.

Later research has shown that the two-step flow theory is really a multistep model—communication going from opinion leaders to an attentive public and ultimately to an inattentive public. However, the basic idea about the role of opinion leaders in communication remains intact. High-technology companies, for example, often design their marketing strategy to first reach respected journalists and experts who really know the industry. They are the opinion leaders who will ultimately tell the public whether the product is any good. A later section discusses adoption theory.

Media Uses and Gratification

Recipients of communication are not passive couch potatoes. The basic premise of uses and gratification theory is that the communication process is interactive. The communicator wants to inform and, ultimately, motivate people to act on the information. Recipients want to be entertained, informed, or alerted to opportunities that can fulfill their needs.

Thus, people make highly intelligent choices about what messages require their attention and meet their needs. That is why people are very selective about what articles they will read in the local daily. The role of the public relations writer, then, is to tailor messages that are meaningful to the audience. Maslow's hierarchy of needs, which will be discussed shortly, relates to the basic needs of individuals.

Cognitive Dissonance

People will not believe a message, or act on it, if it is contrary to their predispositions. A public relations writer must, in this instance, introduce information that causes them to question their beliefs.

This can be done in several ways. First, you can introduce information that says it is okay to change; perhaps the situation has changed because of new discoveries, and so on. Second, you can use sources or testimonials from people the audience trusts.

Media Effects

One theory postulates that the mass media have limited effects. The media may set the agenda in terms of what people think about, but they have limited influence in telling people what to think.

There is also the theory of moderate and powerful media effects. This theory postulates that the media are influential in shaping public opinion when (1) the public has little or no opinion on a subject, (2) the subject is non-ego threatening, and (3) the reader or viewer has no firsthand knowledge of the event or situation. In a highly urbanized and global society, the public is increasingly dependent on the media for information. Because of this, framing theory becomes more relevant.

Framing

The term "framing" was historically applied to journalists and editors and how they selected certain facts, themes, treatments, and even words to "frame" a story that would generate maximum interest and understanding among readers and viewers. For example, how media frame the debate over health care and the policies of health maintenance organizations (HMOs) plays a major role in public perceptions of the problem. Many people, because they lack specific knowledge and experience about an issue, usually accept the media's version of reality.

Framing theory also applies to public relations because, according to more than one study, about half of the content found in the mass media today is supplied by public relations sources. Indeed, Kirk Hallahan of Colorado State University says that public relations personnel are essentially *frame strategists* because they construct messages that "focus selectively on key attributes and characteristics of a cause, candidate, product, or service." This framing, in turn, is echoed in the context and content of stories that the mass media disseminate.

The introduction of the Apple iMac is a good example. The strategy of Apple's public relations firm, Daniel Edelman Worldwide, was to frame the story in the context of Apple's return to prosperity after several years of massive losses, turmoil in the executive suite, and erosion of customer loyalty. The framing of the new iMac, called **product positioning** in marketing, was a success as newspapers used headlines such as "Apple Regains Its Stride" and "Apple's Back on Track." Investor and consumer confidence in the company was restored, and sales of iMacs soared as well.

Diffusion and Adoption

The diffusion theory was developed in the 1930s and expanded on by Professor Everett Rogers of Stanford University. It holds that there are five steps in the process of acquiring new ideas:

1. *Awareness*—the person discovers the idea or product.
2. *Interest*—the person tries to get more information.
3. *Trial*—the person tries the idea on others or samples the product.
4. *Evaluation*—the person decides whether the idea works for his or her own self-interest.
5. *Adoption*—the person incorporates the idea into his or her opinion or begins to use the product.

In this model, the public relations writer is most influential at the *awareness* and *interest* stages of the process. People often become aware of a product, service, or idea through traditional mass outlets such as newspapers, magazines, radio, and television. Indeed, the primary purpose of advertising in the mass media is to create awareness, the first step in moving people toward the purchase of a product or support of an idea.

At the interest stage, people seek more detailed information from such sources as pamphlets, brochures, direct mail, videotape presentations, meetings, and symposia. That is why initial publicity to create awareness often includes an 800 number or an address that people can use to request more information.

Family, peers, and associates become influential in the trial and evaluation stages of the adoption model. Mass media, at this point, serves primarily to reinforce messages and predispositions.

It is important to realize that a person does not necessarily go through all five stages of adoption with any given idea or product. Figure 2.1, for example, shows clearly that some people adopt new technologies earlier than others. A number of factors affect the adoption process. Rogers lists at least five.

- *Relative advantage*—is the idea better than the one it replaces?
- *Compatibility*—is the idea consistent with the person's existing values and needs?
- *Complexity*—is the innovation difficult to understand and use?
- *Trialability*—can the innovation be used on a trial basis?
- *Observability*—are the results of the innovation visible to others?

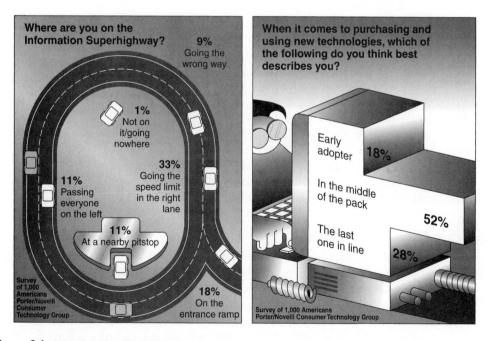

Figure 2.1 Adopting New Technology

People adopt new products and ideas at varying rates. Persuasive writers try to identify and target "early adopters" because they are opinion leaders. This graphic shows the results of a survey about acceptance of new technologies. *(Courtesy of Porter/Novelli Public Relations, New York.)*

You should be aware of these factors and try to overcome as many of them as possible. Repeating a message in various ways, reducing its complexity, taking competing messages into account, and structuring the message to the needs of the audience are ways to do this.

Hierarchy-of-Needs Theory

The hierarchy-of-needs theory has been applied in a number of disciplines, including communication. It is based on the work of Abraham H. Maslow, who listed basic human needs on a scale from basic survival to more complex ones:

- *Physiological needs.* These involve self-preservation. They include air, water, food, clothing, shelter, rest, and health—the minimum necessities of life.
- *Safety needs.* These comprise protection against danger, loss of life or property, restriction of activity, and loss of freedom.
- *Social needs.* These include acceptance by others, belonging to groups, and enjoying both friendship and love.
- *Ego needs.* These include self-esteem, self-confidence, accomplishment, status, recognition, appreciation, and the respect of others.
- *Self-fulfillment needs.* These represent the need to grow to one's full stature—simply as a human being or in terms of some special talent, gift, or interest.

The campaign for the National Turkey Federation (see box on page 45) is a good example of the application of Maslow's concepts. Low-income people got an economical recipe that satisfied basic physiological needs. However, the fancy recipes in upscale magazines were designed to meet the ego and social needs of people who were not worried about food costs.

At times, a public relations or advertising writer can appeal to several needs at once. An ad for a new car, for example, often emphasizes economic, safety, social, and ego needs. For the Baby Boomer who just turned 50, a red sports car may even satisfy self-fulfillment needs.

The main point is to understand that your audience is looking for messages that satisfy needs. If you can identify and articulate those needs, you are well on your way to being a persuasive writer.

Applying Theory to Practice

Understanding the concepts of opinion formation, the process of information diffusion, and the psychological needs of audiences have a great deal of practical applications for the public relations writer.

The diffusion model, for example, points out that mass and direct media are most important in the beginning stages of the process. Although the writer's goal is ultimately to change attitudes and behavior, this is difficult to accomplish unless the audience (1) is highly interested in the message, (2) is predisposed to accept it, and (3) receives reinforcement of the message through opinion leaders and peer groups.

PR Casebook

Tailoring Messages to American Lifestyles

Public relations writers increasingly use psychographics to tailor messages to specific audiences. SRI International, a research organization in Menlo Park, California, has developed a values and lifestyles program known as VALS.

Through extensive research, SRI was able to come up with several lifestyle typologies:

Survivors and sustainers are at the bottom of the hierarchy. Generally they have low incomes, are poorly educated, and are often elderly. These people eat at erratic hours, consume inexpensive foods, and seldom patronize restaurants.

Belongers are family oriented and traditional and tend to be lower- or middle-income people.

Achievers, at the uppermost level of the VALS scale, are often college-educated professionals with high incomes. They are also more experimental and open to new ideas.

A good example of how public relations writing can be tailored to each group is provided by Burson-Marsteller, a public relations firm that handled the National Turkey Federation account. The objective was to increase the consumption of turkey on a year-round basis.

By segmenting the consumer public into various VALS lifestyles, Burson-Marsteller was able to select the appropriate media for specific story ideas. An article placed in *True Experience,* a publication reaching the "survivors and sustainers" group, was headlined "A Terrific Budget-Stretching Meal" and emphasized bargain cuts of turkey. *Better Homes & Gardens* was used to reach the "belongers," with articles that emphasized tradition, such as barbecued turkey as a "summer classic" on the Fourth of July. The "achievers" were reached through *Food and Wine* and *Gourmet* magazines, with recipes for turkey salad and turkey tetrazzini.

By identifying the magazines that catered to these three lifestyle groups and tailoring the information to fit each magazine's demographics, Burson-Marsteller was able to send an appropriate message to each audience. The result was increased turkey sales on a year-round basis.

Consequently, most writers are realistic enough to have the limited objectives of message exposure and accurate dissemination of the message, which coincide with the interest and awareness stages of the diffusion model.

Professor James Grunig of the University of Maryland further applies the diffusion model by saying that the writer has two kinds of audience: passive and active.

Passive audiences have to be lured into accepting your message. Consequently, messages directed to them need to be highly visual, use catchy themes and slogans, and contain short messages. A number of communication tools provide this format: dramatic pictures and graphics, billboards, radio and television announcements, posters, bumper stickers, buttons, and special events that emphasize entertainment.

A variation of the *passive* audience is what Kirk Hallahan of Colorado State University calls the *inactive public*. This public typically has low knowledge and low involvement in the subject—whether it is a political campaign or a new product or service on the market. This presents a massive challenge to the communicator who must devise strategies for effective communication with such publics in

Professional Tips

Effective Communication

Philip Lesly, the late president of Philip Lesly Company, provided the following guidelines for effective, persuasive communication.

1. Approach everything from the viewpoint of the audience's interest. What is on its mind? What is in it for each person?

2. Make the subject matter part of the atmosphere in which audience members live—what they talk about, what they hear from others. That means tailoring the message to their channels of communication.

3. Communicate *with* people, not *at* them. Communication that approaches the audience as a target makes people put up defenses against it.

4. Localize—get the message conveyed as close to the individual's own setting as possible.

5. Use a number of communication channels, not just one or two. The impact is far greater when a message reaches people in a number of different forms.

6. Maintain consistency so that the basic content is the same regardless of audience or context. Then tailor that content to the specific audience as much as possible.

7. Don't propagandize, but be sure you make your point. Drawing conclusions in the information itself is more effective than letting the audience draw its own conclusions.

8. Maintain credibility—which is essential for all these points to be effective.

Source: Adapted from a speech by Philip Lesly as part of the Vern C. Schranz Distinguished Lecturership series at Ball State University.

order even to engage them at the basic level of generating awareness. Indeed, most public relations campaigns for new products and services tend to focus on *passive* or *inactive* publics.

Echoing Grunig's recommendations for communicating with passive audiences can be represented as a chart (see Figure 2.2) that Hallahan has developed showing various communication strategies for enhancing (1) *Motivation*, (2) *Ability*, and (3) *Opportunity* among the *inactive* public. He calls it the **M-A-O model**.

Active audiences, by contrast, are usually aware of the product, service, or idea. They have reached the second stage of the diffusion process, *interest,* and are seeking more detailed information. Appropriate communication tools for them include brochures, in-depth newspaper and magazine stories, slide presentations, videotape demonstrations, short films, symposia and conferences, speeches, and display booths at trade shows.

In most cases, the competent communicator acknowledges the existence of both passive and active audiences by preparing a number of messages that vary in content and structure. A daily newspaper may receive an attractive publicity photo with a short caption, while a specialized trade publication might get an in-depth

**MOTIVATION-ABILITY-OPPORTUNITY MODEL
FOR ENHANCING MESSAGE PROCESSING**

Enhance Motivation	Enhance Ability	Enhance Opportunity
Attract and encourage audiences to commence, continue processing	*Make it easier to process the message by tapping cognitive resources*	*Structure messages to optimize processing*
Create attractive, likable messages (create affect)	Include background, definitions, explanations	Expend sufficient effort to provide information
Appeal to hedonistic needs (sex, appetite, safety)	Be simple, clear	Repeat messages frequently
Use novel stimuli	Use advance organizers, e.g. headlines	Repeat key points within text-- in headlines, text, captions, illustrations, etc.
• Photos	Include synopses	
• Typography	Combine graphics, text, *and* narration (dual coding of memory traces)	Use longer messages
• Oversized formats		Include multiple arguments
• Large number of scenes, elements	Use congruent memory cues (same format as original)	Feature "interactive" illustrations, photos
• Changes in voice, silence, movement	Label graphics (helps identify which attributes to focus on)	Avoid distractions
Make the most of formal features		• Annoying music
• Format size	Use specific, concrete (versus abstract) words and images	• Excessively attractive spokespersons
• Music	Include exemplars, models	• Complex arguments
• Color	Make comparison with analogies	• Disorganized layouts
• Include key points in headlines	Show actions, train audience skills through demonstrations	Allow audiences to control pace of processing
Use moderately complex messages	Include marks (logos, logotypes, trademarks), slogans and symbols as continuity devices	Provide sufficient time
Use sources who are credible, attractive, or similar to audience		Keep pace lively and avoid audience boredom
Involve celebrities	Appeal to self-schemas (roles, what's important to audience identity)	
Enhance relevance to audience—Ask them to think about a question	Enhance perceptions of self-efficacy to perform tasks	
Use stories, anecdotes or drama to draw into action	Place messages in conducive environment (priming effects)	
Stimulate curiosity: use humor, metaphors, questions	Frame stories using culturally resonating themes, catchphrases	
Vary language, format, source		
Use multiple, ostensibly independent sources		

Figure 2.2 M-A-O Model Chart
This chart summarizes the various communication strategies that can be used to reach inactive publics who have little knowledge or interest in a particular issue, product, or service. The object, of course, is to structure messages that attract their attention.
(Copyright Kirk Hallahan, Colorado State University, 1999.)

news release detailing the product's features. On another level, a customer assessing the corporate Web site may review multiple details about the product or service by clicking on multiple links. The strategy of developing multiple messages for a variety of channels is emphasized throughout this book.

PERSUASIVE WRITING

Your purpose is to persuade your target audience. Your message may be delivered in one way, a few ways, or many ways. Techniques for getting your messages into the mass media are detailed in later chapters. As you work on message content, however, keep in mind the concepts of audience analysis; source credibility; appeal to self-interest; clarity of the message; timing and context; symbols, slogans, and acronyms; semantics; suggestions for action; and content and structure.

Audience Analysis

A message, as already stated, must be compatible with group values and beliefs. People who commute by car, for example, become more interested in carpooling

---

Professional Tips

A Behavioral Communication Model

Awareness → Latent readiness → Triggering event → Behavior

Most theories of communication end with the receipt of the message by the receiver. The assumption is that the reader will be persuaded and that the sender's objective will be accomplished.

The behavioral communication model, suggests *PR Reporter*, is better because it forces practitioners to think in terms of what causes people to pay attention to a message or take action. The four-step sequential process is as follows:

1. *Awareness.* The basic purpose of communication is to create awareness, which is the start of any behavioral process.

2. *Latent readiness.* An individual's attitudes and predispositions have a great deal of influence on whether the person is mentally prepared to pay attention to the message and take action on it. There is considerable evidence that receivers don't always respond. They may hear the message but do nothing with it.

3. *Triggering event.* This step gives people a chance to act on their latent readiness. A triggering event is something that stimulates action. It may be a telephone call from a charitable agency asking for a donation, a series of accidents on a stretch of road that makes voters finally vote for costly improvements, or a news conference announcing a new product on the market. Public relations people should build triggering events into their planning; this moves the emphasis from communication to behavior motivation.

4. *Behavior.* Although the ultimate goal is to motivate people to buy something or act in a certain way, they may adopt intermediate behaviors such as requesting more literature, visiting a showroom, or trying the product or idea on a limited basis.

The key is determining exactly what triggering event will cause a reaction on the part of the target audience.

Source: Patrick Jackson, editor, *PR Reporter*.

and mass transit when the message points out the increasing cost of fuel and how gridlock increases every year.

Tapping a group's attitudes and values in order to structure a meaningful message is called **channeling**. It is the technique of recognizing a general audience's beliefs and suggesting a specific course of action related to audience members' self-interests. In this example, the incentive to participate in carpooling or mass transit becomes more motivational than the more abstract concept of saving the environment.

Source Credibility

A message is more believable to an audience if the source has credibility, which is why writers try to attribute information and quotes to people who are perceived as experts. Indeed, expertise is a key element in credibility. The other two elements are sincerity and charisma. Ideally, a source will have all three attributes.

Steve Jobs, president of Apple, is a good example. His success in revitalizing the company in 1999 made him highly credible as an expert on Apple products and a high-tech visionary. In countless news articles and speeches, he also comes across as a personable, laid-back "geek" who really believes that the iMac and the iBook are the best products on the market. Jobs also has that elusive element of charisma—he is self-assured, confident, and articulate. As *Time* notes, he also has his fan club: "adoring legions at MacWorld."

Not every company has a Steve Jobs for its president, nor is that necessary. Depending on the message and the audience, various spokespersons can be used and quoted for source credibility. For example, if you are writing a news release about a new product for a trade magazine, perhaps the best source to quote would be the company's director of research and development. This person is a credible source primarily because of personal knowledge and expertise. If the news release is about the fourth-quarter earnings of the company, the most credible person to quote in the news release would be either the chief executive officer or the vice president for finance, both experts by virtue of their position.

Source credibility also can be hired. The California Strawberry Advisory Board, for example, arranges for a home economist to appear on television talk shows to discuss nutrition and demonstrate easy-to-follow strawberry recipes. The audience for these programs, primarily homemakers, not only identifies with the representative but also perceives the spokesperson to be an expert. Additional credibility is gained if the spokesperson comes across as being sincere about the message.

Sincerity is an important component in celebrity endorsements. Michael Jordan may not be an expert on all the products he endorses, but he has a lot of charisma. Sincerity and charisma are the key elements of using celebrities to provide source credibility.

Celebrities are used primarily to call attention to a product, service, or cause. The sponsor's intent is to associate the person's popularity with the product. This is called *transfer*. Tiger Woods, for example, is considered the most desirable male athlete to be a spokesperson, but he has so many endorsement deals that he is suffering from overexposure. Serena Williams is the most desirable female athlete, and her sister, Venus, is also a strong drawing card.

Popular athletes can lose source credibility because of too many endorsement deals, but this is nothing compared to those celebrities who get involved in scandals and negative publicity. OJ Simpson lost all of his endorsements after being placed on trial for the murder of his wife, and Burt Reynolds was dropped by the Florida orange juice producers after his bitter breakup with Loni Anderson. They thought his marital problems were at odds with their desire to portray orange juice as a healthy, happy, family product.

More recently, Allen Iverson of the Philadelphia 76ers lost considerable endorsement potential after being arraigned on 14 counts of domestic abuse. And Kobe Bryant of the Los Angeles Lakers was dropped by an Italian chocolate spread company after being charged with sexual assault in Colorado.

In sum, the use of various sources for credibility depends in large part on the type of audience being addressed. Surveys seem to indicate that purchasers of athletic shoes don't seem to care about the private lives (and scandals) of celebrities who endorse the shoes they wear, but it may be another matter for a company like McDonalds that is catering to the family market.

Appeal to Self-interest

Self-interest was mentioned in connection with both Maslow's hierarchy of needs and audience analysis. A public relations writer must at all times be aware of what the audience wants to know.

Writing publicity for a new food product can serve as an example. A news release to the trade press serving the food industry (grocery stores, suppliers, wholesalers, distributors) might focus on how the product was developed, distributed, and made available to the public, the manufacturer's pricing policies, or the results of marketing studies that show consumers want the product. This audience is interested in the technical aspects of distribution, pricing, and market niche.

You would prepare quite a different news release or feature article for the food section of a daily newspaper. The consumer wants information about the food product's nutritional value, convenience, and cost, and wants to know why the item is superior to similar products. The reader is also looking for menu ideas and recipes that use the product.

Clarity of the Message

Communication, as already stated, does not occur if the audience does not understand your message. It is important to produce messages that match the characteristics of your target audience in content and structure.

A bar association once thought it was a great idea to produce a brochure to help motorists understand liability in an accident. However, by the time the committee of lawyers added all their legalese, the brochure became useless as an aid to the general public.

One solution to this problem is to copy-test all public relations materials on the target audience. Another solution is to apply readability and comprehension

Professional Tips

Appeals That Move People to Act

Persuasive messages often include information that appeals to an audience's self-interest. Here is a list of persuasive message themes that author Charles Marsh compiled for *Communication World:*

Make money	Satisfy curiosity	Save money	Protect family
Save time	Be stylish	Avoid effort	Have beautiful things
More comfort	Satisfy appetite	Better health	Be like others
Cleaner	Avoid trouble	Escape pain	Avoid criticism
Gain praise	Be individual	Be popular	Protect reputation
Be loved/accepted	Be safe	Keep possessions	Make work easier
More enjoyment	Be secure		

formulas to materials before they are produced and disseminated. Most formulas are based on the number of words per sentence and the number of one-syllable words per 100 words.

In general, standard writing should average about 140 to 150 syllables per 100 words, and the average sentence length should be about 17 words. This is the level of newspapers and weekly news magazines such as *Time.*

Timing and Context

Professional communicators often say that timing is everything. In the earlier example about car commuters, it was pointed out that the best time to talk about carpooling and mass transit to owners of sport utility vehicles is when there is a major increase in gas prices. Another good context is when the state highway department releases a study showing that the average commute on a congested highway from point A to point B now takes 20 minutes longer than it did last year. Both of these situations are good examples of "triggering events," which is described in the box on page 48.

Your message also must arrive at a time when it can conveniently be considered. If it is too early, your audience may not be ready to think about it. April is not the time to talk about winter sports or sports equipment, but October might be just right. Information about income taxes is especially interesting just before the April 15 deadline, but it has no news value after this date. News about a cure for male baldness gets full attention from middle-aged bald-headed men at almost any time.

Symbols, Slogans, and Acronyms

The Red Cross (known as the Red Crescent in the Middle East) is the best-known humanitarian organization in the world. The name is totally unenlightening, but the symbol is recognized and associated with the care and help given by the organization. Flags are symbols. Smokey the Bear is a symbol. Even the Nike Swoosh is a familiar symbol around the world. You are not likely to produce a symbol that will become world famous, but if at all possible, you should try to find something graphic that symbolizes a given organization. This is called **branding**, and corporations often spend millions to establish a symbol that immediately means reliability and quality to a consumer.

Slogans can be highly persuasive. They state a key concept in a few memorable and easily pronounceable words. The American Revolution had the rallying cry of "No taxation without representation," and today's corporations are just as slogan conscious.

Thus, American Express tells us, "Don't leave home without it," Altoids uses "The curiously strong mints," and Hewlett-Packard now uses "invent" with its logo. If you can coin a slogan that expresses the basic idea of what you are trying to promote, it will help you attain your objective.

Acronyms range from the effective to the ridiculous. Coined from the initial letters of the name of some organization or cause, an acronym can be highly useful in some cases. A good acronym is NOW, for the National Organization for Women. It is pronounceable and memorable, and it makes a succinct political point. These women are striving for equality, and they want it "NOW." Another good reason for using acronyms is to shorten a lengthy name. AIDS is much easier to comprehend and write about than "acquired immune deficiency syndrome."

Semantics

The dictionary definition of words may be clear and concise, but there is another dimension to words—the connotative meaning to various individuals and groups of people. The study of meaning given to words and the changes that occur in these meanings as time goes on is the branch of linguistics called **semantics**.

For example, consider the evolution of the word "gay" in American society. The word is traditionally defined as merry, joyous, and lively. Thus, in the nineteenth century, we had the "Gay Nineties" and people often referred to bright colors or sprightly music as "gay." By the 1920s and 1930s, however, "gay" started being applied as a code word for prostitutes who were said to be in the "gay life." From there, it was just a short step for the word to be applied to the "underground" world of homosexuals.

By the same token, the terms "pro-life" and "pro-choice" have very definite connotations to certain groups of people. "Affirmative action" means opportunity to some and exclusion to others. The controversy over politically correct language was cited in Chapter 1. Even the expression "politically correct" has different connotations to different groups of people. To some, it is derogatory, an attempt by radical groups to censor freedom of expression. To others, the concept stands for equality and an effort to eliminate sexism and racism.

To write persuasively and to influence target audiences, you must be sensitive to semantics. The protracted argument between the Republicans and the Democrats over Medicare funding is a good example. The Republicans say they want to "preserve, protect, and strengthen" the program, while the Democrats, and much of the press, portray the Republican plan as meaning major "cuts" in funding. The issue is again a matter of framing.

Professional Tips

Why Marketing Materials Fail to Persuade

Many product news releases and marketing brochures are not very persuasive because some key components are missing. Dianna Huff, a business-to-business marketing writing specialist, gives 10 reasons why marketing materials often remain unread:

Emphasis on the company instead of the customer

It's all right to tell customers about your company and its great manufacturing facility, but it's important to tell customers how it benefits them. Do they get a better product or service? Lower prices? Faster turnaround?

All features, no benefits

Don't let engineers write your copy. Focus instead on how your product or service will benefit your customers.

Copy that fails to say, "What's in it for me?"

Stay away from generalities. Be specific about how the product or service will help the consumer save money, do things easier, or enhance his or her quality of life.

Too much jargon

Make sure phrases and sentences are not corporate or engineering lingo. Translate concepts to basic English.

Redundancies

Are you using the same words or phrases in several places? Edit them out or use other words.

No call to action

The number one rule in promotional writing is to tell potential customers what you want them to do. Pick up the phone? Visit the Web site? Visit a store? Buy the product?

Copy not addressed to target audience

Try to picture a person that represents your audience and write directly to him or her.

Failure to nail down messaging

Don't use vague, meaningless phrases about the product or service. Keep asking management about specific benefits, how the product differs from the competition, etc.

Poor grammar

Yes, people do notice.

Failure to edit or proofread

Ask others to also proofread copy. They will no doubt find typos you missed.

Source: Adapted from *PR Tactics*, April 2002, p. 13.

Suggestions for Action

Persuasive writing must give people information on how to take action, and the suggestions must be feasible.

A campaign by a utility provides a good example. If the company really wants people to conserve energy, it must provide them with information about how to do so. The suggestions may be as simple as turning the thermostat down to 68 degrees, wearing sweaters in the house during the winter months, or purchasing a roll of weather stripping to place around the windows and doors. All these suggestions are within the capability of the utility's customers.

However, if the suggestion is to insulate your house thoroughly, this may not be feasible for consumers with limited incomes. In this case, the utility may accompany the suggestion with a special program of interest-free loans or a discount coupon to make it easier for customers to take the recommended action. In this way, the suggestion becomes feasible to thousands of homeowners.

Environmental organizations, to use another example, make a point of providing information on how to write to your legislator. They provide not only the legislator's address and e-mail but also a sample letter that you can copy. Greenpeace simply mails its members postcards with preprinted messages. All you have to do is sign the postcard and affix a stamp.

Content and Structure

People are motivated by theatrics and a good story. They are moved by bold action and human drama. Your message should go beyond cold facts or even eloquent phrases. If you can vividly describe what you are talking about—if you can paint word pictures—your message will be more persuasive.

A number of techniques can make a message more persuasive; many of them have already been discussed. Here is a summary of some additional writing devices.

Drama Everyone likes a good story. This is often accomplished by graphically illustrating an event or a situation. Newspapers often dramatize a story to boost reader interest. Thus we read about the daily life of someone with AIDS, the family on welfare who is suffering because of state cuts in spending, or the frustrations of a middle manager who is unemployed for the first time in her career. In the newsroom, this is called *humanizing an issue*.

Dramatizing is also used in public relations. Relief organizations, in particular, attempt to galvanize public concern to attract donations. The idea is to personalize suffering and tragedy. Saying that 3 million Africans are starving isn't as persuasive as describing a young mother in Ethiopia sobbing over the lifeless form of her skeletal baby. Readers and viewers can identify with the mother's loss, which graphically illustrates the need for aid. Large numbers alone are cold and impersonal and generate little or no emotional involvement.

A more mundane use of dramatizing is the application story, sent to the trade press. This is sometimes called the *case study technique,* in which a manufacturer prepares an article on how an individual or a company is using the product. Honeywell Corporation, for example, provides a number of application stories about how offices and businesses have saved money by installing Honeywell temperature-control systems. More examples of the application story are found in Chapter 6.

Statistics For some reason, people are awed by statistics. The use of numbers, which appear so precise, seems to convey objectivity, largeness, and importance in a credible way.

Professional Tips

A Persuasion Sampler

A number of research studies have contributed to our understanding of the persuasion process. Here are some basic ideas:

- Positive appeals are generally more effective than negative appeals, in terms of both retention of the message and actual compliance with it.

- Messages presented on radio and television tend to be more persuasive than those seen in print. If the message is complex, however, better comprehension is achieved through print media.

- The print media are more appropriate for conveying detailed, lengthy information; broadcast channels are best for presenting brief, simple ideas. Television and radio messages tend to be consumed passively, whereas the print media allow for review and contemplation.

- Strong emotional appeals and the arousal of fear are most effective when the audience has some minimal concern about or interest in the topic.

- Highly fear-arousing appeals are effective only when some immediate action can be taken to eliminate the threat.

- With highly educated, sophisticated audiences, logical appeals, using facts and figures, work better than strong emotional appeals.

- Like self-interest, altruistic need can be a strong motivator. Men are more willing to get physical checkups for the sake of their families than for themselves.

- A celebrity or an attractive model is most effective when the audience has low involvement, the theme is simple, and broadcast channels are used. An exciting spokesperson attracts attention to a message that would otherwise be ignored.

Source: Adapted from Ronald E. Rice and William J. Paisley, eds., *Public Communication Campaigns* (Thousand Oaks, CA: Sage, 2001).

Toyota, seeking to portray itself as an important contributor to the American economy, placed ads in major metropolitan dailies that used impressive numbers. One ad stated, "Over the last five years Toyota in America has purchased $20 billion in parts and materials from 510 U.S. suppliers. Today, more than half the Toyota vehicles sold in America are built at our plants in Kentucky and California."

Numbers can be effective, but a writer should use them sparingly. A news release crammed with statistics tends to overwhelm the reader. In addition, numbers are somewhat impersonal and don't pack much emotional punch. Consequently, efforts are often made to dramatize the statistic in a way that paints a more vivid picture for readers and viewers.

Gun control advocates, for example, say that 13 children are killed daily by guns in the United States—the equivalent of 365 Columbine High School killings each year. Anti-smoking advocates compare the number of deaths each day attributed to smoking as the equivalent of two loaded 747s crashing every day. On a less horrific note, Kimberly-Clark, the market leader in the sales of toilet paper, said it sold 4.5 billion rolls one year—enough to stretch from the earth to the sun. One can also dramatize statistical percentages by putting them in terms that people can readily understand. For example, one MIT professor was quoted as saying, "You can take a flight every day for 21,000 years before you would be statistically likely to be in a fatal accident."

Surveys and Polls   The public and the media express a great deal of interest in what might be called popularity ratings. During a presidential election campaign, various polls and surveys about who is ahead and why seem to dominate coverage. People are also interested in what product ranks number one in cost or satisfaction or what airline is first in service or leg room.

Polls and surveys, which also use numbers, are related to the persuasion technique called the *bandwagon*. The idea is to show overwhelming support for your idea or product by saying that "four out of five doctors recommend . . ." or that "65 percent of the voters support. . . ." Consequently, everyone should get on the "bandwagon."

Various organizations also use less earth-shaking polls and surveys as a way of getting media publicity and brand recognition. A mattress company once did a poll on how many people slept in the nude. And a music label did a survey on how many CDs college students buy each month. The possibilities are endless, and the use of surveys as publicity opportunities is elaborated upon in Chapter 4.

Examples   A general statement becomes more persuasive when a specific example can clarify and reinforce the core information. A utility company, when announcing a 5 percent rate increase, often clarifies what this means by giving the example that the average consumer will pay about $5 more per month for electricity. The railroad industry, competing with the trucking industry, made the general statement that moving freight by train is three times more fuel-efficient than using trucks. It followed up this statement by giving the example that "the average train can move a ton of freight nearly 400 miles on each gallon of diesel fuel used."

As you read this text, you will notice that the term, "for example," is a frequent phrase. The purpose, of course, is to help you better understand the basic concept and how it is applied to actual situations.

Testimonials   The testimonial is a form of source credibility that can be either explicit or implied. The American Cancer Society has used a woman in her 50s who is dying of lung cancer as explicit testimony about the dangers of smoking. A good example of an implied testimonial is *The Washington Post*'s report that President Clinton's favorite burger was a soy-bean-based veggie product made by Boca Burger Company. Sales of the product immediately boomed. Testimonials are usually given by people or organizations not formally connected with the product, service, or cause.

Endorsements   The endorsement is a variant of the testimonial. Endorsements may be made by individuals, organizations, or media outlets. Star athletes make millions endorsing everything from footwear to soft drinks. Organizations such as the American Dental Association endorse toothpaste brands, and daily newspapers regularly endorse political candidates and community causes.

Emotional Appeals   Persuasive messages often play on our emotions. Fund-raising letters from nonprofit groups often use this writing device, as, for example, the letter from UNICEF in Figure 2.3. The Sierra Club, an organization dedicated to protecting the environment, started one direct-mail letter with the following message printed in boldface type:

> This past July 31, Sierra Club member and volunteer activist Becky Horton of Missouri—in a few terror-filled hours—became a statistic.

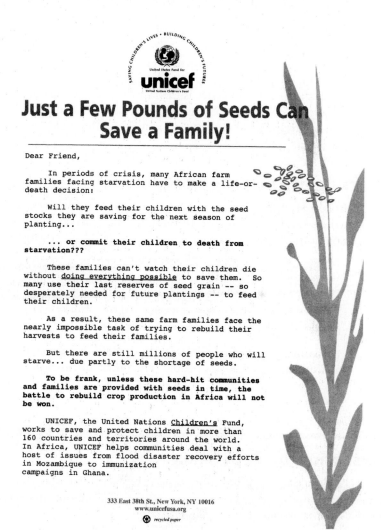

Figure 2.3 Persuasive Techniques
Emotional appeals, combined with statistics and bold type, makes a persuasive message. This four-page letter, which also used two photos, was penned by Hugh Downs, a television personality with high source credibility. A suggestion for action—Please Respond Today—is provided at the end of the letter. *(Courtesy of UNICEF, New York.)*

That day, four hate-driven anti-environmentalists lured her to a remote river access site in order to assault her. They beat her black-and-blue with sticks, then bound her with duct tape to the seat belts of her van. They stuffed and taped a Sierra Club anti-mining brochure in her mouth, taped an anti-environment video to her arm, and smashed the windshield of her van. As they left, they warned her: "Don't bother reporting it to the sheriff . . . he's on our side."

Emotional appeals can do much to galvanize public opinion, but they can also backfire. If the appeal is too strong or shocking, it tends to raise people's ego defenses, and they tune out the unpleasant message. Sometimes the emotional appeal is designed to make people feel guilty. This kind of approach, research studies suggest, is not very effective.

Fear arousal is another form of emotional appeal. An example is "What would happen if your child were thrown through the windshield in an accident?" What makes the question effective is the fact that the message goes on to suggest that a baby, for safety, should be placed in a car seat. Moderate fear arousal, accompanied by a relatively simple suggestion for avoiding the situation, is considered an effective persuasive technique.

THE ETHICS OF PERSUASION

Robert Heath, co-author of *Rhetorical and Critical Approaches of Public Relations,* writes, "A theme that runs throughout the practice and criticism of public relations is its ability to influence what people think and how they act." He continues:

> Even when practitioners' efforts fail to establish their point of view or to foster the interests of their sponsors and influence stakeholders, their comments become part of the fabric of thought and over time add to societal beliefs and actions. Practitioners create opinions, reinforce them, or draw on them to advocate new opinions and actions.

To many observers, persuasion is a somewhat unsavory activity that distorts the truth and manipulates people. The public distrusts professional "persuaders,"

Professional Tips

Persuasion by Repetition

Amateur publicists often make the mistake of failing to reinforce messages. They simply put up one poster or send one news release and call it a day. Remember that repeating the message in various forms is essential for the following reasons:

- Not all members of your audience use the same media channels to get their information.
- Repetition of the message, in various forms, reminds the audience about an idea or product.
- Repetition helps break down earlier resistance to the message.
- Repetition helps overcome competing messages and distractions.

and the media often refer to public relations people and political consultants as **spin doctors**. Yet persuasion is an integral part of society. Everyone uses words and visual symbols to share and evaluate information, shape beliefs, and convince others to do or think things. The ancient Greeks recognized rhetoric, the "science of persuasion," as worthy of study and an essential part of public discourse.

In sum, persuasion is not a nasty concept. It does not have to be manipulative, propagandistic, or full of half-truths. Thomas Collins, manager of public affairs for Mobil Oil Company, sounded this theme when he addressed the annual meeting of the Public Relations Association of Indonesia. He said:

> PR counselors must ensure the messages we create, package, and target are efficient and cost-effective, but they must also be believable. This requires that the images we engineer reflect the reality of our clients' existence. We reject deliberate fabrication because bogus images pollute the public mind and do not serve the public interest, and ultimately undermine the trust we seek. . . . The essential ingredient underlying any successful relationship is trust.

A large measure of public trust, which Collins just described, comes from telling the truth and distributing accurate information. A core value of the Arthur

Professional Tips

An Ethics Test for Public Relations Writers

Persuasive efforts require an ethical framework for decision making. Professors Sherry Baker (Brigham Young University) and David Martinson (Florida International University) have developed a model they call the TARES test. Public relations writers should test their persuasive communication against five basic moral principles:

Truthfulness: Are you just telling the literal truth and not the whole story? "Truthfulness (material and substantial completeness) is essential to ethical persuasion."

Authenticity: Are you intentionally deceiving or manipulating others for the practitioner's or client' self-interest? "A good test for authenticity is whether the practitioner is willing to openly, publicly, and personally be identified as the persuader in a particular circumstance."

Respect: Are you giving respect to your audience as persons of dignity and intelligence? "Respect for others includes facilitating their ability to be informed and to make good choices."

Equity: Are you taking advantage of the public's lack of knowledge or information about a topic, a product, or an idea? "The equity/fairness principle requires, for example, that practitioners avoid fashioning persuasive messages in such a manner as to play upon the vulnerabilities of a particular audience."

Social responsibility: Are your persuasive efforts serving the broader public interest? "Ethically proactive practitioners find ways to make positive contributions to the common good as an integral part of achieving their basic professional objectives."

Source: Baker, Sherry, and Martinson, David L. "Out of the Red-Light District: Five Principles for Ethically Proactive Public Relations." *Public Relations Quarterly*, Fall 2002, pp. 15–18.

W. Page Society, a group of senior communication executives, is to tell the truth by providing "an accurate picture of the company's character, ideals and practice."

The IPRA also has a core tenet in its charter that states, "Each member shall refrain from subordinating the truth to other requirements." And the PRSA states, in part, "We adhere to the highest standards of accuracy and truth in advancing the interests of those we represent and in communicating with the public."

On a more practical note, *PRWeek* writer Anita Chabria simply says, "Do make sure your statements are accurate. The press will pick up on even innocent mistakes as potential lies."

Thus, it can be seen that public relations writers are, by definition, advocates in the marketplace of public opinion. It is their professional and personal responsibility, however, to be persuasive using techniques that are forthright, truthful, and socially acceptable. Professor Richard L. Johannesen of Northern Illinois University lists the following persuasive techniques that should be avoided in persuasive writing:

- Do not use false, fabricated, misrepresented, distorted, or irrelevant evidence to support arguments or claims.
- Do not intentionally use specious, unsupported, or illogical reasoning.
- Do not represent yourself as informed or as an "expert" on a subject when you are not.
- Do not use irrelevant appeals to divert attention or scrutiny from the issue at hand. Among the appeals that commonly serve such a purpose are "smear" attacks on an opponent's character, appeals to hatred and bigotry, innuendo, and "God" or "devil" terms that cause intense but unreflective positive or negative reactions.
- Do not ask your audience to link your idea or proposal to emotion-laden values, motives, or goals to which it is not actually related.
- Do not deceive your audience by concealing your real purpose, your self-interest, the group you represent, or your position as an advocate of a viewpoint.
- Do not distort, hide, or misrepresent the number, scope, intensity, or undesirable features of consequences.
- Do not use emotional appeals that lack a supporting basis of evidence or reasoning and would therefore not be accepted if the audience had time and opportunity to examine the subject itself.
- Do not oversimplify complex situations into simplistic, two-valued, either/or, polar views or choices.
- Do not pretend certainty when tentativeness and degrees of probability would be more accurate.
- Do not advocate something in which you do not believe yourself.

It is also clear that as a writer of persuasive messages, the public relations writer is more than a technician or a "hired gun." Responsibility to client or employer should never override responsibility to the profession and the public interest. This is discussed further in Chapter 3.

However, writers often lack the technical and legal expertise to know whether information provided to them is accurate. Heath explains, "In this regard, they are uneasy partners in the public relations process. They are often given information regarding managerial or operating decisions or practices that they are expected to report as though it were true and just."

This does not excuse writers from ethical responsibility. Heath continues:

> The problem of reporting information that they cannot personally verify does not excuse them from being responsible communicators. Their responsibility is to demand that the most accurate information be provided and the evaluation be the best available.

SUMMARY

- Public opinion is the sum of individual opinions on a subject of importance to those individuals. The purpose of persuasive communication is to sway the opinions of individuals or to motivate them to a specific action.
- Opinions are expressions of attitudes. Individuals get their attitudes from a variety of social, economic, cultural, educational, religious, and political sources and experiences.
- The audience's self-interest is the basis for persuasion. Self-interest includes economic, social, and psychological needs.
- The basic communication model has four elements—sender, message, channel (medium), and receiver.
- Opinion leaders are important in the communication process. They pass on information to their followers and influence the acceptance or rejection of a message.
- People adopt new ideas in a five-stage diffusion process—awareness, interest, trial, evaluation, and adoption.
- Mass and directed media messages are most influential in the awareness and interest stages of the adoption process. Opinion leaders and peers are influential in the later stages.
- People are often galvanized to form opinions and take action after a "triggering event" has called their attention to an idea or a concept.
- According to Abraham Maslow, people have a hierarchy of needs—physiological, safety, social, ego, and self-fulfillment needs.
- A communicator recognizes that there are two kinds of audiences—passive and active (information seeking)—and plans messages and communication channels accordingly.
- Public relations writers, as part of message design, use the technique of framing—selecting certain facts, situations, and context—that are then disseminated by the media.

- The tactics of persuasion are based on psychology. It is vital to understand why your audience thinks as it does and how and when to present your ideas.

- The tactics of persuasive writing include concepts of audience analysis, source credibility, appeal to self-interest, clarity of message, timing and context, use of symbols and slogans, semantics, suggestions for action, and content and structure—including drama, emotional appeal and the use of examples.

- Persuasion should not be manipulative and propagandistic; it should be based on truthful information and the presentation of ideas in the marketplace of public discussion.

ADDITIONAL RESOURCES

Baker, Sherry, and Martinson, David L. "Out of the Red-Light District: Five Principles for Ethically Proactive Public Relations." *Public Relations Quarterly*, Fall 2002, pp. 15–18.

Blumenstein, Rebecca, and Rose, Matthew. "Name That Op: How U.S. Coins Phrases of War." *The Wall Street Journal*, March 24, 2003, pp. B1, B3.

Edgett, Ruth. "Toward an Ethical Framework for Advocacy in Public Relations." *Journal of Public Relations Research*, Vol. 14, No. 1, 2002, pp. 1–26.

Gass, Robert H., and Seiter, John S. *Persuasion, Social Influence, and Compliance Gaining.* Boston: Allyn & Bacon, 2003.

Geary, David L. "The Readability Challenge in Public Relations." *Public Relations Quarterly*, Winter 2001, pp. 37–39.

Huff, Dianna. "Ten Reasons Marketing Materials Remain Unread." *PR Tactics*, April 2002, p. 13.

Lewis, Tanya. "Wary Resignation: When to Quit an Account." *PRWeek*, August 25, 2003, p. 16.

O'Quinn, Ken. "The Art of Writing Well." *PR Tactics*, April 2002, p. 10.

Severin, Werner, and Tankard, James. *Communication Theories: Origin, Methods, Uses,* 5th edition. Boston: Allyn & Bacon, 2001.

Simons, Herbert W. *Persuasion in Society.* Thousand Oaks, CA: Sage, 2001.

St. John, Burton III. "Whither PR Writing? Skills Show Decline, Some Say." *PR Tactics*, April 2002, pp. 1, 22.

Chapter 3

Legal and
Ethical Guidelines

A writer, once he or she has mastered the basics of persuasive writing, also has the responsibility to work within the law and adhere to high professional standards. This chapter establishes that framework, and it appears early in the text for good reasons.

First, you must understand basic legal concepts that provide a framework for all your writing. Ignorance of the law can lead to costly litigation for you and your employer. Second, you cannot produce and distribute publicity materials that are believable unless you have a strong ethical sense of right and wrong. Employers may come and go, but your reputation and credibility become part of you.

EXAMPLES OF LEGAL PROBLEMS

As a public relations writer, you represent the management voice of your organization. What you release is interpreted as the voice of management. Nevertheless, you can be held personally liable for any statements that cause defamation or violate the guidelines of state or federal regulatory agencies. Actions are ordinarily brought against the top officials of an organization, but remember that you can be named as a co-defendant.

To protect yourself, you should be sure that the facts you are given are accurate. It is no excuse to say, "The boss told me that this was so." In court, you must be able to prove that you made a reasonable effort to verify information.

Among the actions for which you might be liable are the following:

- Disseminating information that a court or regulatory agency finds misleading, untrue, or damaging
- Participating in an illegal action
- Counseling or guiding policy to accomplish an illegal action
- Engaging in political lobbying without identifying the source of funds and the special interests involved.

To emphasize the importance of how the law can affect your work, here is a sampling of legal problems that involved public relations and advertising activities of various organizations.

- A Kentucky couple filed a complaint against Merrill Lynch for $240,000 for invasion of privacy, claiming that they were in the background of a photograph used in an advertisement.
- The Federal Trade Commission filed charges against three national diet firms after they failed to provide factual evidence that clients actually achieved weight loss goals or maintained the loss.
- The United Way of America was sued by an 81-year-old man featured on a campaign poster who charged that the picture had been used without his permission.
- A 67-year-old Chicago man sued for invasion of privacy after he appeared in a video news release for a cholesterol-lowering drug because the video producers did not tell him the actual purpose of the taping.
- Mothers Against Drunk Driving (MADD) filed a trademark-infringement suit against a recently formed organization named Dads and Mad Moms Against Drug Dealers (DAMMADD). The lawsuit alleged that the other name was too similar to MADD and would confuse the public. MADD, as an acronym, carries 97 percent name recognition.
- Clothing retailer Abercrombie & Fitch became the target of protests and lawsuits by Asian groups for selling and distributing a T-shirt containing two stereotypical Chinese "coolies" with the caption "Wong Brothers Laundry Service: Two Wongs Can Make It White."
- An executive of Ogilvy Public Relations Worldwide signed a consent decree with the Securities and Exchange Commission (SEC) after he was charged

with insider trading. The SEC complaint claimed the executive's father made $27,000 in illegal profits on stock purchased one day before a news release was issued.

- Enron Corporation and its major executives faced criminal charges for inflating company earnings and financial projections through various communication channels, including news releases.

- A consumer activist sued Nike Corporation for allegedly making false claims about its manufacturing processes and alleged use of "sweatshop labor." The lawsuit, which cost Nike considerable legal expense, centered on whether its advertising and publicity constituted "free speech" or "commercial speech." The case went all the way to the U.S. Supreme Court.

- The Princeton Dental Resource Center paid a $25,000 settlement after the New York attorney general's office charged the organization with making false and misleading claims in its newsletter.

LIBEL AND SLANDER

According to the *AP Stylebook*, "Libel is injury to reputation. Words, pictures or cartoons that expose a person to public hatred, shame, disgrace or ridicule, or induces an ill opinion of a person are libelous." If the statement is broadcast, it may constitute either **libel** or **slander**. If it is made to a third person but neither printed nor broadcast, it may be slander.

Juries award libel damages to the extent that the following four points can be proved by the injured party: (1) the statement was published to others by print or broadcast; (2) the plaintiff was identified or is identifiable; (3) there was actual injury in the form of money losses, impairment of reputation, humiliation, or mental anguish and suffering; and (4) the publisher of the statement was malicious or negligent.

With public figures—people in government, politics, and entertainment—the test is whether the publisher of the statement knew that it was false or had a reckless disregard for its truth. The question of who is a public figure cannot be answered arbitrarily, and the courts are inconsistent on this. It often depends on the context. With private figures—such as corporate executives and even average citizens—the test is whether the publisher of the statement was negligent in checking the truth of the statement. In quoting someone, for instance, be sure you state exactly what was said.

These few highlights only hint at the ramifications of libel law. For your protection and for the protection of your organization, you need to dig deeper into this subject. A good source, and one for your reference shelf, is *The Law of Public Communication* by Kent Middleton, William E. Lee, and Bill F. Chamberlin (Allyn & Bacon, 2003). It includes chapters on libel, privacy, intellectual property, corporate speech, and advertising that are particularly relevant to public relations.

In thinking of libel, you should not confine your precautions to what is printed or broadcast in the mass media. An item in an organization's newsletter or a widely distributed e-mail saying that "Jack was feeling no pain" at the office party could be construed as libel. An unflattering picture of a disheveled employee walking out the door could also be libelous.

Remember that you needn't use a name to commit libel. A recognizable description serves the same purpose. If the subject remains unnamed but the public knows who is being talked about, there may be grounds for a libel case.

In recent years, several lawsuits have been filed because of news releases. In one case, a man sued his former employer after a news release announced that he had been let go after having been investigated for accepting kickbacks from suppliers. In another case, a medical center was sued by another medical facility for implying in a news release that the number of patient deaths at the competing medical center was the highest in the region.

The Fair Comment Defense

These examples provide a warning of what can happen, but this does not mean that an organization has to avoid statements of opinion in public relations materials. Truth is the traditional defense against libel charges, but opinions also have a degree of legal protection under the First Amendment to the U.S. Constitution, which protects the freedom of speech. The legal concept is known as **fair comment privilege**.

In one case, the owner of the New York Yankees was sued for libel by an umpire when a news release from the team called him a "scab" who "had it in" for the Yankees and "misjudged" plays. A lower court awarded the umpire libel damages, but a higher court overturned the judgment by ruling that the comments in the news release constituted protected statements of opinion. A judge also found the Genesis One Computer Corporation innocent of libel when it characterized another firm's breach of contract as a "device" to avoid payment of commissions due Genesis.

If you ever have occasion to write a news release that makes critical comments about another individual or organization, you could use the fair comment defense. However, take several precautionary measures. Experts suggest that (1) opinion statements be accompanied by the facts on which the opinions are based; (2) opinion statements be clearly labeled as such; and (3) the context of the language surrounding the expressions of opinion be reviewed for possible libel implications.

A poor choice of words can literally cost a company millions of dollars. ABC-TV said in a news story that Philip Morris "spiked" cigarettes with nicotine. The unfortunate use of that term resulted in ABC-TV making a public apology and agreeing to pay $15 million to Philip Morris for its legal expenses in bringing the libel suit.

INVASION OF PRIVACY

In recent years, there has been increased sensitivity to invasion of privacy. Laws have been passed and lawsuits have been filed in an effort to protect the privacy of individuals. In general, laws and lawsuits strive to prevent anyone from knowing anything about an individual that the individual does not want known.

Protection of employee privacy can create problems. People are interested in people, and most people are willing to have favorable things said about them. The trick is to include the good things and avoid the others. If John Doe is promoted to a new job, he will be pleased if others know about it. He may be willing to reveal considerable personal detail about himself to help you write an engaging story.

If Doe has two children, he may approve mention of that fact. If one of them has severe handicaps, he may not want that published. If he is married, he may be willing to have that known. If he is in the middle of a divorce, he is likely to prefer no mention.

You can obtain information to flesh out a story by asking questions of each person involved. Elicit facts that are interesting and favorable. After the story is written, show it to the person mentioned. If he or she objects to anything, take it out. Once the material has been approved, get the subject to sign it. A simple "OK—John Doe" on the story will suffice.

There may be times when a reporter will ask you for information about an employee. In general, most companies have adopted a policy of merely confirming that a person is employed and in what position. You can also tell a reporter the date on which the employee first joined the firm.

Under no circumstances should you release an employee's home address, marital status, or number of children, nor should you reveal any aspect of a job performance record. If the reporter wants to know such things, the best approach is to have the reporter contact the employee directly. In this way, the employee knows that an inquiry has been made and can determine what information is to be divulged. It also lets you and the company off the hook in terms of protecting the employee's privacy.

Another way for a company to protect itself against employee invasion-of-privacy suits is to have a standard biographical form completed by the employee. At the top of this form should be a clear-cut statement that the information provided may be used in company publicity and employee newsletters. Such forms, however, should be updated on an annual basis. Old information can be embarrassing and even libelous.

RELEASES FOR ADVERTISING AND PROMOTION

Using names and photos of people in advertising, product publicity, and promotions requires special handling and extra legal attention. These situations are not the same as the **implied consent** that is given when someone poses for a news story in the organization's employee magazine or newsletter.

The courts have consistently ruled that a person's right to privacy is violated when photos or names of individuals are published for commercial purposes or purposes of trade without prior *written* consent. Chemical Bank of New York, for example, used pictures of employees in advertisements without their written permission and was promptly sued for $600,000 in damages for invasion of privacy and "misappropriation of personality."

This situation reinforces the point that everyone whose picture, quote, or name is used in an advertisement or a sales brochure must give explicit written

companies often notified brokerage firms and financial analysts about financial information before informing the general public. The SEC said that this practice fostered an uneven playing field for the buying and selling of stocks.

Under Reg FD, companies are now required to distribute relevant financial information to the public and investors and analysts at the same time. Paul Cordasco, writing in *PRWeek*, explains: "The rule requires a public company to release any information about its business in a manner that allows the general public access to the information at the same time as large institutional investors and analysts."

Under Reg FD, the SEC recommends disclosure to a variety of publics within 24 hours. The Internet and Webcasts, as well as conference calls, can supplement general dissemination through mailed or e-mailed news releases. Cynthia Clark, writing in *The Strategist*, elaborates: "if material information is disclosed intentionally on a conference call, or even in a speech, then the company is required to disclose that information simultaneously with a statement, either through a press release or an SEC filing."

Companies that violate Reg FD run the risk of heavy penalties. In 2002, Siebel Systems paid a $250,000 fine because executives provided bullish future projections at a private brokerage conference for a select group of investors. Schering-Plough, in 2003, was fined $1 million by the SEC for disclosing "negative and material nonpublic information regarding the company's earnings to analysts and portfolio managers."

Professional Tips

Guidelines for Working in Investor Relations

The National Investor Relations Institute (NIRI), an organization of public relations professionals specializing in distributing financial information, has beefed up its ethics code in the wake of financial scandals involving such companies as Enron, World-Com, and Tyco. Investor relations (IR) professionals should:

- Maintain the highest legal and ethical standards
- Avoid even the appearance of professional impropriety
- Ensure full and fair disclosure
- Provide fair access to corporate information
- Serve the interests of shareholders
- Keep track of company affairs and all IR laws and regulations
- Keep confidential information confidential
- Do not use confidential information for personal advantage
- Exercise independent professional judgment
- Avoid relationships that might affect ethical standing
- Report fraudulent or illegal acts within the company
- Represent oneself in a reputable and dignified manner

In general, a company whose stock is publicly traded must immediately publicly disclose the following kinds of "material" news:

- Dividends or their deletion
- Annual or quarterly earnings
- Preliminary but audited interim earnings
- Stock splits
- Mergers
- Changes in top management
- Major product developments
- Major expansion plans
- Change of business purposes
- Defaults
- Dispositions of major assets
- Proxy materials
- Purchases of its own stock

In financial information, accuracy is imperative. Public relations firms have been held responsible for releasing false and misleading information even though they were told by their clients that the facts supplied were correct. The SEC has ruled that anyone preparing or releasing financial news is responsible for making a reasonable effort to ascertain that the information is accurate. You don't have to be an accountant, but you should know how to read a balance sheet and determine whether the information presented is logical and reasonable.

The SEC also expects the information to be easily understandable by the average investor. A company's prospectus for a new stock offering, in particular, must be in plain English rather than the traditional legal jargon. The SEC's booklet on "plain English" even gives helpful writing hints, such as (1) make sentences short, (2) use "we" and "you," and (3) write with active verbs. More information about SEC guidelines can be found at www.sec.gov/consumer/plaine.htm.

Often a company is tempted to report only the good news and bury the bad news. Although this sounds like a good idea to executives interested in the image of the corporation, it is a dangerous practice when it comes to financial news.

Increasingly, courts are applying the "mosaic doctrine" to financial information. Professor Maureen Rubin of California State University, who is also an attorney, explains the concept:

> Under this doctrine, a court may examine *all* information released by a company, including press releases, to determine whether taken as a whole, they combine to create an "overall misleading impression," whether by omission of material information or by inclusion of false information.

Thus a company and its public relations firm may be held liable even if each individual release or other statement is literally true when examined separately.

In other words, companies should avoid the temptation to paint a rosy picture of financial stability if in fact there are problems that stockholders and potential investors need to know in order to make an informed judgment. For example, a company should not announce a new product that is still in the research stage and that will not be available to the public for another year, if at all.

Writers of financial news releases should also be aware of the fact that they have information that is not yet available to the public. If they use this advantage to buy or sell stock in the company in question, they are violating SEC rules on insider trading.

Federal Trade Commission

The Federal Trade Commission (FTC) deals with "unfair methods of competition in commerce, and unfair acts and practices," all of which are illegal. Both advertising and publicity are subject to FTC scrutiny. Also, false advertising and false publicity may be the subject of lawsuits from individuals who may claim injury or deception.

Any product information you release to the public is subject to FTC scrutiny. At first you may think mainly of news releases and advertising, but you should also include letters, booklets, leaflets, brochures, pictures, drawings, audiovisual materials, speeches, and any other type of communication that can reach the public.

Among the areas where deception can occur are these:

- Unsubstantiated claims—statements that you cannot prove
- Ambiguous claims—statements that are confusing
- Fraudulent testimonials—statements that were never actually made
- Puffery and exaggeration—stretching the truth
- Deceptive pricing—concealment of true cost
- Deceptive demonstrations—apparent proof that is not really proof
- Deceptive surveys—for example, "independent" surveys that you have paid for
- Unsound surveys—surveys that are not statistically valid
- Fraudulent contests—contests that were rigged in some way
- Deceptive illustrations—pictures that convey a false impression
- Nonexistent authority—for example, "Doctors recommend . . ."
- Nonexistent surveys—interpretation of a few comments as surveys
- Unfair or misleading comparisons—inaccurate portrayals of superiority over other products

Somewhat related to fraudulent testimonials is the problem of puffery and exaggeration. The film industry, for example, is notorious for taking reviewer's comments out of context. One film critic, for example, reviewed *Foul Play* starring Chevy Chase and Goldie Hawn and was surprised to find himself quoted in newspaper ads describing the film as "good fun." But his intent was different. He told

The New York Times, "I had written that though it was all intended as good fun, it's about as much fun as getting hit by a bus."

Sony Pictures, in 2001, was even found to have concocted quotes from a fictitious movie critic for four of its movies, and Twentieth Century Fox has admitted that they hired actors or paid employees to appear in "man in the street" commercials posing as movie goers. The FTC has guidelines on endorsements and testimonials and promised, due to consumer protest, to review them for stricter enforcement. In other words, be careful taking testimonials of "satisfied" customers or experts out of context.

The FTC interpretation of publicity is based on the "net impression received by the consumer," not just individual facts. Among the types of statements that have been found false or deceptive are these:

- That the product or service is original or the first in the field
- That it is approved by a government agency
- That the product is patented
- That it was developed in a research laboratory
- That the product contains nutritional substances
- That its life or effectiveness is not as claimed
- That a nonexistent or warped survey proved some point
- That the product is misbranded in some way

There are a number of "red-flag" words that the FTC looks for in product advertisements and news releases. They include: *authentic, certified, cure, custom-made, exclusive, famous, first-class, natural, reliable, safe, slightly used, unbreakable,* and *wrinkle-proof.* In recent years, the FTC has even set guidelines for the use of such words as *recyclable* and *biodegradable,* because *green* is a popular marketing buzzword.

Other Regulatory Agencies

Although the SEC and the FTC are the major federal agencies concerned with the content of advertising and publicity materials, you should also be aware of guidelines used by the **Food and Drug Administration** and the **Bureau of Alcohol, Tobacco and Firearms**.

The Food and Drug Administration (FDA) oversees the advertising and promotion of prescription drugs, over-the-counter medicines, and cosmetics. Under the Federal Food, Drug and Cosmetic Act, any person who "causes misbranding" or provides misleading or inaccurate information is liable.

Another policy, the Dietary Supplement Health and Education Act (DSHEA), states that manufacturers of dietary supplements can only claim effects on the "structure or function" of the body and not make claims to mitigate, treat, prevent, cure, or diagnose disease.

The FDA has specific guidelines for video, audio, and print news releases. First, the release must provide "fair balance" by telling consumers about the risks as well as the benefits of the medicine. Second, you must be clear about the limitations of a drug; it may not help people with certain conditions. Third, a news release should be accompanied by supplementary product sheets or brochures that give full prescribing information.

At times, drug companies try to sidestep such requirements by just publicizing the disease. The Glaxo Institute for Digestive Health, for example, distributes material about stomach pain, saying it could represent a serious medical problem. Of course, Glaxo also makes the ulcer drug Zantac.

Another approach, which has come under increased criticism and FDA scrutiny, is the placement of celebrities on television talk shows who are being paid by drug companies to mention the name of a particular drug or health product as they describe their recovery from cancer, a heart attack, or depression. Some programs, such as the *Today* show, have now banned such guests. There's also the published book; the author is a health professional, but the company's public relations staff has written most of the copy.

If you are writing publicity or advertising copy for a product containing alcohol, you should be aware of the laws and regulations under the Federal Alcohol Administration Act. One section prohibits "any statement that is false or untrue in any particular or that, irrespective of falsity, directly, or by ambiguity, omission, or inference, or by the addition of irrelevant, scientific, or technical matter tends to create a misleading impression."

Wineries, for example, have run into problems with the Bureau of Alcohol, Tobacco, and Firearms (BATF) by implying that there are health benefits associated with drinking wine. After intense lobbying by the $9 billion California wine industry, the BATF finally agreed to let wineries label bottles with such statements as "The proud people who made this wine encourage you to consult your family doctor about the health benefits of wine consumption." However, the agency still forbids Geyser Peak winery to use the slogan, "As age enhances wine, wine enhances age." Even if this statement could be proved, the BATF takes the attitude that such claims for alcoholic products should not be allowed.

In summary, a public relations firm and its writers have a responsibility to know all pertinent regulatory guidelines. A number of court cases have determined that you, as the writer, can be held liable for disseminating false and misleading information on behalf of a client. A good knowledge of state and federal laws, plus the guidelines of regulatory agencies, will not only keep you out of trouble but will also help your employer or client avoid costly legal battles.

COPYRIGHT LAW

The purpose of a **copyright** is to secure for the creator of original material all the benefits earned by creating it. Copyrights apply not only to written words but also to illustrations, plays, musical works, motion pictures, sound recordings, graphics, sculptures, pantomimes, and dances.

The Copyright Term Extension Act, passed in 1998 and reaffirmed by the U.S. Supreme Court in 2003, protects original material for the life of the creator plus 70 years for individual works and 95 years from publication for copyrights held by corporations. The previous copyright legislation protected authors for their lifetime plus 50 years. The impetus for a 20-year extension primarily came from the movie industry. Copyrights on the earliest version of Walt Disney's Mickey Mouse, for example, would have expired in 2003 if Congress had not passed the 1998 legislation. Material does not have to be printed or distributed to have copyright protection. As soon as it is created in a concrete form, it is protected, regardless of whether it bears a copyright notice. According to Brad Templeton, an editor of an online newsletter, "The default you should assume for other people's works is that they are copyrighted and may not be copied unless you know otherwise."

Many individuals and organizations continue, however, to put a copyright notice on materials such as brochures, handbooks, and articles. The correct form for a notice is: "Copyright (date) by (author/owner)."

News releases and other publicity materials distributed to the media, although they also have copyright protection, are usually intended for widespread use by journalists. Thus, few if any organizations get upset if all or part of a news release is quoted verbatim in a news story.

Fair Use and Infringement

As a public relations writer, you will also use information and materials from a variety of sources. Therefore, it is important for you to understand thoroughly the dividing line between fair use and copyright infringement.

Fair use of materials, in general, applies for purposes of criticism, comment, news reporting, teaching, scholarship, or research. If you are writing something and want to use a quotation from a copyrighted article or book, you may do so as long as you give proper attribution to the author and the source. In general, you can quote 400 words from a book and 50 words from an article.

If you quote a lengthy passage from an article or a book, however, it is best to obtain permission. Writers should also be careful about using whole paragraphs of copyrighted material with only a few words changed. If the content and structure of the sentences are virtually the same, this constitutes not only copyright infringement but also **plagiarism**, a form of theft and fraud (see Professional Tips on page 77).

Writers of company newsletters and magazines, using information primarily for news reporting purposes, are generally within the boundaries of the fair use concept. Writers who prepare materials that directly support the sales of a product or service (news releases, advertisements, promotional brochures), however, need to be more concerned about copyright infringement.

The use of a selected quotation from an outside source in a product news release or sales brochure, for example, should be cleared with the source. The reason is that you are profiting directly from using someone else's credibility to sell goods and services.

In addition, using selected quotes may distort the author's meaning. For example, a research report may give a new computer product an overall poor performance rating but also mention some good things about the product. To use only the favorable quote from the review in a news release or advertisement, you should clear the quote with the report's authors to avoid possible lawsuits.

Professional Tips

Guidelines for Using Copyrighted Materials

Public relations personnel can avoid costly lawsuits by observing the following guidelines:

- Ideas cannot be copyrighted, but tangible expression of those ideas is protected under copyright law.
- Practically everything, including public relations materials, is copyright protected even if the material includes no copyright notice.
- Fair use requires you to use copyrighted material sparingly: in general, no more than 400 words from a book or 50 words from an article.
- Whenever you are using copyrighted materials, it is necessary to give the source.
- Be careful about using the titles of movies, books, and songs as themes for public relations materials and programs.
- Copyrighted material intended to advance the sales and profits of an organization should not be used unless permission is obtained.
- Copyrighted material should not be taken out of context, particularly if such usage implies endorsement of the organization's products or services.
- Reprints of an article should be ordered from the publisher.
- Permission must be obtained from the copyright owner to use segments of popular songs (written verses or sound recordings).
- Permission is required to use segments of television programs or motion pictures.
- Photographers retain rights to negatives, and permission must be obtained to reprint photos for uses other than those originally agreed on.
- Photographs of celebrities, living or dead, cannot be used for promotion and publicity purposes without permission and payment of licensing fees.
- Permission is required to reprint cartoons and cartoon characters. Cartoons, like other artwork and illustrations, are copyrighted.
- Government documents are not copyrighted, but caution is necessary if the material is used in such a way as to imply endorsement of products or services.
- Private letters and e-mails, or excerpts from them, cannot be published or used in sales and publicity materials without the permission of the letter writer.

Titles of books and plays cannot be copyrighted, but the principle of unfair competition applies nevertheless. Lawyers say that a public relations staff should not copy anything if the intent is to capitalize on or take advantage of its current popularity. The key to a lawsuit is whether an organization is in some way obtaining commercial advantage by implying that a service or product has the endorsement of or is closely allied with the literary property. This is also a problem in using names and logos that closely resemble registered trademarks of well-known companies.

The use of cartoons, illustrations, and photographs from outside sources (either previously published or unpublished) always requires permission. Even if the

Professional Tips

Plagiarism vs. Copyright Infringement

There are some differences between copyright infringement and plagiarism. You may be guilty of copyright infringement even if you attribute the materials and give the source but don't get permission from the author or publisher.

In the case of plagiarism, there is no attempt to attribute the information at all. As the guide for Hamilton College says, "Plagiarism is a form of fraud. You plagiarize if you present other writer's words or ideas as your own." Maurice Isserman, writing in the *Chronicle of Higher Education,* further explains, "Plagiarism substitutes someone else's prowess as explanation for your own efforts."

Today's Internet world has increased the problems of plagiarism because it is quite easy for anyone, from students to college presidents, to cut and paste entire paragraphs (or even pages) into a term paper or speech and claim it is their own creation. Of course, one can also purchase complete term papers online, but that loophole is rapidly shrinking as more sophisticated software programs—such as www.turnitin.com—can now scan the entire Internet for other sources that have the same phrases used in a research paper.

John Barrie, founder of Turnitin.com, told *The Wall Street Journal* that "85 percent of the cases of plagiarism that we see are straight copies from the Internet—a student uses the Internet like a 1.5-billion-page cut-and-paste encyclopedia." Most universities have very strong rules about plagiarism, and it is not uncommon for students to receive an "F" in a course for plagiarism. In the business world, stealing someone else's words and expression of thought is called theft of intellectual property and results in lawsuits.

newspaper photographer takes a photo at your event, you have to get permission from the publication to reproduce it. Copyright infringement also extends to videotaping television documentaries or news programs if the intent is for widespread use of the material to internal or external audiences.

Another category that always requires copyright permission is musical material. The holders of musical copyrights do not permit use of *any* part of their compositions without prior written permission. Quoting even part of a lyric or playing only a few bars of a tune is forbidden. But also keep in mind that most classical music, especially that of the seventeenth and eighteenth centuries, is in the public domain and can be used without permission.

Article reprints also require written permission and, in most cases, the payment of fees. If your company or organization is profiled in a magazine or newspaper, for example, order reprints from the publisher. If you make your own copies for widespread distribution, you are violating the copyright of the publication. Magazines and newspapers, such as *The Wall Street Journal,* have special departments to handle reprint requests in the form of a printed reprint, a PDF, an e-mail, or a Web link. A sample format of a magazine reprint is shown in Figure 3.2.

Even the unauthorized photocopying of newsletters can cost an organization large sums of money. A U.S. district court ordered Labtest International, a New Jersey firm, to pay $111,000 to Washington Business Information, Inc., for re-

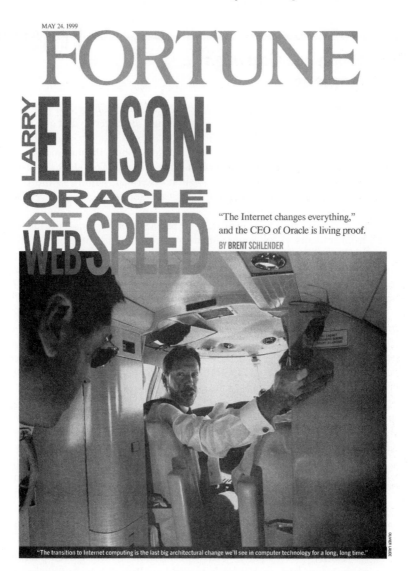

Figure 3.2 "Reprints"
Articles in publications are copyrighted, but organizations can receive "reprints" by paying a fee to the publisher. This article about Oracle's CEO is an example of how favorable publicity can be "recycled" to other audiences.
(Courtesy of Oracle Corporation and Fortune Magazine.)

producing copies of the company's weekly *Product Safety Letter.* Texaco, which was photocopying articles from scientific journals for its engineers, was also ordered by a court to pay damages.

Texaco, as well as Labtest International, could have avoided legal problems if it had paid a licensing fee to the Copyright Clearance Center (CCC). This office,

Professional Tips

Copyright on the Internet

The Internet and the World Wide Web have raised new issues about the protection of ideas and intellectual property. Three issues regarding copyright are (1) the downloading of copyrighted material, (2) the unauthorized uploading of such materials, and (3) how to protect the expression of ideas in cyberspace

The Downloading of Material

In general, the same rules apply to cyberspace as to more earthbound methods of expressing ideas. Original materials in digital form are still protected by copyright, even if they are freely posted. The fair-use limits for materials found on the Internet are essentially the same for materials disseminated by any other means. This includes individual postings on Usenet groups.

The Uploading of Material

In many cases, owners of copyrighted material have uploaded various kinds of information with the intention of making it freely available. This does not mean, however, that they have ceded ownership and put it in the public domain. The major problem arises when you start uploading copyrighted material into Usenet groups and posting it on your Web page. Posting an article from *The New York Times* for the reading pleasure of your friends, for example, is still a violation of copyright law unless you have permission. Sharing your music CDs via the Internet also violates the law.

Federal Legislation/Court Decisions

The U.S. Congress continues to debate legislation about how to best police copyright and trademark infringement on the Internet. One landmark decision by the U.S. Supreme Court (*New York Times v. Tasini*) ruled that although a publisher has a right to print an article submitted by a freelance writer, it does not have the right to post that article online or in a database without first obtaining specific permission from the author. Music labels and film studios are also actively policing the Internet to protect their products from being downloaded without permission or a fee being charged. Unauthorized downloading of material is considered copyright infringement and theft of intellectual property.

Source: Adapted from *Public Relations Strategies & Tactics,* 7th edition by Dennis L. Wilcox, Glen T. Cameron, Phillip H. Ault, and Warren K. Agee (Boston: Allyn & Bacon, 2003).

set up by publishers, licenses the photocopying of materials. The cost of a college course pack, a combination of photocopied articles and book chapters, usually includes a licensing fee levied by the CCC.

Not all publishers, however, are members of the CCC, so it is often necessary to contact a publisher directly for the right to distribute a photocopied article to students, a sales force, or employees.

U.S. government documents are in the public domain and can be used in whole or in part without permission. You could get into legal trouble, however, if a government report is used out of context to imply endorsement of a product.

The Rights of Freelancers

If you work full-time for an employer, your status is considered "work for hire." This means that the employer owns your work and the copyright.

Different rules apply, however, for freelancers and consultants who are hired to do a specific project such as a news release, brochure, newsletter, or even a photograph and computer graphics. Under current federal law, freelancers retain ownership of their work. This means that the original buyer has one-time use of the material and the freelancer can repackage the material and sell it to others.

The concept of one-time rights is important. Traditionally, employers used a particular piece of writing or a photograph in multiple ways without paying the creator any additional money. A picture, for example, might be on the cover of the corporate annual report, show up in the company newsletter, become part of the company calendar, and even be posted on the corporate Web site. According to the law, however, employers should pay the creator each time the material is used. This allows freelancers the opportunity to earn income from the repeated use of their created work.

If an employer wants unlimited rights to use the material, it is necessary to have this discussed and formalized in a letter or contractual agreement before the work begins. Such an agreement transfers all ownership and copyright rights to the employer. Another approach is to sign a licensing agreement with the creator of the work, which spells out the terms of payment for any additional use of the material. Above all, don't ever rely on verbal agreements—not even if the freelancer is your best friend. The specifics of working with photographers, and ownership of negatives, is covered in Chapter 7.

TRADEMARK LAW

An organization's name, products, slogans, and manufacturing processes are usually trademarked. This means that these things are officially registered with the U.S. government (or another national government) and their use is restricted to the owner or manufacturer. A **trademark** is legally protected and should be capitalized whenever it is used.

A trademark is a valuable asset that is zealously guarded by its owners. Sony, Coca-Cola, IBM, Porsche, McDonald's, and Reebok are all registered trademarks. So is the Mercedes-Benz star symbol, as well as slogans such as AT&T's "Reach Out and Touch Someone." High-technology systems may also be trademarked. The term "PhoneMail," for example, is a registered trademark of the Rolm Corporation.

Organizations and companies also are very sensitive to "look-alike" logos and names that could dilute the value of their trademarks. Microsoft, for example, filed a trademark infringement suit against a small software company that called itself Lindows.com. Mothers Against Drunk Driving (MADD) took exception to another nonprofit group, DAMMADD, which focuses on teenage drug abuse. McDonald's continually files suit against restaurants called "Mac Burger," and even Fox News filed suit against an author for using its trademarked phrase "fair and balanced" in the title of a book criticizing the network.

Even public relations firms get cited for trademark infringement. *Entrepreneur Magazine,* for example, successfully sued a firm for changing its name to Entrepreneur PR. In sum, it's important to check with a trademark lawyer before you use a logo or name that is similar to one that has already been trademarked. It can save you considerable time and money in a court of law.

As a public relations writer, it is also important for you to be absolutely clear on how to use an employer's trademarks. Be certain of the rules that apply to the products for which you are responsible. If you worked for the Hewlett-Packard Company, for example, you would need to know whether the company made a "laser jet," "Laser-Jet," or "LaserJet" printer. Failure to use the correct word jeopardizes the trademark and your job.

Organizations and corporations protect their trademarks in various ways. One method is to establish standard policies on how the organization should use and display its trademarked names. For example, at General Foods, the word "Jell-O" is never used alone. Such use would imply that Jell-O is a generic product and that other companies can use the same word. Instead, the usage at General Foods is always "Jell-O brand" gelatin dessert or pudding.

When you write a news release or brochure about your company's product, you must not only capitalize trademarked names and slogans, you must also indicate that they are trademarked by placing the symbol ®, ™, or SM next to them. The ® symbol means that the trademark is registered with the U.S. Patent and Trademark Office, ™ indicates that trademark registration is pending, and SM means that the mark designates a service rather than a product.

Many companies also list trademarked names at the end of any news release in which they appear. This helps ensure that reporters know exactly what words require capitalization in a news story. Motorola, when it announced a new digital wireless phone, ended the news release with the following note: "Motorola, iDen

Professional Tips

Trademarks Require a Capital Letter

Trademarked names are like proper nouns: they are capitalized and should be followed by a generic noun or phrase. The International Trademark Association also recommends that trademarks should never be pluralized, used in possessive form, or used as verbs. Currently, more than 700,000 trademarks are registered with the U.S. government. Here is a sampling of trademarks that are often assumed to be generic words:

AstroTurf	Band-aid	Chap Stick	Day-Timer	DeskJet
Fiberglas	Gatorade	Hula Hoop	Kleenex	Muzak
No Doz	NutraSweet	Plexiglas	Post-It	Rolodex
Stairmaster	Teflon	Walkman	Ziploc	

Source: International Trademark Association, 1133 Avenue of the Americas, New York, NY 10036-6710.

and i1000 are registered trademarks of Motorola, Inc." When several companies or product names appear in a news release, it is also necessary to list their registered trademarks and even indicate if they have pending applications for registration with the U.S. Patent and Trademark Office.

Companies also guard their trademarks by sending advisories to media outlets about proper use of these trademarks, placing advertisements in journalism publications reminding readers of trademarked names (see Figures 3.3 and 3.4), and monitoring publications to ensure that other organizations are not infringing on a trademark. If they are, legal action is threatened or taken.

Be extremely careful not to use another company's trademark improperly or to infringe on it in any way. You may like Garfield and Dilbert, but don't put them on posters advertising the company picnic. They are registered trademarks, like all cartoon characters. If you want to use such characters in company promotions and publicity, you must request permission and pay a licensing fee.

You also can't use the logos or names of amateur or professional athletic teams without obtaining permission and paying a fee. The National Football League and the National Basketball Association, for example, make more than $3 billion annually just licensing team logos and names to a variety of merchandisers, and university sports teams are not far behind them.

Figure 3.3 Trademarks
Trademarked names can lose their protection if people use them as verbs. This advertisement cautions people that they can't go "rollerblading."
(*Courtesy of Rollerblade, Inc.*)

© 1996, 3M. "Post-it" is a registered trademark of 3M.

Figure 3.4 Brand Names
Brand names are important assets. An "R" with a circle around it tells you that it is a registered trademark. This advertisement was placed in a journalism magazine to remind reporters.
(Courtesy of 3M Corporation.)

Payment is also required if you want to use stock photos of current, retired, or deceased actors or entertainers. A company cannot use a picture of KISS, the Marx Brothers, or Elvis Presley—or even dress someone up to look like them for publicity and promotional purposes—without first paying a licensing fee. Even Princess Diana is off-limits; her estate has exclusive rights to approve and license the use of her image for any commercial purpose.

In legal terms, using images of popular personalities, dead or alive, without permission is called **misappropriation of personality**. For example, a $400,000 award given to Bette Midler was upheld by the U.S. Supreme Court. She had brought charges against an advertising agency that used a "sound-alike" singer in a TV commercial. The courts found that Midler's exclusive right to her vocal style had been violated. In another case, lawyers for designer Ralph Lauren filed a trademark infringement suit against a new, upscale magazine, *Polo*. The magazine was ordered to run disclaimers on its cover and table of contents that it was not associated with the designer and his various products.

A take-off on a registered trademark can also get you into trouble. A student at the University of North Carolina found this out the hard way when he decided to produce and sell T-shirts that said "Nags Head, N.C.—King of Beaches" on the front and "This Beach Is for You" on the back. Anheuser-Busch was not amused and slapped him with a lawsuit for infringement on their trademarks, "King of Beers" and "This Bud's for You." The student was eventually vindicated in the federal appeals court, which ruled that his parody couldn't possibly be confused with company trademarks. However, the lawsuit cost the student a lot of money and four years of nerve-racking litigation.

In other trademark suits, the Dallas Cowboys and Converse athletic shoes got into an infringement fight because both use a five-pointed star as a corporate logo. And Phi Beta Kappa, the academic honorary society, took Compaq Computer Corp. to court after the company launched a "Phi Beta Compaq" promotion aimed at college students. Harley-Davidson, however, lost an infringement lawsuit against a motorcycle shop that was named "Hog Farm," because the term "hog" was generally used for big motorcycles long before Harley-Davidson tried to cash in on it.

Social service organizations are not exempt from charges of infringement of registered trademarks. The U.S. Olympic Committee filed suit against the March of Dimes for sponsoring the "Reading Olympics." Under U.S. law, no one can use the word "Olympic" or related words and symbols without the U.S. Olympic Committee's consent.

In sum, become familiar with what might be considered trademark infringement. Even if you are innocent, the money and time spent fighting a lawsuit are rarely worthwhile. Here are some guidelines the courts use to determine if a trademark has been infringed upon:

- Has the defendant used a name as a way of capitalizing on the reputation of another organization's trademark?
- Is there intent to create confusion in the public mind? Is there intent to imply a connection between the defendant's product and the item identified by the trademark?
- How similar are the two organizations? Are they providing the same kinds of services or products?
- Has the original organization actively protected the trademark by publicizing and using it?
- Is the trademark unique? A trademark that merely describes a common product or is a common phrase might be in trouble.

WORKING WITH LAWYERS

You now have an overview of how various laws and government regulations affect your work as a public relations writer and specialist. A basic knowledge of the law should help you do your work in a responsible and appropriate manner, but you also should realize that a smattering of knowledge can be dangerous.

Laws and regulations can be complex. You are not a trained attorney, so you should consult lawyers who are qualified to answer specialized questions regarding libel, copyright, trademarks, government regulation, and invasion of privacy. Your organization's own staff attorneys or outside legal counselors are your first source of information.

At the same time, remember that lawyers can tell you about the law; they should not tell you what to say or how to say it. They are legal experts, but not experts on effective writing and communication. They don't understand that the media want information now, or that "no comment" is perceived as a guilty plea in the court of public opinion.

Indeed, a major area of friction can be the clash between the legal and public relations departments. Lawyers generally prefer to say little or nothing in most situations, whereas the public relations staff perceives its role as providing a steady flow of information and news about the organization to multiple publics. The result is often a never-ending tug-of-war. At the same time, it is essential that the legal and public relations staffs cooperate in the best interests of the organization.

Great care must be taken in releasing information about litigation, labor negotiations, complex financial transactions, product recalls, and plant accidents. Numerous laws and regulations, to say nothing of liability considerations, affect what should or should not be said. Out-of-court settlements, for example, often stipulate that the amount of the settlement will not be publicly disclosed. This is why it is often important to submit a draft news release to legal counsel as a first step.

Your relations with legal counsel will be more pleasant and more productive if you keep abreast of new developments. To do this, you should maintain a file of newspaper and magazine articles that report on legal developments and decisions relating to public relations. This might include new regulatory guidelines, consent decrees, libel awards, trademark infringement suits, product recalls, and court decisions on employee privacy.

To ensure the best cooperation and mutual respect between the legal and public relations functions, here are some guidelines:

- Each department should have a written definition of its responsibilities.
- The heads of both departments should be equal in rank and should report to the organization's chief executive officer or executive vice president.
- Both departments should be represented on key committees.
- The legal counsel should keep the public relations staff up to date on legal problems involving the organization.
- The public relations staff should keep the legal staff up to date on public issues and media concerns that will require an organizational response.
- The departments should regard each other as allies, not opponents.

ETHICS AND PROFESSIONALISM

So far, this chapter has concentrated on the legal aspects of public relations writing. Equally important, however, are the ethical and professional values that you bring to your work.

Professional Tips

Guidelines for Ethical Conduct

Various professional organizations such as the International Public Relations Association (IPRA), the International Association of Business Communicators (IABC), and the Public Relations Society of America (PRSA) have set standards for ethical conduct in public relations. Here are the core values of PRSA that form the foundation of the organization's code of ethics:

ADVOCACY

- We serve the public interest by acting as responsible advocates for those we represent.
- We provide a voice in the marketplace of ideas, facts, and viewpoints to aid informed public debate.

HONESTY

- We adhere to the highest standards of accuracy and truth in advancing the interests of those we represent and in communication with the public.

EXPERTISE

- We acquire and responsibly use specialized knowledge and experience.
- We advance the profession through continued professional development, research, and education.
- We build mutual understanding, credibility, and relationships among a wide array of institutions and audiences.

INDEPENDENCE

- We provide objective counsel to those we represent.
- We are accountable for our actions.

LOYALTY

- We are faithful to those we represent, while honoring our obligation to serve the public interest.

FAIRNESS

- We deal fairly with clients, employers, competitors, peers, vendors, the media, and the general public.
- We respect all opinions and support the right of free expression.

Source: "Public Relations Society of America Member Code of Ethics." *PR Tactics*, January 2002, p. 21.

Ethical considerations, like the law, are often ambiguous and subject to interpretation. Most situations are neither black nor white but rather various shades of gray. Although the public relations writer is an advocate and must convey information in a persuasive way, this does not excuse the presentation of false or misleading information. In sum, you have to ask not only whether something is legal, but whether it is the right thing to do.

James E. Lukaszewski, president of his own counseling and crisis communication management firm, gave the graduates of the New York University Summer Institute Public Relations Program the following advice:

> In my judgment, a successful, important, meaningful public relations career requires self-examination, self-reflection, and a core set of beliefs to guide a constant stream of choices:
>
> - To choose honorable action over something less
> - To choose candor over something less
> - To choose disclosure over something less
> - To choose responsiveness over something less
> - To choose openness over something less
> - To choose what matters over something less
> - Choose the truth no matter what

Unfortunately, such choices often involve personal conflict and the age-old question, "What is truth?" An employer or a client, for example, may think that it is in the organization's interest to hide information that may be detrimental to its reputation or sales. As a public relations writer and practitioner, do you go along with the organization's wishes, or do you adhere to your own personal standards of truth?

The answer depends in large part on how you view your role. Some writers consider themselves technicians whose responsibility is to prepare materials as the organization or client wants them, even if the result is dishonest or misleading. They are the literary equivalent of "hired guns," available for any and every cause. Professionalism to them means writing good, persuasive copy, even if they don't believe in what they are writing.

Other writers feel that they serve as lawyers in the court of public opinion. All parties, they believe, are entitled to tell their side of the story and to be represented by public relations counsel. In this mode, the writer's obligation is to present the best possible defense of the client. Thus, a public relations firm should have no qualms about representing a foreign government accused of human rights violations, a racist hate group, or a cigarette company. After all, the First Amendment guarantees freedom of speech.

Although both views are common in the public relations industry, organizations such as the Public Relations Society of America and the International Association of Business Communicators argue that these approaches are self-defeating and lead to widespread public distrust of public relations activities. Professionalism and public credibility, many professionals say, hinge on other considerations.

Fraser Seitel, former vice president for public relations at Chase Manhattan Bank and now head of his own consulting firm, contends that public relations people should stand up for something, maintain high communications standards, and never compromise their standards. "We must take pride in the communications products for which we are responsible. If the trend continues of PR people becoming image mercenaries, accepting any client regardless of character or conscience, as long as he or she pays the freight, then all of us lose," Seitel warns. "We aren't in the business of confusing or distorting or obfuscating or lying."

As for being a lawyer in the court of public opinion, there is widespread disagreement. Jack O'Dwyer, editor of a public relations newsletter, holds that public relations is not like the law:

> The public accepts the fact that disreputable interests have the right to legal counsel but the public does not believe they also have the right to PR. A courtroom is a highly controlled setting where one legal counsel will battle it out with another under supervision by an expert judge who enforces ground rules. But PR people usually work for organizations and there may be no expert PR help on the other side.

In other words, although all parties have the right to express their side of the story, you are under no obligation to work on behalf of any organization or cause. Public relations firms, like attorneys, may turn down clients if they feel that such representation violates their own values and professional standards. Patrice Tanaka, CEO of PT&Co., said it best in an interview for *PRWeek:* "Our reputation is more valuable than a fee that any one client pays us. We can't support an indefensible position simply for the sake of a fee." In sum, your personal integrity may outweigh any immediate financial loss.

Porter/Novelli, for example, decided to resign a $3 million account for a gun industry trade group after the Littleton, Colorado, school shooting tragedy. On the other hand, one of Burson-Marsteller's biggest clients is Phillip Morris. The activist group, Infact, says the large public relations firm is the "evil force" behind the company's efforts to mislead the public and "destroy anyone who dares to challenge them."

Making an ethical decision on the kind of organization or cause that you want to have as an employer or a client, however, is only one part of the equation. Moral and ethical decisions also have to be made almost daily about the content and structure of various messages. Do you say that an executive has resigned "for personal reasons" even though you know that the person was fired for incompetence? Do you exaggerate the number of people attending an event? Do you say that a product is safe even though tests have revealed a potentially dangerous design flaw? Do you write about a company's restructuring to be more profitable without mentioning the layoff of 1,500 employees?

There are no easy answers to such questions. The simple axiom, "Always tell the truth," understates the complexity of the decision process. For example, Chapter 1 makes it clear that public relations writing is not journalistic reporting of all the unvarnished facts about a situation; information should be placed in a context that helps the organization achieve its objectives. In addition, it is often impossible to say everything about a particular subject in a single message.

David Martinson, a professor of public relations at Florida International University, puts the ethical dilemma succinctly. How, he asks, "does the practitioner respond when trying to determine whether or not to release information—or how much of it to release?" Then he answers, "By determining whether the information should be communicated. The practitioner must have an objective standard to use in determining which information should be released to all seriously interested parties." He suggests that public relations personnel should apply the concept of *substantial completeness,* defined as "the point at which a reasonable reader's requirements for information are satisfied."

Martinson continues:

> A practitioner adopting a policy of substantial completeness will release that information which the public needs to make an informed decision. In conceding that all information regarding a particular matter might not be released because in many cases that is impossible, no suggestion is made that only that information most favorable should be released. Those who release only favorable information may not be lying in a formal sense, but they certainly are not contributing to a process whereby concerned publics can make an informed decision—they clearly have not adopted a policy of substantial completeness.

At times there also are competitive, legal, and proprietary reasons why an organization does not want to distribute information or answer press questions. In

PR Casebook

Questions of Ethical Practice

Some public relations practices have raised controversy and debate. What do you think of the following techniques from the standpoint of ethics and professional responsibility to the public?

Front Groups
What do the Coalition for Vehicle Choice, Americans for Medical Progress, People for the West, and the Consumer Alliance have in common? They are all front groups formed and funded by special interests but named to give the impression that they are organized by citizens and volunteers to promote the public welfare. People for the West, for example, is a coalition of cities and mining companies that are lobbying to open up more public land for development. Is the formation of such groups, with high-sounding names, a legitimate and ethical activity?

Pay for Play
A Baltimore hospital pays a local television station to have their experts interviewed on news programs. In another situation, a public relations firm funnels money to a public radio station on behalf of its client, the Pennsylvania Department of Environmental Protection (DEP), with the understanding that the station's news reporters will do specific types of stories. Such practices threaten to undermine the credibility of the news and the institutions involved. Does this deceive the public by blurring the line between news and advertising?

De-Positioning
A public relations firm, on behalf of a client, sends out news releases bashing the competition. It also plants rumors in the media about a competitor's poor financial health, the reliability of a company's products, and generally tries to slow a competitor's launch of a new product or whatever the competitor is trying to do. The public relations firm, in the meantime, rushes to get the client's new products, services, or ideas out before the competitors do—whether they are ready or not. Is this good business practice? Does it cast public relations in a negative light?

this case, the best approach is to be candid. Jerry Dalton, former national president of the Public Relations Society of America, says that organizations "should state that they will not discuss what they are doing and then give an honest reason why they have taken this seemingly hard-line decision."

Simply refusing to comment, for good reason, is not considered lying by journalists who responded to a survey conducted by Professor Michael Ryan of the University of Houston and Professor Martinson. However, both journalists and public relations people consider it lying if (1) you give evasive answers to questions or (2) you say that rumors about a situation are wrong when they are in fact correct.

Questions of ethics and professionalism are raised throughout this textbook as they relate to various aspects of public relations writing and media techniques. Chapter 7, on photographs and artwork, for example, discusses the ethical implications of altering photos through computer manipulation. Later, in Chapter 11, ethical dealings with the media are discussed.

Providing a framework for many of these discussions are the codes of ethics for various organizations. The box on page 86 highlights the core values of professional practice for the Public Relations Society of America. Take the time to read and understand it.

SUMMARY

- You are legally and ethically responsible for the information that you produce and distribute.
- You should know the dividing lines between libel, slander, and the concept of fair comment.
- Employees, as well as outsiders, have a right to privacy that can be violated through the careless release of personal information.
- You must have written permission to use an individual's quotes and photographs for promotional or advertising purposes.
- Regulatory agencies such as the SEC and the FTC have guidelines and rules concerning the content and release of information about products and services.
- Copyrights are simple, easy to get, and dangerous to infringe. Don't plagiarize. Understand thoroughly the limitations of fair use.
- Trademarks are valuable assets. It is your responsibility to protect and use them correctly.
- The use of trademarked names and cartoon characters often requires the payment of licensing fees.
- Written contracts or letters of agreement are necessary for the employment of freelance writers and other outside consultants.
- Lawyers and legal staff members are valuable resources for understanding the various legal implications of public relations activities. They are allies, not enemies.

- Public relations writers are more than wordsmiths and technicians; they have a moral and ethical responsibility to communicate in a fair and truthful manner.

- Ethics are vital for professionalism. You must do more than just obey the law. You must also consider your personal values and the public interest.

ADDITIONAL RESOURCES

Bunker, Matthew D., and Bolger, Bethany. "Protecting a Delicate Balance: Facts, Ideas, and Expression in Compilation Copyright Cases." *Journalism and Mass Communications Quarterly*, Vol. 80, No. 1, Spring 2003, pp. 183–197.

Calabro, Sarah. "Clippings and the Copyright Conundrum." *PRWeek*, July 15, 2003, p. 18.

Clark, Cynthia. "What Every Public Company Must Know About Disclosing Information." *The Strategist*, Fall 2000, pp. 34–38.

Dinan, Jacques. "More than a Profession." *IPRA Frontline*, September 2002, p. 4.

Gower, Karla K. *Legal and Ethical Restraints on Public Relations*. Prospect Heights, IL: Waveland Press, 2003.

Greenhouse, Linda. "20-Year Extension of Existing Copyright Is Upheld." *The New York Times*, January 16, 2002, p. A22.

Houston, Allen. "Ducking Beneath the FDA's Communications Barriers." *PRWeek*, February 25, 2002, p. 9.

Huff, Dianna. "Give Credit Where Credit Is Due: Proper Attribution for Communicators." *PR Tactics*, February 203, p. 19.

Isserman, Maurice. "Plagiarism: A Lie of the Mind." *Chronicle of Higher Education*, May 2, 2003, pp. B12–13.

Kruckeberg, Dean. "The Public Relations Practitioner's Role in Practicing Strategic Ethics." *Public Relations Quarterly*, Fall 2000, pp. 35–39.

Lohr, Steve. "Glass Panes and Software: Windows Name Is Challenged." *The New York Times*, December 30, 2002, p. C2.

Lukaszewski, James E. "Surviving the Moral And Ethical Jungle: How To Build The Definitive Moral Compass." *PR Tactics*, February 2002, pp. 18–26. Several articles on the PRSA code of ethics.

Martinson, David L. "Ethical Decision Making in Public Relations: What Would Aristotle Say?" *Public Relations Quarterly*, Fall 2000, pp. 18–21.

McGuire, George. "Intellectual Property Issues for PR Professionals." *PR Tactics*, December 2000, p. 6.

Parkinson, Michael. "The PRSA Code of Professional Standards and Member Code of Ethics: Why They Are Neither Professional or Ethical." *Public Relations Quarterly*, Fall 2001, pp. 27–31.

Weidlich, Thom. "Earnings Releases and the Right Balance." *PRWeek*, April 14, 2003, p. 18.

Chapter 4

Finding and Generating News

A major purpose of many public relations programs is to provide information to the media in the hope that it will be published or broadcast. The resulting coverage is called publicity. The public relations writer who writes and places stories in the media is commonly referred to as a publicist.

An effective publicist needs to know three things, which are discussed in this chapter. First, be thoroughly familiar with journalistic news values and tailor your stories accordingly. Second, know where to find news in the organization and how to extract the angle that would be most interesting to journalists and the public. Third, become a problem solver and come up with creative publicity tactics that effectively break through the forest of competing messages.

BARRIERS TO MEDIA COVERAGE

There are several barriers to getting publicity in the media, including the following:

1. *Media gatekeepers.* Reporters and editors decide whether an organization's information qualifies as news and is worthy of being published or broadcast. They may choose to change the order of the information, delete parts of it, or even completely rewrite it. Thus a two-page news release from a company may be published as a full story, a one-paragraph news item, or not at all. In sum, publicists control what is sent to the media, but they have no control over what is ultimately printed or broadcast.

2. *Shrinking news holes.* The number of media entities has skyrocketed in recent years, which has resulted in an intense scramble for advertising revenues to pay the bills. Particularly hard hit have been newspapers and magazines, which often have to reduce the number of pages in an issue. This reduction also affects the amount of space (called the **news hole**) that is available for news and editorial matter. The result is increased competition in getting your publicity accepted and published. A newspaper or trade magazine editor, for example, has hundreds of news releases and story ideas for every edition, and can use only a few. Much of this book is designed to improve your ability to generate the kind of news that editors will use.

3. *Changing nature of the mass media.* The mass media are becoming increasingly fragmented, meaning that they no longer offer the opportunity to reach everyone in a single effort. The "one size fits all" news release is dead. As mentioned in Chapter 1, today's public relations writer must be adept at preparing a news release in a variety of formats—for print, broadcast, video, direct mail, Internet, and the World Wide Web.

4. *Information overload.* Our society is experiencing widespread information clutter. The decline of the mass media has been accompanied by a proliferation of more specialized media—suburban weeklies, trade newspapers and magazines, cable channels, online networks, and the Internet—all of which compete for the individual's attention. As a consequence, your organization's news, even if it is published or broadcast, may never get the audience's attention.

Despite these barriers, the news media are indispensable if the organization's objective is to inform, persuade, and motivate various audiences. You, however, must recognize the barriers and take several steps to make your efforts more effective. They include (1) targeting the right media with your information, (2) thinking continuously about the interests of the readers or listeners, (3) keeping in mind the objectives of the client or employer, and (4) exercising creativity in thinking about how to present information that will meet the requirements of media gatekeepers. Don't try to blanket the media with a blizzard of news items.

To work effectively, you must understand what makes news and how to find or create news.

WHAT MAKES NEWS

Students in newswriting classes are taught the basic components of what constitutes "news." Public relations writers, or publicists, must also be familiar with these elements if they are to generate the kind of information that appeals to **media gatekeepers**. Aspects of news include *timeliness, prominence, proximity, significance, unusualness, human interest, conflict,* and *newness.*

Timeliness

Timeliness may be the most important characteristic of news. By definition, news must be current.

One way to make news timely is to announce something when it happens. An organization usually contacts the press as soon as an event occurs—the issuing of the quarterly earnings report, the appointment of a chief executive, the layoff of workers. Any delay in conveying this information could result in its being rejected as "old news."

A second aspect of timeliness is offering information linked to events and holidays that are already on the public agenda. Auto clubs and insurance companies, for example, have excellent placement success with articles about safe driving just before the Labor Day or July Fourth holiday weekend.

Halloween is another timely holiday. The American Academy of Ophthalmology issues a news release warning that "some ghoulish things can happen to your eyes" unless you take some precautions. The same theme is sounded by the American Optometric Association, which says that masks can be very scary if they limit your peripheral vision. Of course, the American Association of Orthodontists, which knows about candy and teeth, sends out a news release about the "tricks treats can play" and offers orthodontic tips.

At Thanksgiving, Butterball Turkey achieves a publicity bonanza by operating a Turkey Talk-Line and Web site *(www.butterball.com)*, which is used by about 200,000 novice cooks each year. Information about Butterball's hotline, plus articles about how to cook a turkey, also receive considerable print coverage. One story that receives media pickup is a summary of what questions callers asked last year; 15,399 callers, for example, asked, "What is the best way to thaw a turkey?"

Christmas is the major season for purchasing children's toys, so the media are receptive to news releases from toy manufacturers about new products on the market. In fact, Duracell capitalizes on the holiday gift-giving season with its annual "Duracell Kids" Choice Toy Survey. It publicizes a "Top 10" toy list based on a survey of children in YMCA afternoon programs. Of course, Ameritech sends out publicity material about its home security systems that will protect your packages under the tree, and the American College of Gastroenterologists reminds you to see a doctor if all the holiday food and drink causes stomach problems.

A third approach to timeliness relates to current events and issues that are on the public's mind. Any research study or new drug relating to cancer usually receives extensive play in the media. There is also great public debate about the cost of health care, so pharmaceutical firms tailor their news releases around the idea that new "wonder drugs" are a cost-effective way to reduce hospital stays.

Although current issues provide a useful springboard for tailoring an organization's publicity to what is on the mind of editors and the public, Don Hewitt, creator of CBS's *60 Minutes,* says there must be more to it than a current issue or topic. He was quoted in the *Boston Globe,* saying, "I had producers say, 'We've got to do something on acid rain.' I say, 'Hold it. Acid rain is not a story. Acid rain is a topic.' We don't do topics. Find me someone who has to deal with the problem of acid rain. Now you have a story."

A fourth approach to timely distribution of news releases is to relate the organization's products or services to a current event. As Joshua Harris Prager wrote in *The Wall Street Journal,* "In the public relations business, the name of the game is finding a hook that links your press release to the news."

An example is Mary Kay Cosmetics. It used the news that American troops in Afghanistan and Iraq were suffering chafed skin and sunburn because of the desert conditions. It got media publicity by shipping more than 15,000 tubes of shaving cream, skin lotion, sunblock, and lip protector to the soldiers' relatives in the hope that they would forward them on to the troops.

A more questionable use of timely news events was a news release of French's Mustard that some journalists called a "flag-waving" exercise. The company issued a news release with the headline "The Only Thing French about French's Mustard Is the Name" when a number of Americans were advocating the boycott of French goods because France didn't support the invasion of Iraq by the United States.

The release further stated that "Robert T. French's All-American Dream Lives On" and explained that the mustard company was named after an American that founded the company in 1904. Some journalists understood that the news release was timed to fend off the French backlash but thought the company's assertion, "There is nothing more American," was somewhat misleading because the parent company of French's Mustard is a British firm.

A popular movie can also provide a timely opportunity. *The Lord of the Rings* trilogy was filmed in New Zealand and, after the film won an Oscar for cinematography, the New Zealand government launched an international public relations and advertising campaign billing the nation as "best supporting country."

New Zealand hopes to capitalize on the popularity of the hit movie series by marketing the country around the world as a destination for family tourism and a great location for Hollywood productions. There already are tours for Hobbit fans, and the New Zealand tourist Web site announces "Experience New Zealand, Home of Middle Earth."

Timing is everything, but sometimes events cause havoc with even the best-laid plans. The Hong Kong Tourist Board had just launched a campaign to attract more tourists when the SARS epidemic hit and more than 100 people in China and Hong Kong died from the mutant strain of pneumonia. Unfortunately, it was too late to change or recall advertisements in international magazines promising that "Hong Kong Will Take Your Breath Away."

Prominence

The news media rarely cover the grand opening of a store or anything else unless there is a prominent person, with star power, involved. For example, an electron-

- *Other published materials*—Copies of the organization's brochures, speeches, slide presentations, videotapes, and sales material

In addition to reviewing all of these sources, which are available primarily in published form, you must also play the role of roving reporter. Talk to a variety of people, ask a lot of questions, and be constantly on the lookout for something new or different. Most news stories don't come to you; you have to seek out stories. Most people have no clue whether an event or a situation is newsworthy, so you must be alert to clues and hints as well as hard facts.

A new process or technique may be just business as usual to a production manager, but it may lead you to several possible stories. For example, AlliedSignal received news coverage for a new fiber by pointing out that it could be used in automobile seat belts to slow the movement of a passenger's upper body in a collision. The company publicist did two things to make this story newsworthy. First, she related the new fiber to a use that the public could readily understand. Second, she arranged and distributed a photo (see Figure 4.2) that had good composition and human interest.

A change in work schedules may affect traffic and thus be important to the community. Personnel changes and promotions may interest editors of business

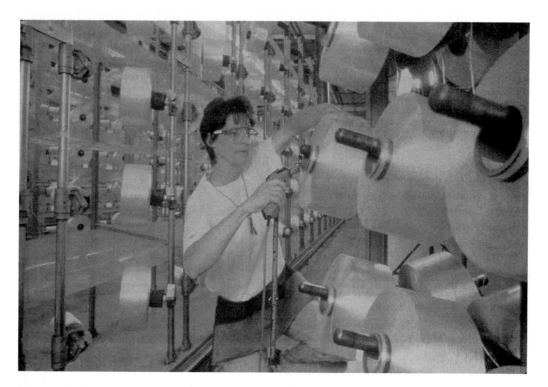

Figure 4.2 Using Interesting Photographs
Action photos in a work setting can add visual context to a new product. AlliedSignal distributed this photo to announce a new fiber that will be used in seat belts.
(Courtesy of AlliedSignal and its public relations firm, jmc Communications.)

and trade papers. A new contract, which means hiring new employees, might be important to the regional economy. By the same token, the loss of a major contract—and its implications for the employees and community—also qualifies as significant news.

External News Sources

Ideas on how to get your organization into the news can come from almost any source.

You might attend a Rotary Club meeting and hear a speaker talk about the national need to train more engineers in the computer sciences. That might spur you to investigate how the problem affects your employer or client. This, in turn, might lead to the idea that you could generate some media coverage by telling the media what your company is doing about the problem in terms of providing college scholarships or even recruiting engineers from other nations. Or perhaps you might offer the media an interview with the company president, who can articulate some solutions to the problem. Another approach might be to have the CEO write an **op-ed** piece for the local daily or even *The Wall Street Journal.* Op-eds are discussed in Chapter 8.

As discussed earlier, you should always think about how you can use news events to create publicity. In order to do this, you need to read, listen to, and watch the news for events and situations that may affect your organization. As Michael Klepper, a New York publicist, says, "This requires becoming a media junkie, which is an absolute necessity for anyone wanting to be successful in the media relations part of the business."

Reacting to a news event is exactly what the Child and Family Services of New Hampshire did when the media reported that a newborn baby had been abandoned. The day the story hit, Renee Robertie, communications director of the agency, faxed all state dailies, radio, and television stations the options a mother experiencing a crisis pregnancy would have if she had called Child and Family Services. This got an immediate media response, and there were many stories of the "What a mother can do" type, which prominently featured the services of the agency. Robertie adds, "The key to success is being prepared so when something like this happens, you are able to step in as the voice of authority and provide reporters with good data and **soundbites** at a moment's notice."

All news events can be used to create news, but you must think of applications to your particular organization and industry on a moment's notice to take advantage of timeliness, which is a core news value. That's the hard part. To help you do this, we will discuss creativity and brainstorming later in this chapter.

Other external sources that you can tap for ideas are polls and surveys, census reports, trade media, financial analyst reports, findings of governmental commissions, sales figures for entire industries, and updates on competitors.

Professional periodicals and newsletters serving the public relations industry should not be overlooked. They often include results of surveys indicating what the "hot" topics are in the media.

A national survey of newspaper editors by News USA, a news release and feature article distribution firm, illustrates the point. The survey, reported in *PR News,* found that the topic of health generated the most interest on the part of editors. In descending order were the topics of senior citizens, medicine, agriculture, environment, food, education, consumer issues, recreation, and finance. A survey of food editors by another firm indicated that low-fat and fat-free recipes and information were "hot" topics.

Public relations newsletters also give tips about what specific publications and editors are seeking. For example, *Jack O'Dwyer's Newsletter* reported that the editor of *Interactive Age* "is interested in getting news about companies involved in Internet banking and financial services." Tip sheets are discussed further in Chapter 10.

HOW TO CREATE NEWS

There is no hard-and-fast definition of what is news. A Hearst editor once declared, probably with more truth than he realized, "News is what I say it is." This is still true, and it is also still true that a lot of "news" comes from the planning and stage managing of events.

Historian Daniel Boorstin coined the term **pseudoevent** to describe events and situations that are created primarily for the sake of generating press coverage. Two early examples, which are still going strong, are the Miss America pageant and the Academy Awards.

The original idea behind the Miss America contest was a creative solution to the question posed by most tourist resorts: "How do we extend the summer season past Labor Day?" The contest was not only good for business in Atlantic City, it also provided the American public with a form of entertainment.

PR Casebook

The Hollywood Walk of Fame as Pseudoevent

A good way for an actor to get at least 15 seconds of media attention is to be accepted into Hollywood's Walk of Fame. Photos of the actor accepting his or her "star" usually make it into most newspapers and entertainment magazines, even though the "honor" seems to be a bit jaded these days.

Such superstars as Julia Roberts, Al Pacino, or Eminem haven't been inducted into the Walk of Fame, but Kevin Bacon was inducted just before his new movie, *Mystic River*, was released.

John Lippman, a reporter for *The Wall Street Journal*, puts it succinctly: "No star gets considered unless a sponsor agrees to pay a $15,000 fee once they're selected. That's usually a movie studio—which means that the milestone these days often boils down to a publicity campaign tied to a new movie." He quotes Eddie Michaels, a Hollywood publicist, who says, "I've been in meetings where they say, 'We're going to have this poster, this outdoor campaign, and a Hollywood Boulevard star.'"

The Walk of Fame, sponsored by the Hollywood Chamber of Commerce as a vehicle of civic pride and tourism, may not attract the likes of Madonna right now, but she may be interested later in her career when her own "star" starts to fade.

The Academy Awards, another American institution, also had its beginnings as a publicity stunt. Lisa Bannon, a reporter for *The Wall Street Journal*, explains the background of what is now a $100 million industry with a worldwide audience:

> What began at the Hollywood Roosevelt Hotel in 1929 as an experimental publicity stunt for the movie industry has grown into the largest entertainment event of the year. It not only provides enough money to run the nonprofit Academy of Motion Picture Arts and Sciences all year, it can double a winning film's box-office revenue, showcase jeweler and designer wares, boost catering careers, and buoy myriad other businesses along the way.

Indeed, creativity and vision are essential attributes for work in public relations, but such things are difficult to teach and even more difficult to learn. Hal Lancaster, author of a "Managing Your Career" column in *The Wall Street Journal,* says creative people share some common traits: "keen powers of observation, a restless curiosity, the ability to identify issues others miss, a talent for generating a large number of ideas, persistent questioning of the norm, and a knack for seeing established structures in new ways."

One way to increase your creativity is to use a checklist. Judith Rich, former executive vice president of creative services for Ketchum Communications, gives her version of such a list:

- Be open to new experiences.
- Recognize and challenge your own creative ability.
- Don't negate the importance of right-brain thinking.
- Encourage your mind to work in different ways.
- Interesting comments are more creative than critical ones.
- Creativity depends more on motivation and mental effort than on any other factor.
- Don't just look for information in the "normal" places.
- Kids are the most creative people around. Listen to them.
- Don't let the "habit" approach interfere with your natural urge to be creative.
- Listen to "outsiders"—they may give you the inside track on a creative solution.
- Draw heavily on personal resources—remember the content of your dreams. Your unconscious may sometimes solve your conscious concerns.

Brainstorming

Public relations firms such as Ketchum generate creative ideas by conducting **brainstorming** sessions. The point of such a session is to encourage everyone to express any idea that comes to mind. An idea may be totally impractical and off the wall, but no one is allowed to say "it won't work" or "that's a stupid idea." This inhibits creative thinking and people's willingness to participate.

All ideas, regardless of their merit, can be placed on a flip chart or white board. As the team looks at all the ideas, new ideas that combine and refine the original list are usually generated. Another approach is to give everyone three colored dots and ask them to place the dots next to the three ideas they believe are best, based on feasibility, cost effectiveness, and timeliness. Then you emphasize and shape the ideas receiving the most dots.

If you have a large team of people trying to come up with creative ideas, a similar approach is to give everyone 25 to 50 note cards and ask them to jot down one idea per card. By a system of sorting, you can come up with five or six common ideas that bear further discussion.

You can do problem solving and create news in a variety of ways. The next several pages highlight the creative tactics of (1) special events, (2) contests, (3) polls and surveys, (4) top 10 lists, (5) stunts, (6) product demonstrations, (7) rallies and protests, and (8) personal appearances.

Professional Tips

Thirty-Two Ways to Create News for Your Organization

1. Tie in with news events of the day.
2. Cooperate with another organization on a joint project.
3. Tie in with a newspaper or broadcast station on a mutual project.
4. Conduct a poll or survey.
5. Issue a report.
6. Arrange an interview with a celebrity.
7. Take part in a controversy.
8. Arrange for a testimonial.
9. Arrange for a speech.
10. Make an analysis or prediction.
11. Form and announce names for committees.
12. Hold an election.
13. Announce an appointment.
14. Celebrate an anniversary.
15. Issue a summary of facts.
16. Tie in with a holiday.
17. Make a trip.
18. Make an award.
19. Hold a contest.
20. Pass a resolution.
21. Appear before a public body.
22. Stage a special event.
23. Write a letter.
24. Release a letter you received (with permission).
25. Adapt national reports and surveys for local use.
26. Stage a debate.
27. Tie in to a well-known week or day.
28. Honor an institution.
29. Organize a tour.
30. Inspect a project.
31. Issue a commendation.
32. Issue a protest.

Source: Dennis L. Wilcox, Glen Cameron, Phillip H. Ault, and Warren K. Agee. *Public Relations: Strategies and Tactics,* 7th ed. (Boston: Allyn & Bacon, 2003).

If It's May, It's National Asparagus Month

National organizations and trade groups often designate a day, a week, or even a month to focus on a cause, an industry, or even a product. May is a popular month, with such designations as National Barbecue Month, National Paint Month, National Physical Fitness and Sports Month, and even National Arthritis Month.

The National Asparagus Association selected May because it marks the peak of asparagus production. By promoting the month, the trade group hopes to encourage consumption of its product at home and in restaurants. Surveys show that more meals are eaten out on Mother's Day than on any other day, and the asparagus association makes a special effort to encourage restaurants to put its product on the menu.

The warm weather in May also prompts the National Paint and Coating Association to sponsor National Paint Month. As a spokesperson says, "It's the time of the year when people are thinking about home improvements, and hence it is the perfect month to alert the public to the power of paint."

If a special day, week, or month is well organized and promoted, it can provide a focus point for media coverage on an annual basis. Breast Cancer Awareness Week, for example, was started almost 20 years ago by ICI Pharmaceuticals with the assistance of its public relations firm, Burson-Marsteller. The week is still going strong with a coalition of 17 organizations supporting a variety of educational efforts and events during the designated week. As a result of continued media coverage, the majority of American women now recognize the phrase "early detection."

However, experts say Breast Cancer Awareness Week is an exception in a very crowded field. "Clients often think these national days are a fantastic way to get publicity when in fact it is one of the least interesting kinds of news you can present to the media," says Audrey Knoth, VP at Pennsylvania-based Goldman & Associates.

If you want to create a special day, week, or month for your client, *PRWeek* suggests the following tips:

- Do have an educational component or call to action.
- Do make sure the campaign has a human element.
- Do find credible experts and partners for the media to interview.

You should also select a date that isn't already taken by multiple other organizations. A good source is *Chase's Calendar of Events* (in print or at www.chases.com) and the book *Holidays and Anniversaries of the World*.

Special Events

Any number of events are created or staged to attract media attention and make the public aware of a new product, service, or idea. This goes back to the communication theory concept in Chapter 2 of the "triggering event" that becomes the catalyst for individuals to adopt new ideas or modify their behavior.

It is less certain, however, what exactly constitutes a "special event." Some say an event out of the ordinary is always "special," whereas others say that any event is "special" if the organizers are particularly creative at organizing it. At times, things that occur on a routine basis can become the focus of media coverage if some creativity is exercised. A new store may quietly open its doors for business, or it can have a "grand opening" with a celebrity cutting the ribbon and a circus in the parking lot.

New product launches are often accompanied by special events or activities. When Coca-Cola introduced its new Vanilla Coke, for example, the company held its first public tasting at the Vanilla Bean Cafe in Pomfret, Connecticut, where 500 guests gulped down about 40 cases in minutes. And General Mills launched its new *Berry Burst Cheerios* at the Great Mall of America in Minneapolis with a concert by David Cassidy, a former teen heartthrob, who gained fame with the song "I Think I Love You."

News conferences can also be a "special event" if a major product is being introduced. Gillette introduced its Mach 3 razor at news conferences held on the same day throughout the United States, Canada, and Western Europe. On the same day, the company sent samples of the Mach 3 products to influential men in entertainment, sports, and politics so they could become the first to try the new product and talk about it.

Another approach was teaser cards sent to some 300 television talk show hosts, news anchors, meteorologists, and radio DJs in all major markets, challenging them to go to work unshaven, where they would receive a special gift of Mach 3 products along with a media kit. Media participation included David Letterman using the product in a skit and a woman shaving her legs on *CBS This Morning*. One week after the Mach 3 introduction, it was the best-selling razor on the market.

A major special event category is anniversaries. Major milestones in the age of a product, an institution, or a service are often the "triggering event" that provides the "news hook" for extensive media coverage. Detroit, for example, held a year-long celebration of its 300th birthday, and a resort hotel in Florida celebrated its 75th anniversary by inviting all the couples married there back for a three-day celebration. The Museum of Art in Dallas celebrated its 100th anniversary by keeping the museum open 100 hours straight for a series of events occurring at all hours of the day.

The 100th anniversary of Harley-Davidson in 2003 was a major publicity bonanza for the company. The motorcycle manufacturer, considered an American icon, held a big celebration in its hometown of Milwaukee that attracted 250,000 bikers and fans of "hogs" from around the world. A Saturday parade included 10,000 motorcycles, and *The New York Times* called the celebration "a huge choreographed event that turned the company's hometown into a sea of roaring motorcycles, hard rock bands, scruffy beards, leather vests, chaps and bikinis and, of course, all products Harley."

The New York Times gave the Harley-Davidson celebration about 80 column inches, including six photos. Other major dailies around the nation also gave the event considerable space, and it was a favorite topic on network television news shows. The event had all the ingredients of a good story—250,000 bikers, all sporting black leather and bandanas, are highly visual—to say nothing of the biker weddings in the park, the showing off of tattoos, the blessing of bikes by a Catholic bishop, and the entire carnival atmosphere.

Maytag Man Celebrates 35 Years of Being Lonely

Anniversaries of advertising campaigns can also be a powerful magnet for media coverage if some creative effort is used.

Maytag, an Iowa-based manufacturer of appliances for more than 100 years, decided to celebrate the 35th anniversary of Ol' Lonely, the Maytag repairman, who has been featured in its advertising since 1967. Ol' Lonely has become one of the most popular campaigns in the history of advertising.

The objective of the anniversary celebration was (1) to increase Maytag brand awareness and reinforce positioning of Ol' Lonely and (2) stimulate preference for the Maytag brand. The audience was married women, aged 25–64, who were somewhat affluent and college educated.

A number of tactics was used. The company created 900 commemorative "Ol' Lonely tool box" media kits, which included media materials, a CD of historical advertisements, and a commemorative Ol' Lonely bobble-head plastic model. It also distributed tips from Ol' Lonely on how to deal with loneliness, booked a 25-city satellite media tour with an actor portraying Ol' Lonely and his apprentice, and hired a university professor to give media interviews about how brand icons affect consumers.

The campaign, conducted by Carmichael Lynch Spong public relations firm, generated 516 placements on television shows and in newspapers and magazines. In addition, the company's Web site received nearly 40,000 inquiries.

Figure 4.3 Ol' Lonely Celebrates 35 Years
Anniversaries provide a news hook for media coverage. Here, Maytag's Ol' Lonely and his apprentice blow out the candles on a cake as part of the public relations campaign.
(Courtesy of Maytag and its public relations firm, Carmichael Lynch Spong.)

Many newspapers, as part of the story, also gave a short history of the company and mentioned Harley-Davidson's considerable success as an American icon. It is the top seller of heavyweight motorcycles in North America and has a particular niche of selling to aging baby boomers who are affluent enough to plunk down $15,000 for a motorcycle. Although the "hog" is historically associated with James Dean and his movie *The Wild One,* the reality is that most of the "bikers" gathered in Milwaukee had receding hairlines (average age 46) and earned an average income of $78,300. Not exactly the demographics of a Hell's Angel.

Creating a compelling special event is more art than science. However, reporter Anita Chabria of *PRWeek* says an event or a publicity stunt should do more than grab media coverage. She writes, "While their wacky or weird imagery may draw camera crews quicker than an interstate pile-up, the end result is that consumers receive a message about the brand identity."

Chabria gives three tips to public relations staffs:

1. Think about how the event will reflect on the brand identity and what message it will send to the consumers.

2. Create fun and engaging visuals for the media that will look good on camera.

3. Make sure you give the media a very clear idea of what those visuals will be in advance of the event.

Contests

The contest is a common device for creating news. In fact, it is often advised that "if all else fails, sponsor a contest."

There are contests of every kind. At the local level, the American Legion sponsors high-school essay contests on citizenship, and Ford Dealers enthusiastically sponsor safe-driving contests for teenagers. There are also numerous Elvis look-alike contests, tractor pulls, and beauty pageants, and eating contests. See Figures 4.4 and 4.5 about a shrimp eating contest.

Here are some other creative examples:

- Dove Deororant sponsored a Most Beautiful Underarms pageant at Grand Central Station in New York, and Miss Florida received the crown. The contest received airtime on *Today, Fox & Friends,* and mentions on the news shows of 400 television stations.

- The Palo Verdes Art Center (PVAC) in California held a fund-raiser in which the prize was a donated house valued at $1.17 million. Raffle tickets were $150 each, and 16,000 people from as far away as the Virgin Islands purchased them. The art center's innovative fund-raiser received considerable media coverage in Southern California, but it was also the subject of national coverage, including NBC's *Today* show.

- Georgia-Pacific wanted to revitalize its Brawny paper towel brand, so it sponsored a contest for consumers to nominate men they felt had the Brawny Man's essential characteristics—strength, dependability, toughness, and ruggedness. More than 500 articles were written about the contest, and the company had a 7 percent rise in sales for the Brawny brand.

OLD BAY

FOR IMMEDIATE RELEASE

Contacts: Amanda Hirschhorn
Hunter Public Relations
212/679-6600 x239 or ahirschhorn@hunterpr.com

Laurie Harrsen
McCormick & Company, Inc.
410/527-8753 or laurie_harrsen@mccormick.com

Old Bay® Casts Net For National Peel & Eat Shrimp Classic
Contestants Attempt to Reel in a $10,000 Grand Prize

HUNT VALLEY, Md. (March 17, 2003) – Shells will be flying as 10 lucky finalists vie for a $10,000 grand prize in the **Old Bay® Peel & Eat Shrimp Classic**, Friday, August 29, 2003, in Baltimore, Md., the birthplace of Old Bay. Old Bay Seasoning, a unique blend of a dozen herbs and spices and a Chesapeake Bay cooking tradition for over 60 years, is once again casting its net in search of America's biggest seafood lovers and Old Bay fans. Last year's winner, John Meitl, set the bar very high, by peeling and eating 87 Old Bay-steamed shrimp in the 10-minute competition – that's nearly nine shrimp per minute!

To enter the contest, which begins on March 17, 2003, Old Bay fans across the country must do their best job to persuade judges that they live, sleep, eat and breathe seafood; describe the lengths they'd go to for a taste of Old Bay (including favorite or unusual recipes); and make a case for why they deserve to compete in the Old Bay Peel & Eat Shrimp Classic.

- more -

ZESTY • BOLD • DISTINCTIVE
Same great taste for over 60 years!
211 Schilling Circle • Hunt Valley, MD 21031
1-800-632-5847 • www.old-bay.com

2/Old Bay® Casts Net For National Peel & Eat Shrimp Classic

Twenty-five semi-finalists will be selected from all the entries by a panel of independent judges. Descriptions will be evaluated based on the following criteria: creativity (35%), persuasiveness (35%), and originality of Old Bay usage (30%). Each semi-finalist will win a trip to compete in one of five regional Old Bay Peel & Eat Shrimp contests in the following cities, based on his/her geographic location.

- Northeast Regional Semi-Finals – New Jersey Seafood Festival; Belmar, NJ, June 7, 2003
- Midwest Regional Semi-Finals – 2003 Comerica Taste Fest; Detroit, MI, July 5, 2003
- West Coast Regional Semi-Finals – QFC Bite of Seattle; Seattle, WA, July 19, 2003
- Southwest Regional Semi-Finals –Tasting Texas Food & Music Festival; Houston, TX; July 26, 2003
- Southeast Regional Semi-Finals – Miami, FL, August 2, 2003

The winner of each regional contest will receive a $500 cash prize. Additionally, the winner and first runner-up from each regional contest will win a trip to Baltimore, MD, to compete in the national final – the Old Bay Peel & Eat Shrimp Classic – on Friday, August 29, 2003. The person capable of peeling and eating the most Old Bay-seasoned shrimp during the competition will win the $10,000 grand prize.

To enter, submit a 100 word or less description online at www.old-bay.com or by US mail. All entries must be postmarked by May 16, 2003. Finalists will be notified on or about May 30, 2003.

To receive an official entry form and contest rules, visit www.old-bay.com or call 1-800-MEAL-TIP (1-800-632-5847).

Figure 4.4 Contests Create News
This news release announces the Old Bay Peel & Eat Shrimp Classic and gives information about entering the contest. Due to the success of the first contest, Old Bay has decided to make it an annual event.
(Courtesy of Old Bay Seasoning and its public relations firm, Hunter Public Relations.)

PR Casebook

Eating Contests: The Newest Competitive Sport

A thin man, Takeru "Tsunami" Kobayashi of Japan for the third straight year won the 2003 annual Nathan's Famous hot dog eating contest in New York by downing 44 hot dogs in 12 minutes. That's one every 16 seconds.

He and thousands of other competitive eaters compete under the regulations of the International Federation of Competitive Eating (IFOCE). The organization is the brainchild of a New York publicist, George Shea, who got started by representing Nathan's back in 1988. He discovered that an eating contest is an excellent way of attracting media attention and, since then, has built Nathan's hot dog contest to be the World Cup of food gluttony.

Today, Shea is chairman of IFOCE, which sanctions more than 150 eating events worldwide. The hot dog contest at Nathan's began in 1916, but Shea is credited with expanding the concept to include contests for all kinds of food consumption—from chicken wings to pickled eggs and reindeer sausage. The IFOCE has attracted a variety of corporate sponsors for regional contests that lead to national play-offs. There is even *The Glutton Bowl: The World's Greatest Eating Competition*, which is aired on Fox Television.

Figure 4.5 Contestants Really Shell Out
Old Bay Seasoning's Peel & Eat Shrimp Classic was held in Baltimore and showcased 10 contestants from across the country competing for $10,000 and the title of America's biggest seafood fan. The event was featured on the *Today* show and CNN.
(Courtesy of Old Bay Seasoning and its public relations firm, Hunter Public Relations.)

- American Standard, a manufacturer of bathroom fixtures, wanted to capture the remodeling market, so it created America's Ugliest Bathroom contest. Consumers could enter by submitting a photo and a 100-word essay. About 1,500 homeowners entered the contest, and the winner received a new bathroom. More than 90 stories, reaching 19 million people, were written about the contest.

Polls and Surveys

The media seem to be fascinated by polls and surveys of all kinds. Public opinion is highly valued, and much attention is given to what the public thinks about issues, lifestyles, political candidates, quality of products and so on.

Author Peter Godwin, writing in *The New York Times Magazine,* says the public fascination with polls and surveys is "a uniquely American trait—a weakness for personal comparative analysis." He continues, "It's the reason we devour surveys about success, weight, love, family and happiness. And why not? Political polls tell us only how one candidate is faring against another. Polls

Do You Have a Messy Apartment? Win a Prize

The annual Messiest College Apartment competition is sponsored by Apartments.com as a way of generating business for its online apartment listings service.

The company started the contest several years ago, offering $10,000 to the most artfully filthy collegiate dive in a bid to entice affluent 20- to 30-year-old renters to visit its Web site. About 38 million people visited the site to cast their votes. In the second year, thanks to extensive publicity in the broadcast media, 110 million people visited the site and voted.

The third year of the contest was also a great success. The two-person public relations staff of Apartments.com made the rounds on radio talk shows, and TV stations were provided video clips of the previous year's finalists for Messiest College Apartment. In addition, the firm made use of Wireless Flash News, an online newswire that provides features and entertainment news to radio outlets.

When the finalists were announced, the publicity focus was on the finalists' home markets—Los Angeles, Chicago, and Minneapolis. The marketing director of Apartments.com told *PRWeek*, "The finalists got more coverage than the winner because people want to know who in their hometown is the messiest and make sure their kids get the title." Each finalist did between 30 and 40 radio interviews.

Arrangements were also made to give NBC's *Today* show the exclusive story on the winners of the contest, which included a live feed from their ultra-messy LA apartment near the UCLA campus. The contest also generated 57 broadcast placements, and the Web site recorded almost 83 million votes.

If you really work on creating a messy apartment, you too can be a winner.

---

about other people's personal lives let us gauge how we're faring relative to our friends and neighbors."

Given this media and public interest, any number of organizations are willing to oblige by conducting polls and surveys on a range of topics. Larry Chiagouris and Ann Middleman, in a *Public Relations Quarterly* article, say "publicity-driven research" is one of the most effective ways for an organization to get media coverage and position themselves as a market leader. In addition, surveys have high credibility because quantitative data is perceived as accurate.

Bausch & Lomb is a good example. It wanted to position itself as a new player in the dental product field, so it commissioned a national periodontal awareness survey. The results were published in a front-page story in a leading medical journal and in the dental trade press. The general public was reached with articles such as "dumb about gums" in the *Chicago Tribune*, which was syndicated nationally.

In another example, MCI WorldCom wanted to publicize its worldwide network conferencing capabilities, so it commissioned a study to find out the cost of meetings and business travel on productivity. The survey, among other things, found that the typical business professional attends more than 60 meetings a month, and more than a third of them are rated unproductive. Also, in-person meetings are up to seven times more expensive than conference calls.

PR Casebook

Corporate News Bureaus Generate News

A number of companies have formed corporate news bureaus and "institutes" to distribute research studies and lifestyle information as a method of generating media placements.

Reebok, for example, has the Aerobic Information Bureau, and Quaker Oats has organized the Gatorade Sports Science Institute. Schering Corporation, manufacturer of Chlor-Trimeton allergy tablets, serves the pollen-conscious public with its Allergy Season Index.

The allergy index relies on the forecasts of allergists in 35 metropolitan areas to let the public know what parts of the country will experience high concentrations of pollen and other allergy-provoking substances. "Local papers and news shows jump on it because they see it as a service to the public," says Chlor-Trimeton product manager Lauren Raabe. Such coverage also helps the visibility of the company.

Reebok, through its information bureau, distributes the results of scientific studies about aerobics and the use of proper gear for exercise. The information is factual and devoid of brand names, but it does position the company as an expert in the market when media stories attribute the study to the Reebok Aerobic Information Bureau.

The Kellogg Company, manufacturer of breakfast cereals, also gets a publicity dividend by providing general information about healthy diets under the banner of the Kellogg Nutrition Project.

News stories in the national press, as well as business periodicals, generated about 65 million **impressions**. Even more important, MCI WorldCom's market share of teleconferencing market increased from 21 to 28 percent. Samples of the publicity materials sent out by MCI WorldCom are shown in later chapters.

Not all surveys, however, are serious research. Scope mouthwash, for example, did a survey of 1,000 men and women to compile a list of "least kissable" celebrities, which included actress Rosie O'Donnell. Nair for Men conducted a survey of 1,000 women and found 90 percent of women between the ages of 18 and 44 find back hair on a man unattractive. However, only four in 10 women felt comfortable asking their significant other to do something about it. Nair, which sells products to remove body hair, also sent the press a compilation of "unusual facts" about hair. Blondes, for example, have an average of 140,000 hairs on their head compared with brunettes who have an average of 108,000. That's one reason, says the fact sheet, that blondes have more fun.

Food & Wine magazine, along with America Online, also did a survey and announced to the world that the supermarket checkout line is the most popular choice for where to meet a mate. It also found, in its admittedly unscientific poll, that whipped cream is the sexiest food but that chocolate mousse is better than sex. Meanwhile, Old Spice ranked 51 cities by perspiration propensity and found that San Antonio was the "sweatiest" summer city in America. Old Spice gained additional media publicity, especially among radio DJs, by sending a case of its new Red Zone antiperspirant to the mayor of San Antonio.

Professional Tips

Tips for Conducting a Survey

A survey of topical interest can generate considerable publicity for an organization. Mark A. Schulman, president of a market research and opinion polling firm in New York, gives these tips:

- Choose a topic that captures the interest of key targets and the media.
- Results must not appear to be self-serving. Journalists look for balance. Don't shy away from some negative findings.
- Find the story hook in advance by doing some preliminary research, often focus groups.
- Choose a sample size that will be credible. Don't skimp on sample size and undercut the project's appeal to media outlets. Sample the appropriate target groups.
- Put a human face on the percentages. Sprinkle some respondent quotes into the report.
- Plan your media strategy at the beginning of the process, not as an afterthought. Build excitement in the survey by including in the press kit some additional background material and sources to help the press build the story. Provide a list of outside experts who can be interviewed.
- Provide key press contacts with an advance peek in exchange for premium coverage.
- Don't sit on your data. Release it quickly. News events can make even the best study stale.
- Release all the results, not just the ones that are favorable to your client.

Guidelines for release of survey results are issued by the American Association for Public Opinion Research (www.aapor.org) and the Council of American Survey Research Organizations (www.casro.org). You should always include information on the method of interview, the number of people interviewed, dates, and the exact question wording. Journalists may not use this information in their stories, but it gives them confidence that the survey findings are credible.

Source: O'Dwyer's PR Services Report, May 2002, p. 33.

Nancy Hicks, a senior vice president of Hill & Knowlton, says surveys and polls can be marvelous publicity opportunities if a few guidelines are followed. In an article for PRSA's *Tactics*, she suggested:

- *The topic.* It should be timely, have news value, and fit the needs of the organization.
- *The research firm.* It should be one that has credibility with journalists. That's why many commissioned surveys are done by the Gallup Organization or similar nationally known firms.
- *The survey questions.* They should be framed to elicit newsworthy findings.

Hicks also suggests paying attention to how the material is packaged for the press. "The lead in the news release should feature the most newsworthy findings, not what is of most interest to the sponsoring organization," says Hicks.

Media kits should include background information on the organization and on the research firm, a summary of the major research findings, and simple charts and graphs that can be easily reproduced as part of a news story. Media kits are discussed further in Chapter 8.

Top 10 Lists

Surveys and polls, although credible, take time and can be expensive. A less expensive way to create news of this sort is to simply compile a "Top 10 List."

Fashion institutes issue lists of the "Top 10 Best Dressed Women," and environmental groups compile lists of the "Top 10 Polluters." Newspapers and magazines also get into the act by compiling a list of the "Top 10 College Basketball Players," or the "Top 10 Newsmakers" of the year.

Briggs & Stratton, a leading manufacturer of lawnmowers and other outdoor power equipment, builds its brand identity with an annual list of the "Top Ten Lawns in America." The 2003 awards were given to beautiful lawns with a view, and the Great Lawn of New York's Central Park was the company's top pick. According to the news release, "The Great Lawn is a newly restored blanket of green grass that attracts both native New Yorkers and visitors to Central Park year-round. . . . The view of the New York City skyline, which provides the lawn's setting, makes jaws drop." See Figure 4.6 for the first page of the news release.

There are endless possibilities for top 10 lists. A San Francisco public relations firm even got 8 inches in *The Wall Street Journal* for its "Top 10 most humiliating public relations gaffes of the year." First place went to the District of Columbia Housing Authority, which issued a news release about a drug bust the night before the raid was planned. The dealers heard about it on the radio and failed to make an appearance.

Product Demonstrations

The objective of a product demonstration is to have consumers or media representatives actually test or sample a product. One computer company, for example, demonstrated its new notebook computer by taking reporters on chartered flights from New York to Los Angeles and letting each reporter use the product during the trip.

A cosmetic company, Styli-Style, introduced its newly designed flat makeup pencil at a New York champagne bar. It hired celebrity makeup artist Mally Roncal to demonstrate the various colors and to also apply makeup to the various journalists and guests attending the event.

Another kind of makeup was done by PetSmart, a pet-supply chain. PetSmart publicized a grand opening of a store by offering its pet grooming services to some of the local Humane Society's grubbiest guests and then putting them on display for adoption. It was a win-win situation. The idea clearly demonstrated the value of its grooming services and also placed the new store in a favorable light because of its community outreach. Even a television news reporter covering the event took a dog home after his wife saw a made-over mutt on television.

For more information:
Tom Ryan
(414) 227-2254
tryan@ckpr.biz

Anita Fisher
(414) 256-1169
fisher.anita@basco.com

For Immediate Release

**Briggs & Stratton Rolls out the Green Carpet
For 2003 National Top Ten Lawns With A View Winners**
Central Park's Great Lawn Claims Top Spot in Sixth Annual Contest

Milwaukee (April 21, 2003) — Lawns around the country are turning green with envy as Briggs & Stratton Corporation announces the 2003 National Top 10 Lawns with a View. Central Park's Great Lawn in New York City claimed the top spot in the annual ranking compiled by the small engine manufacturer, state tourism officials and lawn experts.

Since 1998, Briggs & Stratton has honored impressive public lawns around the country. This year, the Milwaukee-based company is honoring beautiful green spaces located in, or overlooking, impressive scenery. The 2003 Top 10 national winners, which can be found at www.toptenlawns.com, were chosen from regional winners in the East, West, South and Midwest. The 2003 national Top 10 Lawns with a View include:

1. Central Park's Great Lawn – New York, New York
2. Nelson-Atkins Museum of Art – Kansas City, Missouri
3. Piedmont Park – Atlanta, Georgia
4. Minneapolis Sculpture Garden – Minneapolis, Minnesota
5. International Peace Garden – Dunseith, North Dakota
6. Bicentennial Mall State Park – Nashville, Tennessee
7. Bascom Hill – Madison, Wisconsin
8. Esplanade – Boston, Massachusetts
9. Washington Park – Portland, Oregon
10. Pebble Beach Golf Links – Pebble Beach, California

The Great Lawn is a newly restored blanket of green grass that attracts both native New Yorkers and visitors to Central Park year round. Although the well-kept turf impresses those who visit, the view of the New York City skyline, which provides the lawn's setting, makes jaws drop. This winning combination made the Great Lawn Briggs & Stratton's top pick.

-more-

Mailing Address: Post Office Box 702   Milwaukee, Wisconsin 53201-0702
General Offices: 12301 W. Wirth Street   Wauwatosa, Wisconsin 53222-2110   Telephone: 414/259-5333   www.briggsandstratton.com

Figure 4.6 Top 10 Lists Are a Media Favorite
This is the first page of the news release issued by Briggs & Stratton announcing the "Top Ten Lawns With a View." The second and third pages of the news release gave brief descriptions of the 10 winning lawns. The company also distributed color slides of each lawn.
(Courtesy of Briggs & Stratton, Milwaukee, WI.)

A lighthearted but equally effective demonstration of proof was a "wedding kiss workshop" sponsored by a lipstick manufacturer. To demonstrate its smearproof lipstick, the company used the two stars of the off-Broadway hit *Tony and Tina's Wedding,* who were introduced as kissing experts. During the one-hour workshop, staged exclusively for media representatives, actors demonstrated kissing techniques and five brides-to-be competed for the title of "best kisser." The story made *The Wall Street Journal* and *CNN News.*

Auto manufacturers do "product demonstrations" by inviting journalists to test-drive a new model. Hotels and resorts invite travel writers to spend a weekend at the facility. Food companies do demonstrations by getting representatives on cooking and home shows. Weber Grills, for example, hired a well-known chef to give tips on talk shows about the proper way to barbecue.

Stunts

Journalists often disparage publicity stunts, but, if they are highly visual, they often get extensive media coverage.

One popular theme is doing something that qualifies for the *Guinness World Records*. Thus, newspapers print photos and television stations use video clips of "the world's largest quiche Lorraine," "the world's largest apple pie," "the world's largest ice cream cake," or even "the world's longest salad bar." See Figure 4.7 for the world's largest chocolate.

Nintendo of America also got media publicity by the setting the world record the largest bowl of pasta. It filled a 10-foot-diameter bowl with 1.5 tons of spaghetti and then invited fans to literally dive in. The stunt was to promote the release of the new game *Mario Sunshine*. Another videogame maker took a different approach. Acclaim Entertainment offered to pay a couple $10,000 if they named

Figure 4.7 World's Largest Chocolate
Hershey Foods Corporation announced the addition of dark-chocolate kisses to its menu by creating the largest Hershey's kiss ever made. The kiss, weighing in at 6,759 pounds and standing nearly seven feet tall, was unveiled to the press and the public in New York. It was made with the help of pastry chefs from the French Culinary Institute and a stack of 10-pound chocolate blocks 53 layers high. The measurements were sent to the *Guinness World Records* for inclusion as the world's largest chocolate candy.
(Courtesy of Hershey's Corporation and its public relations firm, Edelman Public Relations.)

their newborn after the hero of its new game, *Turok: Evolution*. So if you ever meet someone by the name of Turok, you know how the person got his or her name.

Baskin-Robbins made a 5.5-ton cake in one of the hottest spots on earth, Dubai, to celebrate international ice cream month. In the case of the salad bar (see Figure 4.8 for the **media advisory**), Hidden Valley Ranch salad dressings spon-

---

GREAT PHOTO OPPORTUNITY
FEATURE STORY/ KICKER STORY

C-Band Feed Thursday, May 27th 3:30-4:00PM (ET)

World's Longest Salad Bar
Comes to Central Park May 27th

Stretching 1 1/2 Football Fields, The World's Longest Salad Bar is a Candidate for The Guiness Book of World Records

In honor of their 25th anniversary and to kick-off the 1999 summer picnic season, Hidden Valley Ranch is bringing the world's longest salad bar to Central Park. Any New Yorker with a hearty appetite will be treated to a free lunch featuring more than **17,000 pounds** of lettuce, tomatoes, carrots, mushrooms and an assortment of other fresh vegetables -- topped with Hidden Valley's Original Ranch Dressing.

The event is open to the public from 11:30AM - 1:00PM and will benefit City Harvest, the nation's largest food assistance program. Hidden Valley will donate all surplus produce from the 160-yard salad bar to the 475 New York City food agencies in the City Harvest network designed to help feed the hungry. The world's longest salad bar is co-sponsored by the Produce for Better Health Foundation National 5-A-Day Program and City of New York Parks and Recreation.

The World's Longest Salad Bar will be at The Literary Walk in Central Park -- Entrance is on 66th and 5th Ave.

VNR & B-Roll Hard Copy Available Upon Request:
- Shots of salad bar, various produce varieties
- Close-up of participants
- Soundbites From:
  - **_Julia Erickson_**, Executive Director, City Harvest, Inc.
  - **_Josie Welling_**, Brand Manager, Hidden Valley Ranch
  - **_Nolan Henson_**, Son of the Hidden Valley Ranch Dressing creator, Steve Henson
  - **_Mara Wilson_**, child celebrity, chef and actress
  - **_Justin Miller_**, world's youngest chef

Satellite C-Band Feed: **Thursday, May 27th** • 3:30 - 4:00 PM (ET) • **GE 2** • Transponder 18 • DL Freq. 4060 H • Audio 6.2/ 6.8

For Technical Information: Quicklink (212) 947-4475
For Story Information: Randy Hurlow at Publicis Dialog (206) 270-4642, (206) 648-3403 (pager)
For Hard Copy: Jennifer Burd at Target Video News (212) 889-2323

Figure 4.8 **World's Longest Salad Bar**
Publicity stunts attract media attention. This media advisory alerts the press about photo and video opportunities relating to the World's Longest Salad Bar.
(Courtesy of Hidden Valley Ranch and TVN Productions.)

sored the event in New York's Central Park. It took 17,000 pounds of vegetables to make the salad, which, of course, was topped with Hidden Valley's Original Ranch dressing.

Other kinds of stunts that are also events can be staged. A German software firm, for example, celebrated its listing on the New York Stock Exchange by converting a block of New York's financial district into a "beach party." It took 60 tons of sand, 5,000 beach balls, and several volleyball nets to accomplish the transition. Because of the visual element, the company received more extensive coverage than just a short paragraph on the business page.

Rallies and Protests

A rally or protest may be a large event, such as the "Million Man March" that took place in Washington, D.C., or it could be as small as a group of high school students showing support for a fired coach.

Few television stations or newspapers can resist covering a rally or a protest demonstration, each of which has high news value from the standpoint of human interest and conflict. Moreover, a rally or protest is highly visual, which is ideal for television coverage and newspaper photographs. (See Figure 4.9 for an example of a newspaper photograph showing demonstrators at the World Trade Organization (WTO) in Seattle, Washington.) The United Farm Workers (UFW), for example, organized a march on California's capital to pressure the governor to sign a controversial bill allowing the UFW to have a neutral arbitrator on contract talks with growers. *PRWeek* reported, "The 10-day, 165-mile march elicited plenty of ink for the UFW." In addition to considerable coverage in the California press, the march was a news item on such national media as CNN, *The New York Times*, and the Associated Press (AP).

Although television often gives the impression that demonstrations are somewhat spontaneous events, the reality is that they are usually well planned and organized. The manuals of activist groups, for example, give guidelines on everything from contacting potential participants via an e-mail network to appointing "marshals" who will assure that the protestors won't destroy property or unnecessarily provoke police confrontations. The idea is to make a statement, not create a riot that will damage the organization's cause.

In addition, the media should be contacted in advance to ensure coverage. More than one rally has been rescheduled to accommodate the media. Prominent people and celebrities, if possible, should be asked to join the march or give a talk at a rally. Prominence, as activists know, is another important news value.

Lawsuits are often an extension of rallies and demonstrations. After a six-month campaign against KFC, for example, the People for the Ethical Treatment of Animals (PETA) generated additional publicity by filing a lawsuit against the company claiming that the fast-food giant is misleading the public by denying it mistreats chickens headed for its restaurants. The lawsuit, filed in Los Angeles, claimed that the more than 700 million chickens slaughtered each year for KFC outlets "often endure intense suffering for most, or all of their lives." KFC denied

Figure 4.9 Rallies and Demonstrations
Rallies and demonsrations are highly visual and have the news value of conflict. Demonstrators in Seattle, Washington, protesting the policies of the World Trade Organization (WTO), for example, got more media coverage than the conference itself.
(© AFP/Corbis.)

the charges and said it was committed to the well-being and humane treatment of poultry.

Personal Appearances

Two kinds of personal appearances generate news. First is the kind where news is incidental to something else. Second is the appearance where news is the only objective. Most typical of the first type is the situation where someone makes a speech to an organization. If the president of the XYZ Company addresses the local chamber of commerce, he will be heard by all who attend the meeting.

The audience for the speech, however, may be greatly increased if the media are supplied with copies of the speech, a news release, or several **soundbites**. As a general rule, every public appearance should be considered an opportunity for news both before and after the event. And, of course, there should always be an effort to get reporters to attend the meeting and get the story themselves.

Appearances where publicity is the sole objective take several forms. One is an appearance on a radio or television talk show. There are numerous opportunities for appearing on such shows. For example, more than 1,000 radio stations (out of 10,000) in the nation now emphasize talk instead of music.

Local TV stations and cable systems have their shows, and there are national shows such as *Meet the Press, Oprah Winfrey, Larry King Live,* and the *Today* show. The American Fly Fishing Trade Association (AFFTA), for example, scored a coup by getting on three major television shows in a three-day period.

First was the *Letterman* show, where Sister Carol Anne Corley ("the Tying Nun") enlightened the host about some of the finer points of the sport. The next morning, two AFFTA representatives—clad in boots, waders, and vests—garnered prime time in front of the *Today* show window in New York's Rockefeller Plaza. Two days later, on the opening day of the trout fishing season, Estee Lauder model and fly-fishing instructor Karen Graham bellowed "Good morning, America" for the ABC cameras and gave a clinic for members of the media. Chapter 9 discusses how to get on such shows.

Another approach is the media tour. Increasingly, this is done via satellite and the Internet to save travel time and costs. The **satellite media tour** (SMT), explained further in Chapter 9, is essentially the process of placing a spokesperson in a television studio and arranging for news anchors around the country to do a short interview via satellite. It is the same process that news programs use to get reports from their correspondents in the field.

A good example of an SMT is when the "Melissa" computer virus swamped e-mail systems around the nation. Within hours, an Internet security company was able make an expert available for satellite interviews by television news anchors throughout the United States. The interview supplemented the stations' coverage about the virus and told viewers what to do to avoid "Melissa." Another SMT, sponsored by Cook's Champagne, was done by champion skater Todd Eldredge to raise money for cancer research.

There is also the **cyber media tour**. Michael Dell, CEO of Dell Computer and a leader in the high-technology industry, used this technique to promote his new book, *Direct from Dell: Strategies That Revolutionized an Industry*. He did a series of pre-booked interviews online with journalists. The event was also digitized and streamed live over the Internet, where it was available to consumers and other journalists. The CEO of Advanced Micro Devices (AMD), W. J. "Jerry" Sanders, also used a cyber media tour. The company used a video-conference and an Internet webcast, among other tactics, to announce a new microprocessor chip.

SUMMARY

- A major objective of many public relations programs is to get publicity for the employer or client.

- Publicity is not an end in itself. It is a means to help achieve organizational goals and objectives.

- Publicists should thoroughly understand the basic news values of (1) timeliness, (2) prominence, (3) proximity, (4) significance, (5) unusualness, (6) human interest, (7) conflict, and (8) newness.

- The first step in preparing publicity is to be thoroughly familiar with the company or organization.

- A public relations writer should constantly monitor current events and situations that may affect the organization and provide opportunities for publicity.

- Problem-solving skills and creativity are required to generate publicity.

- Creative solutions can be developed through brainstorming sessions.

- Some opportunities for generating publicity include (1) special events, (2) contests, (3) polls and surveys, (4) top 10 lists, (5) stunts, (6) product demonstrations, (7) rallies and protests, and (8) personal appearances.

- The satellite media tour and the cyber media tour are now used by organizations to book a spokesperson on a television or radio news program.

ADDITIONAL RESOURCES

Ballard, Chris. "That Stomach Is Going to Make You Money Someday." *The New York Times Magazine,* August 31, 2003, pp. 24–27. Eating contests.

Brooke, James. "New Zealand Markets Itself as Film Land of the 'Rings.' *The New York Times,* December 31, 2002, pp. C1, C4.

Chabria, Anita. "Pulling a Stunt That Will Whip Up the Media." *PRWeek,* September 23, 2002, p. 22.

Chabria, Anita. "The Right Way to Seize the Day." *PRWeek,* December 3, 2001, p. 18. Creating special days, weeks, and months.

Davey, Monica. "Harley at 100: Mainstream Meets Mystique." *The New York Times,* September 1, 2003, p. A1, A10.

Dobrow, Larry. "Keeping Tabs on the Talent." *PRWeek,* September 3, 2001, p. 25. Using celebrities as spokespersons.

Frank, John N. "Duck Tape Reaps Rewards of Sticking to Innovative PR Plan." *PRWeek,* August 5, 2002, p. 10.

Grisdela, Margaret. "Create Surveys That Get the Press Calling." *PR Tactics,* April 2003, p. 11.

Kaufman, Frederick. "Fat of the Land." *Harper's,* October 2003, pp. 65–67. Eating contests.

Kuczynski, Alex. "Treating Disease With a Famous Face." *The New York Times,* December 15, 2002, Section 9, p. 1. Celebrity endorsements.

Lippman, John. "Hollywood Report: A Tame Walk of Fame." *The Wall Street Journal*, October 3, 2003, p. W1.

Schulman, Mark A. "PR Surveys Break Through the Clutter." *O'Dwyer's PR Services Report*, May 2002, p. 33.

Trickett, Eleanor. "Brainstorming Ideas for a New Campaign." *PRWeek*, November 18, 2002, p. 20.

Chapter 5

News Releases and Fact Sheets

A basic news release and fact sheet are basic elements in almost every publicity plan. There are, however, two sobering facts. First, various studies have found that between 55 and 97 percent of all news releases sent to media outlets are never used. Second, there is massive competition for the attention of reporters and editors. Many publications receive 300 to 500 news releases a week. The two major electronic distributors, Business Wire and PR Newswire, transmit more than a thousand releases a day.

Given the odds, this means you must do three things if your release is to stand a chance of being published. First, you must follow a standardized format. Second, you must provide information (in the news release or fact sheet) that will interest the audience. And third, your material must be timely.

This chapter outlines how to prepare news releases and fact sheets that will meet these criteria. In several examples, the news release and the fact sheet from an organization are paired so you can clearly see the difference between the two formats. The primary emphasis of this chapter is on the development of the standard printed news release, but many of the basic elements discussed also apply to the formatting of news releases for electronic distribution via the Internet and the World Wide Web.

It is pointed out, for example, that an e-mailed news release should be much shorter than a standard news release. Chapter 9 will discuss how to prepare materials for radio and television stations.

THE VALUE OF NEWS RELEASES AND FACT SHEETS

So why write a **news release**? The primary reason, of course, is to help achieve organizational objectives. The adoption theory model discussed in Chapter 2 points out that people start the process of decision making after awareness has been created.

News releases and fact sheets, when they form the basis of stories in the news columns of newspapers and magazines or are part of a TV news hour, create awareness about ideas, situations, services, and products. A new product on the market, or an appeal for Red Cross blood donations, is brought to the attention of the public. A manufacturer of a potato-chip maker, for example, sold out its entire stock after *The New York Times* included parts of a news release and a fact sheet in an article about new kitchen gadgets.

News releases are also cost-effective. Almost any organization, from a garden club to IBM, can create and distribute news releases at nominal cost compared to the cost of buying advertising. There is also the factor of credibility. News releases appear in the news columns of newspapers, and studies consistently show that people consider information in a news story much more believable than an advertisement.

In one such study, the Wirthlin Group surveyed a sample of 1,023 adults. Almost 30 percent of the respondents said that a news article would affect their buying decisions, whereas only 8 percent indicated that an advertisement would.

PLANNING A NEWS RELEASE

Writing a news release requires the tools and equipment described in Chapter 1. The following sections discuss the selection of paper, some fundamentals about word processing a release, and the style you should follow. But before writing anything, the public relations writer should complete a planning worksheet.

The Basic Questions

Your planning worksheet should answer the following questions.

- What is the subject of the message? What is the specific focus of this release?
- Whom is this message designed to reach? For example, is it aimed at local citizens, or is it mainly for executives in other companies who read the business page and might order the product?
- What is in it for this particular audience? What are the potential benefits and rewards?
- What goal is the organization pursuing? What is the organization's purpose? Is it to increase sales of a product? Position the company as a leader in the field? Show company concern for the environment?
- What do you want to achieve with the news release? Is the objective to inform, to change attitudes and behavior, to increase attendance at a local event?
- What themes should this news release highlight? How can they be tailored to the format of a specific publication and its readers?

These questions enable you to select and structure the content of a news release from a public relations perspective. The release can still meet the journalistic goal of presenting information objectively and in correct newspaper or broadcast style, but it must also be carefully crafted to include key messages. This kind of planning is the major difference between writing as a journalist and writing as a public relations person.

At the same time, however, you must think like a journalist. In terms of format and content, a news release should be the same thing as a news story. Many of the same rules apply, including the news values discussed in Chapter 4. Like a journalist, a public relations writer needs to include the five Ws and H: *who, what, when, where, why,* and *how.* If you have the answers to these questions at your fingertips, you are ready to begin.

Selection of Paper

The standard paper for a news release in the United States is plain white and measures 8.5 by 11 inches. This is called "letter size" and is sold in packages of 500 sheets (called a "ream") at office supply stores. The paper should be 20- or 24-pound weight and designed for multiple purposes—inkjet printers, laser printers, plain-paper fax machines, and high-speed photocopy machines. In Europe and most of Asia, the standard letter size paper is A4—about 1 inch longer and a bit narrower than the U.S. letter size.

The use of colored paper for a news release does not get much support from experienced publicists, despite the logic that a colored release will stand out from the mass of white paper that piles up in a newsroom. Most editors say that news value is the major factor—not the color of the paper. If color does strike your fancy, use pastel colors such as ivory, light blue, light green, or pale yellow. Don't use dark colors; they make words hard to read. The same goes for brilliant colors such as shocking pink, Day-Glo green, or bright yellow. The editor wants facts, not a rainbow.

At the same time, however, you should be alert to opportunities for some creativity. Amann & Associates, a Virginia-based public relations firm, sent news releases on light blue paper with a bottom border of colorful tropical fish because the client was Tetra Systems, a manufacturer of fish food. The approach was effective because the paper gave the effect of looking into an aquarium.

Spacing and Margins

Double-spacing is the standard for printed news releases distributed via fax or regular mail. Double-spaced copy is easier to read at the draft stage, and editors have traditionally found that the extra space allows them to do editing and rewrites.

However, if you are distributing news releases or fact sheets via e-mail and the Internet, single-spacing is the standard format. See Figures 5.3 and 5.4 for examples. You may electronically send a double-spaced news release to an electronic distributor such as Business Wire or PR Newswire, but they will reformat it to single-spacing for distribution directly to a newspaper's computer. Editors, by calling up the news release or fact sheet on their computers, can change the format to anything they want. See Figures 5.5 and 5.11 for examples of electronic news releases distributed by U.S. Newswire, a division of Medialink Worldwide.

In sum, if your news releases are mailed or faxed to a variety of publications, double-space them. If you are distributing via e-mail and the Internet, single-space them.

Standard margins for a printed news release are 2 inches from the top of the page and about 1.5 inches from each side and the bottom of the page. If you have a letterhead, start writing copy about 2 inches below it. See Figure 5.1 for an example of a well-formatted standard news release.

Some other formatting rules for a printed news release are as follows:

- Use 10- or 12-point standard type. Courier and Times Roman are popular fonts because they are easy to read. Avoid "squeezing" copy to fit on one page by reducing the size of type: this is self-defeating.

- Don't split sentences or paragraphs between pages.

- Never hyphenate a word at the end of a line. Unjustified right margins are acceptable.

- Number the pages of a news release.

NEWS RELEASE

Contact: Lynn Barrett
802-258-3992
prime@sover.net

Sue Bohle
310-785-0515 ext 223
sue@bohle.com

National Historic Landmark, Greenfield Village, Re-Opens after $60 Million Facelift
Record Numbers Expected at World's Largest Outdoor History Museum

Dearborn, MI, May 27, 2003 – The national historic landmark, Greenfield Village, will re-open on Tuesday, June 10, after a $60 million facelift, nine months of construction and a new infrastructure. The restored and renovated Greenfield Village at The Henry Ford opened in 1929. It is a national treasure representing more than 300 years of America's past and 83 historic structures.

"There's nothing else like Greenfield Village in the world." said Steven Hamp, president of The Henry Ford. "It is the world's largest outdoor history museum with live presenters, rides, activities and cuisine that altogether give the visitor a truly amazing experience. We are very excited to reopen this amazing 90 acres of American history reaching back to the 17th century. We not only have the sights, sounds and sensations of America's past, but we have real ties with real people who brought the richness of American invention, innovation and tradition."

The Village will bring American experiences to life with seven new themed districts, a new entryway, restaurants and shops. These districts better organize the three centuries of America's traditions and technology presented daily at Greenfield Village. They include: Working Farms, Liberty Craftworks, Main Street, Edison at Work, Porches and Parlors, Henry Ford's Model T, Railroad Junction. (See details on theme districts attached.)

more

1900 Avenue of the Stars, Suite 200 · Los Angeles, CA 90067 · *telephone* (310) 785-0515 · facsimile (310) 277-2066 · www.bohle.com

Page Two
Greenfield Village Re-Opening

In addition to the new districts, changes made to this National Historic Landmark include a new open, airy entryway, which will mean shorter ticket lines and less congestion between ticket holders and ticket buyers who are making their way into the outdoor history attraction.

Before entering the village, visitors will step into the new Josephine F. Ford Plaza with its Neo-Georgian architecture, popular in Henry Ford's day. Beautiful brickwork and inspirational landscaping make this gathering space reminiscent of Market Square in Portsmouth, New Hampshire, in the 1790s. The plaza features a new fountain and a newly remodeled and enlarged Greenfield Village Store, now accessible with or without village admission.

Once visitors enter the village proper, they will be guided by new way-finding signage and newly paved roads and sidewalks. More than 300 historic lampposts, cast from original molds, have been installed to provide much needed visibility for evening programming and events.

The Henry Ford, located in Dearborn, Michigan was founded in 1929 by automotive pioneer Henry Ford. This history destination includes Henry Ford Museum, Greenfield Village, The Henry Ford IMAX Theatre, The Benson Ford Research Center and The Ford Rouge Factory Tour (opening in spring 2004). The Henry Ford, America's greatest history attraction, is the historic destination that brings the American experience to life. For more information and admission prices please visit the website www.thehenryford.org.

\#\#\#\#\#

Figure 5.1 The Traditional News Release
This print release about Greenfield Village is a good example of a well-structured and well-formatted news release. The headline gives the key news, and the lead paragraph is a good length.
(Courtesy of the Bohle Company, Los Angeles.)

- Place a slug line (a short description) at the top of each page after the first one. This identifies the story in case the pages get separated.
- Write "more" at the end of each page if the news release continues.
- Write one of the old journalistic terms "-30-," "end," or "###" at the end of your news release.

Use AP Style

The *Associated Press Stylebook* is the standard reference for writing news releases because most American newspapers use "AP style" or some variation of it. If a news release conforms to AP style, it makes the work of reporters and editors much easier.

Lorry Lokey, general manager of Business Wire, says that thorough knowledge of AP style helps tailor your news release to the person who ultimately decides if it is published. He says, "Editors are your customers, to put it bluntly; you are trying to sell them on your 'story.' Put roadblocks in their way via faulty style and they are likely to take their business to someone else's release."

Lokey also complains that public relations writers don't seem to notice that most newspapers keep paragraphs limited to less than six typeset column lines. Instead, far too many news releases have paragraphs that are six to 10 typed lines, the equivalent of nine to 18 newspaper column lines. More aspects of style are discussed later in this chapter.

TYPES OF NEWS RELEASES

A news release can be prepared on virtually any subject that would affect or interest a general or specialized audience. Indeed, in the course of a year, an organization prepares and distributes news releases on a variety of subjects. There are five basic types of news releases, although the lines between them often blur. They are (1) announcements, (2) spot announcements, (3) reaction stories, (4) bad news, and (5) local news.

Announcements

Announcements herald such occurrences as personnel appointments, promotions, and changes; new products or services (if they are really new and interesting); reports of sales, earnings, acquisitions, mergers, events, awards, contests, policy changes, employment opportunities, anniversaries, price changes, new employees, layoffs, construction, openings and closings of facilities, contracts received (or canceled) and legal actions.

A good example of an announcement release is Figure 5.2, Korbel's "perfect marriage proposal" contest.

In general, it is a good idea to have announcements made by the highest-ranking person in the organization. As pointed out in Chapter 4, prominence is a news value. The president of a company making an announcement garners more news interest than a vice president or a department manager. However, when it comes

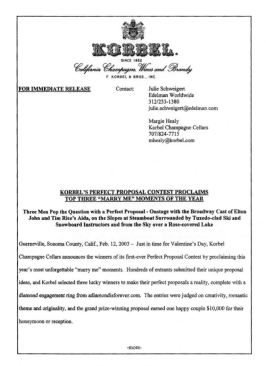

Figure 5.2 An Announcement Release
Korbel Champagne Cellars used a series of news releases to announce a contest for the "perfect marriage proposal." This release announces the top three winners of the contest, which attracted more than 500 entrants. Shown is the first two pages of a three-page release that profiles the three winning couples.
(Courtesy of Korbel Champagne Cellars and its public relations firm, Edelman Worldwide.)

to localizing news, the local plant manager is more prominent to the local press than the company president whose office is in a distant city.

Spot Announcements

When things due to some outside action or influence happen to an organization, a spot news release may be in order. When a storm disrupts the services of a public utility, a fire or an accident stops work, a flood closes roads, a strike closes a factory, such incidents can lead to the issuance of a release that tells what has happened and what effect it is having.

If the affected organization does not give the news to the media, reporters will write their own stories and may do a poor job because they don't have all the facts. In many cases, follow-up stories must be released later. These may carry additional detailed information and report on progress toward solving the problem.

Reaction Releases

Reaction releases are used when something is done or said that may harm an organization—for example, a charge that a factory has unsafe working conditions, a lawsuit claiming injury, or a finding that a certain food additive may cause cancer.

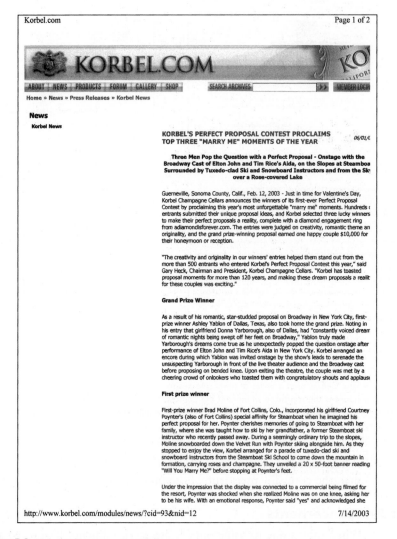

Figure 5.3 News Release on the Web
The printed news release, shown in Figure 5.2, was also posted on the Korbel Web site (korbel.com).
Although the copy is the same, notice the single-spaced formatting of the release on the World Wide Web.
(Courtesy of Korbel Champagne Cellars, Guerneville, CA.)

When a government agency decides to stop funding a particular activity, the people affected by the cutback will issue reaction releases proclaiming that the project is essential and that no budget cuts should be made.

Another use of the reaction release is to hitch on to something that, though not harmful to the organization, has some bearing on it. For instance, if the Environmental Protection Agency announces an easing of controls, an affected company might issue a release stating that it will continue its policy of nonpollution and outline that policy. See Figure 5.5 for a typical reaction news release.

The fact sheet document:

FOR IMMEDIATE RELEASE   F. KORBEL & CROS, INC.

Julie Schweigert
Edelman Worldwide
(312) 233-1380
julie.schweigert@edelman.com

Margie Healy
Korbel Champagne Cellars
(707) 824-7715
mhealy@korbel.com

"Korbel's Perfect Proposal Contest" Program Fact Sheet

- Korbel invited Americans to enter their dream proposal scenario at Korbel.com, from June 1, 2002 – December 15, 2002. More than 500 entries were received, and three lucky winners were selected to win their ultimate dream proposal for their significant other, including a diamond engagement ring. One lucky couple will win the grand prize of $10,000 for a honeymoon or reception.

- This year's winning proposals will be taking place in Colorado, Minnesota and New York. The three winning proposals will be kept a secret from the "intendeds" and brought to life just before Valentine's Day, 2003.

- The contest was open to Americans age 21 years of age or older, as of June 1, 2002, except where prohibited.

- Entries were judged on creativity, originality and romantic theme by an expert panel of judges.

- Korbel plans to conduct Korbel's Perfect Proposal Contest annually. More information on the contest is available at Korbel.com.

- Korbel Champagne Cellars has been producing fine California *méthode champenoise*-produced champagne for more than 120 years. Korbel's premium portfolio includes Korbel Brut, Extra Dry, Brut Rose, Sec, Blanc de Noirs, Chardonnay Champagne, Rouge Vintage Dated Natural, Blanc de Noirs and Le Premier.

###

Figure 5.4 Korbel Fact Sheet
The media, in addition to receiving various news releases about Korbel's "perfect proposals contest," also received a basic fact sheet about the event and how it was organized.
(Courtesy of Korbel Champagne Cellars and its public relations firm, Edelman Worldwide.)

Bad News

Some organizations suppress news that might reflect badly on them. This is a sure way to make things worse. People will talk, rumors will spread, and investigative reporters will take a major interest in exposing the "cover-up."

The only way to make the best of such a situation is to confront the issue. A release giving facts and the organization's point of view should be drafted immediately. If reporters ask for more information, it should be given to them.

Another approach is to bury bad news within a story. One corporation started a news release about its year-end results by reporting "progress in our strategic program by divesting companies outside our core consumer business." In the second paragraph, the company said it had declared dividends on preferred stock. The news that the company had a loss of $109 million didn't come until the second

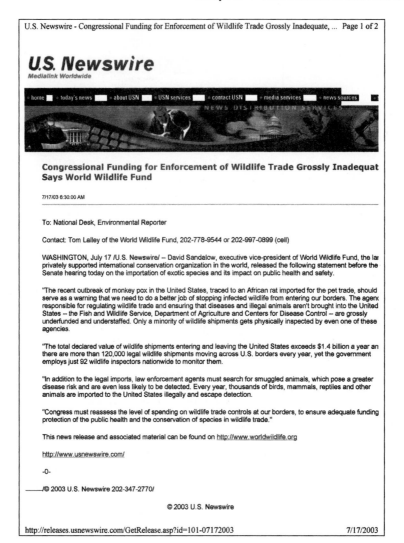

Figure 5.5 Reaction News Release
Organizations often respond to events or statements by high-level government officials, especially if it concerns their industry, cause, or product. This news release reflects the reaction of the World Wildlife Fund to government proposals regarding the importation of exotic species. This release, distributed via e-mail and the World Wide Web, is formatted for the medium. It is only five paragraphs, and it refers readers to the full news release and supporting materials on the organization's Web site.
(Courtesy of U.S. Newswire, a division of Medialink Worldwide.)

page, and it wasn't until the fourth page that the company said it was omitting its dividend on common stock.

This approach to reporting bad news may slip by some journalists, but most alert reporters will detect the clumsy attempt and make a mental note that all future company news releases should be taken with a grain of salt. As discussed in Chapter 3, a professional public relations writer should convince the company that such a news release is not only unethical, but also can violate state and federal regulatory agency guidelines.

Local News

The most common reason that news releases don't get used is the absence of a local angle. Although many publications and broadcast outlets serve a national audience, the reality is that most media outlets serve local audiences.

A case in point is the *Grosse Pointe* (MI) *News,* a weekly newspaper serving an affluent suburb of Detroit. John Minnis, news editor of the paper, and Cornelius Pratt, a professor of public relations at Michigan State University, found that the newspaper received 189 news releases in a single week. Of that number, 65 (34 percent) were selected for publication. Overall, 57 percent of the releases printed were chosen for their local angle.

The two researchers, who reported their findings in *Public Relations Quarterly,* concluded, "Location, location, location is the axiom of real estate agents. In public relations, it should be localization, localization, localization."

There are two ways to localize. One is to use the names of local people; the other is to use information that is of local significance. The computer makes it possible to easily alter a basic news release by inserting information that emphasizes the local angle. An example of this was how to "localize" the insurance award in Chapter 4.

The technique of "hometown" releases is used by many organizations. Colleges and universities, for example, often prepare individualized releases about entering freshmen for newspapers in their hometowns. The Defense Department also sends releases about the positive accomplishments of enlisted men and women to their hometown media. In one recent year, the U.S. Navy prepared and distributed 1.13 million "hometown" releases.

Localizing information is another way to get releases published. An airline, for example, usually issues a quarterly summary giving the total number of passengers, the number of flights, and other statistical details. This information, by itself, does not have much local interest except in the city where the airline is headquartered. You can, however, gain more publicity by extracting local statistics from the general report. For example, the media outlets in Boise, Idaho, would get a "localized" release from the airline that would give the number of passengers boarding the plane in Boise and the most frequent destinations. The release might also give the number of flights per month out of Boise. The last part of the news release would give the overall statistics for the airline.

Any number of state and national organizations also "localize" information. The National Association of Realtors, for example, may break down national statistics by city. Editors in Tucson get a release about the real estate market in their area, while media outlets in Dayton get another "localized" version.

TYPES OF FACT SHEETS

A fact sheet often accompanies a news release. See Figure 5.4 for the fact sheet that accompanied the Korbel Cellars news release in Figure 5.2. It is essentially what the name implies—a list of facts in outline or bullet form that a reporter can use as a quick reference when writing a story. A fact sheet may form the basis of a whole story for a reporter, or the reporter may use just one or two of the facts provided to supplement the information in the news release.

There are several kinds of fact sheets. You can write one for an upcoming event, for example, that uses boldface headings to give (1) the name of the event, (2) its sponsor, (3) the location, (4) the date and time, (5) the purpose of the event, (6) the expected attendance, (7) a list of any prominent people attending, and (8) any unusual aspects of the event that make it newsworthy.

A fact sheet on an organization may use headings that provide (1) the organization's name, (2) products or services produced, (3) its annual revenues, (4) the total number of employees, (5) the names and short biographies of top executives, (6) the markets served, (7) its position in the industry, and (8) any other pertinent details. Some organizations use the term "corporate profile" or "backgrounder" to describe these aspects.

The third kind of fact sheet is simply a summary of a new product's characteristics. A fact sheet for a company's new snack product, for example, might give such details as (1) nutrition information, (2) the production process, (3) pricing, (4) availability, (5) convenience, and (6) how it serves a consumer need. A good example of such a fact sheet is in Figure 5.7, which was prepared by Pillsbury Deluxe Classics Cookies. In addition to the fact sheet, the media also received a basic news release (Figure 5.6) and a product publicity photo (Figure 5.8).

A fact sheet can be compiled on almost anything. Even a simple one, covering the five Ws and H, can be helpful to journalists who want a quick reference to basic information. Fact sheets often accompany media kits, which are discussed in Chapter 8.

A variation on the traditional fact sheet is information presented in a question-and-answer format. This format, often used on Web sites and the Internet, is called a **FAQ**. This is cyberspace jargon for "Frequently Asked Questions." Hewlett-Packard, for example, supplemented its Internet news release on its new ScanJet 4670 with a FAQ that answered typical consumer questions about the new product. When you write a FAQ, try to place yourself in the shoes of the consumer who is hearing about the product for the first time. What questions would you ask?

FAQs on Web sites also give consumers, as well as editors, the opportunity to click on various links (video, audio, photos, product specifications) to get even more information about a product.

PARTS OF A NEWS RELEASE

A news release has six basic components: (1) letterhead, (2) contacts, (3) headline, (4) dateline, (5) lead paragraph, and (6) body of text.

Letterhead

The first page of a news release is usually printed on an organization's letterhead. Letterheads give the name of the organization, its complete address, telephone numbers, fax numbers, e-mail addresses, and even Web sites. If the organization

September 4, 2002   Contact: Marlene Johnson
                                            General Mills, Inc.
                                            763.764.2481
                                            marlene.johnson@genmills.com

                                            Heidi Geller
                                            General Mills, Inc.
                                            763.764.5836
                                            heidi.geller@genmills.com

                                FOR IMMEDIATE RELEASE

**SATISFY YOUR ADULT-SIZED COOKIE CRAVING WITH NEW
PILLSBURY® BIG DELUXE CLASSICS™ COOKIES**

Adults love cookies just as much as kids. And, now, there are convenient, fresh-from-the-oven cookies with truly adult flavors. Pillsbury, the leading brand of refrigerated cookies, has introduced Big Deluxe Classics™ Cookies, a new line of larger-size, premium, ready-to-bake refrigerated cookies in rich flavor combinations designed for grown-ups.

"Adults are avid cookie fans," says Jennifer Jorgensen, associate marketing manager for the General Mills' refrigerated cookie business. She reports that adults eat two thirds of all cookies consumed in the U.S. "The new Big Deluxe Classics™ line is the first refrigerated dough product to provide the kind of generous-sized, indulgent cookies that adults like."

The Pillsbury® Big Deluxe Classics™ line features cookies that bake to 3 to 3½ inches in diameter and are more than 50 percent larger than current ready-to-bake cookies.

                                -more-

-2-

They're made with intensely satisfying, quality ingredients and are available in four indulgent flavors. Premium Blend Chocolate Chip combines two kinds of classic, mouth-watering chocolate – semi-sweet and milk chocolate chips. White Chunk Macadamia Nut is packed full of rich, white chunks and lightly roasted macadamia nuts. Peanut Butter Chocolate Chip blends a dense peanut butter cookie with semi-sweet chocolate chips. And Oatmeal Raisin marries sweet California raisins and rolled oats with a hint of cinnamon.

The cookies come in convenient resealable packages, so you can bake all of them at once or savor them one warm, tender cookie at a time. They're easy to prepare, too. Simply place the pre-formed cookie dough rounds on a cookie sheet and bake 12 to 16 minutes. Each 18-oz. package contains 12 cookies. They cost approximately $2.99 per package.

Part of the General Mills portfolio of brands, the Pillsbury® brand is the leader in the refrigerated baked goods category with a full range of products, including cookies, biscuits, breads, pizza crust and sweet rolls.

                                XXXX

Figure 5.6 New Product News Release
General Mills, Inc. introduced its Pillsbury Big Deluxe Classics brand ready-to-bake refrigerated cookies with a basic, well-written news release sent to food editors at daily and weekly newspapers across the country. It was part of a media kit that included the news release, a fact sheet (see Figure 5.7), and two slide photos of the packaging for the cookies. The media kit folder was no ordinary folder. It was cut to look like a giant cookie with a bite missing, and it even had a chocolate scent to enhance its impact on food editors. The new product story received 11.5 million media impressions, with 82 percent of the food editors' product reviews being positive. In addition, nearly 95 percent of the stories mentioned the product's convenience, while 33 percent mentioned the four flavors available to consumers. The media kit received a bronze anvil from the Public Relations Society of America (PRSA).
(Courtesy of General Mills and its public relations firm, Morgan & Myers.)

Figure 5.7 Fact Sheets Provide the Basics
A good fact sheet give the basics to a reporter or editor in an outline format. This fact sheet accompanied the news release about Pillsbury Big Deluxe Classics that was mailed to food editors across the country (see Figure 5.6).
(Courtesy of General Mills and its public relations firm, Morgan & Myers.)

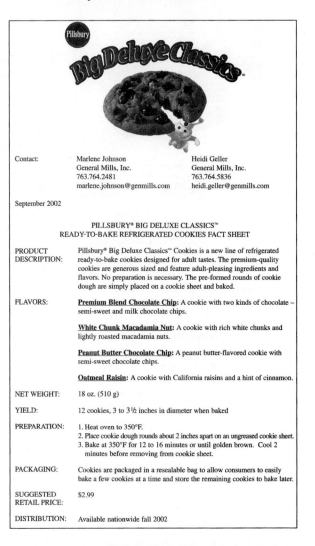

Contact: Marlene Johnson   Heidi Geller
                General Mills, Inc.   General Mills, Inc.
                763.764.2481   763.764.5836
                marlene.johnson@genmills.com   heidi.geller@genmills.com

September 2002

PILLSBURY® BIG DELUXE CLASSICS™
READY-TO-BAKE REFRIGERATED COOKIES FACT SHEET

PRODUCT
DESCRIPTION: Pillsbury® Big Deluxe Classics™ Cookies is a new line of refrigerated ready-to-bake cookies designed for adult tastes. The premium-quality cookies are generous sized and feature adult-pleasing ingredients and flavors. No preparation is necessary. The pre-formed rounds of cookie dough are simply placed on a cookie sheet and baked.

FLAVORS: **Premium Blend Chocolate Chip:** A cookie with two kinds of chocolate – semi-sweet and milk chocolate chips.

                White Chunk Macadamia Nut: A cookie with rich white chunks and lightly roasted macadamia nuts.

                Peanut Butter Chocolate Chip: A peanut butter-flavored cookie with semi-sweet chocolate chips.

                Oatmeal Raisin: A cookie with California raisins and a hint of cinnamon.

NET WEIGHT: 18 oz. (510 g)

YIELD: 12 cookies, 3 to 3½ inches in diameter when baked

PREPARATION: 1. Heat oven to 350°F.
                    2. Place cookie dough rounds about 2 inches apart on an ungreased cookie sheet.
                    3. Bake at 350°F for 12 to 16 minutes or until golden brown. Cool 2 minutes before removing from cookie sheet.

PACKAGING: Cookies are packaged in a resealable bag to allow consumers to easily bake a few cookies at a time and store the remaining cookies to bake later.

SUGGESTED
RETAIL PRICE: $2.99

DISTRIBUTION: Available nationwide fall 2002

does not have a letterhead, you should use a larger or different font in your computer to create one.

Many organizations tailor a letterhead specifically for news releases. In addition to giving the organizational information, the term "News Release" or something similar appears as part of the letterhead. A good example is the Bristol-Myers news release in Figure 5.9.

The term "For Immediate Release" also appears near the letterhead of many releases, but many publicists say that this is just a tradition and not really necessary. New York public relations counselor Alan Hirsch told *Jack O'Dwyer's Newsletter,* "Using 'for immediate release' on any news announcement is extreme ignorance because the term is obsolete and has no meaning. Media don't hold up the news any more. . . ."

Figure 5.8 Product Photos Reinforce Brand
Product news releases and fact sheets are often accompanied by photos that show a picture of the product and its packaging. This helps reinforce the brand and also gives consumers a chance to acquaint themselves with what "package" to look for on the store shelf. The Pillsbury Deluxe Classics Cookies photo (see Figures 5.6 and 5.7) was featured in about two-thirds of the new product stories about the new refrigerated cookies.
(Courtesy of General Mills and its public relations firm, Morgan & Myers.)

That may be true in the age of instant global communication, but there are times that a writer will request a specific release time. For example, you may write: "For Release after 9 p.m. January 16." This often occurs when the release concerns a speech by someone or an award that is announced at a certain time.

The primary reason is that unplanned things happen. The speaker or award recipient, because of a plane delay or another emergency, may not show up. In such a case, the media would look foolish reporting a speech or an award that was never given.

At times, you may also wish to indicate that an advance news announcement is "embargoed" until the organization makes a formal announcement at a news conference. The idea behind this is that a particular news outlet won't "scoop" the opposition by broadcasting or publishing the announcement ahead of time. This approach, however, is risky unless you get an ironclad agreement by a news organization to honor your request. This is usually done *before* you send them the advance news release or press kit. If they decline to honor your embargo, you then have the option of not sending them any advance information. In general, publicists use the embargo sparingly—usually in the case of announcing a major new product, a merger between two major companies, or a change in executive leadership.

Professional Tips

Rules for Writing a News Release

All news releases should be "news centered" according to Schubert Communications, a Pennsylvania public relations firm. Lisa Barbadora, director of public relations and marketing content for Schubert, gives these rules for writing news releases:

- Use short, succinct headlines and subheads to highlight main points and pique interest. They should not simply be a repeat of the information in the lead-in paragraph.

- Do not use generic words such as "the leading provider" or "world-class" to position your company. Be specific, use phrases such as "with annual revenues of."

- Do not use describe products using phrases such as "unique" or "total solution." Use specific terms or examples to demonstrate the product's distinctness.

- Use descriptive and creative words to grab an editor's attention, but make sure they are accurate and not exaggerated.

- Do not highlight the name of your company or product in the headline of a news release if it is not highly recognized. If you are not a household name, focus on the news instead.

- Tell the news. Focus on how your announcement affects your industry and lead with that rather than overtly promoting your product or company.

- Critique your writing by asking yourself, "who cares?" Why should readers be interested in this information?

- Do not throw the whole kitchen sink into a release. Better to break your news into several releases if material is lengthy.

- Do not use lame quotes. Write like someone is actually talking—eliminate the corporatese that editors love to ignore. Speak with pizzazz to increase your chances of being published.

- Target your writing. Create two different tailored releases that will go out to different types of media rather than a general release that isn't of great interest to either group.

- Look for creative ways to tie your announcement in to current news or trends.

- Write simply. Use contractions, write in active voice, be direct, avoid paired words like "clear and simple," and incorporate common action-oriented phrases to generate excitement. Sentences should be no longer than 34 words.

- Follow the *Associated Press Stylebook* and specific publications' editorial standards for dates, technical terms, abbreviations, punctuation, spellings, capitalization, etc.

- Do not use metaphors unless they are used to paint a clearer picture for the reader.

- Do not overdo it. It's important to write colorfully, to focus on small specific details, to include descriptions of people, places, and events, but do not write poetry when you want press.

- Do not be formulaic in your news release writing. Not every release must start with the name of the company or product. Break out of the mold to attract media attention.

- Do not expect editors to print your entire release. Important information should be in the first two paragraphs.

- Make it clear how your announcement is relevant for the editors' readers.

Source: Walker, Jerry. "18 Simple Rules for Writing a News Release." *O'Dwyer's PR Services Report,* November 2002, pp. 32–33.

Contacts

The contact person is listed directly after the letterhead. The contact person is often the writer of the news release, but it might be the director of public relations or another executive.

Include the contact person's full name, telephone number, fax number, and e-mail address. The Korbel release in Figure 5.2, for example, lists a contact for the public relations firm handling the account and the organizational contact. Thus, we have the following information:

> Contact: Julie Schweigert
> Edelman Worldwide
> 312/233-1380
> Julie.schweigert@edelman.com
>
> Margie Healy
> Korbel Champagne Cellars
> 707/824-7715
> mhealy@korbel.com

If a public relations firm has prepared the release, the contacts for both the firm and the client organization are usually given. If the news release is distributed nationally, or even internationally, it often is a good idea to also provide an after-hours number to accommodate time zone differences.

When a contact is given on a news release, it is assumed that he or she is qualified to answer any reporter inquiries about the subject of the news release. It is also important that the person be readily available to take phone calls and respond immediately to e-mail inquiries. Reporters often complain that the contact is impossible to reach, or doesn't seem to know anything more than what is already stated in the news release. So, if you are listed as a contact, make sure you are thoroughly prepared and can respond almost immediately. Many stories never see the light of day simply because a reporter couldn't reach a contact before the publication's deadline.

As a contact, however, you will often be busy with other projects and unable to just sit by the phone waiting for a call that may never come. If you are away from your phone, it is common practice to leave a voicemail message that gives reporters on deadline your pager or cell phone number. Another approach is to give the caller the name and telephone number of another person who can be contacted in your absence.

Headline

Most news releases, particularly product-related ones, carry a brief headline. This usually appears in boldface and in a slightly larger type than that used in the body of the news release. Thus, if the body is in 12-point type, the headline often is in 14- or 16-point type. If you are sending an e-mail release, however, keep the headline and the body of the text in the same type size and font. This is because not all e-mail systems support different text codes.

The purpose of the headline is to give an editor or journalist a quick indication of what the news release is about. Headlines are supposed to give the "bottom line," the most newsworthy aspect of the story. Headlines should be factual, devoid of hype, and to the point.

Here are some examples:

Merck Develops New Drug for Asthma Sufferers

LSI Logic Selects New President

HP Announces Its First Organizer

Theater Company Stages "Guys and Dolls"

Increasingly, news releases include a subheadline after the main one. This provides additional key information to journalists and editors as they scan virtually hundreds of news releases in a short amount of time. Here are some examples of using a subheadline:

Wal-Mart Announces Plans for Chicago Discount Store

Store on North and Kilpatrick Avenues Could Open Spring 2005

Dieting Can Be Dangerous to Your Bones

New Analysis Reveals Important Role of Milk for Dieters

National Historic Landmark, Greenfield Village,

Re-Opens after $60 Million Facelift

Record Numbers Expected at World Largest Outdoor History Museum

Note that these headlines are written in the active present tense. Avoid past tense; it gives the impression that the news item is not timely. If you do use a headline, place it two or three lines above the first line of the news release.

You should also notice that all of the examples above have a single subject or focus. Media trainer Jerry Brown says, "One message is better than two. Two are usually better than three. If you have more than three messages for a story, you're not focused enough." This idea of a single message is explored further when we discuss lead paragraphs in a news release.

Dateline

The dateline appears at the start of the lead paragraph, which is discussed in the next section. The dateline is simply the city and state where the release originated, plus the date. Here are some datelines from the news releases used in this chapter:

Dearborn, MI, May 27, 2003. . . .

Guerneville, Sonoma County, Calif., Feb. 12, 2003. . .

WASHINGTON, July 17. . . .

NEW YORK, N.Y., June 4, 2003. . . .

Global companies often use the day first, followed by the month and the year (28 April 2004). This sequence is used by almost every nation in the world except the United States, which has a tradition of using month, day, year. By spelling out the month, the date is clear whether you use the U.S. style or the international method. If you simply write, "4/12/99," there can be confusion. Are you saying "April 12" (U.S.) or "December 4" (international sequence)?

Another approach to the dateline is simply to put the date on the release above the contact's name. Those who favor this approach say a dateline should not clutter up the lead paragraph.

The Lead

The most important part of any release is the lead paragraph. In one or two sentences, you must give the reader the basic details of the story. Marvin Arth, author of *The Newsletter Editor's Desk Book*, says, "The trick to good lead writing is to focus immediately on the most newsworthy point of the story and to reserve other details until later in the story. Try to reduce the essence of the news to a single sentence or even a single word."

There are two basic types of leads. First is the summary lead, which includes the key information in a brief statement. For example:

- Coldwell Banker Corp., one of the nation's largest residential real estate brokerage firms, is re-entering the commercial real estate business. It plans to sell franchises in more than 100 U.S. markets.

- Vanderbilt University's Owen Graduate School of Management is the recipient of a $33.5 million gift. It is one of the biggest single donations ever given to a business school.

Professional Tips

Types of News Release Leads

Following are examples of several kinds of leads:

- *Straight news lead* (who, what, when, where):

    The History Center of Murray College will open the school year Sept. 21 with a barbecue at 11 a.m. in Martin Murphy Historical Park, 235 E. Woodward Ave., in Des Moines.

- *Modified straight news lead* (stressing a major theme):

    A Chicago thoracic surgeon who plans to focus study on national health insurance programs has been named president of the Cook County Medical Society.

- *Informal lead* (designed to arouse interest):

    The sky will be ablaze with the crackle of scale-model machine-gun fire this weekend at the Hill Country Air Museum in Morgan Hill. (Story about a model airplane exhibit.)

- *Feature lead* (often used in magazine articles or human interest newspaper features):

    Jan Talbott is into the bike craze in a big way. (Story about a custom bicycle built to accommodate a 6-foot, 6-inch man.)

- The Molson Companies, Canada's biggest brewer, has agreed to sell most of its chemicals unit, the Diversey Corporation, to Unilever for $780 million.

The second type is the interest or feature lead, which raises the reader's curiosity. Essentially, the lead is a "hook" that encourages the reader to read the second paragraph for more information. For example:

- Lots of people are talking about a surge in business these days. Those people are not in commercial real estate.
- Want a newspaper? A sandwich? An umbrella? In a few years, if the Metropolitan Transportation Agency has its way, commuters may be buying them with the same cards they pass through the subway turnstiles to pay their fares.
- The patient was getting the best care the local doctors could provide. But this case needed outside expertise, and a long-distance phone call was not an option. (Story about a satellite medical service.)

Inexperienced writers often have the mistaken impression that a lead should answer all six journalistic questions. However, trying to do this often results in a tangle of dependent clauses and convoluted sentences that are difficult to read. Michael Ryan, writing in *Public Relations Quarterly*, gives an example of such a lead paragraph:

A conference addressing the issue, "Maternal and Child Health: Making Indigent Health Programs Work," will be held on Thursday, March 20, 9:00 a.m. to 12:30 p.m. in the Jefferson Davis Hospital Board Room, 1801 Allen Parkway. The Houston conference is the fourth in a series of 20 regional meetings cosponsored by the March of Dimes and the Children's Defense Fund of Texas.

The solution, in this case and others, is to put only the most important element of the story in the lead paragraph. The other Ws, or the H, can be woven into the succeeding paragraphs. Here are examples of leads that emphasize only one element:

Who: Recording artist Lisa Atkinson will lead a sing-along and entertain preschool children. . . .

What: "Fire, Earth, and Water," a major exhibit of pre-Columbian sculpture from the Land Collection, opens Friday. . . .

When: November 15 is the last date for filing claims for flood damage caused by. . . .

Where: A golden retriever has won Best of Show honors at the 90th Golden Gate Kennel Club Dog Show.

Why: Farnell of Britain will merge with Premier Industrial of Cleveland. The deal, valued at $2.8 billion, is an effort to consolidate the worldwide distribution of electronics equipment.

How: Flextime, the system that permits employees to set their own starting and stopping times, has reduced labor turnover at Kellogg Enterprises by. . . .

The mechanics of a lead paragraph are relatively simple. Use strong declarative sentences, keep the number of dependent clauses to a minimum, keep it to five lines or less on your computer screen, and rewrite if any sentence comes out more than three lines long. All this helps the reader to grasp the key information quickly, even if they don't read the rest of the story. In addition, you should avoid the following pitfalls that lead to weak leads:

Prepositional phrases: At a meeting held in the . . . , or For the first time in history. . . . These phrases, used at the beginning of a lead paragraph, tend to weaken the force of the sentence.

Participial phrases: Meeting in an atmosphere of confidence,

Dependent clauses: That all high school students be required to. . . .

Clutter: Joe Gonzales, a veteran retailer and former mayor, at a meeting of the Chamber of Commerce to. . . .

Body of Text

The lead paragraph is an integral and important part of the text. As such, it forms the apex of the journalistic "inverted pyramid" approach to writing. This means that the first paragraph succinctly summarizes the most important part of the story and succeeding paragraphs fill in the details.

There are three reasons for using the inverted pyramid structure. First, if the editor or reporter doesn't find something interesting in the first few lines, he or she won't use the story.

Second, editors often cut the length of an item, and they start at the bottom. In fact, Business Wire estimates that more than 90 percent of news releases printed are rewritten in much shorter form than the original text. If the main details of the story are at the beginning, the release will still be understandable and informative even if most of it ends up in the trash basket.

A third reason for using this structure is that the public does not always read the entire story. Statistics show, for example, that average readers spend less than 30 minutes reading a metropolitan daily newspaper. This means that they read a lot of headlines, some beginning paragraphs, and a few stories in their entirety. If they read only the headline and the first paragraph, readers should get the main facts.

Once the lead is written, you must add information until the story is complete. Michael Ryan, professor of communication at the University of Houston, says a news release should have four basic paragraphs. His model:

- Paragraph One
  a. Most important facts of release
  b. Attribution, less essential information
- Paragraph Two
  a. Essential background material, names of key characters or sources, a second important element

   b. Names of secondary characters or sources
 • Paragraph Three
   a. Elaboration on material in paragraph one
   b. Background material, attribution
 • Paragraph Four
   a. Most important material in sentence
   b. Background material, attribution

This model does not mean that all news releases should be four paragraphs long. Ryan points out that there could be several paragraphs of the same kind in a news release. For example, your particular news release may require more background or include several important and interesting supporting quotations. Thus, in order to tell the story fully, you may use several "3" paragraphs.

The basic idea, however, is to use a structure that enables you to write a succinct news release that includes all the important and interesting information. There is no rule that news releases should be a specific length, but most writers strive to tell their stories in one or two pages. Space and time are always a premium in the news business, so reporters appreciate news releases that are short and to the point.

The body of the news release should also include your employer or client's stock symbol and stock exchange if it is a publicly traded company. Lorry Lokey, general manager of Business Wire, says this is a good idea if you are distributing news releases electronically because full-text is sent to more than 300 databases and Internet news systems. These databases often use the stock symbol as a way of indexing information about companies and industries. It is also a good idea to include an organization's Web site and major e-mail address somewhere in the news release so reporters and even customers can easily access important background information.

If stock symbols and Web sites cannot conveniently be placed within the context of a news release, the information is often found in a standard paragraph at the end of the news release. This paragraph, known in the trade as **boiler-plate**, is standardized copy used in every news release. In addition to stock symbols, etc., this standard paragraph also gives some basic information about the company so reporters get some idea about the size and purpose of the organization.

Wal-Mart, for example, sent a news release about the opening of a new store in Chicago and even localized its standard paragraph at the end of the release to make it more relevant to local editors. The writer of the release wrote:

> Wal-Mart currently has more than 38,000 associates living and working in Illinois at its 81 Wal-Mart Discount Stores, 33 Supercenters, 27 SAM's Clubs and 3 Distribution Centers. In the last fiscal year, Wal-Mart spent almost $20 billion dollars with various Illinois-based suppliers, including Kraft Foods, Land O'Frost, Inc. and Wahl Clipper Corporation.
>
> With annual sales of $244.5 billion, Wal-Mart Stores, Inc. operates more than 2,870 Discount Stores, Supercenters, and Neighborhood Markets, and more than 520 SAM's Clubs in the United States. Internationally, the company's securities are listed on the New York and Pacific stock exchanges under the symbol WMT.

Another approach is provided by Toshiba, which sent out a news release on a new product, the Tablet PC. Its boiler-plate paragraph at the end of the release stated:

> Toshiba Computer Systems Group is a division of Toshiba America Information Systems, Inc. ("TAIS"), a leading vendor for portable computers. In addition to notebooks, the company offers portable and wireless accessories, Pocket PCs, projectors and mobile server computing solutions for business customers under the Toshiba brand name. For more information call 1-800-TOSHIBA or visit the company's Web site at www.csd.toshiba.com.

Other supplemental information at the end of a news release might include a listing of trademarked names used in the release. This alerts the reporter to what products and services must be capitalized. See Figures 5.9 and 5.10 showing capitalization of products and brand names. Thus, there will be a notation such as "Windows is a U.S. registered trademark of Microsoft Corp." This was discussed previously in Chapter 3.

When the release is completed, it should be checked and double-checked. Facts, figures, spelling, punctuation, grammar, sentence and paragraph length, clarity, and adherence to approved news style must be considered. Quotations and the spelling of names must be checked with extra care. A sure way to create ill will is to issue a release that is inaccurate.

.....NEWS.....NEWS.....NEWS.....NEWS.....NEWS....

Bristol-Myers Squibb Company

FOR IMMEDIATE RELEASE

Contact: Julie Keenan
             Corporate Affairs
             609-252-3732
             julie.keenan@bms.com

RELIEF FOR TENSION HEADACHE PAIN
- Bristol-Myers Squibb Launches Excedrin® Tension Headache -

(NEW YORK, N.Y., June 4, 2003) – Bristol-Myers Squibb Company (NYSE: BMY), a leader in headache management, today launched Excedrin® Tension Headache. This multi-ingredient pain reliever provides fast relief of head, neck, and shoulder pain associated with tension-type headache, the most common form of headache pain.

"As Americans become more health-conscious, they are also becoming more aware of the causes and symptoms of their headache pain," says R. Michael Gallagher, D.O., FACOFP, director of the University Headache Center at the University of Medicine and Dentistry of New Jersey. "Excedrin Tension Headache provides doctors and patients with an effective treatment for tension-type headache pain, including neck and shoulder pain."

Tension-type headache affects approximately 93 percent of American adults. Episodic tension-type headaches often happen during or around periods of stress or emotional upset, but the cause of tension-specific headaches remains unknown.

Most people who experience tension headaches feel pain on both sides of their head and describe it as a "squeezing pressure" or a "tight band." The pain can range from mild to severe and can occur continuously or intermittently. The exact location of a tension headache can change (i.e., top, sides, back, forehead), and many people also experience stiffness and tightness in their neck and shoulders.

To better understand the health impact that stress and tension has on the U.S. population, Bristol-Myers Squibb provided an unrestricted educational grant to the National Consumer League (NCL) to conduct an independent national survey. The NCL is expected to release the results of the study later this month.

- more -

- 2 -

About Excedrin® Tension Headache

Excedrin Tension Headache provides relief for the head, neck, and shoulder pain of tension-type headache. Excedrin Tension Headache is available in the pain reliever section of grocery, drug and mass-merchandise stores and is supplied in 24-, 50-, and 100-count cartons. Each Excedrin Tension Headache easy-to-swallow Geltab or caplet contains 500 mg acetaminophen formulated with 65 mg caffeine, a trusted formulation for the treatment of tension-type headache.

Excedrin Tension Headache is the latest addition to the Excedrin portfolio, building on more than 40 years of headache treatment innovation by Bristol-Myers Squibb. In 1960, Bristol-Myers Squibb introduced Excedrin® Extra Strength for headaches, a multi-ingredient formulation headache treatment product. In 1969, the company launched Excedrin® PM, the first nighttime headache product. Bristol-Myers Squibb was also a pioneer in launching Excedrin® Migraine, the first over-the-counter migraine product, approved by the FDA, in 1998, and Excedrin® QuickTabs, a convenient, melt-in-your-mouth headache pain reliever, in 2002. For more information about Excedrin® brand products, visit www.excedrin.com.

Bristol-Myers Squibb is a pharmaceutical and related healthcare products company whose mission is to extend and enhance human life.

Visit Bristol-Myers Squibb on the World Wide Web at www.bms.com.

# # #

Figure 5.9 Product Trademarks Are Important
Many product names carry a registered trademark symbol so reporters and editors know that it is always capitalized. Stock exchange symbols are also used, either in the body of the news release or as part of the standard boiler-plate paragraph at the end of the release.
(Courtesy of Bristol-Myers Squibb Company.)

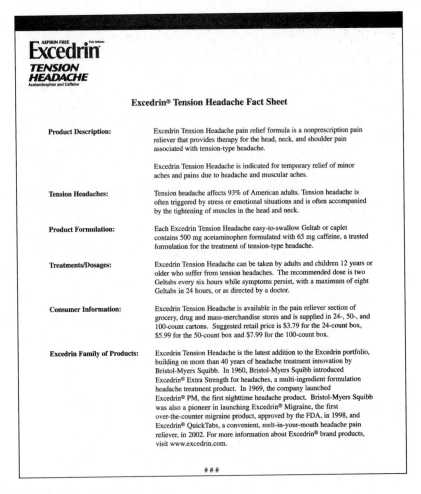

ASPIRIN FREE Pain Reliever

Excedrin

TENSION HEADACHE
Acetaminophen and Caffeine

Excedrin® Tension Headache Fact Sheet

Product Description:	Excedrin Tension Headache pain relief formula is a nonprescription pain reliever that provides therapy for the head, neck, and shoulder pain associated with tension-type headache.
	Excedrin Tension Headache is indicated for temporary relief of minor aches and pains due to headache and muscular aches.
Tension Headaches:	Tension headache affects 93% of American adults. Tension headache is often triggered by stress or emotional situations and is often accompanied by the tightening of muscles in the head and neck.
Product Formulation:	Each Excedrin Tension Headache easy-to-swallow Geltab or caplet contains 500 mg acetaminophen formulated with 65 mg caffeine, a trusted formulation for the treatment of tension-type headache.
Treatments/Dosages:	Excedrin Tension Headache can be taken by adults and children 12 years or older who suffer from tension headaches. The recommended dose is two Geltabs every six hours while symptoms persist, with a maximum of eight Geltabs in 24 hours, or as directed by a doctor.
Consumer Information:	Excedrin Tension Headache is available in the pain reliever section of grocery, drug and mass-merchandise stores and is supplied in 24-, 50-, and 100-count cartons. Suggested retail price is $3.79 for the 24-count box, $5.99 for the 50-count box and $7.99 for the 100-count box.
Excedrin Family of Products:	Excedrin Tension Headache is the latest addition to the Excedrin portfolio, building on more than 40 years of headache treatment innovation by Bristol-Myers Squibb. In 1960, Bristol-Myers Squibb introduced Excedrin® Extra Strength for headaches, a multi-ingredient formulation headache treatment product. In 1969, the company launched Excedrin® PM, the first nighttime headache product. Bristol-Myers Squibb was also a pioneer in launching Excedrin® Migraine, the first over-the-counter migraine product, approved by the FDA, in 1998, and Excedrin® QuickTabs, a convenient, melt-in-your-mouth headache pain reliever, in 2002. For more information about Excedrin® brand products, visit www.excedrin.com.

#

Figure 5.10 Excedrin Fact Sheet
This fact sheet was distributed with the news release (Figure 5.9) about a new headache remedy on the market. Its subheads and short explanations make it relatively easy to comprehend for the consumer. *(Courtesy of Bristol-Myers Squibb Company.)*

PLACEMENT

A news release does no good unless it is published. Getting something published is called **placement**, and is discussed thoroughly in Chapter 10. Placement depends on delivering the story to the right gatekeeper through the right channels at the right time.

Andy Marken, president of Marken Communications, gives the secret of successful placement. He told *Jack O'Dwyer's Newsletter*:

It's quite simple for anyone who is doing PR to gauge the editorial requirements of a given publication or group of publications. All one has to do is skim a few issues and study the editorial direction and emphasis. Then, if the publicity writer

Professional Tips

How to Write an Internet-Ready News Release

The traditional news release on an 8.5- by 11-inch page is often posted on the Internet or e-mailed to editors, and distributors such as PR Newswire or Business Wire still send lengthy news releases to print publications and broadcast outlets.

Increasingly, however, it's recognized that such releases are not really compatible with on-line distribution that requires messages to fit the instant communication of the Internet and World Wide Web. B. L. Ochman, writing in *The Strategist*, suggests that you should "Think of the electronic news release as a teaser to get a reporter or editor to your Web site for additional information." He makes the following suggestions:

- Use a specific subject line that identifies exactly what the news release is about.
- Make your entire release a maximum of 200 words or less, in five short paragraphs. The idea is brevity so reporters see the news release on one screen and don't have to scroll. If a journalist has hundreds of e-mails in their inbox, scrolling becomes a real chore.
- Use bulleted points to convey key points.
- Write only two or three short sentences in each of the five paragraphs.
- Above the headline, or at the bottom of the release, be sure to provide a contact name, phone number, e-mail address, and URL for additional information.
- Never send a release as an attachment. Journalists, because of possible virus infections, rarely open attachments.

Ochman concludes, "Write like you have 10 seconds to make a point. Because online, you do." See Figure 5.11 on page 150 for a sample Internet news release.

Source: Ochman, B.L., "The Death of the Traditional News Release." *The Strategist,* Summer 2000, pp. 16–18.

is worth his or her salt, he or she will provide news releases that have style, content, and the necessary current angle to satisfy the publications' requirements.

At times, tailoring a news release to a specific publication can also mean distributing the information in several languages. Pacific Gas & Electric, in an effort to reach its diverse customer base in the San Francisco Bay region, often includes Spanish and Chinese print and broadcast media in its distribution. But instead of sending an English news release, PG&E goes the "extra mile" and also translates the material for these media. This is not only effective media relations, it also ensures that the information is communicated accurately.

Gatekeepers

You must get the story to the editor or reporter who is most likely to be interested in the particular subject. Thus anything about food would go to the food editor,

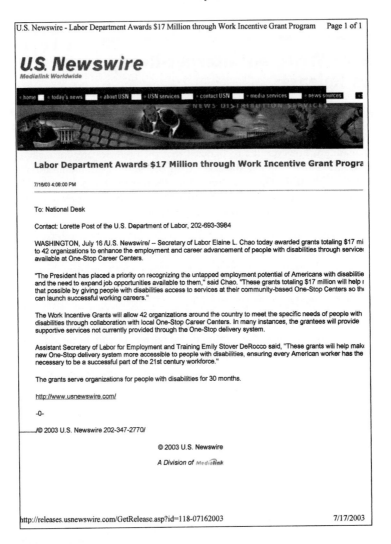

Figure 5.11 News Releases for the Internet Age
Less is best when it comes to news releases distributed via e-mail and the Internet. This release is a good format. The headline gives the basic information. There is a contact person and a telephone number before a five-paragraph story. Such stories basically are designed to fill one screen so readers don't have to scroll. If reporters want more information, a URL is given at the end of the release.
(Courtesy of U.S. Newswire, a division of MediaLink.)

and anything about entertainment would go to the entertainment editor or reporter. Large papers have many editors; smaller papers often have editors covering several subjects.

You can find editors' names in the media directories (see Chapter 10). For weekly newspapers and most magazines, your contact is the editor, although some large magazines have a large number of specialized editors.

There is some controversy about the practice of sending a news release to more than one person at a paper. If two editors or reporters come up with the same story, each may feel duped. One way to avoid this is to send the release to your #1 prospect and provide copies—marked "F.Y.I." ("for your information")— to any others who might be interested. The original would show who got copies, and copies would show to whom the original was sent.

Deadlines

News releases must be timely. The media thrive on late-breaking information and want to know about events when they happen, not a week later. If it is not possible to get routine information distributed right away, a common technique is to make sure that there are no references to specific dates in the release. The announcement of a new company president or a major contract, for example, would not say that the news is two weeks old.

Important late-breaking news can always be e-mailed, telephoned, or faxed to a newspaper at the last minute and get published. Evening papers go to press around noon. The deadline for late-breaking news is variable but is usually early in the morning. Morning papers go to press in the evening, sometimes as late as 10 or 11 p.m., so you could get late-breaking news considered as late as 6 p.m.

Most news releases, however, deal with routine announcements that are not hot news. In this case, media outlets like to receive information with plenty of lead time. Publicity about an upcoming event, for example, should be sent to gatekeepers at least two weeks ahead of time so that editors can process the information and get it into the newspaper in a timely fashion. If a major event is planned, editors appreciate as much advance information as possible so that they can plan their coverage.

Monthly trade magazines usually need information six to eight weeks in advance, and monthly consumer magazines often work five or six months in advance. These publications often deal with feature-type stories rather than straight news releases; these are discussed further in Chapter 6.

News releases to local television and radio stations should arrive at least two or three days in advance. Public service announcements should be sent to radio and television stations at least six weeks in advance. These are discussed further in Chapter 9.

Getting Maximum Results

Whenever you take the time and energy to develop a news release, you should think of how you can produce several releases emphasizing various angles of the same topic or subject.

If Susan Chang has been appointed president of Mammoth Manufacturing Company, there are several media outlets for this story: local news media, the trade magazines serving the industry, her college alumni publication, and the publications of organizations to which she belongs.

In each case the release would be individualized, but all would contain information about the Mammoth Manufacturing Company. Individualizing requires writing the release to fit the medium to which it will be released. For a metropolitan daily, the release should be about one paragraph long—unless the company is of great importance, in which case the release may be longer and give more details. The release may also be longer for trade publications, hometown papers, and organizational publications.

Surveys also lend themselves to developing several releases from basic data. Grant/Jacoby, Inc., of Chicago, for example, emphasized key findings of MCI's "Meetings in America" survey in several news releases. Here are the lead paragraphs in three of these releases:

- Business professionals spend nearly three hours out of every workday in business meetings, and corporate America is paying a heavy price. Research released today by network MCI Conferencing shows the cost of meeting face-to-face is up to seven times higher than meeting via conferencing technology.

- If traveling to business meetings is stressing you out, you are not alone. In research released today by network MCI Conferencing, almost one-fourth of professionals surveyed say they are more stressed out when required to travel to business meetings. Causes of this stress include spending time away from family, arranging to take care of personal responsibilities, and keeping up with work at the office.

- American professionals have a confession: most of them daydream during business meetings. In survey research released today by network MCI Conferencing, more than 90 percent of respondents admit their minds have wandered during meetings and almost 40 percent say they have dozed off. A poorly planned meeting could be the reason.

These featurized leads, using survey findings of general interest, are good examples of using a newsworthy angle to attract the interest of reporters and editors at business and lifestyle publications. MCI's objective, of course, was to use the survey as a vehicle to convey its key message—that its network teleconferencing services can reduce the stress and high cost of business travel.

SUMMARY

- The term "news release" is now preferred over the older term "press release." The latter term has the connotation of being directed only at print media. Today's releases are distributed through a variety of electronic and print channels.

- The media are flooded with hundreds of news releases. To beat the odds and get space or time, your release must be newsworthy, timely, and well written.

- News releases are a basic element of almost every publicity plan. When published or broadcast, they can raise public awareness and influence decision making.

- Planning worksheets and answering the five Ws and H are the basic first steps in writing a news release.

- News releases should be produced on letter-size white paper and conform to Associated Press (AP) style.

Professional Tips

Ten Classic News Release Mistakes

Alan Caruba, a public relations consultant and publicist for three decades, has prepared this list of 10 "Classic News Release Mistakes":

1. Failure to provide a headline. "It's a news story and headlines articulate the theme. Sub-headlines, too, are useful."

2. Boiler-plate. "A first paragraph that jams in the client's name, their title, the company, its location, etc., while ignoring the primary theme of the release, kills it."

3. Spelling and grammatical errors. "Very harmful to any release because it suggests its writer is either uneducated or the release was not proofread."

4. Punctuation errors. "Because editors and reporters, as well as broadcast news personnel, make their living writing, these mistakes are 'red flags,' raising doubts about the source of the release."

5. Hyperbole. "The word from which we get the term 'hype' in which ordinary things are given extraordinary qualities. It's instantaneously recognizable, creating barriers to credibility."

6. Documentation. "Failure to attribute data to verifiable, independent sources diminishes credibility."

7. Contacts. "Failure to provide the names, phone and/or fax numbers of informed, articulate spokesperson(s) renders a release useless."

8. Too long. "The best releases are the briefest. Too much initial data can be a turn-off. If more is wanted, it will be requested."

9. Localize. "Whenever possible, 'localize' the release."

10. Be accessible at all times. "The best news release makes the media come to you. Opportunity ceases after the third ring of your phone."

- There are several types of news releases: announcements, spot announcements, reaction stories, bad news, and hometown releases.

- There are several types of fact sheets, which often accompany news releases. They can give the basic details in outline form about an event, a new product, or an organization.

- One key to successful news release writing is to emphasize the local angle.

- The news release has six components: organization name, contacts, headline, dateline, lead paragraph, body of text. A seventh component can be a standardized supplemental paragraph at the end of the news release that provides basic information about the organization.

- Contacts listed on a news release should be knowledgeable about the topic and highly accessible to reporters who call for more information.

- Lead paragraphs summarize the basic story in five lines or less. Feature leads should arouse interest and encourage people to keep reading or listening.

- Don't try to get all five Ws and H (who, what, when, where, why, and how) in the lead paragraph. Choose the most important one or two elements.

- Write news releases that will appeal to editors and their audiences. Too many releases please the client or employer, but violate journalistic standards.

- News releases are highly structured pieces of writing. Use inverted pyramid style, with the most important facts first.

- Keep news releases factual. Avoid puffery and hype.

- Fact sheets are organized in outline form for easy reference. Another form of fact sheet is the FAQ, which is used on Web sites and the Internet.

- News releases distributed via e-mail or the Internet should be restructured to be about five paragraphs, or about one computer screen. A link to the organization's Web site should also be included if reporters want additional information.

ADDITIONAL RESOURCES

Amernic, Jerry. "How to Avoid Writing the No-News Release." *PR Tactics,* December 1999, p. 12.

Friedman, Mitchell. "25 Ways to Perfect Your Press Release." *PR Tactics,* July 2002, p. 15.

Green, Sherri Deatherage. "Tailoring the Press Release to Different Audiences." *PRWeek,* April 3, 2000, p. 22.

McCarrren, Bill. "A Press Release Is Undervalued if It's Solely Considered a Sales Tool." *PRWeek,* March 3, 2003, p. 2.

O'Brien, Laurel. "The Value of the Common News Release." *The Strategist,* Winter 2001, pp. 28–31.

Ochman, B. L. "The 'Death' of the Traditional Press Release." *The Strategist,* Summer 2000, pp. 16–18. Writing an Internet news release.

Pelham, Fran. "The Triple Crown of Public Relations: Pitch Letter, News Release, Feature Article." *Public Relations Quarterly,* Spring 2000, pp. 38–43.

Smith, Ronald D. *Becoming a Public Relations Writer.* Mahwah, NJ: Lawrence Erlbaum Associates, 2003.

Treadwell, Donald, and Treadwell, Jill B. *Public Relations Writing: Principles in Practice.* Boston: Allyn & Bacon, 2000.

Walker, Jerry. "Editor Says Releases Are Useless." *O'Dwyer's PR Services Report,* January 2003, pp. 24–25.

Walker, Jerry. "18 simple rules for writing a press release." *O'Dwyer's PR Services Report,* November 2002, pp. 32–33.

Wylie, Ann. "Anatomy of a Press Release: What to Include—and What to Avoid—in a Successful Media Relations Piece." *PR Tactics,* September 2003, p. 9.

Yopp, Jan Johnson, and McAdams, Katherine C. *Reaching Audiences: A Guide to Media Writing.* Boston: Allyn & Bacon, 2003.

Chapter 6

News Features

Feature writing requires writers to shift their thinking. News releases, discussed in the last chapter, require left-brain skills emphasizing logical, sequential, analytical thinking. Feature writing, in contrast, requires right-brain skills such as intuition, image making, and conceptualization.

Facts form the basis of feature writing in public relations, just as they do in news release writing, but the approach is different. This time you are asked to write with more imagination and color. Feature stories should be not only informative but entertaining.

This chapter explores the various types of features that public relations writers can develop and gives tips on writing and placing such features.

THE VALUE OF FEATURES

Perhaps the best way to show the value of news feature stories is to contrast them with basic news releases. The news release emphasizes the timely disclosure of basic information about situations and events. The **feature story**, in contrast, provides additional information and creates understanding in a more imaginative way.

Consider, for example, the appointment of a new company president. The news release will give the basic information in one or two paragraphs. It will give the new president's name and perhaps a brief summary of his or her professional career—all pretty dry, routine stuff. A feature article, however, could give the new president a human dimension. It would focus on his or her philosophy of management, college experiences, hobbies and interests, and vision of the future. Such an article might run 1,500 words instead of two paragraphs.

Features are considered "soft news" rather than "hard news." In journalistic terms, this means that features are not as time sensitive as the "hard" news of quarterly earnings, mergers and acquisitions, contracts, expansions, and layoffs. They entertain, provide background, and give consumer tips. They often show up in the specialty sections of the daily newspaper—entertainment, food, business, real estate, automotive, technology—and most of them originate from public relations sources.

Feature stories come in all sizes and shapes, but all of them have the potential to (1) provide more information to the consumer, (2) give background and context about organizations, (3) provide behind-the-scenes perspective, (4) give a human dimension to situations and events, and (5) generate publicity for standard products and services.

Regarding the last point, many products are not particularly newsworthy and would never get coverage if a feature writer didn't exercise some creativity. Think of the lowly potato, for example. It would seem that no self-respecting editor would be interested in a news release from the National Association of Potato Growers. However, a feature directed to the food editor can generate coverage and also increase sales of potatoes. Some possible features might discuss (1) potatoes as a source of vitamins, (2) potatoes as a low-cost addition to daily nutritional needs, and (3) creative recipes using potatoes as an ingredient. Another possibility is a short history of the potato, its origins, and its economic impact.

Indeed, there is evidence that feature materials are becoming increasingly popular with newspapers and magazines. A survey of trade editors conducted by Rhode Island-based Thomas Rankin Associates, for example, found that more than half of the editors wanted more case histories and technical "how to" features from public relations sources. And Mike Yamomoto, managing editor of CNET, says, "The future of media is a greater concentration on the feature story as a branding vehicle. The challenge for the media is to capture audiences with a unique presentation of information."

The new interest in feature articles, particularly by print media, no doubt is related to where people get their news. Radio, TV, and the Internet now provide the instant "hard" news, so print publications are increasingly shifting their focus to publishing more in-depth stories on news events and features that provide consumer tips. The concept of publishing "news you can use" is referred to as **service**

journalism. According to *News Reporting and Writing* by Brooks, Kennedy, Moen, and Ranly, a key component of service journalism is to demonstrate how the reader can use the information to do such things as (1) save time, (2) make more money, (3) save money, or (4) get something free. In other words, the idea is WIIFM—What's in it for me?

If public relations professionals can keep this axiom in mind, the print media will be more than happy to use your material.

PLANNING A NEWS FEATURE

Coming up with a feature idea takes some creative thinking. There are three things to keep in mind. First, you have to conceptualize how something lends itself to feature treatment. Second, you have to determine if the information would be interesting to and useful for a particular audience. Figure 6.1, for example, is a feature that would be of interest to men who are thinking about proposing. Third,

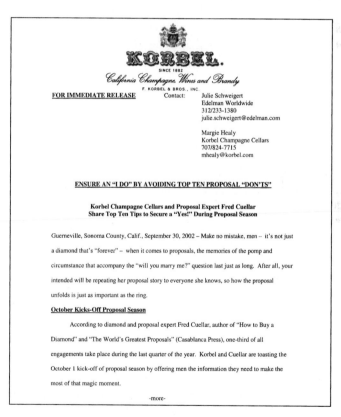

Figure 6.1 Top 10 Lists Are Popular
Korbel Champagne Cellars, as part of its campaign to publicize its "perfect proposal contest," compiled a "Top Ten Proposal Don'ts" as part of a Valentine's Day tie-in. The news feature was distributed to syndicated food and relationship writers, features and lifestyle editors at 200 daily newspapers, and radio DJs in 50 markets. See Figure 5.2 for the release announcing the winners of the contest.
(Courtesy of Korbel Champagne Cellars and its public relations firm, Edelman Worldwide.)

After researching more than 10,000 proposal stories and spending years in the industry advising men on popping the question, Cuellar has compiled this list of mistakes to avoid, ensuring your proposal is blissful:

TOP TEN MISTAKES MEN MAKE WHILE PROPOSING

1. Proposing on a holiday or birthday: Consider picking a day meaningful to your relationship, such as the anniversary of your first date. Your girlfriend wants her day to shine – don't propose on a holiday that can't be yours as a couple.

2. Allowing other women to try on the ring: It's smart to get a second opinion, but don't use your fiancée's friends as guinea pigs. Make sure your fiancée is the first of her friends to see and wear her ring, and let her enjoy the fun of showing it off for the first time.

3. Leaking the news: When you're ready to pop the question, don't spill the beans to too many "confidants." Sharing the news with friends and family is more exciting if you do it together.

4. Forgetting her family: Pull your manners out of the closet and call the appropriate member of her family for "the talk." According to a recent survey conducted by Korbel[1], 42 percent of Americans feel the act of asking a woman's family for her hand – whether it be her father, mother or even a sibling – is still a time-honored tradition.

5. Playing hide and seek with the ring: Imagine this: you're about to propose to your girlfriend when she swallows the ring because you "cleverly" hid it in an ice cream cone or cocktail. Sending your fiancée to the emergency room might not be the best way to start your future.

6. Staging a practical joke: Minutes before the proposal, throwing your girlfriend off by convincing her that you're in jail or that you won't be ready for marriage for years could have unintended consequences.

7. Missing the VIP treatment: Do your research and you'll find that many venues are happy to create a special setting for your proposal. For example, many theaters will schedule private screenings, restaurants can provide champagne toasts and amusement parks can offer private rides.

8. Exhibiting suspicious behavior: As proposal time approaches, make sure your behavior remains consistent with how you act on a daily basis. Repeatedly touching your pocket to make sure the ring is secure and coming up with off-the-wall excuses for your whereabouts can both be giveaways to the bride-to-be.

9. Acting like you settled: A surefire way to ruin any proposal is to start with any of the following statements:
- "You win."
- "We're not getting any younger . . ."

-more-

- "In spite of what my mother says . . ."
- "I have sowed my wild oats."

10. Losing sight of what the proposal is all about: Your proposal will be perfect if it is honest, heartfelt and passionate.

Win Your Perfect Proposal

Once you've planned your perfect proposal using these tips, submit it for consideration in "Korbel's Perfect Proposal Contest." This fall, Korbel and adiamondisforever.com will award three lucky winners their dream proposal, complete with a diamond engagement ring. The grand prize winner will receive $10,000 for a honeymoon or reception.

To enter, log on to www.korbel.com and submit an essay of 250 words or less describing your perfect proposal and why you deserve to have this dream proposal come true for your significant other. Contest is open to Americans 21 years of age or older, and ends December 15, 2002. (Void where prohibited, certain restrictions apply, no purchase necessary. Visit www.korbel.com for a complete set of rules.)

Established in 1882, Korbel Champagne Cellars has been a part of America's greatest celebrations for more than 120 years. Korbel has been a supplier and licensee of the 1996 Olympic Games, the exclusive champagne of the past five Presidential Inaugurations, a supporter of Team Dennis Conner for the 1995 America's Cup and the first global sponsor of *Times Square 2000* – a sponsorship that lasts through 2007. Korbel is an Official Supporter of the 2000, 2002 and 2004 U.S. Olympic Teams and the 2002 Olympic and Paralympic Winter Games. Korbel is the number one selling premium *méthode champenoise*-produced champagne in America.

#

Korbel encourages you to celebrate responsibly.

[1] Source: Korbel Champagne Cellars Proposal Survey. Survey of 1,000 adults conducted by Harris Interactive, April, 2002. Survey findings have a plus/minus three percent margin of error and are projectable nationwide.

Figure 6.1 continued

you must be sure that the feature helps achieve organizational objectives. Does it position the organization in a favorable light? Does it encourage the use of a particular product or service?

Good feature writers ask a lot of questions. They need a natural curiosity about how things work and how things are related to each other. If the company has just produced a new video game, for example, you would find out exactly how the game was developed. By asking questions, you might find out that a 19-year-old computer "nerd" invented the game, or that a new technology was used to create 3-D effects. In each case, you have a potential feature. A story about the inventor would make interesting reading, but so would a story about how the new computer technology could be applied in other fields.

News events and issues can also trigger ideas for feature stories. If Congress passes a law, how does that affect your organization or industry? If media attention is being given to sweatshops in Asia that are producing goods for the American market, perhaps you can develop a feature on how your company assures that its goods are produced in assembly plants that meet minimum pay and working standards. The possibilities are limited only by your own imagination and creativity.

Ways to Proceed

Once you have a feature idea, there are four ways you can proceed. The most common approach is to write a general feature and distribute it to a variety of publications in much the same way as news releases are sent. Another mass distribution method is to have a feature service distribute it for you in **camera-ready** format.

In most cases, features are topic specific and are sent to the editor in charge of a particular section. A feature on the lowly potato is sent to the food editor, but a feature on a new computer video game goes to the computer editor. A feature on how to have a beautiful green lawn, of course, goes to the garden editor. In a more sophisticated version of this approach, newspapers in the same circulation area will receive different features and photos about the same subject. This way, editors know the material is somewhat exclusive to them and won't be showing up in a competing publication.

The second approach is to write an exclusive feature for a specific publication. In this case, you need to target a publication that reaches your selected audience, be they engineers, architects, educators, or purchasing agents. You also need to review several issues of the publication to determine the topics it has covered and the style used in similar articles.

Once you are familiar with the publication, phone the editor, outline the subject in about 60 seconds, and ask if he or she would be interested. You can also send a brief letter. Carol Haddix, food editor of the *Chicago Tribune,* says the ideal PR person "just sends a note explaining his or her idea in a way that is phrased to interest me."

The reason for the short phone call or a note (called a query) is to determine if there is enough interest to justify writing an exclusive feature. Perhaps the editor has recently run several features much like the one you have in mind. Or the editor might suggest another story angle that would appeal to more readers.

Many editors, simply on the basis of a phone call or a brief note, will give you the green light to submit an article for consideration. This does not mean that they are obligated to use it.

Other editors, particularly those for popular magazines, will ask you to submit a proposal that outlines the entire article and explains why the magazine should publish it. A proposal should include the following points:

- Tentative title of article.
- Subject and theme.
- Significance. Why is the topic important? Why should readers know about it?
- Major points.
- Description of photos and graphics available.

The third approach is not to write the feature at all, but to interest a reporter or freelance writer in the idea. You can do this by telephoning the person or by sending what is known as a "pitch letter." You give the idea, provide much of the factual information, provide graphics, or even set up interviews for the publication's reporter, who then writes the story. Pitch letters are discussed further in Chapter 8.

The advantage of this approach is that the publication's staff actually writes the story. Thus, the publication has invested time and money in the story and is more likely to publish it. The disadvantage is that you can't always control how the story will be developed and whether it will advance organizational objectives.

The fourth approach is simply to post the feature on your organization's Web site for possible downloading by journalists and consumers. Hewlett-Packard, for example, has a link on its Web site titled "feature story archive." (See Figure 6.2 for an example of a feature story on this Web site.)

Placement opportunities for features are discussed later in this chapter.

TYPES OF FEATURES

There is no formal classification of feature stories and no practical limit to the variety of stories that can be written. Whenever you find something that can be made interesting to some segment of the public, it may be the beginning of a feature. Some ideas are obvious, but many more can be developed if you hunt for them. Among the most frequently seen features are (1) case studies, (2) application stories, (3) research studies, (4) backgrounders, (5) personality profiles, and (6) historical pieces. These categories are not mutually exclusive, and the lines between them often blur, but some familiarity with them will help you understand the range of possibilities.

Case Study

The **case study** is frequently used in product publicity. The story of how some product solved a problem or how a unique service enabled some organization to save money or improve its own service can be important and interesting.

Feature Story HEWLETT PACKARD Expanding Possibilities

Search

Home

The HP DeskJet 340 on Mount Everest: Taking Portability to New Heights!

Dr. Shani Tan prints a weather report on the HP DeskJet 340C at Everest base camp

Using the same route as Lord Hunt's British Commonwealth team in 1953, the first Singapore team to attempt to scale Mount Everest departed for the Himalayas amidst many cheers and blessings of good luck on March 19, 1998. Along with their supplies and gear, the team packed an HP DeskJet 340 printer.

The 11-person team embarked on their trailblazing adventure with a harrowing flight in an old Russian helicopter to the village of Lukla, Nepal, where the airport consists of a runway that sits on a narrow shelf on the side of the mountain.

In an environment like Mount Everest, where the base camp lies at the lofty height of 5,400 meters (17,717 feet) above sea level, communication with the outside world reaches a critical level. The team regularly checked weather reports as these determined their course of action. This is where the HP DeskJet 340 played its most important role.

Weather reports were printed for easy reference and sharing among the team. The compact, 1.95 kg (4.3 pounds) portable printer performed well even under the most extreme conditions. The high altitude meant extremely low temperatures, low humidity and low pressure. The outside temperature at Everest base camp was a chilling -15 C while the inside tent temperature was only marginally warmer at -5 C. Base camp also experienced severe windstorms, one of which shredded most of the team's tents with its 150 km/hour winds.

"We used the DeskJet 340 to print e-mail and any other interesting stuff, but weather reports, which are of extremely high importance, were the primary function," commented Johann Annuar, the expedition's communications specialist and person in charge of satellite

http://www.hp.com/ghp/features/everest/ 7/15/99

Figure 6.2 Tell a Story About Your Product
A news feature about the toughness or durability of a product often generates media interest if there's an unusual angle. This application story, posted on Hewlett-Packard's Web site, shows how its Deskjet portable printer operated under extremely difficult conditions. Consumers may not be climbing Mt. Everest, but they get the impression that this is an extremely durable and reliable product.
(Courtesy of Hewlett-Packard Company.)

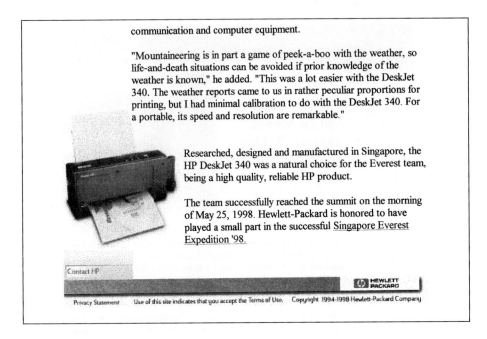

Figure 6.2 continued

Andy Marken, a public relations counselor, writing in the *Public Relations Journal,* says case studies offer excellent exposure because they quickly inform the market of new and different solutions, demonstrate products and services in use, illustrate a company's innovative technology, show acceptance and experience in the marketplace, and encourage readers to relate solutions to their own needs.

A good example of a case study is one distributed by the Hewlett-Packard Company that told how Nissan used HP computer equipment to monitor prototype electronic engine-control systems in its racing cars. The story quotes a Nissan executive saying, "Our jobs are simplified knowing that the engine computer will perform up to specifications under severe race conditions. With HP's help, we can get down to the business of winning races."

A good case study was also developed by Oracle in cooperation with the American Red Cross. It told how a company-developed software program was deployed to locate and re-unite families split up by the war in Kosovo.

Application Story

The **application story** is a lot like the case study. It tells how to use a new product or how to use a familiar product in a new way. Much food publicity consists of application stories—new recipes or new variations on familiar ones. The food pages of newspapers carry many such features. Some are published exactly as received; others are rewritten or combined in a longer feature.

Professional Tips

How to Write a Case Study

A satisfied customer is the key to writing a case history that shows how a company's product or service was used successfully. G. A. "Andy" Marken, president of Marken Communications, gives a list of questions that a public relations writer should keep in mind:

- What can be told about the company, its place in the industry, its size, and other details?
- Why did the company first need the products or services in question?
- Who was involved in the application?
- What did the products or services do for those people? What can they do now, as a result of the products or services, that they couldn't do before?
- How does the solution save time and money and add quality?
- Could the company get the same results with a competitive solution? If not, how does this solution provide savings that couldn't otherwise be achieved?
- What is the customer contact protocol? Who should clear and approve the article?

A feature on home maintenance tips could provide a basis for publicity about a new kind of paintbrush or paint. Wherever there is a product or service that serves some useful purpose, there may be an audience for information about it. Even the Mayo Clinic was able to generate publicity about a book on stress by preparing a story that provided some practical advice (see Figure 6.3).

A variation on the application feature is the technical article. It may describe the technology behind a new product, or it may simply explain how a product can be used in specialized settings. For Hewlett-Packard, such a setting was Mt. Everest. It posted a feature on its Web site telling how a Singapore team climbing the mountain relied on a DeskJet 340, which was able to operate despite the high altitude, windstorms, and below-freezing temperatures. See Figure 6.2 for the text of this article.

Research Study

Surveys and polls, as well as scientific studies, can provide opportunities for features. This is particularly true if the **research study** is about some aspect of contemporary lifestyles or a common situation in the workplace. One study, sponsored by a winery, was about how Americans propose marriage. It found, among other things, that 25 percent of men still propose marriage on bended knee.

Residence Inn, a chain owned by the Marriott Corporation, got extensive coverage with a research study about the effects of long business trips on female managers and executives. The feature concentrated on the research finding that women feel more productive and stimulated by extended business trips than men, who report feeling more lonely and bored.

Deal With Anger and Stress

(WMS) - It's natural to feel angry and stressed once in a while. But it's not healthy to stay agitated, bottle up your anger or express it with explosive outbursts. Here are a few tips from the book "Mayo Clinic on Depression" (ISBN 1-893005-17-8) that can help you deal with anger and stress in a more positive way:

* Identify what triggers your anger and prepare for it.
* Remove yourself from the situation, then choose your response.
* Express your frustration calmly rather than in a verbal outburst.
* Find a constructive way, like writing or dancing, to release the energy produced by your anger.
* Release "hot thoughts" that rekindle anger.

Researchers believe harboring vengeful and painful feelings places your body under continuous stress. In addition to harming your emotional health, holding on to anger may increase your risk of high blood pressure and heart disease.

So, how do you let go? You learn to forgive. Anger may be fueled by a lingering resentment toward someone who wronged you or hurt you. A study of women who survived incest found that those who learned to forgive lessened their anxiety and depression. Forgiving doesn't mean denying or condoning what happened, but it is a way to keep negative feelings from consuming you.

Sometimes simply becoming aware of what causes you stress can make it easier to cope. Your stress may be linked to external factors like work, family or unpredictable events. Or it may stem from internal factors, like perfectionism or unrealistic expectations. Concentrate on those stressors you can change. In situations beyond your control, look for ways to remain calm under the circumstances.

One of the best ways to manage your emotional health is to anticipate and solve potential problems before they become worse. This means embracing habits that support your emotional health, like exercise and good nutrition. Be aware of the warning signs that your emotional health is out of whack, like waking up early in the morning, eating more than usual or irritability over trivial matters. Life naturally brings ups and downs; occasionally feeling sad or blue doesn't mean you're sinking into depression. But if these feelings persist, see your doctor or therapist.

To help you develop healthy habits, Mayo Clinic Health Information is offering a free booklet, "Live Longer, Live Better." Write to Mayo Clinic Health Information -- Live Better Booklet -- OE-6, 200 First Street S.W., Rochester, MN 55905. Or, order the book "Mayo Clinic on Depression," ($14.95 plus shipping, handling and applicable sales tax) by calling (800) 291-1128, extension 124 and receive the booklet free with your purchase.

http://www.metrocreativegraphics.com/031-HealthMindBody/07-HM031112.html   7/28/2003

Figure 6.3 Health Advice for Personal Problems
Surveys show that editors and consumer are very interested in health and medical information that relates to individual concerns. The Mayo Clinic publicized its new book on stress and depression by sending out this news feature giving consumers basic information on how to mange their emotional health. The release is a good example of offering a "reward" (advice) at the beginning and then concluding on how get the "reward" by getting a free pamphlet or ordering the book.
(Courtesy of the Mayo Clinic. Distributed by Metro Editorial Services.)

The feature went on to quote psychologists, female executives, and Residence Inn managers about the findings of the study. According to Marriott, women now comprise 31 percent of all business travel "roomnights."

Backgrounder

There are several kinds of **backgrounders**. One focuses on a problem and how it was solved—by an organization or a product. Often there is considerable historical material and an opportunity for injecting human interest into the story. One example is a story on the reclamation of strip-mined land and how a coal company restored an area to productive use for farming.

Another kind of backgrounder explains where a product comes from or how it is made. A manufacturer of woolens might release a feature on sheep farming

Tension-Type Headache Backgrounder

Introduction

The National Headache Foundation reports that more than 45 million Americans have recurring headaches.[1]

According to the International Headache Society,[2] most headache pain can be classified as one of the "primary headache disorders," tension-type, migraine, or cluster. Of these, tension-type headache is by far the most common, affecting up to 93 percent of American adults.[3]

Description

Tension-type headaches are different for everyone, but they have a number of telltale signs. Most people feel pain on both sides of their head and describe it as a "squeezing pressure" or a "tight band." The pain can be severe, but it is rarely unbearable. The exact location (i.e., top, sides, back, forehead) can change with every headache. Some experience pain intermittently; for others, the pain is continuous. Many people say that tension-type headache also causes stiffness and tightness in their neck and shoulders.

Causes

Even though doctors have learned a lot about headache over the last two decades, the exact cause of a tension-type headache remains unknown. Tension-type headaches are associated with periods of stress or emotional upset. So a bad day at the office, a fight with a spouse, or a major social event are just a few of the many reasons people get tension-type headaches.

Figure 6.4 Backgrounders Give the Additional Details
Ever wonder why you get tension headaches? When Bristol-Myers Squibb introduced its new product, Excedrin Tension Headache, it sent a news release (Figure 5.9) and a fact sheet (Figure 5.10) to the media. The company also sent this backgrounder (only the first page is displayed) on tension headaches giving information about causes and suggestions on relaxation exercises to relieve the pain.
(Courtesy of Bristol-Myers Squibb Company.)

and the differing characteristics of wool from the various breeds, finally leading up to the excellent products made from that wool.

A third approach is to give consumers background information so they can make intelligent purchasing decisions. A Hewlett-Packard feature, for example, sought to educate consumers who were bewildered by the blizzard of conflicting information about buying and using computers. The feature, of course, also positioned HP products as a simple and effective solution. See Figure 6.4 for a backgrounder on a new headache medicine.

Personality Profile

People like to read about people, particularly if they are prominent, in positions of power, or celebrities. A review of any magazine newsstand is a graphic confirmation that the "cult of personality" is alive and well.

Personality profiles about the lives and times of entertainment celebrities are the staple of many magazines, and even the business press prominently displays profiles of "movers and shakers" in the corporate world. A cover article in *Fortune* magazine, for example, was a personality profile on Larry Ellison, CEO of Oracle. Other profiles of prominent executives can also be found in such publications as *Business Week*, *Forbes*, the *New Yorker*, and *The Wall Street Journal*.

In most cases, these profiles are written by journalists with, quite often, a strong assist from public relations personnel who (1) "sell" the idea of a profile,

Professional Tips

How to Write a Personality Profile

A writer attempts to capture the essence of an individual in a personality profile by creating a full-color picture in words. Ragan Communications, Inc., publisher of various newsletters about communication, gives these tips on how to enhance the writing of your profile features:

- **Give the "essence."** Tell the reader who the profile subject is and why he or she is interesting.
- **Take some chances.** A profile is an interpretation, not an official biography. Give the reader a picture of your subject as you see him or her.
- **Get a different view.** Try to see the world through the subject's eyes. A profile works when you understand a person's motivations.
- **Don't write in chronological order.** Most people are more interesting at 40 than they are at 4. Don't begin at the beginning. Write about what makes your subject interesting now.
- **Make your subject reflect.** Ask profile subjects to evaluate themselves, describing good points and bad, high and low points.
- **Don't focus on work alone.** Don't limit your profile to a piece about somebody's job. Try to see the whole person who goes home after work and has an interesting hobby.
- **Describe, describe, describe.** Paint a picture of your subject. Is he or she serious, jovial, upbeat? What kind of personality does the person exhibit under stress, or at play?

(2) make the executive available, (3) provide background information, and (4) even arrange photo shoots.

A person doesn't have to be a CEO, however, in order to qualify for a personality profile. There are any number of employees in any organization who would make an interesting profile because they have an unusual job, an interesting hobby, or have distinguished themselves in some way. Pacific Bell, for example, once distributed a feature on the new manager of the company's Vietnamese Service Center because the woman had a compelling story about her escape from war-torn Vietnam. And Bowling Green State University once got a major feature in the *Chronicle of Higher Education* by profiling the director of the university's research center on fruit flies, which the publication dubbed "Fruit-Fly Capital of the World."

Historical Piece

Anniversaries, major changes, centennials, and many other events lend themselves to historical features. Whenever a significant milestone is passed, there may be an opportunity to report on the history of the organization, its facilities, or some of its people. Stressing the history of an organization lends it an air of stability and permanence. The public can logically deduce that if an organization has lasted "that long," it must have merit.

Betty Skov, director of public relations for Logitech, Inc.—the world's largest manufacturer of the computer mouse—was able to generate a large number of feature stories by discovering that the thirtieth birthday of the mouse was coming up. According to *Ragan's Media Relations Report*, she found the inventor of the mouse and invited him to come see the 200 millionth mouse come off the assembly line. Of course, the press was invited to the celebration.

Another example of a **historical piece** is shown in Figure 6.5 about Maytag's icon, Ol' Lonely. Accompanying this feature was a short, humorous list of how to tell if you are lonely (Figure 6.6).

Historical features are also a staple of publicity about tourism. The Alaska Division of Tourism distributes features about the history of the state to encourage visitors. One article was titled, "Following 19th-Century Russians across Alaska." The lead paragraph was:

> Visitors to Alaska who have forgotten their American history are quickly reminded that the 49th state was once a Russian colony. One reminder is the large number of Russian names sprinkled across the map. . . .

PARTS OF A FEATURE

The formatting of a feature is similar to that of a news release. You should use the organization's letterhead and give the standard information such as contacts, headlines, and datelines. Lines should be double-spaced, and sentences or paragraphs should not break between pages.

The Headline

"Newspaper and broadcast editors pick daily from over 10,000 releases online and on paper . . ." says Ronald Levy, founding president of North American Precis

MAYTAG

Contact:
Jill Spiekerman
Maytag Appliances
641-787-6886
jspiek@maytag.com

John Merritt
Carmichael Lynch Spong
612-375-8528
jmerritt@clynch.com

Still Lonely After All These Years:
Maytag® Celebrates the 35th Anniversary of a
Cherished American Icon – Ol' Lonely®, the Maytag Repairman

NEWTON, Iowa (July 30, 2002) – For 35 years, he's been waiting patiently by the phone, hoping someone will call for his help, but of course, no one ever does, because the company's products are "so darned reliable." He's Ol' Lonely, the dependable Maytag Repairman, and today Maytag Appliances is celebrating the 35th anniversary of the cultural icon who has become the longest-running real-life advertising character in television history.

The first Maytag Repairman commercial premiered on the "Today" show in 1967. Ol' Lonely was a natural outgrowth of the thousands of letters Maytag received about its repair-free washers. Today, the character is known and cherished by millions as the symbol of dependability and icon of loneliness.

"There's something about Ol' Lonely that people just gravitate to," says Bill Beer, Maytag Appliances president. "He has human strengths and weaknesses. People identify with him. They trust him."

Ol' Lonely is among the most enduring cultural icons, according to Christie Nordheilm, an assistant professor of marketing of the Kellogg School of Management at Northwestern University, and a consultant who has created advertising strategies for Nestle, Keebler and Star-Kist Foods. "What makes cultural icons successful is the fierce protection of an idea. Because Maytag has protected and nurtured the Maytag Repairman character all of these years, he's become a friend to consumers. He has definitely become a part of pop culture, and has even showed up in political cartoons."

- more -

403 W. Fourth Street, North ■ Newton, IA 50208 ■ Tel: 641-792-7000

Maytag Repairman 35th Anniversary
Page 2 of 3

Ol' Lonely Through the Years

In the mid-1950s, Maytag began to receive letters from customers who wrote about the reliability of its products. Leo Burnett Company eventually created Maytag's "Dependability" advertising campaign, which launched in 1961. Advertisements began to feature real Maytag consumers, and with each ad came even more letters. "Every time we ran an ad featuring a consumer, we got more letters from people who wanted to tell us about their own positive experiences with our appliances," says Kristi Lafrenz, Maytag brand manager.

A Canadian radio call-in program followed. On the program, an appliance repairman offered advice to consumers in the style of "Dear Abby." The concept was translated to television in 1967, with actor Jesse White appearing as a Maytag Repairman. Titled "Drill Instructor," the commercial showed White preparing trainees to fill their considerable free time with such activities as crossword puzzles, playing cards and beadwork.

By the 1980s, the repairman began to appear in Maytag advertisements accompanied by soulmate and companion, Newton, a sad-eyed Basset Hound named after Maytag's Newton, Iowa headquarters.

Evolving With the Times

After 68 Maytag Repairman commercials, Jesse White retired in 1989 at the age of 70 years old. Maytag chose to continue its campaign, featuring repairman ads with former "WKRP in Cincinnati" actor Gordon Jump. "The repairman concept was so firmly entrenched in people's minds and represented our products so well that we kept on with it," says Lafrenz.

Consumers quickly began to love Jump, who first appeared as Ol' Lonely in 1989 in a spot called "Biker." He was shown riding a bike as a narrator described how "neither rain, nor sleet, nor dark of night can keep the Maytag Repairman from his appointed rounds, even if the only thing he needs to fix. . . is lunch." Jump ended the spot by fixing a hot dog for lunch.

- more -

Figure 6.5 History Can Be a News Angle
Maytag, the appliance manufacturer, has built its entire corporate image and advertising on Ol' Lonely—the service-man who never gets a phone call—for the past 35 years. It celebrated the 35th anniversary of Ol' Lonely with a news feature giving the background and history of this American advertising icon. See Figure 4.3 for a photo of Ol' Lonely and his birthday cake.
(Courtesy of Maytag Appliances and its public relations firm, Carmichael Lynch Spiong.)

Syndicate, but you can get hundreds of placements if you use headlines that "editors find delightful and charming."

"Headlines are vital," says Steven Gossett, editorial manager of PR Newswire's feature news unit. He suggests headlines of 20 words or less, and to use the name of the organization or product if it is well-known. If your client or employer isn't a household name, then the next best approach, says Gossett, is to tell what's new, unusual, different, or important about your product, service, or organization.

> *Maytag Repairman 35th Anniversary*
> *Page 3 of 3*
>
> As Maytag products kept pace with the changing needs of consumers, the Repairman evolved with them. In 2001, the company introduced the Apprentice character, played by actor Mark Devine. The Apprentice came to embody Maytag Appliances' innovations as well as dependability.
>
> Today, the two repairmen appear together in the company's commercials, with Ol' Lonely still looking for ways to pass the time, while the Apprentice works hard to fill his time.
>
> "The two characters approach their jobs differently," says Lafrenz. "The Repairman wants to instill within the Apprentice the same serious sense of responsibility to the Maytag consumer that for decades has kept Ol' Lonely idle, yet alert, waiting by the phone. The Apprentice brings a more proactive and contemporary approach to his job. His days are filled with creative ways of putting Maytag's appliances to the test."
>
> The key to the Maytag Repairman's popularity has been his consistency of character, Beer says. "His endearing human qualities, when combined with a brand known for reliability, are something that never disappoints our customers. People feel like they know him."
>
> **About Maytag**
>
> For the better part of a century, Maytag brand appliances have been synonymous with dependability and quality. Today, Maytag remains one of America's most trusted appliance manufacturers. Based in Newton, Iowa, Maytag Appliances offers a full line of high performance appliances, including the Gemini® double-oven range, Neptune® and Atlantis™ washers and dryers, Wide-by-Side™ refrigerator with ClimateZone™ Technology, and Jetclean® II, the world's first three-rack dishwasher. For more information on any Maytag appliance visit www.maytag.com to purchase an appliance online.
>
> - 30 -

Figure 6.5 continued

There are two kinds of headlines that you can use. The first is the informational headline that gives the crux of the story. Some informational headlines are "Travel Tips: Travel Insurance Offers Peace of Mind on Family Vacations" and "Expert Advice for Buying Power Tools as Gifts." Another informational headline is "Good News for Caffeine Lovers: Study Shows Caffeinated Beverages Hydrate Like Water." The feature, of course, was distributed by Coca-Cola.

The informational news-type headline works well for the results of research studies or when the organization is offering advice and tips (10 tips seem to be the standard) on how to do purchase a product, book a cruise, or even improve your wardrobe. Essentially, these headlines make the promise of a "reward" for the consumer by helping them save money, buy a good product, achieve better health, or prevent illness. Verizon, for example, got extensive media placements by sending out a news feature offering tips on how to help a child succeed in the classroom.

The second kind of headline is one that uses a play on words, alliteration, or a rhyme to raise the curiosity of the editor or the consumer. Ron Levy, mentioned earlier, gives some examples of word play:

Maytag Repairman's Top 10 Signs That You're Lonely

(ARA) — If you think you're the only one who's lonely, think again.

Ol' Lonely®, the Maytag Repairman, has been waiting patiently by the phone since 1967, hoping some consumer would call for his help – but of course no one ever has, because Maytag's appliances are so darned reliable.

That's 35 years of being lonely.

To determine whether you're among the truly lonely, listen to the voice of experience. Here are the Maytag Repairman's "Top 10 Signs That You're Lonely:"

1.   Your back goes out more than you do

2.   You talk to yourself, but even you don't listen

3.   You call the IRS and ask to be audited

4.   You've converted every measurement in your home to the metric system

5.   You look forward to visits from door-to-door salespeople

6.   Your imaginary friends don't want anything to do with you

7.   You call telemarketers to let them know you're home

8.   You look forward to renewing your driver's license

9.   You can twirl pencils in each hand better than a state fair baton champion

10.   You've actually read your life insurance policy

If you're looking for ways to fend off loneliness, visit **www.Maytag.com** to obtain a free Maytag Men screensaver. It'll remind you that you're not the only one who's lonely this summer.

- 30 -

Figure 6.6 Ol' Lonely's Top 10 List
Maytag Appliances, in addition to the news feature shown in Figure 6.5, also prepared a humorous feature on "Maytag's Repairman's Top 10 Signs That You're Lonely." It was distributed in matte format (camera-ready) so editors on small publications could easily publish it. Readers were offered an additional "re-ward" of a free screensaver just by visiting the Maytag Web site.
(Courtesy of Maytag Appliances and its public relations firm, Carmichael Lynch Spong.)

"School Day Stress Busters That Get High Marks" (Procter & Gamble)

"Work and Money Problems Are One Big Headache" (Tylenol)

"Knight of the Road Spend Nights on the Road" (American Trucking Association)

"The Good the Bad and the Bubbly—Celebrating Safely" (American Academy of Ophthalmology)

A sampling of headlines on the feature news Web site of PR Newswire provides additional creativity:

"New Parents Need the Scoop on Cat Litter" (a new cat litter product)

"Help Your Teen Put His Best Face Forward" (a new acne medicine)

"See Your Way Through the Next Power Outage" (a new flashlight)

"New National Water Gardening Group to Dive into Deep End on Important Issues" (organization of a new water conservation group)

Whatever your choice of headline, whether it is an informational one or one that generates curiosity, make sure it grabs the interest of editors and readers.

The Lead

News releases usually have a summary lead that tells the basic facts in a nutshell. The name of the organization is in the lead, and readers will get the key information even if the summary is all they read.

In contrast, the purpose of the lead in a news feature story is to attract attention and get the reader interested enough to read the entire article. A good lead requires creativity on the writer's part because it must intrigue people and appeal to their curiosity. A lead is a promise; it tells people that they will learn something that will be beneficial to them.

The problem-solving angle often makes a good lead. Here is the lead that Plast World used on a feature news release for its product:

> Mom alert! The solution to summer "blahs" and Father's Day gift giving can be found on the shelves of the nearest gift or toy store. GEOMAG, the world's strongest magnetic building system from Italy, is both the perfect gift for dads and the answer to the most irritating summer question. "I'm bored . . . what can I do?"

Here are some other creative and interesting leads that create interest, give information, or promise a benefit:

- Many home improvement enthusiasts will tell you that new tools are at the top of their wish lists. But for those with little knowledge of power tools, shopping for them can be an intimidating and confusing experience. (A feature release by Dremel, a manufacturer of power tools, which gives five tips on shopping for power tools.)

- The joy of the perennial bloom, children's carefree laughter, and a relaxed drive in an old convertible bring to mind the wonderful, cheerful months of summer. The essence of this anticipated season is captured when Filoli, one of America's greatest treasures, hosts its new event, "Summer at Filoli: A Family Celebration," on June 28 from 10 A.M. to 3:30 P.M. (A feature release by Filoli Estate, Woodside, California.)

- Bravo's hit television series, "Queer Eye for the Straight Guy" makes it abundantly clear that most men—whether they think so or not—need serious fashion help. (A feature release by Penguin books about a new book by the show's food expert and a fashion writer for *Esquire*.)

Professional Tips

How to Write a Good Feature Story

An organization may get more media exposure by doing a feature story instead of a straight news release. Fred Ferguson, head of PR Newswire's Feature News Service (www.prnewswire.com), offers the following advice on how to write a feature news release:

- Grab the editor's attention with a creative headline that tells the story.
- Tell the same story in the first paragraph, which should never be cute, soft, or a question.
- Support the lead with a second paragraph that backs it up and provides attribution. Place the product and service name at the end of the second paragraph so it becomes less advertorial.
- Try to keep all paragraphs under 30 words and to three lines. This makes it easier for editors to cut to fit available space, holds the reader's attention, and is attractive in most page layouts.
- Do not excessively repeat the name of the product or service. It dilutes the value of the story.
- Forget superlatives, techno-babble, and buzzwords. Instead, tell consumers why they should care.
- Never say anything is the first or the best, express an opinion, or make claims unless you directly attribute it to someone else.
- Avoid using a self-serving laundry list of products or services.
- Discard a telephone number acronym in favor of numerals. It makes it easier for consumers to make a telephone call for more information
- Don't put the corporate name in all capital letters. It violates AP style.
- Don't give a standard paragraph about the organization at the end of the article.

- For all those hen-pecked, harassed coffee and cola drinkers who've been told caffeine's a diuretic, there's good news. The second of two studies reinforces the findings that all non-alcoholic drinks, including caffeinated beverages, are hydrating. (A feature release by The Coca-Cola Company.)
- Tired of staying up all night assembling your kids' holiday gifts? Does the thought of deciphering lengthy, complicated instructions make your skin crawl? If so, you're not alone. (A feature release by Huffy Sports Company about a "no tools" portable basketball hoop stand.)

A good lead may focus on the most unusual part of the story. Thus a lead introducing a machine that builds curbs without forms could start with these words: "The formless curber lays concrete curbs without the use of expensive forms." This statement is factual and true, but the feature would be much more interesting if it started like this: "It's just like squeezing toothpaste out of a tube. In fact, it works on the same principle. By squeezing the concrete through a die shaped like the final curbing, it is possible to lay concrete curbs without the labor and materials needed for forms." This lead should appeal to the contractor who is a prospective buyer of the machine. It is unusual, it is interesting, and it promises the reward of savings.

Body of the Feature

Chapter 5 pointed out that news releases use the inverted pyramid, presenting the most important facts first and elaborating on them in the succeeding paragraphs. It also pointed out that news releases should be relatively short.

The feature story, in contrast, has none of these constraints. It doesn't need to follow Ryan's four basic paragraphs, and it can be five to eight pages, double-spaced. The practical guide to length is to use enough words to tell the story thoroughly but to stop writing when it is told. Because most features are planned for specific publications, you should look at the average length of features in the chosen medium. Food sections in the newspaper, for example, tend to want features that are 500 to 750 words long.

Feature stories emphasize the following:

- Quotes from people
- Concrete examples and illustrations
- Descriptive words that paint mental pictures
- Information presented in an entertaining way

Keep in mind the use of parallels. A strange subject will be more understandable if it is explained in familiar terms—as in the curbs-as-toothpaste example. In the amplification of that story, the writer would undoubtedly explain how the concrete is squeezed out of the die using a screw like that in a meat grinder, which extrudes the concrete mix and at the same time pushes the machine away from the newly cast curb.

If a feature runs to several pages, insert subheads. The subheads, often bold-faced or underlined, indicate the major sections of the story. Subheads, however, should also provide information. Instead of saying something vague such as "Adaptability," it is better to write "Adaptability at Local Offices."

The body of the story essentially delivers the reward promised in the lead.

Summary

In many cases, the summary is the most important part of the feature. It is often quite brief, but it must be complete and clear. Essentially, it is the core of the idea that the writer wants to leave with the reader.

The Coca-Cola news feature on the study about hydration is a good example. The concluding paragraph says:

> According to Reimers (the person who conducted the study), the bottom line is, "All people need to think about drinking enough fluids to stay hydrated, but people should feel comfortable knowing that part of their requirements are met through foods and the rest can be met by drinking a variety of beverages—both caffeinated and noncaffeinated—with or without water. Choosing the beverages you enjoy can have a positive impact on your hydration status."

The feature release promoting the book co-authored by one of the characters in *Queer Eye* ended with the following paragraph:

Good fashion sense can improve a man's career and love life—for men not born with a flair for style, Ted Allen's *Things A Man Should Know About Style* makes it easy.

See Figure 6.7 for complete release.

And the feature news article that gave tips to travelers on the benefits of travel insurance ended with the following pitch for the insurance company:

Today's News   Page 1 of 2

Feature News

One of 'Queer Eye's' 'Fab Five' Offers Style Tips to Hopelessly Unfashionable Men ... Women Everywhere Breathe a Sigh of Relief

NEW YORK, Sept. 11 /PRNewswire/ -- Bravo's hit television series, "Queer Eye for the Straight Guy" makes it abundantly clear that most men -- whether they think so or not -- need serious fashion help!

Before Ted Allen served as the show's food expert, he shared valuable fashion tips as co-author of Esquire's Things A Man Should Know About Style (Riverhead Trade Paperbacks; $10.95; in bookstores everywhere). Based on the popular column, "Things a Man Should Know ... " in Esquire magazine, the book is a style primer for men that offers the same combination of witty and practical advice that has made the "Fab Five" instant celebrities. When it comes to sartorial savvy, most men could use some help, but why wait for Tuesday nights?

Attention men: "Unless you live in Chicago or Buffalo or International Falls, Minnesota, you must never wear a headband." And by the way, "Casual Friday does not excuse the visibility of chest hair" (from Things A Man Should Know About Style).

Men (and the women who love them) everywhere will appreciate having this indispensable style advice at their fingertips.

* Thinking about changing you hairstyle? The length of one's sideburns is inversely proportional to one's ability to rise in the corporate hierarchy ... unless one works at Graceland.

* Green suits are NOT wearable, are difficult to match ties to, and can cause a short man to be mistaken for a leprechaun.

* Suit trouser bottoms should break on top of your shoe, so that the crease in the leg rumples just slightly. If your suit trouser bottoms are too short, you'll look like Garrison Keillor. If your suit trousers are too long: Charlie Chaplin.

* Toupees and comb-overs betray a level of moral dishonesty equivalent to the practice of buttock augmentation. If you are going bald, cut your hair close to the scalp.

* And fellows, Harrison Ford doesn't look as good with that earring as he thinks he does.

                    Source: Things A Man Should Know About Style

Good fashion sense can improve a man's career and love life -- for men not born with a flair for style, Ted Allen's Things A Man Should Know About Style makes it easy.

SOURCE Penguin Group
Web Site: http://www.penguinputnam.com

Issuers of news releases and not PR Newswire are solely responsible for the accuracy of the content.

http://www.prnewswire.com/cgi-bin/stories.pl?ACCT=106&STORY=/www/story/09-11-... 10/17/2003

Figure 6.7 Popular TV Shows Are a Feature Angle
Penguin books capitalized on the popularity of the *Queer Eye* television show by sending out a news feature on one of the leads who is co-author of a new book, *Esquire's Things a Man Should Know About Style.* The story gave men five fashion tips in a humorous way.
(Courtesy of Penguin Group. Distributed by PR Newswire.)

HTH Worldwide provides travel insurance services and global health and security information for travelers. For more information or for a free quote, visit www.travelhealthinsurance.com or call HTH Worldwide at (866) 501-3254.

Photos and Graphics

A feature story is often accompanied by photos and graphics to give it more appeal. Pacific Bell, for example, sent a photo of the Vietnamese manager with its release to editors. Food producers typically send mouth-watering color photos of prepared food. See Figure 6.8 to see how herb tea can be attractively photographed.

Increasingly, publications are using **infographics**, computer-generated artwork that attractively displays simple tables and charts. *USA Today* pioneered the use of infographics, and newspapers around the nation now use them with great frequency. One key finding of MCI's "Meetings in America" survey, for example, was chosen by *USA Today* for its front-page "USA Snapshot" series. It was a simple bar chart giving the primary reasons why people get stressed about business travel. Leading the list was "time away from family" with 75 percent. Only 20 percent reported stress filling out expense reports. Chapter 7 gives more information about photos and artwork.

PLACEMENT OPPORTUNITIES

The possibilities for feature story placement are endless. Media Distribution Services, a company that sends news releases and feature stories, says there are more than 50,000 print and broadcast media in the United States, and more than 165,000 editors, broadcasters, freelance writers, and syndicated columnists are on its database.

Your challenge is to figure out what kind of publication would be most interested in your feature story. It may be only one particular trade publication, or it may be all weekly newspapers in the country. See Chapter 10 for a discussion of press directories that can help you make that decision.

In general, placement opportunities for the print media include newspapers, general-circulation magazines, specialty/trade magazines, and internal publications. Placement opportunities for broadcast media are discussed in Chapter 9.

Newspapers

The primary use of features generated by public relations personnel is in the special sections of daily newspapers. The food section is a popular place for manufacturers and producers of food products, and the automotive section gets its fair share of features from Ford, General Motors, and Chrysler.

Weekly newspapers are not as specialized, but editors are always on the lookout for features that affect the average citizen. The Internal Revenue Service, the Social Security Administration, and even producers of grass seed often get space because they give tips to the public about how to save on taxes, file for Social Security, or grow a great lawn.

Figure 6.8 Attractive Food Photos Generate Interest
Photos can also serve as news features. This photo from Celestial Seasonings is about its new product,
True Blueberry Herb Tea. It was sent to syndicated lifestyle and food editors as well as food editors on
daily and weekly newspapers. In this case, the news feature was a caption accompanying the photo.
(Courtesy of Celestial Seasonings. Distributed by PR Newswire Photo Service.)

General Magazines

Although it can be argued that there is no longer any such thing as a "general"
magazine, we use the term to mean "popular" magazines such as *Better Homes and
Gardens, Redbook, Popular Mechanics,* and *People.*

These magazines usually have their own staffs and regular freelancers who
write features, but they do rely on public relations sources for ideas and information. Thus *Seventeen* magazine might carry an article about the difference between

suntan lotions and sunscreens. Most of the information would probably have originated with a sunscreen manufacturer that hired a public relations firm to create publicity and increase sales to female teenagers.

Specialty/Trade Magazines

There are two kinds of magazines in this category. The first is magazines that serve particular interest and hobby groups. There are magazines for golfers, surfers, car buffs, stamp collectors, scuba divers, joggers, gardeners, and even soap opera fans. The list of hobbies and interests is endless.

Whenever your organization has something bearing on a special field of interest, there may be a theme for a feature—and it is possible to write more than one feature on the same subject. With a new line of golf clubs, one story might tell how the line was developed under the guidance of a well-known player; another might deal with unusual materials and manufacturing techniques; and a third could describe the experiences of several golfers with the new clubs. Each of these stories might be placed with a different golf magazine.

The second category is publications that serve a particular industry. There are, for example, about 2,600 publications covering the computer industry. The advent of the Internet has spawned a whole new set of publications.

Another thing to remember in preparing features for business or trade publications is that a given subject might be of interest in several fields. The remodeling of a hotel could lead to features for a number of unrelated publications. Engineering magazines could be interested in structural problems and solutions, architectural magazines might use stories about design and decoration, travel publications might use stories about the renaissance of an obsolescent favorite, and hotel supply magazines might use stories about new carpeting, furniture, kitchen facilities, and so on.

Internal Publications

Many internal publications use material from outside sources. The most likely prospects are those where there is a built-in interest. A feature telling how something produced by your organization is helping another organization has innate interest. For example, you might have a feature describing exactly how your company makes the special insulating material that the XYZ Company is using to produce cold-weather footwear. The XYZ Company newsletter or magazine might welcome such a piece.

SUMMARY

- News feature writing requires right-brain thinking—intuition, image making, and conceptualization.
- A feature story can generate publicity for "ho-hum" products and services. It also can give background, context, and the human dimension to events and situations.

- Features and background stories are part of a trend in the print media to do what is called service journalism—"news you can use."

- Feature writing uses the "soft sell" approach. The name of the organization, the product, or the service may appear only once or twice. Stay away from hype and provide editors with information that is factual and informative.

- A good feature writer is curious and asks a lot of questions. He or she can conceptualize and see possibilities for the development of a feature article.

- There are four approaches to feature writing: (1) distribute a general feature to a variety of publications; (2) write an exclusive article for a publication; (3) interest a freelancer or reporter in writing a story; and (4) post feature articles on the organization's Web site.

- There are several types of features: (1) case study, (2) application story, (3) research study, (4) backgrounder, (5) personality profile, and (6) historical feature. Features can also be a blend of several types.

- Feature stories are formatted much like news releases in terms of using letterheads, contacts, headlines, and datelines.

- A feature should use extensive quotes, concrete examples, highly descriptive words, and information presented in an entertaining way.

- Photos and graphics are an integral part of a feature story package.

- There are numerous placement opportunities for feature articles in specialty newspaper sections (food, real estate, etc.), general-circulation magazines, special-interest magazines, business and trade magazines, and internal publications.

ADDITIONAL RESOURCES

"Editors Run More 'Free' Features." *Jack O'Dwyer's Newsletter*, May 21, 2003, p. 3.

Ferguson, Fred. "Creating Feature Stories That Get Coverage." *PR Tactics*, December 1999, pp. 14–15.

Friedlander, Edward Jay, and Lee, John. *Feature Writing for Newsapers and Magazines.* New York: Addison Wesley Longman, 1996.

Levy, Ronald N. "Media Opportunity: Use Your Head." *Public Relations Quarterly*, Summer 2003, pp. 27–28. Headlines for news features.

Levy, Ronald N. "Survival for PR." *Public Relations Quarterly*, Winter 2001, pp. 45–36. News features about prevention of illness.

Levy, Ronald N. "PR Skill: Present the Client in Perspective." *Public Relations Quarterly*, Spring 2000, pp. 23–24. News features about organizations.

Chapter 7

Photos and Graphics

Photographs and graphics are important components of news releases and feature stories. They add interest and variety, and they often explain things better than words alone.

Helen Dowler, director of photo services at PR Newswire, told *O'Dwyer's PR Services Report*, "Images should be an integral part of every PR plan. Photos alone, or with a press release, will increase interest in a story. In fact, if your picture illustrates a story well, it can be the deciding factor for an editor on whether to report on a story or someone else's."

Today, the digital revolution has made it relatively easy to provide photos and graphics to the media almost instantly via the Internet and the World Wide Web. Thom Weidlich, a reporter for *PRWeek*, explains: "These days, seemingly nothing could be simpler than supplying a newspaper, magazine, or other publication with a needed photo; just attach a jpeg to an e-mail and whisk it through cyberspace. And yet, it appears that many PR pros are still in the dark when it comes to providing photo editors with what they want—both the technical formats and the subject matter."

This chapter explores the elements that make a good publicity photo or graphic and explains how to prepare the material for media consideration. Its purpose is not to make you a professional photographer, but to give you a better working knowledge of what constitutes a good photo and how to work with photographers to achieve maximum media placement results.

ELEMENTS OF A GOOD PUBLICITY PHOTO

The adage says that a picture is worth a thousand words. A picture in a newspaper or magazine often takes the same space as a thousand words, but it has much more impact.

Studies have shown that more people "read" photographs than read articles. The Advertising Research Foundation found that three to four times as many people notice the average one-column photograph as read the average news story. In another study, Professor Wayne Wanta of the University of Missouri found that articles accompanied by photographs are perceived as significantly more important than articles without photographs. This also applies to graphics, which will be discussed later in the chapter.

Publicity photos, however, are not published if they are not high resolution and don't appeal to media gatekeepers. Although professional photographers should be hired to take the photos, the public relations writer often supervises their work and selects what photos are best suited for media use. Therefore, you need to know what makes a good publicity photo.

This section discusses such factors as (1) quality, (2) subject matter, (3) composition, (4) action, (5) scale, (6) camera angles, (7) lighting, and (8) color.

Quality

The visual quality of a photo is very important. Indeed, a common complaint of editors is the poor content and technical quality of publicity photos. They look for the key elements of good contrast and sharp detail so the photo reproduces well on a variety of papers, including grainy newsprint. You must also consider that photos are often reduced in size or, on occasion, enlarged when they are published. If they have good resolution to begin with, they will hold their quality.

It wasn't too long ago that the traditional approach was to submit photos printed on glossy paper in an 8- by 10-inch or 5- by 7-inch format. Basic mug shots (head and shoulders) were often submitted in a 4- by 5-inch format. Today, nearly all professional photojournalists use digital cameras, and the traditional process of taking photos on film, developing the film, and making prints has practically disappeared. In fact, 2003 marked the year that digital cameras began to outsell film cameras.

Although the process of taking photos has radically changed, the key elements of a good photo remain the same. Photos must have high resolution and sharp detail to be used. This is particularly pertinent because some quality is sacrificed when photos are downloaded from Web sites or sent to editors as part of e-mail attachments.

Web sites, for example, sacrifice quality for the speed of download, so they typically want images at 72 dpi (dots per inch). Newspapers want photos at around 150 to 200 dpi, and magazines need at least 300 dpi. Distribution services, such as NewsCom, generally distribute publicity photos in a 300-dpi format to accommodate the needs of almost any publication—from monthly glossy magazines to small weekly newspapers.

Digital photos also lose some quality as they are transformed into other formats. The photo may look great on your computer screen, but it may not come out exactly the same when you make a print of it, despite the advertising claims of printer manufacturers. You can also distribute digital photos on a CD or even as 35-mm slides, which will be discussed later in the chapter.

Subject Matter

There is a wide variety of subjects for a publicity photo. On one level, there are somewhat static photos of a new product or a newly promoted executive. On another level, photos are used to document events such as a groundbreaking or a ribbon-cutting ceremony.

Trade magazines, weekly newspapers, and organizational newsletters often use the standard "grip and grin" photo of a person receiving an award, a company president turning the first shovel of dirt on the site of a new building, or the traditional "ribbon-cutting" ceremony to open a new store. These shots have been a traditional staple of publicity photos for years, and there is no evidence that they are going out of fashion. At the same time, you should be aware that such photos are becoming tired clichés, and editors want more unusual or artistic material.

Group pictures nearly always present a problem; it is relatively easy to violate the concepts of newsworthiness, action, and central focus. There is often the danger of showing too many people, so a good rule is no more than three or four people in any one photo. Such a rule provides for more action, keeps the picture simple, and makes every face easily identifiable.

A common mistake is to please everyone by having people pose for a group photo. This might mean the entire board of directors, 60 real estate salespeople, 125 college graduates, or even all 250 members of a club. A group photo may be legitimate when you want to give a souvenir of a particular meeting or conference or provide documentation for a specialized publication such as a fraternal or alumni magazine. However, pictures of this kind should not be sent to general-circulation newspapers and magazines.

One way to handle large groups is to take a series of small group pictures of individuals from the same town or company. These then let you multiply the coverage by localizing the event for hometown newspapers or employee publications.

In organizing these photo shoots, you should make sure that there is activity in the picture: people talking to each other, looking at a display, or shaking hands with a notable person in an informal pose. The people should not be lined up looking at the camera. A common composition is to show three people all talking or listening to a fourth person who is at the left of the picture. This fourth person may be a keynote speaker, the president of an organization, or someone who has just received an award. Such a composition can provide a focus.

In a group situation, it is extremely important to take down the names and titles of people as they are photographed. This will make your job much easier later on, when you have to write the caption. Don't rely on memory—yours or anyone else's.

Composition

We have already discussed ways to compose photographs of groups. Inherent in all this is the concept of keeping the photo simple and uncluttered.

A look at the family album will illustrate the point. We have Aunt Minnie and Uncle Oswald looking like pygmies because the family photographer also wanted to include the entire skyline of New York City. Consequently, Aunt Minnie and Uncle Oswald are about 35 feet from the camera.

In most cases, the photographer should move into, not away from, the central focus of the picture. If the purpose is to show a busy executive at his or her desk, the picture should be taken close up so that the subject fills most of it. Sufficient background should be included to provide context, but it is really not necessary to show the entire surface of the desk—including the disarray of papers, picture of spouse and kids, and paperweight from a recent convention. All this conflicts with what the viewer is supposed to focus on in the picture.

Another reason for moving in on the subject and minimizing the background or foreground is to achieve good composition. That picture of Aunt Minnie and Uncle Oswald also shows the Empire State Building growing out of Uncle Oswald's head.

Experts have made the following suggestions about composition and clutter:

- Take tight shots with minimal background. Concentrate on what you want the reader to get from the picture.
- Emphasize detail, not whole scenes.
- Don't use a cluttered background. Pick up stray things that intrude on the picture.
- Try to frame the picture.
- Avoid wasted space. There should not be a large gap between an object, such as an award, and the person's face. In the case of a group picture, people should stand close to each other.
- Ask subjects wearing sunglasses to remove them.

All this advice is logical, but there may be times when the background plays an important role. If the purpose of the photo is to show someone in his or her work setting, it is important to capture a sense of the person's environment. A photo of a manager in management information systems, for example, might show him or her surrounded by three or four computers and a stack of printouts. Phil Douglis, a widely known photographic consultant who writes a regular column in IABC's *Communication World*, calls it the "environmental portrait." He continues, "Such portraits blend posed subjects with their supporting context to symbolize jobs, capture personalities, and ultimately communicate something about them to readers."

Action

Action is important because it projects movement and the idea that something is happening right before the reader's eyes. A picture of someone doing something— talking, gesturing, laughing, running, operating a machine—is more interesting than a picture of a person standing still and looking at the camera. Douglis, the

Selecting the location or setting of a picture is important if you want good, sharp results. For example, if you know that the people involved will be wearing light colors, you should not use a white background. Conversely, don't select a dark background if your photo subjects will be wearing dark clothing. In both cases, the result will be "floating heads," because the clothing will blend into the background. In all situations, you want to strive for high contrast between the background and the individuals being photographed.

Color

In the past, the vast majority of publicity photographs were produced in black and white because they were economical, versatile, and acceptable to most publications. However, color photographs are now commonplace and used by all kinds of publications as printing technology has become more sophisticated and less expensive.

Color can be used in at least three types of publications: in leaflets or brochures, in magazines that publish color photos, and in special sections of daily and weekly

Professional Tips

How to Take Product Photos that Get Published

- Show the product in a scene where it would logically be used. If it is used in an office, show it in an office.
- Clean up the area where the picture is to be taken. Remove any litter or extraneous items. Repaint if necessary.
- If people are in the picture, be sure that they are dressed for the situation. They should wear the kind of clothing that they would wear while using the product.
- Put perspective into the photo so viewers will know how big the item is. Show a hand, a person, a pencil.
- If you plan to use a digital camera for publicity photos, experts recommend a top-of-the line product to ensure maximum quality and resolution.
- Don't accept anything but the best in photographs. They have a potential shelf life of five years; many may be used by others to illustrate books or brochures. Give them quality.
- Take at least two photos—vertical and horizontal—of each new product. This makes them adaptable to a variety of situations. When possible, show the product in use. Application stories need illustrations.
- If there are other products in the picture, be sure that the new one is in the dominant position.
- The setting should be realistic, with everything hooked up and ready to go.
- Every picture must have an identifying caption.
- Be sure that the background contrasts with the product. Make the product stand out.
- Check your models. Look at complexions. Is there anything that would ultimately require retouching? Are neckties straight? Is hair combed?

newspapers. Color is now commonly used in the food, business, sports, entertainment, and travel sections of newspapers. If a publication does want a black-and-white photo, color photos can easily be converted with a minimal loss of quality.

Everything that has been said about composition and quality should be underlined in relation to color pictures. To be used, they must be outstanding in both interest and technical quality.

The preferences of various publications vary; many consumer and trade publications still prefer color slides or a CD, whereas newspapers have a strong preference for digital files that can be downloaded from the Web site of an organization or a distributor such as NewsCom. Some publications may even prefer glossy photos that can be scanned, but this is increasingly a rarity in the instant world of the Internet. The best procedure is to make photos and graphics available in several formats to accommodate different publication preferences. Most media directories, discussed in Chapter 10, usually indicate the photo preferences of the publication.

Professional Tips

Photo Advice from the Experts

The following 10 tips were given by three photo experts at a workshop sponsored by MediaLink/WirePix at the National Press Club in Washington, D.C.

- Remember that photographs, even for publicity, are not advertising. Make sure you identify the news value of the story you want to illustrate.
- Wire services like AP get a thousand or more photos a day. Your photo needs to tell a story quickly and creatively, and have real news value to make the cut.
- Capture images that tell your story at a glance. If your story is you're donating money to build homes for the homeless, get a photo of people building homes, not a "grip and grin" check presentation.
- Write a complete and proper caption. Don't be misleading.
- Identify the audience you are trying to reach. Photos for newspapers and trade publications are different than ones for annual reports or brochures.
- Get stories out in a timely fashion. Day-of-event photos are important. Use a respected distributor who is experienced with newsroom operations.
- Try to create photos that have a shelf life and can be used for other projects down the road.
- If you are organizing a press event, make sure you provide the media, both print and broadcast, with a visual opportunity. Talking heads at the podium are not visual.
- Don't try to over-brand the photo. It should look spur-of-the-moment, even if it isn't.
- PhotoShop is a wonderful tool. Don't abuse it by altering reality in your photos.

Source: Walker, Jerry. "Photo Editors Give Tips for Shooting PR Photos." *O'Dwyer's PR Services Report,* August 2001, pp. 41–42.

WORKING WITH PHOTOGRAPHERS

It is important to use a skilled photographer with professional experience. Too many organizations try to cut corners by asking some amateur in or associated with the organization to take pictures. This may be all right for the company newsletter, but publicity photos sent to the media must be extremely high quality if they are going to be competitive with the hundreds of other photos that are readily available.

It will cost more money to hire a professional photographer, but at least you won't end up with pictures that are unusable. Another reason is that it is better business practice to use a professional who has high-quality equipment. You can give direction to a photographer who is being paid, whereas it may be awkward to tell the boss's nephew or a colleague that the results are unacceptable.

Finding Photographers

You should have a file of photographers, noting their fees and particular expertise. If you have no such file built up, you might consult colleagues to find out if they can make any recommendations. If you are unfamiliar with a photographer's work, ask to see his or her portfolio. This is important because photographers are skilled at different things.

A good portrait photographer, for example, may not be good at photographing special events. A news photographer, by contrast, may be an expert at special events but unable to take good product photographs. In sum, you should find the special photographer you need for each kind of job. A photographer skilled in digital photography, for example, should be used if you definitely plan to distribute the resulting photos via e-mail, an electronic news service, or a Web site. This saves considerable time and expense in converting slides or prints to digital format by using a scanner connected to your computer.

The three experts at a workshop sponsored by MediaLink/WirePix (see Professional Tips on page 189) say that PR people should always ask three questions of a prospective photographer before hiring him or her: (1) Do you shoot digital? (2) Can you show me examples of other similar photos you have taken? and (3) What contacts do you have with the media and how will you help me distribute the photo once it has been shot?

Contracts

Any agreement with a photographer, as Chapter 3 pointed out, should be in writing. A written document helps you to avoid misunderstandings about fees, cost of prints, and ownership of the negatives.

A letter of agreement with a photographer should cover the following matters:

- The photographer's basic fee for taking pictures and a statement of exactly what this includes (developing the film, making prints, and so on).
- Costs of prints or transparencies. (Most photographers charge for each item ordered.)

- Who will supervise the photographer. Will you or someone else in the organization help the photographer set up shots?

- Who pays expenses—mileage, food, lodging—while the photographer is on assignment.

- Who will retain the negatives or the digital disk. Photographers generally want to retain all images. This gives them the opportunity to collect additional fees if you use the images for other purposes.

- Nature of use. Does the organization have unrestricted use of the photograph, or does it have to get permission from the photographer each time it wants to use the shot?

- Photographer's use of negatives or digital images. Can the photographer sell prints to outside parties, either individuals or other organizations?

The last point can be a bone of contention and create poor public relations for an organization. It is not uncommon for a photographer to expand the revenues from a photo session by contacting people in the pictures individually and asking if they want to purchase copies.

Before you hire a photographer, you should clearly establish whether it is all right for the photographer to make additional money selling prints to individuals. In many cases, the organization wants exclusive rights to all photographs and their distribution for purposes of its own public relations outreach.

The Photo Session

You will save time and money if you plan ahead.

- Make a list of the pictures you want. For pictures of people, arrange for a variety of poses.

- Know who you need, where and when you need them, and what props will be required.

- Notify people whose pictures are to be taken. Get releases if needed (see Chapter 3).

- Be sure that the location for the photo session is available, clean, and orderly.

- Consider lighting. Will the photographer have everything needed, or should you make preparations?

- Have everyone and everything at the right place at the right time.

- Tell the photographer what you need, not how to do the job.

Cropping and Retouching

A film photographer usually produces a series of contact sheets or proofs that show all the pictures on a roll of film. Digital photos, of course, can be viewed on your computer. This gives you an opportunity to review everything available and decide which pictures you want.

In most cases, the quality and composition of the photos can be improved through editing. The process is called **cropping** and **retouching**. Cropping is editing the photo by slicing off parts of the picture that you don't want. Eliminating parts of the photo permits a tighter focus on the key elements. A photo of the CEO talking to a major stockholder, for example, may also include the waiter clearing a table at one side. It is relatively easy to "crop out" the waiter and any other surrounding background.

The second technique, retouching, is usually done to alter the actual content of the photo. Let's assume the photo just mentioned was also taken in such a way that a basket of flowers on the stage behind the CEO looks like it is planted on top of his head. In such a situation, cropping may not be the answer because it also would scalp the top of the CEO's head. The solution, of course, is to simply eliminate the flowers through "airbrushing" or digital manipulation.

The film photographer has traditionally done the cropping and retouching of prints in the darkroom. Back in the old days, photographers spent countless hours working with negatives to get the best print possible—and to even "airbrush" away the flaws and imperfections of someone's face. *Playboy* magazine photographers, of course, spent considerable time perfecting entire bodies.

Today, all of this has radically changed because of sophisticated software programs such as Adobe's PhotoShop that allow even amateurs to crop and retouch photographic images at will. Too much "red eye" in the subject's eyes? No problem. The background is a bit dark or the sky not blue enough? With a few key strokes, the problem is solved. Indeed, amateur photographers armed with digital cameras and software programs can manipulate and improve the quality of their photos with relative ease.

Ethical Considerations

Cropping and retouching are common and uncontroversial practices in photography, but there are increasing ethical and legal concerns about the ethical boundaries of altering photographic images.

An original photograph, for example, can be scanned or downloaded. An editor can then call up the image on the computer screen and make any number of alterations. For example, a person's dark suit can be changed to a light tan, and a shadow on a person's face can be removed. The editor can also change the background from a plain wall to an oak bookcase or even a desert by merging the photo with another one stored in the computer's memory. An output device generates the new image on a printed page.

Advertising and public relations people often use computer alteration to enhance the quality of publicity photos. Thus the directors are shown with the company's production line behind them, even though the original photo was taken in a studio. Or a new product is enhanced by blacking out the background and putting more light on the actual product.

The examples cited so far are relatively harmless, but news editors worry about additional liberties that may be taken. For example, *National Geographic* provoked a major outcry when it used a computer to move two of the pyramids of Giza closer together so that they would fit on the magazine's cover.

PR Casebook

The Ethics of Manipulating a Photo

The new admissions brochure at the University of Wisconsin displayed a happy group of students attending a football game at their home stadium. The original photo contained no black faces, but university officials desperately wanted their admissions materials to reflect a diverse student body. So, using photo-design software, the director of university publications and the director of undergraduate admissions asked their staff to add one.

Meanwhile, at the University of Idaho, the top of the university's Web site showed another group of smiling students. The original photo contained only white students, so the university digitally pasted the face of one black and one Asian onto white bodies.

What is your opinion of these actions? Did the universities violate the boundaries of ethical responsibility? Both universities no doubt have blacks and Asians in the student body, so is it really a "lie" to alter the photographs to reflect student diversity? If you were asked to insert a black or an Asian into a picture to show ethnic diversity, would you do it? Why or why not?

Source: Adapted from an article written by Roger Clegg, *Chronicle of Higher Education*, November 24, 2000, p. B17.

Sensational tabloid newspapers have also come under fire for computer merging of photos to show celebrities who have never met talking or embracing each other at an intimate dinner party.

Photographers also worry about the new computer technology because their photos can be altered and used without permission or the payment of royalties. One photographer's picture of a racing yacht was used on a poster after the art director changed the numbers on the sail and made the water a deeper blue. This raises the issue of who owns such a new "original" picture.

Computer alteration of a photo is a judgment call that you, as a public relations specialist, will have to make. You have a professional responsibility to honor the original photographer's work and present accurate information; if an altered photo misleads and deceives the public in a significant way, do not use it.

WRITING PHOTO CAPTIONS

All photos sent to the media need a **caption**. This is the brief text under the photo that tells the reader about the picture and its source.

This does not mean describing a photo. Some novice caption writers make the mistake of writing, "Pictured above . . ." or "This is a picture of. . . ." Don't write the obvious; write to provide context and additional information that are not readily apparent by looking at the picture.

Most captions, when they accompany a news release, are two to four lines long. In fact, one study by Gallup Applied Science showed that two-line captions are the most effective. This guideline, however, does not apply to **photo news releases**. PNRs, as they are called, are simply photos with longer captions that are distributed to the media without any accompanying news release—the caption tells the entire story.

According to Deborah S. Hauss, writing in *PRWeek*, "Photo news releases enable PR pros to get pictures out more quickly and stand out amidst a sea of written press releases. . . . Sometimes all it takes to capture the media's attention is a visually compelling image and a short caption." A good example of a PNR distributed via Medialink Photography is Figure 7.5, about Vlasic Pickles.

Regular captions and PNRs are written in the active, present tense. Don't write "The park gates were opened by Mayor Jones"; say instead, "Mayor Jones opens the park gates." You should use active, present tense when describing activity in the picture, but you can shift to past tense when you begin to give the context or situation. For example:

- John Iwata, vice president of IBM, speaks to employees at the company's plant in Dayton. He was in town as part of a multi-city tour to promote total quality management (TQM).
- Northern Telecom's Donald Jones explains the Norstar system to Gussie Brown, chairperson of the Urban League. In the past year, the company has donated 100 systems to community agencies.
- Brian Mueller, who once taught in traditional classrooms, runs an online program for the for-profit University of Phoenix that takes courses to students around the country.
- At the Warren Hotel in Spring Lake, N.J., the new young crowd fills the tables for drinks on the lawn.
- Jack Valenti, head of the Motion Picture Association of America, mingles with Army recruiting officers Wednesday at the University of Southern California. The Army signed a $44.3 million contract with USC to establish a research institute that will draw on the entertainment industry and computer experts to develop advanced military simulations.

On the other hand, a caption for a head-and-shoulders picture of a person (a mug shot) can be even shorter. The caption may contain just the person's name.

Captions for publicity photos of new products should include a key selling point. For example:

- New HP keyboard makers it easier than ever for consumers to maximize their Internet experience. . . .
- Pasteurized Eggs, L.P. has developed an all-natural pasteurization process for in-shell eggs that prevents salmonella-causing bacteria from forming. The new safe eggs will display a USDA certified pasteurized shield and will be introduced from Boston to Washington, D.C. in October.

There is some argument about stating "from left to right" in a photo caption. To many people this seems redundant because people read copy—and probably scan photographs—from left to right anyway. If there are two or three people in the picture, it is assumed that you are identifying them from left to right. You can also indicate identity by the action taking place in the picture—for example, "John Baroni presents Nancy Southwick with a $5,000 scholarship at the annual awards banquet."

Figure 7.5

The Photo News Release

Photos sent to the media with a long caption can serve as a stand-alone, visual news release.

Medialink Photography, which produces photos and distributes them for clients, had an interesting assignment. How can you visually portray a new product for Vlasic Pickles in an interesting and unusual way that will grab the editor's attention?

The photographer, Jim Sulley, created the eye-catching photo above by carefully staging pickle slices on a large piece of glass. The resulting photograph won a CIPRA (Creativity on Public Relations Award) for outstanding news photography.

Here is the text of the caption that was sent with the photo:

> Frank Meczkowski, product development director for Vlasic, inspects his latest pickle invention, Hamburger Stackers, at the company's headquarters in Cherry Hill, NJ. The all-natural 3.5 inch diameter pickle slices are made from specially grown cucumbers to cover an entire hamburger. This week marks International Pickle Week, celebrating a food that's been around for more than 4,000 years and is still being perfected today. *(Jim Sulley/Medialink Photography)*

The photograph was produced and distributed via satellite and the Web to U.S. print and Internet newsrooms.

In general, the most important person in the photograph should be the first person at the left side of the picture. This ensures that this person is mentioned first in the photo caption. The most important person may alternatively be in the center of the picture, surrounded by admirers. In this case, you can write,

"Sharon Lewis, the singer, is surrounded by adoring fans after her concert in Denver." Any reader should be able to figure out which person in the picture is Sharon Lewis.

However, the terms "left," "right," and "center" are perfectly acceptable if better clarity is achieved. Here is an example from *The New York Times*:

> Ha Jin Jhun, center, president of the Hangul and Computer Computer Company of South Korea, met with other company executives in Seoul last week. In just a year, Hangul has returned from the brink of bankruptcy.

Distribution of Photos and Captions

Digital technology makes photos and captions relatively easy to distribute. All you need is a computer, a high-speed modem, a broadband or DSL line, either e-mail or file transfer (FTP) software, editing software, and a scanner for digitizing hard copy photographs a minimum of 200 dpi.

Photographs and captions can then be e-mailed, posted on a Web site, or distributed via one of the major services such as PR Newswire, Business Wire, and Medialink Photo almost immediately. (See Figure 7.6 for the format of a photo and caption distributed by NewsCom.) In fact, Court Mast, president of Mast Photography in San Francisco, says, "I can put a photo on the desks of 80 percent of the editors in the nation in about one hour." Using the Internet as a distributor of publicity materials is covered more fully in Chapter 10.

Captions, as indicated by Figure 7.6, are posted on Web sites or distributed as part of the photograph. In other words, editors (and consumers) are usually given a thumbnail of the photograph and the caption. If they want to see the enlarged photo, they click on the appropriate link.

News releases and features distributed to the media via regular mail (yes, newspapers still receive many print news releases), e-mail, or through an electronic news service often have URLs that editors can use to download photo and graphic packages related to the news release. Many companies and organizations also operate a "press room" on their Web sites that includes a gallery of various photographs and graphics that can be downloaded.

On occasion, organizations will send color slides to a publication. Showtime, for example, placed two slides in plastic holders and attached it to a page titled "The Incredible Mrs. Ritchie Photo Caption". General Mills, in its media kit for the Pillsbury Deluxe Classics Cookie, also enclosed two color slides showing the packaging of the new product. If you send slides to a publication, however, make sure they are clearly marked with your organization's name and numbered so editors can match them with the appropriate caption.

Graphics

Photographs are not the only art form that you can use for publicity purposes. Charts, diagrams, renderings and models, maps, line drawings, and clip art are widely used.

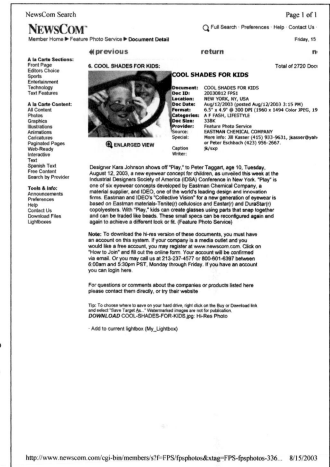

**Figure 7.6 Photo Distributed via
the Internet**
A number of vendors are in the business
of distributing photos and news releases
to the media and the public. This page
gives editors a thumbnail photo and its
caption for their review. If they are interested, they can download the actual photo
and caption for use in their publications.
The column on the left shows various categories of materials available. Most companies and organizations use the services
of a distributor who has the technical expertise to efficiently reach newsrooms on
a daily basis.
*(Courtesy of NewsCom and its client,
Eastman Chemical Company.)*

Many of these visuals can be formatted on your own computer using various
software applications, but you should also consider using graphic artists and commercial illustrators. This is particularly true if you are preparing material for distribution to the media. As with photographers, ask to see illustrators' portfolios
before you commission a particular assignment.

Charts

The primary reason for using charts is to make figures understandable. There are
three basic charts for this purpose, and each seems to work best for certain kinds
of information.

- *Pie chart.* Ideal for showing what part of a total is used for each of several
  purposes. An organization may use such a chart to show how a budget or
  revenues are divided.

- *Bar chart.* Ideal for showing comparisons between years in such things as income, population, sales, and prices.

- *Graph.* Somewhat like a bar chart, but better suited for showing changes over a long period of time. A simple graph may track sales and profits in relationship to each other.

Today, with computer graphics, charts are being dressed up to be more appealing and decipherable. Reading a copy of *USA Today* makes the point. Instead of showing a simple bar chart or graph, an attempt is made to incorporate representations of the subject into the chart.

A logging company, for example, might produce an **infographic** that uses trees instead of bars to show the number of trees planted annually. A chocolate company might use chocolate bars to show growth of sales over a five-year period.

Infographics can be prepared on paper, posted on a Web site, or sent to editors on a diskette. Large dailies usually have their own graphics departments and make their own infographics. However, many smaller dailies and thousands of weeklies have no such capability, so they are less adverse to using material from outside sources.

Diagrams

Diagrams are most valuable in showing how something works. The functioning of an engine, the attachment of some accessory, the use of some product—all can be made clearer with a diagram.

In planning diagrams, you should not only check with the engineers but should also pretest the final diagram on potential readers for comprehension and understanding. The key to effective artwork, particularly diagrams, is simplicity.

Renderings and Models

A rendering is an architect's drawing that shows how a finished structure will look. Increasingly, such artwork is being produced by computer drawing programs or the alteration of photos.

Photos of scale models are also used to give readers a thorough understanding of what is being built or renovated. Both renderings and scale models are widely used in news and feature stories about construction projects. The availability of such artwork often makes the difference between a major news story and a brief mention.

Maps

Maps can show where a road is to be built, how to get to a meeting, how traffic is to be routed, or which streets will be closed or opened. They can explain the site of a proposed housing development, the location of a dam, or the borders of a new lake created by a dam.

For your purposes, maps should, as far as possible, show the details necessary to understand the situation but avoid clutter and irrelevant information. Too much detail makes a map difficult to read. Remember, maps sent to the media are often reduced, so small type or thin lines may not reproduce.

Line Drawings and Clip Art

Cartoons are a form of line art, but most people think of line art as drawings of symbols, designs, and objects. These drawings are still made by artists using paper and ink, but the process is now available to almost anybody with a personal computer.

Barnaby Feder, a *New York Times* reporter, summarizes the state of the art as follows:

> Today's PC graphics programs typically come with hundreds or even thousands of stored images, called clip art, that users can put into their graphics as building blocks. Photographs, shots from video clips and animation can be pasted in as well. Users can also choose from virtually infinite varieties of color and quickly change perspectives, shading, overlapping images and other features.

Some popular art software programs are QuarkXPress, PageMaker, and Adobe's GoLive. **Clip art** can be ordered on floppy disk or CD from a number of specialty companies. CD-ROM technology has increased the variety of type fonts and line drawings considerably. One popular and easy-to-use program is Broderbund's Print Shop, which claims more than 100,000 ready-to-use graphics. There are smaller clip art files embedded in the latest versions of Microsoft Word, WordPerfect, and AppleWrite.

Line drawings and clip art are used primarily for organizational advertisements, leaflets, brochures, and newsletters. They can also be used to illustrate press kits, position papers, and camera-ready features sent to the media.

PHOTO AND ART FILES

A properly indexed and rigidly controlled illustration file is a necessity. Without this, negatives, digital images, or artwork will be lost. Historically important pictures will lose their identity and be useless because everyone who knew what they meant is dead or gone from the organization.

Digital photos should be stored on the organization's file server with readily identifiable headings. In addition, back-up CDs or DVDs should be made. Corporate files may be identified by names such as "J. Gladwyn Jones, Chairman," or topical areas such as "Employee Recognition Banquet," "Grand Opening of Lansing Store" or "Scale Model of Springfield Office Bldg."

It is important to place in the file all pertinent data such as the date the picture was taken, the location, photo releases from people portrayed, complete names and titles of people shown, the name and address of the photographer, and restrictions on use of the picture.

SUMMARY

- Photographs and graphics add appeal and increase media usage of news releases or features.
- A public relations writer should be familiar with the elements of a good publicity photo: quality, subject matter, composition, action, scale, camera angle, lighting, and color.

- Publicity photos should be sharp, clear, and high contrast.
- Photos should be creative. Traditional pictures of "ribbon cuttings" no longer work.
- A publicity photo should have no more than three or four people in it. Save the large-group shot for the photo album.
- Photos with action and informality are more interesting than rigid, posed shots.
- Use professional photographers if you plan to send materials to news organizations.
- Crop photographs to remove clutter and get a tighter focus on the main subject.
- Photo captions are short, use present tense to describe the action, and provide context.
- Photos and graphics can be distributed by regular mail, e-mail, electronic news wires, and Web sites.
- Digital cameras are increasingly being used for taking publicity photos; they can be taken and distributed almost instantly.
- Charts, diagrams, maps, etc., should be simple and uncluttered.
- Through computer technology, charts can be made more visually attractive. They are often called "infographics."
- It is important to keep a well-organized photo and graphics file for reference purposes.

ADDITIONAL RESOURCES

Atkinson, Claire. "Smile! The Art of Working with Professional Shutterbugs." *PRWeek*, June 5, 2000, p. 20.

Clegg, Roger. "Photographs and Fraud Over Race." *Chronicle of Higher Education*, November 24, 2000, p. B17.

Douglis, Philip N. "Digital Photojournalism: More Choices, Lower Costs, Quicker Results." *IABC Communication World*, February–March 2002, pp. 30–31.

Londner, Robin. "Every Picture Sells a Story." *PRWeek*, November 12, 2001, p. 22.

Parrish, Fred S. *Photojournalism: An Introduction*. Belmont, CA: Wadsworth Publishing, 2002.

Walker, Jerrry. "Releases with Photos Pack a One-Two Punch." *O'Dwyer's PR Services Report*, June 2003, pp. 24–25.

Walker, Jerry. "Photo Editors Give Tips for Shooting PR Photos." *O'Dwyer's PR Services Report*, August 2001, pp. 41–42.

Weidlich, Thom. "Providing Quality Photos Puts Your Story in Sharper Focus." *PRWeek*, August 18, 2003, p. 18.

Whittle, Scott. "Digital Photography Can Improve Your Chances for Media Placement." *O'Dwyer's PR Services Report*, May 2003, p. 29.

Chapter 8

Pitch Letters, Advisories, Media Kits, and Op-Ed

Public relations people work with the media in many ways. This chapter explores other kinds of written materials that are prepared and distributed to the mass media, primarily for the purpose of encouraging and facilitating media coverage.

The first section discusses how to write effective letters that persuade reporters and editors to cover your product, service, or event. In the trade, this is called making a pitch—thus the term **pitch letter**. Next, the format and writing of **media advisories** are discussed. These are used to let assignment editors know about a newsworthy event or an interview of opportunity that could lend itself to photo or video coverage. On occasion, publicists also prepare **media kits**, also referred to as press kits, that contain such items as news releases, photos, backgrounders, and even product summary sheets. They are often assembled for the introduction of new products. Finally, this chapter explores the writing and placement of what are called **op-ed** articles. The term "op-ed" is shorthand for "opposite the editorial page." These articles, carefully crafted, are short, persuasive essays stating a particular point of view on an issue, cause, or societal concern. **Letters to the editor** also are discussed at the end of this chapter.

PITCH LETTERS

Pitch letters have one fundamental purpose. They are supposed to convince an editor that a staff reporter should be assigned to do a print or broadcast story on your product, service, or event. They also are used to convince a radio or television producer to book your spokesperson on a talk show. See Figure 8.1 for an example of a well-organized letter to an editor.

pca
PHARMACEUTICAL CORPORATION OF AMERICA

June 4, 2003

Julie Sevrens-Lyons
Health & Fitness Reporter
San Jose Mercury News
750 Ridder Park Drive
San Jose, CA 95190-0001

Dear Julie:

More than 45 million Americans suffer from headache. Consumers often hear about migraines and other more severe types of headache. But the most common type of headache, tension headache, which impacts almost all of us, is rarely the focus of media coverage.

Tension headache affects 93% of American adults. Tension headache is often triggered by stress or emotional situations and is often accompanied by the tightening of muscles in the head and neck. As Americans become more health-conscious, they are also becoming more aware of the causes and symptoms of their headache pain. That is why Bristol-Myers Squibb Company today launched **Excedrin® Tension Headache**, a nonprescription pain reliever that provides fast relief of the head, neck, and shoulder pain associated with tension-type headaches.

During National Headache Awareness Week (June 1-7), consumers are urged to take control of their headaches. Clinical studies have demonstrated the effectiveness of **Excedrin® Tension Headache** in providing fast, effective relief with a multi-ingredient formula.

R. Michael Gallagher, D.O., FACOFP, director of the University Headache Center at the University of Medicine and Dentistry of New Jersey, is available to discuss tension-type headache and treatment options.

Enclosed is new information about **Excedrin® Tension Headache,** as well as background material on tension-type headache. If you have any questions or would like to schedule an interview with Dr. Gallagher, please contact me at (732) 819-0170 or abbe@thekirstengroup.com.

I look forward to speaking with you soon.

Sincerely,

Abbe Kirsten Schiffman

Abbe Kirsten Schiffman

2000 Lenox Drive – Suite 100 Lawrenceville NJ 08648   Tel: 609-896-4738   Fax: 609-896-4789

Figure 8.1 The Basic Pitch Letter
Pitch letters are possible story ideas for a publication or broadcast show. This one, on behalf of a new product, Excedrin Tension Headache, first establishes the idea that such headaches are a widespread problem and worthy of the editor's consideration. It also uses a tie-in to National Headache Awareness Week and offers an expert who can be interviewed. It ends with information on a contact if the journalist or editor wants to follow up. See the news release (Figure 5.9), the basic fact sheet on the product (Figure 5.10), and the backgrounder (Figure 6.4).
(Courtesy of Bristol-Myers Squibb Company.)

As you might guess, there is considerable competition to get the attention of an editor or broadcast producer. According to *Ragan's Media Relations Report,* a typical example is *Barron's.* Richard Rescigno, managing editor of this influential business weekly, gets about 30 to 35 calls from public relations people each week. In addition, he receives more than 200 "pitches" by mail and e-mail every week. Rescigno estimates that only 1 or 2 percent of all the ideas that are pitched actually result in stories. Another 5 percent serve as supporting material for larger stories. "PR people have to have a high tolerance for rejection," he told *Ragan's* reporter.

Given these statistical odds, it is important that you understand the components of an effective pitch letter that will substantially increase your odds for getting a story published or broadcast. A good pitch has three phases: (1) researching the publication or broadcast show, (2) writing the letter or making the call, and (3) follow-up.

Researching the Publication

Perhaps the most important component is the first phase—doing your homework. Pitch letters must be customized to a particular editor and publication. There is no such thing as a "one size fits all" pitch letter that is appropriate for all media.

Lynn Lipinski, a senior media specialist for GCI public relations in Los Angeles, writes in *PR Tactics,* "You must . . . familiarize yourself with the publication's style, format, readership, deadlines, and regular features. Media guides can provide the basic information about a publication, but the only way to truly know if it is right for your client is to read it."

In addition to media guides, which are detailed in Chapter 10, public relations writers rely upon "media profile" reports that are published by such publications as *PRWeek, Ragan's Media Relations Report, Bulldog Reporter,* and *O'Dwyer's Newsletter.* These articles give the background of the publication, the key editors, the kinds of stories they want, and how to make a "pitch."

PRWeek, for example, has a "media profile" practically every week about a particular publication. One article was about *Parade* magazine, which is distributed in Sunday newspapers, reaching about 75 million people each week. *PRWeek* advised its readers, "Editors prefer e-mail pitches that are short, sweet, and to the point. Don't send attachments or samples until they are asked for. Don't send mass e-mails, and know what is appropriate for the magazine. You have to prove that you've read *Parade.*"

Even publications that appear to focus on the same subject matter often don't have the same audience characteristics. Tripp Whetsell, a New York public relations counselor, writes in *PR Tactics,* "Even if you're pitching the same story about prostate cancer to *Esquire, Men's Journal,* and *GQ,* don't automatically assume that the content is the same just because all three are men's magazines." The same goes for broadcasting; Fox News targets 30- to 40-year-olds, whereas CNN draws viewers with an average age of 60.

Lipinski adds, "Read articles written by the reporter you are pitching. Familiarize yourself with the reporter's style, interests, background, and regular beat." At the same time, she urges would-be writers of pitch letters to be aware of current issues, business trends, and societal issues, so you can angle your pitch within the framework of a larger picture. If the company is expanding by purchasing smaller companies, perhaps the story can be pitched from the angle that it is an example of consolidation in a particular industry.

Relating a product to a trend line is how Fineberg Publicity, a New York firm, convinced *Hard Copy* to do a three-minute segment on its client, Jockey International. The news hook was the "slit skirt" trend in the fashion industry and how women were buying stylish hosiery to complement their skirts. The show showed celebrities wearing Jockey's hosiery products.

Preparing the Pitch Letter

Once you've done your research and have ascertained what kind of pitch would be most appropriate for a particular publication or broadcast show, the next step is to write a succinct, attention-grabbing letter. As Richard Rescigno of *Barron's* notes, you have about 60 seconds (either in a letter or a telephone call) to grab an editor's interest.

Therefore, the first rule of a pitch letter is brevity—one page or less. Second, the advice of Whetsell about good writing should be followed: "Your sentences should be clean, sharp, and to the point. Your syntax, as well as your spelling, should be flawless. Don't give journalists a reason not to take you and your clients seriously by being sloppy."

Third, a pitch letter should have an enticing lead. That means that you should avoid beginning a pitch letter with something trite such as "I'm writing to inquire if you would be interested in a story about . . ." That's a good way to turn off an editor.

Ragan's Media Relations Report has published several articles on how to write pitch letters and create great opening lines. Here are some examples of opening lines that generated media interest:

- "How many students does it take to change a light bulb?" (Story about a residence hall maintenance program operated by students who receive financial aid).

- "Would you like to replace your ex-husband with a plant?" (Story about a photographer who is expert at removing "ex's" and other individuals out of old photos).

- "Our CEO ran 16 Boston Marathons. . . . And now he thinks we can walk a mile around the river." (Story about a CEO leading employees on a daily walk instead of paying for expensive gym memberships or trainers.)

- "You are cordially invited to the Dirtiest Event in Boulder." (This pitch added some "sex," but the story was really about staging a coal-dumping event to show people how much fossil fuel it takes to heat an average house. The slightly "smutty" approach worked; major dailies and television stations covered the coal dumping.)

- "For almost 25 years, Jack Osman has been drinking shots of oil. He also sings songs about such foot-tapping topics as breakfast and grease. And sometimes, just for fun, he cooks down ground beef to find out its fat percentage." (Pitch about the availability of a nutrition professor to give media interviews on diet and health.)

As these examples show, a pitch letter should immediately raise curiosity or get to the point as soon as possible. Here is a letter written by Michael Klepper, owner of a New York public relations firm, that netted eight minutes on NBC's *Today* show.

> Plastics!
>
> How can we get rid of them? Some environmentalists say we can't. Ralph Harding says we can. He is executive vice president of the Society of Plastics Industry. He has just returned from Europe where they easily dispose of plastics in modern incinerators.
>
> I'll call you in a week to see if the *Today* show would be interested in talking to him.

Klepper, who has written hundreds of pitch letters in his career, adds, "The pitch letter should be newsy, not groveling. It shouldn't read 'respectfully submitted' or 'I need this one' or 'my client is breathing heavy.' You are never asking for a favor; you are submitting good, topical, newsworthy material that is directed to a decision maker."

A good example of a succinct pitch letter is one written by Samantha Schoengold of Fineberg Publicity in New York, on behalf of her client, Danskin Plus clothes. It was sent to Sharon Lee in New York, who produces the 5 p.m.

Professional Tips

Writing The "Perfect" Pitch

Stephen Miller, assistant to the technology editor at *The New York Times,* offers these suggestions for making what he calls the "perfect pitch":

- Find out what the reporter covers and tailor your pitch accordingly.
- Find out how the reporter prefers to be contacted—paper, fax, or e-mail.
- Make sure you're pitching news or a new trend.
- Offer help on trend stories even if your client or employer isn't the focus.
- Don't call during deadline unless you've got breaking news.
- Don't call to find out if the release has arrived.
- Don't send clips of other stories about your client.
- Don't call to find out when or if the story has run.
- Relationships are everything. If you get the trust of the reporter, don't abuse it.
- Don't lie. Advise your clients or employer not to either.

local news program on WCBS-TV. The major highlights of the letter are summarized by *O'Dwyer's PR Services Report* as follows:

> Did you know that most women in the United States are a size 14 or larger? These women are not necessarily overweight; they can be tall or just big boned, and they have long been forgotten and overlooked by most fashion manufacturers.
>
> Danskin caters to women of all ages and sizes by addressing and dressing their fitness and fashion needs. . . .
>
> Let our Danskin Plus expert, Phyllis Moroney, offer her advice on fashion, fitness and health for the larger size woman. We can create a fashion segment incorporating Danskin Plus styles to show the different ways it can be worn from the office to the gym or just to hang out in. . . .

The television station, as a result of this letter, aired a segment on "The forgotten woman." See Figures 8.1 and 8.2 for examples of other pitch letters.

Melvin Helitzer, author of *The Dream Job: Sports Publicity,* says a pitch or query letter should have the following six elements:

- Enough facts to support a full story
- An angle of interest to the readers of that specific publication

Professional Tips

Guidelines for Pitching Stories by E-Mail

Publicists frequently pitch story ideas by e-mail. In fact, many editors prefer this method over letters, faxes, or even phone calls.

However, it's important to remember some guidelines:

- Use a succinct subject line that tells the editor what you have to offer; don't try to be cute or gimmicky.
- Keep the message brief, one screen at the most.
- Don't include attachments unless the reporter is expecting you to do so. Must reporters, due to virus attacks, never open attachments unless they personally know the source.
- Don't send "blast" e-mails to large numbers of editors. E-mail systems are set up to filter messages with multiple recipients in the "To" and "BCC" fields—a sure sign of spam. If you do send an e-mail to multiple editors, break the list into small groups.
- Send tailored e-mail pitches to specific reporters and editors; the pitch should be relevant to their beats and publications.
- Personally check the names in your e-mail database to remove redundant recipients.
- Give editors the option of getting off your e-mail list; it will make your list more targeted to those who are interested. By the same token, give editors the opportunity to sign-up for regular updates from your organization's Web site. If they cover your industry, they will appreciate it.
- Establish an e-mail relationship. As one reporter said "The best e-mails come from people I know; I delete e-mails from PR people or agencies I don't recognize."

- The possibility of alternative angles
- An offer to supply or help secure all needed statistics, quotes, interviews with credible resources, arrangements for photos, and so on
- An indication of authority or credibility
- An offer to call the editor soon to get a decision

Pitch letters can be sent via regular mail, faxed, or even e-mailed. Part of your homework is finding out how editors want to receive pitches. If you do use e-mail, you should review the Professional Tips box on page 207.

Follow Up Your Letter

Once you have e-mailed, faxed, or sent a pitch letter to an editor or broadcast producer, it is important to follow up. It is not good enough to end a letter by volunteering to answer a reporter's questions, which many releases do. A better approach is what Julie Schweigert of Edelman Worldwide wrote at the end of her pitch letter for Korbel's "perfect proposal contest" (Figure 8.2). She takes the initiative in a nice way by writing "I will contact you next week to follow-up, but in the meantime you can reach me at 312/233-1380 with any questions." Remember, in public relations, keep the ball and the responsibility for follow-up in your court.

In your follow-up, the reporter may ask you to send more information. If that is the case, make sure you provide all the information within one or two days. You should also ask how he or she would like to receive the information—by e-mail, fax, U.S. mail, or special messenger. Editors all have their own preferences.

Reporters and editors can also be quite blunt and tell you in no uncertain terms that they aren't interested. Or they may be more polite and say they have already done a similar story recently, so they are not interested at the moment. But you can impress them, and even change their minds, if you have done your homework and can say accurately why your story is different from the last three articles about similar subjects.

Follow-up, however, often means that you graciously accept "No" for an answer. Don't keep pitching the idea or arguing with the editor over the merits of the story; it is better to cut your losses and keep the door open for future pitches to the same editor. You must continually develop good, productive relationships with the reporters you typically pitch; you won't win all the time, but you will improve your batting average by remaining cordial and gaining trust as a good resource person.

MEDIA ALERTS

Media alerts are also called **media advisories** because they tell assignments editors about upcoming events that they might be interested in covering from a story, photo, and video perspective.

The most common format uses short, bulleted items rather than long paragraphs. A typical one-page advisory might contain the following elements: a one-

Edelman

DATE

EDITOR
ADDRESS

Dear FIRST NAME,

Have you heard about the guy who mowed "Will You Marry Me?" into his lawn? How about the practical joker who "accidentally dropped" a fake diamond ring overboard, only to watch his girlfriend jump off their sailboat to retrieve it? According to author and marriage proposal expert Fred Cuellar, these heartfelt and often unexpected moments — from the traditional on bended knee to the offbeat, where anything goes— happen more frequently on Valentine's Day than during any other day of the year.

With so many upcoming proposals in the works, Korbel Champagne Cellars has partnered with Cuellar to outline the "Top Ten Signs He's about to Pop the Question." Women around the country can use this handy checklist of clues to see if their boyfriends are planning to pop the question this Valentine's Day.

We can help you create a terrific story for your readers -- whether it's a "be prepared" piece, or even an article for guys on how to avoid the hints they may be unintentionally giving their girlfriends. We have the results of a proposal survey to offer you, as well as an interview with Cuellar, who is available to discuss this information with you.

I will contact you next week to follow-up, but in the meantime you can reach me at 312/233-1380 with any questions.

Cheers!

Julie Schweigert
On behalf of Korbel Champagne Cellars

200 East Randolph Drive
Chicago Illinois 60601
Tel +1 312 240 3000
Fax +1 312 240 2900
www.edelman.com

A Daniel J Edelman Company

Figure 8.2 Korbel's Pitch Letter
Another example of an effective pitch letter is one prepared by Edelman Worldwide on behalf of its client, Korbel Champagne Cellars. It starts with a human interest lead, provides some advice, ties the event to a special day (Valentine's Day), offers some interesting survey results, and offers an expert to interview. See the basic news release (Figure 5.2), a sample fact sheet (Figure 5.4), and a feature release (Figure 6.1).
(Courtesy of Korbel Wine Cellars and its public relations firm, Edelman Worldwide.)

line headline, a brief paragraph outlining the story idea, some of journalism's five Ws and H, and a short paragraph telling the reporter who to contact for more information or make arrangements.

Figure 8.3 about Old Bay Seasoning's shrimp eating contest is a good example of formatting and content. Note that the journalistic "who" is used as a lead followed by the components of what, when, and where. Given the highly visual as-

Figure 8.3 Media Advisories Alert the Media
Assignment desks at newspapers, magazines, and broadcast outlets want highly visual stories. A shrimp eating contest is such an opportunity. This advisory not only gives reporters the basic information, but the time and place of the event. If you can't make it to Baltimore, a satellite feed is available. See Figure 4.4 for the basic news release. *(Courtesy of Old Bay Seasonings and its public relations firm, Hunter Public Relations.)*

****** MEDIA ALERT ******

WHO:	Old Bay® Seasoning, a unique blend of a dozen herbs and spices and a Chesapeake Bay cooking tradition for over 60 years, conducted a search for America's biggest seafood lovers and Old Bay fans.
	More than 1,600 people across the country entered by briefly describing, in 100 words or less, why they are America's biggest seafood fanatics and Old Bay fans, and provided their favorite or unusual uses for Old Bay.
WHAT:	Ten lucky finalists from across the country were selected to vie for a $10,000 grand prize in the first-ever **Old Bay® Peel & Eat Shrimp Classic** – a ten-minute, timed tournament to see who can peel and eat the most Old Bay-seasoned shrimp.
WHEN:	The contest will kick-off Labor Day Weekend On Friday, August 30, 2002, from 11:30 AM – 12:30 PM.
WHERE:	Harborplace Amphitheater (outdoors) 200 East Pratt Street Baltimore, Maryland
SPECIAL GUEST:	Tory McPhail, executive chef at Commander's Palace restaurant in New Orleans, and rising star in the culinary industry, will be master of ceremonies for the event.
	Local dignitaries
CONTACT:	Amanda Hirschhorn, Hunter Public Relations 212/679.6600, ext. 239 or ahirschhorn@hunterpr.com, event day cell 914/475.4074

SATELLITE FEED INFORMATION FOLLOWS

FRIDAY, AUGUST 30, 2002
FEED TIME: 3:30 - 3:45 PM ET(FED IN ROTATION)
COORDINATES: C-BAND: TELSTAR 4 (C) /TRANSPONDER 11/AUDIO 6.2 & 6.8
DL FREQ: 3920 (V)

pects of this event, a number of television stations showed up with camera crews. See Figures 4.4 and 4.5 for a news release and a photo of the event.

Another example of a media alert for an event is the "world's longest salad bar," which is shown in Figure 4.8. It was written in such a way that local reporters knew the details of "when" and "where" and television stations in other cities knew how to get video footage and soundbites via satellite.

Media alerts are often used to announce the time and location of a press conference. The Center for Global Development, for example, sent such an advisory to print and broadcast assignment desks via U.S. Newswire to let journalists know that the organization was having a news conference to discuss President Bush's trip to Africa and the policy issues involved.

A third kind of media advisory is one that lets reporters and editors know about an interview opportunity. Korbel Champagne Cellars, for example, let journalists know that its "marriage proposal" expert was available for interviews during a two-week period in July. The "interview opportunity" (see Figure 8.4) even suggested five other timely topics that he could discuss.

The fourth kind of advisory alerts the press to a local angle as part of a national story. Korbel Cellars (see Figure 8.5) sent print media and broadcast stations in the Dallas area an announcement that a Dallas couple was one of the three finalists in its "perfect proposal contest." Also made available to the press (see Figure 8.6) was a photo of the actual marriage proposal on the stage of the Palace

---

**** Timely Interview Opportunity ****

Marriage in America – State of the "Union"
Careers, Divorce Fears, Biological Clocks and Diamonds
All Play a Part in the BIG DECISION

WHAT: The HOT topic of the summer is marriage in America. The news has been full of stories about men's fear of marriage, the downside of living together before the wedding and the earlier and louder clicking of women's biological clocks! Reports are indicating men and women are not only waiting to tie the knot, but both have varying views on who should propose, who wears the ring and when to, if ever, get married! With the average age for a first marriage the oldest in history -- 27 years old for men and 25 years old for women -- there is no doubt that proposing the big leap into marriage is something to think about.

This week, experts across the country are discussing Americans' marriage trends at the "Smart Marriages" Conference in Washington, D.C. Topics like engagement, cohabitation and divorce are all up for debate.

WHO: Fred Cueller, author of, *How to Buy a Diamond* and *The World's Greatest Proposals*, is an expert on diamonds, proposals and marriage. He can share with your viewers his views on marriage in America and discuss the most popular proposal and engagement ring trends of the year.

Cuellar can also discuss:

- How will marriage change as couples marry later in life and often remarry?
- Are men still proposing to women – if so, how?
- What about male engagement rings – are they the newest trend?
- What are some of the most unique proposal ideas encountered?
- What are men really saying and thinking about rings, proposals and marriage?

WHEN: July 9, 2002 – July 24, 2002

Additional Information: Cueller and Korbel Champagne Cellars are searching for the nation's most unique wedding proposal ideas in the first annual "Perfect Proposal Contest." Three winners will receive a diamond ring and the counsel of a professional wedding planner to make their proposal plan a reality. The grand-prize winner will receive $10,000 toward a luxurious honeymoon or reception.

To schedule an interview or receive more information, please call:
Julie Schweigert at 312.233.1380, julie.schweigert@edelman.com

Figure 8.4 Advisories Offer Interview Opportunities
Informing journalists about the opportunity to interview an expert is often done through a media alert, or advisory. Here Korbel Champagne Cellars gives some interesting facts about the "state of marriage" and offers TV reporters a chance to do an interview as a news feature segment. The advisory also suggests some topics—with the idea of exploring trends.
(Courtesy of Korbel Champagne Cellars and its public relations firm, Edelman Worldwide.)

Figure 8.5 Localizing Is Important for Coverage

Korbel Cellars (see Figures 8.2 and 8.4), as part of its national media campaign to publicize the "perfect proposal" contest, also sent an advisory to local media about a finalist couple living in the area. This advisory was targeted to all media in the Dallas area and was prominently marked "Local Couple" to encourage coverage. The "local angle" is a strong selling point for editors on an otherwise "ho hum" story. See Figure 8.6 for the local photo angle. *(Courtesy of Korbel Champagne Cellars and its public relations firm, Edelman Worldwide.)*

> ****** LOCAL COUPLE WINS ULTIMATE MARRIAGE PROPOSAL ON BROADWAY IN NEW YORK CITY – INTERVIEW OPPORTUNITY FOR FEBRUARY 12 - 14******
>
> ATTN:
> PHONE:
> FAX:
> FROM: DEVIN COLLINS, ph. 312/616-1697
>
> ### LOCAL COUPLE ANNOUNCED AS FIRST-PRIZE WINNERS IN NATIONAL CONTEST
>
> Ashley Yablon of Dallas, TX was one of three first-prize winners in Korbel's Perfect Proposal Contest -- from more than 500 entrants, Ashley's romantic, creative and heartfelt proposal idea for his girlfriend Donna was selected to come to life among the bright lights of Broadway.
>
> We coordinated the surprise proposal for Donna after a performance of Aida at the Palace Theatre in New York City. Ashley truly stole the show, earning his own standing ovation as he popped the question onstage, with help from the cast. Prior to proposing, Yablon serenaded his intended in front of a live theater audience – the audience was so moved, they can be heard singing right along with him.
>
> Today, all three first-prize winning proposals were revealed to the nation, just in time for Valentine's Day, and Ashley and Donna were named Grand Prize Winners. They will be awarded $10,000 to a reception or honeymoon.
>
> Please let me know if you would like to discuss the proposal and program further – we have video footage available for you to review if you're interested. Ashley and Donna are available for Valentine's Day-week interviews to discuss this exciting experience.
>
> **To schedule an interview or receive more information, please call:**
> **Devin Collins, 312/616-1697, devin.collins@edelman.com**

Theatre in New York where Aida was playing. And finally, the advisory let the editors know that the couple were available for interviews.

MEDIA KITS

A media kit, also commonly referred to as a "press kit," is usually prepared for major events and new product launches. Its purpose is to give editors and reporters a variety of information and resources that make writing about the topic easier for the reporter.

The basic elements of a media kit are (1) a main news release; (2) a news feature; (3) fact sheets on the product, organization, or event; (4) background information; (5) photos and drawings with captions; (6) biographical material on the spokesperson or senior executive; and (7) some basic brochures. All materials should be clearly identified; it's also important to prominently display contact information such e-mail addresses, phone numbers, and Web site URLs.

Such a list is a good starting point, but remember that each press kit you produce will no doubt have variations depending on the event or the product. A good example of a typical press kit is one produced by Microtune, Inc., to announce a new microchip technology for TV tuners. Inside the two-pocket folder were the following items:

- A news release with the headline, "Microtune Revolutionizes Traditional Tuner Industry with the World's First TV Tuner on a Single Chip."

Figure 8.6 A Photo Is an Extra Bonus
The play may be the thing, but it's even better if the drama of a marriage proposal is part of the final act. National media, as well as the Dallas media, received a photo of the actual marriage proposal on the stage of the Palace Theatre in New York after a performance of Aida. Ashley proposed to Donna while members of the cast looked on.
(Courtesy of Korbel Champagne Cellars and its public relations firm, Edelman Worldwide.)

- Two slide photos of the new microchip relative to the size of a coin and a match.
- Three short (about three pages) backgrounders on such topics as "Market Issues Solved by the MicroTuner," "Industry Challenges of the Digital Media Era Requires Revolutionary Solutions," and "Technology Backgrounder: World's First Single-Chip TV Tuner."
- A five-page Microtune corporate profile that gave the mission, business, products, product benefits, technology, customers, management, and head-quarters address.
- A two-page Microtune "fast facts" that gave a thumbnail sketch of the company, its products, and its management team.
- A one-page listing of quotes from experts in the industry praising the new microchip.
- A four-page, glossy product information sheet.

We have already discussed news releases and basic fact sheets in Chapter 5, but here is some additional information about **corporate profiles** and **backgrounders** that are often included in press kits such as those of Microtune, Inc.

Corporate Profile

A **corporate profile** is similar to a fact sheet about an event or product, which was discussed in Chapter 5.

A corporate profile gives an overview of the organization. Such "fact sheets" should describe the organization—its nature and objectives, main business activity, size, market position, revenues, products, and key executives. Profiles may be several pages, or simply one page. See Figure 8.7 for an example of a corporate profile.

A variation on the corporate profile is a compilation of interesting facts about an organization. Disneyland, for example, not only gives in-depth information about the Disney organization and its popular rides, but also various "Fun Facts." Did you know, for example, that in one year, Disneyland guests buy 4 million hamburgers, 1.6 million hot dogs, 3.4 million orders of French fries, and 3.2 million servings of ice cream?

Cirque Du Soleil, an artistic performance company, also gives out some impressive numbers on a fact sheet distributed with its elaborate media kit. It has 2,500 employees, including 500 artists, representing more than 40 nationalities and 25 languages. The total audience for more than 240 engagements in 90 cities, since 1984, is more than 37 million. In 2003, more than 7 million people attended various performances of the eight productions that were running at the time.

A major reason for including a corporate profile in a press kit is to give reporters and editors background information about your organization. There are literally thousands of companies in the world that make arcane products and aren't household names, so it is important to "educate" reporters about your client's or employer's particular niche in the marketplace. Are you a small, insignificant company—or the market leader and a major player? Oracle, for example, is widely known in the high-technology industry as one of the world's leading software companies (second only to Microsoft), but the business reporter on a small-town daily may not know this. Once she does know this, through a corporate profile, she may be more inclined to use the story because Oracle is an industry leader. Remember the journalistic news value—prominence.

Indeed, *The Wall Street Journal* gets so many company news releases that one screening device is to ignore companies unless they are publicly traded, generate substantial revenues, or are the market leader in a particular industry. A corporate profile outlining your size and significance often makes the difference between whether your new product announcement is used, or thrown in the trash.

Alcon, for example, is a Swiss firm specializing in medical equipment; it isn't exactly a household name, even among *Wall Street Journal* staffers. Consequently, its corporate profile (Figure 8.7) and a one-page biography (Figure 8.8) on the senior vice president for U.S. sales were important components of the media kit that acquainted editors with the company and its products.

Backgrounder

Many organizations also prepare what is known as a **backgrounder**. The purpose, quite literally, is to give journalists additional background on a new product, a new medical procedure, a new service, or any number of other topics that help re-

Figure 8.7 Corporate Profile Gives the Basics

Media kits often include a basic fact sheet that gives a brief overview of the company or organization. This gives reporters and editors, who may be unfamiliar with the organization, an opportunity to assess whether or not the organization deserves coverage on the basis of its size and relative position in the industry. This profile, for example, makes the point that the company has 43 percent of the ophthalmic surgical market.

(Courtesy of Alcon Corporation.)

Corporate Headquarters
Bösch 69, CH-6331 Hünenberg, Switzerland

U.S. General Office
6201 South Freeway, Fort Worth, Texas, 76134

Company Profile
Alcon develops, manufactures and markets ophthalmic pharmaceuticals, ophthalmic surgical equipment and devices, contact lens care products and other consumer eye care products that treat diseases and conditions of the eye. With the exception of eye-glasses and contact lenses, Alcon operates in all areas of ophthalmology. Its broad range of products represents the strongest portfolio in the ophthalmic industry, and it has leading market share across most major product categories. In addition, Alcon has been listed on *Fortune* magazine's annual survey of the 100 Best Places to Work in the U.S. for five consecutive years.

Company History
Alcon was founded in 1945 when two pharmacists, Robert Alexander and William Conner, opened a small pharmacy in Fort Worth, Texas, combining the first syllables of their last names to call it ALCON. After strong growth, leadership in the ophthalmic market was well established when, in 1977, Alcon was wholly acquired off the New York Stock Exchange by Nestlé S.A. (the world's largest food company). Alcon re-entered the NYSE 40 times larger than when it left it, when it completed an IPO of a portion of its shares on March 21, 2002.

Incorporated in Hünenberg, Switzerland, with its U.S. general office in Fort Worth, Texas, Alcon has operations in more than 75 countries. Its products are sold in more than 180 countries and it has a highly skilled workforce of more than 11,500 employees worldwide. Competing in a large and growing $11 billion market place, global sales represent 17% of the ophthalmic pharmaceutical market, 43% of the ophthalmic surgical market and 18% of the ophthalmic consumer market, making Alcon the largest specialty ophthalmic company worldwide.

Financial Information
Alcon is traded on the New York Stock Exchange: ticker symbol ACL. Sales for 2002 totaled $3.01 billion.

Management Team
- Tim Sear, Chairman and CEO
- André Bens Ph.D., Senior Vice President, Global Manufacturing and Technical Support
- Gerald Cagle, Ph.D., Senior Vice President, R&D
- Jacqualyn Fouse, CFO and Senior Vice President, Finance
- Fred Pettinato, Senior Vice President, International
- Cary Rayment, Senior Vice President, U.S. Operations

Board of Directors
- Tim Sear, Alcon, Chairman of the Board
- Werner Bauer, Nestlé S.A.
- Peter Brabeck-Letmathe, Nestlé S.A.
- Francisco Castañer, Nestlé S.A.
- Dr. Wolfgang H. Reichenberger, Nestlé S.A.
- Lodewijk J.R. de Vink, Global Healthcare Partners
- Philip H. Geier, Jr., The Interpublic Group

Web Site
www.alconinc.com

Figure 8.8 Executive Profiles Help Establish Credibility

Often accompanying a corporate profile is a short biography of the senior executive. It gives a human face to the organization and, like the corporate profile, helps establish credibility among journalists. "Bios" focus on a person's professional career but also can include some personal information in the final paragraph.

(Courtesy of Alcon Corporation.)

Cary Rayment
Senior Vice President
Alcon United States

Cary Rayment has served as Senior Vice President, Alcon United States since January 2001. In this position, he has responsibility for the U.S. Surgical, Pharmaceutical, and Consumer business units.

Cary began his career with the Kendall Company in 1974, where he served in a variety of sales and marketing positions. In 1984, he joined CooperVision IOL as Director of Sales and Marketing, and was promoted to Vice President of Marketing.

He joined Alcon in 1989 (following the acquisition of CooperVision IOL) as Vice President, Marketing, Surgical Products. Since that time, his responsibilities have continued to increase in diversity as well as scope. He served as Vice President and General Manager, Surgical Products 1991-1995; was named Vice President and General Manager, Managed Care in 1996; became Vice President, International Marketing in 1997 (adding responsibility for Alcon Japan in 1998); and returned to the Surgical Division as Vice President and General Manager in 2000.

Cary holds a BS in Education from the University of Washington in Seattle, as well as an MBA from the University of Kansas in Lawrence, Kansas. He is a graduate of the Harvard Program for Management Development.

Cary is a member for the Board of Directors for the ASCRS Foundation as well as the Board of Directors for the United Way of Metropolitan Tarrant County, serving as Chairman of the United Way's Diversity Committee. He is also active in his local community of Colleyville, where he and his wife Janet reside. As an avid golfer and sports fan, Cary enjoys any opportunity to practice his swing or to cheer on his favorite team, the Washington Huskies, during football season.

porters better understand a concept. Backgrounders must be accurate, complete, and objective to have credibility.

Backgrounders were also briefly discussed in Chapter 6, *"News Features."* The example given was information provided by Excedrin Tension Headache about what causes tension headaches and how to do relaxation exercises (Figure 6.4). Another product backgrounder concerned a new, highly sophisticated lens removal system for cataract surgery. Alcon, the manufacturer, provided a background sheet on what a cataract was (the clouding of the eye's lens) and what age groups are usually affected (senior citizens). Another background sheet gave information about the procedure for removing a cataract.

Shire Pharmaceuticals Group, in a media kit to medical and health reporters, announced a new drug to combat Attention-Deficit/Hyperactivity Disorder (ADHD) in children. This is pretty complicated stuff, even for health reporters, so the company also provided a backgrounder on the disorder. It used a Q & A format with such questions as "What is ADHD?" "Who is affected by ADHD?" and "What are the causes of ADHD?" Shire also provided a backgrounder on the development of its new medicine to help children with ADHD, Adderall XR.

Other backgrounders may not be about a product, but rather a company. A good example is a backgrounder from Sun Microsystems that outlined the history of the company and how it became a *Fortune* 500 company within 10 years of its founding. The difference between a "corporate profile," discussed earlier, and a "backgrounder" is usually one of style. A profile is usually a series of bullets or facts about the organization. A backgrounder is more leisurely; it's a narrative that can run three to five pages and even have quotes.

Not all backgrounders need to be technical, or dull. Cadbury Adams USA launched a new product, Dentyne Fire, that the company touted as "the first intense cinnamon pellet gum in the Dentyne product offering." In addition to providing a sample of the gum in its media kit, Cadbury also included a backgrounder on "The history of chewing gum." In case you are interested, it all started when people in ancient Greece and the Middle East chewed the resin from the mastic tree.

Compiling a Media Kit

The contents of a media kit, which has been discussed previously, are usually placed inside a folder of some kind. There are virtually hundreds of folder formats, and Figure 8.9 is just a sampling from a 26-page catalog of one supplier.

The folder selected depends a lot on what exactly you plan to include in it. The typical media kit folder is 9 by 12 inches and has four sides—a cover, two inside pages (often with pockets to hold news releases, etc., in place), and a back cover that gives the name and address of the organization. You also can include clear plastic holders (affixed to one of the inside pockets) to hold color slides. Another common feature is to include slots on one of the inside pockets where you can insert your business card.

You can also order standard media kit folders that include slots for CDs, which can include photos, artwork, video clips, soundbites, and computer-generated graphics. Electronic media kits will be discussed shortly.

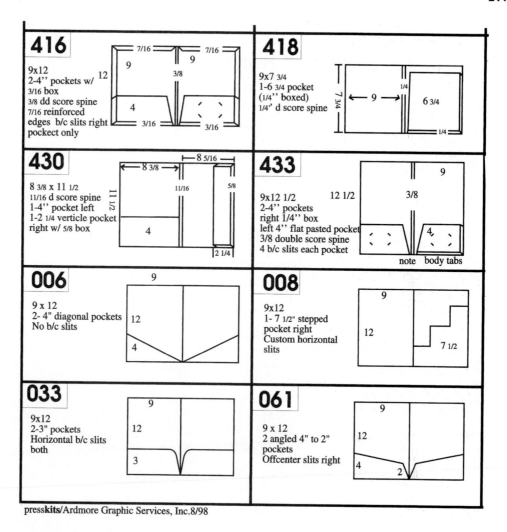

presskits/Ardmore Graphic Services, Inc.8/98

Figure 8.9 Media Kit Folders
Media kits have multiple components so a folder is often designed to hold all the materials. The exterior of a media kit is usually 9 × 12 inches. The most common approach is to have a folder with "pockets."
(Courtesy of Ardmore Graphic Services, Inc., Walpole, MA.)

There are also custom-designed folders, which package the contents of a media kit creatively. Crayola, for example, created a colorful media folder to publicize its 25-city bus tour celebrating the 100th anniversary of the company. The package was a self-mailer (see Figure 8.10) that unfolded into a large round sheet two feet in diameter that featured artwork done with a rainbow of crayon colors. The packet also included a colorful news release (localized for each city) and two backgrounders. One interesting piece of trivia: "Since 1903, more than 120 billion crayons have been sold throughout the world. End to end they would circle

Professional Tips

Compiling the "Perfect" Media Kit

Kristin Zhivago, editor and publisher of *Marketing Technology,* is still looking for the "perfect" media kit. She, however, has compiled a "don't" list of things to avoid if you are preparing one:

- Don't use Velcro on pockets or elastic bands around your kit. It sends one message: "Don't open me."
- Don't load your kit down with everything you ever produced. If you have over 10 items, you're begging the editor to toss half your kit contents into the trash.
- Don't emphasize your glossy pieces. Instead, use releases, backgrounders, and white papers.
- Don't use vertical or fancy pockets.
- Don't use a gatefold (three-panel) folder. They are impossible to open when they are sitting in a press kit bin. A two-pocket folder can easily hold your 10 items.
- Don't worry about "wrecking" your fancy folder cover with an information-rich, specific sticker. Use the sticker to announce new products or event-related information.

Source: O'Dwyer's PR Newsletter, April 15, 1998.

Figure 8.10 A Colorful Approach
Media kits often use standard 9 x 12 folders, but Crayola had a different idea. It created a colorful media kit that, when opened, unfolded into a large circular poster two feet in diameter. The news release and other materials were enclosed. The kit cover, in multiple colors, perfectly fit the organization's major business—crayons.
(Courtesy of Binney & Smith, Inc.)

the earth 200 times." Media kits should reflect the image and products of a company; the colorful Crayola media kit is a classic example.

Maytag Appliances also compiled a media kit for its 35th anniversary celebration of its advertising icon, Ol' Lonely. Previous chapters have reprinted parts of the media kit (a photo, a news feature, and a fact sheet), but the media kit itself was a major piece of creativity. It was packaged in a repairman's toolbox, which included media materials, a CD of historical advertisements, a commemorative Ol' Lonely bobble head, and a video. See Figure 8.11 for a photo of the media kit. Again, the organization spent the time to design a media kit that reflected the subject matter.

Compiling and producing a media kit is time-consuming and expensive, particularly if you customize the folder and produce various brochures. It is not uncommon for press kits to cost $8 to $10 each by the time all the materials are produced and the folder cover is prepared. Consequently, press kits should be distributed selectively and only to reporters who regularly cover your employer or client.

Media kits represent a valuable opportunity to get publicity placements, but several surveys of editors indicate that such kits often miss the mark. They are too

Figure 8.11 Media Kit as Took Kit
Maytag Appliances packaged its media kit celebrating the 35th anniversary of its advertising icon, Ol' Lonely, as a serviceman's tool kit. The kit, sent to key editors, contained everything from a basic news release to a CD of historical highlights to a doll in the replica of Ol' Lonely. See Figure 6.5 for the feature news release.
(Courtesy of Maytag Appliances and its public relations firm, Carmichael Lynch Spong.)

large, contain too many sales brochures, include poor-quality photos, and have poorly written news and feature stories.

Apple Computer, for example, once won a "dubious achievement" award from a group of journalists for regularly distributing press kits the size of phone books. Other companies are roundly criticized for emphasizing packaging and ignoring the content. Other criticisms are expressed in the box, "Compiling the 'Perfect' Media Kit," on page 218.

You should keep press kits slim and cost-effective; they should not be repositories for all the company's product brochures. Provide reporters and editors with information that is simple, factual, and relevant to their audiences. Give them story ideas, local angles, photos, and interesting infographics based on solid research. Briggs & Stratton (see Figure 8.12) compiled such a media kit for its "Top Ten Lawns in America" announcement.

Figure 8.12 The Grass Is Greener over There
Here is the cover of the Briggs & Stratton media kit announcing its sixth annual "Top Ten Lawns." It portrays a framed picture of Central Park in New York, which was rated number one in the list of lawns with a view. It is another good example of how the cover of a media kit directly relates to the product or event.
(Courtesy of Briggs & Stratton.)

Electronic Media Kits

Today's media kits are not restricted to bulky folders. Increasingly, organizations are using electronic press kits. EPKs, as they are called, can be placed on an organization's Web site or even directly e-mailed to a reporter or editor.

Kits and news releases sent in PDF format are ideal for small businesses with limited resources because they can be reproduced from printed materials at nominal cost and they can be read using Adobe's free Acrobat Reader software by virtually every computer user, according to Jonathan Gill, a senior account executive at Eric Mower & Associates in Buffalo. CD-ROMs and Web-based media kits involve more expense, but add more flexibility in terms of graphics, photos, video, illustrations, and audio elements, says Gill.

Movie studios, in particular, are using satellite transmissions, Web sites, and CDs to promote new films by providing film clips, interviews with the stars, and production facts (see Figure 8.13 showing the digital media or kit for a film). Recording companies are doing the same thing with music videos. Even electronic game producers, such as Electronic Arts (EA), effectively use CD format to show entertainment reporters and editors simulations from the various games.

Shel Holtz, author of *Public Relations on the Net*, says organizations often fail to understand the medium. Instead of taking full advantage of the technology, some organizations merely post news releases with some stock photos. The EPKs

Figure 8.13 Digital Media Kits
These are also called electronic press kits (EPK). They can contain standard news releases, photos, video clips, fact sheets, biographies of senior executives, etc. CDs are increasingly being used instead of printed materials. *(Courtesy of New Line Home Entertainment.)*

for NASA's space shuttles, he laments, "are nothing more than long, linear paper documents—good text-based information with no photos of the astronauts or vehicles involved." Sun Microsystems, on the other hand, has a good EPK for its Java platform. Holtz says, "it includes a glossary, a primer on Java, a collection of marketing documents, and a timeline of Java's first 800 days. Reporters also have access to an archive of Java-related FAQs." Novell, another high-tech company, even has PowerPoint presentations in its EPK.

Holtz concludes, "The access to information offered by online press kits is a good first step, but the techniques will provide real value over old models only when we begin tapping into the differences between the Web and print, and using them to create something more than an online version of our old brick-and-mortar kits." Web pages, and using them for media kits, are discussed more thoroughly in Chapter 13.

OP-ED

The term "op-ed" literally means "opposite the editorial page." The concept originated at *The New York Times* some years ago and has now spread to many major newspapers and magazines across the country. The purpose of op-ed articles is to present a variety of views on current news events, governmental policies, pending legislation, and social issues.

From a public relations standpoint, op-ed provides an excellent opportunity for individuals and organizations to reach an audience of readers who also tend to be opinion leaders. Indeed, if an organizational executive wants to become a spokesperson for a particular industry or cause, public relations counsel often recommends writing one or more op-ed pieces.

This was the case in Minneapolis when a former mayor was asked by a development company and its public relations firm to write an op-ed piece supporting the immediate opening of a $134 million entertainment complex in the downtown area.

About the time that the Block E complex was ready to open and tenants were to move in, a political controversy about the wisdom of the building the complex in a tight economy started to surface. Even the City Planning Commission was threatening to call public hearings and delay issuing occupancy permits.

McCafferty Interests, the developer of the complex, sought the services of Carmichael Lynch Spong public relations to devise a strategy to get the Block E project back on schedule and to dampen the "political bickering." The firm's recommendation was to place an influential thought piece in the *Minneapolis Star Tribune*, Minnesota's leading newspaper, under the by-line of former Mayor Sayles Benton who was a strong supporter of the project.

Carmichael Lynch Spong researched past media coverage of the Block E complex, compiled historical data, and consulted with Ms. Benton to develop a persuasive op-ed piece under her by-line article titled "Block E Deserves to Shine." It was published in the *Star Tribune* with two photos, one showing the derelict neighborhood in 1982 and a current photo showing the new complex.

The op-ed reached an estimated audience of 2.3 million residents in the Twin Cities, and it turned the tide in terms of public support for the project. The *Star Tribune* also wrote an editorial supporting the Block E complex after the op-ed piece was published, and even the City Planning Commission changed its mind. Due to these efforts, the complex opened on schedule.

Universities and think tanks such as the Brookings Institution also make considerable use of op-ed pieces to gain visibility and position the organization as a leader. The public relations department of Washington University in St. Louis, for example, got 426 placements in one year by sending op-ed articles written by 62 faculty members.

The op-ed pages of *The New York Times, The Wall Street Journal,* and the *Washington Post* are the best known and the most prestigious in terms of placement. They regularly carry op-eds written by ambassadors, former presidents, CEOs of major corporations, senators, and a host of other prominent or influential people. The competition is steep; *The Wall Street Journal* receives about 500 to 700 op-ed articles a month and has space for only a few of them.

Your employer or client may not be a former ambassador or a general, but that should not discourage you from submitting op-ed pieces to these three newspapers and to other U.S. dailies. Editorial page directors are always looking for fresh insights from those who have expertise or experience on a particular topic of current public concern. Indeed, op-eds must have a current news angle to fulfill the journalistic requirement of timeliness.

In addition, you should not overlook the trade press. Publications that serve a particular industry or profession also use commentaries and short opinion articles. A company's head of research, or the vice president of human resources, might have something to say that would be interesting to the readers of these publications.

Public relations writers often do the initial work of drafting an op-ed for a client or employer. Another way to approach it is to ask a person for notes from a recent speech. Speeches to organizations are often recycled as op-eds to newspapers.

Op-eds, by definition, are short and to the point. The most effective in terms of placement are 400 to 750 words, which is about three to four word-processed pages, double-spaced. Various publications establish their own guidelines for length. The *Atlanta Journal and Constitution* prefers 200 to 600 words, while the *Washington Post* wants submissions 600 to 700 words. *The Wall Street Journal* will consider op-eds 700 to 1,500 words long.

Such restrictions in length mean that you must write well in terms of organization and conciseness. Jennie Phipps, in an article on how to write an op-ed for *PRWeek,* gives the basic format:

> Start with a catchy lead paragraph that is about 30 words. Use the second 35- or 40-word paragraph to explain further what you said in the first graph. The third graph is the nut graph—that's the place where you make your point, preferably in a sentence or two. Use the next half-dozen or so paragraphs to support your point—logically and with verifiable statistical information and quotes from experts. Banish the phrase "I think" altogether. Throw in humor whenever possible. Wrap it all up with a concluding graph that clearly ties back to the nut graph.

Good advice. But there are some other guidelines to keep in mind. As in pitch letters, you need to do some homework on the audience and geographic reach of the targeted publication. It is also wise to read the editorial pages of the publication and find out, either from the newspaper or a media directory, how op-ed submissions are handled. Some editorial page directors prefer an e-mail or fax query outlining the subject of the proposed op-ed piece and the credentials of the author. Others simply want a brief phone call and a pitch in 60 seconds or less.

If the editor is interested, he or she will most likely ask you to submit the op-ed for consideration. This gives you the "green light" to proceed with this particular publication because you at least have an editor's commitment to review the piece. This is important because an op-ed should be submitted to only one publication at a time; it is not like a news release that is distributed to numerous publications.

You can always retool the basic op-ed for submission to other publications, but each publication expects exclusive rights to the piece you send them. In fact, publications "lock up" these exclusive rights by paying op-ed authors, even if they are CEOs or millionaires in their own right. *The New York Times* pays $150+, and *USA Today* pays $300+. Smaller dailies often pay less.

Professional Tips

Writing the "Perfect" Op-Ed

- Daily newspapers prefer articles of about 400 to 750 words, which is about three double-spaced pages.
- Concentrate on presenting one main idea or a single theme in your op-ed.
- Have a clear editorial viewpoint. Get to your point in the first paragraph, and proceed to back up your opinion.
- Use facts and statistics to add credibility to what you say. Double-check your facts before using them. John Budd, chairman of The Omega Group, says, "Ratio of opinion to fact should be about 20% to 80%."
- Don't ramble or deviate from your principal points. An op-ed is not an essay that slowly builds to its point.
- Use short, declarative sentences. Long, complex sentences and paragraphs cause readers to tune out.
- Be timely. The article should be about a current social issue, situation, or news event.
- Avoid the use of "I" in stating your opinion. Write in journalistic third person.
- Use active verbs; avoid passive tense.
- Describe the background of the writer in the cover letter to the publication. This helps editors determine the person's qualifications.
- Don't do a mass mailing of an op-ed piece. Standard practice is to offer the piece to one publication at a time.
- Query editors before sendng an op-ed; it will save you time and energy.

Op-Ed: A Case History

Perhaps the best way to explain the mechanics of what is entailed in an op-ed is to give an example of one that appeared in *The Wall Street Journal*. It was by-lined by Eric A. Benhamou, chairman and CEO of 3Com Corporation.

According to Leslie Davis, group manager of corporate public relations for 3Com, the idea of an op-ed came about because the company and the industry were actively involved in the issue of gaining more government support for corporate research and development (R&D) through tax credits. There was already pending federal legislation and some media coverage regarding the issue. As Davis says, "You have to select an issue that's timely, and there's some controversy about it."

Corporate public relations worked with Alexander Communications of Washington, D.C., to prepare a first draft for Benhamou to review and edit. In the meantime, the op-ed editor of *The Wall Street Journal* was queried by phone to determine if there was an interest in the topic and the key themes. The editor was interested because of its timeliness, so the article was faxed almost immediately. Within a week, the piece appeared.

The following is the op-ed piece that was faxed by 3Com to *The Wall Street Journal:*

R&D Needs Washington's Support
By Eric A. Benhamou

It may sound strange to hear a Silicon Valley executive credit the birth of such industries as the Internet and local-area networks to the prescience of the U.S. government.

But in many respects it is the government that has provided the seeds, and the industry that has provided the water and light, to cultivate the technological innovations that are improving the nation's economy and quality of life. Unfortunately, from 1987 to 1995, federal investment in basic research shrank by 2.6 percent a year. As a fraction of gross domestic product, the federal investment in research and development is about half of what it was 30 years ago.

Meanwhile, the information technology sector alone has more than doubled its annual R&D investment over the past 10 years to a current level of $30 billion. In this searing-hot competitive environment, however, most of these expenditures must be allocated to short-term product development. It isn't feasible for the private sector to assume responsibility for long-term, high-risk research when shareholders require solid quarterly returns on investment.

A newly released study by the council on competitiveness confirms these findings and highlights both the long-term returns from, and the dangers of being complacent about, the U.S. investment in R&D. For every dollar spent on basic research, we can expect a 50 cents per year increase in national output.

Let's look at just a few of the transforming events of the industry-government partnership in R&D. Thirty years ago, federally supported research into the nature of genetic material conducted at Stanford University and the University of California, San Francisco, led to the discovery of recombinant DNA technology—the foundation of genetic engineering and of the biotechnology industry.

It was federal investments in research performed at the Defense Advanced Research Projects Agency in the 1960s that provided a technological launch pad for the Internet. And in the 1980s, scientists at the National Science Foundation's supercomputer center at the University of Illinois perfected the graphical Web browser, transforming the Internet from a research tool into a mass medium and creating hundreds of billions of dollars in new wealth.

The Technology Network, known as TechNet, consisting of 140 of the new economy's leaders, have called for a joint commitment by government and industry to increase federal funding for basic science, engineering, and technology research and enact a permanent R&D tax credit.

The federal government should ensure consistent increases in funding for fundamental research. Top priorities for funding increases should include the Defense Advanced Research Projects Agency and the National Science Foundation, which provides 25 percent of all federal support for basic research at academic institutions. Congress has taken a step toward strengthening the federal commitment to basic research with the recent introduction of two important pieces of legislation. The first, sponsored by Reps. James Sensenbrenner (R., Wis.) and George Brown (D., Calif.), would double the federal investment in basic information technology research over five years. The second, sponsored by Sens. Bill Frist (R., Tenn.) and Jay Rockefeller (D., W.Va.) would double basic research funding across a range of federal agencies over a decade.

To spur additional private-sector research, Congress should make the R&D tax credit permanent. For almost 20 years the credit has provided a powerful incentive for increasing research by American industry. But uncertainty over whether the credit will be extended each year makes it difficult for companies to invest in longer-term research. Coopers & Lybrand estimates that a permanent R&D Credit would result in an additional $41 billion in R&D investment between 1998 and 2010.

Research and development funding is our seed corn. Without it there is no future harvest. Industry and government must make a joint commitment today to reinvest the fruits of America's technological and economic leadership in R&D policies that will ensure our nation's continued growth and prosperity into the next millennium.

Mr. Benhamou is chairman and CEO of 3Com Corp., a member of the board of TechNet and a member of the President's Information Technology Advisory Committee.

Letters to the Editor

The next best thing to an op-ed article is a published letter. Letters are generally shorter than op-ed pieces. They focus primarily on rebutting an editorial, clarifying information mentioned in a news story or column, or adding information that might not have been included in the original story.

Burton St. John III, writing in *PR Tactics,* calls a letter to the editor an **LTE**. He says, "LTEs often react to negative editorials, unbalanced news stories or unfavorable letters from other readers. But, increasingly, newspapers are running letters when an organization has positive news to share—perhaps recognizing important civic contributions by their employees or stating public support for an important community movement like downtown development."

An example of a good LTE, reprinted in *PR Tactics,* is the following:

Advertising Mail Has Value

I note with considerable consternation the repeated use of the term "junk mail" in your recent article concerning expanded recycling services in St. Paul. The truth is that most Americans, most of the time, use advertising mail.

According to the *Guide to Mail Order Sales,* $200 billion a year is generated by advertising mail for business and charities. According to the American Newspaper Association, the typical Sunday newspaper is 67 percent advertising. How would you react if a third party referred to the *Star Tribune* as a "junk news-paper." Just doesn't seem right, does it?

Peggy Larson
Postmaster, St. Paul

There is limited space for letters, so you should follow closely any guidelines that the publication has established. Most newspapers and magazines publish these guidelines as part of an LTE page. *Time* magazine, for example, gives the follow-ing information:

Letters to the Editor should be addressed to Time Magazine Letters, Time & Life Building, Rockefeller Center, New York, NY 10020. Our fax number is (212) 522-8949. Correspondence should include the writer's full name, address and home telephone, and may be edited for purposes of clarity or space. Our E-mail address is Letters@time.com

Many of the op-ed guidelines apply, but here are some that relate directly to letters:

- Keep it short. A letter of 200 words or less has a much better chance of being published than one with 500 words.
- Be temperate and factual. Don't call the editor or the author of an article names or question their integrity.
- Identify the subject in the opening paragraph. If your letter is in response to a specific article, refer briefly to the article and the date it appeared.
- State the theme of your letter in the second paragraph. Do you agree, dis-agree, or want to clarify something?
- The next several paragraphs should give your viewpoint, supported by con-vincing facts, examples, or statistics.
- Close. At the end of your letter, give your name, title, organization, and tele-phone number. Publications often call to confirm that you wrote the letter.

Another aspect of the editorial page, working with the publisher and editor to have the publication write an editorial supporting your idea or project, will be dis-cussed in Chapter 11.

SUMMARY

- The purpose of a pitch letter is to convince editors and reporters to cover an event or do a story.
- Pitch letters to editors must be brief, raise interest, and come immediately to the point.
- Pitch letters are customized to each editor based on the publication's con-tent, demographics, and circulation.

PR Casebook

Form Letters not Welcome

Letters to the editor are a good way for individuals or organizations to express their opinions, but a number of newspapers across the country are complaining about "Astroturf" letters. In other words, a letter that purports to be the opinion of an individual letter writer but is actually a form letter prepared by an organization or a cause.

The issue came to light when newspapers, such as the *Boston Globe*, unwittingly published letters that were written not by local residents who signed them, but by the Republican National Committee. The same letters, all praising President Bush, also appeared verbatim in newspapers across the country, each signed by a person in that paper's area.

Another spat of such "letters" also surfaced when it was discovered that soldiers serving in Iraq were sending letters to their hometown newspapers about the great progress that the military and the Bush administration was making in Iraq. The only problem was that all the letters were practically identical, which indicated an organized effort by the Pentagon to have soldiers sign a basic form letter.

As a result of what the newspapers call "fake" letters, many have now instituted policies that original authorship of letters must be confirmed. The *Boston Globe*, for example, even runs online searches of key phrases in a submitted letter in order to determine if a nearly identical missive was already published in another paper. Editors are also issuing alerts on a 600-member e-mail list run by the National Conference of Editorial Writers to catch "Astroturf" letters.

Organizations such as Planned Parenthood and the National Republican Committee say the newspaper ban against form letters is unfair. They say that organized letter-writing campaigns have been around for decades and that people don't always have time to compose their own letters. Shane Kinkenon, vice president of public relations for Grassroots Enterprise, told *PRWeek*, "Just because a person doesn't write the letter doesn't make the opinion any less valid."

Boston Globe ombudsperson, Christine Chinlud, acknowledges that this is a valid point, but says a newspapers's letters to the editor column should be a forum for heartfelt personal views—not a bulletin board for public interest organizations.

What do you think? Would you use the tactic of writing a basic form letter that individuals could sign and send to the newspaper as a "letter to the editor"? Why or why not?

- The purpose of a media alert is to tell assignment editors about an upcoming event or interview opportunity.
- Media alerts about upcoming events should include the five Ws and H in outline form.
- Media kits are packets of material that may include news releases, photographs, feature stories, fact sheets, position papers, backgrounders, and brief biographical sketches.
- Electronic press kits (EPKs) are prepared in CD format. They can include all the information in a printed media kit, but also include audio soundbites, video clips, and product demonstrations.
- Corporate profiles are an overview of the organization. They can give the size of an organization, its major products and services, and the number of employees.

- Backgrounders are documents that give the history, need, and development of a particular product or service. They may also show how the organization's product or service solved a particular consumer need, or even the technology behind the development of a product.
- Op-ed articles are a good way for individuals and organizations to gain visibility among opinion leaders and position themselves as leaders of an industry.
- Op-ed pieces should be relatively short—400 to 750 words.
- A letter to the editor is an effective way of refuting or elaborating on previous news coverage and opinion columns.
- Letters to the editor should be even shorter than op-ed pieces. About 100 to 200 words is the maximum length.

ADDITIONAL RESOURCES

"Digging up the AstroTurf: Newspapers Declare War on 'Fake' Letters to the Editor: PR Pros Stress Letters that Add a Personal Touch." *Ragan's Media Relations Report*, February 17, 2003, p. 3.

"Great Opening Lines: Boost Your Chances at Coverage by Writing Pitch Leads that Get Reporter's Attention." *Ragan's Media Relations Report*, February 3, 2003, pp. 1, 6.

Green, Sherri Deatherage. "Coaxing Scribes to Cover a Product Launch." *PRWeek*, July 24, 2000, p. 20. Reporters dread pitches for new products.

" 'Know the Show, Keep Pitches Short,' Producers Tell PCNY." *O'Dwyer's PR Services Report*, November 2000, p. 48.

Lee, Jennifer. "Editors and Lobbyists Wage High-Tech War Over Letters." *The New York Times*, January 27, 2003, p. C10.

Quenqua, Douglas. "*Boston Globe* to Ban Form Letters from Advocates." *PRWeek*, February 10, 2003, p. 10.

Seitel, Fraser P. "Letters to the Editor." *O'Dwyer's PR Services Report*, May 2003, p. 32.

"Study: Media Are Turned off by Blind Pitches." *O'Dwyer's PR Services Report*, January 2002, p. 29.

Todorova, Aleksandra. "Inbox of Tricks for Sending a Pitch." *PRWeek*, July 22, 2002, p. 18.

Ward, David. "Op-eds Remain a Coveted Voice for News Analysis." *PRWeek*, March 31, 2003, p. 12.

Chapter 9

Radio, Television, and Webcasting

Radio and television, including new developments in Webcasting, offer many opportunities for the public relations writer who wants to reach both mass and specialized audiences effectively.

Broadcasting and its various forms are important because they serve as the primary source of information for most of the population. More than 80 percent listen to the radio daily, and people still spend more time watching television than surfing the Internet.

Writing and preparing materials for electronic and digital media, however, requires a special perspective. This chapter explains how to write for the ear, integrate audio and visual elements into a script, and harness the power of satellite and digital communications to conduct media tours that can reach a global audience. It also tells you how to get your spokesperson on broadcast talk and magazine shows.

RADIO

Radio, lacking the glamor of television and the popularity of the Internet, is not always the first medium that public relations people think of when planning an information campaign.

On a local level, however, radio is a cost-effective way to reach large numbers of people in various age, ethnic, and income groups. Radio benefits by its ability to be heard almost anywhere. It is the only mass medium, for example, that can reach millions of Americans as they commute to and from work in their cars. In addition, the miracle of the transistor brings radio to mail carriers on their routes, carpenters on construction sites, homeowners pulling weeds in their gardens, and exercise enthusiasts working out at a gym or jogging. Each week, radio reaches 94 percent of Americans ages 12 and up, with a total audience of 223 million.

Approximately 13,500 radio stations are on the air in the United States, ranging from low-powered outlets operated by volunteers to large metropolitan stations audible for hundreds of miles. In addition, radio stations are increasing their audience reach through the Internet. An estimated 2,000 now have an Internet presence, and many are concurrently broadcasting and Webcasting their programming. Webcasting is discussed further at the end of the chapter.

The station's format often determines the nature of the audience. There are "top 40" stations for teenagers, all-news stations for commuters, classical stations that appeal to an older and better-educated group, and stations that play "adult contemporary" for aging baby boomers. One popular format is "country," which reaches a variety of age and occupational groups.

A public relations practitioner should study each station's format and submit material suitable to it. There is little sense in sending information about senior citizen recreational programs to the news director of a hard rock FM station with an audience made up primarily of teenagers.

You can determine the demographics of a station by consulting radio and television directories or by contacting the station's advertising and marketing department. One common source of advertising rates and demographic data is published by Standard Rate and Data Services. Another source is the *Radio Marketing Guide and Fact Book for Advertisers.* See Figure 9.1 for an example of a radio station listing from *Bacon's Media Directories.*

Radio News Releases

Although radio station staffs often find themselves rewriting print releases to conform to broadcast style, the most effective approach is to send news releases that are formatted for the medium. Radio is based on sound, and every radio release must be written so that it can be easily read by an announcer and clearly understood by a listener.

Format There are several major differences between a radio release and a news release prepared for print media. Although the basic identifying information is the same (letterhead, contact, subject), the standard practice is to write a radio release using all uppercase letters in a double-spaced format. You also need to give the

```
┌─────────────────────────────────────────────────────────┐
│ Programs:                                                │
│ Dow Jones Money Report                                   │
│                                        Fax: (609) 520-5773│
│ Air Time: Mon-Fri, Hourly, 60 seconds                    │
│ Profile: Business/Finance, Personal Finance; Format: Talk.│
│ Can Use: Guests; Contact Method: Fax.                    │
│ Focus: 60-second vignette covering a broad range of personal│
│ finance and investment topics which can interest anyone from the│
│ everyday consumer to experienced investors. Subjects include│
│ advice, trend information, economic news, new products and│
│ services, corporate developments, technology, the Internet,│
│ E-commerce, mortgage rates and small business news.      │
│ Show Personnel:                                          │
│ Managing Editor  . . . . . . . . . . . . . Patrice Sikora  (609) 520-4477│
│                              patrice.sikora@dowjones.com │
│   Contact Notes: Mon-Fri, Preferred order: Fax, Phone, U.S. Mail, E-Mail.│
│   Evergreen material is accepted on slow news days and seasonal features│
│   are always of interest; allow 1-month lead time for seasonal pitches. Also,│
│   surveys work well for this brief report, especially if your research│
│   uncovers a workplace trend or offers personal finance insight.│
│ Assignment Editor . . . . . . . . . . . . . . . Pat O'Neill  (609) 520-4356│
│                                  pat.oneill@dowjones.com │
│   Contact Notes: Mon-Fri, Preferred order: Phone, Fax, E-Mail. Serves as│
│   Afternoon Newsroom Editor. Do not include him on your mass mailing│
│   list. Instead, phone during business hours keeping in mind to time your│
│   call for off-air time.                                 │
│ Assignment Editor . . . . . . . . . . . . . Ian MacLeod  (609) 520-4000│
│                                  ian.macleod@dowjones.com│
│   Contact Notes: Mon-Fri, Preferred order: Phone, Fax, E-Mail. Do not│
│   include him on your mass mailing list. The most effective way of pitching│
│   your idea is through a phone call during normal business hours. Make│
│   sure you place your call when he is off-air. Fax and e-mail is also│
│   accepted.                                              │
└─────────────────────────────────────────────────────────┘
```

Figure 9. 1 Media Directories Profile Radio Sites
A publicist has more success placing materials on the radio if he or she knows the format and demographics of the station. Armed with such information, the publicist can tailor the material and also find out who should be contacted. This is an excerpt from the Wall Street Journal Radio Network. *(Courtesy of Bacon's Media Directories.)*

length of the radio release. For example, "RADIO ANNOUNCEMENT: 30" or "RADIO ANNOUNCEMENT: 60." This indicates that the announcement will take 30 or 60 seconds to read.

The timing is vital because broadcasters must fit their messages into a rigid time frame that is measured down to the second. Most announcers read at a speed of 150 to 160 words per minute. Because word lengths vary, it is not feasible to set exact word counts for any length of message. Instead, the general practice is to use an approximate line count. With a word processor set for 60 spaces per line, you will get the following lengths:

- 2 lines=10 seconds (about 25 words)
- 5 lines=20 seconds (about 45 words)
- 8 lines=30 seconds (about 65 words)
- 16 lines=60 seconds (about 125 words)

There are also differences in writing style. A news release for a newspaper uses standard English grammar and punctuation. Sentences often contain dependent and independent clauses. In a radio release, a more conversational style is used and the emphasis is on strong, short sentences. In fact, you can even write radio copy using incomplete or partial sentences, as you would do in a normal conversation. This allows the announcer to draw a breath between thoughts and the listener to follow what is being said. An average sentence length of 10 words is a good goal.

Here is a an example of a 60-second news feature (153 words) distributed by North American Precis Syndicate for the National Automotive Parts Association (NAPA):

CAR CARE CORNER

YOU CAN KEEP YOUR CAR, AND YOUR FAMILY ON THE ROAD TO SAFETY EVEN IN ROUGH WEATHER, IF YOU HEED A FEW HINTS. FIRST, HAVE YOUR BATTERY AND CHARGING SYSTEM TESTED BY A CERTIFIED TECHNICIAN. AN OLD BATTERY MAY FAIL IF IT HAS TO RUN LIGHTS, HEATER, DEFROSTER, DEFOGGER, AND WIPERS WHEN THE TEMPERATURE IS LOW. HAVE YOUR ANTIFREEZE CHANGED BY AN AUTOMOTIVE TECHNICIAN EVERY TWO YEARS. STEER CLEAR OF LOW TIRE INFLATION. A 30-DEGREE DROP IN TEMPERATURE CAN MAKE A FOUR TO FIVE POUND DIFFERENCE IN PRESSURE. LOW PRESSURE TIRES DON'T MEET THE ROAD PROPERLY OR SHED WATER EFFECTIVELY. CHECK TIRE WEAR. PUT A PENNY IN THE

Professional Tips

How to Write a Radio News Release

- Time is money in radio. Stories should be no longer than 60 seconds. Stories without actualities (soundbites) should be 30 seconds or less.
- The only way to time your story is to read it out loud, slowly.
- A long or overly commercial story is death. Rather than editing it, a busy radio newsperson will discard it.
- Convey your message with the smallest possible number of words and facts.
- A radio news release is not an advertisement; it is not a sales promotion piece. A radio news release is journalism—spoken.
- Announcers punctuate with their voices; not all sentences need verbs or subjects.
- Releases should be conversational. Use simple words and avoid legal-speak.
- After writing a radio news release, try to shorten every sentence.
- Listeners have short attention spans. Have something to say and say it right away.
- Never start a story with a name. While listeners are trying to figure out who the person is, they forget to listen to the sentences that follow.

Source: News Broadcast Network, New York.

TREAD WITH LINCOLN'S HEAD DOWN. IF THE TOP OF HIS HEAD SHOWS,
YOU NEED NEW TIRES. YOU CAN LEARN MORE FROM THE EXPERTS AT
THE NATIONAL AUTOMOTIVE PARTS ASSOCIATION AT W-W-W—DOT—
N-A-P-A—ONLINE—DOT-COM.

Notice the spaces in the Web site address. This alerts the news announcer to
read the URL slowly so people can remember it. The same rule is applied to telephone numbers. Oftentimes, a number or URL is repeated a second time for listeners who are in the process of grabbing a pencil and pad.

Audio News Releases

Although news releases in broadcast style can be sent to radio stations for announcers to read, the most common and effective approach is to send the radio
station a recording of the news announcement.

An audio news release, commonly called an **ANR**, can take two forms. One
simple approach is for someone with a good radio voice to read the entire announcement; he or she may or may not be identified by name. This, in the trade,
is called an **actuality**. The second approach is a bit more complicated, but relatively easy to do. In this instance, you use an announcer but also include a **soundbite** from a satisfied customer or a company spokesperson. This approach is better
than a straight announcement because the message comes from a "real person"
rather than a nameless announcer. These combination announcements are also
more acceptable to stations because local staff can elect to use the whole recorded
announcement, or take the role of announcer and use just the soundbite.

Format   The preferred length for an ANR is one minute; however, shorter tapes
can be used. It is advisable to accompany any sound tape with a complete script of
the tape. This enables the news director to judge the value of the tape without listening to the tape.

Here is the script of an ANR that includes a soundbite from a spokesperson.
TVN Productions in New York produced it on behalf of its client, Hidden Valley
Ranch (see Chapter 4, Figure 4.8, for the media advisory about the event):

World's Longest Salad Bar: 60 Seconds
THIS IS A TVN REPORT. WHAT IS 160 YARDS LONG, BOASTS
MORE THAN 17,000 POUNDS OF PRODUCE AND IS FREE TO ANYONE
WHO HAS AN APPETITE FOR HEALTHY LIVING? WHY, IT'S THE
WORLD'S LONGEST SALAD BAR, OF COURSE, AND IT'S HAPPENING
THURSAY, MAY 27TH IN NEW YORK CITY'S CENTRAL PARK TO KICK
OFF MEMORIAL DAY WEEKEND. JOSIE WELLING OF HIDDEN VAL-
LEY RANCH EXPLAINS:

"Ranch dressing is as much an American original as Central Park and
Memorial Day Weekend, which is why we decided to bring them together for a
good old-fashioned Memorial Day picnic. It's also a great way to celebrate our
25th anniversary."

THE SALAD BAR FEATURES COUNTLESS VARIETIES OF FRUITS,
VEGETABLES, GREENS AND GARNISHES, AS WELL AS 20 DIFFERENT
SPECIALTY SALADS ALL FEATURING HIDDEN VALLEY ORIGINAL

RANCH DRESSING—A PRODUCT WHICH TURNS 25 THIS YEAR. THE
EVENT IS EXPECTED TO BE RECOGNIZED BY THE GUINNESS BOOK OF
RECORDS AS—YOU GUESSED IT—THE WORLD'S LONGEST SALAD BAR.

Notice that the above script is written in a somewhat breezy manner, reflecting the nature of the event. The World's Longest Bar is a fun and oddball event. Organizations announcing new products, on the other hand, tend to be more low-key and play it straight. A good example is the ANR, with a soundbite, that the World Resoures Institute used to announce the publication of a major report. The following report (56 seconds) was produced by WestGlen Communications and distributed in MP3 format by North American Network, Inc.:

ANNOUNCER:
A LANDMARK REPORT RELEASED THURSDAY (JULY 10TH) CALLS FOR
FUNDAMENTAL CHANGES TO HOW DECISIONS ARE MADE—AND WHO
MAKES THEM—CONCERNING THE WORLD'S NATURAL RESOURCES. THE
REPORT—**WORLD RESOURCES 2002–2004: DECISIONS FOR THE EARTH—
BALANCE, VOICE, AND POWER**—STRESSES THAT THESE CHANGES ARE
URGENTLY NEEDED, IN ORDER TO ARREST THE GROWING DETERIORATION
OF THE WORLD'S ENVIRONMENT. **WORLD RESOURCES INSTITUTE**
PRESIDENT JONATHAN LASH. . .

LASH:
**"DESPITE 10 YEARS OF RESOUNDING DECLARATIONS AND
INTERNATIONAL ENVIRONMENTAL AGREEMENTS,
ENVIRONMENTAL PROBLEMS ARE STILL GETTING WORSE IN MUCH
OF THE WORLD. THE BEST WAY TO CHANGE THOSE TRENDS IS TO
INFORM PEOPLE, EMPOWER THEM, AND GET THEM ENGAGED."**

ANNOUNCER:
THE REPORT CALLS FOR THE INCLUSION OF THE PUBLIC IN THE DECISION-
MAKING PROCESS; STRENGTHING THE CURRENT LOOSE INTERNATIONAL
SYSTEM OF ENVIRONMENTAL GOVERNANCE; AND BETTER DISCLOSURE
FROM BUSINESS. IT WARNS THAT NON-GOVERNMENTAL ORGANIZATIONS
SHOULD ADHERE TO THE SAME STANDARDS OF ACCOUNTABILITY AND
TRANSPARENCY THEY ARE ASKING FROM GOVERNMENT AND
BUSINESSES.

Production   Every ANR starts with a carefully written and accurately timed script. The next step is to record the words. In doing this, it is imperative to control the quality of the sound. A few large organizations have complete facilities for this; some get help from moonlighting station employees; but most people use a professional recording service.

The recording services have first-class equipment and skilled personnel. They can take a script, edit it, eliminate words or phrases that will not be understandable, record at the proper sound levels, and produce a finished tape suitable for broadcasting. They can find an announcer of whatever type is best suited to the kind of message to be delivered, and they can produce many copies of a tape.

Radio news stories can be produced on cassette or CD-ROM. The most common method, and the most economical, is a CD. If you are doing a national distribution, you also can use MP3 format. You can find a recording service by asking your colleagues for recommendations or by looking under "Recording Services" in the Yellow Pages.

Delivery   Various radio stations, like newspapers, have preferences about how they like to receive audio news releases. One survey by DWJ Television, however, showed that 71 percent of the radio news directors prefer to receive actualities by phone. This is particularly true when there is a late-breaking news event. When a forest fire threatened California's Napa Valley, a large winery featured its president in a topical actuality. He reported that the fire had not endangered the grape crop and went on to forecast an excellent harvest. When the tape was offered by telephone to 50 or so radio stations, almost 40 accepted it for use.

Another method of delivery is via satellite or the World Wide Web. Figures 9.2 and 9.3 show a "radio newsfeed" from Medialink in both English and its Spanish version.

Use   Producing audio news releases is somewhat of a bargain compared to producing materials for television. When Sears distributed a radio news release re-

Figure 9.2 Radio News Release
This is a script for a radio news release that was made available via satellite. It was part of a Cigna public relations campaign to reach Americans making health-care decisions. Medialink produced and distributed three English and three Spanish audio news releases that summarized results from a Cigna survey regarding awareness of health-plan services. See Figure 9.3 for the Spanish version.
(Courtesy of Cigna and its producer/distributor, Medialink.)

Medialink *Radio Newsfeed*

Audio & Scripts available 24/7 at 1-888-727-2948, press # 7
Download audio files in .wav, .mp3 or .ra formats at www. newstream.com
(click *Medialink Radio* button on right hand side)
Also available via satellite:
ABC Radio: Satellite: GE-8, transponder: 23
Provider: ABC NY Service: Sat Srvs 03 L/R (RIGHT channel), 4:45 am - 5:00 am et
Westwood One/CBS StarGuide 2: GE -8, transponder 21 Channel 43
5:30 – 5:45 am ET & 8:15 – 8:30am ET

August 26, 2002

WORRIED AT WORK
New Survey Shows American Workers Are Stressed Out But Can Take Simple Steps to Ease Workplace Tension

SUGGESTED ANCHOR LEAD: If you're feeling stressed out at work, you're not alone. A new survey shows economic uncertainty, dwindling retirement savings, and ongoing terrorist concerns have American workers increasingly stressed out. But as Roberta Facinelli explains, employees and employers alike can do things to counteract all this tension. (:60)

SCRIPT: If you're like most American workers, you're facing increased stress on and off the job. In fact, according to a new nationwide study conducted by employee assistance experts at CIGNA Behavioral Health, almost half of employees surveyed have been tempted to quit their jobs over the past year, have quit, or are planning to soon given the series of pressures they're facing. But according to CIGNA's Dr. Jodi Aronson Prohofsky, there are things you can do to ease workplace tension.

CUT (Aronson Prohofsky): Simple changes in your lifestyle can help reduce stress. Exercising more often, volunteering, making time to read or engaging in a favorite hobby are all easy steps we can take. Many of us also take time out for reflection and meditation to deal with daily pressures.

SCRIPT: Employees often find workplace support programs a good place to start, so check with your employer. Many provide programs such as counseling services, flexible work schedules as well as nutrition and health programs – all of which can help re-energize stressed out workers to achieve a better work-life balance. I'm Roberta Facinelli.

SUGGESTED ANCHOR TAG: If you're interested in learning more about workplace stress reduction tips, visit www.cignabehavioral.com.

Produced for CIGNA Behavioral Health
For more information on this story, contact ------

708 Third Avenue , New York, NY 10017 212-682-8300   800-843-0677 Fax 212-682-2370 www.medialink.com

Figure 9.3 The Hispanic Market Is Important

This is the Spanish version of the audio news release in Figure 9.2. Public relations writers can expand the potential audience by thinking about other languages. There are 37 million Hispanics in the United States, and they possess buying power of more than $580 billion. In addition, Spanish-language publicity materials have another potential audience of 450 million in Latin America. In seven major markets, including Los Angeles, New York, and Miami, the Spanish language Univision cable channel ranked number one for adults 18–34.

(Courtesy of Cigna and its producer/distributor, Medialink.)

Medialink *Radio Newsfeed*

Atención salas de redacción:
Audio y Libretos Disponibles en Radio Noticias de Medialink
NUMERO GRATIS: 1-800-801-1106, presione # 1
Periodistas y estaciones de radio inscritas para este servicio pueden bajar los archivos de audio para este reportaje en el siguiente sitio
www.newstream.com (haga click en Medialink Radio en Español)

Agosto 30 del 2002
EL ESTRES EN EL TRABAJADOR
Nueva encuesta indica que el estrés es una gran preocupación para muchos empleados, pero existen opciones para aliviar la tensión

INTRODUCCIÓN SUGERIDA: Si estás sufriendo de estrés, no estás solo. Una encuesta nacional, indica que los problemas económicos, la pérdida de ahorros para la jubilación, y las continuas amenazas terroristas, tienen a muchos trabajadores preocupados e insatisfechos. Pero como nos explica Lilian Carbone, hay varias opciones para quienes padecen de los síntomas del estrés.

LIBRETO: Casi la mitad de la gente empleada ha pensado en abandonar su trabajo. O, de hecho, ya lo ha hecho. Esa es la conclusión de una encuesta nacional, dirigida por CIGNA Behavioral Health, que ha identificado las causas de tal comportamiento en las presiones laborales y sociales que diariamente agobian al trabajador. Pero como explica Aaron Gallegos de CIGNA, existen métodos con qué aliviar el estrés en el trabajo.

SONIDO(Gallegos): Un simple cambio en su estilo de vida puede ayudarle a combatir el estrés. Por ejemplo hacer ejercicios, trabajar como voluntario, leer, o dedicarse a un hobby son maneras de liberar las tensiones laborales y ocuparse de su bienestar físico y mental.

LIBRETO: Hay programas de consejería en muchos sitios de trabajo con asesoría en nutrición y salud, y horarios flexibles, que ayudan al empleado a encontrar un balance entre su vida personal y profesional. Le Reportó Lilian Carbone.

SUGERENCIA PARA EL CIERRE: Para obtener más información sobre el estudio y sugerencias para una mejor calidad de vida visite el sitio en la red www.cignabehavioral.com

Producido para Cigna Behavioral Health
Para más información sobre esta nota, llame a —
708 Third Avenue, New York, NY 10017 212-682-8300 800-843-0677 Fax 212-682-2370 www.medialink.com

sponding to charges of overcharging customers at auto repair centers in California, the cost of preparing and distributing a national release was $3,900. Ford spent $3,500 for a news release on battery recycling as part of Earth Day festivities. However, Ford also got 624 broadcasts and reached more than 5 million people with the message.

Despite the cost-effectiveness, you should still be selective about distribution to stations that have an interest in using such material. Radio releases, like news releases, should not be shotgunned to every radio station.

You also need to monitor usage. Many organizations send a return postcard on which the station can report use. However, News Broadcast Network estimates that usage cards generate only a 5 to 7 percent response rate. Other organizations simply call the station and ask how many times a particular story or announcement aired. By using Arbitron ratings, which give estimated audience figures, public relations people can then calculate how many listeners were exposed to the message. Evaluation procedures are discussed in Chapter 19.

The use of audio news releases is increasingly popular with radio stations. Thom Moon, director of operations at Duncan's American Radio, *Quarterly*, told *PRWeek* that he thinks the major reason for this is the consolidation of ownership in radio broadcasting (Clear Channel now owns 1,200 stations), which has resulted in cost cutting and fewer news personnel.

Jack Trammell, president of VNR-1 Communications, told *PR Reporter*, "They're telling us they're being forced to do more with less. As long as radio releases are well produced and stories don't appear to be blatant commercials, newsrooms are inclined to use them." Trammell conducted a survey of radio stations and found that 83 percent of the newsrooms use radio news releases (RNRs). And 34 percent say RNRs give them ideas for local stories. The editors look for regional interest (34%), health information (23%), and financial news (11%). They also like tech stories, children's issues, politics, seasonal stories, agriculture, and local interest issues.

A good example of "localizing" a story is the ANR that Moultrie News Generation produced about the need for air bags and seat belts that was distributed around Memorial Day weekend (a heavy traffic time). To localize the story for individual markets, the release included statistics for each area.

Some Tips   Trammell, in an article for *PR Tactics*, gives some additional "rules" for successful radio and television story placement:

- **Topicality**. Stories may fail every other judgment criteria and still get airtime simply because they offer information on a hot topic. *Newsroom Maxim:* News is about issues that matter to the majority of our listeners or viewers.

- **Timeliness**. Stories should be timed to correspond with annual seasons, governmental rulings, new laws, social trends, etc. *Newsroom Maxim:* The favorite word in broadcasting is "now" followed by "today" and then "tomorrow." The least favorite word is "yesterday."

- **Localization**. Newsrooms emphasize local news. A national release should be relevant to a local audience. Reporters are always looking for the "local angle." *Newsroom Maxim:* If it's not local, it's probably not news.

- **Humanization**. Show how real people are involved or affected. Impressive graphics and statistics mean nothing to audiences without a human angle. *Newsroom Maxim:* People relate to people—and animals.

- **Visual appeal**. Successful stories must provide vibrant, compelling soundbites or video footage that subtly promotes, but also illustrates and explains. *Newsroom Maxim:* Say dog, see dog.

Public Service Announcements

Public service announcements are another category of material that public relations writers prepare for radio stations.

A **public service announcement (PSA)** is defined by the Federal Communications Commission (FCC) as an unpaid announcement that promotes the programs of government or voluntary agencies or that serves the public interest. In general, as part of their responsibility to serve the public interest, radio and TV stations provide airtime to charitable and civic organizations, although there is no legal requirement that they do so. Thus, a PSA may be a message from the

American Heart Association about the necessity of regular exercise or an appeal from a civic club for teacher volunteers in a literacy project.

According to DWJ Television, a video producer, PSAs give various governmental and nonprofit organizations an opportunity to use the same channels of communication as major business advertisers but at only a fraction of the cost. DWJ further states, "It is not unusual for a television campaign, produced and distributed on a budget of $25,000 to $40,000, to get airtime that would have cost $1 to $5 million or more for paid advertising."

Profit-making organizations do not qualify for PSAs despite the "public service" nature of their messages, but sometimes an informational campaign by a trade group qualifies. For example, the Aluminum Association received airtime on a number of stations by producing a PSA about how to recycle aluminum cans. Before the announcement was released, the association received an average of 453 calls a month. Five months after the PSA began appearing, the association had received 9,500 calls at its toll-free number. The PSA was used in 46 states, and 244 stations reported 16,464 broadcasts of the announcement.

This example shows the potential effectiveness of PSAs. Remember, however, that others are aware of the potential; therefore, many PSAs are available to the stations. Only those that are timely and of high recording quality stand a chance of being used.

Here are a few more points to remember about PSAs:

- Only nonprofit, civic, and voluntary organizations are eligible to use PSAs. Announcements by profit-making organizations are considered advertisements, and stations charge regular advertising rates for carrying them.

- Since the deregulation of the broadcasting industry, stations feel less pressure to provide a community service by running PSAs for nonprofit groups. Although a station's renewal of its license is still based to a certain extent on serving the local community, there is no minimum standard for broadcasting PSAs.

- Few PSAs are aired during periods of peak listening, when a station can run revenue-producing advertisements. However, WestGlen Communications did an analysis of PSAs used on radio stations and found that most of them (69 percent) aired PSAs during the daytime hours, thus somewhat deflating the perception that most PSAs are run in the wee hours of the morning, when only insomniacs are listening.

Format   PSAs, like radio news releases, are written in uppercase and double-spaced. Their length can be 60, 30, 20, 15, or 10 seconds. And unlike radio news releases, the standard practice is to submit multiple PSAs on the same subject in various lengths. The box on page 241 shows several PSAs from the American Red Cross in various lengths.

The idea is to give the station announcer flexibility in using a particular length to fill a particular time slot throughout the day. DWJ Television, a producer of PSAs, further explains: "Some stations air PSAs in a way that relates length to time of play, for example placing one length in their early news shows and another in the late news show. Supplying both lengths allows a campaign to be seen by people who only watch one of these shows."

Here are basic 15- and 30-second PSAs that were distributed by the Social Anxiety Disorder Coalition:

0:15

> ANNCR: RESEARCHERS IN BOSTON ARE LOOKING FOR PEOPLE—AGE 18 THROUGH SENIORS—FOR A STUDY INVESTIGATING A NEW DRUG THAT MAY HELP PEOPLE WITH GENERALIZED ANXIETY DISORDER. IF YOU HAVE OVERWHELMING AND PERSISTENT WORRIES, YOU MAY QUALIFY. CALL 1-800-221-1923.

0:30

> ANNCR: HAVE YOU EVER BEEN SO WORRIED THAT IT AFFECTS YOUR ABILITY TO SLEEP, CONCENTRATE, AND CARRY ON WITH DAILY ACTIVITIES? IF SO, YOU MAY BE ONE OF THE MILLIONS SUFFERING FROM GENERALIZED ANXIETY DISORDER. RESEARCHERS IN BOSTON ARE LOOKING FOR MEN AND WOMEN—AGE 18 THROUGH SENIORS—SUFFERING FROM THESE SYMPTOMS FOR A STUDY INVESTIGATING A NEW DRUG THAT MAY HELP THEM. FOR MORE INFORMATION, CALL 1-800-221-1923.

Another message, prepared by the same organization for television, is shown on page 253. In this case, entertainer Donny Osmond delivered a video message about getting help for social anxiety disorder.

Production   PSAs can be delivered in the same way as radio news releases. You can just mail the scripts and let the station announcer read them as needed. Or you can record your own PSAs, using a good production house, and distribute cassettes or a CD. Once a recording is made, it can also be transmitted via telephone.

Use   Almost any topic or issue can be the subject of a PSA. However, stations seem to be more receptive to particular topics. A survey of radio station public affairs directors by WestGlen Communications, a producer of PSAs, found that local community issues and events were most likely to receive airtime, followed by children's issues. The respondents also expressed a preference for PSAs involving health and safety, service organizations, breast cancer, and other cancers.

The majority of respondents also prefer PSAs that include a local phone number rather than a national toll-free number. Because of this preference, many national groups such as the American Cancer Society or the American Red Cross have a policy of distributing scripts to chapters that can be localized.

Other studies have shown that an organization needs to provide helpful information in a PSA and not make a direct pitch for money. Radio stations tend to shun PSAs that ask people for money directly. A more subtle approach is to tell people about the organization and give them a phone number or a Web site to get more information.

Professional Tips

Offer PSAs in Varying Lengths

It is important to write public service announcements of varying lengths. This gives the radio or television station the opportunity to vary the message and use the appropriate one for the time available. Keep in mind that you should use active voice and simple sentences. Never use a clause between a subject and a verb. Here are some radio PSAs from the American Red Cross:

20 Seconds

Ever give a gift that didn't go over real big?

One that ended up in the closet the second you left the room?

There is a gift that's guaranteed to be well received.

Because it will save someone's life.

The gift is blood, and it's desperately needed.

Please give blood. There's a life to be saved right now.

Call the American Red Cross at 1-800-GIVE LIFE.

30 Seconds

Ever give a gift that didn't go over real big?

One that ended up in the closet the second you left the room?

There is a gift that's guaranteed to be well received.

Because it will save someone's life.

The gift is blood, and the need for it is desperate.

Over 20,000 people must choose to give this gift every day.

We need your help.

Please give blood. There's a life to be saved right now.

Call the American Red Cross at 1-800-GIVE LIFE.

This public service message brought to you by the Advertising Council and the American Red Cross.

60 Seconds

We want you to give a gift to somebody, but it's not a gift you buy.

We want you to give a gift, but not necessarily to someone you know.

Some of you will be happy to do it. Some of you might be hesitant.

But the person who *receives* your gift will consider it so precious, they'll carry it with them for the rest of their life.

This gift is blood / and every day in America, thousands of people desperately need it.

Every day, we wonder if there will be enough for them.

Some days, we barely make it.

To those of you who give blood regularly, the American Red Cross and the many people whose lives you've saved would like to thank you.

Those of you who haven't given recently, please help us again.

There's a life to be saved right now.

To find out how convenient it is to give blood,

Call the American Red Cross today at 1-800-GIVE LIFE. That's 1-800-GIVE LIFE.

Tag

This public service message has been brought to you by this station, the Advertising Council, and the American Red Cross.

PR Casebook

Adding Music and Sound to a PSA

You can make your radio PSA more interesting if you take the time to incorporate music and other sounds (SFX) to the speaker's script (VO). The Santa Clara County (CA) Network for a Hate Free Community distributed this PSA in a CD format to radio stations in the area:

DON'T TEACH HATE (60 SECONDS)

MUSIC: MUSIC BOX VERSION OF "WHEELS ON THE BUS"

SFX: BABY TALK, CHILDREN LAUGHING

VO: **AT SIX WEEKS BABIES LEARN TO SMILE.**

SFX: BABY COOING

VO: **BY SIX MONTHS THEY WILL RESPOND TO DIFFERENT COLORS.**

SFX: BABY LAUGHING

VO: **AT SIXTEEN MONTHS, THEY DEVELOP A SENSE OF SELF.**

SFX: BABY SAYS "MINE!"

VO: **AT WHAT AGE DO THEY LEARN TO HATE?**

SFX: (PAUSE—MUSIC STOPS)

SFX: HORN HONKS, BRAKES SLAM.

            ANGRY MAN'S VOICE: JEEZ, FREAKIN' FOREIGNERS, TOO

            DAMN STUPID TO OPERATE A CAR. YOU OKAY, BACK THERE,

            SPORT?

(MUSIC UP)

BABY'S VOICE: I'M OKAY DADDY.

VO: **THEY LEARN TO HATE WHEN YOU TEACH THEM. YOUR**

            CHILDREN ARE LISTENING AND THEY'RE LEARNING

            FROM YOU. INSULTS AND SLURS BASED ON RACE,

            RELIGION, DISABILITY, GENDER OR SEXUAL ORIENTATION

            TEACH CHILREN IT'S OKAY TO HATE. HATE IS THE ENEMY

            IN SANTA CLARA COUNTY AND YOU ARE ON THE FRONT

            LINE. To report a hate crime or to receive services, call the Santa

            Clara County Network for a Hate Free Community at (408) 792-2304.

Some Tips   Phil Rabin, writing in *PRWeek*, gives some tips for successful PSAs—whether they are for radio or television. You should:

- Do your research so your PSA achieves an identified goal for your organization.
- Keep it simple. The short length of PSAs means that you must minimize the points you want to make.
- Send broadcast PSAs in different lengths and print PSAs in different sizes.
- Establish an effective tracking system.

- Try to localize your PSAs, and a local number is often more effective than a national toll-free number.

Radio Media Tours

Another approach in radio is the **radio media tour (RMT)**. Essentially, this can be described as a spokesperson conducting a series of round-the-country, one-on-one interviews from one central location. The publicist pre-books telephone interviews with DJs, news directors, or talk show hosts around the country, and the personality simply gives interviews on the phone, which is recorded for later use or broadcast live.

A major selling point for an RMT is its relatively low cost and the convenience of giving numerous interviews from one central location. David Thalberg, vice president of Ruder/Finn, told *Ragan's Media Relations Report*, "You don't have to go to a TV station, and you don't have to put on a suit. Your client can do the interview over the phone, seated in his or her office, with all the supplementary material he or she needs to come across as authoritative and informed."

Laurence Mosowitz, president of Medialink, echos this aspect of convenience. He told *PRWeek*, "It is such an easy, flexible medium. We can interview a star in bed in his hotel and broadcast it to the country. Radio is delicious."

A major multinational pharmaceutical concern, Schering-Plough, used an RMT to point out that most smokers in the United States fail to recognize the warning signs of chronic bronchitis. The RMT was picked up by 88 stations with a listenership of more than 2.8 million. This RMT was done in conjunction with a **satellite media tour (SMT)** for television stations. SMTs are discussed in the next section of this chapter.

TELEVISION

The fundamental factor that separates television from the other media and gives it such pervasive impact is the visual element. The combination of color, movement, sound, and sight on a screen in your own living room is hard to resist. No wonder the medium is the primary source of news, information, and entertainment for most people. In fact, the National Association of Broadcasters (NAB) says local TV news attracts 150 million viewers. Network news reaches 30 million, prime-time national cable, 3 million, and regional cable, 31 million. The average daily per-household hours of television use in the United States is still more than seven hours a day, despite the advent of the Internet.

There are almost as many television stations (1,500) in the United States as there are daily newspapers (1,532), and there are numerous opportunities for the placement of public relations materials at the local and network level. However, you need to know how a television station is organized and who is in charge of various programs. The titles may vary somewhat, but the following positions are common at both radio and television stations:

- *General manager.* This person, comparable to the publisher of a newspaper, determines general policy and manages all the departments.

- *Program director.* This person decides which programs to produce and broadcast—including news, public affairs, and entertainment programs.
- *Directors and producers.* These people moderate the various interview and talk shows that are the staple of many stations. They are comparable to the section editors of daily newspapers.
- *News director.* This person, comparable to the managing editor of a newspaper, manages the entire operation of gathering and producing newscasts.
- *Assignment editor.* This person, comparable to the city editor of a newspaper, assigns reporters and camera crews to cover news stories.
- *Reporters.* These are the people who write and report the news, as well as the sound and camera technicians who accompany them on assignments.
- *Public affairs or public service director.* This person is the station's public relations representative. Duties may include working with community organizations to broadcast public service announcements and organizing public affairs programming.
- *Promotion director.* This person promotes the station by sponsoring contests and events, often in partnership with other community groups.

You may have reason to contact all of these people at one time or another. Specific placement opportunities for talk shows, call-in programs, product placement, community calendars, and other messages are discussed later in the chapter. Here, we focus on working with television news directors, assignment editors, and reporters to generate news coverage of your organization or client.

There are four approaches to getting your news story on local television. First, you can send the television station the same news release that you send to the local print media. If the news editor thinks the topic is newsworthy and lends itself to visual representation, he or she may tell the assignment editor to have a reporter and camera crew follow up on the news release.

Second, you can prepare a media alert or advisory advising the news department about the particular aspect of an event or occasion that would lend itself to video coverage. These media alerts can be sent via e-mail, fax, or even regular mail.

A third approach is to phone or e-mail the assignment editor and make a "pitch" to have the station do a particular story. The art of writing pitch letters was discussed in Chapter 8.

The fourth approach is to write and produce a **video news release (VNR)** that, like an audio news release, is formatted for immediate use with a minimum of effort by station personnel. The VNR also has the advantage of being used by numerous stations on a regional, national, or even global basis.

Video News Releases

An estimated 5,000 VNRs are produced annually in the United States. Large organizations seeking enhanced recognition for their names, products, services, and causes are the primary clients for VNRs. The production of VNRs can more easily be justified if there is potential for national distribution and multiple pickups by television stations and cable systems.

VNRs are not cheap. A typical 90-second VNR, says one producer, costs a minimum of $20,000 to $50,000 for production and distribution. Costs vary, however, depending on the number of location shots, special effects, and staff required to produce a high-quality tape that meets broadcast standards.

One producer, WestGlen Communications, advertises a basic VNR package for $19,950 that includes (1) consultation on story concept and news positioning; (2) production; (3) script, one-day shoot, edit, and voice-over; (4) distribution; and (5) distribution to newsrooms, satellite feed, and two days of pitching assignment editors to use it. Other producers, such as Medialink, TVN Productions, DWJ Television, and DS Simon Productions offer similar packages.

Because of the cost, you must carefully analyze the newsworthiness of your information and consider whether the topic lends itself to a fast-paced, action-oriented visual presentation. If you have nothing to show except talking heads or graphs and charts, you should think twice about producing a VNR.

You should also consider whether the information will be current and newsworthy by the time a VNR is produced. On the average, it takes four to six weeks to script, produce, and distribute a high-quality VNR. In a crisis situation or for a fast-breaking news event, however, VNRs can be produced in a matter of hours or days.

A good example of rapid response is Pepsi. Within a week of news reports that syringes and other sharp objects had been found in cans of Diet Pepsi, the soft-drink company produced and distributed a VNR showing that the insertion of foreign objects into cans on their high-speed bottling lines was virtually impossible.

This VNR reached an estimated 186 million television viewers and helped avoid a massive sales decline of Pepsi. Subsequently, Pepsi commissioned three more VNRs on such subjects as a message to consumers from Pepsi's president, a surveillance camera catching an alleged tamperer, and a "thank you" to consumers for their support. According to Medialink, the producer and distributor, the VNRs were seen by an aggregate of 500 million viewers on 3,170 news programs. See the box on page 246 for a list of other VNRs that received significant coverage.

Format   Essentially, a VNR is a television release converted to a finished tape that can be broadcast. The standard length is 90 seconds, which is preferred by the overwhelming majority of TV news directors. Some features, however, can run up to two minutes.

Writing a script for a VNR is a bit more complicated than writing one for an audio news release because you also have to visualize the scene, much like a playwright or a film writer. Adam Shell, editor of *PR Tactics*, describes the required skills:

> Producing a VNR requires expert interviewing skills, speedy video editing, a creative eye for visuals, and political savvy. The job of the VNR producer is not unlike that of a broadcast journalist. The instincts are the same. Engaging sound bites are a result of clever questioning. Good pictures come from creative camera work. A concise, newsworthy VNR comes from good writing and editing. Deadlines have to be met, too. And then there's all the tiny details and decisions that have to be made on the spot. Not to mention figuring out subtle ways to make sure the client's signage appears on the video without turning off the news directors.

PR Casebook

VNRs Reach Millions of People

Here's a list of the top 10 video news releases (VNRs) that, according to Nielsen Media Research, were used by television stations in a recent year:

- **Insurance Institute for Highway Safety (IIHS):** The crashworthiness of large pick-up trucks (213 million viewers, 1,855 airings)
- **British Airways:** Improvements to the Concorde (191 million viewers, 214 airings)
- **Buena Vista Film Studio:** Pearl Harbor world premiere (190 million viewers, 204 airings)
- **Insurance Institute for Highway Safety (IIHS):** SUV bumper crash test (157 million viewers, 1,332 airings)
- **Motorola:** The role of mobile phones (146 million viewers, 92 airings)
- **Insurance Institute for Highway Safety (IIHS):** Crash-test results of Dodge Grand Caravan/Hyundai Elantra (139 million viewers, 1,309 airings)
- **Ericsson:** Consumer-oriented technology products (130 million viewers, 181 airings)
- **European Space Agency:** The first European astronaut (121.6 million viewers, 298 airings)
- **Taco Bell:** The re-entry of 15-year-old space station Mir as part of a product promotion (121 million viewers, 1,615 airings)
- **Novartis:** FDA approval of Gleevec oral therapy drug (120 million viewers, 1,062 airings)

Overall, the top 10 VNRs reach a total global audience of more than 1.5 billion viewers in the United States, Canada, Europe, Asia, and Australia.

Perhaps the best way to illustrate Shell's comments is to show a typical VNR script. Figure 9.4 shows one produced by DS Simon Productions for Nextel's nationwide service for cell phones. Figure 9.5 is the VNR script produced by TVN Productions for Hidden Valley Ranch when it constructed the World's Longest Salad Bar in New York's Central Park. See page 234 for the ANR version.

Production Although public relations writers can easily handle the job of writing radio news releases and doing basic announcements for local TV stations, the production of a video news release is another matter. The entire process is highly technical, requiring trained professionals and sophisticated equipment. Consequently, the public relations writer serves primarily as an idea creator and a facilitator.

He or she may come up with the idea, write a rough script (storyboard) outlining the visual and audio elements, and make arrangements for a video production and distribution service to produce the video. Such firms are listed in the Yellow Pages under "Video" and "Television." The advertisements in public relations magazines (see Chapter 1) are also a good source.

It is important to keep in mind that the video producer follows the basic **storyboard** (outline of who and what should be included) to achieve the organiza-

Suggested Lead: Imagine if the walkie-talkies you played with as a kid could talk to anyone across the country instantly. Now, you can. Gerry Gardner reports.

Video	Audio
	(1) Announcer: Digital cell phones with walkie-talkies are being used by businesses and consumers to make170 million direct connect calls every day. Now, for the first time, this push to talk service is available nationwide.
Jane Zweig Analyst, The Shosteck Group	**(2) Jane Zweig, Analyst:** *Coast to Coast is important for the business user because it extends their productivity. It extends the way they do business, who they do business with and when they do it.*
	(3) Announcer: The first nationwide push to talk service, developed by Nextel, works for RKA Petroleum, who relies on instant communication.
Keith Albertie RKA Petroleum	**(4) Keith Albertie (verbatim):** *Nationwide will be absolutely huge. The direct connect throughout different states will help us out tremendously. If we've got a customer in Chicago, we've got a customer in Indiana, in Ohio, we've got can contact the driver right now and find out what's going on.*
	(5) Announcer: Research shows that when equipped with a phone offering both "push-to-talk" and cell service users are three times as likely to use the walkie-talkie feature over their regular cell phone. A big reason is that the calls are shorter and more direct.
Drew Caplan Vice President, Nextel	**(6) Drew Caplan, Nextel:** *The average direct connect call is about 30 seconds long compared to the average interconnect call which is around two minutes long.*
	(7) Announcer: Some tips before "pushing to talk." First, make sure the service you select connects calls in less than a second and allows for group calls. Make sure you have a variety of choices about the models and price plans.

Figure 9.4 VNR Scripts Must Include Video and Audio

Nextel publicized its coast-to-coast "walkie-talkie" service with a video news release (VNR). Notice the two-column format for the script showing the video and audio components. This VNR has many "talking heads" as the video component, and not much action. You should note the additional "soundbites" at the end, which are included in the B-roll and can be used by the television station as part of its own story.

(Courtesy of Nextel and its producer/distributor, DS Simon Productions.)

	(8) Drew Caplan, Nextel(verbatim): *The biggest issue for people is how quickly is the call going to be connected. And under our nationwide system that happens in less than a second.*
	(9) Announcer: If you're currently one of the more than 11 million Nextel subscribers you can add Nationwide Direct Connect service without changing your phone or phone number. A big plus after hours.
	(10) Jane Zweig, Analyst: *The business user is business by day consumer at another time so it extends their whole lifestyle in the way they communicate with others they care about.*
	(11) Announcer: Great for business traveler Joyce Golden who keeps in touch with her family while on the road.
Joyce Golden Business Traveler	**(12) Joyce Golden:** I'm able to talk to them any time of day or night, whether I'm on the East coast or the West coast. I simply push that little button on the side and they're available because their cell phones are on constantly.
Phone	**(13) Announcer:** I'm Gerry Gardner.

Additional Soundbites:

Jane Zweig
Analyst, The Shosteck Group

So it's been very effective to generate new business, to firm up existing relationships and it's been very successful.

Push to Talk right now is a very hot buzzword. Everyone talks about it. Everyone has a different definition of it and how it will be explored, who it is targeted to. Certainly, Nextel today has seen success in its use with the business market. As the technology becomes more widely distributed to the corporate users, to kids, to family use, then the technology will grow and will grow in importance.

Drew Caplan,
Vice President, Nextel

When coast to coast is fully operational, anyone will be able to connect in less than a second. Whether you're right next door or New York to Hawaii.

Nationwide Direct Connect has been in development and test for five years. It is going to be available to all of our customers by the end of this summer.

This is massive. We carry over 170 million direct connect calls each day. 60 billion last year, and we only anticipate that's going to keep on growing with Nationwide Direct Connect.

Roger Albertie
President CEO
RKA Petroleum

They'll direct connect me. Say Dad I have this problem. You've probably solved this problem in all the years you've been in business so maybe you can help me through this. So it really works out. Direct Connect is just great for us.

Joyce Golden
President, JCG Associates
Business Traveler

It's going to save a lot of time. Time that we can always touch base at any given moment and we can always be in touch at any time of day.

tional objective, but will usually videotape many minutes of footage and use the editing room to make the finished 90-second product.

Consequently, it is not necessary to write a prepared script for everyone who appears on video. It is better, and more natural, to have them talk informally in front of the camera and then use the best soundbite.

Medialink, a major producer and distributor of VNRs, gives some tips about the production of VNRs that best meet the needs of TV news directors:

- Give TV news directors maximum flexibility in editing the tape using their own anchors or announcers. This can be done by producing the VNR on split audio (the announcer track on one audio channel and the natural sound

Figure 9.5 VNR for the World's Longest Salad Bar
This example, about the World's Longest Salad Bar, is another format where the audio is on the left and the visual elements are listed on the right.
(Courtesy of TVN Productions, New York.)

Suggested Anchor intro:
Thousands of picnic lovers got an early start to the Memorial Day weekend today when they gathered in Central Park to help set the record for the World's Longest Salad Bar. The event was organized by Hidden Valley Ranch in honor of the 25th anniversary of ranch dressing. Here is Jennifer Morrow with more on this story.

AUDIO:	VISUALS:
VO: What is 160 yards long, boasts more than 17,000 pounds of produce, and free to anyone who has an appetite for healthy living?	Montage of Deputy Parks Commissioner Garafola officially opening the line for the Salad Bar, pull back to see the tons and tons of food and crowd people.
VO: Welcome to the World's Longest Salad Bar, where organizers hope to be recognized by the Guinness Book of World Records.	Dolly shot/steady cam of first table laden with food, then accelerate film speed to show one end of the salad bar to the other.
VO: The salad bar features 65 varieties of fruits, vegetables, greens and garnishes as well as 20 different specialty salads. All topped with ranch dressing--a product which turns 25 this year.	Close-up of various produce varieties with a bottle of Hidden Valley Ranch dressing in the background.
Soundbite (Nolan Henson, HVR): "We never thought it would ever get this big. I always dreamed that this would be a national institution and my dream has come true"	Nolan Henson Ranch Dressing Founding Family Member
VO: Co-sponsored by the Produce for Better Health Foundation, today's event also benefits City Harvest, a leading non-profit hunger assistance organization.	Various shots of the park site; bandshell, the band playing music; the people walking away from the salad bar with plate laden with food.

Soundbite (Julia Erickson): "We are really delighted that a company with such a great reputation as Hidden Valley Ranch would celebrate its anniversary by wanting to help feed hungry people."	Julia Erickson Executive Director City Harvest, Inc.
VO: Ranch dressing may be 25 years old, but there's no generation gap here when it comes to enjoying a fresh summer salad.	"Mr. Produce Guy" on roller skates goes up to a bunch of kids standing on line to pour ranch dressing on their salads.
Soundbite (Participant): "I'm going to try a little bit of everything as long as I can fit it in my stomach!"	Random salad bar participant

Suggested anchor close: Event organizers estimate that more than 5000 people turned out for the event. To obtain a copy of Original Ranch Recipes contact Hidden Valley Ranch at 1-800-537-2823.

Additional Soundbites:

Josie Welling, Brand Manager, Hidden Valley Ranch:
"Ranch dressing is as much as an American original as Central Park and Memorial Day weekend, which is why we decided to bring them all together here for the World's Longest Salad Bar."

Justin Miller, World's Youngest Chef:
"Ranch Dressing is the only dressing I eat. Ever since I was five, it has been the only dressing I ever ate."

of the VNR on another). This way, the producer has the option of "stripping" the announcer's voice.

- Produce the VNR with news footage in mind. Keep soundbites short and to the point. Avoid commercial-like shots with sophisticated effects.

- Never superimpose your own written information on the actual videotape. TV news departments usually generate their own written notes in their own typeface and style.

- Never use a stand-up reporter. Stations do not want a reporter who is not on their staff appearing in their newscast.

- Provide TV stations with a local angle. This can be done by sending supplemental facts and figures that reflect the local situation. These can be added to the VNR when it is edited for broadcast.

- Good graphics, including animation, are a plus. Stations are attracted to artwork that shows things in a clear, concise manner.

Pintak Communications, of Washington, D.C., adds to the Medialink list of suggestions. The firm says that VNR disasters can be prevented if you do the following:

- Use outside experts to give credibility. A VNR with only corporate spokespeople is not a good idea. In addition, don't clutter up the VNR with an excessive number of corporate logos.

Professional Tips

The Jargon of Writing for Video

Do you know where your SOT is? Do you need a CU or a V/O for your script? The video industry has its own vocabulary, and you should be familiar with it when writing storyboards and scripts. Here are a few of the most common terms:

- **A-roll** Video that contains the audio portion. This may be an announcer speaking or a quote from someone being interviewed.
- **B-roll** Only the video portion, without sound.
- **CU** Close-up shot of a person or object. An MCU is a medium close-up.
- **Dub** A duplicate of an audio- or videotape.
- **On cam** Person or object is on camera—part of what is being videotaped.
- **Pan** Moving the camera (while shooting) from side to side.
- **SOT** Sound on tape. Usually refers to an interview.
- **Super** Printed material, usually words, to show the name of a person, a telephone number, or a location.
- **V/O** Voice-over. A story where someone off-camera, usually an announcer, reads a portion of the video story. Sometimes listed as ANNCR:V/O.
- **Zoom** Changing the camera angle by going from a wide shot to a close shot, or vice versa.

- Avoid commercialism and hype. The VNR is a news story, not a corporate advertisement.
- Avoid overproduction. Slick dissolves and flashy effects are great for music videos, but news producers equate it with advertising.

Delivery   Your VNR package should also include two or three minutes of **B-roll**, or background pictures, for use by the TV news producer in repackaging the story. Typical B-roll includes additional interviews, soundbites, and file footage. Notice the extra soundbites at the end of the VNR for Nextel and the World's Longest Salad Bar. A Nielsen Media Research survey of 130 TV news directors, for example, found that almost 70 percent wanted a VNR with a B-roll attached.

An advisory will accompany the VNR package or will be sent to news directors before the actual satellite transmission of the video to the station. The advisory, in printed form, should contain the basics: the key elements of the story, background and descriptions of the visuals, editorial and technical contacts, satellite coordinates and date and time of the satellite transmission.

A survey by VNR-1 Communications, a producer of VNR packages, found that many newsrooms prefer to receive VNR advisories by fax rather than e-mail or wire service announcements. Jack Trammell, president of VNR-1, says that because a fax is on paper it tends to be passed around a newsroom so a number of news staffers see it.

Satellite distribution is the most cost-effective way of distributing VNRs on a national or global basis. In addition, it is the preferred method of most news directors. Virtually every television station in the country now has at least one satellite-receiving dish.

Analog satellite feeds have been the standard since the 1980s, but the new standard is now digital delivery via satellite. As Katie Sweeney, writing in *PR Tactics*, explains, "The digital advantage is that TV producers don't have to down-link a VNR at a scheduled time from a satellite feed. Instead, the VNR file is sent directly to an assignment editor's desktop where the editor can preview it and decide whether to download it at any time." Editors are able to elect content and drag-and-drop files to other station systems, such as editing suites and play-to-air servers.

All this sounds like an Internet-based system, but this is a misconception. As Michael Hill of News Broadcast Network, a VNR distributor, writes in *PRWeek*, "This system is not Internet-based. It uses dedicated digital satellites, down-link dishes and servers to quickly move video from our clients to TV station newsrooms."

Delivery of VNRs via a digital satellite was still fairly new in 2003, but many experts predicted it would make analog satellite feeds obsolete within a year. Others, however, cautioned that digital would not completely replace the old methods. Gerri Ford Kramer, senior vice president of DWJ Television, told *O'Dwyer's PR Services Report*, "We haven't abandoned satellite feeds or hardcopy distribution. We still need to reach the newsrooms that aren't using Pathfire's systems and news producers who may be slow to change."

VNRs and other publicity materials can also be distributed via Web-based systems, and this will be discussed in the section on Webcasting.

VNRs can also be distributed by mail, but this is time-consuming and expensive. Multiple videotapes must be produced and mailed. The preferred format is 3/4-inch VHS cassette, but Beta-format tapes are still used. Many stations, for example, are now capable of using DVDs. Essentially, you should check with a station to determine what format they prefer. Failure to do so can mean that all your hard work is thrown in the trash just because you didn't pay attention to this little detail.

On occasion, however, VNRs that are not time-sensitive can be mailed to selected stations. These are known as **evergreens** because they are always in season. A VNR on general research into AIDS could be held by a producer for use in an eventual series, or a VNR from the U.S. Forest Service on how to prevent fires could be held in reserve until summer, when the danger is highest.

Mail distribution is also used for what is known as **stock footage**—standard video shots of a company's production line, headquarters, or activities that the station can store until the company is in the news. Then, as the anchor gives the news, the viewer sees the stock footage on the screen. A news story about an electric power plant, for example, may use stock footage from the utility company showing interior scenes of the facility.

Use VNRs are widely used by television stations and cable systems, particularly in smaller markets. A survey by WestGlen Communications, for example, once found that 90 percent of TV stations regularly use outside-produced video for newscasts. This optimistic statistic, however, is tempered by the reality that TV stations today receive so many VNRs that they are drowning in them.

A survey by KEF Media Associates in Atlanta, for example, found that almost 90 percent of the local TV newscasts in the top 100 markets devoted less than 5 percent of their airtime to VNR material. In a 44 minute news hour (allowing for advertising), that represents only two or three minutes. At the same time, some stations in top markets receive more than 100 VNR pitches a week, which graphically illustrates the stiff competition any VNR has for being used at all.

In other words, VNRs go through the same gatekeeping process as news releases and features submitted to newspapers and magazines. Emil Gallina, a senior vice president of Hill & Knowlton's Electronic Media Services, once made the comparison in a *Communication World* article:

> Video releases look like TV news in the same way that press releases read like newspaper articles. And the moving pictures we distribute for television are the equivalent of the 8 by 10 glossies we send to newspapers and magazines. Their purpose is the same: to encourage coverage and to provide materials the reporter might not otherwise obtain . . . They are merely one source of raw material from which news reports can be created.

PR Casebook

VNR Helps Company Launch New Product

One effective way to launch a new product is to produce a video news release. Kimberly-Clark introduced the world's first disposable swimpants for toddlers using such a technique.

Its public relations firm, Meltzer & Martin, was given a budget of $27,000 and charged with creating a newsworthy VNR to make parents of children 6 months to 48 months old aware of the new product, Little Swimmers. WestGlen Communications was hired to produce the video, which was titled, "Preparing Your Children for Their First Swimming Experience." Key product benefits such as "diaper-like protection" and "won't swell or fall apart in the water" were part of the VNR. It was distributed a week before Memorial Day weekend.

The VNR was used by 126 television stations in 41 markets, and it reached an audience of more than 4 million. Soon after, retailers reported that they couldn't keep enough of the product on their shelves. More important, sales of Little Swimmers were 50 percent above Kimberly-Clark's first-year sales projections. The company won several product-of-the-year awards as well as a Bronze Anvil award from the Public Relations Society of America (PRSA).

The comparison is appropriate, but many public relations practitioners worry about the expense and whether the potential audience reached is worth the investment. A single VNR can cost $20,000 to $50,000 or more to produce and distribute. And even if it is used, the typical VNR rarely reaches millions of people. A well-done VNR, according to surveys, usually gets 40 to 50 station airings with an audience of 2 to 3 million people. This is a far cry from the blockbusters like the Insurance Institute for Highway Safety that garnered 213 million viewers with a VNR about the ability of pick-up trucks to survive crashes.

Consequently, it is important that you undertand the value, purpose and limitations of VNRs. Before you commit the money to have a quality VNR produced and distributed, you should first assess (1) the news value of the topic, (2) whether the topic lends itself to a visual treatment, and (3) whether this is a cost-effective method of reaching your target audience.

There are other, more cost-effective ways to achieve broadcast coverage. One is the satellite media tour, which will be discussed shortly.

Some Tips Ron Piedrahita, vice president of production for Medialink, gives 10 ingredients for successful VNRs in an article written for *PR Tactics*:

- Newsworthiness.
- Tell a story.
- Use footage that is difficult for newsstations to obtain.
- Provide animation.
- Humanize with patients and consumers affected by the product.
- Incorporate industry leaders.
- Include research and statistics.

- Tie-in VNRs with current news.
- Reach out to Hispanic markets.
- Consider global interest.

Public Service Announcements

Television stations, like radio stations, use public service announcements on behalf of governmental agencies, community organizations, and charitable groups. In fact, a survey by News Broadcast Network found that the typical TV station runs an average of 137 PSAs per week as part of its commitment to public service. DWJ Television, another video producer, says 70 percent of television PSAs are used between the hours of 7 A.M. and 1:30 A.M., with about 40 percent of this number used between 6 P.M. and 12:30 A.M. See Figure 9.6 for an example of a standard television PSA.

Many of the guidelines for radio PSAs, which were discussed previously, apply to television PSAs. They must be short, to the point, and professionally produced. Television is different, however, in that both audio and visual elements must be present. Thus, the soundbites or actualities must have someone with not only a good voice but also an attractive appearance. Many times, television PSAs use a well-recognized celebrity or spokesperson.

On page 240, a radio PSA was given for the Social Anxiety Disorder Co-alition. For a television PSA, however, the group used entertainer Donny Osmond to deliver the message. Here is the text, produced by TVN, Inc., of New York:

> **Social Anxiety Disorder PSA: 30 Seconds**
> **Donny Osmond on camera:** A FEW YEARS AGO I COULDN'T HAVE WALKED ONTO THIS STAGE WITHOUT FEELING LIKE I WAS DYING INSIDE. THIS WASN'T ONLY A FEAR OF PERFORMING. CERTAIN SIMPLE ACTIVITIES, SUCH AS GOING TO THE MALL OR INTERACTING WITH STRANGERS WOULD PARALYZE ME WITH FEAR.
>
> I'M TALKING ABOUT A MEDICAL CONDITION CALLED SOCIAL ANXIETY DISORDER. WHEN THE FEAR OF BEING EMBARRASSED OR HUMILATED IN FRONT OF OTHER PEOPLE CONTROLS YOUR LIFE.
>
> OVER 10 MILLION PEOPLE HAVE THIS DISORDER. I GOT HELP. YOU CAN TOO.
>
> **Voice-Over Narrator** (Below information will be featured as a slate): IF YOU THINK YOU HAVE SOCIAL ANXIETY DISORDER CONTACT THE SOCIAL ANXIETY DISORDER COALITION.
>
> - A Public Service Message
> - Social Anxiety Disorder Coalition
> - 1-800-934-6276
> - www.allergictopeople.com
>
> (INSERT LOGOS AND/OR NAMES OF THE COALITION MEMBERS)

The Osmond PSA is known in the trade as the **talking head**. This means that the format is relatively simple; it involves just one person speaking to the camera.

Figure 9.6 Television PSAs Need a Visual Element
This example shows a simple 60-second television public service announcement (PSA) that includes one slide, or visual. These materials are often made available to TV stations to fill air time at the end of a local show and before the beginning of the next program. *(Courtesy of North American Precis Syndicate, which produced and distributed this PSA on behalf of Student Loan Funding Resources.)*

ON TAPE
TV TAKES

NORTH AMERICAN PRECIS SYNDICATE, INC.
350 Fifth Avenue • New York, NY 10118-0110 • (212) 867-9000

CALCULATING COLLEGE COSTS

While many Americans identify the first three months of the year as the time to file taxes, a growing number of parents and students consider it an even more critical time to handle other financial matters, like applying for financial aid to enter college in the fall.

Here's a tip from Student Loan Funding Resources, a national expert in student financial aid. The first step during this key time of year is to send in a free application for federal student aid.

To better assist those who have financial aid or student loan questions, leading companies like Student Loan Funding offer online tutorial services and live phone counseling free of charge. In addition, they provide information and applications for specific loan products.

For a free copy of Student Loan Funding's booklet called Student Financial Aid: A Primary Guide, which assists students in planning out their financial aid needs, call toll-free 1-8-7-7--4-7-7--7-5-3-7. Or visit w-w-w--dot--student-loan-funding--dot--com.

There are no other visual cues such as other scenes or action. A more sophisticated, and more complex, approach is to involve action and a number of scenes to give the PSA more movement and appeal.

When there are a number of elements, the script begins to look more like a page from the manuscript of a play. In film and video production, it is often called a **storyboard**. Its purpose is to provide dialog but also to describe the scenes and visual aspects so a camera crew knows the general outline. A good example of a storyboard is one created by writer Jeff Goldsmith for the American Cancer Society. He created a parody using the motif of a television game show primarily to reach teenagers about the dangers of smoking. Here is the storyboard:

Cancer Cash
SHOT 1: Medium shot of a group of smoking teens. They look at the camera as an overly enthusiastic announcer's voice speaks from off-screen.
ANNOUNCER: You love Brown Mountain cigarettes!
SHOT 2 and 2A: Quick pops of the 'guy' and 'gals' nodding and smiling to reveal their ugly yellowed teeth during narration.

Professional Tips

PSA Survey Gives Some Insights

WestGlen Communications conducted a survey of radio and television public affairs directors to find out what they wanted in a public service announcement (PSA). Here are some of the survey results:

- **Length**: Thirty seconds is the perfect length for TV, with 40 percent of the stations preferring them. Almost 75 percent of the radio stations prefer 30-second spots.

- **Format**: Practically all TV stations prefer "hard copy" tape because satellite equipment is often in use for news and other programming. Most want Beta or Beta SP format. More than 75 percent of the radio stations prefer a CD.

- **Chance of getting aired**: TV stations air about one-third of the spots they receive. Radio airs about 40 percent of the PSAs they receive.

- **Event-driven spots**: Do you have an upcoming event or special awareness day? Almost 50 percent of TV stations want PSA four weeks in advance. About 40 percent of radio stations say they can work with two weeks advance, but 50 percent prefer three or four weeks.

- **Local contact**: TV stations (65 percent) say it's irrelevant if the spot has a local number or a national, toll-free number. Radio stations (61 percent) say they prefer to use a local number.

- **Factors in air play**: Both TV and radio, with overwhelming majorities, say "relevance" is the most important factor, followed by familiarity with the organization. Less than 2 percent of the TV and radio stations say a celebrity spokesperson is a factor in air play.

- **Pet peeves**: For TV, it's the wrong format (39 percent) compared to too many follow-up calls (18 percent). Radio said receiving the PSA was the number one complaint (25 percent), followed by too many follow-up calls (20 percent).

- **TV issues**: Almost half of the TV stations like closed-caption captioning for PSAs. About 25 percent find storyboards very important.

- **Radio issues**: PSA usage occurs most in evening (35 percent) and overnight (31 percent) followed by mid-day (18 percent). Mornings are the least popular time (6 percent).

ANNOUNCER: And we love our customers!

(Cheesy 'game-show' styled music up full.)

SHOT 3: Close up on a pack of 'Brown Mountain' cigarettes.

ANNOUNCER: That's why we're giving you Cancer Cash!

(During this narration a hand yellowed by habitual smoking, has dug through the pack and taken out the dollar-like 'cancer cash' coupon.) FLASH TO:

SHOT 4: Medium shot of three showgirls next to a spinning coffin on a showroom styled set.

ANNOUNCER: You can exchange Cancer Cash for some of these free gifts.

SHOT 5: During the following narration the camera starts in close on a pair of hands holding a cigarette. Ash flies away as a football swishes into frame and is caught by the hands. Camera quickly zooms out into a topview to reveal a football player wearing a hard yellow-plastic (sportsman-like) 02 mask with matching tanks. He runs around during the narration.

ANNOUNCER: 500 coupons gets you this sporty oxygen mask! Built strong for a busy person just like you.

The football player gives a 'thumbs-up' to the camera) DISSOLVE TO

SHOT 6: Close-up of a beautiful sunset over the ocean. Camera pulls back to reveal a smiling bathing-suited model reclining in a sun chair. She's on her side facing the camera, with a cigarette in her hand and a tracheal-tube in her neck! The trach-tube leads to a ventilator, which stands next to an E.K.G. machine directly behind her.

ANNOUNCER: 4000 coupons gets you this beautiful lung ventilator with matching tracheal tube!

(Close up of her smiling at camera, her tracheal tube protruding from her neck.)

SHOT 7: Medium shot of a young chemo-patient sitting in a chair. A lit cigarette is in his hand. Cancer Cash falls through the frame.

ANNOUNCER: And, for a limited time, you can exchange Cancer Cash for a discount on chemotherapy!

(The kid inhales a cloud of smoke and, as he finishes this, he fades away. The American Cancer Society logo comes up full on the chair.)

ANNOUNCER: Smoking. Nobody's a winner.

(Fade to black)

The parody was a bit too controversial for some television stations. Several networks, including ABC, refused to run it. However, Tony Fox of Comedy Central thought it was perfect. He told *PRWeek,* "We look for PSA's that are relevant to our audience and have a lighthearted or funny approach. This fits both bills." See Figure 9.7 above for a video still of a Cancer Cash coupon.

Other PSAs, less controversial, often get considerable airtime. A series of PSAs on anxiety disorders, which was profiled in this chapter, got more than 100,000 air plays. A Salvation Army PSA series reached more than 43 million Americans.

Figure 9.7 Cancer Cash
This video still is from the public service announcement (PSA) by the American Cancer Society. The PSA was a parody on television game shows and designed to reach a youth audience.
(Courtesy of American Cancer Society.)

The National Organization on Fetal Alcohol Syndrome (NOFAS) reported a 400 percent increase in calls to their hotline in the 2–3 day period following a PSA featuring TV star Laura San Giacomo. Many PSAs also seem to stick in people's minds. "McGruff, the Crime Dog," is recognized by 98 percent of children between the ages of 6 and 12.

Satellite Media Tours

The television equivalent to the radio media tour (RMT) is the **satellite media tour (SMT)**. This is essentially a series of pre-booked, one-on-one interviews from a fixed location via satellite with a series of television journalists and, sometimes, talk show hosts.

The SMT concept started in the mid-1980s when companies began to put their CEOs in front of a television camera. The public relations staff would line up reporters in advance to interview the spokesperson via satellite feed during allotted timeframes and, in this way, television journalists across the country could interview them personally. For busy CEOs, the satellite was a time-efficient way of giving interviews. All they had to do was visit a corporate or commercial television studio near their office. See Figure 9.8 for an illustration of how a satellite media tour works.

Today, the SMT is a staple of public relations and the television industry. One-on-one interviews, as well as news conferences via satellite, are widely used. In fact, a survey by WestGlen Communications found that nearly 85 percent of the nation's television stations participate in satellite tours, including stations in the top 10 markets. Reporters, in general, like SMTs because they can ask their own questions and get an exclusive interview with a source anywhere in the

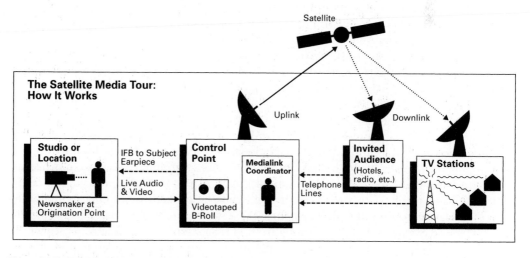

Figure 9.8 The Mechanics of an SMT
Satellite media tours are efficient and save traveling time. This illustration shows the mechanics of an SMT. The process is interactive because the spokesperson and the interviewer can talk as if they were in the same room.
(Copyright: Medialink, New York.)

world. This is in contrast to the VNR, which is a set piece much like an ordinary news release.

The easiest way to do an SMT is simply to make a spokesperson available for an interview. Celebrities are always popular, but an organization can also use articulate experts in its subject area. Essentially, the spokesperson sits in a chair or at a desk in front of a television camera. Viewers usually see the local news anchor asking questions and the spokesperson on a newsroom monitor, via satellite, answering them in much the same way that anchors talk with reporters at the scene of an event.

Basically, the format is two talking heads—the news anchor and the spokesperson. An example of such an SMT is when the "Melissa" virus hit computers. An Internet security company offered one of its computer experts via an SMT, and a number of news anchors around the country supplemented its news coverage by interviewing him via satellite. Good publicity for the company, and good information for the consumer.

Although **talking heads**, as they are known in the industry, are often used for SMTs, today's most successful SMTs are more interactive and dynamic. As Sally Jewett, president of On-The-Scene Productions, told *PRWeek,* "It's important to offer reporters something beyond the talking head, especially since competition is increasing as more firms realize the benefits of SMTs."

One approach is to integrate additional video into the SMT. As discussed in the section about VNRs, this is called **B-roll** material. Essentially, video footage of an event or activity is run while the spokesperson talks off-screen. For example, Abbott Labs hired Simon Productions to do an SMT on a new product for diabetics. While the spokesperson was talking about the new product, Simon showed people using it, being checked out by a doctor, and eating the "wrong" foods.

WestGlen Communications, in a survey of television news directors, found that almost 95 percent of the stations prefer B-roll footage to accompany the interview. "Stations like to put together a background piece to air prior to the interview," says Annette Minkalis, senior vice president of WestGlen's broadcast department. She adds, "Many stations prefer B-roll to be provided in hard copy three to four days in advance of the tour. Having footage in advance, as opposed to having it fed during the interview, gives stations time to prepare the story, especially in a live interview." At times, an SMT is also coordinated with the release of a VNR about the same topic.

Another popular approach to SMTs is to get out of the television studio and do them on location. When the National Pork Producers Council wanted to promote outdoor winter grilling, its public relations staff hired a team from Broadcast News Network to fire up an outdoor grill in Aspen, Colorado, and put a chef in a parka to give interviews, via satellite, while he cooked. In another example, the Hawaii Tourism Board targeted television stations in New England on a cold winter day with an SMT originating from Hawaii's sunny and attractive beaches.

Log Cabin Syrup, a division of Aurora Foods, opted for an even more remote locale to do an SMT. WestGlen Communications organized an SMT from the north rim of the Grand Canyon to show Log Cabin's sponsorship of a project called "Restoration of America's Log Cabins." The SMT, and a VNR, featured interviews with a restoration team that was restoring a 1930s log cabin. Of course,

PR Casebook

Satellite Media Tour Talks Turkey

How do you get media coverage for a new plastic wrapper product? One successful solution was a satellite media tour (SMT) originating from Berkeley Plantation, the site of the first official Thanksgiving in America.

Amann & Associates, a public relations firm in Virginia, came up with the idea to link the new wrapper with Thanksgiving. According to Elinor Mutascio, vice president, "the whole focus of the product is sandwiches, so we came up with the idea of using the wrappers for turkey leftover sandwiches."

That idea, in itself, was hardly newsworthy, so that's when the Berkeley Plantation was chosen as a site for an SMT. The spokesperson was Sissy Biggers from the TV Food Network, who would give interviews and conduct demonstrations. The SMT, which ran six hours, was done on November 19, and Biggers conducted 47 interviews with TV journalists across the country. They were made aware of the SMT through notifications that were accompanied by coolers filled with turkey sandwiches.

Reynolds, on the day of the SMT, got more than 3,000 calls to its product hotline and 10,000 hits on its Web site. Nothing like talking turkey.

the grandeur of the Grand Canyon also made the site attractive, despite the considerable logistical details of providing satellite links to the remote location. However, Michael Hill of News Broadcast Network told *O'Dwyer's PR Services Report,* "A remote location adds value to the story itself, and increases the likelihood—and quality—that the SMT will be picked up by the media."

Organizing an SMT from a remote location, however, does involve more planning. Here are some tips from various production companies:

- Do a site survey. Figure out the logistics for sound, lighting, telephones, and satellites.
- Make contingency arrangements in case of bad weather.
- Make sure your spokesperson is adaptable and prepared to answer all sorts of questions.
- Arrange for necessary permits and permissions if using public or private property.
- Make sure the location has some tie-in with your subject.
- Make certain that the location is free from general public access to avoid background distractions.
- Be conscious of other complications, such as noise from honking horns and even air traffic.

Another aspect to consider is whether the SMT has enough news value to justify its cost. In general, an SMT costs about $10,000 to $25,000 for a 21-city tour. If it is done outside a television studio, costs can rise substantially depending on the location and logistics involved. Given the cost, many organizations try to get

Professional Tips

Guidelines for a Successful SMT

Anecdotal evidence indicates that four out of five pitched Satellite Media Tours don't get aired. You can increase the odds if you follow these "do's" and "don'ts" compiled by *PRWeek*:

DO

- Include a relevant angle for the stations in every market you pitch.
- Use an interesting, visually appealing background or set. It often makes the difference between your SMT getting on the air or not.
- Get stations involved by sending them items that will help them perform and promote the interview.
- Respect producer's wishes when they tell you they will get back to you. Incessant follow-up will only annoy those who you are trying to convince.
- Localize your SMT. If local audiences aren't going to be interested, neither are the producers airing the story.
- Be clear in your pitch. Provide producers with the who, what, when, and why right away.
- Use credible, knowledgeable spokespersons who project confidence and are personable.

DON'T

- Let the SMT become a commercial. If producers think there is the possibility of too many product mentions, they won't book it.
- Be dishonest with producers about the contents of your SMT.
- Pitch your SMT to more than one producer at a station.
- Be conservative with amount of talent. A boring medical SMT will pack more punch if you present a patient along with the doctor.
- Surprise the producer. Newscasts are planned to the minute and unexpected events (spokesperson cancels) will not be appreciated.

maximum benefit by combining an SMT with audio news releases (ANRs) and video news releases (VNRs).

News Feeds   A variation on the SMT is a news feed that provides video and soundbites of an event to TV stations across the country via satellite. The news feed may be live from the actual event as it is taking place (real time), or it could be video shot at an event, edited, and then made available as a package.

In either case, the sponsoring organization hires a production firm to record the event. DWJ Television, for example, was hired by Christie's to cover the auction of 56 outfits worn by women at Academy Award ceremonies. DWJ engineers managed everything from setting up cameras and lighting to troubleshooting problems for crews during the auction.

The event, which benefited the American Foundation for AIDS Research, was made available in real time to television stations around the country and the world via satellite. Stations could air the whole auction, or simply make a video clip for use in later newscasts. Stations in nine of the top 10 markets used the news feed, which reached almost 12 million viewers.

An example of a packaged news feed is one done for Korbel Champagne Cellars to announce the three winners of its "perfect marriage proposal" contest. Edelman Worldwide, the public relations firm, worked with distributor WestGlen to offer TV stations video clips and soundbites showing the three winning proposals—which ranged from a proposal at a Broadway production to tuxedo-clad men skiing down a Colorado slope armed with roses and, of course, champagne. See Figure 9.9 for a copy of the news feed advisory sent to TV producers.

Figure 9.9 Satellite News Feed

Korbel Champagne Cellars, through WestGlen Communications, sent an advisory via fax and the Internet to let editors know about the availability of visuals regarding the finalists for the "perfect proposal" contest. B-roll and soundbites from the couples were made available so "clips" could be added to the nightly news. Please see previous chapters for illustrations of other Korbel publicity materials. *(Courtesy of Korbel Champagne Cellars and its public relations firm, Edelman Worldwide.)*

SATELLITE NEWS FEED

Wednesday, February 12, 2003 *(do we need to list other dates and times?)*
X:00 – X:15 p.m. ET

KORBEL'S PERFECT PROPOSAL CONTEST PROCLAIMS TOP THREE "MARRY ME" MOMENTS OF THE YEAR

THREE MEN POP "THE PERFECT PROPOSAL" –
ON STAGE WITH THE CAST OF BROADWAY'S AIDA; ON THE SLOPES
SURROUNDED BY TUXEDO-CLAD SKI INSTRUCTORS; FROM THE SKY ON
ROSE-COVERED LAKE

Just in time for Valentine's Day, Korbel Champagne is announcing the winners of its first-ever Perfect Proposal Contest by proclaiming this year's most unforgettable "marry me" moments. Three lucky winners were chosen from hundreds of entries to make their perfect proposals a reality, complete with a diamond ring:

- **Celebrity-Studded Proposal Onstage at Elton John and Tim Rice's Aida, New York, NY**
  Ashley Yablon, of **Dallas, TX,** truly stole the show, earning his own standing ovation as he popped the question onstage, with help from the cast of Broadway's AIDA. Prior to proposing, Yablon serenaded his intended in front of a live theater audience – the audience was so moved, they can be heard singing right along with him.

- **Tuxedo-Clad Ski Instructors Aid Ski Slope Proposal, Steamboat, CO**
  This inventive perfect proposal took place on a ski slope and enlisted a parade of tuxedo-clad, ski and snowboard instructors from the Steamboat Ski School. As Brad Moline, of **Fort Collins, CO,** snowboarded down the mountain with his girlfriend, the parade of instructors skied down the mountain in formation, carrying roses and champagne, and unveiled a massive 20 x 50 foot banner emblazoned with the words "Will you Marry Me?" to help this future groom pop the question.

- **Saying it with Roses Via Aerial Proposal, Minneapolis, MN**
  Drew Mitchell, a **Minnetonka, MN**, native and current resident of **White Plains, NY**, took his girlfriend sky-high in a chartered plane so she could see his perfect proposal from the air. Using 5 x 8-foot rose-covered lettering, Mitchell spelled out his intentions on frozen Bryant Lake in Minnesota, as family and friends waited to celebrate with the happy couple on the ground.

> **WHAT WE HAVE: B-roll** with **visuals** from each proposal, including cast of Aida onstage introducing groom-to-be, groom-to-be singing in front of live Broadway audience, tuxedo-clad Steamboat ski and snowboard instructors coming down the slopes in formation with roses and "Will You Marry Me?" sign, aerial shot of rose petals spelling "Will You Marry Me" on frozen lake as well as footage of each perspective groom popping the question. **Soundbites** from all the "Perfect Proposal" couples and reactions from the intendeds.

RECEIVE VIA SATELLITE: C-BAND

Wednesday, February 12   X:00– X:00 p.m.   Telstar X, Transponder X, D/L Freq. XXX (X)

FOR MORE INFORMATION OR TO RECEIVE A HARD COPY PLEASE CONTACT:

PERSONAL APPEARANCES AND PRODUCT PLACEMENTS

Radio and television stations, as well as cable systems, increasingly operate on round-the-clock schedules. They require a vast amount of programming to fill all the time available.

So far in this chapter we have concentrated on how to prepare and generate timely material for newscasts. Here we will present an overview of other placement opportunities in broadcasting, from getting people booked on talk shows to having a popular sitcom use your employer's or client's product on the show.

In these cases, your contact is no longer the news department but the directors and producers of various specialty features and shows. Your most valuable communication tools are the telephone and the persuasive pitch letter (see Chapter 8).

Before using either tool, however, it is necessary to do your homework. You must be familiar with a show's format and content, as well as the type of audience that it reaches. You can obtain this information in several ways.

One method is to study the station and descriptions of its shows in a broadcast directory. Directory listings can tell you program format, types of material used, and the name of the director or producer. Directories are discussed in the next chapter, but see Figure 9.10 for an example of a television station listing.

A second approach is to watch the program or feature and study the format. In the case of a talk or interview show, what is the style of the moderator or host? What kinds of topics are discussed? How important is the personality or prominence of the guest? How long is the show or a segment? Does the show lend itself to demonstrations and visual aids? The answers to such questions will help you tailor your phone calls and pitch letters to achieve maximum results.

Talk Shows

Radio and television talk shows have been a staple of broadcasting for many years. KABC in Los Angeles started the trend in 1960, when it became the first radio station in the country to convert to an all-news-and-talk format. Today, more than 1,110 radio stations have adopted the format. Other stations, of course, also include talk shows as part of their programming. In fact, it is estimated that there are now more than 4,000 radio talk shows in the United States.

The same growth rate applies to television. Seven years after KABC started the talk show format, Phil Donahue began his TV show. Today, there are more than 20 nationally syndicated talk shows and a countless number of locally produced shows. For the past decade, the number one syndicated daytime talk show has been the *Oprah Winfrey Show*, attracting about 8 million viewers on a daily basis. On the network level, three shows are the Holy Grail for publicists: NBC's *Today*, ABC's *Good Morning America*, and CBS's *Early Show*. Collectively, these three shows draw about 14 million viewers between 7 and 9 A.M. every weekday. As *PRWeek* says, "there's simply no better way to hit millions of consumers in one shot."

WWBT-TV, Channel 12

P.O. Box 12
Richmond, VA 23218-0012
5710 Midlothian Turnpike
Richmond, VA 23225-6120

(804) 230-1212
Fax: (804) 230-2793
News Phone: (804) 233-1212
News Fax: (804) 230-2789
Home Page: www.nbc12.com
Network: **NBC**

Owner: Jefferson Pilot Communications
Type of Video News Releases Used: Digital Video
General Management/News Executives:
General Manager . . . . John R. Shreves
Operations Manager . . . . Henry Boze
Program Director . . . . JoAnn Cardwell
News Director . . . . Nancy Kent
Assistant News Director . . . . Woody Coates
News Assignment Editor . . . . Craig Harrison
Public Service Director . . . . Treeda Smith
Advertising Sales Manager . . . . Ellen Shuler
Promotion Director . . . . Jo Ann Cardwell
Sports Director . . . . Ben Hamlin
Meteorologist . . . . Jim Duncan

Programs:

12 News at 11
Air Time: Mon-Fri, 11:00 PM
Profile: News/Weather/Sports
Anchor . . . . Gene Cox
Anchor . . . . Sabrina Squire
Producer . . . . J.W. Barnes
Sports Reporter . . . . Ben Hamlin
Meteorologist . . . . Jim Duncan

12 News at 6
Air Time: Mon-Fri, 6:00 PM
Profile: News/Weather/Sports
Anchor . . . . Gene Cox
Anchor . . . . Sabrina Squire
Producer . . . . Libby McDaniel
Sports Reporter . . . . Ben Hamlin
Meteorologist . . . . Jim Duncan

12 News at Noon
Air Time: Mon-Fri, 12:00 PM
Profile: News/Weather/Sports
Anchor . . . . Colleen Reilly
Guest Contact . . . . Laura Reed

12 News Today
Air Time: Mon-Fri, 5:35 AM
Profile: News/Weather/Sports
Anchor . . . . Mark Hubbard
Anchor . . . . Andrea McDaniel
Producer . . . . Brandon Richardson

First at Five
Air Time: Mon-Fri, 5:00 PM
Profile: News/Weather/Sports
Anchor . . . . Gene Lepley
Anchor . . . . Sabrina Squire
Producer . . . . Frank Jones

First News
Air Time: Mon-Fri, 5:30 PM
Profile: News/Weather/Sports
Anchor . . . . Gene Cox
Producer . . . . Holly Walker

Figure 9.10 Profile of a TV Station
Media directories are excellent sources to find the names of personnel in charge of various departments and programs. They also give information about the preferred format of VNRs and the focus of most programs. Personnel and format change often, so that's why most directories are published on an annual basis and have daily Web site updates.
(Courtesy of Bacon's Information, Inc.)

The advantage of talk shows is the opportunity to tell your views directly to the American public without the filter of journalists and editors interpreting and deciding what is newsworthy. Another advantage is the opportunity to be on the air for longer than the traditional 30-second soundbite in a news program.

You may never have the opportunity to book a guest on the *Today* show but you should be aware of such shows and their ability to reach large audiences. Talk shows and public affairs programs on local radio and television stations, as well as a proliferation of cable channels, provide excellent placement opportunities for organizational spokespersons talking on any number of topics.

Here are some questions you might ask when thinking about placement on a talk show:

- Is the topic newsworthy? Do you have a new angle on something in the news?

- Is the topic timely? Can you tie the idea to some lifestyle or cultural trend?

- Is the information useful to the viewers? How-to ideas may be welcomed.

- Does your spokesperson have viewer appeal? A celebrity may be acceptable, but there must be a logical tie-in to your organization and to the topic to be discussed. A professional athlete might be plausible talking about running shoes but out of place in a discussion about the economy.

- Can the spokesperson stay on track? It is easy for celebrities to get involved in discussions of their professional activities and personal lives.

- Can you keep the speaker from stressing the commercial angle? Most talk show hosts will allow a brief mention of a brand name or sponsor identifi-

PR Casebook

Networks Clamp Down on "Stealth" Guests

Actress Lauren Bacall, appearing on NBC's *Today* show, talked about a dear friend who had gone blind from an eye disease and urged the audience to see their doctors to be tested for it. She also mentioned a new drug, Visudyne, that was a new treatment for the disease.

Meanwhile, over at ABC's *Good Morning America* show, actress Kathleen Turner was telling Diane Sawyer about her battle with rheumatoid arthritis and mentioned that a drug, Enbrel, helped ease the pain. A month later, Olympic gold medal skater Peggy Fleming appeared on the show to talk about cholesterol and heart disease. Near the beginning of the interview, Fleming said, "My doctor has put me on Lipitor and my cholesterol has dropped considerably."

What the viewing audience didn't know was that each of these celebrities were being paid hefty fees by drug companies to mention their product in prime time. Indeed, even the talk show hosts apparently didn't know until *The New York Times* wrote an investigative piece on drug companies using "stealth marketing" tactics to get product mentions on regular news and talk shows.

As a result, CNN and other networks issued a new policy that viewers will be told about a celebrity's ties to corporations. A CNN spokesperson, quoted in *Jack O'Dwyer's PR Newsletter*, said "We decided it was important for our viewers to be aware of that as part of any future interviews or features about a celebrity."

Tim Bruno, a producer on the *Today* show, says publicists should "tell the truth." He adds, "Be sure to disclose if your client is a paid spokesperson for a product. . . ."

cation. If your speaker gets too commercial, the entire interview may be deleted—and your organization may land on the list of those who will not be invited back.

When you know the answers to these questions, you will be ready to look for a booking—or several. Here are some tips that should help:

- Be sure that your speaker fits the program. If he or she isn't a fast thinker, avoid shows full of rapid exchanges and loaded questions.
- Be sure that you know the requirements of the program and the abilities of your spokesperson.
- Plan to use visuals if possible. Charts, diagrams, samples, and videotapes may help the producer decide.
- Deal with only one person on the program. But you may certainly approach producers of other programs on the same station.
- Be careful about exclusivity. Some stations will refuse to book a guest who appears on a competing station. Find out before you commit. By committing to one station, you may miss an opportunity to get on others.
- Plan variations so that you can offer the same person to different shows or different stations without giving the same thing to each.
- Prepare your speaker.

After you have done your homework on the format of a radio or television talk show, contact the show's producer or associate producer. If it is a network or nationally syndicated show, the contact person may have the title of talent coordinator or talent executive. Whatever the title, these people are known in the broadcasting industry as **bookers** because they are responsible for booking a constant supply of timely guests for a show.

You can place a phone call briefly outlining the qualifications of your proposed speaker and why the person would be a timely guest, or you can write a one-page pitch letter (see Chapter 8) that convinces the producer to book the guest. In many cases, the booker will ask for videos clips of the spokesperson on previous TV shows, and even newspaper clips relating to past interviews. As mentioned previously, the more you know about the format and the audience of the show, the better you can tailor a persuasive pitch.

It is also important to be honest about the expertise and personality of your client. According to Marsha Friedman of Event Management Services in Clearwater, Florida, which specializes in booking guests, talk show producers often complain that guests often bear little resemblance to their publicist's pitch. And Barbara Hoffman, producer of *Doctor to Doctor,* told *O'Dwyer's PR Newsletter* that the best pitches come from publicists whose "clients are always exactly what they say they are, always prepared, interesting, on time, and always have something unusual or cutting edge to offer my program."

In general, talk shows book guests three to four weeks ahead of time. Unless a topic or a person is extremely timely or controversial, it is rare for a person to be booked on one or two days' notice. Keep this in mind as you plan talk show appearances as part of an overall public relations plan.

calendar" that would list upcoming plays, musicals, and art shows. By the same token, a rock music station might have a "concert calendar" that lists upcoming rock concerts.

You write a calendar announcement in much the same way as you write a radio news release. The announcement should be to the point. It should give the name of the event, the sponsoring organization, the date and time, location, cost, and a telephone number listeners can call for more information.

Here is an example of a typical announcement for a community calendar. Notice that phonetic spelling is given for some names to help the announcer.

- *10 seconds*: The Amadeus (ah-ma-day-us) Quartet will perform at Mills College on Sunday, May 11. Phone area code 510-793-7043.

- *20 seconds*: The Amadeus (ah-ma-day-us) Quartet will perform at the Mills College auditorium on Sunday, May 11, at 3:30 p.m. The program for this Chamber Music Concert will include compositions by Mozart, Britten, and Beethoven (bay-toe-ven). For information, phone area code 510-793-7043.

- *30 seconds*: The Amadeus (ah-ma-day-us) Quartet will perform at the Mills College auditorium on Sunday, May 11, at 3:30 p.m. In its thirty-fourth year with the same personnel, the Amadeus Quartet offers the widest active repertory among the world's string quartets. Their program for this Coleman Chamber Music Concert will include compositions by Mozart, Britten, and Beethoven (bay-toe-ven). For information, phone area code 510-793-7043.

Community calendar items should be sent to the station via mail or fax at least three weeks in advance.

Editorials

Many radio and television stations regularly broadcast editorials on topics of public interest. They are usually delivered by a representative of the station's management and aired as part of the news program. The editorial is clearly identified as a statement of opinion.

Statements of support, from either newspapers or broadcast stations, can be a valuable aid to your organization if the objective is to influence public opinion and generate community support. For example, you might propose an editorial against a new state tax on the grounds that it will discourage business development.

On a less controversial level, many stations are routinely asked to air editorials supporting the programs of community organizations. Thus the station encourages everyone to participate in the United Way campaign or give donations to the local food bank.

If you are seeking editorial endorsement from a station, write a persuasive letter to the general manager, outlining the reasons for your point of view and explaining why the station should do an editorial. A personal interview with the station manager, if possible, may also be beneficial.

By contrast, if the station airs an editorial that your organization disagrees with, it is appropriate to let the station know that you have a rebuttal. The station may offer you free-speech time or may include your comments in a future editorial.

Free-Speech Messages

Free-speech messages are guest editorials. They are expressions of opinion presented by an individual or a group on a topic of general public interest. The topic must be timely and relate to a contemporary issue. For example, an individual or a group may wish to record a free-speech message about the city council's lack of support for public libraries or make a statement about the necessity of passing legislation to provide universal health insurance.

There is no automatic right to deliver a free-speech message. The radio or television station reserves the right to review the message for libel or slander, as well as the choice of words. The station also decides when to air the message and how many times.

If you want to record a free-speech message, you usually contact the station's public service director. One approach is to write a letter outlining the topic and its importance to the station's audience. If your proposal is accepted, the next step is to record the message at the station or by telephone. Free-speech messages are usually short, ranging from 30 to 90 seconds.

Feature Films and Videos

Television stations and especially cable systems require a vast amount of programming to fill their schedules. Short features of two or three minutes and full-length productions that run 20 minutes or more are often used to fill gaps in the programming day.

Many of these **fillers** are produced and distributed by businesses, nonprofit organizations, trade associations, and professional groups. For maximum acceptability, they must be relatively free of commercial hype and must concentrate on informing or educating the viewing audience.

Some typical features available for use by television stations and cable systems are:

- *Waltzing Matilda*, a 32-minute travelog on Australia, sponsored by the Australian Tourist Commission
- *Rethinking Tomorrow*, a 28-minute report on energy conservation, sponsored by the U.S. Department of Energy
- *Oil over the Andes*, a 27-minute account of the building of an oil pipeline, sponsored by the Occidental Petroleum Company
- *Noah Was an Amateur*, a 27-minute history of boat building, sponsored by the National Association of Engine and Boat Manufacturers

Getting such films and videos distributed requires some method of informing the broadcast stations of their availability. You can handle this yourself by writing to media outlets and having them fill out an order card, but it is more efficient to use a distribution service. These organizations can distribute your materials by mail or satellite, depending on the preferences of the TV stations or cable systems that order them. In addition, these distribution services have an established program that can place your films and videos with schools, clubs, special-interest groups, and civic groups.

WEBCASTING

This chapter has emphasized radio and television, but it would be incomplete if the Internet was not mentioned as a major vehicle for distributing information and reaching millions of people. Indeed, it is now possible for journalists and the public to access audio news releases (ANRs), video news releases (VNRs), satellite media tours (SMTs), and online news conferences via their computers.

One important development has been the advent of Web-based news sites. There are now more than 6,000 news sites, and the number grows each day. In addition, WestGlen communications says "more than 50 percent of the 110 million users of the Internet in the United States use this medium as a source of news and information."

MSNBC.com, for example, reaches 4 million viewers a day, which few daily newspapers in the United States can match. Dean Wright, editor-in-chief of MSNBC.com, told *Jack O'Dwyer's Newsletter*, "No one would seriously suggest that the daily newspaper is irrelevant. But the Web is something that can't be ignored. The message I have for PR pros is, if you want to reach out to a highly desirable demographic—people at work—then you must include the Web in your plans."

Elizabeth Shepard, editor-in-chief of Epicurious.com and Concierge.com, agrees. She says Epicurious, the longest running and largest food site on the Internet, gets 20 million page views per month. She told *Jack O'Dwyer's Newsletter*, "People contact me about new restaurant openings or special tasting menus, new wines that are launching in the U.S., or special distribution of wines in certain areas." Needless to say, if your client or company is in the food or wine business, Shepard should be on your list to receive publicity materials.

Many news Web sites, of course, are extensions of a particular newspaper, magazine, radio or television station, or even a television network. That means that the materials used in these traditional mediums may also wind up on their Web sites. Articles from *Gourmet*, *Bon Appetit*, and *Parade*, for example, can be found on Epicurous.com, but most of these sites also have editors who are looking for original material. This means that you should also pitch to news Web sites in the much the same manner that you would for traditional media (see Chapter 8).

Organizational Web Sites

In previous chapters, we said that it is common for news releases, graphics, and even video clips to be posted on an organization's Web site. Such materials enable journalists to download the material and the public to access the material. Now, most organizations also are posting SMTs, news feeds, and online news conferences on the Internet to reach an ever-expanding audience through continuous audio and video.

According to Medialink, the process for converting audio and video news releases into an Internet format is a relatively easy process. The steps are as follows:

1. Your printed news release or media advisory is converted to HTML format, the standard language of the Internet.
2. Your video or audio is digitally encoded from the original video. Beta format is better than VHS, cassette, or CD.
3. The elements are posted on a dedicated Web page, with headlines supporting the text and graphic images.
4. Hyperlinks from this page, and your company or client home page, help direct visitors to the site.

Webcasts can also used for live events such as news conferences and new product introductions that are made available in real time to online journalists, consumers, employees, or other key audiences.

Marc Wein, president of Murray Hill Studios in New York, told *PR Tactics* that any media relations tool that makes it easier for reporters to cover an event will likely generate wider press coverage. He added: "We did one press conference where almost nobody showed up; we did a live stream onto the Web and we had dozens of reporters watching it."

Six Flags Magic Mountain in Valencia, California, for example, produced a VNR about a new ride, but it also digitized the video B-roll of the actual ride and distributed it via a Web site. Visitors to the site could experience the ride from their own PC screen in full motion and full sound.

In another application, Orbis Broadcast Group produced a health-care VNR for television stations, but also included information on how viewers could find additional information at a Web site. When viewers went to the site, they were able to take part in chat sessions with physicians, attend virtual press events, and find other consumer-friendly health information provided by leading health-care organizations. Indeed, one advantage of the Internet is the opportunity for consumers to get more information about a product and even engage in interactive discussion with company representatives about it.

Sometimes a Webcast is done in conjunction with a telephone conference call. XM Satellite Radio, for example, sent out a media advisory about a conference call to announce and discuss its third quarter financial results. The company provided a call-in telephone number, but also stated, "The conference call can also be accessed via a live Webcast on the company's Web site, located at www.exradio.com. The Webcast will be archived on the company's Web site." In other words, journalist were given three options to get the information: telephone conference call, Webcast in real time, or the archive on the Web site if they want to review it later. See Figure 9.11 for a sample of a Webcast media alert.

PR Newswire
United Business Media

Close Window

Jul 28, 2003 16:38 ET

Webcast Alert: The Reader's Digest Association Announces RDA Q4 2003 Financial Release Conference Call Webcast

PLEASANTVILLE, N.Y., July 28 /PRNewswire-FirstCall/ – Readers Digest Association (NYSE:RDA) announces the following Webcast:

What: RDA Q4 2003 Financial Release Conference Call

When: 07/30/03 @ 8:30 a.m. Eastern

Where: http://www.firstcallevents.com/service/ajwz386584443gf12.html

How: Live over the Internet -- Simply log on to the web at the
           address above.

Contact: William Adler
           Director, Corporate Communications
           914-244-7585
           william.adler@readersdigest.com

If you are unable to participate during the live webcast, the call will be archived at http://www.rd.com/.

The Reader's Digest Association, Inc. is a global publisher and direct marketer of products that inform, enrich, entertain and inspire people of all ages and all cultures around the world. Worldwide revenues were $2.4 billion for the fiscal year ended June 30, 2002. Global headquarters are located at Pleasantville, New York.

(Minimum Requirements to listen to broadcast: The Windows Media Player software, downloadable free from http://www.microsoft.com/windows/windowsmedia/EN/default.asp and at least a 28.8 kbps connection to the Internet. If you experience problems listening to the broadcast, send an email to webcastsupport@tfprn.com, and The Real Player software, downloadable free from http://www.real.com/realone/index.html?lang=en&loc=us)

Audio: http://www.firstcallevents.com/service/ajwz386584443gf12.html

Source: Reader's Digest Association, Inc.

CONTACT: William Adler, Director, Corporate Communications, The Reader's Digest Association, Inc., +1-914-244-7585, william.adler@readersdigest.com

Web site: http://www.rd.com/

Close Window

http://media.prnewswire.com/en/jsp/includes/contents/printable.jsp?resourceid=2501119   7/28/2003

Figure 9.11 Webcast Alert
Reporters and editors are regularly informed via fax and the Internet about opportunities to sit in on live Webcasts so they don't even have to leave their offices for a news conference.
(Courtesy of Reader's Digest Association and its distributor, PR Newswire.)

SUMMARY

- The broadcast media are important channels of communication, but using them requires thinking in terms of sound and visual elements.

- Radio releases are similar to press releases, but they require more concise writing and a conversational tone.

- Audio news releases (ANRs) are more effective than written releases because they are formatted for immediate use.

- Public service announcements (PSAs) are short broadcast announcements used by nonprofit groups and public agencies.

- Radio media tours (RMTs) are a cost-effective way to reach many stations with exclusive interview over a wide geographic area.

- Television is an excellent medium of communication because it combines the elements of sight, sound, motion, and color.

- Television news releases must contain both sound and visual elements such as graphics, slides, or videotape. A TV release can consist of a written script plus the accompanying graphics, but it will be more acceptable if it is on videotape.

- Video news releases (VNRs) are now standard in the industry and are widely used by TV stations and cable systems.

- VNRs require professional preparation and high technical quality. To be used, they must be newsworthy and timely. Satellite distribution is the most cost-effective method.

- Satellite media tours (SMTs) are widely used in the broadcast industry. A popular format is setting up interviews from a location that reinforces the story.

- A good, persuasive query or pitch letter is used to get placements on news programs and talk shows.

- Talk shows offer numerous opportunities for reaching mass and specialized audiences.

- Organizations and groups can get exposure by making use of community calendars, free-speech messages, radio promotions, and creative publicity ideas.

- The Internet will play an increasingly important role in the distribution of electronic materials to journalists and the public. Online news conferences, for example, are already standard.

ADDITIONAL RESOURCES

Calabro, Sara. "How Planning Can Add Value to a VNR." *PRWeek*, October 7, 2002, p. 18.

Calabro, Sara. "Choosing the Right Vendor for Your VNR." *PRWeek*, July 29, 2002, p. 36.

Calabro, Sara. "Channel Vision: What TV Stations Want." *PRWeek*, June 24, 2002, p. 34.

Calabro, Sara. "Getting a Hit on the Radio." *PRWeek*, June 17, 2002, p. 18.

Chabria, Anita. "For $200, How Do You Get a Product on a Game Show?" *PRWeek*, October 21, 2002, p. 20.

Chabria, Anita. "Cingular Climbs High on *Spider-Man's* Back." *PRWeek*, July 22, 2002, p. 19.

Chabria, Anita. "PR Firms Vie for Hollywood Product Placement Power." *PRWeek*, May 13, 2002, p. 9.

Chabria, Anita. "Getting a Product in Front of the Cameras." *PRWeek*, May 6, 2002, p. 18.

Chabria, Anita. "Winning over Radio Stations." *PRWeek*, April 8, 2002, p. 18.

Dembo, Mark. "Don't Let Broadband Leave You Behind: Keeping up With High-Speed Technology." *PR Tactics*, June 2003, p. 20.

Eisenstadt, David. "How to Make Video News Releases Work." *Public Relations Quarterly*, Winter 2002, pp. 24–25.

Fowler, Geoffrey A. "Hollywood Ending: Stapler Becomes a Star." *The Wall Street Journal*, July 2, 2002, pp. B1, B4.

Gaschen, Dennis J. "What TV Stations Really Think About VNRs." *PR Tactics*, June 2001, p. 10.

Griffo, Paul. "The Top Five VNR Myths." *PR Tactics*, June 2001, p. 18.

Hazley, Greg. "Broadcast PR Divided over Digital's Arrival." *O'Dwyer's PR Services Report*, April 2003, pp. 10, 14.

Hill, Bob. "A Guided Tour: Tips for SMT Spokespeople." *PR Tactics*, July 2003, pp. 15, 17.

Lewis, Lidj. "Capturing Premium Airtime: PSAs Can Score if Done Right." *O'Dwyer's PR Services Report*, April 2002, p. 8, 14.

Londner, Robin. "Action Stations: Getting SMTs on the Air." *PRWeek*, February 4, 2002, p. 18.

Marshall, Norm. "Brands on the Movie Screen." *IPRA Frontline*, June 2002, p. 9.

Petersen, Melody. "Heartfelt Advice, Hefty Fees: Companies Pay Stars to Mention Prescription Drugs." *The New York Times*, August 11, 2002, pp. C1, C14.

Purushothaman, Shoba. "Resuscitate Your VNR Using B-roll." *PR Tactics*, June 2003, p. 26.

Quenqua, Douglas. "Production, Subject, Audience: Getting a PSA on Air." *PRWeek*, March 3, 2003, p. 18.

Quenqua, Douglas. "When Bush Lobbies Barlett: How Issues Get Written into Prime-time TV Scripts." *PRWeek*, May 20, 2002, p. 15.

Rafe, Stephen C. "Being Assertive: Handling the Hot Questioner During Interviews." *PR Tactics*, December 1999, p. 17.

Sweeney, Katie. "What's Next for VNRs? The War Is Over, But Stations Are Still Choosy about What to Air." *PR Tactics*, June 2003, p. 19.

Shortman, Melanie. "Get on a Morning Show, and You'll Rise and Shine." *PRWeek*, February 17, 2003, p. 18.

Trammell, Jack. "Five Rules for Television and Radio Placements." *PR Tactics*, June 2003, p. 21.

Walker, Jerry. "Ten Tips for Making a Good Impression in a TV Interview." *O'Dwyer's PR Services Report*, July 2003, p. 32.

Walker, Jerry. "Getting a Story through a Busy TV Newsroom." *O'Dwyer's PR Services Report*, May 2003, pp. 31, 33.

Walker, Jerry. "Entertainment Shows Make Pitch for Exclusives." *O'Dwyer's PR Services Report*, March 2003, pp. 32–33.

Chapter 10

Distribution: Snail Mail to the Internet

An important part of any publicity effort is the distribution of information to the appropriate media and audiences.

The first part of this chapter explains the format and content of media directories, which are available in print, CD, and online versions. They provide the foundation for the compilation of any media list, and they must constantly be revised to provide up-to-date information. Tip sheets and editorial calendars are also valuable adjuncts to media directories because they provide information on personnel changes in the media and what kinds of information editors are currently seeking.

Many distribution methods are available. Regular mail and fax, despite the advent of newer technologies such as the

Internet, are still alive and well. They are, however, supplemented by such methods as electronic wire services, feature placement firms, CD-ROM, e-mail, and the Web.

The Web, in particular, is perceived as the ultimate distribution channel. It is forecast that nearly 1 billion people, or about 15 percent of the world's population, will be using the Internet by 2005. Despite this impressive figure, the traditional media—radio, television, newspapers, and magazines—continue to be a significant force.

Each method has its advantages and disadvantages, and this chapter will help you to select the distribution channels that are most appropriate for your message.

FINDING THE MEDIA

Previous chapters emphasized that an essential part of public relations writing is making sure that the right media—and the right audience—receive your material.

Indeed, a common complaint of editors is that they receive reams of news releases that are not relevant to their publication or their audience. A second major complaint is that news releases are often sent to the wrong person. Compounding this problem is the estimate that nearly one-third of all journalists change their job or beat every 90 days.

So how do you find the right medium and the correct, current contact person? How do you reach every daily newspaper real estate editor in the nation? How do you contact every Spanish-speaking radio station in Texas? How do you know what specialized trade publications would be interested in your company's new product?

Finding media, their addresses, and the names of editors would be nearly impossible if not for the existence of media directories in print and electronic form.

Media Directories

Directories vary in format and scope. However, a common denominator is that they usually give such essential information as (1) names of publications and broadcast stations, (2) mailing addresses, (3) telephone and fax numbers, (4) e-mail addresses, and (5) names of key editors and reporters. Many directories also give a profile of the media outlet in terms of audience, deadlines, and placement opportunities.

Bacon's Information, Inc. publishes a comprehensive 10-volume set of directories, which is available in print and through its MediaSource online service. Its four core directories are *Newspaper/Magazine, Radio/TV/Cable, Media Calendar,* and *Internet Media.* Specialty directories are *Computer and Hi-Tech, Medical & Health, Business Media, New York Publicity Outlets, International Media,* and *Bacon's Directories QuickSearch,* which is only available online.

Bacon's says that all of its directories combined feature nearly 80,000 media outlets, cover more than 600,000 beats, and include more than 120,000 profiles of journalists.

Other major directories include Burrelle's, which has an online database that includes contacts at daily newspapers, magazines, radio, nondaily newspapers, and television and cable. See Figure 10.1 for a screen shot showing how the database is organized. MediaMap also has a comprehensive online database that claims to include 175,000 journalist contacts at 45,000 print, broadcast, and online media outlets.

Although print and CD directories are still popular for quick reference (see Figure 10.2), online databases have the advantage of always being up-to-date with the latest information because they are updated on an almost daily basis. A Bacon's promotional letter, for example, claims that its staff makes about 4,500 updates on a daily basis. In one year alone, the company advertises that it made more than 1 million updates to its database, which is the sales reason you need to purchase a new directory every year.

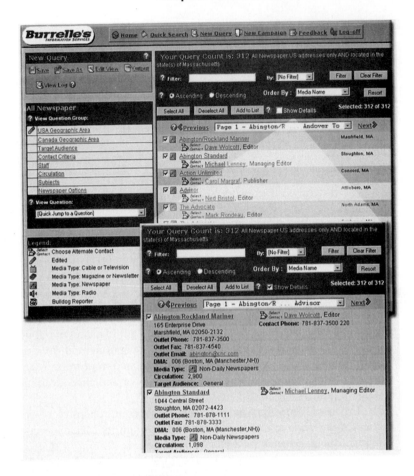

Figure 10.1 Media Directories Online
Burrelle's, which also offers media monitoring services, has an online database that allows public relations writers to find basic information about newspapers, magazines, radio, television, and cable outlets. One major advantage of online databases is up-to-date information and the ability to build a media list for your specific needs.
(Courtesy of Burrelle's Information Services.)

Media directories have been compiled for particular cities or metropolitan areas, ethnic media, and even international media. Bacon's has its *New York Publicity Outlets*, and the *Hispanic Media and Markets Directory* is also available. On the international level, there are directories such as *Benn's Media Directory* and *Ulrich's International Directory*.

Software programs and online databases allow you to rapidly compile a tailored media list for your messages, print out mailing labels, or even e-mail or fax your news release directly to a journalist. For example, if you need a list of business editors in four markets at dailies with a circulation above 50,000, you can

The Wall Street Journal Radio Network
PO Box 300
Princeton, NJ 08543-0300
4300 Route 1 & Ridge Road Bldg 1
South Brunswick, NJ 08852

(609) 520-4000
Fax: (609) 520-4044
News Phone: (609) 520-4100

E-Mail: wsjradio@dowjones.com
Home Page: www.wsjradio.com

Profile: Network providing hourly business and financial news reports transmitted live via satellite 24 times daily from the Wall Street Journal's newsroom. Also airs regular programming spotlighting money news and consumer trends, in addition to a show dealing with the problems associated with balancing work and family. Additionally, the network provides business news script services with the aid of the vast resources of the Dow Jones Co.

Management/News Executives:
Broadcast Services Executive
Director . . . . Paul Bell (212) 597-5606
Fax: (212) 597-5756
paul.bell@dowjones.com
Mailing Address: 1155 Avenue Of The Americas Fl 8
New York, NY 10036-2711

News
Managing Editor . . . . Patrice Sikora (609) 520-4477
patrice.sikora@dowjones.com
Contact Notes: *Preferred order:* E-Mail, Fax. As the Managing Editor, Sikora gathers information on Stocks, Business, Personal Finance, Consumer news and Economic news and updates. Topics of interest include the regional Economy and breaking Technology. Send press releases and information via e-mail or fax. With all other inquires she can be contacted via phone.
Editor . . . . Pat O'Neill (609) 520-4356
pat.oneill@dowjones.com
Contact Notes: Mon-Fri, *Preferred order:* Phone, Fax. Serves as Afternoon Newsroom Editor. Do not include him on your mass mailing list. Instead, phone during business hours keeping in mind to time your call for off-air time.
Editor . . . . Ian MacLeod (609) 520-4000
ian.macleod@dowjones.com
Contact Notes: Mon-Fri, *Preferred order:* E-Mail, Fax. As a News Editor of the network in New Jersey, MacLeod is the main contact for breaking news concerning Business, Consumerism and Workplace issues. He is interested in receiving information concerning different areas of Business such as Accounting, Corporate Finance, Economic Developments, Management Issues, International and Domestic Trade, Investments, Electronic Commerce, Computer News and coverage, Mergers and Acquisitions and Entrepreneurism. Send press releases via e-mail or fax and questions to his e-mail address.
Editor . . . . Jeff Bellinger (609) 520-4389
jeff.bellinger@dowjones.com
Contact Notes: *Preferred order:* E-Mail. As Morning News Editor for the network in New Jersey, Bellinger is the main contact for breaking news concerning Business, Consumerism and Workplace issues. He is interested in receiving information concerning different areas of Business such as Accounting, Corporate finance, Economic developments, Management issues, International and Domestic trade, Investments, Minority and woman based Businesses, Electronic commerce, Computer news and coverage, Mergers and acquistions and Entrepreneurism. Send all press releases and questions via e-mail.

Figure 10.2 Profiles and Contact Notes Are Important
A comprehensive media directory does more than just give you the name and address of a publication or a broadcast service. It also provides a thumbnail sketch of the publication or program. In addition, you can get the names, telephone numbers, and e-mail addresses of key news personnel and their particular interests.
(Courtesy of Bacon's Information, Inc.)

compile it with a few keystrokes on your computer. With a few more keystrokes, you can print out the entire list on mailing labels or send the news release to Bacon's or Burrelle's via e-mail for distribution to selected media.

Maintaining up-to-date media lists is a mundane and tedious job, but the computer has considerably improved the process. Many organizations use the commercial databases just described, but a number also maintain their own media lists using such programs as *Professional File* for PCs and, for Apple, *dBase Mac* or *File Maker.*

The concept of distribution codes, or various media lists, is important. An organization, for example, may set up several mailing lists. List One may include only local media in the organization's headquarters city. List Two might include local media in cities where the organization has manufacturing plants. List Three might include statewide media. List Four might include regional and national media. List Five might include trade and business media covering your industry.

After writing a news release, a public relations writer fills out a distribution form that indicates which media should receive the news release. If the story has only local significance, you would check "List One" so the mail room will know what mailing labels to use. In small organizations, you might even print off the address labels on your own computer.

A note of caution: Once compiled, media lists must be constantly updated. If you're using a print directory or CD-ROM version, remember that last year's edition is obsolete. That's why organizations buy new editions every year or subscribe to regular updates of basic databases.

Many professional publicists, in order to ensure total accuracy, also take the time to call the media outlet and double-check an editor's name before sending out an important news release. Bill Clapper, a public relations practitioner, posted a note on PRFORUM that sums up the problem. He wrote, "I think we buy fancy software that can sort, slice, and dice all the media in the galaxy. But it doesn't guarantee that my press release will get to the right person in a timely manner. Only way to do that is to call and find out who the business editor is today."

If you have compiled your own media list, you also must constantly and regularly update its accuracy. Whenever and however you learn of a change, correct your mailing list immediately. Nothing annoys an editor or reporter more than a useless news release, but a close second is a release sent to someone who hasn't been around for months—or years.

Some public relations people try to solve this problem by addressing envelopes to titles instead of people. For example, a news release will be sent to the "news editor" or the "features editor" of a publication. Although this seems a logical approach, recipients react much as they do to junk mail addressed to "occupant."

Editorial Calendars

Not only do media directories help you find the names and addresses of media gatekeepers, several of them also tell you when to approach publications with specific kinds of stories.

Trade publications and business periodicals, in particular, tend to operate on what is known as an **editorial calendar**. That means that certain issues have a special editorial focus. Special issues are used to attract advertising, but news stories and features on the subject are also needed.

For example, a high-technology magazine may have a special issue on laptop computers planned for April. Companies who manufacture laptop computers will no doubt want to advertise in that issue. If you're in the public relations or marketing communications department of the company, this special issue should also alert you that the publication is also open to news and feature stories about laptop computers.

Indeed, one of your major duties for a client or an employer is to review the editorial calendars of various publications to determine stories and features that might be submitted to coincide with the editorial focus of a particular issue. It also pays to check your local daily to get a list of special supplements planned for the year. Doing this sort of homework will dramatically increase your story placements.

Periodicals often set their editorial calendars a year in advance, and many keep the same special-issue calendars from one year to the next. Several media directories provide the editorial calendars of publications, including Bacon's and MediaMap.

Tip Sheets

Another good way to find media personnel who might have an interest in your material is **tip sheets**. These are weekly newsletters that report on recent changes in news personnel and their new assignments, how to contact them, and what kinds of material they are looking for. Some even tell you how to pronounce people's names.

Public relations newsletters such as *Bulldog Reporter*, *Jack O'Dwyer's Newsletter*, *Ragan's Media Relations Report*, *PRWeek*, and *PartyLine* provide regular tips as part of their content. Here's a sample from *Bulldog Reporter*:

> Ms. Nancy Cooper
> *Newsweek*
> Senior Editor
> (212) 445-4355
> nancy.cooper@newsweek.com
>
> Cooper oversees *Periscope*, a front-of-the-book section, which features brief reports and news. She wants to know about national trends, breaking news, and people to "watch." In particular, tell her about medical breakthroughs, crime, politics, new products, books, film, and the arts. If including photos in your release, make sure they're in color. Send all materials via e-mail.

Bulldog Reporter also publishes a *National PR Pitch Book* that profiles about 35,000 journalists and their publications. It gives names of publications or broadcast outlets, complete staff listings, gender identification, direct phone and e-mail addresses, and even tips from the journalists themselves on how to pitch them. Here is an excerpt on a profile of an editor from *The Wall Street Journal*:

> When calling Ms. Levy, ask her if she is on deadline first, and respect her request to contact her later. Pet peeves include misspelling her name. E-mail is the preferred method for all pitches.

Armed with this kind of information, a public relations professional considerably increases the odds of getting a media placement. Tip sheets allow you to use the rifle approach, instead of shotgunning material all over the country in the hope that some editor, somewhere, is interested in your material.

DISTRIBUTION OF MATERIALS

The vast majority of publicity materials have traditionally been distributed through four methods: (1) mail, (2) fax, (3) electronic wire services, and (4) feature placement firms. All four are still being used today, but distribution has also been revolutionized by the CD, e-mail, and the World Wide Web. This section discusses each distribution channel from the standpoint of its advantages and disadvantages, starting first with the oldest distribution channel (regular mail) and moving up to instant global communication via the Web.

Mail

A widely used distribution method, even in the Internet age, is still regular mail. It is often referred to as **snail mail** by dedicated users of the Internet, but newsrooms still receive thousands of news releases and media kits via this method every day. It is delivered by the U.S. Postal Service or by private companies such as Federal Express, Airborne Express, and DHL Worldwide.

In fact, some surveys indicate that journalists still prefer to receive information on paper. One study, by Jim Rink of *PRBytes* (online newsletter), surveyed 250 journalists from a cross-section of print and broadcast outlets and found that 80 percent of the respondents ranked mail number one in terms of preference for unsolicited PR materials, even if it was time sensitive. In second place was fax, followed by e-mail in third place. Another survey, by Bennett & Company, found that 82 percent of the respondents said mail was still acceptable to them; 27 percent even said they preferred it over e-mail.

Although other studies show that journalists distinctly prefer e-mail over a large margin (see section on e-mail), the survey data cited above seems to indicate some second thoughts. As one survey respondent noted, "E-mail isn't as good as it was. Haven't you heard? SPAM is driving us crazy just like you." Another one wrote, "After 9/11, all I wanted was e-mail. Now, I want only fax. I get hundreds of e-mails weekly and I seldom read any but those from people I know."

Most organizations and public relations firms continue to mail print media kits even when they have companion electronic versions. Daniel Cantelmo, writing in *Public Relations Quarterly*, says there are some good reasons for this. He quotes, for example, one senior editor for a high-technology magazine who said, "In 5 or10 minutes I can go through 25 printed press kits . . . and pick out exactly what I need. If I had to go through 25 CDs or online press kits, it would take hours. I don't have the time."

In sum, the U.S. Postal Service continues to be a cost-effective method for distributing news releases, media kits, fact sheets, position papers, and other background materials. However, they must always be sent first class mail or by overnight express. It is never acceptable to send materials by second- or third-class mail.

Many organizations also use services such as Federal Express on a routine basis to mail everything from letters to packages. Overnight delivery is usually guaranteed, and these services are quite adequate for sending materials on a regional, national, or even international level. Another advantage is sophisticated tracking so you know exactly when a package was delivered.

Some publicists think that delivery by overnight service increases an editor's perception of the material's importance and newsworthiness, but the widespread use of these services has pretty much eliminated any feeling that the material is special or urgent. In fact, most editors say they treat such envelopes just like any other mail that is delivered to their desks from the mail room.

Mailing can be done by the organization. All you need is a good address list, properly prepared labels, and a postage meter. If you mail in the morning, chances are good that media in the area will receive the material the next working day. Letters sent nationally are received in two or three days. However, if you are mailing materials to international media, you will be better off using another channel of distribution such as fax, electronic wire services, or e-mail. These will be discussed shortly.

Another approach to mailing is to use a distribution firm, also called a **mailing house**. A number of firms serve the public relations industry, including Media Distribution Services (MDS) and Bacon's, which were discussed in the last section. MDS (www.mdsconnect.com), for example, has centers in 10 U.S. cities and offers full-service printing, production, and mailing of everything from news releases to media kits, newsletters, and brochures.

Fax

Sending timely news releases and media advisories by facsimile transmission is often done. A **fax** is as quick as a telephone call and has the advantage of providing information in written and graphic form.

Ideally, the fax is used only if there is a late-breaking news development or you are sending a media advisory about an upcoming event. The reality is that modern technology has made it possible to send faxes to every media outlet in the country within minutes. One fax distribution service, for example, claims that it can transmit information over as many as 1,000 phone lines simultaneously.

This is called **broadcast fax** or **bulk fax**. Political candidates, for example, use bulk fax extensively to let media editors know their latest statements on the economy, health care, and a host of other public issues. They also used bulk fax to provide media alerts about upcoming speeches, rallies, and public appearances.

Sending bulk faxes, however, is not popular with editors. In fact, many newspapers actively discourage faxes of routine news releases and even change their fax numbers on a regular basis to avoid reams of "junk" faxes—which are like "junk" mail. Another approach tried by more than one daily is to have 900 numbers so the publicists are charged for sending unsolicited faxes.

But the problem still remains. George Condon, Washington bureau chief for Copley News Service, told *Jack O'Dwyer's PR Services Report* that "Junk faxes are one of our biggest problems. There is nothing more annoying to me than having those faxes clog up our machines."

The opposite of sending bulk faxes is **fax on demand** (FOD). In this situation, a reporter can call an 800 number and, through a series of custom-designed prompts, ask for various organizational materials to be sent by fax. This service helps reporters on deadline if they can't reach an organizational spokesperson.

Kmart Corporation is a good example. It provides a toll-free access number to reporters who regularly cover the organization. By dialing certain extensions, reporters can automatically have the material immediately sent to the newsroom by fax. Also available are executive biographies, information about earnings, fact sheets, and position papers. Such materials can also be downloaded from a Web site, which will be discussed shortly.

Fax material only if the medium specifically requests it or gives permission in advance. Check with your regular media contacts to ascertain whether they want material sent by this method and under what circumstances.

Professional Tips

Selecting a Distribution Channel

This chapter gives a number of channels for the distribution of media materials. That still leaves the question, "What channel should I use for my material?" The answer is not simple. It depends on the purpose and objectives of your message—and who you want to reach with it. Here are some general tips.

- **Mail:** A common method for distribution of routine materials to local and regional media. Mailing houses are effective for mailing media kits on a regional or national basis.

- **Fax:** Good for sending media advisories and alerts, late-breaking important news. Not recommended for mass distribution of news releases.

- **Electronic wire services:** Best for distribution of financial news to large newspapers and major broadcast outlets on a national or international basis where immediate disclosure is needed. National announcements of major new products can also be sent via electronic news wires.

- **Feature placement firms:** Good for reaching suburban newspapers and small weeklies. Best for feature-type material, when you want to create awareness and visibility for a product or organization.

- **CD-ROMs:** Best used for background material, such as corporate profiles, executive bios, and product information sheets. Increasingly being used in place of printed media kits.

- **E-mail:** Good for suggesting story ideas to journalists and editors, answering media questions and queries, and sending news releases—but only if the journalist prefers or requests it.

- **Web sites:** A place to post news releases and background material for possible reference by reporters and the public.

- **Usenet:** A good place to post messages and engage in dialogue with the public and media personnel. Not recommended for posting news releases or other press materials.

- **Listserv:** An ideal way to reach journalists who cover specific topics and beats. News releases are automatically e-mailed to "subscribing" journalists who have requested to be on your Listserv.

Electronic Wire Services

Although mail and fax distribution will be with us for the foreseeable future, many organizations now use electronic news release distribution. This is particularly true for corporate and financial news that require, according to Securities and Exchange Commission (SEC) regulations, immediate timely disclosure to media over a wide geographic area.

The two major newswires are *Business Wire* (BW) and *PR Newswire* (PRN). Each organization transmits more than 15,000 news releases monthly to daily newspapers, broadcast stations, trade publications, and online news services. Other major distributors are *US Newswire,* a division of Medialink Worldwide, and *Internet Wire,* which exclusively use Web portals. There is no paper involved. Your news release automatically enters the appropriate databases and computer queues, which can be accessed with a single keystroke.

Using their PCs, editors and reporters can call up your news release for review. They can edit it on the screen, write a headline for it, and then push another key to have it printed in the right typeface and column width. Of course, they can also push the delete key and send the whole release to the electronic trash can.

The advantage of electronic distribution services is timely and immediate delivery of your material in a format that can be easily used. Mailed releases, by contrast, must be processed manually. They can be scanned electronically and placed in a computer file, but most of the time they are simply used as background material as reporters write stories on their PCs.

BW and PRN can customize the distribution of your news release to specific media. They can send your news release to every daily newspaper in Ohio, or you can send it to a select list of financial publications in North America, Europe, and Asia. They can also distribute full-text news releases and color photos to African-American and Hispanic publications, or a select list of high-tech trade magazines. Both BW and PRN also offer clients the additional opportunity of distributing their news releases to such online services as America Online, MSN MoneyCentral, and Yahoo!.

Indeed, news releases can be transmitted with an increasing number of bells and whistles. Business Wire, for example, now offers a service called "Smart News Release." In other words, the basic news release can be imbedded with visuals and audio. According to Janet Lynn, a BW vice president: "Included within the release are high-resolution photos, streaming audio, streaming video, and spreadsheets. All a person visiting our Web site has to do is click on any of these options and be hyperlinked to their choice." See Figure 10.3 for an annotated version of Business Wire's "smart" news release. Another example is provided in Figure 10.4.

It should also be noted that the news release isn't just for the press anymore. The public can also access Business Wire (www.businesswire.com) and PR Newswire (www.prnewswire.com) online to read news releases and other materials that have been distributed to the media.

According to Michael Lissauer, senior vice president of marketing for Business Wire, "The press release is reaching an additional audience today. Press releases were always aimed at the media, which would interpret those releases, write what they wanted to write based on those releases, that was what consumers ultimately

Business Wire Sample News Release

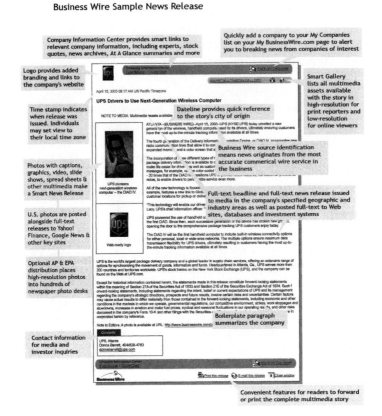

Figure 10.3 Electronic Wire Services
Several services distribute electronic news releases directly to a publication's servers via phone lines or satellite. This illustration identifies the various elements of a Business Wire "smart" news release that embeds such elements as photos, graphics, video, spread sheets, and slide shows into the basic news release. Journalists can access these elements with a simple click of the mouse.
(Courtesy of Business Wire.)

saw. But with the advent of the Internet, the target audience can see press releases in their original form." The *Holmes Report* also noted that "by appearing on wires such as Business Wire, press releases are being read by potential investors, by potential customers, and even employees."

Cost   National distribution of a "smart news release" can cost up to $1,000, but a basic 400-word news release transmitted to major media in all 50 states is about $600. A regional news release is about $250 to $400, and a statewide release is between $125 and $225. Distribution to media in a single city, such as Cleveland, is about $125.

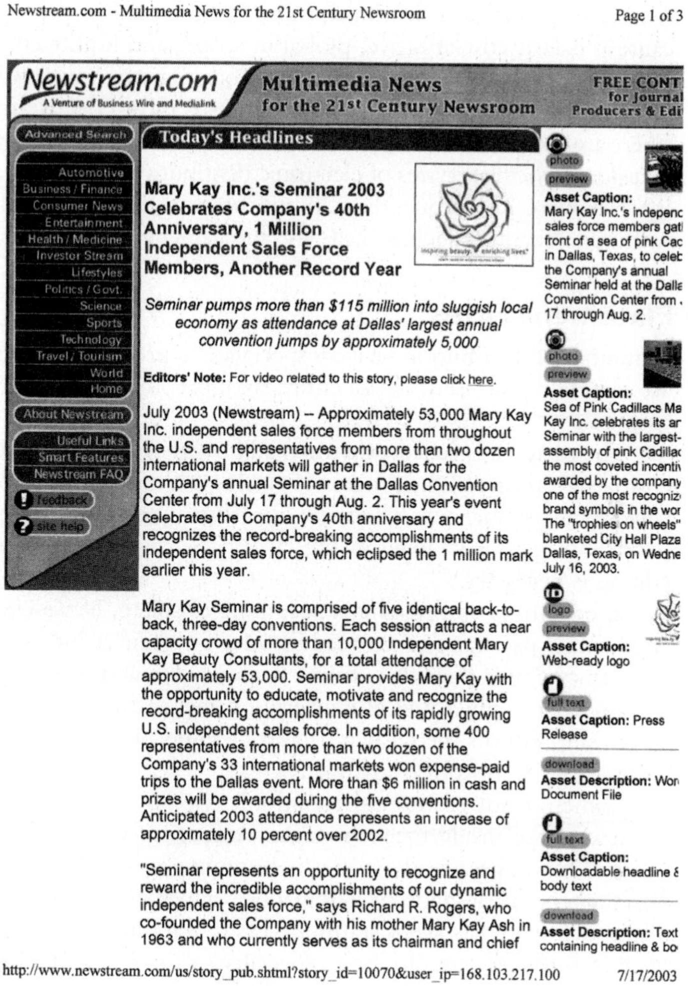

Newstream.com
A Venture of Business Wire and Medialink

Multimedia News
for the 21st Century Newsroom

FREE CONT
for Journal
Producers & Edi

Advanced Search

Automotive
Business / Finance
Consumer News
Entertainment
Health / Medicine
Investor Stream
Lifestyles
Politics / Govt.
Science
Sports
Technology
Travel / Tourism
World
Home

About Newstream

Useful Links
Smart Features
Newstream FAQ

feedback
site help

Today's Headlines

Mary Kay Inc.'s Seminar 2003 Celebrates Company's 40th Anniversary, 1 Million Independent Sales Force Members, Another Record Year

Seminar pumps more than $115 million into sluggish local economy as attendance at Dallas' largest annual convention jumps by approximately 5,000

Editors' Note: For video related to this story, please click here.

July 2003 (Newstream) -- Approximately 53,000 Mary Kay Inc. independent sales force members from throughout the U.S. and representatives from more than two dozen international markets will gather in Dallas for the Company's annual Seminar at the Dallas Convention Center from July 17 through Aug. 2. This year's event celebrates the Company's 40th anniversary and recognizes the record-breaking accomplishments of its independent sales force, which eclipsed the 1 million mark earlier this year.

Mary Kay Seminar is comprised of five identical back-to-back, three-day conventions. Each session attracts a near capacity crowd of more than 10,000 Independent Mary Kay Beauty Consultants, for a total attendance of approximately 53,000. Seminar provides Mary Kay with the opportunity to educate, motivate and recognize the record-breaking accomplishments of its rapidly growing U.S. independent sales force. In addition, some 400 representatives from more than two dozen of the Company's 33 international markets won expense-paid trips to the Dallas event. More than $6 million in cash and prizes will be awarded during the five conventions. Anticipated 2003 attendance represents an increase of approximately 10 percent over 2002.

"Seminar represents an opportunity to recognize and reward the incredible accomplishments of our dynamic independent sales force," says Richard R. Rogers, who co-founded the Company with his mother Mary Kay Ash in 1963 and who currently serves as its chairman and chief

photo
preview

Asset Caption: Mary Kay Inc.'s independ sales force members gath front of a sea of pink Cad in Dallas, Texas, to celeb the Company's annual Seminar held at the Dalla Convention Center from . 17 through Aug. 2.

photo
preview

Asset Caption: Sea of Pink Cadillacs Ma Kay Inc. celebrates its ar Seminar with the largest-assembly of pink Cadillac the most coveted incentiv awarded by the company one of the most recogniz brand symbols in the wor The "trophies on wheels" blanketed City Hall Plaza Dallas, Texas, on Wedne July 16, 2003.

logo
preview

Asset Caption: Web-ready logo

full text

Asset Caption: Press Release

download

Asset Description: Wor Document File

full text

Asset Caption: Downloadable headline & body text

download

Asset Description: Text containing headline & bo

http://www.newstream.com/us/story_pub.shtml?story_id=10070&user_ip=168.103.217.100   7/17/2003

Figure 10.4 An Internet News Release
News releases distributed via the Internet and e-mail often use longer headlines so recipients know exactly what the story is about. This one is five lines long, followed by a secondary headline of three lines. The release, distributed by Newstream.com (a venture of Business Wire and Medialink), also contains elements of a "smart" news release by giving reporters the opportunity to click on photos, the organization's logo, or even a video of the event.
(Courtesy of Newstream.com)

Business Wire also has worldwide distribution packages. If you want the whole planet to get your news release, it can be arranged for about $6,000. Individual nations are much cheaper; a news release to media in Australia is about $400. Ethnic media can also be reached. The Black PR Wire is $475 per release, and the national Hispanic PR Wire is $375 for a 400-word release.

In other words, using an electronic distribution service can be very cost-effective and about the same as first-class mail on a local, state, or national level.

As a result, electronic distribution has been touted as the wave of the future because it is fast, cost-effective, global in scope, and highly compatible with the extensive use of the computer in processing today's news. You should be aware, however, that electronic distribution of news releases is most effective to reach major media. There are thousands of weekly newspapers, trade publications, and broadcast stations that don't use the services of electronic distribution firms such as Business Wire and PR Newswire. Consequently, you still have to supplement electronic distribution with other channels such as mail, fax, and camera-ready feature placement firms.

Feature Placement Firms

A number of distribution services specialize in preparing columns and features that are camera-ready—sent out as entire layouts complete with headlines, photos, and graphics.

The material is called **camera-ready** because a camera makes a negative of the entire page as part of the process of getting pages ready for offset printing. A newspaper editor simply cuts the article out from a glossy sheet of paper (called a **repro proof**) and pastes it down in the layout. No headline writing, picture sizing, or editing is necessary.

Even cutting and pasting is becoming obsolete. News USA and others, for example, now package camera-ready stories for their clients on CD-ROMs that editors can pop into their PCs. Editors receive a new disk every month.

Another popular way of delivering camera-ready materials is to post them on a Web site. Editors then download articles and high-resolution photos and graphics that they want to use.

Camera-ready stories are commonly used by weekly and daily newspapers to fill news space inside the newspaper. According to the distribution services, the demand for camera-ready stories is booming as a result of rising costs and fewer staff writers. Thousands of newspapers, which receive the stories free, find that using such materials keeps staffing costs to a minimum and fills their inside pages. Such features are often found in specialty sections of a newspaper: auto, food, real estate, travel, computing, etc.

The primary use of a feature placement firm is to distribute features and other information that is relevant over a period of several months. In the business, these stories are often called **evergreens**. Popular camera-ready items are about food, travel, health, education, special events, and consumerism. Here are some headlines of typical feature stories prepared for various clients:

- "What to Do About Childhood Cancer" (National Childhood Cancer Foundation)
- "Experts Warn: Itching Can Signal Serious Illness" (GenDerm Corporation)
- "How to Protect Your House When You Go on Vacation" (Schlage Lock Company)

Trade groups, national charitable organizations, national membership organizations, state tourism departments, and a number of corporations use camera-ready releases to create awareness and visibility. The most successful ones emphasize consumer tips and keep commercialism to a minimum. In fact, most camera-ready features only mention the organization once or twice in the entire article. See Figures 10.5 and 10.6 for examples of a camera-ready feature distributed on behalf of a software publisher.

AROUND THE HOUSE
Start Buttoning Up Your Home for Winter

By Jeff Keller
For News USA

(NU) - As the weather cools, your attention should focus on winterizing the home. Here are some tips that you should follow before the cold winds arrive.

Replace screens with storm windows and shut off outside water. Add an extra layer of insulation in the attic if necessary. Check crawl spaces.

Replace worn caulk around windows and doors, wall and roof vents, skylights and chimneys and wherever electrical wiring, pipes or ducts exit. Caulk reduces drafts and caulk for a tight seal. Place caulk where the old caulk that has cracked. Place weather stripping length wide.

Last winter, in the northeast, a split-level home reduced 50 percent of heat loss. Though some walls usually will be insulated, some problems...

reduce heating costs.

3M window insulator kits were applied to all windows and patio doors. The plastic film also was used to cover an air conditioning...

AROUND THE HOUSE
New Adhesives Repair Common Household Items

NewsUSA

By Jeff Keller
For News USA

(NU) - In the movie "The Graduate," the central character, while contemplating a career, is told to remember one word - plastics.

While plastics have become a large part of everyday life, many people do not have confidence in the store-bought adhesives designed to repair household items made from plastic.

"Consumers often become frustrated because they can't locate a durable adhesive to repair broken plastic items," said Gretchen Hauble of 3M. "They are forced to discard an item and purchase a replacement when a quick fix would suffice if a repair adhesive could be found."

3M, known for adhesives technologies found on everything from repositionable notes to construction materials, has developed a new line of retail adhesives to repair everyday plastic and vinyl items.

Rigid plastic repair. A unique surface primer and adhesive work together to repair breaks and cracks in rigid plastic items such as toys. It works fast on all household plastics, forming a long-lasting, rigid repair.

Flexible plastic repair. A unique surface primer and adhe-

sive patches work together to repair tears, breaks and cracks in flexible plastic items when the repair usually would flex and break. Unlike other adhesives, the patches bond to all plastics, including polyethylene and polypropylene. Uses include refuse containers and lawn furniture.

Plastic repair wrap. A unique surface primer and self-fusing wrap work together to provide a strong and durable repair of hard-to-fix items such as vacuum cleaner hoses and laundry baskets.

Inflatable plastic repair patch. A self-adhesive patch provides strong repair of rips, tears and punctures of everyday vinyl inflatable items such as air mattresses and pool toys. It bonds to wet or dry surfaces, forming an airtight repair that is faster and easier than vinyl strips with glue.

Inflatable plastic repair sealer. Repairs seam failures and small punctures of vinyl items such as air mattresses and pool toys. The liquid sealer bonds to dry surfaces to form an airtight seam.

These products can be found in your local retail stores.

Jeff Keller can be heard nationwide every Saturday morning on the "Mr. Handyman" show. Check local radio listings for time and station.

AROUND THE HOUSE
Hate Paint Stripping Jobs? Try Stripping Tanks

By Jeff Keller
For News USA

remover, a water-based remover that does not present the handling difficulties of other more hazardous strippers.

Due to the large size of the project, Camp Pendleton's environmental group also had to consider the impact that the stripper and removed paint might have on local water treatment facilities. Military personnel decided to collect the residue instead of flushing it down the sewer. The 3M stripper, however, is biodegradable when washed down the drain with water after completing small projects around the home.

At home, when stripping wood, the product is applied with a brush and removed with putty knives and stripping tools. The military, however, has large vehicles, and a lot of them - more than 4,000 - so the stripper is applied with power sprayers. It is removed, along with the latex camouflage coat, with water from high-pressure nozzles.

Though the war ended in 1991, no doubt soldiers at Camp Pendleton and other bases still are removing camouflage from jeeps, tanks and other equipment. They try to squeeze in a couple of vehicles between drills, meals, sleep and the coveted three-day pass.

Jeff Keller can be heard nationwide every Saturday morning in the "Mr. Handyman" show. Check local radio listings for time and station.

Figure 10.5 Camera-Ready Features Are Popular
Both corporations and nonprofit organizations use feature services to write, format, and distribute materials that can be used over a period of months. The material is called "camera-ready" because it is already prepared in a newspaper column format and "ready" to be used. This series of articles for client 3M gave tips on household repairs because the company makes a number of products in this area. This particular series ran for two years and was used by a variety of daily and weekly newspapers.
(Courtesy of NewsUSA.)

NEWS OF COMPUTERS

Computer Care 101: Ensuring A Healthy Relationship Between You And Your Computer

(NAPS)—As last year's PC prices dropped to less than $1,000 for a complete system, there is a good chance you received (or bought) a computer this past year. In fact, the number of PC users is increasing dramatically as novices receive their first systems and families add second and third computers to their homes. With the face of the "PC Nation" changing to reflect the growing number of new users, it's vital to remember that computers need a certain amount of care and preventive maintenance to ensure a healthy and long-lasting relationship.

Whether you use your computer to surf the Net, e-mail your friends and family, play games or write documents, you want a computer that functions properly. Symantec, the world leader in utility software for business and personal computing, recommends the following essential items to keep you and your computer operating smoothly and efficiently. These items are available nationwide at most computer stores:

• Surge Protectors: With so many peripherals plugged in to the same outlet, it is important to utilize a surge protector to guard against fatal, data-destroying electrical overloads.

• Floppy Disks or Zip Drives: All computer users should back up and save important data in the event of an unrecoverable system crash.

• Dust Guards: A computer cover and can of compressed air can go a long way in keeping vital parts of the computer and keyboard dust-free.

• Wrist Rests: These helpful products are important to utilize while operating the keyboard, especially for people who are prone to sore wrists or who have carpel tunnel syndrome.

• An Integrated Software Utility Suite Such as Norton SystemWorks: The first integrated utility suite, Norton SystemWorks provides everything a user needs to keep their computer working. The suite includes the following applications: Norton AntiVirus for total protection—even against Macro viruses; Norton Crash Guard to quickly recover from a system crash and save your work; Norton Web Services to search the Web and install the latest software and hardware upgrades; Norton Utilities to provide continuous correction of hardware and software problems and disk repair; and Norton CleanSweep to safely, quickly and easily remove pesky and unwanted files. In addition, Norton System Works is a great value with more than $500 worth of products available for less than $70.

No matter what you use your computer for, the above items are sure to give you peace of mind as well as a long-lasting, healthy relationship with your computer.

To find out more about software suites and Norton SystemWorks, visit Symantec's website at www.symantec.com.

Figure 10.6 Features Must Be Informative, Not a Sales Pitch
Distributors of camera-ready features are adept at writing materials that focus on consumer tips instead of a commercial pitch. In general, the name of the sponsoring organization should be buried in the middle of the story or at the end of it. The idea is to create brand awareness and credibility, but to do so in a subtle way.
(Courtesy of North American Precis Syndicate (NAPS).)

Camera-ready features are relatively short. A one-column feature is about 225 words, and a two-column story is about 350 words. To attract editor and reader interest, most also include a photo or a graphic of some kind. Radio stations receive short spots professionally voiced on CD, and TV stations often receive video features on Betacam tape.

Cost Several companies deliver camera-ready features. North American Precis Syndicate (NAPS) (www.napsinfo.com) is one of the oldest and largest in the business, but there are also other national firms such as Metro Editorial Services (www.metrocreativegraphics.com) and NewsUSA (www.newsusa.com).

NAPS, for example, distributes its client features to 10,000 daily and weekly newspapers across the country and says that an organization typically will get 100 to 400+ placements. The cost for a two-column feature, which includes writing, formatting, and distribution, is about $5,550; a one-column feature is about $4,000. A camera-ready release to a television station (four slides, plus a script) costs about $6,500 for distribution to 1,000 TV stations. According to NAPS, the client typically receives 100 to 150+ placements. NAPS also prepares and distributes radio releases to about 6,500 stations and claims clients receive about 400 to 500+ placements. The cost of a radio release is about $5,000.

NewsUSA specializes in packages of multiple releases. It, for example, will send 26 different camera-ready features over the course of a year to 10,500 newspapers for about $80,000. The same number of radio features will cost a similar amount. Of course, there is always the success story. NewsUSA prepared and distributed 23 camera-ready features for American Century Investments and received a total of 4,304 placements, representing 242 million potential readers. You should note, however, that audience size is based on the total circulation of the newspaper, not how many people actually read the feature.

In addition to regular mailings, distribution services prepare camera-ready stories on a central theme. Metro Publicity Services, for example, has mailings on everything from Mother's Day to Fall Home Improvement. Many of these articles show up in advertising supplements of daily newspapers. For example, the home improvement supplement might use a camera-ready story from a paint manufacturer offering tips on what kind of paint would be best for a bathroom or kitchen.

CD-ROM

The technology of using digital compact disks (CD) and read-only memory (ROM) is well advanced in the reference field. As mentioned at the beginning of this chapter, most media directories are now available on CD-ROM, as well as many standard encyclopedias, games, and software programs.

The use of CD-ROM for the distribution of publicity materials, however, is still developing. A major limiting factor in the past was that most editors and reporters didn't have CD-ROM drives on their desktop PCs, but this has rapidly changed.

The music, TV, and movie industries have made extensive use of CD-ROM for media kits. The disks, which are mailed to editors and reviewers at thousands of publications, contain high-resolution photographs, bios, and press releases about new music videos, TV series, and films. Also included are digital video clips of the shows, the stars, and the producers. Media personnel can access the information and then select only the items they want (see Figure 8.13).

ABC network, for example, found this distribution less costly and more effective than using paper media kits. Cal Vornberger, president of Tumble Interactive Media in New York, told *Jack O'Dwyer's Newsletter*, "Instead of assuming the cost, the time and the logistics to reproduce thousands of photographs and press releases and collate them together in a mailer, the information is programmed once on high-resolution digital images and printable versions of the press releases. . . ."

As media outlets upgrade their computers to include CD-ROM drives, the expectation is that this medium of distribution will increase. "CD-ROM will increase in prominence," says Brian Croft, a consultant with the Toronto office of Towers, Perrin.

One idea is that organizations will use CD technology to store and distribute background material about the organization to interested editors and reporters. A CD library would eventually replace the old method of simply storing media kits and other material in file cabinets.

A recent development is the digital media kit that is a CD-ROM product about the size of a credit card. It holds up to 30 megabytes of information, enabling MPEG video, audio, multimedia, printable documents, and electronic graphics. It can be played on a CD-ROM or DVD drive.

E-Mail

Electronic mail, or **e-mail**, is the oldest feature of the Internet. It was first developed in the 1970s to send messages on closed networks, and even today many organizations maintain their own e-mail systems for internal communications.

System networks, however, can also be linked with other networks on the Internet, thus creating the opportunity to communicate with anyone in the world in real time. The most popular feature of the Internet is the ability to send instant personal messages to any number of people around the world.

Indeed, it was once estimated that 7.3 billion messages were sent each day in the United States. And, as of late 2003, the combined e-mail account holders of the three major providers—AOL, Microsoft, and Yahoo!—stood at 200 million. It is no wonder that servers get bogged down and countless messages get lost forever in cyberspace.

Having an e-mail address seems to be almost universal. People put it on their business cards, organizations publicize their e-mail addresses, and media personnel increasingly rely on e-mail to get news releases, media advisories, and other communications.

Although some surveys indicate that many editors and reporters don't mind mailed news releases or even prefer it, most surveys indicate that e-mail is the preferred distribution method. Even the Bennet & Company survey of 150 travel and high-technology journalists, which was mentioned earlier, found that 47 percent of the respondents chose e-mail as the preferred means of getting information.

Vocus Public Relations found an even higher percentage in its survey of 142 newspaper and broadcast journalists. According to *PR Reporter*, "While spam is a problem, 83 percent still choose e-mail as their preferred way of receiving news releases over fax and mail."

The Vocus survey also found that 43 percent of the respondents selected "e-mail with attachments" as their most preferred method for receiving news. This statistic contradicts the usual advice, which is to never send attachments. The survey did, however, find that almost the same percentage of respondents preferred e-mail with links. In fact, Vocus concluded "We suspect it (links) will quickly succeed the preference for attachments in e-mail."

If you do use links, however, Vocus recommends that it's better to link journalists to a customized Web site that pertains to the news release. All too often, the only link is the organization's home page, and reporters have to do more clicking to find the actual material.

If you do send an e-mail news release, here are some general rules:

- Write a subject line that says something. There's no better candidate for the delete button than "press release."
- Put useful information—not contact numbers—at the beginning of a news release.
- Don't send attachments unless requested. File attachments often carry viruses.
- Don't send HTML e-mail messages.
- Provide links to a Web site that contains additional information and graphics.
- Use an extended headline at the top of the news release to give the key message or point.
- Try to use bullets for key points.
- Keep it short; reporters hate to scroll through multiple screens.
- Don't mass distribute releases; it's called spam.
- Don't rely entirely on use of e-mail for distribution of news. Support it with fax or hard copy distribution.
- Use blind copy distribution, and don't reveal your entire mailing list. No reporter wants to know they are part of a mass mailing.
- Remember to provide contact e-mail addresses and phone numbers.
- Continually update your e-mail addresses.
- Make sure your news release is factually correct and free of any spelling, grammar, or punctuation errors.

There are several advantages to e-mail. Ron Solberg, one of the pioneers in using new technologies for public relations purposes, wrote in *Public Relations Tactics*:

Reporters receiving news releases by e-mail don't have to re-key your words. They can easily save or discard the document. And if a reporter wants to keep the release for future reference, it's more convenient to store it on their computer's hard drive than in an overstuffed file drawer. In addition, any copy you key in and send directly to a reporter by e-mail will appear on his or her computer screen exactly as you sent it. There is less opportunity for re-keying error if the reporter uses a quote from your electronic news release in a story.

Advocates of e-mail also say it is less intrusive than a phone call. If a reporter or editor receives the message at deadline, they can read it at a more convenient time. Others say e-mail is much more efficient and less annoying to editors than faxes. E-mail also eliminates telephone tag. Reporters and public relations personnel can easily engage in an e-mail dialogue, posting messages on each other's computer, instead of trying to reach each other by telephone and leaving messages on voicemail.

The downside, of course, is the problem of getting noticed in a deluge of 200 or 300 e-mails that typically flood an editor's "in box" on a daily basis. The Vocus study, for example, found that 17 percent of the respondents received over 200 e-mail releases a week, another 33 percent received 100 to 200 releases a week.

Spamming has become a common complaint among journalists. Spam, broadly defined, is unsolicited e-mail, and many journalists say there is little difference between mass e-mails from pubic relations firms and those from organizations that want to enhance your physical attributes with various potions. Consequently, public relations professionals increasingly are finding that their news releases are blocked as anti-spamming software becomes more sophisticated.

Jennifer Martin, corporate communications manager for CipherTrust, has one solution: "Try to go through and personalize each e-mail, and don't blind copy a press release."

The World Wide Web

The fastest growing part of the Internet is the **World Wide Web**. Indeed, the number of sites on the "Web" continues to increase in geometric proportions. By the beginning of 2000, an estimated 250 million Web pages were being accessed by more than 3,000 search engines. Nearly 90 percent of the Fortune 500 companies had a Web site, and thousands of other organizations had established a Web presence, to say nothing of an almost countless number of individuals. With the advent of e-commerce, the number of Web sites is expected to continue growing geometrically.

Essentially, the World Wide Web (WWW) is a collection of computerized documents that individuals, nonprofit agencies, government agencies, and businesses want to make available to Internet users. Each collection is called a **Web site** or a **home page**.

A Web site, from a public relations standpoint, can be a distribution system in cyberspace. Organizations, for example, use their Web sites to post news releases, corporate backgrounders, product information, position papers, and even photos of key executives or plant locations. The public, as well as media personnel, can access the information and download selected materials into their computers. They can even get a hard copy through a laser or inkjet printer. Organizations use their Web sites in different ways. Here's a sampling:

- Federal Express uses its Web site for investor relations. Stock prices, analyses of company performance, the annual report, and other financial information are available.
- Rutherford Hill Winery in California used a Web site to give a video tour of the winery.
- L. L. Bean has a Web site that gives a history of the company, how it hand-sews its shoes, and a list of attractions at 900 state and national parks.
- SGI, Inc., posts a variety of messages on its Web site. Users can get a company profile, recent news releases, sales brochures, a list of special-interest groups, the company's annual report, financial performance, and the addresses of various sales offices.

In many cases, an organization's Web site is hyperlinked to other Web pages and information sources. A user can jump immediately to a related Web site by clicking a mouse on various icons. Business Wire's Web site, for example, is hyperlinked to the home pages of various organizations that use its distribution services.

Various surveys indicate that journalists use Web sites to retrieve current news releases and other materials. One survey of high-tech publications by Tsantes & Associates, a Silicon Valley-based PR firm, found that reporters spend up to five hours a day on the Web gathering background material for various stories. They also use Web sites to access current and archived news releases about a company, download graphics, and even e-mail the company requesting more information. See Figure 10.7 for an example of a "newsroom" page on a corporate Web site.

John Tsantes, president of Tsantes & Associates, told *PR Tactics*, "The press no longer have to pick up the phone to research stories. The Web has in effect reduced the amount of one-on-one communication between journalists and PR practitioners." However, journalists are not completely happy with the arrangement. The Tsantes survey also found that the major complaint of journalists was that organizational Web sites often failed to provide media contact names for additional follow-up questions.

Web sites, as a form of communication, have the following advantages.

- A great amount of material can be posted. There is no space or time limitation.
- You can reach niche markets and audiences on a direct basis without going through mass media.
- The cost is low for worldwide distribution.
- You can update information quickly, without having to reprint brochures and other materials.
- The media and other users can access details about your organization 24 hours a day from anywhere in the world.

The last point is important when it comes to late-breaking news. On more than one occasion, the media already had a story, but the organization's Web site did not mention it. When TWA Flight 800 exploded after taking off from New York, neither the airline's nor Boeing's Web sites acknowledged it for days. The

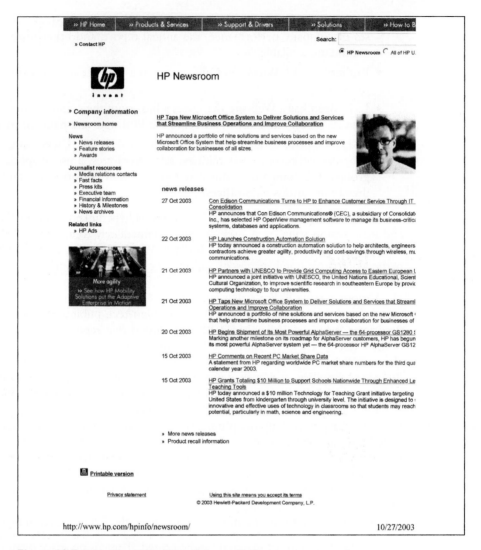

Figure 10.7 Web Sites Offer News Releases Online
Many corporations include a "newsroom" as part of its home Web site. With a few clicks, a journalist doing research can access everything from the organization's executive profiles to the most recent news releases. A good "newsroom," according to surveys, should provide a link to personnel in media relations who can answer questions from reporters. This page shows the "newsroom" home page of Hewlett-Packard (HP).
(Courtesy of Hewlett-Packard Company.)

tragedy dominated the news, but at the cyberspace addresses of the firms involved, it was a crash that didn't happen. This extreme example is why it's important to daily update material on a Web site. Reporters seeking additional information will look for it and, if it isn't there, this essentially is a corporate "no comment."

PR Casebook

A Web News Conference

MCI WorldCom used its Web site to conduct a news conference about its research findings on "Meetings in America." The company, working with Grant/Jacoby Public Relations, developed a PowerPoint presentation that was made available on the MCI WorldCom Web site.

About 35 reporters nationwide logged on to the site to view the presentation while listening in on a separate audio conference call. After the presentation, the phone lines were opened for questions. The names of reporters and their publications were captured when they logged on, so MCI WorldCom knew exactly who was on the call and with whom to follow up. The Web news conference resulted in stories published by *The Wall Street Journal, USA Today,* and *The Chicago Tribune,* among others.

Neal Lulofs, a senior marketing manager at MCI WorldCom Conferencing, told *PR Tactics,* "If we had opted for an in-person news conference, we might have been limited to reporters in a particular city. But the journalists we needed to reach were scattered across the country. Through a Web-based news conference, we could reach all of them simultaneously with detailed, thought-provoking information that also demonstrated the advantages of meeting in cyberspace."

Competition to attract users, or **hits**, to a Web site is intense, and the public relations writer must think in visual terms. It is not enough just to post the company's annual report or corporate profile on the home page in its original printed form. Instead, the material must be reduced to highly graphic displays and the writing must take the form of soundbites.

Anyone browsing the World Wide Web will testify that the majority of home pages are visually boring and not worth a second look. In order to avoid the pitfalls of having such a home page, experts offer this advice.

- Define the objective of the site.
- Design it with the audience in mind.
- Don't just place existing materials on it; redesign the material with strong graphic components.
- Update the site constantly. This is the real cost of a home page.
- Don't overdo the graphics. Complex graphics take a long time to download.
- Make the site interactive; give the user buttons to click on for exploring various topics.
- Use feedback (an e-mail address or computer bulletin board) to evolve the site.

Cost   Although you can design your own Web site and even uplink it to the World Wide Web, experts recommend that you hire professionals who are experienced in the field of graphics and interactive media. A good site on the Web will cost between $20,000 and $50,000 to set up. Then you must maintain the site and replace materials on a periodic basis. In fact, experts say that the only way you can get users to revisit the site is by constantly changing the information. General Electric, fully realizing this, spends $10,000 a month to maintain its Web site.

Chapter 13 explores in greater detail the mechanics of creating and maintaining a Web site for an organization.

Usenet and Listserv

No one knows for sure, but experts estimate there are more than 10,000 discussion groups (also called "newsgroups" or "bulletin boards") on the Usenet portion of the Internet. Basically, **Usenet** is an international meeting place where people gather (but not in real time) to discuss events and topics in specialized areas.

Chapter 1 outlined some Usenet groups that specialize in public relations topics. Other groups may focus on topics such as the environment, television shows, baseball, and frisbee. There are also numerous discussion groups about sex and pornography that have become a political issue, with some people lobbying Congress to pass legislation to forbid "indecent" material.

From a public relations standpoint, Usenet is a good way to distribute information to users who are interested in your organization. In fact, many organizations create their own bulletin boards, often within their own Web sites, for the purpose of posting messages and getting feedback from users. Organizations can also post messages on more generalized bulletin boards.

A good example of how this works is Slocan Forest Products, a Canadian company, which was threatened by a hostile takeover bid. In order to drum up support to remain independent, the president of Slocan posted messages on various computer bulletin boards that reached stockholders, the business community, the press, environmental groups, and government regulatory agencies. He also posted his own personal e-mail address so people could comment directly on the takeover bid. The hostile bid was beaten back.

Organizations also use the Usenet to monitor issues and what people are saying, electronically sampling public opinion to determine how people feel about various issues that affect the organization. See Chapter 19 for information on eWatch (www.newcast.com/ewatch), a specialty company that monitors Usenet groups and what is said about various products, organizations.

Listserv is similar to Usenet, but instead of messages being posted to a bulletin board, items are sent directly to users via e-mail. The advantage of a Listserv is that it eliminates the need for journalists to initiate access a particular Web site. Since almost every company now has a Web site, it is unlikely that a reporter will make this effort unless there is a major news event involving the company.

Listserv, however, automatically sends information via e-mail to anyone who has asked to receive information on a selected topic. Edelman Worldwide (www.edelman.com), as noted previously, has a Listserv on its Web site so a reporter can "subscribe" to information about his or her specialty area, whether it be food, autos, or health care. If a reporter signs up for information regarding the auto industry, for example, Edelman automatically forwards any news releases from its clients involving that industry.

Internet Wire (www.internetwire.com) operates on a similar basis. The company says it can reach more than 20,000 individual editors and reporters by e-mail every business day. Depending on the topic of the news release, Internet Wire can e-mail news releases to a particular segment of the media, such as technology, finance, entertainment, travel/leisure, education, government, and sports. In the trade, this is called **vertical communication**.

THE CONTINUED ROLE OF TRADITIONAL MEDIA

There is no doubt that the Internet has radically changed the way public relations professionals distribute information. It offers many new distribution and placement opportunities, but the public relations writer should not completely ignore the traditional media.

You should keep in mind that the Internet, despite its rapid adoption, hasn't yet replaced—if it ever will—traditional media. In fact, the AOL–Time Warner merger seems to indicate more convergence than the disappearance of such traditional media as newspapers, magazines, radio, and television.

Carole Howard, long-term vice president of public relations for *Reader's Digest*, told *PR Reporter:*

> It's easy to get drawn into the hype. Yet it's important to remember that the Net is just another tool in your arsenal. It may be the latest—but it's not necessarily the greatest distribution vehicle for every publicity opportunity.

One problem with the Internet is its current reach and audience. Although an estimated 200 million individuals in the United States now have Internet access at home, it is still important to remember some of the following figures:

- The total weekday readership of 1,469 daily newspapers in the United States is more than 125 million, and total Sunday readership is more than 136 million.
- 10 million families are heavy readers of magazines.
- Families still watch more than seven hours of television daily, and the Super Bowl still garners about 120 million viewers on a Sunday in January.
- Radio reaches over 150 million Americans daily.

In other words, the Internet has not replaced traditional media. Even Americans online still devote considerable time each week to watching television (15.6 hours) and listening to radio (12.6 hours) than they spend online (7.1 hours). In addition, Internet users still devoted 4.0 hours to newspapers and 3.4 hours to radio each week, according to *The Wall Street Journal.*

Daniel Eisenberg, writing in *Time* magazine, noting the irony of all this, commented, "Although network television loses viewers every year, ABC can still produce an audience of 18 million in a prime-time hour. Try to get that many visitors to your website in a day or a week."

Although the Internet has no time or space constraints, this is a double-edged sword. On one hand, publicists are thrilled that the public can now access the full text of news releases—instead of shortened versions (or no mention) in the news media. However, the flip side is that millions of documents are added daily to the Internet and no one has the time or ability to cope with absorbing this mountain of information.

The traditional media, in such an information glut, perform the valuable function of distilling and synthesizing information so people can easily access it at home, on a bus, or even on a Stairmaster in a health club.

W. Russell Neumann, writing in *The Future of the Mass Audience* (Cambridge University Press) adds:

> People will continue to rely on the editorial judgment of established news media to relay what are deemed to be the significant headlines of the world and the nation. Packaging, formatting, filtering and interpreting complex flows of information represent the valued-added components of public communications. In a more competitive, complex and intense communication environment, that value-added component will be equally important to the individual citizen, if not more so.

There's also the matter of credibility. Publicity materials in the mass media have increased credibility because media gatekeepers, a third party, have already decided that the information is newsworthy. Two media researchers, Robert Merton and Robert Lazarsfeld, termed this the status conferral role of the press. Other researchers say media coverage of your organization represents an implied third-party endorsement by the press. No such status conferral occurs when anyone can post anything and everything on the Internet.

A study by Ogilvy Public Relations Worldwide, for example, concluded that although the use of the Internet is skyrocketing, trust of it is not. Only 45 percent of Americans profess trust for information garnered from the 'Net, while 96 percent feel traditional news sources are reliable. Some 30 percent of Americans also consider local TV highly influential when making spending decisions, which is seven times those naming the Internet.

In sum, the Internet has been added to your tool box as another way to distribute information to the traditional mass media and the public. It is not, however, a tool that replaces all existing tools. In fact, Dan Cantelmo, president of Media Distribution Services (MDS), told *PR Tactics*, "The use of paper in the form of news releases and press kits is at least 10 times what it was a decade ago. We're a long way from a paperless PR world."

SUMMARY

- Media directories, in print, CD-ROM, or online, are essential tools to compile media lists and distribute information to them.
- Media lists and e-mail addresses must be constantly updated and revised; journalists move around a lot.
- Publicists use editorial calendars to find out what special editions or sections various publications are planning for the year.
- Tip sheets let publicists know what kind of material a publication or broadcast station is seeking for a particular purpose.
- Mailing labels must be accurate; they should be addressed to a specific editor by name and include such details as the floor or suite in an office building.
- The vast majority of news releases and other press materials are still mailed, via either the U.S. Postal Service or commercial vendors such as FedEx.

- Some surveys indicate that editors and reporters still prefer receiving publicity materials in the following descending order: mail, fax, and e-mail. Other surveys, however, show e-mail as the first choice of journalists.
- The fax machine is a good way to send media advisories and late-breaking news releases. However, it is not wise to mass distribute routine news releases by fax.
- New technology allows firms such as Business Wire to send your news releases electronically to the computers of the mass media throughout the world.
- Camera-ready features are widely used by newspapers and other media outlets because they reduce staff costs and fill space. Feature service firms distribute camera-ready articles on paper, diskettes. CDs, or online.
- E-mail is now a popular way of communicating with reporters and editors about possible story ideas. It works best, however, when the publicist and the reporter have already established a working relationship.
- The World Wide Web allows an organization to establish its own "home page" to post a variety of materials, which can be accessed by the press and the public.
- A good Web site is highly visual and interactive, with short blocks of text.
- Publicists can use Internet discussion groups to post information and receive feedback. Listserv allows organizations to e-mail materials directly, on a daily basis, to journalists who "subscribe" to the service.
- The Internet is a supplemental tool for distributing information; it doesn't replace traditional mass media.

ADDITIONAL RESOURCES

Calabro, Sara. "For Wires, Looking after the Media Is a Priority." *PRWeek*, July 28, 2003, p. 18.

Calabro, Sara. "Beyond the Wire: Enhancements in News Delivery." *PRWeek*, February 13, 2003, p. 18.

Calabro, Sara. "Wires: The Next Generation." *PRWeek*, April 8, 2002, p. 17.

Cantelmo, David P. "How PR People Distribute—and the Media Prefer to Receive—News Releases and Other Public Relations Information: The Myths vs. the Reality." *Public Relations Quarterly*, Fall 2001, pp. 15–18.

Duke, Shearlean. "E-Mail: Essential in Media Relations, but No Replacement for Face-to-Face Communication." *Public Relations Quarterly*, Winter 2001, pp. 19–21.

Leggiere, Cybil. "At the Crossroads: PR Links to the Web." *PRWeek*, January 29, 2001, pp. 25, 27, 29.

Londner, Robin. "The Wires and Wherefores of Pricing." *PRWeek*, February 11, 2002, p. 18.

Londner, Robin. "Good News for Newswires." *PRWeek*, May 28, 2001, p. 19.

Chapter 11

Working with the Media

Media relations is the core activity in many public relations jobs. In fact, one survey of 539 large companies by the Public Affairs Group (PAG) found that media relations was the #1 job responsibility of their public relations staffs. In most cases, public relations personnel are the primary contact between the organization and the media. Consequently, it is important to discuss the concepts of effective media relations and how to establish a good working relationship with journalists.

Public relations professionals and journalists have long had a love–hate relationship. There are flashpoints of friction and distrust, but there is also the realization that they are mutually dependent on each other. A national survey of journalists by a New York public relations firm is indicative. Two-thirds of the journalists said they don't trust public relations people, but 81 percent say they need them anyway.

This chapter explores the symbiotic relationship between publicists and journalists from several perspectives. First, we discuss how each depends on the other. Second, we examine some areas of friction such as excessive hype, advertising influences, sloppy reporting, and tabloid journalism.

We then give some guidelines for giving effective media interviews, organizing news conferences, and conducting various kinds of media tours. The chapter concludes with a list of media relations tips and how to handle crisis situations. By keeping these guidelines in mind, you will build a trusting and productive relationship with journalists.

MEDIA DEPENDENCE ON PUBLIC RELATIONS

The reality of mass communications today is that reporters and editors spend most of their time processing information, not gathering it. And, although many reporters deny it, most of the information that appears in the mass media comes from public relations sources that provide a constant stream of news releases, features, planned events, and tips to the media.

Gary Putka, the Boston bureau chief of *The Wall Street Journal*, admits that "a good 50 percent" of the stories in the newspaper come from news releases. His assessment is backed up by several research studies.

One such study goes back to 1973, when L. V. Sigal wrote *Reporters and Officials: The Organization and Politics of Newsmaking*. He studied 1,200 *New York Times* and *Washington Post* front pages and found that 58.2 percent of the stories came through routine bureaucratic channels, official proceedings, news releases and conferences, and other planned events. Just 25.2 percent were the products of investigative journalism, and most of these were produced by interviews, the result of routine access to spokespersons. Sigal explained, "The reporter cannot depend on legwork alone to satisfy his paper's insatiable demand for news. He looks to official channels to provide him with newsworthy material day after day."

More recent studies have the same basic finding. Jericho Promotions (New York) sent questionnaires to 5,500 journalists worldwide and got 2,432 to respond. Of that number, 38 percent said they got at least half of their story ideas from public relations people. The percentage was even higher among editors of lifestyle, entertainment, and health sections of newspapers.

PRWeek conducted a national survey and found that almost 60 percent of the responding journalists used news releases "all the time" or "often." And 30 percent acknowledged that they relied more on public relations sources than they did five years earlier. Another survey by Bennett & Company (Orlando) found that nearly 75 percent of the responding journalists said they used public relations sources for up to 25 percent of their story information.

Perhaps another indication of the media's reliance on public relations sources is the extensive use of "spokespeople" as primary sources in news stories. Journalists often use "spokesman" or "spokeswoman" as a code word for public relations personnel who provide information. Bob Williams, an ethics fellow at the Poynter Institute for Journalism, conducted a computer search of articles in the top 50 U.S. newspapers for references to "spokesperson" or similar terms. He found that the term appeared 501,101 times in 2000, up 81 percent from the 292,308 times in 1995.

All this amounts to what O. H. Gandy calls "information subsidies" to the press. In his book, *Beyond Agenda Setting: Information Subsidies and Public Policy*, he explains that material such as news releases constitutes a "subsidy" because the source "causes it to be made available at something less than the cost a user would face in the absence of a subsidy."

In other words, public relations materials save media the time, money, and effort of gathering their own news. Indeed, no medium—including *The New York Times*—has enough reporters to cover all the available news. As one editor of the *San Jose* (CA) *Mercury News* once said, publicists are the newspaper's "unpaid reporters."

Despite such statements, most journalists are loath to admit any reliance on public relations sources because they think it reflects negatively on their abilities as reporters. Denise E. DeLorme and Fred Fedler comment on this in a *Public Relations Review* article that gives a historical analysis of journalist hostility to public relations. They wrote:

> In one contradiction, journalists wanted information to be easily available, yet resented the men and women who made it available. By the mid-twentieth century, journalists were dependent upon PR practitioners for a large percentage of the stories appearing in newspapers. But admitting their dependence would shatter cherished ideals. Journalists were proud of their ability to uncover stories, verify details, and expose sham. Thus, they were unlikely to admit their dependence, lack of skepticism, failure to verify, and failure to expose every sham.

PUBLIC RELATIONS DEPENDENCE ON THE MEDIA

The purpose of public relations, mentioned in the early chapters of this book, is to inform, shape opinions and attitudes, and motivate. This can be accomplished only if people receive messages constantly and consistently.

The media, in all their variety, are cost-effective channels of communication in an information society. They are the multipliers that enable millions of people to receive a message at the same time. Through the miracle of satellite communications and the Internet, the world is a global metropolis of shared information.

Thousands of publications and hundreds of radio, television, and cable outlets enable the public relations communicator to reach very specific target audiences with tailored messages designed just for them. In addition, Bacon's Information has an *Internet Media Directory* containing nearly 6,000 online news outlets, all but 400 of which are tied to traditional print or broadcast outlets. Demographic segmentation and psychographics are now a way of life in advertising, marketing, and public relations.

The media's power and influence in a democratic society reside in their independence from government control. Reporters and editors make independent judgments about what is newsworthy and what will be disseminated. They serve as filters of information, and even though not everyone is happy with what they decide, the fact remains that media gatekeepers are generally perceived as more objective than public relations people, who represent a particular client or organization.

This is important to you because the media, by inference, serve as third-party endorsers of your information. Media gatekeepers give your information credibility and importance by deciding that it is newsworthy. The information is no longer from your organization but from *The New York Times*, *The Wall Street Journal*, or CNN.

AREAS OF FRICTION

The relationship between public relations and the media is based on mutual cooperation, trust, and respect. Unfortunately, certain actions compromise the relationship. On the public relations side, these actions often involve the use of excessive hype, not doing the necessary homework, and making a nuisance of themselves. Perhaps Peter Himler, executive vice president of Burson-Marsteller public relations in New York, said it best: "Overt commercialism, hyperbole, artificiality and manipulation are the best ways to turn off a reporter and, in so doing, damage the fragile, but vital relationship between our two professions."

On the journalistic side, these actions include name calling, sloppy/biased reporting, and tabloid sensationalism. Both groups face the issue of improper advertising influence, which tends to undermine the credibility of the news coverage.

Hype and Other Irritations

As noted in Chapter 5, journalists receive hundreds of news releases every month. Far too many of them contain hype words such as "unique," "revolutionary," "state-of-the-art," and "sophisticated." Journalists, dulled by the constant flow of news releases that sound like commercials, generally conclude that the majority of publicists are incompetent. In fact, the *PRWeek* survey mentioned previously found that slightly more than 50 percent of the responding journalists thought "poorly written materials" was a major problem with public relations.

Although this complaint was near the top of the list, almost 60 percent of the journalists thought the biggest problem was public relations people who were "unfamiliar with our editorial requirements and format." Other major complaints, in descending order, were (1) too many unsolicited e-mails, faxes, and phone calls, (2) don't know the product or service, (3) repeated calls and follow-up, (4) spokespersons not available, and (5) don't meet publication deadlines. Some of these issues are discussed in greater detail later in the chapter.

Using Gimmicks to Sell a Story   Journalists also resent the gimmicks that often accompany news releases and media kits. T-shirts, coasters, caps, paper-weights, pens, and mugs have historically been the most popular items, but *PRWeek* columnist Benedict Carver says these items are dull and overdone: "Everyone has 50 mugs and T-shirts."

Consequently, public relations people and their marketing counterparts try to come up with more creative gimmicks that, in theory, will make their media kit stand out from all the others that arrive daily in the newsroom. Mindbridge Software, for example, wanted to raise the profile of the company's efficiency-improving products so it sent custom-printed rolls of toilet paper to reporters. The catchphrase printed on the toilet paper, next to the company logo, was "Helps you with the bottom line."

Other creative, and sometimes bizarre, methods of catching an editor's eye have included the following:

- A new lightbulb along with a new lamp to test its use
- A miniature Harry Potter broomstick wrapped in a scroll announcing a press luncheon and movie screening
- Two volleyballs emblazoned with details of a press event to announce the creation of a new professional women's volleyball league
- Four popcorn balls to announce the opening of a new roller coaster

Journalists often refer to such items as "trash and trinkets." Most items are innocuous, but some are downright tasteless or show poor judgment. A movie studio, for example, once sent editors a box of sirloin steaks to announce its cannibal-themed movie, *Ravenous*. And publicists for the book publisher Harlequin decided to announce a new book, *Fish Bowl*, by sending journalists fish bowls containing Betta Splendens, also known as "Siamese fighting fish." The gimmick made the press all right; PETA, the animal rights organization, fired off a public letter demanding that the book publisher and its public relations firm desist from using live animals in promotions.

Although many publicists think sending such gimmicks helps separate their media kits and releases from the pack, most journalists say they are a waste of time. In a national survey by Bennett & Company, an Orlando public relations firm, only 16 percent of the responding journalists ranked gimmicks as a good way of gaining attention.

June Kronholz, education reporter at *The Wall Street Journal*, told *PRWeek*, "Trinkets won't sell a story." As for the idea that promotional items will influence journalists to use a story, Kronholz says, "No one's going to buy anyone with a coffee mug. What PR people know and what they're counting on is that we'll open the boxes first. But they think that if we open the package first, we'll give it more consideration, and that's not true."

Matt Lake, a senior editor at C-Net, an online publication in San Francisco, was even more blunt. He told *The Wall Street Journal*, "These things are really stupid."

However, if you do decide to include a promotional item with your news release or media kit, *PRWeek* recommends the following guidelines.

- Make sure there is a "news hook" and a clear connection between the promotional item and the news you are announcing.

- Try to send items that reporters can use. Otherwise, they may be viewed only as an annoyance that takes up space.

- Consider creative packaging instead of a promotional item. A brightly colored envelope is likely to be opened before a white one.

- Think simply. Rather than sending a basketful of items, consider sending one item that represents the message you are trying to convey.

As a general rule, the value of such gimmicks and giveaways should not exceed $10 or $15. This helps avoid conflicts with a media outlet's ethics guidelines, which often limit the value of items that can be accepted. Some newspapers even have a policy that forbids staff to accept any promotional item.

Name Calling

The excesses of hype and promotion have caused many journalists to openly disdain public relations as nothing but covert advertising, deception, and manipulation. Or, as one columnist wrote, public relations people make their living by "sticking Happy Faces over unpleasant realities."

As a consequence, journalists tend to stereotype public relations people as "flacks," a derogatory term for press agents. It is somewhat like calling all lawyers "ambulance chasers" or all reporters "hacks."

While some reporters still use the term "flack" or "flak" to describe anyone in public relations, concentrated efforts by the public relations community have made the practice less common. *The Wall Street Journal*, for example, finally adopted a policy that forbids the use of the word "flack" by reporters in their stories. Unfortunately, reporters at other publications haven't gotten the word or have decided to update the word "flack" with the term "spin doctor." They use "spin" and "public relations" in the same breath. Such name calling by reporters impedes mutual respect and cooperation.

Sloppy/Biased Reporting

The quality of reporting does not seem to inspire much confidence among public relations people and organizational executives. One survey, for example, found that 82 percent of executives think news coverage today reflects the reporter's personal opinions and biases. Another survey of *Fortune* 500 communications executives found that 43 percent of them would give reporters a "B" grade, and another 38 percent would give reporters a "C" grade on covering their companies.

The biggest complaint of the *Fortune* 500 communication executives is that journalists are perceived as having no background in the subject they cover or are considered biased. These findings echo a survey some years ago by the American Management Association. It found that the majority of the public relations directors who participated thought that sloppiness on the part of reporters was the major reason for inaccurate stories. Reporters were also faulted for not doing their homework before writing a story, having a tendency to sensationalize, and making simplistic generalizations.

On the other hand, business executives often don't have a clear idea of how the media operate and what they need to write a fair, objective story. Many times, for example, executives give vague answers and stonewall reporters—and then complain that the story is not totally accurate. Executives also don't seem to realize that news stories go through various levels—writing, editing, headline writing, and placement—that are done by several people. This, of course, increases the chance of distortion.

You can reduce the percentage of sloppy reporting by doing three things:

- Educate executives about how the media operate and how reporters strive for objectivity. That means other viewpoints, sometimes unfavorable, will be in a story.

- Train executives to give 30-second answers to questions. This reduces the possibility of answers being garbled and distorted.

- Provide extensive briefing and background material to reporters who are not familiar with the topic or the organization.

- Familiarize executives with basic news values. Even *The Wall Street Journal*, says Senior Editor Dennis Kneale, looks for stories with "conflict, drama, and obstacles. . . . Our readers love to read about people, and about how egos and ambitions are shaping companies."

Tabloid Journalism

Newspapers and broadcast shows are not all alike, and the level of commitment to journalistic standards ranges from wholehearted to nonexistent. For example, *The Wall Street Journal* is highly praised for its objective and fair reporting, whereas the *National Enquirer* and the *Star* are famous for manipulated photos and headline stories based on hearsay.

The same situation exists in television. Shows such as *Access Hollywood, Jerry Springer Show, Jenny Jones,* and the *Ricki Lake Show* are known as "tabloid television" and "trash TV" because they concentrate on the sensational and have used the facade of traditional journalism on what is pure entertainment. This has been called "journaltainment."

The proliferation of tabloid television and its gloves-off approach means that you have to be very careful. Professor Fran Matera of Arizona State University, writing in *Public Relations Journal*, puts it succinctly:

> Tabloid journalists, no matter how pleasant, are not your friends. They are often there to trick or trap your client. They are looking for the one killer shot where they catch you or your client stammering and fumbling. That's what sells, and earns the reporter accolades.

Organizations are even becoming more wary of traditional shows such as *60 Minutes, 20/20,* and *Dateline NBC.* In the race for ratings, these shows have started to offer more sensationalism and to manipulate events for greater effect. As mentioned earlier, NBC was sued by General Motors and had to make an on-air apology for rigging a sequence that showed gas tanks on GM trucks exploding. The people responsible were all fired.

Such lapses of journalistic standards are a major concern for the media because the antics of an isolated few affect the credibility of all journalists.

Your challenge is to make sure you don't paint all media with the same brush. You should continue to give service to responsible journalists and provide information. However, if a reporter has a reputation for sensationalism, you are probably better off by refusing to be interviewed or to provide information.

If you do decide to work with a tabloid television reporter, Professor Matera provides some pointers that can help you keep control of the situation:

- Never do an adversarial interview alone. One option is to have a media-savvy lawyer sit in on the interview.

- Research the interviewer's record before facing the camera. Know his or her method of questioning.

- Don't accept any document on camera. Surprise documents can be used to trip up subjects and make them look foolish.

- Get a commitment that you will be able to respond to accusations made by others, as part of the story.

- If cornered, counterattack. Take the offensive and accuse the reporter of unprofessional conduct, incompetence, or a lack of understanding of the subject.

Advertising Influence

It is a fact of economic life that most media are dependent on advertising revenues for survival. Increased competition, coupled with a recession in the magazine industry, has made competition for ad dollars stiffer than ever.

"As a result," writes *Wall Street Journal* reporter Fen Montaigne, "some publications are feeling more pressure to please advertisers, either by running positive spreads on them, plugging them into captions, or including them in roundups of the best new products to buy."

Although mainstream news periodicals and daily newspapers generally keep a high wall between the news and advertising department, this is not always the case in the trade press and among specialized magazines. Beauty, fashion, auto, and home decorating magazines, for example, are well known for running fashion layouts and other features that prominently promote their advertisers. *Architectural Digest*, for example, actually has a policy of mentioning only advertisers in the magazine's captions for photo layouts. And Linda Wells, editor of *Allure*, told *The Wall Street Journal*, "We write about people who advertise in the magazine. That's what magazines do."

Influencing News Content On another level, large advertisers also have been known to influence story content in magazines and broadcast shows. Chrysler, for example, once insisted that magazines carrying the company's ads had to give the auto maker summaries of upcoming issues or advance warnings about controversial articles—so Chrysler could decide whether to pull its ads from a particular issue. The practice got considerable publicity and criticism after Chrysler cancelled its advertising in *Esquire* magazine because the editor decided to publish a novella about a gay man ghosting college term papers in exchange for sex.

But columnist Max Frankel, writing in *The New York Times Magazine*, says many corporations do the same thing. He writes, "Many airlines demand that the *Times* yank their ads if they appear near news of an air crash. Department stores take a dim view of showing their goods in the vicinity of news about discount stores. Supermarkets want a neighborhood of recipes, far from famines."

Buying Product Reviews   There's also concern that product reviews are influenced by advertisers. The editors of *PC Magazine*, for example, are often paid consultants on developing products that later go on to win the magazine's highly sought "Editor's Choice" award. In the car industry, automotive editors often serve as paid consultants to major auto companies that they also write about. It raises the question whether the "car of the year" is really chosen on the basis of performance, or on advertising and consulting contracts.

A Question of Ethics   All this, of course, raises troubling questions about journalistic ethics and integrity. The editors and reporters on specialty publications loudly proclaim that advertising and consulting assignments don't affect their editorial judgment, but their protestations seem a bit hollow and hypocritical.

The situation also affects public relations personnel. If the public increasingly takes a skeptical view of what they read and hear, the value of the media as an objective, independent source of information is compromised. Thus, messages from organizations won't have the same impact and believability that the media now bestow on such messages.

Advertising influence also presents practical problems for the public relations practitioner. How do you sort out the publications that are "for sale" and those that maintain high ethical standards? Should you build an advertising budget into your plans to pave the way for product reviews in some specialty publications?

If a publication insists that you buy an ad to get news coverage, should you go along with it? The PRSA Code of Ethics (Chapter 3) states that you should not engage in any activities that would "corrupt" the channels of communication. Is buying a full-page ad in a publication or paying an editor a consulting fee a violation of professional ethics? Or is it just good business?

WORKING WITH JOURNALISTS

There will always be areas of friction and disagreement between public relations people and journalists, but that doesn't mean there can't be a solid working relationship based on mutual respect for each other's work. Indeed, one definition of public relations is the building of relationships between the organization and its various publics, including journalists.

Press interviews, news conferences, media tours, and other kinds of gatherings provide excellent opportunities to build these working relationships. They are more personal than just sending written materials and allow reporters to get direct answers from news sources.

Company executives who are prone to stage fright may view such contact with the media as a nightmare. They fear that they will say something stupid, be misquoted, or be "ambushed" by an aggressive reporter who will slant the interview to imply that the organization is guilty of some wrongdoing.

Nevertheless, regular one-on-one contact with journalists helps the organization accomplish the objectives of increasing visibility, consumer awareness, and sales of services or products. They key is preparation. As book author Dick Martin points out, "In dealing with the press, as in any other business dealing, preparation is compulsory." The following discussion will provide tips and techniques to make sure that you or your organization's executives are prepared to meet the press.

Media Interviews

An old public relations joke goes, "You know you're going to have a bad day when your secretary tells you that Mike Wallace of *60 Minutes* is in the lobby."

A local newspaper or television reporter can cause the same sort of discomfort, particularly if he or she shows up unannounced. However, most press interviews are set up in advance. You can pitch a possible interview, or they can be requested by a reporter who is looking for credible experts to fill out a story.

There are many tip lists on how to conduct media interviews, but some points are worth noting here. First, if a reporter calls to request an interview, you should interview the reporter first. Some common questions are:

- Who are you?
- What is the story about?
- Why did you call me?
- What are you looking for from me?
- Who else are you speaking with?
- Are you going to use my comments in your story?
- When is the story going to run?

By asking such questions, you can decide if you are qualified to answer the reporter's questions or whether someone else in the organization would be a better source. You may also decide that the context of the story is not appropriate for your organization and decline to be interviewed. For example, the reporter may ask you to comment on some topic that has nothing to do with your organization.

One danger in a telephone interview is that you may be caught off guard and will not have time to formulate your thoughts. Before you know it, you and the reporter are chatting away like old friends about a number of topics. This is fine, but do remember that your name and a quote will probably appear in the article or as a soundbite on a newscast. It may be used accurately, or it may be completely out of context.

A better approach for a major interview, whether initiated by you or the reporter, is to schedule it in advance. If you know the purpose of the story, you can better prepare yourself or other spokespersons for the session.

Professional Tips

You Have the Right to Remain Silent

Most media guidelines emphasize that public relations personnel should always be helpful to and cooperative with the media. However, there are times when the best course of action is to remain silent.

Ron Levy, former president of North American Precis Syndicate and a lawyer, says public relations people should remain silent when:

- You don't know the answer.
- Management prefers that the answer come from someone who is an expert on the subject.
- You think the reporter will twist or distort your answer.
- Management says any answer to a particular question should be checked with legal counsel.
- The question deals with proprietary information that would benefit competitors.
- The inquiry is about the personal lives of employees.

Here are some tips, compiled from a number of sources, on how to handle interviews with print or broadcast personnel:

- Anticipate questions and plan answers. Be totally familiar with facts, figures, details that will help you sound credible.
- Prepare for the worst. Think of every question that might possibly be asked, reasonable or unreasonable. Then prepare answers for each.
- Be sure to state your key points early in the interview. Use examples and anecdotes. Don't tell half-truths. Don't exaggerate. Don't brag about your organization or its products or services.
- Answer questions, but link them to your message whenever possible.
- Be quotable. Say it briefly, clearly, and directly in 30 seconds or less.
- Speak conversationally and use personal anecdotes when appropriate.
- Don't let reporters put words in your mouth. Rephrase their words, avoiding negative ones.
- Don't lie. If you know information that's not appropriate to give out at that moment, say so.
- Don't ever say "no comment." It makes you sound guilty. Try to give the reporter a reason you can't comment, and offer alternative information if appropriate.
- There is no such thing as "off the record." Assume anything you say will appear in print or broadcast.
- Don't answer hypothetical questions.
- Don't speak ill about the competition or other individuals.

- Dress and act appropriately. Don't distract your listeners with defensive non-verbal language such as crossing your arms.

- Watch for loaded questions. Take time to think. Don't repeat a derogatory remark; shift to another subject.

- Always answer positively. It's the answer that counts, not the question.

- Watch your attitude. Don't be arrogant, evasive, or uncooperative. Don't argue. Don't use jargon. Don't lose your temper.

- Avoid memorizing your statements, but do use notes for reference. Speak from the public viewpoint; it is the public's interest that is important. Look at the interviewer when he or she is asking a question, but face the camera when you are answering a question being recorded by a television crew.

- Be cooperative, but don't surrender. Watch for presumptive questions: "Why are you resisting the efforts to control pollution?" "Why do you charge such outrageous prices?" Deny the statement and shift to another topic.

- If a question is unfair or too personal, say so and refuse to answer. You are not required to answer every question.

- Don't challenge figures unless you know for certain they are wrong. Remember that there are too many ways to cite statistics.

- Discuss only activities and policies that lie within your area of responsibility.

- Admit that you don't know the answer if that is the case. If you promise to provide more information later, make sure you do.

- Smile. Be as relaxed and informal as possible. A humorous remark may be used if it is appropriate, but don't be facetious; you might be misunderstood.

Other media training experts have added to and elaborated on this list. One common suggestion is to provide reporters with company background materials in advance. This will help them get facts and names correct. Body language is important. Be confident and relaxed, always look a reporter in the eye, keep your hands open, smile and lean forward when you're talking. The idea, says Stephen Rafe of Rapport Communications, is to be assertive and avoid being defensive, passive, submissive, or aggressive.

There are additional tips that apply to interviews on broadcast talk shows. Ketchum Communications gives the following advice:

- Say it in 60 seconds.
- Deliver your message with sincerity.
- Know your facts.
- Rehearse your message.
- Stay alert.
- Participate in discussion.
- Get your message across.

- Don't get mad.
- Don't look at the camera.

Grooming and dress are also important in a television program. Men should wear conservative suits. A sports jacket might be permissible in some cases, but it must not be loud. Wild plaids or violent colors won't do. Suits should be dark; if there is a pattern, it should be so subdued as to be almost invisible. Men should avoid white shirts. Pale blue, gray or tan with no noticeable pattern is best. Flashy rings, large cuff links, and big belt buckles are unacceptable. If a man has a dark beard, a shave just before the appearance is a good idea. For any television appearance, the producer may suggest some makeup. This should not be resisted; even the nation's presidents have used it.

Women should dress conservatively in dresses or suits. Makeup should be the kind that is normally worn for business. Any jewelry that dangles, jingles, or flashes is taboo.

Another important point is that the speaker is "on stage" at all times. A surreptitious scratch or adjustment of clothing may be seen by some members of the audience or picked up by a TV camera. A speaker should assume that an inelegant gesture will be seen.

News Conferences

A news conference is a setting where many reporters ask questions. It is called by an organization when there is important and significant news to announce, news that will attract major media and public interest.

Bulldog Reporter, a media relations newsletter, gives the following list of instances that are appropriate for news conferences:

- An announcement of considerable importance to a large number of people in the community is to be made.
- A matter of public concern needs to be explained.
- Reporters have requested access to a key individual, and it is important to give all media equal access to the person.
- A new product or an invention in the public interest is to be unveiled, demonstrated, and explained to the media.
- A person of importance is coming to town, and there are many media requests for interviews.
- A complex issue or situation is to be announced, and the media need access to someone who can answer their questions.

The two major reasons for having a news conference are to give all media an opportunity to hear the announcement at the same time and to provide a setting where reporters can ask follow-up questions. Many announcements, particularly ones involving research breakthroughs, major corporate decisions, and crises, raise numerous questions as reporters seek information on all aspects of an issue or event.

Professional Tips

Attribution in Interviews

A person being interviewed by a reporter should be familiar with the four levels of attribution. Guy L. Smith, head of his own public relations firm in New York, gave this explanation to *O'Dwyer's PR Services Report:*

- *On the record.* Everything you say can be attributed to you, either with quotes or paraphrased. ("We are not raising prices," says Betsy Knoop . . . .)
- *Background.* You can be quoted directly, but your name is not used. ("We are not raising prices," a Widget executive said.)
- *Deep background.* No quotes can be used. (A Widget executive said no price rise was being considered.)
- *Off the record.* There can be no direct or indirect quote of the information provided, nor can any of the information provided be attributed in any way to you, either directly or indirectly. (An industry source said . . . .)

Smith also advises that you take the time to make sure both you and the reporter have the same understanding of these terms before you proceed with any interview. It avoids unpleasant arguments later.

Other media relations experts take a cautious approach: they say it's better to assume that anything you say will be reported. It's risky to assume that a reporter will remember exactly what was "on the record" and what was "background" or "off the record."

Your role as a public relations professional is to determine when and if a news conference is needed. All too often, executives in an organization want to call a news conference to stir up publicity and make routine announcements that can just as easily be handled with a news release. Not only is this an expensive proposition, it also alienates the media, who have better things to do than attend news conferences when there is no news.

Scheduling a News Conference   The conference should be scheduled at a time that is convenient for the reporters—that is, with an eye on the deadlines of the media represented. In general, Tuesday, Wednesday, or Thursday mornings are best for dailies and broadcast media. This allows sufficient time for reporters to get stories in the next morning's daily or on the 6 P.M. news. If the primary audience is the trade press—reporters representing publications in a particular industry— late afternoon news conferences may be more convenient.

Avoid Saturdays and Sundays, as well as major holidays. Most media operate with skeleton staffs on these days and hence don't have the personnel to cover news conferences. Also, avoid news conferences after 5 P.M. Major newspapers and broadcast outlets are unionized, and they prefer not to pay reporters overtime.

Another consideration, which often can't be planned for, is to schedule the news conference on a day when there are not other major announcements or news events. In many major cities, for example, local bureaus of the Associated Press (AP) keep a "day book" of upcoming events, including news conferences that have already been scheduled by various organizations.

Selecting a Location   A location for a news conference must meet several criteria. First, it must be convenient for the media invited and relatively close to their places of work. Second, the room selected must have the necessary facilities to accommodate both print and broadcast media.

Organizations often use hotels and conference centers for news conferences, as well as the corporate headquarters. It is important for the room to have plenty of electrical outlets, particularly for radio and television crews. Television people may prefer a room on a ground floor near an entrance so that they can park a mobile communications center outside the room. In some cases, they will want to run cables from the truck to the room for live broadcast.

Live radio can involve microwave, cellular phone, or land-line transmission. Radio reporters will want a room with phone jacks or a bank of phones nearby.

You should make the room available one or two hours in advance so that radio and television crews can set up. You should have a general seating plan to make sure that the equipment doesn't obstruct the view or hinder the work of the print reporters. An elevated platform for TV cameras in the back of the room is helpful. See Figure 11.1, which shows a news conference in session.

If you think journalists from out of town would be interested in the news conference, it is now a standard procedure to hire your own video and audio crew to provide a transmission via closed-circuit television or the Internet. When the music industry announced a new copyright protection plan to allow music to be distributed on the Internet, 2,500 journalists and industry experts received press materials and heard the announcement online through their personal computers. Only 25 reporters actually attended the event, which was held in New York City.

Another consideration is to have several smaller rooms reserved nearby for exclusive interviews with a company representative after the general news conference.

Invitations   The invitation list should include all reporters who might be interested. It is better to invite too many than to omit some who may feel slighted.

Invitations take various forms, depending on the event and the creativity of the public relations person. The standard approach is a letter that can be delivered by first class mail, e-mail, fax, or even messenger. A second approach is a more formal invitation that incorporates some graphic elements. This approach is often used for new product announcements, acquisitions, and mergers.

A third approach is the stunt. When Swatch invited reporters to a news conference announcing a new line of divers' watches, it had people in SCUBA gear deliver aquariums containing invitations.

If the news conference will also be broadcast live via satellite to reporters in various cities, a satellite distribution firm will send a media advisory. Silicon

Figure 11.1 News Conferences
A good way to reach many reporters at the same time is to have a news conference. A brief statement or presentation is given, and the majority of the time is spent answering reporters' questions. Here, Sen. Hillary Clinton gives an impromptu sidewalk news conference.
(© Reuters News Media, Inc./Corbis.)

Graphics, for example, held such a news conference when it announced a joint business venture with movie producer Steven Spielberg. A video feed from a news conference was discussed in Chapter 9.

Use the telephone or e-mail if the conference is being scheduled on short notice. In any case, the invitation should state the time and place, the subject to be discussed, and the names of the principal spokespeople who will attend.

Print invitations should be sent 10 to 14 days in advance and should be marked "RSVP" so you can make appropriate decisions regarding the size of the meeting room, the number of media kits needed, and what special equipment will be required. Reporters are notorious for not responding to RSVPs, so it is standard procedure to phone or e-mail them several days before the event and encourage their attendance.

Handling the Conference   It is important that a news conference be well organized, short, and punctual. It is not a symposium or a seminar. A news conference should run no more than an hour, and statements by spokespeople should be relatively brief, allowing reporters time to ask questions.

You should brief your employers or clients on what they are going to say, how they are going to say it, and what visual aids will be used to illustrate their announcement. Reporters should receive copies of the text for each speech and other key materials such as slides, overheads, charts, executive bios, and background materials. These are often given to reporters in the form of a media kit, which was discussed in Chapter 8.

Coffee, fruit juice, and rolls can be served prior to the opening of a morning news conference. Avoid trying to serve a luncheon or cocktails to reporters attending a news conference. They have deadlines and other assignments and don't have time to socialize.

After the Conference   At the conclusion of the news conference, the spokespeople should remain in the room and be available for any reporters who need one-on-one interviews. This can be done in a quiet corner or in a room adjacent to the site.

As the public relations person, you should be readily accessible during the remainder of the day in case reporters need more information or think of other questions as they prepare their stories. You should know where the spokespeople are during the day and how they can be reached, just in case a reporter needs to check a quote or get another.

Another duty is to contact reporters who expressed interest but were ultimately unable to attend. You can offer to send them the printed materials from the news conference and, if you have recorded the news conference, offer excerpts of videotape or soundbites. Another possibility is to arrange a one-on-one interview with one of the spokespeople. In media relations, as stated previously, service is the name of the game.

Teleconferences

A variation of the news conference is the teleconference or Webcast. The technology is simple: a speakerphone hookup and a conference call linking reporters throughout the country. See Figure 9.11 for a Webcast alert.

According to a survey by the National Investors Relations Institute (NIRI), almost 75 percent of the *Fortune* 500 companies use large-scale conference calls to announce and disseminate quarterly financial results. In addition, NIRI estimates one out of three U.S. businesses use teleconferences at least once a month.

A teleconference or Webcast can be effective for several reasons. First, it is a cost-effective way to interact with reporters on a somewhat one-to-one basis. Second, it is convenient for the media. Rather than taking time to travel to and from a news conference, reporters can participate from their desks. Third, conference calls can be scheduled much more easily than a regular news conference or a meeting.

Here are some guidelines for holding a teleconference or Webcast:

- Invite reporters to participate in advance.

- The teleconference or Webcast should last no more than 45 to 60 minutes.
- Remember time zones when scheduling a teleconference.

Media Tours

An alternative to the news conference, which is held in one location, is the media tour. Unlike the satellite media tour (SMT) that was described in Chapter 9, this involves personal visits to multiple cities and a number of media throughout the region or the nation. Although the ultimate purpose of any media tour is to generate news coverage for the client or employer, there are two approaches. The first has the immediate objective of generating coverage; the second is focused on providing background and establishing a working relationship.

Generating Stories   Getting people on talk or interview shows was discussed in Chapter 9. In many cases, the spokesperson for an organization goes on a media tour and is booked on locally produced broadcast shows in various cities. The publicist also will arrange local print media interviews. This concept, already mentioned in Chapter 4, capitalizes on the idea that a "local" angle often gets more media attention.

A good example of how this works is a marketing communications program conducted on behalf of Step Reebok, an adjustable device for step training. The objective was to promote the product and physical fitness in general.

Rich Boggs, founder of Sports Step and creator of the adjustable step, was an ideal spokesperson. He was once an overweight, three-pack-a-day smoker who completely changed his lifestyle and now has a strong commitment to health and fitness.

Boggs went on a 14-city media tour to promote step training and his product. Because physical fitness was topical and trendy, he was able to get on 24 different TV news and talk shows, four of which were national. He also gave 21 radio interviews and was the subject of more than 20 newspaper feature articles.

The media tour, a key element in an overall marketing communications program, led to a 45 percent increase in sales of Step Reebok. A comparable advertising campaign would have cost almost $750,000.

Relationship Building   The second kind of tour is longer range in terms of results. An organization's officials visit key editors for the purpose of acquainting them with the organization and what products or services they provide. Unlike the first kind of tour, which focuses on the general media, these tours primarily involve publications that cover specific industries. At times, a media tour is also used to reach financial analysts who track a specific industry and make stock recommendations.

It would be difficult to get representatives from national business and trade publications to visit the offices of a small company. Yet by taking the president, the director of public relations, and perhaps the chief financial officer to the publication, it is possible to arrange for a one-on-one meeting with the editors. Your presentation may not result in a story immediately, but you will have laid the groundwork for future coverage. See the "PR Casebook" for a case study of a media tour.

The Role of a PR Firm   Public relations firms often are hired to arrange media tours. Their job is to (1) schedule appointments with key editors, (2) conduct media training for the organization's spokespeople, (3) prepare an outline of key talking points, (4) make airline, hotel, and local transportation arrangements for each city, and (5) prepare a briefing book about the background of the editor and the publication that will be visited. Excerpts from such a book are shown in Figures 11.2 and 11.3. Of course, an account executive from the public relations firm goes on the media tour and coordinates all the logistics.

Previews and Parties

Three basic situations warrant a press preview or party: (1) the opening of a new facility, (2) the launch of a new product, and (3) announcement of a new promotion for an already established product.

PR Casebook

A Media Tour Pays Off

Handspring, Inc. faced a challenge. Although the company was already established in the media as a leading innovator of handheld computing products, it needed a strategy to launch its new Treo product line. With such respected giants as Nokia and Ericsson commanding this market, how could a small handheld computer manufacturer compete?

Handspring and its public relations firm, Switzer Communications, decided that an aggressive media tour—including product demonstrations—conducted with a wide range of media and financial analysts, would be vital to the launch of the Treo product line and subsequent product reviews. The objectives were (1) position Handspring as a leading innovator of new products and technologies, (2) launch and establish credibility for a new communicator product line, and (3) educate consumers about the extension of product lines, not a replacement for current products.

Switzer Communications organized a media tour that included a broad range of publications, including technology, business, and consumer-focused media, through an extensive series of briefings. The tour, which took place several weeks before the product was actually available for purchase, consisted of a 10-day sweep of the West and East coasts, including Boston, New York, Washington D.C., Los Angeles/San Diego, and the San Francisco/Bay Area. In addition, Switzer organized briefings with top wire syndicates, online news and trade sites, and daily newspapers on the Thursday and Friday before the Monday launch to secure announcement-day coverage.

The media tour gave journalists an early preview and demonstration of the Treo product line. According to Switzer, publications with a combined circulation of 43 million covered the launch of the new product line. Ellen Sheng of *The Wall Street Journal*, for example, reported, "Shares of Handspring, Inc. sprang up as much as 53 percent Monday following announcements that its highly anticipated integrated wireless device would be on the market."

The media tour had a budget of $60,000. According to Switzer Communications, the return on investment (ROI) was 717 print impressions per PR budget dollar. The coverage not only boosted sales but also the value of the company's stock.

Thursday, April 22

Breakfast is on your own. Please check-out on Thursday by 8:45 a.m. Car service will pick you up at the upper ramp mezzanine level entrance of the hotel at 9:00 a.m.

Car Service
Music Express
1-800/255-4444
Confirmation #772388
Pick up from the Grand Hyatt is at 9:00 a.m.

- *Fortune Magazine* **10:00 a.m.**

Directions from the Grand Hyatt New York to *Fortune Magazine*: Approx. 5 minutes

Go Southeast on E 44TH ST towards 2ND AVE. Turn RIGHT onto 2ND AVE. Turn RIGHT onto E 42ND ST. Turn RIGHT onto 6TH AVE.

1271 Avenue of the Americas
New York, NY
212/502-1212

- *Computer Shopper* **11:30 a.m.**

Directions from *Fortune Magazine* to *Computer Shopper*: Approx. 5 minutes

Go Northeast on 6TH AVE towards W 51ST ST. Turn LEFT onto W 51ST ST. Turn LEFT onto BROADWAY -BROADWAY becomes JACK DEMPSEY COR. Turn LEFT onto W 48TH ST. Turn RIGHT onto 7TH AVE. 7TH AVE becomes ACTOR SQ. Stay straight to go onto 7TH AVE. 7TH AVE becomes BROADWAY. BROADWAY becomes GREELEY SQ. Turn LEFT onto W 32ND ST. Turn LEFT onto PARK AVE.

One Park Avenue
11th Floor
New York, NY
212/503-3900

Figure 11.2 Media Tours
A briefing book, often prepared by a public relations firm, gives organizational spokespersons a schedule of appointments and directions to a publication.
(Courtesy of Copithorne & Bellows public relations, San Jose, CA.)

Journalists are often invited to tour a new facility before it is open to the general public. This allows them to prepare stories that will appear one or two days before the grand opening. From a public relations standpoint, this kind of coverage helps generate public awareness of the new facility and often increases opening-day crowds. Press previews are routine for a new corporate headquarters, hospital wing, shopping mall, department store, restaurant, even a new toxic waste dump. In most cases, the press gets a background briefing, a media kit, and a tour.

Demonstrations of new products also lend themselves to press previews. See Figure 11.6 on page 328 for a press invitation to an amusement park. This is particularly true in high technology, where sophisticated products can be put through

---

Fortune Magazine

Jane Hodges   Thursday, 10:00 a.m.

Overview

Fortune Magazine is a magazine written for the business and investor community. *Fortune*'s mission is "to be the world's most influential source of ideas, explanations, and solutions for decision makers." The magazine's focus is on management and competition: how an industry will shake out, who's competing with whom, and who will end up on top. *Fortune* reports on successful enterprises, people, strategies, trends, management styles, and technology in the American business community. Stories often profile people or companies that are doing innovative things with computers or with the business of technology to turn a better profit. *Fortune* stories also deal with emerging technologies and how they have contributed to a business person's success. Computer and technology coverage appears throughout the magazine in the context of business stories. Computer coverage most often appears in the Information Technology, Managing, and First sections.

Editorial Profile

Jane Hodges is a reporter at *Fortune Magazine*. Prior to *Fortune,* Hodges was a reporter for *Advertising Age*. She was also a freelance writer.

Figure 11.3 Know the Publication
Briefing books also give organizational spokespersons a brief background of the publication where they will make a presentation. A brief background on the reporter often is included.
(Courtesy of Copithorne & Bellows public relations, San Jose, CA.)

their paces by the engineers who developed them. Many companies have a press preview of their products just before a major trade show. The advantage is that reporters from all over the country are already gathered in one place.

New campaigns for old products also generate their share of press previews and parties. The Champagne Wine Information Bureau, for example, invited food and wine journalists to a tasting at the Bubble Lounge in New York to kick off Champagnes Week, a nationwide promotion.

Planning a press preview is like planning any other event (see Chapter 17). Great attention must be paid to detail and logistics to ensure that the guests have a positive experience. See Figure 11.4 for an example of a digital press invitation to a product preview.

Of course, even the best plans sometimes go awry. The staff of Daniel Edelman Public Relations was red-faced when a USAir 757 flight crew did not

TOSHIBA
INVITATION

The evolution of Technology is often thought to occur on the edge. Come join us for a preview of Toshiba's Tablet PC in the epicenter of the hottest trends in business and technology....New York City.

Teaming up with Microsoft, Toshiba has redefined the way users think about and use their PC.

Come experience the evolution of mobile computing.

Figure 11.4 Invitation to a Media Preview
Reporters are often given an advance opportunity to see a new product before it appears in the stores. Toshiba sent this e-mail invitation to selected reporters to show off its new Tablet PC in Times Square. The advantage of such an invitation is that journalists can instantly RSVP. See Figure 1.1 for a product photo of the Toshiba Tablet PC.
(Courtesy of Toshiba and its public relations firm, Benjamin Weber Shandwick.)

show up to fly a plane for a demonstration of In-Flight Phone's new air-to-ground communication system. On board waiting for the demonstration were more than 100 newspeople who had been brought to Washington, D.C., to cover it.

Previews may also include a cocktail party or a dinner. One national company combined a press preview of its new headquarters building with a party that included cocktails and dinner. This kind of event falls into the category of relationship building and networking. It allows company executives to mingle and socialize with reporters in a casual atmosphere. Ultimately, this helps executives feel more relaxed when a reporter they already know wants to interview them for a story. Unlike news conferences, press previews are often held after "working hours," when reporters are not on deadline.

Press Junkets

A variation on the press preview is the press tour. Such events, in the trade, also are called **junkets**. Within the travel and tourist industry, they are called **fam trips**, which is shorthand for familiarization tour (see Figure 11.5). By whatever name, they usually involve invitations to key reporters and experienced freelance writers for an expense-paid trip to witness an event, view a new product, tour a facility, or visit a resort complex.

Here are some examples of press tours:

- Joe Boxer Corporation took 150 fashion and lifestyle reporters on an all-expense-paid weekend trip to Reykjavik, Iceland, to unveil its new line of underwear and pajamas.
- Weber-Stephens Products took 25 journalists on a four-day trip to the Bahamas to launch its new line of charcoal and gas grills.
- Ford Motor Co. took 14 auto editors and journalists on a five-day trip to France, where it was unveiling a new model at the Paris auto show.

Figure 11.5 Press Junkets
An important tool in travel promotion is the familiarization trip, often called a "fam" trip. Travel writers are taken as guests to inspect a travel destination such as a resort complex.
(© Edeleman)

- The Australian Tourist Commission regularly invites groups of travel writers "down under" to acquaint them with the country's natural wonders.

Although all-expense-paid junkets are a well-established practice, journalists remain somewhat divided about the ethics of participating in them. Some feel the acceptance of free trips is a corrupting influence on journalistic freedom. Some large media organizations, such as *The New York Times, Conde Nast Traveler*, and *USA Today* even have policies against free trips. They see no reason why a reporter has to travel all the way to Iceland for the unveiling of a new underwear line. Other organizations, such as *The Chicago Tribune* and CNN, will not accept expense-paid trips but will pay a discount "press rate" on airfares and hotel rooms if they think the tour is sufficiently newsworthy. Still other media outlets, smaller and less wealthy, have no qualms whatsoever about accepting free trips.

As a consequence, public relations people must consider carefully all aspects of sponsoring a junket and whether the cost is justified in terms of potential benefits. One of the most important things to remember, says Andrea Graham in *O'Dwyer's PR Services Report*, "is that a sponsored trip is not accepted in exchange for a rave review. It's simply a means of facilitating a writer's research." In other words, there is no guarantee that a story will be written or that it will be positive.

To be effective and generate good media relations, a press tour must be well planned and organized. There must be a legitimate news angle, and it should not be just a vacation with plenty of free food and booze. Lavish entertainment and the giving of expensive gifts are frowned upon in the ethics code of the Society of Professional Journalists (SPJ) and the Public Relations Society of America (PRSA). Journalists, although they may attend, generally "bad-mouth" the affair if they think there has been an overt attempt to "buy" favorable coverage.

What PR Firms Do   Public relations firms often are hired to organize media tours. Their job is to take care of virtually everything—airline tickets, press kits, itineraries, hotel rooms, local transportation, event tickets, menus, and even special requests from somewhat jaded journalists who expect first-class treatment. According to Teri Grove, owner of a Denver firm specializing in travel tourism, "Hosting a press trip is extremely labor intensive, since no detail can be overlooked during the trip, from the moment guests are greeted at the airport to their departure."

Editorial Board Meetings

The key editors of a newspaper or a magazine meet on a regular basis to determine editorial policy. Your client or employer, on occasion, may wish to meet with them as part of an overall strategy of developing long-term relationships. Editors usually are long-term employees of a publication.

Charitable agencies, for example, often meet with a local newspaper's editorial board to request coverage and editorials supporting a particular community cause—such as a fight against illiteracy or a drive to donate food to the homeless. Corporations and trade groups also meet with editorial boards to give background briefings on complex issues or why some pending legislation is good or bad from

Figure 11.6 A Creative Press Preview Invitation
Six Flags Marine World used the creative approach to invite journalists to a press review of a new roller coaster. This invitation was attached to a bright yellow Hoola-Hoop that was delivered by messenger to newsrooms in the San Francisco Bay Area. Reporters were given three choices of preview times and were offered satellite uplinks, video, and still photographs.
(Courtesy of Six Flags Marine World.)

their perspective. Of course, political candidates also seek meetings with editorial boards in the hope of persuading the publication to endorse their candidacy.

In general, you contact the editorial page director and request a meeting with the publication's editorial board. Most editors want a tightly written, one-page letter outlining who you represent, what issues you would like to cover, and why your representatives are the best qualified to discuss the issue. Don't weigh down your first letter with a media kit or other background information.

Once you have an appointment, you should develop a message that focuses on three or four key points. You should also decide in advance what you want to accomplish in the meeting. Do you simply want the editors to know about your viewpoint so it can perhaps be incorporated into future news stories and editorials, or do you want them to write an editorial supporting you?

The best approach is to have a well-informed senior person from your organization give the presentation. This may be the company president, but it can be an expert in a particular field such as law, accounting, environmental standards, technology, etc., depending on the issue. In general, your role as the public relations person is not to give the presentation but to make arrangements for the meeting, prepare the background materials, and help your spokesperson prepare for it.

PR Reporter gives the following tips for meeting with editorial boards:

- Conduct a practice session before the meeting, responding to difficult questions; it helps to know something about previous editorial positions.
- Take no more than four people. Well-known experts with credentials are great as long as they can explain their views simply.
- Don't expect more than a half-hour.
- Bring the same materials you would have sent had there been no meeting.
- Leave videos at your office (they won't watch them).
- Offer to submit an op-ed piece if the editors do not adopt your position.
- Write a follow-up note offering further information and the names of third-party experts that can be contacted.

Ann Higbee, managing partner at Eric Mower and Associates, sums up the value of editorial boards. She writes, in *PR Tactics*, "Building good working relationships with the editorial board can help your organization get credit for the positive things it does and lays the groundwork for public understanding in tough times."

A MEDIA RELATIONS CHECKLIST

Many checklists and guidelines for dealing effectively with the media have been compiled. Most of them are well tested and proven, but you must always remember that there are no ironclad rules. Media people are also individuals to whom a particular approach may or may not be applicable. Here's a list of general guidelines, many of which will sound familiar to you from reading previous chapters

- **Know your media.** Be familiar with the publications and broadcast media that are used regularly. Know their deadlines, news format, audiences, and needs. Do your homework on other publications and broadcast shows before sending a pitch letter or news material.
- **Limit your mailings.** Multiple news releases are inefficient and costly, and they alienate media gatekeepers. Send releases only to publications and broadcast outlets that would have an interest in the information. You are not running a mass-mailing house.

- **Localize.** Countless surveys show that the most effective materials have a local angle. Take the time to develop that angle before sending materials to specific publications.
- **Send newsworthy information.** Don't bother sending materials that are not newsworthy. Avoid excessive hype and promotion.
- **Practice good writing.** News materials should be well written and concise. Avoid technical jargon and hype.
- **Avoid gimmicks.** Don't send T-shirts, teddy bears, balloon bouquets, or other frivolous items to get the attention of media gatekeepers.
- **Be environmentally correct.** Avoid giant media kits and reams of background materials. Save trees.
- **Be available.** You are the spokesperson for an organization. It is your responsibility to be accessible at all times, even in the middle of the night. Key reporters should have your office and home telephone numbers.
- **Get back to reporters.** Make it a priority to make a quick response to any media inquiries. One survey of journalists found that this was the #1 rule to establishing a good working relationship with reporters. Quick response is even more necessary when you are working with an online publication, because they work within a very tight time frame.
- **Answer your own phone.** Use voice mail systems as a tool of service, not as a screening device. Reporters (like other people) hate getting bogged down in the electronic swamp of endless button pushing.
- **Be truthful.** Give accurate and complete information even if it is not flattering to your organization. Your facts and figures must be clear and dependable.
- **Answer questions.** There are only three acceptable answers: "Here it is," "I don't know but I'll get back to you within the hour," and "I know but I can't tell you now because. . . ." "No comment" is *not* one of the three alternatives.
- **Avoid "off-the-cuff" remarks.** Don't say anything to a reporter that you would not wish to see in print or on the air.
- **Protect exclusives.** If a reporter has found a story, don't give it to anyone else.
- **Be fair.** Competing media deserve equal opportunity to receive information in a timely manner.
- **Help photographers.** Facilitate their work by getting people together in a central location, providing necessary props, and supplying subjects' full names and titles.
- **Explain.** Give reporters background briefings and materials so that they understand your organization. Tell them how decisions were reached and why.
- **Remember deadlines.** The reporter must have enough time to write a story. One good rule is to provide information as far in advance as possible. In addition, don't call a reporter at deadline time.

- **Praise good work.** If a reporter has written or produced a good story, send a complimentary note. A copy to the editor is also appreciated.
- **Correct errors politely.** Ignore minor errors such as misspellings, inaccurate ages, and wrong titles. If there is a major factual error that skews the accuracy of the entire story, talk to the reporter who wrote the story. If that doesn't work, talk to the editor or news director.

Media Etiquette

The points above constitute the core of effective media relations, but here are some additional tips about basic media etiquette that should be observed. Failure to do so often leads to poor media relations.

Irritating Phone Calls   Don't call a reporter or an editor and say, "Did you get my news release?" You should assume that it was received if you used a regular channel of distribution such as first-class mail, a courier service, fax, or e-mail.

Unfortunately, the practice of phoning reporters with such an inane question is widely used as a pretext for calling attention to the news release and making a pitch for its use. Although the approach seems logical, and some publicists strongly defend callbacks as an obligation to their employer or client, surveys continue to show that such calls are a major irritant to journalists. The *PRWeek* survey mentioned earlier in this chapter found that "repeated calls and follow-up" was one of the top five complaints journalists had about public relations people.

However, if your boss still insists on doing callbacks, it's better to call a reporter to offer some new piece of information or a story angle that may not be explicit in the news release. The telephone call then becomes an information call instead of a desperate plea to read the release and use it.

If you do call a journalist, the best time is usually in the morning. Never call when a publication is close to deadline unless you have late-breaking news.

Inappropriate Requests   Don't call reporters to ask them when a story will be used. Most reporters don't know when the story will be used, or even *if* it will be used. Editors make that decision based on the space and time available.

In addition, don't ask the publication or broadcast station to send you a news clipping or broadcast segment. If you want such materials, make arrangements with a clipping service or broadcast monitoring firm.

Finally, don't ask to see a story before it is published or broadcast. The media, citing policy and the First Amendment, usually refuse. It is permissible, however, to ask a reporter if you can check any quotes attributed to you. In many cases, you will still get a frosty no.

Lunch Dates   Don't take a reporter to lunch unless the purpose is to discuss a possible story or to give a background briefing on some upcoming event. In other words, a lunch should have a business reason. You need to be well informed about the product or idea and be organized. Reporters don't like to waste time in idle chitchat, nor are they impressed by dining at an expensive restaurant.

Setting the Record Straight

News coverage isn't always objective, factual, or accurate. Mistakes happen, and it is likely that you or your employer will have complaints about inaccurate and unfair news coverage. Here are several steps you can take.

Ascertain the facts. Analyze the offending article or broadcast news segment. What exactly is inaccurate, incomplete, or unfair about it? If it's simply a matter of not liking the tone of the story, there probably isn't much you can do about it. Oftentimes, organizational executives think any article that doesn't praise the organization is unfair and biased. If it's a matter of inaccurate information or something taken out of context that distorts the true picture, you should document the correct facts to make a convincing argument.

Talk to the reporter. Call the reporter and politely point out the inaccuracies. The reporter may correct the information in subsequent articles or broadcasts. Many newspapers also print corrections under the rubric of a clarification.

Talk to the editor. If you don't get satisfaction from the reporter, and the complaint is a major one, you may wish to write a letter to the editor and request publication. Another approach is to request a meeting with the editor and the reporter.

Go public. An old adage holds that you should never pick a fight with anyone who buys ink by the barrel; nevertheless, many companies take the offensive and make every effort to inform key publics about their side of the story. Letters can be sent to community opinion leaders, employees, or even stockholders, depending on the story. Another approach is to purchase advertising to rebut the allegations.

File a lawsuit. The last resort is to file a lawsuit if legal counsel believes that the newspaper or broadcast outlet has intentionally distorted the truth. A threatened libel suit often encourages the media outlet to print a correction or an apology. A lawsuit also gets media coverage, which gives the organization a platform to inform the public about inaccuracies in the original story.

If you do have lunch, give the reporter the opportunity to select the restaurant and pay for his or her portion of the meal. Many publications have strict rules forbidding reporters to accept free lunches. Others, of course, have no such restrictions. In your case, it is always acceptable to ask and then do whatever feels comfortable for the reporter.

Gift Giving Many organizations like to give reporters a souvenir for attending a preview or party. Gifts can be appropriate if they have nominal value, such as a coffee mug, a T-shirt, or even a CD. However, it is not wise to give expensive gifts because it raises questions of "influence buying." In any case, the gift should be available at the door, and reporters should be given the option of taking the gift or bypassing it.

Some organizations also send reporters Christmas gifts or even birthday presents, but this is becoming a rarity. This may be the custom in China, where reporters expect everything from watches to free Internet access, but American and Western European reporters think such a practice is a thinly veiled attempt to influence coverage.

There is also the problem of "gifts" that are actually outright bribes. In nations where there is a strong tradition of an independent press, giving money in unmarked envelopes to a reporter is considered unethical, illegal, and unprofessional. The International Public Relations Association (IPRA) has gone on record in strong opposition of "paying for play," but reporters in many nations—including the new nations of the former Soviet Union—say such "bribes" are an economic necessity because the wages are so poor.

Some public relations personnel take the attitude of "when in Rome, do as the Romans do." Most, however, refuse to provide "bribe" money because it violates their personal ethics and those of the national and international professional organizations such as the IABC, PRSA, and IPRA.

In the United States and Western Europe, bribes are not an issue because they are rarely offered. Journalism periodicals rarely, if ever, report that some reporter was offered $1,000 to do a story. Instead, the focus is on "gift giving" and whether it buys "influence." Most reporters say it doesn't.

Janelle Brown, an Internet news service reporter, posted a story on Salon.com about all the gifts that landed on her desk during the Christmas season. She notes, "More often than not, the thought of all that marketing money being blown on undeserved presents leaves me slightly nauseated. If a company really wanted to stand out this holiday season, it could put all those funds toward a better cause: a hefty donation toward a deserving charity. It may not make headlines, but then neither do all the baubles they send us."

In other words, gifts to reporters are rarely appreciated, or are they necessary to generate a good working relationship.

CRISIS COMMUNICATION

A good working relationship with the media is severely tested in times of crisis. All the rules and guidelines stated previously about working effectively with the press are magnified and intensified when something out of the ordinary occurs and thus becomes extremely newsworthy.

There are many dimensions of what constitutes a crisis for a company or an organization. Pacific Telesis, the parent company of Pacific Bell, defines a crisis as "an extraordinary event or series of events that adversely affect the integrity of a product; the reputation or financial stability of an organization; or the health of well-being of employees, the community, or the public-at-large."

Here is a sampling of major crises that have hit various organizations:

- The safety of Dow-Corning's silicone gel breast implants came under fire from both the medical community and thousands of women who claimed that they were harmed by the product.
- Sears was charged by consumer agencies in several states of defrauding customers and making unnecessary repairs at its auto centers.

- An outbreak of food poisoning, leading to the death of a two-year-old, was traced to contaminated beef served by Jack-in-the-Box restaurants in Washington State.

- Odwalla, the natural juice maker, had to recall most of its product line after several cases of *E. coli* poisoning—including one death—was linked to its unpasteurized apple juice.

- Microsoft, charged with monpolistic practices by the U.S. Department of Justice, received considerable unfavorable publicity that threatened its corporate reputation and credibility.

These situations, no matter what the circumstances, constitute major crises because the reputation of the company, industry, or product is in jeopardy. Economic survival is at stake, and a company can lose millions of dollars overnight if the public perceives that a problem exists.

Johnson & Johnson, owner of the maker of Tylenol, saw the brand's market share shrink from 37 percent to barely 6 percent in a matter of days after capsules laced with cyanide killed seven people in Chicago. By the time it was established that someone had tampered with the product after it had reached store shelves, the

PR Casebook

A Utility Uses Online Crisis Management

An energy crisis in California resulting in rolling power blackouts. One of the largest corporations in the U.S. filing for bankruptcy protection. The political crisis surrounding deregulation of the California electricity industry.

This is what Pacific Gas & Electric Company (PG&E) faced, and one of its solutions to fully informing consumers about what the company was doing about these crises was a revamped Web site (www.pge.com). The site was originally designed to provide functionality and interactivity to enhance customer service; people could pay their utility bill, sign up as a new customer, or close an account online.

However, with rolling blackouts and the deterioration of the utility's financial situation as the state government failed to solve deregulation problems, the Web site also became a major source of company information about these issues.

Harry Tuttle, manager of strategic communications, began to post power system status, safety information, and background information on the energy shortage. This information, along with news about the bankruptcy, was posted "above the scroll" on the home page, ensuring that what readers wanted was easy to find and access. In addition to the latest information, there was substantial detail on these topics to help frame and provide context.

The response to the site from customers and the media was favorable. At one point, hits on the Web site reached 20 million. Site tracking showed that nearly 50 percent of viewers were coming to the site for the purpose of viewing energy-crisis information. The media also used the site to get updated information and daily news releases. For their convenience, a pop-up window on the home page scrolled the latest news on the issues from both the utility and other sources.

One key element of crisis communications is to establish a consistent stream of information to concerned citizens. The PG&E site accomplished this.

ordeal had cost the company more than $50 million to recall the product and test all its manufacturing processes.

During such times of crisis, the media can be adversaries or allies. It all depends on how you and your organization manage the crisis and understand the media's point of view. Keep in mind the following guidelines developed by *PR Newswire*:

- "No comment" fuels hostility. Even a simple "Can I get back to you?" can be misconstrued as evasive.

- Always try to be helpful. Too many executives are so guarded in conversations with reporters that they miss opportunities to get their own case across.

- Be familiar with print and broadcast deadlines. Calling a news conference on or after a deadline may hurt your organization's chance to get fair or full treatment.

- Get to know the journalists in your area before a crisis hits. That way, they will already know something about you and your company, and you will have an idea of how they work.

The key to successful dealings with the media during a crisis is to become a credible source of information. *PR Newswire* suggests the following:

- Appoint a spokesperson whom the media can trust and who has authority to speak for the company. It also is a good idea to designate one spokesperson, so that the organization speaks with one voice.

- Set up a central media information center where reporters can obtain updated information and work on stories. You should provide telephone lines so reporters can talk with their editors or send e-mail messages. Provide fax machines and computers for their use. Provide food and transportation if necessary.

- Provide a constant flow of information, even if the situation is unchanged or negative. A company builds credibility by addressing bad news quickly; when information is withheld, the cover-up becomes the story.

- Be accessible by providing after-hours phone numbers or carrying a cellular phone with you at all times.

- Keep a log of media calls, and return calls as promptly as possible. A log can help you track issues being raised by reporters and give you a record of which media showed the most interest in your story.

- Be honest. Don't exaggerate, and don't obscure facts. If you're not sure of something or don't have the answer to a question, say so. If you are not at liberty to provide information, explain why.

These guidelines reflect plain common sense, but when a crisis hits, it is surprising how many organizations go into a defensive mode and try to stonewall the media. Dow-Corning, for example, got considerable negative coverage by treating the media as an enemy. Corporate spokespeople accused the media of reporting only the "sensationalistic, anecdotal side of the breast implant story, which has un-necessarily frightened women across the country." At a news conference, the head of Dow's health-care business continued the attack by telling the assembled re-porters that they took "memos out of context and distorted reality." It would be an understatement to say that this is a poor way to get the press on your side.

Jack-in-the-Box also violated the tenets of crisis communications in the first days of the reported food poisonings. The company initially said "no comment" and then waited three days to hold a news conference, at which the company pres-ident tried to shift the blame to the meat-packing company.

David Vogel, a business professor at the University of California in Berkeley, says, "There are two principles: accept responsibility and take action." Even if you are not directly at fault, the organization should take responsibility for its product and the public safety.

Johnson & Johnson did this with Tylenol, but Dow-Corning chose to defend its product even after evidence had mounted that the company knew the product had a history of causing medical problems. Experts also say that Jack-in-the-Box fumbled early on by not showing concern for the poisoned customers. The com-pany would have won more public goodwill and favorable press coverage by more quickly offering to pay all medical bills, which it eventually did.

Pacific Telesis, perhaps learning from the mistakes of others, emphasizes two considerations in its crisis-management plan:

- Demonstrate our commitment to good corporate citizenship by taking prompt and decisive actions to control problems in our operations.

- Communicate swiftly, constantly, and consistently to all appropriate audi-ences in clear, straightforward, nontechnical language.

SUMMARY

- Journalists depend on public relations sources for receiving most of their in-formation; public relations people rely on the media for widespread distri-bution of information.

- The most common complaints journalists have about public relations peo-ple, according to a *PRWeek* survey, are (1) lack of familiarity with editorial requirements and format, (2) poorly written materials, (3) too many unso-licited e-mails and phone calls, (4) lack of knowledge about their product or service, and (5) repeated calls and follow-ups.

- Gimmicks, such a T-shirts and coffee mugs, are not well received by re-porters and editors.

- "Flack" or "flak" is a disparaging term for a press agent or publicist.

- The major complaint about journalists is that they are sloppy in their accu-racy and often don't take the time to do their homework.

- Publications and broadcast programs that engage in sensational journalism require special handling and precautions. Declining an interview is always an option.

- Media credibility is undercut when publications link advertising contracts with the amount of coverage that an organization receives.

- Spokespersons for an organization should prepare carefully for media interviews. Media training is essential to assure a positive outcome.

- News conferences should be held only if there is significant news that lends itself to elaboration and questions from journalists. News conferences can also be held via teleconferences or online.

- Media tours involve travel to major cities and setting up appointments with local media outlets. One purpose is to generate coverage; another is to acquaint editors with your product, services.

- Previews and parties are acceptable ways of giving executives and reporters a chance to know each other better. Gifts are not necessary.

- Press tours, often called junkets, should be used only if there is a legitimate news story or angle. Avoid junkets that simply wine and dine journalists.

- A meeting with a publication's editorial board is a good way to establish rapport and long-term relationships.

- There are many guidelines for how to conduct effective media relations. The bottom line is to be accurate, truthful and provide outstanding service.

- Don't irritate reporters by asking, "Do you get my news release? Also, don't ask to see an advance copy of the story or when a story will be published.

- If you need to set the record straight, begin with the reporter who wrote the story.

- Crisis communications is a test of excellent media relations. You need to work closely with the media to assure that the public is fully informed.

ADDITIONAL RESOURCES

Adams, Bill. "Media Training Is Not Enough When Preparing Executives for the Press." *PR Tactics*, May 2003, p. 18.

Bernheimer, Mark. "Confessions from a Former Reporter." *PR Tactics*, December 2002, p. 16.

Bernstein, Jonathan. "The 10 Steps of Crisis Communications." *PR Reporter*, March 3, 2003, pp. 1–2. Tips & tactics.

Bollinger, Lee. "Public Relations: Business and the Press." *Public Relations Quarterly*, Summer 2003, pp. 20–22.

Burnett, James. "Poynter Study Finds Increased Media Reliance on Spokespeople." *PRWeek*, March 25, 2002, p. 1.

Creamer, Matthew. "Repairing Relationships with Reporters." *PRWeek*, March 23, 2003, p. 26.

DeLorne, Denise E., and Fedler, Fred. "Journalists' Hostility toward Public Relations: An Historical Analysis." *Public Relations Review*, Vol. 29, 2003, pp. 99–124.

Grove, Aimee. "Make the Media Sit up and Listen." *PRWeek*, January 15, 2001, p. 22.

Himler, Peter. "Building Relationships with Reporters." *O'Dwyer's PR Services Report*, December 2002, p. 28.

Howard, Carole M. "When a Reporter Calls." *PR Tactics*, December 2002, p. 10.

Kornecki, Bob. "Building Trust: Challenges and Opportunities for the PR Profession." *The Strategist*, Spring 2003, pp. 28–31.

McGaugh, Scott. "Media Training the Media." *PRTactics*, December 2001, p. 13.

McLoughlin, Barry. "The Truth About Media Training." *PR Tactics*, December 2002, p. 12.

Seitel, Fraser. "Media Relations 'Don'ts' for PR Pros." *O'Dwyer's PR Services Report*, January 2002, p. 30.

Trickett, Eleanor. "The Sink or Swim World of Exclusive Stories." *PRWeek*, October 28, 2002, p. 18.

Trickett, Eleanor. "Corrections and the Pursuit of Accuracy." *PRWeek*, June 3, 2002, p. 18.

Trickett, Eleanor. "Making Friends and Influencing Papers." *PR Week*, February 25, 2002, p. 18. Pitching to editorial writers.

Trickett, Eleanor. "Building Relationships with Reporters." *PRWeek*, January 14, 2002, p. 22.

"Trinkets and Trash: What Reporters Think of Promotional Freebies and Whether They Help your Company Get Ink." *Ragan's Media Relations Report*, February 17, 2003, pp. 1, 6.

Walker, Jerry. "Media Coach Puts Clients in Reporters' Shoes." *O'Dwyer's PR Services Report*, February 2003, p. 28.

Walker, Jerry. "Reporters Tell PR Pros: Hold the Spam." *O'Dwyer's PR Services Report*, July 2002, p. 30.

Chapter 12

Newsletters, E-zines, and Brochures

The newsletter, e-zine, and brochure are major communication tools in any organization.

They are designed for a specific audience, such as employees, or for a variety of groups that may include stockholders, community opinion leaders, government officials, suppliers, or customers. As such, they serve as effective channels of continuous information about the organization. They also have the advantage of reaching their audiences without the filtering process of mass media reporters and editors who, as noted in Part 1, control the distribution of the message and the content.

This chapter gives a brief overview of what is involved in the writing and production of these publications. We will examine the editor's role and the content, design, production, and distribution of these periodicals in print and electronic form. We will then turn our attention to the writing of brochures and the basics of desktop publishing.

THE VALUE OF PRINT PUBLICATIONS

The Wall Street Journal, several years ago, announced in a page 1 headline that "Employee Newsletters Are Rapidly Becoming Obsolete." The article pointed out that organizations were switching to other communication tools—internal TV, e-mail, and Web pages—to inform employees and even external audiences.

Although the new technologies are being used with increased frequency by all organizations, most professional communicators agree with Mark Twain, who once said, "The reports of my death are highly exaggerated." Indeed, newsletters and magazines in print form—as well as brochures in countless formats—are still alive and well in the age of cyberspace.

There are several reasons why printed publications continue to be produced in vast quantities. Many organizations, for example, still find printed periodicals more efficient in reaching their entire workforce. This is particularly true of many companies that have field staff and plant workers who have limited access to electronic communications via computer. The problem is well defined by Libby Howell, administrator of corporate communications for Southwest Gas Corporation, who was quoted in *PR Tactics:* "The schism between PC-dependent employees and so-called 'blue collar' workers is widening daily, providing corporate communicators with the serious challenge of how to best reach these disparate groups."

In order to reach all its workers, Mobil Oil (now ExxonMobil) produced a magazine six times a year for its 43,000 employees in 125 countries. According to Gary Grates, writing in IABC's *Communication World*, the print publication is extremely popular because "it keeps employees feeling connected, no matter where they are—on a rig, at a refinery, or at the company's corporate offices."

Grates, who is now executive vice president for executive communication at General Motors, also gives a second reason why printed newsletters and magazines continue to thrive. He says, "A printed publication is unique; employees can hold it, touch it, mark it up, pass it around, take it home, and refer back to it." He quotes another senior communication executive who says, "There's just something about a well-written newsletter or magazine that gives you a real feel for an organization—it's not a feeling you get with e-mail or a fax or any of the more immediate types of communication."

Echoing this thought is Karen White, corporate communications specialist for Alpha Therapeutic Corporation. She told *PR Tactics*:

> There's something about a well-designed newsletter printed on quality paper that gives you a feel for an organization. It has a personality. This is something you can't communicate as easily on a computer. It's a way to recognize employees. Whether it's an employee anniversary, an award ceremony, or the winning softball team, people like to see their names and photos in print. When people appear in the employee newsletter, they want to take them home to their families and post them on bulletin boards at work. It's not as permanent with a video or computer message.

Last, but not least, many organizations continue to publish high-quality publications because the look and feel of them, coupled with the content, make a powerful, positive impression on clients, prospective customers, and opinion leaders. In other words, a well-designed and well-written publication conveys the image that the organization is highly successful, well managed, and a market leader.

Accenture, for example, launched a new magazine for its employees when it began a campaign to reinforce its new brand positioning and personality. New typography, photos, and stories reflected and reinforced the idea that the company was composed of professionals who brought "insights, practical know-how, and integrated capabilities to help clients achieve success."

Another premier publication is *Promise*, published by St. Jude's Children's Hospital in Memphis. According to Elizabeth Jane Walker, publications manager:

> The magazine serves as the hospital's external platform to educate the public about the innovative research and excellent medical care happening at St. Jude. The publication tells the public who we are—a world-class biomedical research institution as well as children's hospital that treats patients regardless of their families' ability to pay. Promise puts a 'face' to our work—introducing readers to individual patients who benefit directly from the research and clinical care at St. Jude.

See Figure 12.1, which shows a cover from the issue of the magazine and its lead feature story about a patient. The story received a Bronze Anvil for excellence from the Public Relations Society of America (PRSA).

Although it is clear that print publications are not "obsolete," or doomed to extinction anytime soon, they are changing to accommodate the realities of the digital revolution. E-mail and the company **intranet** are excellent channels for giving late-breaking news and daily updates, but newsletters and magazines are better vehicles for in-depth analysis and feature articles. Gary Grates, already mentioned, says, "Today's employee publications are less about immediacy and more about providing analysis, rationale, and specifics. And the content reflects this; instead of news briefs and time-sensitive announcements, included are stories in depth, profiles and lighter feature articles."

Adding to this thought is Mary Hettinger, a communications specialist for Staples, Inc. She is quoted in *PR Tactics*: "The role for printed publications should be to expand on news with more feature-oriented articles—describing the company's goals and direction; educating employees on the business they are in so they can excel; recognizing and profiling model employees; conveying the leader's personalities; showcasing how the company is a good corporate citizen. . . ."

Echoing Hettinger's thoughts, Paul Sanchez wrote in *Communication World*, "Communicators and senior management must work to establish proactive, well-defined communication strategies that engage and align employees with the organization's business goals. A closer tie between business and communication strategies will help the work force understand and support the direction of the organization."

These comments make it clear that organizational newsletters and magazines, and even brochures, have a strategic role to play in advancing the organization's goals and objectives. This means that the editors of these publications have several roles to play.

Into the Light

Katelyn Atwell journeys out of the shadows with the help of her faith, family, friends and St. Jude caregivers

By Elizabeth Jane Walker

One chilly day last December, Sharon Atwell stood, transfixed, watching her youngest daughter carry the Olympic torch through the streets of Memphis. Amid a deafening tumult of cheers, shouts, sirens and applause, 15-year-old Katelyn Atwell waved serenely at the crowd and, with a radiant smile, quietly passed the Olympic flame to her mother.

Only two years earlier, Katelyn's own flame had almost been extinguished by a bacterial infection that had catapulted her into the yawning void of a coma. Her journey back to the light has been slow, tortuous, and—in the words of many St. Jude researchers and health care providers—miraculous.

The candle flickers

Long before she ever held an Olympic torch, Katelyn Atwell had acquired the discipline and tenacious spirit of an athlete. A competitive swimmer, she spent countless hours in the pool, testing her limits. That same sense of determination also pervaded other aspects of Katelyn's life. When her family moved from Florida to Tennessee, the outgoing youngster joined the band and the flag squad at her new school, and helped lead a children's choir at church. Life was good; life was busy. Then her back began to hurt, and Katelyn went to the doctor. Soon the diagnosis came back: acute lymphoblastic leukemia.

In June of 1999, Katelyn began treatment at St. Jude Children's Research Hospital. But after two weeks of chemotherapy, she complained of a chill. Immediately, her physician prescribed three antibiotics and admitted her to the hospital. "We rarely see meningitis in our patients, and even if it were meningitis, with three antibiotics, she should have been covered," recalls Jeffrey Rubnitz, MD, of Hematology–Oncology. But then Katelyn started having seizures. The doctors found that she had *Bacillus cereus* meningitis, an infection so rare that only six cases had been documented in medical literature. Two days later, she was critically ill on a ventilator. She slipped into a coma. Everyone thought she was going to die.

Everyone except Katelyn's mother, father and sister. During the five months Katelyn spent in the Intensive Care Unit (ICU), Katelyn's mother never left her side, constantly optimistic and determined, clinging to her faith in the midst of staggering odds. "I think Katelyn's mom almost willed her to live," observes Robert Tamburro, MD. "A lot of times, people are unrealistic or irrational, and act upbeat because they haven't really accepted how serious the situation is. That was never the case with Katelyn's family. They said, 'We're going to stick with our faith and be as upbeat and positive for Katelyn as we can, because that's what she's going to need.' "

Sharon watched as scientists and clinicians joined forces to fight for Katelyn's life. "The people at this hospital don't accept defeat gracefully," Sharon says. "When you present them with challenges, they really

Figure 12.1 Magazines Set Tone and Image

St. Jude's Children's Research Hospital sends its glossy magazine, *Promise*, to more than 12,000 readers who include top-level donors, elected officials, medical reporters, and employees. The publication puts a "face" on the organization's work by showing donors how their dollars are saving the lives of children around the world. The best way to do that is to introduce them to a patient whose story is compelling and memorable. "Into the Light," which is reprinted here, received a Bronze Anvil in the feature story category from the Public Relations Society of America (PRSA).

(Magazine cover and story courtesy of St. Jude's Children's Research Hospital, Memphis, TN.)

go to battle. It was a hospital-wide effort. Our doctors would be beeped by scientists in the Danny Thomas Research Tower, who would say, 'I've been researching Kate's situation. Have you tried this or that?' Every department was doing everything they possibly could—researching and calling other hospitals to see if they could find anyone who had ever had this infection before."

At one point, a prominent neurosurgeon arrived to provide a second opinion on Katelyn's condition. "He looked at the diagnosis, he saw the type of infection that she had, he looked at the CAT scan, and he told me, 'You might as well kiss this baby goodbye and call your family in, because there is no hope for her,' " Sharon recalls. "I believe with all my heart that if she had been in any other hospital than St. Jude, they would have taken his word for it, and Katelyn would have passed away. But the folks at St. Jude said, 'You know, we're not ready to believe that yet,' and they called in someone else."

Because of increased pressure within her brain, Katelyn underwent dozens of operations to insert drains, shunts and remove cysts. The trauma to her brain prompted what doctors called autonomic storms. Her temperature would plateau at 108 or 109 degrees for more than 12 hours. Her heart rate would sky-rocket, and her blood pressure would increase to 200/185. The storms would abate for a couple of hours, and then they would resume with increased ferocity. "We didn't think she was going to make it," says ICU nurse Peggy Derringer. "And we thought that if she did make it, the damage to her brain would be so profound that her quality of life would be terrible." But Katelyn did not die. She remained in a coma for more than a year.

Fanning the flame

During that year, Sharon and Ray Atwell and their older daughter, Crystal, prayed relentlessly and celebrated each achievement, no matter how small. They relied on their faith, friends and family for support. Through the Internet, people around the world heard about Katelyn and began to pray for her. Sharon sent out regular "Kate Update" e-mails to an ever-increasing number of "prayer warriors." A huge map on the wall of Katelyn's room marked the cities and towns where people were praying for her. "I wanted Katelyn to know when she woke up how many people were praying for her to be well," explains Sharon.

The medical staff taking care of Katelyn were astonished by her family's unwavering optimism and faith. "There was always a family member at Katelyn's bedside, encouraging her, playing her favorite music, doing passive range of motion exercises," recalls Stephen Thompson, MD.

Katelyn's caregivers received support, as well. "Whenever I'd operate on Katelyn, I'd get e-mails literally from all over the country—people saying, 'We're praying for you; we're praying for Katelyn,' " recalls Stephanie Einhaus, MD. "It was incredible."

Sharon compares Katelyn's battle with *Bacillus cereus* meningitis to a roller coaster ride. As soon as doctors would rectify one problem, another would arise. She would begin to rally and then she would have a stroke. Or she would get a viral infection. Or she would have a seizure. But a year into Katelyn's coma, her condition began to improve. Although she was blind and nonverbal, she began to respond to her family with hand squeezes, blinks or nods.

In a June 2000 "Kate Update," Sharon wrote, "It was one year ago today that the Atwell family got on this roller coaster ride called the cancer express. It has more corkscrew turns, downward spirals, upside down turns, only to be shot straight up into the heavens or to find yourself plummeting down into the bowels of the earth. For a very long time I prayed every day for God to get us to the exit ramp, but we never did see it. . . . We are now on a very smooth ride, every once in a while a whoop-tee-doo, but for the most part just an enjoyable, slow ride going forward."

Dividing light from darkness

One evening, four months after writing that e-mail, Sharon was tucking Katelyn into bed. After a goodnight kiss, she said, "I love you Katelyn." As she backed away, Sharon saw her daughter silently mouth the words, "I love you, too." Within days, Katelyn began to lip sync her favorite songs. In November of that year, her sight suddenly returned. In December, she began eating for the first time in a year and a half. Slowly, steadily, Katelyn began to surface. "I remember the first time she came to my office after she woke up," says Einhaus, who performed dozens of operations on Katelyn's brain. "She had started to communicate. I cried; it touched me that much. Many neurosurgeons had told me, 'You're wasting your time op-

Figure 12.1 continued

erating on her. She's not going to wake up.' But we just plugged along, hoping that she might. Then all of a sudden she woke up. It was a bit miraculous, to be perfectly honest."

Everyone who took care of Katelyn was astounded at her recovery. "You know, the word 'miracle' is sometimes thrown around too freely in the world of medicine," observes Tamburro. "But certainly with Katelyn, I think it's appropriately used. To see the way she's progressing is nothing short of miraculous."

Thompson, who spent many nights sleeping outside Katelyn's door in the ICU, keeps a picture of Katelyn on his desk. "This is probably one of the most satisfying recoveries I've ever seen in a patient I've cared for," he says.

"Hers is truly a miraculous recovery." Derringer, who has worked as an ICU nurse for 12 years, says the faith of Katelyn and her family, combined with aggressive medical care, made the difference. "She's one of our true, bonafide, no-way-she-should-be-here miracles. And that's the truth," Derringer says.

As Katelyn began to surface, she quickly regained her competitive spirit and sense of humor. The rehabilitation specialists who had worked tirelessly with Katelyn during her coma now began to help her relearn the most basic tasks. With the daily help of physical, occupational and speech therapists, she began to make progress. She began to sit alone, then talk, then stand. In September, she had her last dose of chemotherapy. Two months later, she walked with her walker from Rehabilitation Services to the St. Jude reception desk, as St. Jude staff and patients lined the corridors and filled the lobby, cheering.

On Friday, December 14, Katelyn carried a flaming torch through the streets of Memphis.

"I stood at the corner of the street, watching this huge entourage of people coming my way," wrote Sharon in a "Kate Update." "I stood there praising God for how great he truly is. Who would have ever thought two years ago that she would be coming toward her mother with torch in hand, waving at everyone with the biggest smile possible on her face? A vision of her in ICU with all the tubes and machines popped into my head, and then I looked at her coming toward me, and I almost lost it."

Katelyn seems unaware that she has become a symbol of hope and faith to others. "Every time I see Katie, my heart just swells," says Derringer. "Doctors, nurses, respiratory therapists, we all light up when we see Katie. When she walks into the ICU, we look up and say, 'Ah! We're so glad you're here!' She gives us inspiration, and she lifts our spirits."

Let your light shine

During the past year, a silent girl with a blank stare has evolved into a vivacious teenager who greets everyone she meets with a broad smile and enthusiastic greeting. At any moment, Katelyn might break into a praise song, a joke or a pithy commentary. "There's me as a body-woddy," says Katelyn, as she marvels at the emaciated stranger depicted in her mother's photo album. I don't remember diddly squat. All I remember is loud, annoying beeps."

Katelyn doesn't mourn about the time she has lost; she is too busy setting, meeting and exceeding goals. Today she is dressed for physical therapy in a navy sweatshirt, Florida Gators sweat pants and blue glitter nail polish. Sunlight streams through the windows of Rehabilitation Services, falling in a bright strip across the linoleum floor. For Katelyn, walking is still hard work, a task that demands intense concentration. Brow furrowed, head bowed, muscles quivering, she takes one step, a deep breath, then another.

"C'mon, girly girl! You can do it!" urges Sharon. Panting, Katelyn steps into the light, moving forward, ever forward. Instilled with determination, upheld by faith and propelled by the sheer power of a mother's love.

Figure 12.1 continued

THE DUAL ROLE OF THE EDITOR

Editing a sponsored publication has been described as something of a high-wire act. You must produce an e-zine or newsletter that advances and promotes management's organizational objectives. After all, management is the publisher of the periodical and is paying all the bills. Indeed, a weekly newsletter or a monthly magazine is the most expensive component of a communications budget for most organizations.

In addition, you have a responsibility to serve the interests of the employees or other constituents. Some public relations texts consider public relations personnel, including periodical editors, as "boundary spanners," who must continually make sure that the views of various publics are heard in the management suite.

There is also the matter of editorial freedom. Many editors, particularly former newspaper reporters, think that they have the right to decide what stories will be covered and in what context. They resent management trying to use the publication as a propaganda tool and resist anything that smacks of editorial interference, including story ideas that support organizational objectives.

The dilemma many editors face is how to balance the needs of management, the interests of readers, and their own journalistic standards. Some never do solve the dilemma and stick to folksy stories that please many and offend none. Actually, the balancing act can be done if the editor is able to understand that the needs of all three are interrelated.

Take company strategies and goals. These are usually based on broad concepts such as human resources, corporate image, business expansion, competitiveness, productivity, marketing, and economic development. Communication goals should be based on corporate goals, so the editor may decide to support the goal of increased competitiveness by publishing at least six stories during the year about the organization's market share and what factors are involved in making the organization more competitive.

These stories, if done well, should also interest employees because they are concerned about job security and making sure that the company remains competitive. If the company is successful, it could also mean bonuses and higher pay scales.

Even if management has set broad or specific goals for the year, it is usually the editor who decides how the periodical can support each goal. In this case, the editor can choose any number of journalistic treatments, including the angle of what's in it for employees. Stories about competitiveness don't have to be propaganda. They can be written with the same degree of objectivity as any article in an independent publication.

Mission Statement and Editorial Plan

The best editors, the ones who regularly win awards, seem to understand the purpose of their publication. One technique is to develop a concise, simple mission statement of 25 words or less. The statement should cover the publication's general content, its audience, and its strategic role.

Writing a mission statement is tough. *Dallasite,* an employee newsletter of Texas Instruments (TI), first started out with a somewhat broad mission statement: "The *Dallasite* will serve TI by reporting news about the corporation, its people and its goals."

The advent of "bottom-line" economics in the late 1990s, however, created a need for a more precise mission statement. It now reads: "We want the *Dallasite* to be a tool that helps employees understand TI's goals and how they can help achieve those goals."

Professional Tips

Story Ideas for Newsletters

Periodicals carry a variety of feature articles and news stories. Here are some ideas from *Communication Briefings* for your newsletter or magazine.

- Feature a day in the life of an employee. Describe what the person does and how his or her work ties into the organization's goals.

- Select a current issue affecting the organization and give an in-depth analysis of the situation.

- Interview long-term employees or managers. Have them discuss how things have changed, and link the changes to the organization's strategy and industry developments.

- Offer "how to" tips on writing memos, choosing a health plan, or even selecting a child-care center.

- Show how the functions of each department affect the others. Follow a typical customer going through all the channels to show the importance of teamwork.

- Profile customers. Describe how a customer problem was solved. Use quotes from the customer and the employee problem solver.

- Interview 10 employees about their opinions on key issues or events. Use short quotes under pictures of the employees, along with their names and job titles.

Another example is the goal for GuideOne's *Going for Great!* magazine. It is to "provide all targeted audiences with in-depth information about current business initiatives, strategic planning, industry changes and education, and other key data that contribute to GuideOne's success, while building trust throughout the organization."

Charlotte Forbes, senior vice president of Stromberg Consulting, sums up the bottom-line approach. She told *PRWeek*, "Corporations need to think of a newsletter as something that can inform, educate, and hopefully drive action, as opposed to being a reporter of facts, after the fact."

It is also a good idea to prepare an annual editorial plan. Bobby Minter, of Publication Productions in New York, says you need to map out what kind of articles and other material you will prepare for the entire year. This will enable you to develop story ideas that complement the organization's objectives for the year. Bell Atlantic and NYNEX, for example, merged and faced the daunting problem of integrating a combined workforce of 140,000 employees. To energize and rally their support for the new company, corporate communications identified several key needs that could be addressed in various employee publications:

- The need to explain the strategies of the new Bell Atlantic and to illustrate how the company is using these strategies to be a leader in an industry undergoing constant, dramatic change.

- The need to communicate the ways in which Bell Atlantic is positioning itself against our competitors, and to point out how individual employees can support our efforts.

- The need to create a corporate source of information that could be the primary vehicle for news about the company and the industry—supplanting the external media and union sources that had become a principal source for some employees during the merge process.

- The need to quickly foster teamwork and enthusiasm about the new company among employees, many of whom had strong loyalties to their former company and harbored suspicions of being "taken over" by their merger partner.

The primary vehicle chosen for communicating these core strategies was *The Wave*, a four-page weekly tabloid, mailed to all employees. According to Ken Terrell, director of employee media for Bell Atlantic, "Virtually all of the material in *The Wave* is based on our core strategies. Our approach is to depict various groups and individuals that are successfully putting these strategies into action. We use devices such as highlight boxes, bullet points, special column headings, graphics, and **pull quotes** to emphasize key strategic information." A front page of *The Wave* is shown in Figure 12.2.

Bell Atlantic supplements *The Wave* with a daily bulletin covering company and industry issues that is available to subscribers via fax, e-mail, or voice mail. It also is posted on the corporate intranet. The use of multiple communication channels, to ensure reaching everyone, is a tactic used by many organizations.

NEWSLETTERS AND MAGAZINES

The content of periodicals, in broad terms, is news and information. That is why many of these publications are called newsletters—they essentially are messages from the organization to various publics who want news and information.

Civic and professional groups use newsletters to inform their members of upcoming meetings and events. Nonprofit organizations send donors and prospective contributors information about the agency's programs and needs and recognize the efforts of current volunteers. See Figure 12.3 on page 350 for an effective magazine that reaches donors. Companies keep wholesalers informed about new product developments and offer ideas on how to market existing products.

The four-color magazine of the Department of Conservation and Land Management (CALM) in Western Australia is an example of the multiaudience publication. *Landscope* is sent to key groups who can influence the operations of the Department—government, industry, community opinion leaders, educators, the media, employees and other Western Australians with an active interest in the management of the natural environment.

As such, *Landscope*'s broad editorial goals are geared to the Department's strategic plan. According to Ron Kawalilak, director of corporate relations at CALM, this is: "to increase community awareness, understanding and support for

Wireless 'Net Access
Our Italian wireless investment is the first with wireless voice access to the Internet. **3**

Voice Mail vs. Breast Cancer
A new program enlists our Home Voice Mail product in the fight against breast cancer. **3**

Hispanic Achievers
Two employees were among those honored as National Hispanic Corporate Achievers. **4**

http://cwm.bell-atl.com/emplcomm

June 14, 1999   **News and Information for Bell Atlantic Employees**

Different Strokes: Technician Mike Harbold's workdays are decidedly different these days as he prepares for a shot at his fourth Olympic team. As his number here indicates, Harbold is a top U.S. prospect in sprint kayaking.

Uncharted Waters

Technician Is First Employee-Olympian in Training

It's Monday at 7 a.m. and rush-hour traffic is backing up over the bridges into Washington, D.C. On the placid Potomac River below, by contrast, Bell Atlantic technician Mike Harbold is a solitary figure as he begins another workday.

Harbold is skimming swiftly over the water in a featherweight racing craft, a one-man kayak, powered by his own rapid, precise strokes. There are few service orders or morning meetings in Harbold's work life these days — and no regular paychecks

either. But still, his hours on the river are fulfilling a commitment to Bell Atlantic.

Harbold is the first of a new, and likely rare, breed of employee at Bell Atlantic: a bona-fide world-class athlete who's been given unpaid time off and support funds to focus on training for a shot at the U.S. Olympic Team.

When the 31-year-old Harbold joined the company two years ago as a cable-splicing technician, he had already been a member of three U.S. Olympic teams, competing in sprint kayaking in the singles ('88), doubles ('92), and four-man ('96) events.

"It was time to start thinking about things like benefits and saving for retirement," said Harbold, whose wife, Alexandra, is also a two-time Olympian in sprint kayaking.

During eight-years of world-class competition, Harbold was consistently at the top rung of his sport, but near the bottom of the economic ladder.

He supported himself in a variety of interim jobs: coaching, carpentry, iron working, airplane building, selling plastics, doing freelance desktop publishing. "I created ads and gift certificates for a bagel com-

(Continued on page 2)

National 411 Calls Reach 10 Million

Late last week, a Bell Atlantic customer made the 10-millionth request for a telephone number using our new National 411 Directory Assistance service.

"We're logging close to 140,000 National 411 requests per day, proof that our customers appreciate the easy access and accurate listings they get from our service," said Walter Abernathy, director-product development, Operator Services.

Customers participating in Bell Atlantic's on-going customer satisfaction surveys give National 411 glowing praise (see box).

As part of our Customer Care and quality-assurance programs, approximately 1,500 directory assistance customers are interviewed each month.

"It's great being able to call 411 for everything and not have to find area codes," one customer said.

"It was nice to be able to get information from anywhere in the country," said another. "Things are handled very nicely and very promptly."

Bell Atlantic began a state-by-state rollout of National 411 in January and now provides the service in 12 of our 14 serving areas. To get a telephone number for any directory listing in the country, customers only need to dial 411 — just as they do to request local phone numbers — and provide the state, city and listing they want. There's no need to know the area code for the listing.

Since the service was launched, customers no longer need to dial the distant city's area code plus 555-1212 for the listing they want, nor do they need to dial long 10-10 numbers to get national listings. Listings provided by using these methods come from long-distance companies. Long-distance companies used to purchase the lookup services from local telephone companies, but have begun providing the service themselves. They charge a single price, up to $1.40, for both local and long-distance listings.

Our National 411 requests cost 95 cents per call and customers can request two listings. Requests for local listings are billed automatically at low rates set by state regulators that range from 20 cents per call to 45

(Continued on page 4)

Why Customers Like National 411

- You don't need to know the area code for the listing.
- You dial 411 for both local and national listings.
- Our operators use various tools and customer dialog to ensure accuracy.
- Our operators provide "polite," "courteous," and "fast" service.

Judge Agrees: AT&T Can't 'Lock and Block' Its Cable Systems

A recent federal court ruling could derail AT&T's strategy of imposing an old-style, closed cable model into the new world of Internet and data. The court ruled that the city of Portland, Ore., can require AT&T to open its recently acquired cable lines to competing Internet service providers.

The ruling comes as AT&T has completed a buying and deal-making spree with cable companies that will give it access to more than 60 percent of U.S. homes. Portland required AT&T to open its network as part of its review process

when AT&T bought local cable provider TCI.

AT&T faces similar review procedures across the country. Additionally, some cities have "me too" clauses in their agreements with AT&T that require the company to give them the same provisions if another community strikes a better deal.

Because cable firms currently do not have to open their networks to competitors, as the Bell companies do, the fear is that AT&T will have unchecked control over broadband pipes into a large percentage of the nation's homes.

Voice, video, data, and Internet services are expected to travel through those pipes. Bell Atlantic has argued that if we have to open our networks to competitors, AT&T and other cable companies should do so as well.

Jim Cullen, Bell Atlantic president and chief operating officer, said the court's decision mirrors the legitimate concern of many consumers and virtually all information-service providers that cable networks will be 'locked and blocked.'

"It reflects Bell Atlantic's goal of competitive parity in the regulation of all

broadband services," Cullen said, "and it reflects Bell Atlantic's operating principle that all networks should be open to both affiliates and non-affiliates.

"It's the height of hypocrisy for AT&T to say that open networks and wholesale discounts should apply to companies like Bell Atlantic but not AT&T," Cullen said.

AT&T said it would appeal the ruling. Internet service providers and companies such as America Online, which have been pressing Congress and regulators for access to cable systems, hailed the ruling.

The Wave: (703) 974-3444, (703) 974-8436 (Fax), 1310 North Court House Road, 9th Floor, Arlington, VA 22201, Editor: Ken Terrell. If your address label is incorrect, update your job profile sheet.

Please recycle

Figure 12.2 Newsletters Should Reflect Corporate Objectives
The Wave, a four-page tabloid published by Bell Atlantic, was created to create a sense of teamwork and enthusiasm among 140,000 employees after Bell Atlantic and NYNEX merged. The masthead doubles as a teaser for major stories inside the publication.
(Courtesy of Bell Atlantic, Arlington, VA.)

CALM's nature conservation and natural land management programs, services and policies, and to promote wider cooperation in the prevention and solution of conservation and land management problems in Western Australia."

To accomplish this goal, the 56-page quarterly generally follows a standard pattern:

- **Cover story:** Emphasizing CALM's activities in the area of broad public interest
- **Six or seven features:** Articles covering CALM activities in nature conservation and wildlife management, forest resource management, and management for tourism and recreation
- **In Perspective:** A column written by CALM's chief executive and letters to the editor
- **Bush Telegraph:** Short articles on natural history topics of interest
- **Endangered:** A one-page article on an endangered plant or animal and what CALM is doing to preserve it
- **Urban Antics:** A one-page article on a WA natural history topic aimed primarily at schoolchildren

Meeting Audience Interests

Every sponsored periodical is unique, but there are some general guidelines that can be applied. The International Association of Business Communicators (IABC) and Towers, Perrin, Forster & Crosby, a consulting firm, surveyed 40 companies and 45,000 employees to determine what topics employees were most interested in. The top five choices were (1) the organization's future plans, (2) personnel policies and procedures, (3) productivity improvement, (4) job-related information, and (5) job advancement information. The last five choices on the 17-topic list were (1) personnel changes and promotions, (2) financial results, (3) advertising and promotion plans, (4) stories about other employees, and (5) personal news such as birthdays and anniversaries.

It must be noted, however, that the range of high to low interest was from 95 percent to 57 percent—still more than half for the last choice. The study does indicate, however, that today's employees are more concerned about the health and direction of their companies than they are about the fact that someone in the accounting department just celebrated a wedding anniversary or won a bowling tournament.

Michael C. Brandon, director of internal communication for Northern Telecom, Nashville, Tennessee, puts it more bluntly. He wrote in IABC's *Communication World* that today's employee communications need to do more than make employees feel good. He continued:

> Communicators can no longer permit bowling leagues, birthdays and babies to dominate the pages of the company newsletter. Instead, employee communication must deliver business information critical to the organization's success. The most critical information employees need is about the organization's objectives. If em-

PR Casebook

A Well-Designed Magazine Generates Members and Donations

Z, the magazine of the Cleveland Zoological Society, is designed to educate Zoo Society members about Cleveland Metroparks Zoo and the organization's joint conservation goals, as well as to boost member retention and donations.

The publication does this by offering timely information about zoo animals, programs, and special events, updates on membership services, and information on an array of donor programs aimed at supporting the zoo.

Z is published twice a year, and each issue is planned with input from the zoo's marketing and animal care divisions. It includes information on topics of interest to members and donors such as new exhibits, animal acquisitions, upcoming events, and endangered species.

Z has been an excellent public relations and marketing communications tool for the zoo. Since 1997, the total number of member households has grown 66 percent. In addition, membership revenue has almost doubled from $1.1 million to $2.1 million. Membership in the ZooKeeper's Circle, a group of major donors, grew by 85 percent, from 350 members to 650.

The magazine, because of its success, was awarded a Bronze Anvil by the Public Relations Society of America (PRSA).

Photo of magazine cover courtesy of Mary L. McMillan, director of finance and operations for the Cleveland Zoological Society.

Figure 12.3

ployees are to maximize effectiveness, management must strive for alignment between the organization's goals and the individual objectives of the employees.

A survey of employees at one corporation by Dallas consultant Tom Geddie indicates that editors should always start with the assumption that employees want answers to the "what's-in-it-for-me" questions. The number-one information concern for 30 percent of employees was the internal work environment and how their work was important to the company. Another 22 percent wanted to know about the company's financial health and the prospects for continued employment. Another 17 percent each were interested in information about improving the day-to-day work process and hearing about annual priorities and goals. It is clear that a publication's content should not only address management's objectives, but that the information must be relevant to the needs of the readers. How to package this content in an attractive, eye-appealing form is discussed next.

Design

More than one communications expert has pointed out that a publication's design should reinforce the content and also reflect the organization's personality. The idea is that content and design should work together to achieve a complete message.

Consequently, periodicals have distinct "personalities" that reflect their organizations. Reebok International has an employee tabloid that features modern typefaces, cutaway photos of athletes in action, and brown as a dominant second color. Stories are set in large type, ragged right, surrounded by a lot of white space. The publication, in sum, projects ruggedness and the great outdoors

On the other hand, *One Lime Street,* published by Lloyd's of London, is a 24-page newsletter with simple headlines, pages jam-packed with small type, and mug shots. It is a rather conservative publication, again reflecting the nature of the financial and insurance business.

AT&T *Now* is an eight-page tabloid that portrays a modern, up-to-date corporation. Jean Hurt, editor, describes the publication in the following way:

> In order to be an inviting, employee-focused publication, we feature many names and faces. We bring AT&T's strategy to life by showing how AT&T people contribute to it. The look is contemporary and clean. Vibrant color and photography, particularly large front-page photos, add interest and help us compete against overflowing in-boxes and commercial media. Liberal use of call-outs, headline decks, and sidebars serves the reader who prefers to scan. To better link our stories to the company's strategy, we accompany many stories with a small box containing a strategic summary.

Hurt adds, "A monthly print publication, distributed to 50 states and more than 50 countries can't deliver fast-breaking news. The company's Intranet and a daily e-mail newsletter do that. The value we add is 'second-day' perspective, interpretation, graphic appeal, and creative packaging to encourage readership and sharing with others."

Format   Newsletters are easy to produce, are cost-effective, and can reach any number of small, specialized audiences. Word processing programs such as *MacWrite* and *Microsoft Word* make it possible for almost anyone to produce a simple newsletter with mastheads, a two- or three-column format, and clip art or scanned photos. The use of desktop publishing software such as *PrintShop,* *Illustrator* and *InDesign* is discussed shortly.

The most popular format for a newsletter is letter-size, 8.5 by 11 inches. Organizations from large corporations to the local garden club use two- to-four page newsletters to reach employees, customers, and members. Although this format is workable, it has greater design limitations than the larger tabloid format, which is 11 by 17 inches. This format, often called a **magapaper**, allows a great deal of flexibility in design and can contain more graphic elements.

Professional Tips

How to Create Attractive Publications

Newsletters and brochures should be designed to convey information in an attractive, un-cluttered way. Here are some general guidelines.

Copy

- Less is better. Write short, punchy sentences. Keep paragraphs short.
- Use informative subheads to break up copy blocks.
- Use bullets to list key points.
- Use news summaries and news briefs.

Layout

- Don't cram the page with copy; allow for plenty of white space.
- Organize layout from left to right and top to bottom. Most people read in this sequence; don't confuse them with another arrangement.
- Avoid large blocks of reverse type (white on black). It's difficult to read.
- Facing pages should be composed as two-page spreads; that's how readers see them.
- Use graphics and photos to balance blocks of copy.
- Make photos and illustrations as large as possible. Whenever possible, use action-oriented photos.

Type

- The best type size for text is 10 or 11 point with 2 points of leading. If the target audi-ence is senior citizens, increase the type size to 12 or 14 point.
- Use serif type for text. It is easier to read. Headlines can be set in sans serif type.
- Use a minimum number of fonts and type families. A three-ring circus of type is poor design and just confuses people.
- Use boldface sparingly. Use for subheads and a few key words only. Don't use for an entire paragraph.
- Use italic type for emphasis sparingly, if at all.
- Avoid all caps in headlines. Caps and lowercase is more readable.

Color

- Use black ink for stories. If you use a second color, apply it as a highlight to frame a story, a quote (set in larger type), or an entire page.
- Headlines can utilize color, but the ink should be on the dark side.
- Avoid using extensive color on low-quality paper. Reproduction and clarity of images suffer.
- Eliminate complex screens. A color or graphic behind a block of copy often makes the type difficult to read.

The magazine, usually in an 8.5- by 11-inch format, often is an organization's top-tier publication. Magazines are the most expensive to produce because they are printed on glossy paper, have up to 56 pages, and include multiple displays of computer graphics and full-color photographs. Accenture's magazine, mentioned previously, has an annual budget of $700,000. Boeing Co. spends $500,000 annually on its quarterly *Aero* magazine.

Magazines concentrate on in-depth stories about people and industry trends. Stories, unlike the shorter articles found in newsletters and newspapers, are much longer and tend to be more thoroughly researched.

In sum, you have the option of the standard newsletter, the magapaper, or the magazine. It all depends on the purpose of the publication, the kind of messages you want to send, and the target audience. Budget is a major consideration.

Layout   Layout is a plan showing the arrangement of the material in the publication—the size and location of such items as stories, regularly appearing columns, headlines, photographs, and artwork.

There is no exact rule for any of these items. The most important stories, of course, should be placed on the front page. If a story is fairly long, it can be continued on a later page. There are two advantages to this. First, you can give several stories visibility on the cover if you continue stories on other pages. Second, continuing a story on an inside page encourages the reader to go beyond the first page. Another rule of thumb is to place important stories on the inside right page of a publication, because this is where people look first when they turn the page.

Most periodicals have a layout that is somewhat standardized, so that each issue of the publication has the same look and feel. This is called a **template**. A template starts with the **masthead**, or the name of the publication. It is always in the same type font and has the same graphics. Other items that may remain the same in every issue are the location of the major story on the front page, boxes giving a list of stories inside the issue, or the placement of a standard column or update of late-breaking news items.

AT&T Now, for example, has a template that calls for a large photograph on the cover of every edition. GuideOne Insurance publishes a 16-page color magazine, *Going for Great!*, for its employees and agents that also has a standard pattern for each issue. An employee profile, for example, is always on page 14, and an explanation of a company's core value is always on the back cover.

The idea behind a template is that the readers rapidly learn where to find specific kinds of information in the publication. Readers of *Time* magazine, for example, always know that the "People" section is in the back of the publication, and the page has a highly recognized format that does not vary. If the editors of *Time* arbitrarily placed "People" at random every issue, readers would get extremely frustrated trying to find it. Helping readers find information, issue after issue, is why newspapers have a template that divides the paper into sections—business, sports, computing, entertainment, lifestyle, etc.

Although the basic layout of a periodical should be the same from issue to issue, each issue will vary, depending on the length of the articles, the availability of good illustrations, and the relative importance of the stories.

Keep the following ideas in mind as you do the layout for a newsletter or magazine:

- Use white space. Don't think you need stories or illustrations covering every single part of the page.
- Vary paragraph length. If your copy looks as dense and forbidding as the Great Wall of China, your readers will be intimidated. Make paragraphs seven lines long or less to create even more white space.
- Break up longer stories with boldface subheads.

- Create bulleted lists. Any sentence containing a sequence of three or more items is a good list candidate. Listing also frees up more white space.

- Use only two or three typefaces, to give consistency to your periodical. The variety comes in using different type sizes, not a different type family.

- Keep articles relatively short for maximum interest. If *USA Today* can summarize a world crisis in four paragraphs, you can cover the company picnic in the same amount of space.

- Inside pages should balance one another. If you use a strong graphic on one page, you should balance it with a large headline or a graphic on the facing page.

- Use headlines that give information, not just labels such as "Company Picnic" or "New Vice President." (See the section on headline writing.)

The traditional method of layout, which is still helpful in this age of computers, is to work with a blank template and sketch out where stories, headlines, and artwork will be placed. This method helps you conceptualize the entire issue and how the various stories you have planned might be incorporated. This can be done with a sheet of paper and a pencil, or you can call up the template on the computer and sketch out the contents electronically. After the section on brochures, we will discuss the whole concept of desktop publishing—and all that it entails.

Illustrations   Photos and artwork were discussed extensively in Chapter 7. Many of the concepts presented there also apply to sponsored periodicals.

All publications need strong graphic elements to attract the television generation of readers. Photos must be tightly composed or cropped for impact, and a good photo should be used in as large a format as possible. A common criticism of organizational periodicals is that they use tiny photos awash in a sea of type.

Computer-generated graphics and imported clip art are commonly used in periodicals. Clip art is available on CD-ROMs. In addition, if you see something in another publication or book, you can use a scanner to import it into your computer. (Be certain not to violate copyright laws, which were discussed in Chapter 3.) A better use of scanners is to import graphic designs commissioned by the organization.

Headlines   Writing good headlines takes practice. The headline is an important component of any story because it is an attention-getting device. According to *Communication Briefs*, 70 to 90 percent of readers look at headlines. Subheads attract 60 to 90 percent of the readers, and photos also rank high with the same percentage. About 40 to 70 percent will read a lead paragraph, but only 5 to 10 percent of the potential readers read the text of a story. In today's culture of information overload, headlines are the real workhorses of effective communication.

A title or a label may identify a particular feature of the publication—for example, a regular column by the president of the company could be labeled

"President's Corner." For news stories, however, a sentence or capsule headline should be used. Here are a few examples from the American Express employee newspaper, *Dateline International:*

An era ends with the closing of TRS's first operations center

American Express's presence during Olympics is more than fun and games

New American dream defined by old values

The style used in these headlines is known as **downstyle** because only the first word and proper nouns are capitalized, just as in a sentence. A large number of newspapers and magazines now use this style.

A more traditional style is upper- and lowercase. In this style, all words except articles, short prepositions, and conjunctions have initial caps—for example, "New American Dream Defined by Old Values."

Both styles are acceptable; it is a matter of preference. All uppercase letters in a headline is not recommended, because the words appear as blocks and individual letters lose their identifiable characteristics. If you want to emphasize something, it is better to use a larger type size than to use all capital letters.

Headlines should be written in active voice because it makes the news story more timely. Figure 12.4 gives some headlines from various newsletters and magazines. Notice the variety of styles, the use of smaller explanatory heads, and the active voice.

Here is a headline written in passive voice: "Gift awarded to 4-H Club." Notice how much better and more timely it sounds when you write the same headline with an active verb: "Chapter awards gift to local 4-H Club."

Another way to get more information into a headline is to use what is called a **kicker**. A kicker is set in smaller type above or below the main headline. Here is an example:

ANOTHER DELAY

EPA HEARING SET FOR JUNE 5

In writing headlines that require two or more lines, you should avoid splitting ideas between lines. Here is one humorous example:

PASTOR LEAVES FOR GOOD

FRIDAY SERVICES AT PRISON

You should also avoid ending lines with a preposition. Here is a sample of a poor headline and how it can be changed:

POOR: Fredericks plans to

take 6-month leave

BETTER: Fredericks to take

6-month sabbatical

After writing a headline, it is always a good idea to review it for context, use of the correct word, and whether it conveys the right impression. Here are several

New Faces, Bright Ideas

These talented Generation Xers were recruited for the ingenuity and initiative they bring to the company

HISTORY

Keep on truckin'

By Cornelia Bayley

A traveling museum-on-wheels celebrates the development of HP's inkjet printing technology.

A Bright Future

1,500 girls look ahead by joining their parents at work

Fast Response On Short Runs

Boscobel Opens To Serve Changing Marketplace

Figure 12.4 Headlines Should Provide Information
Most people read headlines, but rarely entire articles. Therefore, it is crucial for headlines to convey a key message. Here are some sample headlines from various publications. Notice that kicker heads and secondary headlines combine to give the essence of the story. They also are written in active, present tense.

somewhat humorous headlines found in the nation's newspapers by the *Columbia Journalism Review:*

First female Marines train for combat with men

Denver Chapter will have senator for breakfast

UMaine women selling fast in Portland

Yellow perch decline to be studied

Red Tape Holds Up New Bridge

Panda Mating Fails; Veterinarian Takes Over

Writing headlines requires that you know the width of the space allocated for each headline. In a word processing software program, you simply set the margins and keystroke the headline you want. If it doesn't fit the space allocated to it in your mock-up or in the desktop publishing layout, you can easily enlarge or reduce it until it fits. Selection of type fonts will be discussed shortly.

ELECTRONIC NEWSLETTERS

Many organizations supplement their printed publications with electronic newsletters. These are also known as **e-zines** (the hyphen is optional), and their primary advantage is instant dissemination of information.

Unlike print publications that go through a number of production steps, editors of an e-zine do everything on the computer. With one mouse click, the newsletter is instantly sent via e-mail or an organization's intranet to everyone on the "subscriber" list.

The second advantage of e-zines is cost. The cost of paper, printing, and postage is eliminated. An average printed newsletter might cost up to 50 cents per individual copy, whereas an e-zine typically costs less than 5 cents per "copy."

In sum, electronic newsletters are fast, efficient, and inexpensive. However, they do have limitations. Most rely on a simple format—text only, limited use of color, limited graphics, no photos or fancy design effects. This is because e-zines, especially those using e-mail as a distribution method, are received on a variety of e-mail systems around the world, many with limited graphic capabilities. Extensive graphics and color make the download time much longer.

According to *PR News*, rule number one for e-zines is to keep them short. It adds, "The whole document should be between three and five pages. Articles within them should be news-driven, not feature-y, and should only run a few paragraphs. Think bullet points that can link to a more in-depth article on your Web site."

Nabisco E, the weekly electronic newsletter of Nabisco Corporaton, follows this advice. The maximum length of any story is 10–12 lines. The editor, Vic DePalo, says, "You do lose readers if you put in a long, complex story." According to the experts, readers rapidly tune out if they have to scroll through a long story or a multiple-page newsletter.

Since you have only about 10 lines, the writing style is more informal than in regular print publications. You can be more conversational and use less formal English than is expected in a print publication. This is not to say, however, that you don't need to craft well-written sentences. Every word counts, and it's important to keep sentences short and to the point.

Writing an e-zine is a lot like writing for radio or television, which was discussed in Chapter 9. Long, complex sentences are out, and you need to start stories with summary headlines that convey the key information in the story. Various surveys show that people, more often than not, just scan messages instead of reading them.

Using an Intranet

Much of the above advice about the content and format of an e-zine has been in the context of electronic newsletters that are disseminated via e-mail to lists of

Professional Tips

Some Basics about Writing an E-Zine

Most e-zines are sent as text files, the lowest common denominator on the Internet. Using text files allows you to reach the widest possible online audience because they can be read by almost any e-mail system. If you are producing an e-zine for an intranet system, however, you can be more creative about color and graphics because you will know the capabilities of your system.

Here are some basic formatting guidelines for text files:

- Use a text editor to create your files. If you are a Windows user, you can use Notepad. Text editors support monospacing or fixed-width fonts that use the same amount of space for every character instead of letters such as "i" or "w" being spaced proportionally.

- Use 65 characters to accommodate the widest range of e-mail programs. Hit ENTER at the end of each line instead of relying on word-wrap formatting. Without hard line breaks, your e-mail message will wrap in places that you had not anticipated and your message might look jumbled.

- Use spaces for indentation. Stay away from your TAB key. The length of a TAB key is set by the recipient, and if they have different spacing, your e-zine format will be altered and perhaps even appear disjointed.

- Avoid using ALL CAPS. If you want to highlight a word or phrase, surround the **word** in asterisks. Your readers will find it easier to understand the emphasis.

- A popular font for e-zines is 10-point Courier New.

For more information on writing and producing e-zines, visit www.ezineuniversity.com, which offers templates and basic information. Additional resources are also available at www.ezine-tips.com.

"subscribers" outside the organization. They may be registered users of a product, members of a professional group, or simply people who are interested in a particular subject. MediaMap, for example, e-mails a weekly newsletter to public relations practitioners who have signed up to receive it.

Many corporations, however, have established intranets for communicating with their employees. Essentially, an **intranet** works on the same principles as the Internet, but it is a private network within an organization for the exclusive use of employees and perhaps some other audiences such as suppliers. Intranets, because they are closed systems and the technical standards are set by the organization, are able to produce much more sophisticated electronic newsletters.

A good example of what is possible on an intranet is the daily online publication of Hewlett-Packard Company (HP). *hpNow* is an attractive newsletter that includes (1) color, (2) graphics, (3) photos, and (4) links to thousands of archived pages that contain everything from past issues to news releases, speeches, organizational charts, and employee awards. Figure 12.5 shows the home page of *hpNOW*.

Lia Kakuk, editor of *hpNOW*, says the publication is sent daily to 140,000 HP employees in 37 nations. A typical issue will have about three to eight stories,

Figure 12.5 Online Publications Can Be Published Daily
One advantage of online publications, often called e-zines, is that daily editions can be created and published faster than printed ones. Also, if you have employees around the world, an online publication reaches everyone at the same time. This is the home page for *hpNOW*, which is sent daily to 140,000 employees.
(Courtesy of Hewlett-Packard Company, Palo Alto, CA.)

ranging from one paragraph to 2,000 words. Feature stories about HP products and how they are being used in a variety of ways is a prominent feature of the publication. One article, complete with color photos, discussed the role of HP computers in the making of a Dreamworks' animated film. The lead to this highly interesting application story was as follows:

> When DreamWorks set sail on a voyage to animate *Sinbad: Legend of the Seven Seas,* the studio knew only HP could deliver the necessary computing prowess to bring the legend to life.

More information about online newsletters as part of organizational Web sites are discussed in Chapter 13.

BROCHURES

Writing brochures, like producing newsletters and magazines, requires the coordination of several elements. These include message content, selection of type, graphics, layout, and design. It also requires working with designers and printers.

Brochures are often called booklets, pamphlets, or leaflets, depending on their size and content. A pamphlet or booklet, for example, is characterized by a book-like format and multiple pages. An example is the corporate annual report, required by the Securities and Exchange Commission (SEC). Such reports are discussed in Chapter 14.

A leaflet, however, is often described as a single sheet of paper printed on both sides and folded into three panels (see Figure 12.6 for a typical format). There are also handbills and flyers, which are printed on one side only and are often found on bulletin boards and a surprising number of telephone poles. For purposes of this section, however, the common term "brochure" will be used.

Brochures are used primarily to give basic information about an organization, a product, or a service. Organizations mail them or hand them out to potential customers, place them in information racks, hand them out at conferences, and generally distribute them to anyone who might be interested. Whenever an organization needs to explain something to a large number of people—be they employees, constituents or customers—a brochure is the way to do it.

Planning

The first step in planning a brochure is to determine its objective. Such items are always prepared to reach a specific audience and to accomplish a definite purpose, so these questions should be asked:

- Who are you trying to influence and why? Be as specific as possible in identifying the people you must reach.

- What do you want the piece to do? Be clear about the desired effect. Do you want to impress, entertain, sell, inform, or educate?

- What kind of piece do you need to get your message across? Should it be a simple flier, a pocket-size brochure, a cheaply produced leaflet for widespread public distribution, or a fancy four-color brochure for only key customers or opinion leaders?

Factors such as budget, number of copies needed, and distribution method must be considered. In addition, you should think about the method of printing. There are various levels of printing quality that you can use, depending on the answers to the above three questions. Authors Beach, Shepro, and Russom refer to four levels in their book, *Getting It Printed*:

- **Basic:** This is quick copy, such as fliers, simple business forms, and one-color leaflets. Copy shops such as Kinko's and PIP are commonly used.

Professional Tips

How to Produce a Publication on Time

Producing a newsletter or brochure requires setting up a timetable of activities that must be done. One approach is to determine when you want to distribute the finished product and work back in time:

- What is the mailing or distribution date?
- When does printing have to be completed?
- When is the final press proof due?
- When are the proofs and color keys due?
- When do camera-ready materials have to be delivered to the printer?
- When does production begin?

- When do layout and design begin?
- When are final copy and graphics due?
- When does content have to be finalized?
- When is senior management review?
- When are copy revisions due?
- When is first-draft editorial copy due?
- When is the editorial plan due?

- **Good:** This is material that requires strong colors, black-and-white photos, and exact alignment or registration of graphic elements.
- **Premium:** This requires a full-service printer, expensive paper, and high-end graphic elements.
- **Showcase:** Everything from design to paper and specialty inks are first class. Best for portraying an organization as well managed and successful.

Writing

Once you have a general idea of what format you will use to communicate with your audience, you need to think about how that format will shape your writing. If you decide that a simple flier is needed, you will have to be concise and to the point. Fliers, for example, contain the basic five Ws and H—and not much more, because the type must be large and the space (usually an 8.5- by 11-inch piece of paper) is limited.

On the other hand, a simple brochure that has four to six panels folded to a pocket-sized format (4 by 9 inches) or will be mailed in a standard business envelope (#10) can contain more detailed information. Figure 12.6 shows four ways that a simple brochure can be folded.

Whatever the format, you should keep it in mind as you write copy. The most common mistake of novice public relations writers is to write more than the proposed format can accommodate. A second major mistake is to try to cram everything in by reducing type size or margins instead of editing, thus creating a mass of dense type that nobody wants to read. Indeed, the most difficult concept to learn is that less is best. Copy should be short and should have plenty of white space around it. This means ample margins, space between major subsections, and room for appropriate graphics.

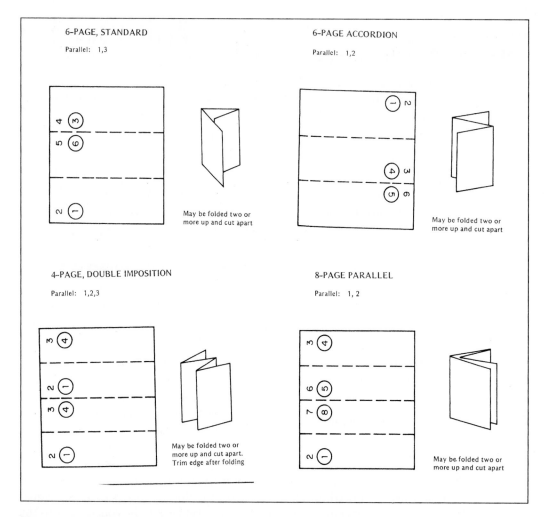

Figure 12.6 Brochures Can Be Folded in Creative Ways
These diagrams show how a single piece of paper, printed on both sides, can be folded into four, six, or eight panels (or pages). Each panel has its own number. The circled "1" is the cover, and the "2" is the reverse panel.
(Courtesy of Baum Folder Company, Sidney, OH.)

The concepts of good writing, elaborated in previous chapters, are the same for brochures. Short, declarative sentences are better than compound sentences. Short paragraphs are better than long ones. Major points should be placed in bulleted lists or under subheads. It is always a good idea to pretest brochure copy on members of the target audience to be sure that it is understandable and that you have included all the necessary information.

Research Gathering information for use in a leaflet or brochure may involve anything from asking a few questions to conducting a major survey. In most cases, the needed information can be found within the organization.

Keeping in mind the subject and purpose of the proposed publication, start by talking to the people in the organization who know the most about the subject. Tell them what you want to accomplish, and ask for information that will enable you to prepare a clear explanation of the subject. Often, all the needed information can be obtained from one source.

A good way to decide what to include in a brochure is to put yourself in the position of a member of the prospective audience. Ask every question that this person might have about the subject. The answers can constitute sections of the pub-

Professional Tips

How to Write an Effective Brochure

Shannon Ganun, a writer and designer in Virginia Beach, Virginia, says any effective brochure has some key elements. This is her list, adapted from an article she wrote in *PR Tactics*.

- **Write in terms of benefits to the reader.** How will he or she benefit from the product or service? Resist the temptation to talk about the company and how wonderful it is. Such statements do not engage the client or customer.

- **Prioritize your message in two or three key points.** Communications research suggests that people are able to digest and remember only a few points. Write your key points from the standpoint of what the reader want to know about your product or service. To be credible, back up your key points with proof. If you say your product is the safest on the market, how are you going to prove that point?

- **Tell the complete story in headlines.** Most people only skim materials. Therefore, you should get your key messages across in bold headlines and subheads that the reader will likely read.

- **Include specific facts and figures.** Use statistics and facts to enhance your credibility. For example, "Our clients averaged a 20 percent return on their investments last year," or "All our doctors are board certified."

- **Use testimonials.** Use excerpts from letters and e-mails sent by satisfied customers. This, of course, requires you to get permission first. If you don't have any testimonials, send a short note to customers asking them to write a few words about your product or service. Be clear about your intention to use their comments in a brochure.

- **Offer more information.** You can only have so much copy in a brochure. Use collateral pieces such as a "Frequently Asked Questions" or a list of 10 reasons why your product or service is needed. Focus on what additional information the reader wants to know; leave out the sales talk.

- **Use positive language.** The copy should be positive, interesting, and vivid. Use the active voice because it is more compelling, and it also requires fewer words. Instead of saying, "The following services are available through XYZ company," say "XYX company offers the following services."

- **Guarantee your products or service.** Ensure that the buyer will be satisfied. Include specific guarantees or at least emphasize how you will make sure the customer is satisfied.

- **Tell the next step.** Give the reader information about how to order or get more information. Give your e-mail address, Web site, and telephone number.

lication. You can even use the questions as subheads. Many successful brochures have consisted entirely of questions and answers.

Putting It Together   Brochures vary so widely that no general guide is applicable. Each has a different audience, a different purpose, and a different format. It is imperative to use words that your readers will understand. If you have to explain a technical topic, check with the experts once you have put the story into everyday English, to be sure you've got it right. For any but the briefest publications, you will need to prepare an outline. This should cover all the main points to be included, and it should list the illustrations to be used.

As you write and plan the layout of the publication, remember to include visual variety in your pages. Illustrations, blocks of copy, and headlines not only serve the direct purpose of communication, but can also make the pages attractive and interesting. Some writers recommend preparing a complete layout before starting to write. Others prefer to develop the layout after the writing is finished. A practical compromise is to prepare a rough layout before writing and then to revise it as the writing progresses.

Choosing the Format   Before deciding on the format of printed materials, get samples of items like those you want to produce. Note how they were done and be guided by them. There are several basic formats, which have already been mentioned. The next step up is to do a brochure that has six panels (two folds) or eight panels (three folds), which is shown in Figure 12.6. Brochures with multiple pages, however, need to be bound. The binding may be **saddle-stitched**, which means the pages are stapled together on the centerfold. Magazines, for example, are usually bound in this way. If the booklet is large, it may be stapled on the side (**side-stitched**) or spiral-bound.

Preparing a Layout   The layout is the plan for the finished piece. It may be rough or comprehensive, but it must be accurate enough for the person who assembles the parts to do exactly what you want. The first step in making a layout is to prepare a **dummy**—a blank-paper mock-up of the finished product. It should be made of the paper to be used in the printed piece and should be the same size. If the piece is to be a booklet, the dummy should be stapled just as the finished booklet will be. If it is to be a brochure, the dummy should be folded the same way.

With the dummy at hand, you can now plan where everything is to go. For a leaflet, the layout will be complete—it will indicate what is to go on each page. For a small booklet, the layout will also be complete, but if there are many pages, you will need to design only the cover and sample pages of the body.

The layout indicates both type and illustrations. Thus a page layout might show various blocks of copy, headlines, and the location of illustrations for that page. For very simple jobs, you may make the layout yourself; however, most printers are able and willing to do this for you, especially on big jobs.

Production

With the copy written, illustrations selected, and general format decided, it is time to think about producing the newsletter, magazine, or brochure. Here we give you only the highlights. For full information, see *Pocket Pal,* published by the International Paper Company.

Printing Processes   Five main processes are used: offset lithography, letterpress, gravure, screen printing, and thermography.

- **Lithography** is the most popular form of printing. It is based on two premises. First, grease and water do not mix. Second, ink is "offset" from the plate to a rubber blanket, then from the blanket to the paper. Offset printing has two advantages: (1) make-ready or press preparation is minimal and (2) a wide range of paper qualities can be handled.
- **Letterpress** is the oldest printing method, and it was the most popular before the advent of offset printing. It uses the relief method from cast metal type or plates on which the image or printing areas are raised above the non-printing areas. Letterpress images tend to be crisp and sharp.
- **Gravure (intaglio)** uses a sunken or depressed surface for the image and is excellent for printing newspaper supplements and catalogs where color is used.
- **Screen printing (silk screen)** is simply ink with the consistency of paint, forced through a fine silk or Dacron mesh by a squeegee. A stencil on the screen controls which areas receive ink and which do not. Screen printing is versatile and is ideal for short runs. T-shirts are printed this way.
- **Thermography (raised)** gives an embossed effect to stationery, invitations, and business cards. Ink is raised to create texture on the paper.

Finding a Printer   A variety of printers and printing processes are found in every city. In even the smallest town, there is likely to be at least one printer who does offset printing.

Having located some prospects, you should meet with them to discuss your particular needs and their capabilities. Look at samples of their work. Find out what various services cost. It is particularly important to find out what software publishing programs they use, and what format is preferred for submission of copy and artwork.

Most printers today are computerized, and the most common software programs used are *InDesign, Quark Xpress,* and *PhotoShop.* Therefore, if you are submitting digital files to them via e-mail or CD-ROM, they should be compatible with the printer's system. The computers of most commercial printers, for example, can't read files created on programs such as *Microsoft Publisher* or *PrintShop.* You also have to ask whether a printer's system is PC- or Mac-based.

Paper

The weight of the paper may range from very light (such as bond) to very heavy (such as cover stock). There is also a range of weights within these classes. Usually, the heavier the paper within a class, the more it costs. Thus a 100-pound cover is more expensive than a 50-pound cover. These weights are based on the actual weight of 500 sheets of that paper in the standard sheet size. For

One note of caution: People are so impressed with the variety of type styles available that they try to use too many in a given publication. Novice desktop publishing enthusiasts tend to go overboard, and the result is a mishmash of conflicting styles that almost guarantees reader confusion.

Printers' Measurements   The beauty of word processing programs such as *Microsoft Word* is your ability to make a variety of type fonts scalable to any size. In desktop publishing, you can select one type style and size for the headline and another type and size for the body text. If a headline or text copy doesn't quite fit the layout, a few clicks on the mouse will reduce it until it fits. You, of course, have to consider readability, which is discussed shortly.

We are so used to just clicking on a type size such as 14, 16, 24, 36, etc., that some historical background is needed. Printers have always measured type size in **points,** and the standard set long ago was 72 points to the inch. In other words, a 72-point headline is 1 inch high. A 36-point headline is $^1/_2$ inch high. And, of course, copy set in 18-point is $^1/_4$ inch high.

Many printers still measure the length of a typeset line by **picas**. There are 6 picas to an inch, so a 24-pica line is 4 inches wide. The column width in Bell Atlantic's *Wave* (Figure 12.2), for example, is 18 picas—or 3 inches. Please note, however, that many experts say column widths should be no more than 12–14 picas and no less than 8 picas. Picas are also used to measure the depth of a block of copy. Thus a story that is 42 picas deep will measure 7 inches.

Another term used in typesetting is "em," which is a square of the size of that particular type (or roughly the space taken up by the upper-case letter "M" in that point size). A 12-point em is about $^1/_6$ inch high and $^1/_6$ inch wide. The use of ems is largely limited to indicating paragraph indention. A very narrow indention might be 1 em. A wide indention could be 4 or 5 ems. The em is always related to the size of type being used in the body text of the material being typeset.

Desktop publishing software has eliminated the need to be totally conversant in points, picas, and ems—but you should be familiar with the terms and what they mean when you are talking with a printer. A list of such terms is found on page 369.

Readability   Legibility is affected by the typeface. Times Roman letter is more legible than Old English letter. Readability is affected by the legibility of the type and by letter spacing, line spacing, the length of the lines, the color of paper and ink, the kind of paper, and the total amount of reading matter involved. A brochure could be effective with headlines in 18- or 24-point Times Roman, but using this size type for body text in a 16-page booklet would not work.

The only purpose for printing anything is to get it read. Accordingly, any printed material should be planned with readability in mind. Select a legible type and, if necessary, use letter spacing to spread headlines. Use line spacing to improve the readability of lowercase body copy. Keep the length of lines short enough that each can be read as one unit. As a general rule, try to use type no smaller than 10 point for text copy. If your target audience is over 50 years old, you might want to use 12 point type, or even 14 point.

Professional Tips

The Jargon of Printers

When working with graphic designers and printers, you need to know some basic terms.

- **Bleed** An element that extends beyond the trimmed edge of a finished page. Most often used in the context of a photo going to the edge of the page.
- **Dylux** The final proof of composed film work, made on photosensitive paper. It is used to check the position of page elements and allowances for folding and binding.
- **Camera-ready** Description of artwork that is suitable for photographic reproduction on film or a printing plate.
- **Mechanical** Type, photos, line art, and so forth, assembled on a single board to be used for reproduction by a printer.
- **Plus cover** Indicates that a brochure or booklet has a cover, usually a different paper stock, that is added to the total pages in the piece. For example, "16 pages plus cover."
- **Self-cover** A designation indicating that a brochure has the same paper for the inside pages as for the cover.
- **Scoring** Creasing sheets of paper to make folding easier.
- **Electronic files** The copy, layout, artwork, etc., of a brochure or newsletter on diskette; used in desktop publishing to transfer files to a printer's computer system.

Ink and Color

Technological advances in printing now make it easy and economical to use color in all kinds of publications. The use of color, either by choosing colored paper or various inks, not only makes the publications more attractive, but studies show that it improves reader comprehension and a willingness to read the material.

Mario Garcia, a nationally known graphic designer, told *PR Tactics*, "The color is the first thing people notice when a publication lands on their desk. People attach meaning to the publication based on the colors they see."

In many respects, color also conveys the image and values of the organization. If the organization is somewhat conservative and traditional, it's best to stick with soft pastels and earth colors. Garcia, for example, used champagne and sky blue shades when he redesigned *The Wall Street Journal*. This approach also is more pleasing to an older and more traditional audience, which the newspaper serves. On the other hand, *USA Today*, with a younger audience and considerable reliance on newsstand sales, uses a lot of bright colors throughout its pages to attract readers.

Color is used in photos, graphics, headlines, background screens (text boxes), and even body type. A good example of effective color is the magazine of GuideOne Insurance, *Going for Great!* A two-page article about drunk driving and underage drinking, for example, used light pink as a background screen with the body text in dark blue. The headline and subheads were in red ink, so the light pink was simply a 10 or 20 percent screen of this basic color. A one-line kicker headline was in white reversed through a screen of dark blue, which matched the body text.

Having used this example of color, it is important to note that black continues to be the most used color for body text in newsletters, magazines, and brochures. There are two reasons for this. First, black provides the strongest and clearest contrast on white or pastel paper. In other words, black type is much easier to read than text in hot pink or another vivid color. Second, printers typically have presses set up for black ink, so the cost is less than using multiple colors.

With any ink, however, you must consider the color of the paper on which it will be printed. No color will read well against a dark-colored stock. Black ink on dark green paper, for example, makes the copy almost impossible to read and causes eye strain. Consequently, the best choice is white paper or something in a pastel or neutral shade.

Listen to the advice of your designer and printer. They are much more knowledgeable about how inks and paper go together for maximum effectiveness and readability. A printer's input is particularly important if you plan to use full-color photography.

DESKTOP PUBLISHING

The word "layout" is more accurate than "publishing," because desktop software programs don't "publish" anything; what they do is allow a person to provide a commercial printer with electronic files that, linked together, provide the text, artwork, photos, and design of your publication.

Today, practically all newsletters, magazines, and brochures are produced through desktop software programs. The biggest advantage of desktop publishing, according to most surveys, is keeping control over the stages of publication preparation, from the writing of copy to camera-ready output.

Desktop software allows you to manipulate text and artwork in a number of ways. You can (1) draw an illustration and then reduce or enlarge it, (2) use different type fonts and sizes, (3) vary column widths, (4) shade or screen backgrounds, (5) add borders around copy, (6) import graphics and photos from other sources, and (7) print out camera-ready pages that can be photocopied or printed on an offset press.

There are, however, at least three levels of desktop publishing software. At the very basic level, *Microsoft Word* or Apple's word processing program has templates for creating basic newsletters and fliers. With a scanner and some creativity, you can create simple documents that are quite adequate for the local garden club or a campus club.

The second level is programs such as *Microsoft Publisher* or Broderbund's *PrintShop,* which give you increased capability to design newsletters, brochures, and banners using an extensive library of layout templates and clip art. Small businesses and real estate agents, who need a neighborhood newsletter or a flier announcing an event, often use these user-friendly software programs to create materials that can be produced in limited quantities on your printer or at the local photocopy shop.

The third, and most sophisticated, level is programs such as *InDesign* and *Quark Xpress.* They often are used in conjunction with high-level illustration programs such as *Adobe Illustrator, Freehand,* and *PhotoShop.* Most commercial printers and professional designers use these programs so, if you are submitting electronic

Professional Tips

How Much Will It Cost?

Printers need detailed specifications before they can tell you how much your publication will cost. When you contact a printer, Media Distribution Services (MDS) in New York says you should be prepared to provide the following information:

- Size of piece
- Print quantity
- Number of colors
- Type and quantity of photos and illustrations
- Number of folds
- Whether there are "bleeds"
- Type of binding
- Quality and weight of paper
- Whether there will be die cuts or embossing
- Delivery deadlines

It is also a good idea to show printers a "dummy" or sample of what your piece will look like, so they can see what you require. This preliminary "look-see" will help them spot potential problems.

files to them, you need to make sure you are using the same software. In other words, be aware that you can't use *Microsoft Publisher* to prepare electronic files if the printer or designer is set up for *Quark Xpress*. The two are not compatible.

Although desktop publishing has made it possible for public relations writers to do their own layouts and to prepare materials in a more attractive manner, experts caution that you need more than writing skills. You also need design and layout skills to come up with a camera-ready layout that meets professional standards. As one public relations practitioner observed, "These skills are not necessarily found in a single person under normal circumstances."

In other words, having access to sophisticated software and computer hardware is not a substitute for well-trained technicians and graphic designers who know what to do with the technology. Not everyone is a good designer, and one of the by-products of desktop publishing is the "garbage dump document," put out by people who know nothing about design. In many cases, they are so bedazzled by the technology at their fingertips that they commit the sin of using a dozen typefaces in a single newsletter.

There's also the question of how you want to spend your time. You can write and edit the copy, take all the photos, design the periodical, and prepare the camera-ready artwork—but that doesn't leave much time for other public relations duties.

Consequently, public relations writers often work closely with professional designers who are responsible for putting all the components of a publication together. If you work with a designer on a project, Media Distribution Services (MDS), a New York printing and distribution firm, outlines the basic approach:

- Prepare your manuscript in word processing software that is compatible with the designer's computer system.
- Prepare the manuscript along the same guidelines as you would for traditional copy, using whatever graphic capabilities are available to indicate type

PR Casebook

Brochures Help Raise $5 Million

Catholic Charities, in the Archdiocese of Minneapolis and St. Paul, had a challenge. The group wanted to raise an additional $1 million from the private sector to help fund its services to the poor and homeless. Since other nonprofits and foundations were also soliciting funds, Catholic Charities knew it would take something "special" to meet its goal.

That something "special" was the development of two award-winning brochures that were written and designed by Schermer Kuehl, a marketing design firm in Minneapolis. One brochure, designed for donors who give between $2,500 and $50,000 per year, was a 9- by 12-inch, spiral-bound view book on glossy paper that emphasized the theme, "Putting a Face on the Poor."

Dramatic full-page, black and off-white photos showed individuals who needed help. In one photo, a close-up of a mother and child, the caption read, "I want the best for her ... because I've seen the worst." A fold-out page gave information on how Catholic Charities helped homeless and low-income single mothers. In this way, each of the charity's services was effectively communicated.

A second brochure, designed for donors in the $500-to-$2,500 range, was 8.5 by 11 inches with two folds (see Figure 12.8). It carried out the theme and graphics of the more elaborate brochure, but the copy focused only on an overview of the services that Catholic Charities offered. In both cases, according to Chris Schermer, a principal in the design firm, "The strategy was to show the emotional appeal, as well as provide detailed information to show that there is a need, and what CC was doing to address those needs."

The brochures, each designed for a well-defined audience, hit the mark. The campaign was a major success, raising more than $5 million. In addition, the brochures won numerous awards for design and achieving results.

Figure 12.8 An Award-Winning Brochure
The cover for the brochure of Catholic Charities in Minneapolis/St.Paul attracts interest because of strong graphics. This brochure, plus a larger, more elaborate one on the same theme, raised more than $5 million to help homeless and low-income families.
(Courtesy of Catholic Charities and Schermer Kuehl Marketing Design, Minneapolis, MN.)

sizes, type styles (italics, etc.), and other simple design elements such as bullets and dashes.

- E-mail the manuscript to the designer or send it on a disk. Fax or deliver a rough layout of the printed piece for general guidance. Don't waste time and money trying to design the piece yourself.

- Once the designer has done his or her job, request a printout so you can proofread and check everything. If you make any changes, request another proof to ensure that the changes were made.

- After you have given final approval for the piece, the designer then sends the electronic files to the printer. The electronic files should contain all the necessary components to print the piece, such as a "read me" file detailing all applications and fonts. It is also a good idea to send a laserprint of the final layout and any notes you have for the printer.

SUMMARY

- Printed materials such as newsletters, magazines, and brochures are still important communication channels in the Internet age.

- An editor must serve the dual role of meeting management expectations and employee needs.

- A publication's format and content should reflect the organization's culture, goals, and objectives.

- Today's employees want periodicals that address their concerns about the economic health of the organization and their job security.

- Every publication should have an overall mission statement. An annual editorial plan outlines the kind of stories and features that will support the organization's priorities.

- Periodicals are designed to reflect how the organization wants to be perceived.

- The newsletter is the most common organizational publication. Magazines usually are the most expensive publication and are often sent to both internal and external audiences.

- Headlines should be written in active voice and provide key messages.

- Most electronic newsletters sent by e-mail consist of simple online text that can be easily downloaded. Stories should be 10 to 12 lines long. They are fast and cost-efficient, but they don't replace print periodicals.

- Electronic newsletters sent on an organization's intranet system often contain more color, graphics, and photos.

- Brochures vary in format and size from a single sheet of paper folded into panels to multiple-page pamphlets and booklets.

- Writing and designing a brochure requires you to know its purpose, the target audience, and the most cost-effective format.

- A brochure requires simple sentence construction, informative headlines, liberal use of subheads, and short paragraphs.

- The most common mistake of novice writers is to write too much copy for the space available. A brochure page crammed with type is a turnoff.

- Factors such as cost, distribution, and estimated life span of the brochure help determine the format of the printed piece and the kind of writing required.

- It pays to prepare a dummy or mock layout of the brochure before you begin writing.

- Offset lithography is the most versatile and popular form of printing today.

- A printer needs to know all the specifications of a planned piece before he or she can give you a cost estimate.

- There are various grades of paper, each designed for specific kinds of jobs.

- There are various type classes and families. Stick to fonts that are highly readable. Use decorative type and italics sparingly.

- Black ink is the most popular and readable color. Use spot color to make your publication more attractive.

- Although you may be able to write and design a simple flier or brochure, experts recommend hiring a professional graphic designer for bigger jobs.

- Desktop publishing is now widely used for preparing newsletters, magazines, and brochures.

- Desktop publishing requires the preparation of extensive electronic files that show the links between copy, graphics, photos, headlines, and layout.

ADDITIONAL RESOURCES

Battenberg, Erik. "Design Guru Tells All: Tips for Publication Redesigns." *PR Tactics*, July 2002, pp. 1, 13.

Creamer, Matthew. "Inside Story: The Role of Employee Newsletters." *PRWeek*, August 4, 2003, p. 18.

Dysart, Joe. "E-Mail Newsletters Dymystified." *PR Tactics*, June 2003, p. 6.

Kappel, Don J. "So. . . . You Want a Brochure." *Public Relations Quarterly*, Summer 2003, pp. 43–44.

Nemec, Richard. "The Perfect Couple: Design and Writing Will Forever Be Inseparable." *Communication World*, April/May 2001, pp. 20–23.

Sanchez, Paul. "How to Craft Successful Employee Communication in the Information Age." *Communication World*, August/September 1999, pp. 9–15.

Somerick, Nancy M. "Practical Strategies for Avoiding Problems in Graphic Communication." *Public Relations Quarterly*, Fall 2000, pp. 32–34.

Stewart, Joan. "Creating Your Own Ezine." *PR Tactics*, December 2001, p. 15.

Zapotocky, Debra. "Making the Most of Graphic Design." *PR Tactics*, March 2002, p. 22.

Chapter 13

The World Wide Web

The World Wide Web, as part of the Internet, is an important communication tool for public relations practitioners. Over 60 percent of Americans now have Internet access and 40 percent of them have been online for more than three years, according to the Pew Internet and American Life Project.

In addition to the World Wide Web, it should be noted that more than 90 percent of U.S. enterprises—including quite small ones—now have internal Web sites and portals that are called **intranets**. Consultant John Gerstner, writing in *Communication World*, notes, "More than 75 percent of all Web servers being installed are for intranet purposes, and the market for intranet applications, platforms and related technology is substantially outstripping that for the public Internet and all other IT areas." Chapter 12 discussed e-zines, or online publications, which are often part of organizational intranets.

The Web and organizational intranets, like newsletters and brochures, are controlled mediums because the sender of the message has control over the content that reaches the receiver. Indeed, it can be said that the World Wide Web is the first public medium to reach a mass audience without the message being filtered by editors in traditional mass media. Before the Web, advertising was the only way to send a controlled message to the general public through a mass medium.

This chapter focuses on the World Wide Web from a public relations perspective. Although many of the concepts presented also are applicable to intranets, this chapter discusses (1) how journalists use Web sites for information, (2) creating a "news room" for the media, (3) writing for the Web, (4) designing a Web site, (5) working with computer experts to build a Web site, (6) the components of Webcasting, (7) attracting visitors to a Web site, and (8) tracking Web site visitors.

THE GROWTH OF THE WORLD WIDE WEB

The worldwide adoption of the Internet has taken less time than the growth of any other mass medium. Marc Newman, general manager of Medialink Dallas, says, "Whereas it took nearly 40 years before there were 50 million listeners of radio and 13 years until television reached an audience of 50 million, a mere four years passed before 50 million users were logging on to the Internet since it became widely available."

The growth of the Internet and the World Wide Web continues at an astounding rate, and any figures given today are out of date almost before they are published. Yet some figures are worth noting. According to the Computer Industry Almanac (2002), at the end of 2000 home use of the Internet was about 500 million worldwide. The United States led Internet users with an estimated 140 million online by the end of 2000.

In terms of U.S. college students, Greenfield Online (2001) reported that around 84 percent of them had Web access from some campus location. It is estimated by International Data Corporation that nearly 1 billion people, about 15 percent of the world's population, will be using the Internet by 2005.

The World Wide Web has also grown by geometric leaps. *Time* magazine proudly announced in 1999 that there were 800 million pages stored on the World Wide Web. By 2002, however, this number had mushroomed to more than 3 billion pages, and another 2.5 million Web pages were being added every day. The Web, according to two professors of information management at the University of California at Berkeley, now contains 17 times what is contained in the Library of Congress' print collection.

The exponential growth of the World Wide Web is due, in large part, to its unique characteristics. The box on page 378 compares the differences between "traditional media" and the "new media," but here are some of the major characteristics of a Web site that enable public relations people to do a better job of communication:

- Information can be updated quickly.

- It allows interactivity; viewers can ask questions about products or services, download information of value to them, and let the organization know what they think.

- Online readers can dig deeper into subjects that interest them by linking to information provided on other sites, other articles, and sources.

- Online information is not limited by the space constrictions of print.

- It is a cost-effective method of disseminating information on a global basis to the public and journalists.

Public relations personnel, of course, do their part in contributing to the popularity of the Internet and increasing the content of the World Wide Web. Michael Ryan, at the University of Houston, conducted a survey of 150 practitioners and

Professional Tips

Traditional Media vs. New Media

The World Wide Web is today's new medium. Many of its characteristics can be better understood by comparing it with traditional mass media. Kevin Kawamoto, at the University of Washington, compiled this chart for a Freedom Forum seminar on technology.

Traditional Mass Media

Geographically constrained: Media geared to geographic markets or regional audience share; market specific

Hierarchical: News and information pass through a vertical hierarchy of gatekeeping and successive editing

Unidirectional: Dissemination of news and information is generally one-way, with restricted feedback mechanisms

Space/time constraints: Newspapers are limited by space; radio and TV by time

Professional communicators: Trained journalists, reporters, and experts tend to qualify as traditional media personnel

High access costs: Cost of starting a newspaper, radio, or TV station is prohibitive for most people

General interest: Many mainstream mass media target large audiences and thus offer broad coverage

Linearity of content: News and information are organized in logical, linear order; news hierarchy

Feedback: Letters to the editor, phone calls; slow, effort heavy, moderated and edited; time/space limited

Ad-driven: Need to deliver big audiences to advertisers to generate high ad revenues; mass appeal

Institution bound: Much traditional media are produced by large corporations with centralized structure

Fixed format: Content is produced, disseminated, and somewhat "fixed" in place and time

News, values, journalistic standards: Content produced and evaluated by conventional norms and ethics

New Media

Distance insensitive: Media geared toward needs, wants, and interests, regardless of physical location of the user; topic specific

Flattened: News and information have the potential to spread horizonally, from nonprofessionals to other nonprofessionals

Interactive: Feedback is immediate and often uncensored or modified; discussions and debate rather than editorials and opinions

Less space/time constraints: Information is stored digitally; hypertext allows large volumes of info to be "layered" one atop another

Amateurs/nonprofessionals: Anyone with requisite resources can publish on the Web, even amateur and nontrained communicators

Low access costs: Cost of electronic publishing/broadcasting on the Internet is much more affordable

Customized: With fewer space/time restraints and market concerns, new media can "narrowcast" in depth to personal interests

Nonlinearity of content: News and information linked by hypertext; navigate by interest and intuition, not by logic

Feedback: Electronic mail, posting to online discussion groups; comparatively simple and effortless; often unedited, unmoderated

Diverse funding sources: While advertising is increasing, other sources permit more diverse content; small audiences OK

Decentralized: Technology allows production and dissemination of news and information to be "grass-roots efforts."

Flexible format: Content is constantly changing, updated, corrected, and revised; in addition, multimedia allows the integration of multiple forms of media in one service

Formative standards: Norms and values obscure; content produced and evaluated on its own merit and credibility

found widespread use of computers for a variety of purposes. He reported in *Public Relations Quarterly:*

> . . . 99 percent of practitioners said computers are used in their offices to access the World Wide Web; 61 percent said computers are used for Web page maintenance; 58 percent said they are used for Web page development; 57 percent said they are used for surveillance of companies; 49 percent said they are used for exploring data bases at other sites; and 39 percent said computers are used to monitor government activities.

Ryan also noted, "Nearly 48 percent of survey respondents agreed that their public relations department's Web site is "very important" in supporting public relations objectives, and more than 46 percent said the site is "important."

A growing number of public relations firms, like other businesses, also have established Web sites to promote and market their services. Stovin Hayter, a columnist for *PRWeek,* thinks too many of them are too "brochure-like" and sales oriented, but he likes Porter Novelli's (www.porternovelli.com) site because it has a section devoted to a project titled "Kids Think Link." This involved PN staff in a dozen nations teaching kids to use Net tools such as e-mail, bulletin boards, and the Web for research and communication.

Hayter notes, "The result is a Web site that demonstrates an enthusiasm for and an active commitment to the new media. It shows a company that doesn't just tell its clients to get involved in their surrounding communities—it does it itself." Tips on how to create an effective Web site will be discussed shortly.

THE WEB: A MAJOR SOURCE FOR JOURNALISTS

Although an organization's Web site is designed to bypass the traditional media and reach a variety of audiences directly, it is also a major source of information for journalists working for online publications or the traditional mass media.

A national survey of newspapers, for example, found that 92 percent of U.S. daily newspapers used the World Wide Web for news gathering. Another national survey by Middleberg Associates (www.middleberg.com) found that journalists rank the Internet and the World Wide Web second after the telephone as a source of information. The consulting firm also found that: "Growth in Internet access among journalists increased significantly in the past few years, and now approaches universality."

Studies also show that journalists are spending more time using the Internet and the World Wide Web to research stories. A survey of the National Association of Science Writers (NASW), for example, found that nearly all (97 percent) of the journalists had indirectly used information from a Web site in a story, as background or in a paraphrase. About 75 percent had directly used information from the Web.

Middleberg and Ross have conducted the most extensive research on journalists and the Web. In their 2000 annual media survey, 91 percent of the editors at daily newspapers and magazines said they or their staff use online services for article research. The Middleberg survey also indicated that 75 percent of the journalists use the World Wide Web on a daily basis. Other findings indicated that journalists spend 8.7 hours a week on the Internet at work and another 4.7 hours from home.

Journalists use the Web to find specific information. According to Tsantes & Associates, which has done an annual survey of high-tech reporters for the past several years, the primary reason why journalists go online is to get contact information—the phone number or e-mail address of someone who can answer their questions or be interviewed on the phone. At the same time, more than one survey has indicated that the leading complaint of journalists is not being able to find such information on organizational Web sites. One study, for example, found that almost 90 percent of the sites had news releases, but only 60 percent listed media contact information.

Journalists, even if they get frustrated about the lack of telephone numbers and e-mail addresses for press contacts, still make great use of background information on Web sites. According to a research paper by Louisa Ha of the Gallup Organization and Cornelius Pratt of Michigan State University, "Journalists use the Web to find people and news story sources, conducting background research about business and individuals, identifying news story ideas, and locating public and private information stored in digital form."

More specifically, reporters often seek news releases, company product information, data sheets, backgrounders, and information on product pricing and availability. See Figure 13.1 for a typical news release on a corporate Web site. The Middleberg survey of 2,500 business editors also found that the Web is one of the first places that many individuals go for up-to-the-minute information. It notes, "When reporting a breaking story after hours, journalists try for the source first, almost every time, but indicate they turn to company Web sites second for information." This information reinforces the idea that media advisories and news releases on Web sites need to be updated on a daily basis, which will be discussed shortly.

In sum, the Web has become a major source of information for journalists. According to *NetMarketing*, companies are sending out fewer media kits and getting fewer phone inquiries as a result of putting material on Web sites. As Rick Rudman, president of Capital Hill Software, told *PR Tactics*, "The days of just posting press releases on your Web site are gone. Today, journalists, investors, all audiences expect to find media kits, photos, annual reports, and multimedia pres-entations about your organization at your press center. Get ready!"

One downside of this, however, is the reduction of one-on-one contact between public relations personnel and media representatives, because reporters no longer have to use the phone to research stories. John Tsantes, president of Tsantes & Associates, says, "This presents a challenge for PR pros to change the way we work and communicate with the press, and really validates the use of the Internet in PR programs." At the same time, Don Middleberg says ". . . building relationships with the media remains the core value of public relations. . . ."

In other words, the Web facilitates the flow of information, but it does not replace the need for public relations practitioners to have regular personal contact with reporters. A large percentage of reporters, according to the Middleberg survey, still get their story ideas through personal contact with sources.

Creating a Press-Friendly Web Site

A good Web site, however, can do much to cement a good relationship with the media if it fulfills the needs of journalists who cover your organization.

Figure 13.1 News Releases on the Web
Journalists often review and download news releases posted on organizational Web sites. This release, from IBM's press room, is a typical example. The key information is included in several headlines at the top of the release for fast review. The page itself has several navigation features. On the left, a journalist can access current and past news releases by month, topic, and country. There are also links to photos, biographies, contacts, and even a link so the journalist can send an e-mail query about some aspect of a news announcement. *(Courtesy of IBM Corporation, New York.)*

Debbie Neville, who works for O'Keeffe & Company in McLean, Virginia, writes in *PR Tactics,* "The media, often frustrated with today's information overload from PR professionals, are looking for one-stop sources that can deliver comprehensive information—on demand. To this end, corporate Web sites can be powerful communicaton tools." In other words, an organization's Web site should have pages dedicated specifically to journalists. On home pages, the link often is called a "newsroom" or "press room." Figures 13.2 and 13.5, for example, show the opening pages of the Hewlett-Packard and Cisco Systems newsrooms.

Joanna Schroeder, who wrote a master's thesis at Iowa State University on journalists' use of Web "press rooms," conducted a survey and made a list of what materials in a "press room" were most useful to them:

- **Contact information:** "The most important element journalists are looking for when they visit your Web site is updated contact information," says Schroeder. Journalists want a contact name, title, phone number, pager number, after-hours number, and e-mail address. In addition, they want the contact information in a prominent place on the Web page.

- **Search tool:** Journalists want the most recent news releases first, but they also want a navigation tool that allows them easy access to past news releases.

- **Company background:** Journalists want news articles about the company, position papers on industry issues and initiatives, industry events, and trade show documents. They also like links to outside sources about the company.

- **Financial data:** They also seek quarterly financial reports, stock quotes, and annual reports as well as links to SEC filings, outside financial data, and analyst coverage.

- **Company history and executive profiles:** Materials commonly found in media kits, including company fact sheets, logos, executive head shots, and executive profiles are also sought. See Figure 13.3 for an example of an executive profile.

- **News:** Current, up-to-the-minute news is important as well as links to specialized news services that cover the industry.

- **Multimedia:** Video and audio clips were ranked in the survey as the least useful information that journalists needed. In addition, even multimedia news release were not that popular despite the promotional efforts of Business Wire and PRNewswire.

- **Graphics and usability:** Schroeder says, "Your site should be quick to download. If that means fewer graphics, then move these pictures to a photo gallery. Use a simple color scheme with a white background. A Web page should easily fit on a user's computer screen because journalists (as well as anyone else) hate to scroll. It's also important to have a simple, clear navigational system so items are easy to identify and find."

- **Downloadable material:** Journalist also want product publicity photo, logs, and other artwork that can be easily downloaded in PDF or TIFF files with a minimum of 300 dpi, which meets the requirements of most publications.

If your organization is global in scope, with facilities in many nations, many experts also recommend that the "press room" include a link that allows reporters to access company information relevant to their own countries. IBM, in Figure 13.1 has such a link. *Interactive Public Relations*, a newsletter published by

Figure 13.2 A Corporate Newsroom

Many organizational Web sites have "newsrooms" or "press rooms" primarily designed to serve journalists. This is the home page of Hewlett-Packard's newsroom. It lists the most recent news releases by date so journalists can easily click on the one that involves their beat. The left column gives more links. Journalists can access archived news releases, features, media relations contacts, media kits, biographies of key executives, and financial information.

(Courtesy of Hewlett-Packard, Palo Alto, CA.)

Figure 13.3 Executive Profiles Are a Standard Feature

The HP Newsroom includes short profiles of the management team. These profiles serve as background for journalists who need to check exact titles or the spelling of names. This Web profile is about Carly Fiorina, chairman and chief executive officer of Hewlett-Packard Company.

(Courtesy of Hewlett-Packard, Palo Alto, CA.)

Lawrence Ragan Communications (www.ragan.com) notes, "Putting the release online in more than one language will let foreign journalists know they are an important audience to your company and client, and will allow them to access your news as it happens."

WRITING FOR THE WEB

So far, we have discussed what journalists want from a Web site and what elements should be in the "press room" of an organization's Web site. As a public relations writer, you will be responsible for preparing much of the material that the media and the public will read at your Web site. Therefore, we now turn our attention to how to write Web-based material.

Two basic concepts are important. First, there is a fundamental difference between how people read online and how they read printed documents. According to a study by Sun Microsystems, it takes 50 percent longer for an individual to read material on a computer screen. As a consequence, 79 percent of online readers scan text instead of reading word by word.

Second, the public relations writer needs to know the basic difference between linear and nonlinear styles of writing. Printed material usually follows a linear progression; a person reads in a straight line from the beginning of the article to the end of it. Nonlinear means that items can be selected out of order; a person selects a note card out of a stack. Online reading, say the experts, is nonlinear; people seek out particular "note cards" about an organization, a product, or a service. One person clicks the tab for price and availability of a product, while another clicks for more information about how to use the product in a specific situation.

This technique is called **branching**. Michael Butzgy, owner of Atomic Rom Productions in Cary, North Carolina, explains in *Communication World*, "Branching allows you to send users in specific directions. The basic idea behind branching is to eliminate the need for viewers to scroll down a long linear document." In another *Communication World* article, Jeff Herrington, owner of his own Dallas public relations firm, says:

> Rather than organize information so it runs linearly from the top of the screen to past the bottom, we want to layer the information in sections that sit like index cards in a file box, one screen behind the other. The first card (or screen) of information contains within it all the links to all the cards (or screens) behind it, and so on. That way, the online user rarely, if ever, has to perform the tedious and time-consuming task of scrolling.

Helen L. Mitternight, owner of her own communications firm in Annandale, Virginia, explains nonlinear writing in yet another *Communication World* article:

> Think of it as writing in chunks, with each idea or information contained in each "chunk" (or component of your writing) complete unto itself. Identify elements of your writing that contain a single unit of information and recast it into a "chunk" that can both stand alone and work with the rest of your online piece. And, even more than most writing, shorter is better. Documents written for the Web should be 50 percent shorter than their print counterparts, according to the Sun Microsystems study.

Professional Tips

Writing for a Web Site

Diane F. Witmer, in her textbook, *Spinning the Web: A Handbook for Public Relations on the Internet,* says writing for the Web is much like any other writing project. You need to follow many of the same basic guidelines, but also be aware that the text will be read on a computer screen. Witmer gives 10 basic tips:

- As with all effective public relations writing, your text must be mechanically excellent, and free of any grammar, punctuation, spelling, or syntax errors.
- Avoid "puff" words, cliches, and exaggerations.
- Keep the sentences short, crisp, and to the point.
- Use active verbs and avoid passive voice.
- Support main ideas with proper evidence.
- Keep individual paragraphs focused on one central idea.
- Make sure each paragraph logically follows the one before it.
- Set the reading level appropriate to the readership; use short words and sentences for young and inexperienced readers.
- Avoid a patronizing tone by talking "with" rather than "at" the reader.
- Avoid jargon, acronyms, and other specialized language that may confuse the reader.

How short is "short"? Herrington, mentioned already, says sentences should be less than 20 words long, and only two or three sentences should be used in a paragraph. An entire topic should be covered in two or three paragraphs, or about the length of one screen. This approach, he says, recognizes the fact that people scan material and dislike scrolling to view other links to the topic.

Other experts also offer tips for writing online. *Communication Briefings,* for example, says you should limit line length to fewer than 60 characters. It further states, "Long text lines are hard to read and give your Web site a claustrophobic 'filled-up' look that discourages visitors from remaining." Other tips offered by the newsletter: (1) use subheads to break long articles into shorter chunks, (2) insert extra space between paragraphs because it adds visual contrast, (3) avoid distracting backgrounds that make type difficult to read, and (4) avoid using "yesterday," "today," or "tomorrow"; use the day of the week or dates.

Shel Holtz, author of *Public Relations on the Net,* also offers a number of writing tips:

- **Write the way you talk.** Injecting more personality into the copy will make it easier for people to invest the time in reading it.
- **Limit each page to a single concept.** Provide links to related ideas, allowing the reader to decide which information to pull.
- **Use a lot of bullet-point lists.** Lists are easy to scan, but they also force readers to absorb each item one at a time.

- **Make sure each page provides the context readers need**. You have no way of knowing whether they followed your path to get to this page.
- **Limit the use of italics and boldface**. Italics and bold draw attract attention, so use them only to highlight your key points.
- **Don't overuse hyperlinks within narrative text**. Each hyperlink forces the reader to make a choice between continuing to read or following the link. Collect your hyperlinks at the bottom of the page, after the narrative.
- **Make sure your hyperlinks are relevant**. Think about your audience and what they are looking for; don't include gratuitous links simply because you can.
- **Provide feedback options for readers**. Feedback can lead you to make revisions and updates that keep the writing current and relevant.

The box on page 386 expands on what Holtz and others have said about writing for a Web page.

All too often, however, Web sites violate many of these guidelines because public relations writers don't understand the medium and simply post printed materials to a Web page without making any changes. This is a big mistake, according to Nick Hernandez, project manager for Frito-Lay. He told *Web Content Report*, "Placing the text from a printed brochure onto a Web page word-for-word doesn't work. It's just static text." He says such a document really needs hyperlinks, graphics, and animation to attract interest and readership.

Ideally, at the very least, a public relations writer should edit articles, brochures, and handbooks into bit-sized chunks so the online reader isn't faced with constant scrolling. One relatively simple approach is to give the reader an executive summary of the material—in one screen or less—and then provide a link to the entire document if it isn't too long.

The ideal way, of course, is to do what Hernandez at Frito-Lay suggests; convert the entire document to nonlinear style and make it more digestible through graphics and various links. A company's annual report, for example, would get virtually no readership on a Web page if it was a replica of the 36-page printed version. Consequently, a company such as SGI (formerly Silicon Graphics, Inc.) formats its annual report in nonlinear style.

According to Richard Koreto, writing in the *Journal of Accountancy*, key sections of the annual report are given their own Web page, with links joining the whole report together. Readers can jump from page to page based on subheadings rather than flipping through the entire printed report, scanning for the section they are interested in. Likewise, some companies have provided links to other sites of importance, such as the SEC, within the e-report.

Some companies have even taken advantage of the fact that a Web site gives them the opportunity to expand on information. Intel, for example, adds audio and video clips to its annual report on the Web. More material on corporate annual reports is found in Chapter 14.

News releases, feature stories, media advisories, and position papers posted to Web sites tend to be full-text files. There are two major reasons for this: (1) they are relatively short, and (2) reporters often download them and save them for quick referral while they are working on a story. See Figure 13.1 for the first page of a news release posted on IBM's Web site.

Posting a news release to your Web site is relatively easy. You create your document as you usually do, but instead of saving it as a Word, WordPerfect, or WordPro file, you save it as an HTML file. Any one of the office suites—Microsoft Office, Corel's PerfectOffice, or Lotus Smartsuite—is capable of publishing documents to your Web site. There are other aspects of a Web site, which will be discussed next.

BUILDING AN EFFECTIVE WEB SITE

"You have 10 to 12 seconds to 'hook' an Internet surfer onto your Web site, or else they'll click onto something else," says consultant Gordon MacDonald in an interview with *O'Dwyer's PR Services Report.*

For this reason, considerable attention is given to Web design so a site can compete with the thousands of other Web pages that are readily accessible with the click of a mouse. The idea is to create a Web site that is attractive, easy to navigate, and offers relevant information. We have previously discussed how a Web site can be media-friendly, so this section discusses additional aspects of creating a Web site for your organization.

MacDonald, in his interview, says building a good Web site requires four key skills. They are:

- First, you must have the "vision" of how you want your organization to be perceived by the public.
- Second, you need a copywriter to write the text.
- Third, you need a graphic artist to add the visual element.
- Finally, you need a computer programmer to put the ideas together in HTML code for the Internet.

MacDonald mentions having a "vision" for the Web site. Other experts, such as Ralph F. Wilson of Wilson Internet Services, describes the first step as deciding what you want the Web site to accomplish. In most cases, an organization wants a Web site to accomplish multiple objectives—and keeping the press informed is only one of them.

Marketing is a common objective. Organizations, in the stampede to cash in on e-commerce, often want to sell products and services directly from a Web site. Other marketing approaches might be to create a Web site where potential customers can learn about the organization and gain a favorable impression, or to develop a qualified list of prospects for goods or services. Web pages with a strong marketing emphasis may have several main sections, such as (1) about the organization and its reputation for service and reliability, (2) a list of product lines, (3) technical support available to customers, (4) how to order products or services, and (5) various services available.

Another preliminary step before creating a Web page is to spend some time thinking about your potential audience and their particular needs. It is one thing to decide what the organization wants to accomplish; it is quite another thing to place yourself in the minds of the audience and figure out how they will use your

PR Casebook

Web Site Is an Important Communication Tool

Large corporations aren't the only ones that use Web sites. Many nonprofit organizations and governmental agencies also use them to communicate with the public.

One such organization is the Contra Costa Water District (www.ccwater.com). Its site says, "The mission of the CCWD Web site is to provide the effective services and information that Contra Costa Water District constituents require."

This mission is fulfilled in several ways. Visitors find current information on major water district construction projects, up-to-date reports on fishing at the Los Vaqueros Reservoir, tips on water conservation, and even an online library that has 44 different district publications available in PDF format.

In addition, the site serves as a major source of information about employment opportunities. Approximately 90 percent of the job applications the district receives each year are filled out online. In one year, for example, almost 2,000 people submitted applications online. Customers also use the Web site to e-mail the district, asking about such things as the safety of water facilities and how to get extensions on paying their bills.

The water district publicizes its Web site by including the URL in all newspaper advertisements and publications. It is also listed on promotional items, the district's job phone

hotline, and at public events sponsored by the district.

The budget for the CCWD Web site is approximately $15,000 annually. This includes Web page design, programming, and implementation of new services.

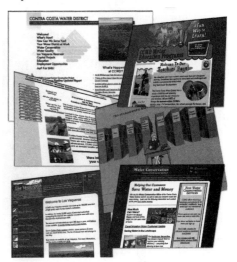

Figure 13.4 Web Pages Must Be Well Designed
An organizational Web page, to attract visitors, should use short blocks of copy surrounded by photographs, graphics, and color. This shows various pages from the Web site of a water district.
(Courtesy of Contra Costa Water District, Concord, CA.)

Web site. Are they accessing your Web site to find a particular product? Are they primarily investors who are looking for financial information? Or are they looking for employment information? Are they likely to download the material and save documents in print form? If that is the case, Diane Witmer in her book, *Spinning the Web: A Handbook for Public Relations on the Internet*, says you need to have ". . . light background and dark text, and avoid Java and JavaScript features that do not print."

Focus groups, personal interviews, and surveys often answer these questions and help you design a user-friendly site. The San Diego Convention Center, for example, redesigned its Web site by forming a customer advisory board of 28 clients that used the facility. Focus group research was held to find out what they wanted to see in an updated Web site.

According to *PRWeek*, "The Customer Advisory Board feedback enabled SDCC to jettison a great deal of the clutter that plagues many sites and focus on exactly what the target audience wanted. Gone was dense copy and hard-to-navigate pages, replaced by hot links to key portions of the site."

Indeed, paying attention to the needs of the audience helps you decide exactly what links you want to list on your home page. HP (see Figure 13.2), for example, has a short but comprehensive list of key links to past news releases, feature stories, media relations contacts, and media kits on its "newsroom" page for journalists. If you look at HP's corporate home page, however, you won't find those links. Instead, there are multiple links to products and various business systems—information that consumers might be seeking.

Such categories, prominently displayed like index tabs, help the user go directly to what interests them. Indeed, being able to navigate a Web site with ease is the key to an effective site. According to *Web Content Report*, "Improved navigation ranks first on nearly every site's priority list. The goal: Fewer required clicks for users to access information because your site loses users at each step in your navigation."

Jakob Nielsen, an Internet consultant, gives a list of additional design elements that increases the usability of virtually all sites (www.useit.com):

- Place your organization's name and logo on every page.
- Provide a "search" tab if the site has more than 100 pages.
- Write straightforward and simple headlines and page titles that clearly explain what the page is about and that will make sense when read out of context in a search engine results listing.
- Structure the page to facilitate scanning and help users ignore large chunks of pages in a single glance. For example, use groupings and subheadings to break a long list into several smaller units.
- Don't cram everything about a product or topic into a single page; use hypertext to structure the content space into a starting page that provides an overview and several secondary pages that each focus on a specific topic.
- Use product photos, but avoid pages with lots of photos. Instead, have a small photo on each of the individual product pages and give the viewer the option of enlarging it for more detail.
- Use link titles to provide users with a preview of where each link will take them, before they have clicked on it.
- Do the same as everybody else. If most big Web sites do something in a certain way, then follow along, since users will expect things to work the same way on your site.
- Test your design with real users as a reality check. People do things in odd and unexpected ways, so even the most carefully planned project will learn from usability testing.

Professional Tips

PR Ethics on the Web

Is it all right for public relations personnel to covertly promote their employers and clients in online chat rooms while posing as average consumers? This and other ethical dilemmas have caused the Arthur W. Page Society, a group of senior communication executives, to formulate some basic principles that should be followed when using the Internet:

Present Fact-based Content

- Tell the truth at all times.
- Ensure timely delivery of information.
- Tell the full story, adhering to accepted standards of accuracy.

Be an Objective Advocate

- Act as a credible information source, providing round-the-clock access.
- Know your subject.
- Rely on credible sources for expert advice.
- Offer opportunities for dialogue and interaction with experts.
- Reveal the background of experts, disclosing any potential conflicts of interest or anonymous support of content.

Earn the Public's Trust

- Simultaneously contact multiple stakeholders with relevant and accurate information.
- Disclose all participation in chat rooms and conferences.
- Correct misinformation that is online.
- Provide counsel on privacy, security, and other trust issues.

Educate the PR Profession on Best Practices

- Compile case studies on the best use of new media.
- Advance and encourage industry-wide adoption of best practices on the Internet.
- Practice principled leadership in the digital world, adhering to the highest standards.

The Page principles have been endorsed by 11 other public relations organizations.

The box on page 392 supplements Schroeder's tips for effective Web design; both go a long way toward generating repeat visitors to your Web site. Forrester Research says there are four main reasons why visitors return to a particular Web site. First and foremost, high-quality content is the main reason. Then, in descending order, are ease of use, quick to download, and frequent updates.

Making the Site Interactive

A unique characteristic of the Internet and the World Wide Web, which traditional mass media does not offer, is interactivity between the sender and the receiver.

One aspect of interactivity is the "pull" concept. The Web represents the "pull" concept because you actively search for sites that can answer your specific questions. At the Web site itself, you also actively "pull" information from the various links that are provided. In other words, you are constantly interacting with a site and "pulling" the information most relevant to you. You have total control over what information you call up and how deep you want to delve into a subject.

In contrast, the concept of "push" is information delivered to you without your active participation. Traditional mass media—radio, TV, newspapers, magazines— are illustrative of the "push" concept, and so are news releases that are automatically sent to media. So are e-mail messages sent to you.

Another dimension of interactivity is the ability of a person to engage in a dialogue with an organization. Many Web sites, for example, encourage questions and feedback by giving an e-mail address that the user can click on and send a message.

One successful application of this is the Web site of the Broward County Public Schools in Ft. Lauderdale, Florida. The school board was working on two new policies, and it realized that not everyone could attend meetings to discuss the proposed policies. Therefore, the decision was made to post the policy drafts on the Web site and allow the public to e-mail their comments and views to the district. Dozens of e-mail messages were received, and the suggestions were used to revise the policies. The Public Relations Society of America awarded the school district a Bronze Anvil for its Web site and noted, "For Broward County Public Schools, interactive is much more than a buzzword, it is a working program to make a school district function better."

Professional Tips

How to Create a User-Friendly Web Site

Developing an effective Web site takes considerable research, planning, and teamwork. Here are some tips from the experts:

- **Know your audience**. Design your site with your shareholders, customers, and the press in mind. Ask them what they want.

- **Teamwork is a must**. Work with other departments, Webmasters, and technical experts from management information systems (MIS) or information technology (IT) to design the Web site jointly.

- **Keep it simple**. Web site graphics should be crisp, attractive, and simple. Elaborate graphics such as large photos and charts slow the download time for users with limited bandwidth.

- **Don't bury data**. Follow the "three-click" rule. Make sure essential data are no more than "three clicks away from your front page."

- **Use HTML for text**. HyperText Markup Language is universally recognized by all Web browsers. It loads quickly and can be read immediately.

- **Use fewer colors**. An attractive site can be created by using a single, strong accent color with black and shades of a second color. Avoid overusing bright colors in backgrounds; they are tiring and it is difficult to read type on such a background.

- **Keep it current**. An out-of-date site undermines the credibility of the organization. Make sure your own data and data from third parties is updated each day.

- **Encourage feedback**. Your Web site should give users multiple ways to reach the organization: phone/fax numbers, e-mail addresses, Web site response form, and a postal address.

Unfortunately, the idea of "interactive" and encouraging feedback is more buzzword than reality on many Web sites. According to reporter Thomas E. Weber of *The Wall Street Journal*, "Many big companies invite a dialogue with consumers at their Internet outposts but are ill-prepared to keep up their end of the conversation." He explains, *"The Wall Street Journal* zapped e-mail inquiries to two dozen major corporate Web sites with e-mail capabilities and found many of them decidedly speechless. Nine never responded. Two took three weeks to transmit a reply, while others sent stock responses that failed to address the query. Only three companies adequately answered within a day."

Weber also quotes another survey that randomly checked the Web sites of 100 large U.S. companies. Only 17 of them sent back e-mail replies, and almost half of the sites didn't include any e-mail capabilities at all. Another survey by Jupiter Communications found that 42 percent of "top-ranked" sites either took longer than five days to reply to customer e-mail, never applied at all, or offered customers no way to make an e-mail query from their Web site.

A delayed response to an e-mail query, or no response at all, damages an organization's reputation and credibility. Ideally, an e-mail query should be answered by an organization within 24 hours. Although it is good public relations to solicit feedback from the public, you should think twice about providing e-mail response forms on your Web site if the organization isn't capable of handling the queries.

Book author Diane Witmer sums it up best: "... double check that the client's staff is both prepared and able to respond quickly to e-mail messages. If the client fails to meet the expectations of Internet users through slow or inadequate responses, the Web site is likely to be more harmful than helpful to the client's reputation."

Using Audio and Video Components

Webcasting has become more common as bandwidth has increased and better technology has evolved. In fact, one survey found that more than 90 percent of public companies use Webcasts at least quarterly.

As discussed in Chapter 9, Webcasting essentially means the delivery of a broadcast (live, delayed, and even abbreviated) over the World Wide Web or even a company's intranet. When this is done in real time, it is called **streaming**. Shel Holtz explains, "you see or hear the files as it reaches your computer without having to wait for the entire file to download first."

Webcasts are often used to report a company's quarterly financial results to business reporters and financial analysts, or even to have the CEO address all employees in locations around the world. They also are used to introduce new products or to give updates on various issues. US Pharmacopeia, for example, used a Webcast to let the media know about the certification of the company's dietary-supplement-verification system. And Office Depot delivered a series of seminars, "Women in Business," via several Webcasts.

Clarkson University in Potsdam, New York, uses its Web site to stream campus events in real time to its alumni and other supporters. One event was a lecture by a Nobel Laureate, Dr. Paul Crutzen, who was visiting the campus to talk about global warming. Another was a "night at the opera" featuring a former opera singer.

Professional Tips

Bloggers of the World, Unite!

Weblogs or "blogs" are now an integral part of the Internet. Essentially, these sites are regularly updated online personal journals (written by "bloggers") with links to items of interest on the Web. In fact, one expert estimates that there are now about 500,000 blog sites, and the number increases daily.

Most bloggers are amateurs, but many also are professional journalists who like to express their opinions, observations, and criticisms about almost everything under the sun. Increasingly, a number of public relations writers are also becoming "bloggers" on behalf of their clients or employers because, as one professional says, "They (blogs) let businesses take their messages right to the public without the TV networks news or the local newspaper having to act as mouthpieces."

Jason Kottke, a San Francisco Web designer and blogger, told *PRWeek*:

> A clever Weblog can combine the information dissemination of traditional Web site with the communication you get with direct mail, e-mail, or an e-mail newsletter. The frequent updates, along with a looser writing style adopted by many Webloggers gives your customers the impression that you're having a conversation with them instead of just shoving information at them in a press release form.

Macromedia, a software publisher, was a pioneer in "corporate blogging" by having employees start Weblog sites touting the company's products. This was criticized by the blogging community, however, because the writers didn't identify themselves as Macromedia employees. Today, the seven macromedia "bloggers" post their comments on a section of the corporate Web site. Jupiter Research was also an early user of blogs—it now has more than a dozen analysts writing blogs.

Public relations personnel are also starting to pitch Weblogs. One public relations firm didn't think a client's minor software upgrade was worth a news release, but staff did send an e-mail to some bloggers covering the industry and got a favorable response. The Heritage Foundation, a conservative think tank, also took the time to e-mail 175 political bloggers and found that most of them would be interested in receiving information from the organization.

Another aspect of blogs, which causes some headaches for public relations staffs, is what the writers say about a company or its products. As *Ragan's Media Relations Report* says, "A prominent blogger who trashes a product, service, or company can do serious damage to sales or public image. Bloggers also frequently post links to mainstream or other news articles—making the reach of offending news coverage that much greater."

Consequently, it is recommended that public relations staffs monitor Weblogs that reach large numbers of consumers or cover a particular industry. Oftentimes, the information being disseminated is untrue or distorted, and it's necessary for the organization to set the record straight. One way of monitoring Weblogs is to look up your brand or company via Google each week. *PRWeek* also notes, "You could also use a blog search engine, such as bloggr.com or portal.eatonweb.com."

To find out more about the content of blogs, or even how to have your very own blog, see the following sites: www.blogger.com (create your own blog); www.weblogs.com (news and links about blogs); and http://blogdex.media (list of blogs and blogging news).

The audience for such events may not be very large, but Karen St. Hillaire, director of university communications, thinks their promotional value makes the cost and effort worthwhile. She told *Interactive Public Relations*, "It is our belief that eventually this medium can be one of the most effective media to communicate with our alumni. It's a wonderful way to reach people who cannot be physically present for an event."

The value of a Webcast is its delivery system—the computer. You could reach more people via a regular radio or television broadcast, but that requires the involvement of media gatekeepers making a decision to use your information, or you could buy the time at expensive commercial advertising rates. Closed-circuit television is another method, but that requires the audience to gather at a specific location to view the program.

If you do use Webcasting for transmitting audio and video, either in real time or as archived material, you should be aware of two aspects. The first one is quality. People expect the same high-resolution quality from the Internet as they see on television, so top-notch lighting, staging, and production are necessary.

The second aspect is understanding the computer capability of the intended audience. Is the Web site easily accessible? Are there enough servers and broadband width available to handle the traffic? Victoria's Secret's first attempt at streaming a live fashion show of lingerie-clad models, for example, crashed because the IT infrastructure was not able to handle the traffic. You also have to be careful about using too many "cool" technologies and graphic programs that are impressive but that take a lot of broadband that older computers may not be able to handle.

Greg Gardner, vice president of marketing for Webcast vendor CCBN, told *PRWeek*, "Don't use *Flash*. There are certain graphics that shouldn't be used because they will just make it more difficult for your audience. And you have to stream in multiple formats and speeds. Companies just don't understand all of the aspects of a Webcast. It's not easy." Medialink gives some additional guidelines to ensure successful transfer of images on the Web or an organization's intranet:

- Minimize fast movements and significant screen shifts.
- Emphasize strong foreground images and avoid shadows.
- Tiny details are often lost through digital encoding; provide sharp, clean screens.
- Audio should be clean and without the clutter of distracting background noise.

Who Controls the Site?

Web sites, as they become more important, seem to generate turf battles within organizations as to who should control the site. One survey of corporate communications and public relations executives by the Institute for Public Relations Research, for example, found that 70 percent of the respondents believed an organization's communications/public relations function should manage and control all content of the Web site.

They argue that an organization's Web site is a communications tool and, since they are the communication experts within the organization, they should decide what messages are communicated. This ensures that key messages are disseminated in the proper format and context to accomplish specific objectives.

On the other hand, personnel in Information Technology (IT) take a different perspective. IT staffers were the first to develop the capabilities of the Internet and the World Wide Web, before anyone else knew they existed. They argue that the Web is simply an extension of their traditional domain, which is the constant upgrading and maintenance of an organization's computer systems.

The reality, of course, is much more complicated. Neither public relations nor IT, in today's content-rich Web, has sole proprietary rights. An organization's Web site serves a number of functions, including marketing. Shel Holtz, writing in *Communication World*, says, "As for the Web, electronic commerce falls in the marketing/sales jurisdiction. While communicators can play a role in both these areas, it is highly unusual to expect . . . sales transactions within the communication department."

At the same time, neither public relations nor marketing personnel have the technical expertise to understand all the technical specifications and computer hardware that is needed to actually make a Web page work. IT people, who are computer programmers and engineers, are the ones best trained to worry about routers, AVI animation files, pixels, Mbone, etc.

The conclusion, then, is that no one department or function should manage and control an organization's Web page. Instead, experts such as Shel Holtz and others say the best solution is a team approach, where representatives from various departments are equals. Holtz elaborates, "The team should take ownership of responsibility for the Intranet or Web site, since teams work better than a situation in which one department retains control and others are merely subservient to the demands of the controlling group."

The advantage of cross-functional teams is that various members bring different strengths to the table. IT can provide the technical know-how, the PR manager can share expertise on the formation of messages, and marketing can provide the perspective of consumer services that can provided through the site. Even Human Resources, as a team member, can contribute ideas on how to facilitate and process employment inquiries.

Although public relations departments rarely control a Web site, surveys do indicate that public relations personnel play an active role in shaping the structure and content of Web sites. One survey of PRSA members found that nearly 54 percent of the respondents said they were "very involved" in determining the objectives of their organization's Web site. In terms of actually getting involved in the construction of a Web site, 49 percent said they were "very involved."

Some companies, such as Visa, solve the problem of turf battles by creating a whole new department that is responsible for all Web and Intranet content. The heads of such departments were once called Webmasters, but such a title seems to have gone out of favor. It implies that someone is a "techie" or computer "geek," which doesn't reflect today's range of skills that are needed to manage a Web site.

According to an article by Nick Wingfield in *The Wall Street Journal*, "Today's corporate sites are no longer cobbled together by an information-systems manger in his spare time, but rather are managed by people who possess a mix of marketing, publishing, and management savvy, as well as the ability to juggle the conflicting needs of the corporation's different departments."

In other words, you don't need to be a programming or computer expert to manage a Web site. You do need, however, to understand the scope of IT activi-

PR Casebook

Maintaining a Web Site Is a Team Effort

Staffing a Web site or company intranet is usually a team effort in most organizations, involving several departments. Jim Rink, who writes a column (prbytes@yahoogroups.com), took a look at two companies, Sears and Aetna.

At Sears, the four divisions of the Public Affairs office—Corporate Communications, Corporate Public Relations, Media Relations, and Government Relations—jointly produce much of the content that is used by the Technology Communications unit.

The company's intranet is only one area of responsibility for this department. Others include photography (which contributes images for the intranet) and Sears TV. There are two full-time staffers with intranet responsibilities. In addition to producing copy, these two staffers also handle all the company's corporate sites, such as the CEO site. They do identify and write news, says Rink, but they also handle submissions from employees throughout the organization.

Aetna Insurance has another structure. Three full-time people work on the communication side of the company's intranet, including two editors and one writer who spends about 50 to 60 percent of his time on intranet-related work. According to Steve Perelman, director of employee communications, "I manage the process, and am pretty involved in story generation, selection and placement."

Other departments that may contribute to the content of a Web site or intranet, through an IT department, might be human resources, sales, and marketing. In general, they generate their own content in the same way that the corporate public relations department is responsible for contributing its own material.

---

ties in the organization and the jargon of the field. This will help you understand what the "techies" and various suppliers are talking about.

Shel Holtz says it's no different than learning the jargon of printing so you can communicate your needs to a printer. He writes, "IT professionals are the printers of the digital, net-worked world. Just as we did with printers, we need to learn enough about computers and networks to be able to work with the IT staff and get the same results." The box on page 400 gives some tips on Webspeak.

Emily Avila, co-author of *Connecting Online: Creating a Successful Image on the Internet*, makes the additional point that public relations people have a responsibility to continually improve and update their knowledge of the Internet and the Web. She says, "If you ever expect your site to move beyond 'brochureware' (also called 'shovelware') where you just shove your existing brochures, catalogs, etc. onto the Web, then we must think in new ways and figure new ways to work."

The Cost of a Site

The cost of creating a Web site depends on its size and sophistication. You can create your own personal Web page for virtually nothing (see "PR Casebook" on page 399), but the costs start going up when an organization wants to create a page as polished as its advertisements in other media.

Do-it-yourself, of course, is the cheapest cash outlay. Back in the old days, all you needed to know was a bit of HTML (HyperText Markup Language) and you were on your way. Today, it's even simpler. Software programs such as *PrintShop Deluxe*, Microsoft's *FrontPage*, and Macromedia's *Dreamweaver* provide the basic templates. You can even save a Microsoft Word document as a Web page.

More sophisticated Web page design, however, is no place for amateurs if you want your site to reflect a professional image and compete with the other millions of sites on the Internet. Ralph F. Wilson, a Web site developer, notes, "To do a really professional job takes professional level graphics software and a great deal of experience. The improving HTML editing software makes it look easy, but professional sites are worth what you pay for them if you're really serious."

Wilson estimates that a small business or organization will pay $300 to $1,500 for a basic Web site. Medium-sized companies may spend $1,500 to $10,000 on Web page design. Large corporations may expect to spend from $10,000 to $500,000 or more. The range in cost, says Wilson, often depends on the number of pages created and the sophistication of such things as graphics, animation, video, and sound. In general, professional Web designers charge $75 to $150 per page.

Peter Temes, a Web consultant, estimates that it costs $50,000 and a full-time staff person to have an adequate home page presence. Indeed, organizations need to consider the cost of maintaining a Web site after it is created. In order for a Web site to be effective, it must be constantly updated with new and fresh information. David Compton, an Internet consultant, estimates that an average-sized organization will pay $12,000 to $20,000 annually to maintain its Web site. A large corporation such as Cisco Systems, on the other hand, spends about $1 million annually to staff and maintain its Web site.

In sum, the decision to have a credible Web presence should not be taken lightly. It requires a serious commitment of time, staff, and money on the part of the organization.

Attracting Visitors to Your Site

Promoters of new sports stadiums often say, "If we build it, they will come." Some "builders" of Web sites believe the same thing, but that is not necessarily true. Unlike sports stadiums, there are literally thousands of Web sites, and an organization has to actively promote its presence on the Web. If you want to attract visitors, you need to do much more than "build" one following the guidelines discussed in the previous pages.

You also have to give a lot of directional signage so people can find your Web site. The two major "directional" signs are hyperlinks and search engines. Most people find Web sites by following links, either from other Web sites or search engines. In fact, one study by the Georgia Institute of Technology found that 85 percent of people begin their online research at a search engine (see Chapter 1).

Hyperlinks According to Joe Dysart, writing in *PR Tactics*, "One of the Web's most powerful promotional tools is also one of its most basic: the hyperlink." In other words, sites that have a lot of links with other sites tend to get more visitors.

In a Media Frenzy, a $100 Web Site Does the Job

What do you do when national and international media descend on your small sheriff's office after a husband is arrested for murdering his wife and her unborn child?

This was the situation for the Stanislaus County Sheriff's Office in Modesto, California, after the much-publicized arrest of Scott Peterson. The invasion of Iraq was winding down, and the mystery of who murdered Laci Peterson became the next story that engaged the public's fascination. Several hundred journalists, TV producers, and photographers descended on Modesto, and the sheriff's office was receiving about 150 media calls a day. Media relations manager, Kelly Huston, and an assistant, were overwhelmed and knew something had to be done to satisfy the media's thirst for information

The answer was a Web site (www.pressupdate.info) that Huston and a 20-year-old volunteer Internet enthusiast put together for about $100, most of which was spent on the domain registration. Among the information included on the site was (1) up-to-date news developments, (2) public court documents, (3) instructions on how a reporter could apply for a press seat in the courtroom, (4) applications for allowing a camera in the courtroom, (5) court-ordered media guidelines, and (6) high-resolution photos of the inside of the jail, etc. In addition, Huston also posted a FAQ, Frequently Asked Questions, to answer most of the common questions. Reporters could also sign up to receive e-mail updates about the case.

The Web site, assembled over a weekend, allowed Huston to handle the hundreds of requests without a large staff or even excessive amounts of overtime. So, the next time hundreds of journalists and millions of dollars in TV and satellite equipment arrive at your doorstep, think about creating a Web site just for the occasion.

You should link your Web site to organizations or topics that have a direct or indirect interest in your organization or the industry. According to Dysart, "Some businesses, for example, exchange links with a few of their suppliers or trading partners. Others offer links to information directories, free map-making services, and the like." Another approach is to piggyback, so to speak, on already well-established Web sites that continually come up first in any search by keywords related to your business. If the link is not a direct competitor, you should make an inquiry about exchanging hyperlinks for the benefit of both organizations.

If your site has many links, it also increases your ranking on search engines, says Jan Zimmerman, author of *Marketing on the Internet*. Dysart says, however, that your links should not be posted on your home page. Otherwise, some of your visitors might get distracted even before they get into your site. He suggests "burying" these links within your Web page. If you are looking for linking partners, he says, "a good source is the Mega Linkage List (www.netmegs.com/linkage), a site that lists more than 1,500 directories, little known search engines, and other clearinghouses where you can post your link."

Search Engines The essential key to the vast, sprawling universe called the World Wide Web is a search engine. There are multiple search engines, many of which were described in Chapter 1, but the major ones are Google, Yahoo!, and

Professional Tips

How to Talk Webspeak

Public relations personnel, when working with Web designers and information technology (IT) staff, need to know some basic terms. Here are some key words from the glossary of *Public Relations on the Net* by Shel Holtz:

Bandwidth: Deals with how much information can be sent—or received—at once. A system with low bandwidth is one that cannot handle the transmission of too much information at any given time. A modem that connects at 28,000 bits per second has only half the bandwidth of one that connects at 57,600 bits per second.

Browser: A computer application that enables you to get to the Web and view pages.

Firewall: A form of technical security that protects computers and networks from hackers, viruses, etc.

GIF: Graphics Interchange Format, a standard graphics file format. It is the predominant format used on the World Wide Web.

HTML: HyperText Markup Language, the standard scripting code used to create Web pages.

Hyperlink: An icon on the Web page that, once clicked on, will link you to another page.

JPEG: Joint Photographic Experts Group, a format for displaying graphic images on Web pages. JPEG files are better for photographs than GIF, which is better for clip art.

IT: Information technology, a common acronym for the departments within organizations that are responsible for computer-related activities. The term also relates to any technology used to create, store, exchange, and use information.

Listserv: Commonly refers to a program that is used to manage e-mailing lists. Users subscribe to the list by sending an e-mail message to the listserv. Any messages sent to the mailing list are distributed by the listserv to all subscribers.

Markup: Characters inserted into text files that are interpreted by a program in order to determine how the text (and other elements) should be displayed.

Palette: The colors that a Web browser is designed to display.

Router: A device or software that determines the next network point to which a packet of information should be forwarded.

Shockwave: A Web plug-in commonly used to add animation and sound to a message.

Streaming: A format for sending video and audio files over the Internet in real time.

URL: Universal Resource Locator. The unique address for a Web site. For example: www.PrandMarketing.com

Wallpaper: The background in which the text or graphics are embedded.

MSN. Fredrick Marchini, in a *PR Tactics* article, writes, "According to IMT Strategies, search engines create more awareness about Web sites than all advertising combined, including banner, newspaper, television, and radio placements."

There are two reasons for the preeminence of the search engine in our daily lives. First, most of us begin online research by typing in a few words and seeing what list of sites Google or another engine generates. Second, one study indicated that about a third of the 175 million U.S. citizens currently using the Internet believe that the first 10 citations contain the names of the major site, service, or product being researched. In other words, if your site is mentioned in the top ten citations—as opposed to being citation number 154 on a 27-page list—you get much greater visibility and traffic.

So how do you get into the top 10 when someone puts in the key words that describe your organization or products? Unfortunately, Virginia, there is no Santa Claus. The answer, for the most part, is money. Search engines are commercial enterprises, so they earn revenue by charging a fee to get listed on their indexes. As Aleksandra Todorova writes in *PRWeek,* "If you want your client's Web site to outscore the competition, the choices are to pay, or pay more."

The most expensive proposition is the concept of "pay-for-position." This is a system of purchasing, more or less in competition with others, the exclusive rights to search words that best describe your organization or products. Say your company, for example, makes ping-pong balls; you would pay Google several cents or even several dollars for each click on "ping-pong," and Google would automatically list your organization in the top ten citations. If you are doing a three-month product publicity campaign, a pay-for-position strategy would be a good approach.

The second method is cheaper. This is called the "pay for inclusion" strategy because you just pay a fee to be listed on search engine indexes. It's something like a lottery, however. You may get listed in the top ten citations on occasion or, then again, you might not. At least it's better than not being listed at all. With this approach, a lot depends on the number of visitors to your site.

A useful resource, says Todorova, for keeping updated on the latest news, tips, and trends on how to get listed on all major search engines is www.searchengine watch.com.

Advertising   Another method of attracting visitors, of course, is a traditional advertising campaign. Victoria's Secret, for example, spent $1.5 million on a Super Bowl TV ad and $4 million on full-page newspaper advertisements to tell the world about its planned lingerie fashion show on its Web site. Traditional media was also the choice of many e-commerce dot.com companies that wanted to create brand awareness for their sites. More than half of the television ads in the 2000 Super Bowl were sponsored by dot.com companies. A year later, many of these companies had disappeared in the dust of the dot.com bust.

You may not have the budget for sexy models or Super Bowl ads, but you should think about advertising your Web site in local newspapers, industry publications, or even on radio, television, and cable. You can also do specialty advertising. If your site has an online "press room," for example, you may wish to advertise this fact in various trade magazines, such as *Editor & Publisher,* that serve the journalism profession. Today, most organizations indicate their Web site URL on print and broadcast ads, including those irritating little pop-up ads that show up on search sites.

Another form of advertising is to place your Web site's address on the organization's stationery, business cards, brochures, newsletters, news releases, promotional items, and even special event signage. In addition, individuals usually have

Professional Tips

Responding to Rogue Web Sites

Not all Web sites are established to promote a product, a service, or the image of an organization. The World Wide Web also has sites that attack organizations for a variety of sins: making shoddy products, exploiting Third World labor, selling unhealthy products, polluting the environment, ripping off the consumer, etc.

Many URLs for these sites, written by disgruntled employees, customers, or social activists, end with "sucks.com," such as www.gapsucks.org, or something similar, such as www.ihate starbucks.com or www.noamazon.com. Others are not so blunt in terms of orientation, such as www.mcspotlight.com or www.walmartsurvivor.com.

In any case, such sites present a public relations challenge to those organizations who are being maligned. Should the organization actively respond to preserve their reputation, or should they ignore such sites? The answer is somewhat mixed.

In general, the rule is to only closely monitor such sites to find out what customers, social activists, and disgruntled employees are saying about you. Such monitoring often detects the "tip of an iceberg" about a problem that the organization should address before the complaint hits the mainstream media, such as *The Wall Street Journal* or *The New York Times*. The issue of Nike using sweatshop labor, for example, was first posted on rogue Web sites before the mainstream media picked up the story.

Monitoring firms such as *PR Newswire Ewatch* and *CyberAlert* can be retained to monitor Web sites, Usenet groups, listservs, and message boards to give you a sense of what is being said about you. The general rule, however, is not to respond to the Web site operator or message board operator unless you want to inform them they are violating trademark rules or engaging in slander that is legally actionable. It is never acceptable to post a response posing as a consumer and not identify yourself as an organizational representative. "Planting information is out of bounds," says Nick Wreden, author of *Fusion Branding: How to Forge Your Brand for the Future*.

PRWeek writer Melanie Shortman says, "It is only appropriate to acknowledge and respond to saboteurs if they break the law or pose an imminent or dangerous threat." She quotes Tony Wright, an account supervisor at Weber Shandwick, who says, "The only times I would ever respond is if the thread of the message is getting out of control. If, all of a sudden there are 50 posts, and everyone is saying something that isn't true, then you can respond."

The main idea is to recognize opinion "I don't like Starbucks" as legitimate free speech, but you should respond if the site says something untrue about the brand, such as "Starbucks buys coffee from the Colombian Mafia, who use the plantations as a front for illegal drug operations."

a standard signature line on their e-mail messages that includes telephone numbers as well as Web site addresses.

Tracking Site Visitors

An important part of Web site maintenance is tracking visitors to your site. Management, given its investment, wants to know if the site is actually working. In other words, how well is it fulfilling its objectives? Is it generating sales leads? Is it selling products and services? Is it helping the organization establish brand identity? Are journalists actually using it to write stories?

Fortunately, the digital revolution allows quick and tangible ways to monitor traffic on any Web site. There are a number of measurement terms used, and it is often confusing as to exactly what each one means.

One term is **hit**. Victoria's Secret, for example, reported that the lingerie fashion show got 5 million hits an hour, which sounds pretty impressive. The term "hit," however, merely describes the number of requests a Web server has received—not the number of actual viewers. In fact, most people trying to log-on to the fashion show never got connected, because the servers were only configured to handle 250,000 to 500,000 simultaneous viewers.

Another term often used is **page view** or **page impression**. These are interchangeable terms tracking the number of times a page is pulled up. Unlike a "hit," one log-in equals one page view. According to Paul Baudisch, general manager of Circle.com, "This term is most often used to describe 'traffic' to a site."

The term **unique visitor** is occasionally used. It basically means first-time visitors to a site. Baudisch says "unique visitor" is good for tracking quantity of viewership, while "page view" is better for tracking brand awareness.

Armed with an understanding of these basic terms, a public relations practitioner can track various dimensions of Web site usage. Each individual page within a Web site, for example, can be tracked for first-time visitors, return visitors, and the length of time a viewer stays on a particular page. This gives you an indication of what information on your Web site attracts the most viewers, and it also may indicate what pages should be revised or dropped.

You can even track the number of people who used a search engine or the actual URL to reach your site. If a high percentage of visitors are going directly to your site, it at least indicates that you've done a good job of publicizing the address.

Web sites can also track the effectiveness of overall advertising, marketing, and public relations efforts. Was there an increase in site visits after the placement of an advertisement in a major trade publication? What about a major story in a business magazine?

Many organizations also use their Web sites to gather names and e-mail addresses by having a simple registration form that viewers must fill out before they can open certain pages in the Web site. As an incentive, organizations run contests and give prizes for those who provide detailed information about themselves. The same kind of information is gathered when viewers request more information or provide comments via links on the site.

Even if you don't "pull" information from a Web site, you leave something behind you. It's called a **cookie**, which is a file that is placed on your hard drive by a Web site you have visited. According to Shel Holtz, "The next time you visit that particular site, it looks for the cookie, which helps the site remember who you are, what you've done on the site before, and any other information you may have stored."

In sum, tracking Internet and Web users is getting more sophisticated by the month. An organization can easily cut and slice data many ways to find out exactly who is being reached, their demographics, and even their product preferences. To marketers, this is a bonanza. For many individuals, it raises major privacy issues. Expect more legislation and court battles in the coming years.

Return on Investment   Web sites require staffing and budget. One good way to convince management that a Web site is well worth the investment and contributes to the "bottom line" is to calculate its **return on investment** (ROI). This means that you compare the cost of the Web site to how such functions would be done by other means.

Hewlett-Packard, for example, says its saves $8 million a month by allowing customers to download printer drivers instead of the company mailing them out on disks. And in the category of sending out news releases, Cisco Systems says news release distribution via its Web site, NEWS@Cisco, saves it about $125,000 annually in distribution wire costs, such as for BusinessWire (see Figure 13.5).

There can also be substantial savings in the area of brochures and printed materials.

Terry Colgan, senior account manager at Oki Business Digital, told *Interactive Public Relations*, "Since I know the cost of printing/warehousing and distributing data sheets, catalogs, and other pre-sales materials, I can calculate ROI based on documents downloaded or ordered via fax. In fact, Oki earned a 285 percent ROI in its very first year on the Web."

Amy Jackson, director of interactive communications at Middleberg Associates, says calculating ROI on your Web site is one of the best ways to evaluate your online success. She told *Interactive Public Relations*, "Companies who invest in developing comprehensive, well-managed online media rooms can save thousands of dollars on printing and faxing costs if the media can readily find what they are looking for on the Web."

SUMMARY

- The worldwide adoption of the Internet and the World Wide Web has taken less time than the adoption of any other mass medium in history.

- The World Wide Web is the first medium that allows organizations to send controlled messages to a mass audience without the message being filtered by journalists and editors. Before the Web, the placement of advertising in the mass media was the only method by which the organization controlled the message.

- Public relations practitioners are heavy users of the Internet and the Web. They disseminate information to a variety of audiences and also use the Internet for research.

- The new media, including the Web, has unique characteristics. This includes (1) easy updating of material, (2) instant distribution of information, (3) an infinite amount of space for information, and (4) the ability to interact with the audience.

- A large percentage of journalists are now online and use the Internet as a major source of information for writing stories.

- Journalists want a Web site to include information on how to contact people in the organization; they also want up-to-date information posted on the Web site at all times.

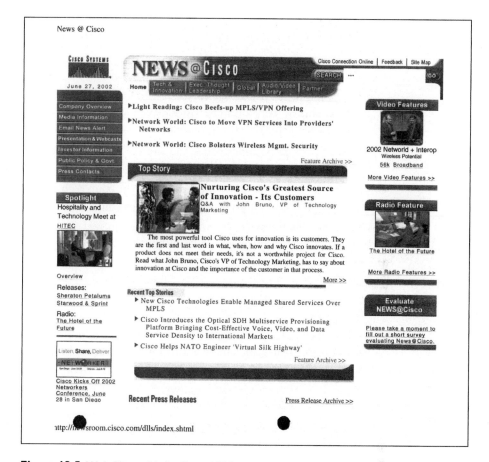

Figure 13.5 Web Sites with Audio and Video
New advances in technology and broadband width have made it possible for organizational Web sites to include more streaming audio and video. On this particular day, News@Cisco (http://newsroom.cisco.com) provided a video link to an archived interview and a radio feature about hotels of the future.
(Courtesy of Cisco Systems, San Jose, CA.)

- Many Web sites include a "press room" or "news room." Current news releases, as well as an archive of past news releases, often are provided. In addition, such a page might include media kits, downloadable graphics and photos, and background information on the company.

- Writing for the Web requires nonlinear organization. Topics should be in index-card format instead of long linear narrative. This allows viewers to click on the information most interesting to them.

- Written material for the Web should be in short, digestible chunks. Two or three paragraphs (or about one screen) should be the ideal length of a news item. Long pieces of information require too much scrolling and turn off viewers.

- Avoid putting "brochureware" or "shovelware" on a Web site. Simply transferring printed documents such as brochures to a Web site creates a boring Web site.

- Two questions should be answered before deciding to create a Web site. What is its purpose, and who is the potential audience?

- Graphics, photos, and sound enhance a Web site, but don't overdo it. Such features cause major delays for viewers who want to download the site.

- Provide hyperlinks to other pages and sites so viewers can dig deeper into a subject.

- Think twice about providing an e-mail link on your Web site if the organization isn't staffed to answer viewer queries within 24 hours.

- Webcasting, the streaming of audio and video in real time over a Web site, is gaining in popularity as the technology improves.

- A Web site should be controlled and maintained by a team of employees representing various departments. Cross-functional teams provide various perspectives and strengths.

- The cost of creating a Web site varies. A small organization may spend $1,500, while a large corporation may spend $1 million. It all depends on the number of pages and the sophistication of the graphics.

- Publicizing and promoting a Web site are necessary to generate traffic. Print and Internet advertising, e-mail, hyperlinks, and putting the URL on all printed material are some ways to promote a site.

- Organizations should track visitors to its site. Today, a variety of methods are used to calculate audience size and demographics.

- One way to show the value of a Web site to an organization is to calculate ROI—return on investment.

ADDITIONAL RESOURCES

Arnold, Matt. "Survive Online Attacks." *PRWeek*, March 12, 2001, p. 17.

"Best Practices: Making Intranet PR More Than a Tech Thing." *PR Reporter*, March 10, 2003, pp. 1–2.

Biersdorfer, J. D. "Building Web Pages Without the Drudgery of HTML." *The New York Times*, December 6, 2001, p. D7.

Burnett, James. "Internet Ethics for PR Professionals." *PRWeek*, January 7, 2002, p. 18.

Callison, Coy. "Media Relations and the Internet: How *Fortune* 500 Company Web Sites Assist Journalists in News Gathering." *Public Relations Review*, Vol. 29, 2003, pp. 29–41.

Dysart, Joe. "Making the Most of Promotional Links." *PR Tactics*, November 2002, p. 21.

Geigel, Sara Means. "Web Writing That Wows." *PR Tactics*, February 2003, p. 15.

Gerstner, John. "Intranets Mean Business." *Communication World*, February–March 2002, pp. 14–17.

Goldsborough, Reid. "Dressing up a Web Site Without Overdoing It." *PR Tactics*, February 2003, p. 6.

Gordon, Andrew. "Getting the Most out of Webcasting." *PRWeek*, April 21, 2003, p. 18.

Graham, Andrea. "Websites Receive a Failing Grade." *O'Dwyer's PR Services Report*, May 2002, pp. 1, 14, 37.

Hachigian, David, and Hallahan, Kirk. "Perceptions of Public Relations Web Sites by Computer Industry Journalists." *Public Relations Review*, Vol. 29, 2003, pp. 43–62.

Horton, James L. *Online Public Relations: A Handbook for Practitioners.* Westport, CT: Quorum Books, 2001.

Jo, Samsup, and Kim, Yungwook. "The Effect of Web Characteristics on Relationship Building." *Journal of Public Relations Research*, Vol. 15, No. 3, 2003, pp. 199–213.

Kent, Michael L., and Taylor, Maureen. "Maximizing Media Relations: A Web Site Checklist." *Public Relations Quarterly*, Spring 2003, pp. 14–17.

Keohane, Kevin. "Our Intranet Looks Great But No One Uses It." *Communication World*, February–March 2002, pp. 18–21.

Levy, Steven. "Will the Blogs Kill Old Media?" *Newsweek*, May 20, 2002, p. 52.

Linkon, Neal. "Increasing Your Web Site Traffic." *PR Tactics*, May 2002, p. 6.

Long, Barbara S. "How to Avoid Common Web Mistakes." *PR Tactics*, November 2002, p. 23.

Miller, Debra. "Measuring the Effectiveness of Your Internet." *The Strategist*, Summer 2001, pp. 35–39.

Momorella, Steve, and Woodall, Ibrey. "Tips for an Effective Online Newsroom." *PR Tactics*, May 2003, p. 6.

O'Dwyer, John. "Intranets Hike Productivity, Build Community." *O'Dwyer's PR Services Report*, March 2003, p. 35.

Outing, Steve. "Savvy Media Relations Skills and a $100 Web Site Help Satisfy an International Press Contingent." *PR Tactics*, July 2003, p. 11.

Scherpereel, Lawrence R., and Skutski, Karl J. "Assessing Your Web Site." *PR Tactics*, March 2003, p. 6.

Schroeder, Joanna. "Keep Journalists Coming Back to Your Online Pressroom." *PR Tactics*, November 2002, p. 20.

Shortman, Melanie. "When Should you Respond to Online Attacks?" *PRWeek*, March 17, 2003, p. 18.

Sims, Maja Pawinska. "Blogging, the Great Untapped Resource." *PRWeek*, June 10, 2002, p. 18.

Todorova, Aleksandra. "Getting Listed on a Search Engine." *PRWeek*, September 9, 2002, p. 18.

Walker, Jerry. "The Internet Brings New Trends to Media–PR Relations." *O'Dwyer's PR Services Report,* May 2002, pp. 36–37.

Weidlich, Thom. "Weblogs: Windows of Marketing Opportunity." *PRWeek*, June 2, 2003, p. 24.

Chapter 14

E-Mail, Memos, Letters, Proposals, and Reports

The public relations writer doesn't always communicate with a large, impersonal audience. He or she also communicates on a more personal level through e-mail, memos, personal letters, talking on the phone, and face-to-face communications.

In fact, public relations personnel spend a large percentage of their working day engaging in interpersonal communications. They are constantly sending, receiving, and replying to e-mail, summarizing the results of client or management meetings, answering voice-mail messages, sending memos to colleagues, writing proposals, preparing position papers, and—at certain times of the fiscal year—heavily involved in preparing the organization's annual report. All this takes organization, efficiency, and communication skills.

This chapter explores the general purpose, format, and organization of all of these activities. Everyone thinks they know how to do e-mail, write a memo, or draft a personal letter, but this chapter will give you insight and guidelines on how to handle these activities in a more efficient and professional manner.

THE CHALLENGE OF INFORMATION OVERLOAD

Today, almost everyone is faced with a mountain of information. According to *The Wall Street Journal*, the Institute for the Future estimates that more than 200 messages are sent and received daily by the average office worker in the United States. Among administrative personnel, the figure goes up to 230.

The messages, in categories ranging from telephone calls to e-mail and pagers, are enough to cause massive information overload as individuals struggle to cope with all the messages that pile up in a day's time. Indeed, e-mail has become so pervasive in many organizations that it now consumes one or two hours a day for many employees.

It takes a lot of time to read all the messages that inundate us, but it also takes considerable time to organize, write, and send all those messages. In many cases, public relations writers are major contributors to information clutter because their jobs involve the writing and dissemination of so many messages. The problem is best expressed by Richard E. Neff, a consultant in Belgium, who writes in *Communication World*, "Writers waste too much time producing texts that waste even more time for readers."

The solution, he says, is to "write smart, simple, and short." Neff continues, "When people write letters and reports that are clear enough and simple enough and accurate enough and short enough—the time it saves the reader is immense." In other words, you should follow the basic guidelines of clarity, completeness, conciseness, correctness, courtesy, and responsibility in all your writing.

- **Completeness**: Whether you are writing a 10-line memo or a 32-page annual report, you must be certain that it contains the information needed to serve its purpose. Ask yourself why you are writing and what your reader wants or needs to know. If more information will aid the reader's understanding, provide it—but don't give your reader a mass of irrelevant material. An outline will help to ensure that your message is on target and complete.
- **Conciseness**: *Less is better.* Conciseness means brevity. Your objective is to be as brief as possible, because people don't have the time or the patience to read through long messages. This means that you need to carefully select words that convey ideas and thoughts in a concise manner. If *USA Today* can summarize a major news event in four paragraphs, so can you.

- **Correctness**: You must be accurate in everything you write. If an item in the mass media contains an error, the blame may be spread among many people. An error in a personalized communication, however, reflects solely on you and your abilities. Be sure that what you prepare is accurate, and you will get credit for being a professional.

- **Courtesy**: These are *personal* communications. Personal names are used extensively, and both senders and receivers have considerable interest in the material. You might think it advisable to make the messages as personal as possible, but don't go overboard. The writing should be polite but not effusive, personal but not overly familiar.

- **Responsibility**: Be prudent and think about how your communication will be perceived by the recipient. A letter or e-mail is a highly visible record of what you say, so be careful about setting the right tone. Do you come across as flippant, arrogant, or defensive? Or do you come across as helpful, sympathetic, and concerned? You are representing your employer or client, so your communications must be in accordance with the organization's policies and procedures.

These general guidelines are helpful in all communications, but now we will discuss the specific techniques of how to prepare e-mail correspondence, memos, letters, proposals, and annual reports.

E-MAIL

Electronic mail, commonly called e-mail, is now a household word and a common activity around the world. According to Rogen International, a research firm, some 4 trillion e-mails are sent worldwide each year from about 600 million electronic mailboxes.

The firm, which interviewed more than 1,400 senior and middle-level executives, also found that the average employee sent about 20 e-mails and received about 30 each day—a six-fold increase since 1995. Executives, however, are receiving considerably more e-mail and are spending an average of 120 minutes a day receiving, checking, preparing, and sending e-mails.

In other words, the sheer volume of e-mail messages is already staggering and multiplying every year. Intel, a global corporation, moves about 3 million e-mails through its system every day. Such a flood of e-mail on a daily basis often overwhelms even the most advanced servers and computer switching equipment—one reason why your e-mail on occasion disappears into cyberspace. Of course, e-marketers have also discovered e-mail, so there is considerable concern, at both the public and legislative level, about how to reduce the amount of spam that clogs up most e-mail systems.

Purpose

According to a survey of communicators in *Fortune* 500 corporations, e-mail (1) reduces the cost of employee communications, (2) increases the distribution of messages to more employees, (3) flattens the corporate hierarchy, and (4) speeds up decision making.

E-mail has other advantages. It is a good way for public relations writers to send media advisories and news releases to the media, disseminate employee newsletters, and even chat with colleagues around the world. E-mail is also effective from the standpoint of (1) keeping up with events, (2) making arrangements and appointments, and (3) reviewing or editing documents. Managers also report that e-mail makes them more accessible and available to their staffs, but that is a mixed blessing. Some managers say e-mail makes them too accessible.

E-mail, however, is not suitable for all person-to-person communications. It is primarily an informal memo system and, at times, it is important to send a more formal letter on nice stationery. A job recommendation or a letter to a disgruntled customer makes a better impression on paper than in an e-mail message, which seems less official and permanent. Writing the personal letter will be discussed shortly.

Also, the experts say that e-mail should never be a substitute for face-to-face communication. More than two-thirds of the respondents in the Rogen International survey say face-to-face is the preferred channel of communication for delivering important information. The study notes, "The good and the bad should be delivered face-to face: 71 percent preferred good news to be delivered that way, as did 81 percent for bad news."

According to *PR Reporter:*

> Similarly, face-to-face should be used for discussing issues of workplace performance or personal confrontation. When it comes to job performance, employees need to be able to probe for answers and clarify responses, which is lost in e-mail dialogue. For other discussions around potential conflicts or misunderstandings, face-to-face is key because e-mail messages can be misunderstood; readers can perceive angry tones, abrupt manners, and even humor incorrectly.

In other words, you should think of e-mail as one of your communication tools—just not the only one. E-mail is a somewhat sterile, mechanistic form of interpersonal communication that can convey routine information very well, but you should also make the time to use the telephone and talk face-to-face with colleagues and customers.

Gerald Goldhaber, professor of Information Studies at the State University of New York, believes e-mail is eroding the art of face-to-face communication. He told *PR Reporter*, "While e-mail might bring people close together, e-mail contacts are not as strong and committed. Therefore, what we tend to have on e-mail are a lot of ephemeral contacts and transactions that don't lead to a richness in human exchange that we get from direct conversation."

Content

Both style and substance are key to effective e-mail. Michael Hattersley, writing in *PR Tactics*, continues, "Although one can be quite informal in a personal conversation or even in a meeting, you never know where an e-mail will end up. Make sure it represents you as you want to be seen. Every written communication should be flawless and represent your best work."

In other words, you can be somewhat informal in an e-mail message, but that does not mean you can be sloppy about grammar, punctuation, spelling, and sentence structure. It also means that you need to think twice about writing something that would be embarrassing to you if the sender decides to forward it to any number of other individuals.

Today's technology means that no e-mail message is secure or confidential. If you are using e-mail at your place of work, be aware that management has the ability to read your e-mail messages even if you erase them. More than one employee has been fired for posting messages that have included crude jokes about ethnic minorities, comments about supervisors who were "back-stabbing bastards," and complaints about management's incompetence. Newer kinds of surveillance software can even log all your keystrokes even if you don't send a message or erase that rant about your "stupid" boss.

Even Bill Gates has found out the hard way that erased e-mail messages can be easily retrieved. The case against Microsoft by the U.S. Justice Department hinged, in part, on what Gates wrote in e-mail messages about the competition. Justice Department lawyers claimed that Gates lied under oath because they were able, through technology, to reconstruct e-mail messages that he had deleted from his computer.

Here are some other suggestions about the content of an e-mail message.

- Use language that falls halfway between formal writing and spontaneous conversation.
- Blunt words and statements assume more importance in electronic form than in a telephone conversation. Temper your language.
- Keep messages, including quoted material, brief.
- Send messages as unformatted text without attachments whenever possible. An attachment drastically decreases the odds that your message will be read.
- Use standard English and abbreviations. Don't use a lot of cryptic symbols as shorthand.
- Copy only necessary people when responding to a group message.
- Double-check who will receive your message before sending it.
- When sending e-mail messages to the media, use blind copy distribution so that the recipients don't know it is a mass mailing.
- Don't be an e-mail junkie. Don't clutter up electronic mailboxes with nonurgent chitchat; it's irritating to receivers.
- Although e-mail is a form of one-to-one communication, it is not a substitute for phone conversations and meetings. They are important for maintaining personal relationships.
- Always reread an e-mail message before sending it. Will the tone or choice of words offend the receiver? Are you coming across as friendly and courteous, or brusque and pompous?
- Always respond to e-mail messages in a timely manner.

Format

Everyone knows how to send an e-mail. All you have to do is sit down in front of the computer, connect to the Internet, and start typing. Right? Although this method may be all right for quick notes among your friends, you should be aware that everyone is getting flooded with e-mails, and your missive is one of many that appears in an inbox that already contains 50, 100, or even more e-mails. Consequently, it is important to know some techniques that can improve the readership of your e-mail.

Subject Line   An e-mail format, after the address, includes a subject line. This is the opportunity to say succinctly what the message is about. Think of the subject line as a form of headline, which was discussed in Chapter 12. If you are announcing an event, don't just do a label line such as "Spring Concert." You have up to 42 characters to give more detail. For example, you might say "Tickets Now Available for May 5 Spring Concert."

If you need a decision or response, say so. The subject line, in this case, might say, "Your plans for attending Spring Concert?" or even "You're invited to attend Spring Concert on May 5." By providing context and more description, the recipient knows exactly what is being discussed or requested.

Salutation   An e-mail is somewhat informal, so it is unnecessary to include the sender's full name, title, organization, and address as you would in a regular letter. It is also unnecessary to say, "Dear. . . ." Just begin with the person's first name. If the e-mail is being distributed to a group, use an opener such as "Team" or "Greetings."

First Sentence or Paragraph   Get to the "bottom line" right away, so the recipient knows immediately what the key message is and what you want him or her to do with it. Avoid starting e-mail messages with such phrases as "I wanted to inform you. . . ."

Body of Message   Think of an e-mail as a memo, which is discussed in the next section. Most experts say the best e-mail messages are short. How short? A good rule of thumb is one screen. That is about 20–25 lines, single-spaced. It is also recommended that there be no more than 65 characters per line. Others recommend that you keep the length of lines even shorter, because people can read material faster in a narrow column (left half of page) than as an entire screen of type.

When appropriate, you can use boldfacing, underlining, and bullets to highlight key pieces of information. The idea, as stated in Chapter 13, is to help the viewer scan the message for the important points. It is also a good idea to include other e-mail addresses or Web sites so a viewer can easily click on them to get more information.

Closing   Include your name, title, organization, e-mail, phone, and fax numbers in a standard signature. This enables the recipient to contact you directly if he or she wants additional information and feedback. It is also a handy reference for them if they print out the message and file it.

Christopher Dobens, a vice president of Creamer Dickson Basford public relations, gives a final bit of advice about e-mail. He writes in *PR Tactics*, "To ensure that my e-mails get read beyond the first line (or even the subject heading), I make sure they are well written. I keep them brief and succinct, and often use creative flair or humor to differentiate them. The tools may have changed and the speed has definitely increased, but there is no substitute for good writing in public relations."

MEMORANDUMS

A memorandum—*memo* for short—is a brief written message, usually a page or less in length. In the past, it was on a piece of paper that was photocopied and distributed to employees through the organization's mail system. Today, the standard method of delivery is e-mail for most routine memos. On occasion, however, memos are still distributed in hard copy if they contain important information

Professional Tips

Mind Your E-Mail Manners

Microsoft Office Online has a column authored by the "crabby office lady." In one issue, she listed the top 10 cyber-discourtesies that are "driving all of us nuts."

- **Avoid the "Reply to All" button**. In most cases, your personal reply to an e-mail doesn't require you to share your thoughts with everyone on the mailing list. Greta, in accounting, probably could care less if you are attending the company picnic.
- **Skip the CAPITAL letters**. By using uppercase letters, it essentially means that you are yelling at the recipient. Save the capital letters unless you really want to shout and seek assistance.
- **Save the fancy stationery**. You don't need pastel backgrounds, smiley faces, and a fancy letterhead to send an e-mail. Keep it simple and uncluttered.
- **Give your response first**. When you reply to an e-mail, make sure your reply is the first thing the recipient reads.
- **Keep forwards to a minimum**. Everyone has already heard the joke.
- **Don't be a cyber-coward**. If you have something to say that is highly personal, scary, sad, angry, tragic, vicious, shocking or any combination of the above, say it in person.
- **Keep the 500KB image file to yourself**. Most e-mail accounts have limited capacity. Don't send your vacation photos to everyone in your address book.
- **Fill out the subject line**. People get plenty of e-mails every day; if you can't take the time to fill out the subject line, I don't need to take time to open it.
- **Avoid HTML format**. The most easily accessible e-mail format around the globe is plain text.
- **Count to 10 before hitting the Send button**. Think twice, or even wait 24 hours, before sending that clever, scathing message to someone and possibly the rest of the world. A "flaming" e-mail often starts more fires than we can put out.

about employee benefits, major changes in policy, or other kinds of information that an individual should retain for his or her records.

Purpose

A memo can serve almost any communication purpose. It can ask for information, supply information, confirm a verbal exchange, ask for a meeting, schedule or cancel a meeting, remind, report, praise, caution, state a policy, or perform any other function that requires a written message.

Many public relations firms require staff to write a memo whenever there is a client meeting, or even a telephone conversation, because it creates a record and "paper trail" of what was discussed and what decisions were made. Copies are often distributed via e-mail to all staff involved in the project, including the client. A memo avoids the problem of someone saying, "I don't remember that," which can lead to disagreements and uneven execution of the plan.

It should be noted, however, that hard copies of memos are often distributed even if it was sent via e-mail. The reason for this is that not everyone pays close attention to the multiple e-mails they receive, and they often overlook or unintentionally delete some of them before they are read. Consequently, many organizations continue to distribute and retain hard copies of important memos even if they are sent via e-mail.

Also, e-mail memos tend to be somewhat ephemeral, so printed copies provide a more concrete record of what was said, announced, or decided upon. Printouts of e-mail memos have also been a good back-up when someone says, "I never received that information."

Content

A memo should be specific and to the point. The subject line, as in e-mail messages, should state exactly what the memo is about. If it is about a meeting, the subject line should state: "Department meeting on Thursday at 3 P.M." If it is a summary of decisions made at a meeting, you could use: "Decisions made at last staff meeting."

The first sentence or paragraph of a memo should contain the key message that would be of most interest to the reader. All too often, first sentences don't provide any meaningful information. *Communication Briefings*, in one article, asked the reader to choose the best opening statement for a memo. Which one of the choices below would you choose?

1. "Kevin Donaldson and I recommend that we cancel the Carstairs account."
2. "Kevin Donaldson and I met yesterday to discuss the Carstairs account."
3. "Kevin Donaldson and I recommend that we cancel the Carstairs account for these reasons."
4. "I've been asked to reply to your request for more information on the Carstairs account."
5. "You'll be glad to know that we finally got the results on the Carstairs account."

Professional Tips

Voice Mail as a Memo System

Memos aren't only in written form. Organizations also use sophisticated computerized telephone answering systems that allow a person to send a voice memo to one, several, or thousands of persons in the organization. This is called *voice mail*.

Advantages

Voice mail speeds the process of getting information; a call is quicker than a memo delivered by interoffice mail. It eliminates "phone tag," because you can leave messages in someone's "mailbox" and that person can respond by leaving a message in yours. Messages are accessed by giving the code number that opens the mailbox—thus, confidentiality is maintained. Another feature of voice mail is the group conference call, which often eliminates the need for meetings.

Disadvantages

Although voice mail has many advantages for internal communication, it often frustrates people from outside the organization who wish to speak to someone. People are also alienated by complicated instructions involving pushing buttons as they work their way down the voice-mail tree, trying to reach the proper department or individual.

Another frustration is leaving repeated messages but receiving no return call. Also, the answering message on voice mail can be long and tedious, giving more information than is really needed.

Making Voice Mail Work

Every voice-mail system should be individually designed for the organization that will use it. Employees should be taught how to use the system and how to record an answering message that is short, concise, and clearly enunciated. Every system should make it possible for a caller to talk to a real person immediately, at the push of a button. It also is suggested that you update your answering message frequently. People also show good manners by letting callers know if they are traveling or when they can reasonably expect a return phone call. In any event, it is common courtesy to return calls as soon as possible.

Both 1 and 3 are better than the other choices because they are specific about a course of action. Number 3 is the preferred choice because it includes "for these reasons"—a phrase that explains "why." All the others are too vague and don't give the reader much useful information.

Format

Every memo should contain five elements. They are (1) date, (2) to, (3) from, (4) subject, and (5) message. This format should be used in e-mail and hard copy memos. Here is an example of a simple memo:

Monday, November 1

To: Public Relations Committee

From: Susan Parker

Subject: Meeting on Monday, November 15

We will meet in the conference room from 3 to 4 P.M. to discuss how to publicize and promote the company's annual employee picnic. The president wants to encourage the families of all employees to attend, so please come prepared to offer your ideas and suggestions.

LETTERS

A letter is a more formal document than an e-mail or even a memo. It is written primarily to individuals outside the organization when a more "official" response is needed. As a public relations writer, you will write two kinds of letters.

One is the single, personal letter to a specific individual. This is the most personal form of letter writing, because a one-to-one dialogue is established between the sender and the recipient, who already have a relationship or mutual interest. A letter, in legal terms, can serve as an official record of a dialogue involving employment, an issue about company policy, or even an answer to a consumer complaint.

The second kind of letter is less personal, because it is often a form letter about a specific situation sent to large numbers of people, such as stockholders, customers, or even residents of a city. These form letters might be considered direct mail (discussed in the next chapter), but they go beyond the common description of direct mail as a form of advertising to sell goods or services, or even to solicit funds for a charitable organization. Form letters, often written by public relations staff and signed by the head of the organization, usually give background or an update on a situation affecting the organization and a particular public.

A good example is a form letter signed by the president of Coca-Cola to stockholders about the recall of some of its products in Belgium and France due to quality concerns. Various negative news reports had caused the stock value to drop, so the president wrote the letter to let the stockholders know what the company was doing to solve the problem. He assured the stockholders that "your company remains totally committed to maintaining the quality of our products, the strength of the brand and the trust of our customers and consumers, as we continue to seize the vast opportunities before us to build value for you."

Whether you are writing a personalized letter or a form letter, here are some general guidelines about their purpose, content, and format.

Purpose

A letter may be used to give information, to ask for information, to motivate, to answer complaints, to soothe or arouse, to warn, to admit, or to deny. In short, a letter can carry any sort of message that requires a written record. It is a substitute for personal conversation, although it is not as friendly as face-to-face conversation. It does have the advantage, however, of allowing the writer to get facts in order, develop a logical and persuasive approach, and phrase the message carefully to accomplish a specific purpose.

Answering a complaint letter is a good example. The specific purpose is to satisfy the customer and retain his or her product loyalty. Although many organizations use standard form letters to answer customer complaints, a more personal approach that specifically deals with the complaint is usually more effective. This is not to say that every letter must be written from scratch. There are often key sentences and paragraphs that can be used or modified that fit the situation. Most letters, for example, will include (1) thanking the customer for writing, (2) apologizing for any inconvenience, and (3) replacing the product or providing a coupon for future purchases.

Content

The most important part of any letter is the first paragraph. It should state the purpose of the letter concisely, so the reader knows immediately what the letter is about. This is the same principle that was discussed in Chapter 5 for the first paragraph of a news release.

From a writing perspective, a declarative statement is best. Instead of writing, "I am writing you to let you know that our company will be contacting you in the near future about your concerns regarding product reliability," you can simply say, "A company representative will be contacting you about our product reliability."

The second and succeeding paragraphs can elaborate on the details and give relevant information. The final paragraph should summarize the important details, or let the recipient know you will telephone if something needs to be resolved through conversation.

Writing a business letter requires clear thought and thorough editing to reduce wordiness. Every time you use the word "I" to start a thought, think about how to remove it. In most cases, starting a sentence with "I believe," "I feel" or "I think" is unnecessary. At the same time, take every opportunity to use the word "you" in a letter. It places the focus on the receiver and his or her needs instead of those of the sender.

The tone of a letter is an important consideration. Readers don't like to be scolded, chastised, or pacified. Try to write positive statements instead of negative ones. Instead of saying, "You didn't follow up with the client," it is better to say, "You need to improve your follow-up with the client." If you are apologizing for something, say so. Don't just say "I'm sorry. . . ."

Format

As a general rule, letters should be written on standard business stationery. The letterhead should be printed and should carry the name, address, and telephone number of the organization. Additional information can include e-mail address, fax numbers, and even a Web site.

Letters should always be word processed. Usually they are single-spaced. Each paragraph should be indented, either by indention or by a line space. One page is the preferred length. A two-page letter is acceptable, but if the letter runs longer than that, consider putting the material in another format that is introduced by a letter of transmittal.

Professional Tips

Handling Correspondence Efficiently

A personal letter is a labor-intensive effort. Here are some ways to increase your efficiency and still keep the personal touch.

- Produce courteous and effective printed forms for repetitive correspondence, such as requests for printed material or acknowledgments of inquiries.

- Develop standard replies for often-asked questions or often-solicited advice where this is a part of the organization's routine business.

- Develop standard formats for certain kinds of common correspondence to enable inexperienced writers to handle them easily and effectively.

- Prepare a correspondence guide containing hints and suggestions on keeping verbiage and correspondence volume down to reasonable and effective levels.

- Place a brief heading on the letter after the salutation, indicating the letter's subject. The heading will give the reader an immediate grasp of the letter's substance and will also facilitate filing.

- Use subheads if the letter is more than two pages long, thereby giving the reader a quick grasp of how the subject is treated and where the major topics are discussed.

- To personalize printed materials, attach your card with a brief, warm message.

- If a letter requires a brief response, it is acceptable to pen a note on the original letter and mail it back to the sender. Retain a photocopy for your files.

The full name, title, and address of the receiver are obvious inclusions, but how do you address the reader? The usual approach is to write "Dear Mr. —" or "Dear Ms. —." The latter avoids the "Miss" or "Mrs." dilemma and is common in business correspondence. You should not use just a first name, such as "Dear Susan," in a greeting unless the person already knows you.

On occasion, you will need to write a letter to an organization on some routine matter and won't know the name of the person. This often occurs when you are requesting information or inquiring about a billing. You can use the traditional "Dear Sir," but this is increasingly inappropriate now that more than half the workforce is female. A better approach is to put your letter in the form of a memo. For example, a letter about a bill might be addressed, "To: Manager, Accounting Department."

Closing a letter is easy: You can write "Yours truly," "Truly yours," "Sincerely," or "Sincerely yours." Some bold correspondents omit both the salutation and the close, since they aren't really necessary.

PROPOSALS

Public relations firms usually get new business through the preparation of a proposal offering services to an organization. In many cases, a potential client will issue a Request for Proposal, known as an **RFP**, and circulate it to various public relations firms. The organization will outline its needs and ask interested public relations firms to recommend a course of action.

In most situations, the public relations firm will prepare a written proposal that will be part of a presentation to the prospective client. A typical public relations proposal might include sections about (1) the background of the firm, (2) the client's situation, (3) goals and objectives of the proposed program, (4) key messages, (5) basic strategies and tactics, (6) general timeline of activities, (7) proposed budget, (8) how success will be measured, and (9) a description of the team that will handle the account. More information about public relations program planning is given in Chapter 18.

Proposal writing, however, is not unique to public relations firms. Any number of outside suppliers and vendors write proposals to provide goods and services to an organization. The proposal may be as simple as a bid to provide goods and services for X amount of money, or it may be much longer, depending on what information the organization needs to make a decision.

Within an organization, proposals are a management technique to consider new programs and policies. Almost anything can be proposed, but to give you a starting point, here are some possible subjects of proposals: to move the office, to adopt a 10-hour workday or a four-day workweek, to provide a child-care facility at the plant, or to modify the employee benefit plan.

Purpose

The purpose of a proposal is to get something accomplished—to persuade management to approve and authorize some important action that will have a long-lasting effect on the organization or its people. By putting the proposal in writing, you let management know exactly what is proposed, what decisions are called for, and what the consequences may be. A verbal proposal may be tossed around, discussed briefly, and then discarded. In contrast, when the idea is in writing and presented formally, it forces management to make a decision.

Before writing a proposal, author Randall Majors says you should ask yourself questions like these:

- What is the purpose of the proposal?
- Who will read the proposal?
- What are the pertinent interests and values of the readers?
- What specific action can be taken on the basis of the proposal?
- What situation or problem does the proposal address?
- What is the history of the situation?
- How much information, and what kinds of information, will make the proposal persuasive?
- What format is most effective for the proposal?
- How formal in format, tone, and style should the proposal be?

Organization

A proposal may be presented in a few pages or multiple pages, depending on the size of the organization and the scope of the proposal. A major proposal could include the following components:

- **Transmittal**—a memo, letter, or a foreword that summarizes why the proposal is being made
- **Table of contents**—a list of all items in the proposal
- **Tables and exhibits**—a list of illustrative elements and where they can be found
- **Summary**—a condensation of the proposal, which gives readers the basic information and enables them to appraise the idea before they go on to the details
- **Introduction**—giving the scope, the approach, how information was obtained and evaluated, limitations and problems to help the reader understand the idea and weigh its impact
- **Body**—a complete, detailed statement of what is proposed
- **Recommendation**—a clear, concise statement of just what is suggested and how it is to be implemented
- **Exhibits and bibliography**—items substantiating the statements in the proposal and assuring the readers that the proposal is based on thorough study of the problem or the opportunity

A more informal proposal, one that is project-oriented, might have the following organizational structure:

- **Introduction**—stating the purpose of the proposal
- **Body**—providing background to the problem situation, criteria for a solution, the proposed solution, a schedule for implementation, personnel assignments, budget, and some background on the proposal's authors
- **Conclusion**—requesting approval or the signing of a contract

ANNUAL REPORTS

The most expensive and time-consuming report prepared by an organization is the annual report. This is a fairly extensive printed document complete with photos, charts, text, and color that resembles an elaborate brochure. Indeed, some textbook writers discuss annual reports as part of a chapter on brochures (see Chapter 12), but it is placed here in this book because, despite its brochure-like nature, it is still called a "report" and has unique characteristics.

First, unlike a brochure, a corporate annual report is a quasi-legal document that is required of all public companies. Much of the financial information in such

Professional Tips

How to Write a Position Paper

Organizations, on occasion, prepare a detailed report about an issue relating to the organization or the industry. Such reports are called *white papers, briefing papers,* and *position statements.* They are often used as background information when executives and public relations personnel talk to the media, or they can also be distributed to opinion leaders and journalists as "backgrounders" about the organization and its position on a particular topic or issue.

Here are some tips for writing a position paper:

- On a cover page, use a title that tells exactly what the paper is about.

- If the paper is 10 pages or more, use a table of contents or an index.

- Include, at the beginning of the paper, a succinct summary of the report's findings or recommendations (often called an "executive summary"). It enables busy readers to rapidly understand the crux of the position paper.

- Avoid cluttering up the basic report, by placing supporting materials and exhibits in the appendix at the end of the report.

- Use subheads, boldfacing, or underlining throughout the paper to break up blocks of copy.

- Use simple graphs, bar charts, and pie charts to present key statistical information.

- Be concise. Don't use excessive words. Check for repetitious information.

- Check for clarity. Is it clear what you want the reader to do with the information?

Meetings in America

A study of trends, costs and attitudes toward business travel, teleconferencing, and their impact on productivity

A networkMCI Conferencing White Paper

Prepared by
INFOCOM
A Division of NFO Worldwide, Inc
Two Greenwich Plaza
Greenwich, CT 06830

Figure 14.1 Position Papers and Reports
MCIWorldCom published this white paper giving the results of a national survey about the cost and efficiency of business meetings as part of a marketing objective to increase the use of the company's teleconferencing capabilities.
(Courtesy of MCIWorldCom, Washington, D.C.)

a report is mandated by the Securities & Exchange Commission (SEC) as a way to ensure corporate accountability to shareholders.

In addition, due to the corporate scandals of such companies as Enron and Worldcom, the U.S. Congress passed the Sarbanes-Oxley Act, which requires the SEC to put in place rules designed to provide investors with information about the audit controls used by public companies. As a result, management must now include a statement in the company annual report stating that it takes full responsibility for maintaining adequate internal controls over financial reporting.

All this legal and financial material, of course, is a fairly dry accounting of how the company did in a previous year. Some public companies merely put a cover on the required SEC financial report and let it go at that. Most companies, however, also use the annual report as a marketing tool that can help build stockholder loyalty, attract new investors, and even increase their customer base. As Bob Butter, associate director of Ketchum's global practice told *PRWeek*, "The annual report is still a company's most rounded corporate capability presentation."

If you work on an annual report, you will be primarily involved with the non-financial part. The report may consist largely of tables, but it is more interesting if it contains items such as a letter from the CEO or details about the products or services and the people who make or perform them. Other topics include plans, problems, opportunities, and prospects.

Other subjects that could be included are construction plans and progress, supplies of raw material, labor and legal problems, manufacturing, personnel, taxes, tariffs, marketing, advertising, social responsibility, and public relations.

Most annual reports are prepared in booklet or brochure form. A few have been printed in a newspaper format, and several have even appeared in comic book format. Foodmaker, Inc., of San Diego, for example, took the comic book approach to talk about its major property, Jack-In-The-Box restaurants. Such an unusual approach to a corporate annual report generated a lot of news coverage and even caused a rise in its stock.

The readers of annual reports are of two sorts: the non-expert individual and the sophisticated financial analyst. The amateur is interested mainly in the quality of the management, earnings, dividends, stock appreciation, and the outlook for the industry. The experts—who advise investors or manage large holdings—want much more information, which they feed into their computers. This difference in information needs presents the organization with a problem. A few hundred people want great masses of data, while thousands don't want the detail.

There are several solutions to this problem. One approach is to design an annual report that gives the financial highlights in easy-to-read charts and graphs at the beginning of the report. This section is often labeled "Financial Highlights." Apple Computer, for example, used 16 pages of 24-point type and color photos at the beginning of its annual report to give key information about finances, markets, and its business strategy for the coming year. The next 32 pages, however, were in 8-point type and crammed with all the statistics that a financial analyst would need.

A second approach is to do a summary annual report of several pages for employees, individual stockholders, and other key publics who are interested in the financial health of the organization but don't want masses of detail. Hughes Aircraft Company, for example, took the innovative approach of producing an artist's version of a reservoir that represented the firm's total assets. The three out-flow pipes from the dam represented current liabilities, long-term debts, and other liabilities.

Preparing an Annual Report

An annual report usually covers every aspect of the organization. Consequently, every department head may want input, and each may have different and emphatic ideas. The task of the public relations people involved is to coordinate, plan, consult, write, design, and produce the report. Tact, perseverance, and determination to get the job done are essential.

Work on the report may start six months before the date of issue. A first step is to establish a budget. Glossy, four-color reports can run $3 to $5 a copy, so it is important to know how many copies you will need. Foodmaker's comic book annual report, mentioned previously, cost $90,000 for 25,000 copies, or $3.60 each. The NIRI's 2002 survey (see "Professional Tips") determined that small-cap companies had average budgets of about $75,000 and were printing around 17,000 reports that averaged 40 pages in length, or about $4.50 per copy. Large companies, such as AT&T with 4 million shareholders, usually economize by cutting down on the number of pages, photos, and fancy graphics.

With a budget established, you can start planning the report. First, you should look at the last report; compare it with those of other organizations; criticize it;

Professional Tips

How to Write an Annual Report

- **Use a theme**. Focus the entire report on a central idea such as quality measurement, productivity, innovation, technical innovation, or employee dedication. Each section should explain how the subject matter contributes to the central theme.
- **Use headings that say something**. Instead of labels such as "Innovation," "Finance," and "Research," use newspaper-type headlines such as "How We Develop New Products" or "Where the Money Goes." For example, IBM used the following headline in one of its annual reports: "Helping Customers with Service and Solutions."
- **Keep the report understandable**. Don't let lawyers and accountants fill the pages with turgid, pompous prose or technical jargon. Remember that an annual report is for stockholders who need simple explanations in common English.
- **Make the shareholder letter say something**. Let the CEO write it in his or her own words. If things are good, say so. If things are bad, don't weasel. Simply say, "This year resulted in lower-than-expected earnings" or "This year was a disappointment."
- **Humanize executives**. Brief biographies can make key people more human and can build confidence in management.
- **Stress uniqueness**. Tell the shareholders what is different about the company. What makes it good or profitable? Why is the company a good investment? How does it compare to competitors, and what is its position in the industry?

think of ways to make it better, more informative, more understandable, more useful. One useful tool is focus groups with analysts and stockholders to find out what they want to see in your upcoming annual report.

There are many sources of information that should be tapped for possible use in writing the report. Especially critical are internal reports, planning documents, market research findings, and capital budgets. You should also review the 10-K (annual) and 10-Q (quarterly) reports filed with the SEC.

When you are thoroughly informed about the situation, you can start consulting with key executives and establishing a theme for the report. Basically, the objective is to inform, but a theme makes the report more interesting and focused. Usually, it focuses on some aspect of the business that the company wants to showcase that particular year. The theme of many corporate annual reports, after the Enron scandal and intense public scrutiny of executive misdoing, was corporate responsibility and accountability. Other examples of themes were "Toward a Healthier World" (Pfizer) which is shown in Figure 14.2, "Helping People in More Ways Than Ever" (Medtronic), "Elevate Expectations" (Conoco Phillips), and "Creating New Value" (Coca-Cola).

When the theme is established, it is time to think of design—how the report will look, what will be included, how the various elements will be treated. You can get some useful ideas by studying the reports that are cited each year by the Financial Analysts Federation.

Design, to a large degree, depends on what the corporation wants to communicate. If it wants to project an image of success and dominance in the marketplace, the report may be a dazzling display of glossy paper, color, and state-of-the-art graphics. On the other hand, if the company did not do so well the previous year, there is a tendency to use only one or two colors, simple graphics, and plain paper, so stockholders don't think the company is wasting money.

A good example of a corporation signaling its transformation from a stodgy, old company to a modern one is IBM. Its annual report several years ago announced on the cover "The New Blue" and featured a young woman in jeans. Inside, other young people in casual attire were pictured instead of the traditional man in a coat and tie. The *Raleigh News & Observer* noted, "those words and pictures . . . emphasize . . . the venerable company's remodeling from a slow, hulking giant that laid off hundreds of thousands of employees in the early 1990s into a leader in technology and marketing again."

Trends in Annual Reports

Annual reports change with the times. They are considered the most important single document a public company can produce, so a great amount of attention is given to content, graphics, and overall design. The objective is to assure that the annual report reflects corporate culture and external economic conditions.

Seven trends in corporate annual reports are discernible:

- **Candor and frankness**. Global competition has caused the shrinkage of corporate profits and major dislocations in many industries. Consequently, many corporations are more candid in their annual reports. St. Paul

Figure 14.2 Annual Reports Enhance Corporate Reputation
An annual report is the most expensive and time-consuming publication of a corporation. It satisfies the requirements of the Securities & Exchange Commission (SEC) regarding financial data and also serves as a capabilities brochure for the organization.
(Courtesy of Pfizer Corporation, New York.) Credits: Design: VSA Partners, New York City. Principal Photograher: Neil Selkirk.

Insurance Company, for example, told annual report readers, "The relentless parade of storms and floods produced the second-worst total catastrophe loss in our 144-year history."

- **Corporate governance and accountability.** All corporations are under intense public scrutiny because of major scandals in financial reporting and ex-

Professional Tips

Profile of Annual Reports

There are about 15,000 public companies in the United States, and each one is required by the Securities & Exchange Commission (SEC) to file an annual report for its investors.

The National Investor Relations Institute (NIRI) conducts an annual survey of annual reports and compiled the percentage of 2002 reports that included the following components:

Primary Audience		Financial performance	30 percent
Institutional investors	88 percent	Future plans	26 percent
Individual shareholders	77 percent	Maintaining/increasing	30 percent
Financial analysts	74 percent	shareholder value	
Employees	58 percent	**Report Content**	
Customers	54 percent	Photographs	82 percent
Primary Development		Charts/graphs	75 percent
Themes		Mission statement	60 percent
Strategic direction	65 percent	Market size/share data	35 percent
Products and markets	44 percent	Margin call-outs	34 percent

ecutives receiving benefits in the millions of dollars. Consequently, many companies are addressing the issue in their annual reports. Leggett & Platt, a diversified manufacturer, stated in its annual report, "Leggett shines under the light of close examination. First, our pension plan remains over-funded in the aggregate despite three yeas of stock-market declines. Few *Fortune* 500 firms can make that statement." And the Pittsburgh-based utility, DQE, even had a code of ethics in its report signed by the senior executives.

- **Web sites**. Many companies now make their annual reports, or some version of it, available online. One advantage is savings on postage and paper costs, but this doesn't mean that the printed version is going out of fashion. Potlatch Paper Company, for example, conducted a survey and found that analysts and portfolio managers want both electronic and print materials. The survey report concluded, "The bottom line is that the (print) annual report is going to persist as the cornerstone communications vehicle for public companies." If you do place the corporate annual report on your Web site, it should be reformatted to be highly visual, entertaining, and interactive.

- **More emphasis on marketing**. Today, the annual report is also used as a marketing tool to increase consumer loyalty and build the company's image. Hewlett-Packard, for example, spent most of one report showing how various businesses and individuals benefited from using HP products.

- **More emphasis on the future**. Last year's financial performance is old news by the time an annual report is published, so many corporations emphasize growth potential and future strategies. Applied Materials, for example, focused on the growing world market for its microchips and information technology.

- **Readability**. Annual reports are becoming more magazine-like, with summary headlines, easy-to-understand charts and graphs, simple question-and-answer sections, and more conversational prose. This reflects the growing trend of distributing the annual report to a variety of publics—customers, current and prospective employees, suppliers, community opinion leaders, and others.

- **Environmental sensitivity**. In an effort to portray themselves as environmentally conscious, many organizations use recycled paper and soybean-based inks for annual reports. In addition, annual reports are becoming shorter, saving more trees.

- **Global approach**. Corporations now have global operations, and the annual report functions as a capabilities brochure that markets a company on a worldwide scale. Some companies even translate parts of their annual report into several languages. The chairman's letter in Nike's annual report was translated into French, Spanish, and Chinese.

SUMMARY

- Information overload is pervasive in our society. You can help reduce clutter by keeping your messages simple, short, and to the point.

- E-mail (electronic mail) is rapid and cost-efficient. It is not, however, a substitute for personal one-on-one communication.

- E-mail is less formal than a letter, but more formal than a telephone call. You can increase the effectiveness of your e-mail messages by (1) providing key information in the subject line, (2) keeping them to 25 lines or less, and (3) using proper grammar, spelling, and punctuation.

- Letters are personalized communication that should be well organized, concise, and to the point. They can prevent misunderstandings and provide a record of an agreement or a transaction.

- Memos should be one page or less and state the key message immediately. A memo has five components: (1) date, (2) to, (3) from, (4) subject, and (5) message.

- Proposals and reports must follow a logical, well-organized format. They are prepared in response to a management request for information in connection with a problem or an opportunity.

- Reports should begin with an "executive summary" or an overview, so people can read the highlights in a few seconds.

- Reports are often called white papers, background briefings, and position papers.

- An annual report is the most expensive and most time-consuming publication published by any organization. It has two main purposes: (1) it satisfies

PR Casebook

Annual Reports on the Web

Many large corporations now post a version of the corporate annual report on their Web site. The reports, however, are reformatted so viewers can click on links that will lead them to the section they want to review. Dow Jones Interactive did a survey of corporate annual reports on the Web and reported the following percentages:

- 93 percent of online annual reports contain a letter to shareholders.
- 85 percent had a board of directors listing.
- 74 percent had a listing of senior officers.
- 75 percent included financial statements.
- 72 percent had an operational review section, either in whole or part.
- 69 percent had a shareholder's information page.
- 64 percent had a management's discussion and analysis of financial conditions.
- 18 percent described the function, effectiveness, and contributions of board members.

SEC regulatory requirements for publicly traded companies, and (2) it is used as a public relations and marketing tool.

- Today's annual reports are designed with a number of audiences in mind. They are more magazine-like, more environmentally correct, and more global in outlook.

ADDITIONAL RESOURCES

Casteel, Lynn. "Investing In an Effective Annual Report." *PR Tactics*, November 2002, pp. 10–11.

Cato, Sid. "The Legible Tangible Annual Report." *PRWeek*, April 22, 2001, p. 26.

Cordasco, Paul. "SEC Augments Sarbanes-Oxley with Additional Rules." *PRWeek*, June 9, 2003, p. 7.

Crowther, Greg. "Face-to-Face or E-Mail: The Medium Makes a Difference." *Communication World*, August/September 2001, pp. 23–25.

"Check Your E-Mail, Please." *PR Reporter*, November 4, 2002, pp. 1–2.

"Don't Believe the Hype: Few Workers Are Overwhelmed by E-Mail." *PR Reporter*, December 2002, pp. 2–3.

Goldstein, Stuart Z. "The Annual Report Isn't What It Used to Be." *Communication World*, February/March 2001, pp. 11–13.

Hafner, Katie. "Billions Served Daily, and Counting: Along E-Mail's 30-Year Path, the Medium Took Shape Early. The Masses Caught Up Later." *The New York Times*, December 6, 2001, pp. D1, D9.

"Making the Telephone Work for You." *Communication Briefings*, June 2003, pp. 8A–8B.

Saunders, Elizabeth. "There's No Stencil for Writing Shareholder Letters, but Buffett's a Good Start." *PRWeek*, June 10, 2002, p. 8.

Seitel, Fraser P. "Answering Customer Complaints." *O'Dwyer's PR Services Report*, March 2003, pp. 31–32.

Weidlich, Thom. "Annual Reports Must Reflect the Times." *PRWeek*, July 7, 2003, p. 22.

"Word-Usage Rules for Writing Strong Memos and Reports." *Communication Briefings*, October 2002, pp. 8A–8B.

Chapter 15

Direct Mail and Advertising

Direct mail and advertising are often used as supplemental communication tools in public relations campaigns. Consequently, it is important for a public relations writer to have a basic understanding of how and when to use these tactics.

Unlike news releases, which are sent to media editors for possible use, direct mail is a cost-effective form of access media. That is, it reaches people as a direct communication from the organization. Advertising, on the other hand, uses the vehicle of mass communication outlets to reach the audience. Basically, it is purchased space in a mass medium. Both direct mail and advertising ensures that the message is exactly as you want it—

in the format that you specify. It also means that you control the exact timing and context of your message.

In this chapter, you will learn the pros and cons of using direct mail and advertising. You also will learn how to create the five basic components of a direct mail package—envelope, letter, brochure, reply card, and return envelope.

Later, you will become acquainted with the five basic types of advertising that can be used in a public relations campaign—image building, financial relations, public service, advocacy/issues, and announcements. You then will be given some tips on how to write an effective ad. The chapter ends with a review of other advertising channels, such as billboards, posters, T-shirts, sponsored books, promotional items, and product placements, that can be used in public relations campaigns.

THE BASICS OF DIRECT MAIL

Letters and accompanying material mailed to large groups of people is a form of marketing called **direct mail.** Although many consumers and the media often refer to it as **junk mail,** it has a long history. According to Media Distribution Services, one of the first examples of "direct mail" was in 1744, when Benjamin Franklin mailed a list of books for sale to a selected list of prospects. Not exactly Amazon.com, but a start.

Since then, the use of direct mail to sell ideas, goods, and services has sky-rocketed. Billions of direct mail pieces are produced each year in the United States, primarily to sell products and services. Indeed, *U.S. News & World Report* says that the average household receives 34 pounds, or more than 550 pieces, of direct mail annually.

Although the major use of direct mail is to sell goods and services, it also has a number of uses as an effective public relations tool. Direct mail, for example, is used by political candidates to inform voters about issues and also to ask for their votes. It is used by charitable groups to educate the public about various social is-sues and diseases, and to solicit contributions. Corporations often use direct mail to notify consumers about a product recall, inform investors about a merger or ac-quisition, or make an apology about a poor service or shoddy goods. Community groups use direct mail to let its members and other interested people know about forthcoming events and the group's stand on important issues. In other words, whenever a number of people can be identified as a key public, it is logical to reach them with direct mail.

Advantages of Direct Mail

Direct mail is a controlled communication medium just like newsletters, brochures, and Web pages.

It allows you to have total control over the format, wording, and timing of a message to audiences as broad or narrow as you wish. Indeed, the three major ad-vantages of direct mail are (1) targeting your communication to specific individu-als, (2) personalization, and (3) cost-effectiveness.

Targeted Audience   An appropriate mailing list is the key to using direct mail as an effective public relations tool. At the very basic level, a mailing list may be a compilation of an organization's members, past contributors, employees, or cus-tomers. Organizations compile mailing lists on all sorts of audiences. In public re-lations, for example, you may compile a mailing list of community leaders. People working in investor relations might have a list of analysts, institutional investors, and stockholders.

You can also rent mailing lists from various membership organizations and media outlets. If you want to send a letter to all dentists in your area, you contact the American Dental Association. If your purpose is to reach affluent individuals, you might rent a list of BMW and Mercedes Benz owners from the state depart-ment of motor vehicles. You can also rent the subscription lists of various news-papers and magazines if you feel that the demographics of the subscribers fit your particular purpose. For about $150, for example, List Services Corp. will provide 1,000 subscribers to *Forbes* magazine with average incomes of $232,000.

Advances in marketing research, including demographics and psychographics, make it possible to reach almost anyone with scientific precision. Thanks to vast data-collection and data-crunching networks, it is now possible to order mailing lists based on people's spending habits, charitable contributions, and even their favorite beer. Every time you purchase groceries with a store discount card, buy a book from Amazon.com, or order something from a catalog, your name and address goes into a marketing database.

Metromail, a division of publishing giant R.R. Donnelley & Sons, is one major supplier of tailored mailing lists compiled from any number of computer databases. One database, for example, has the names and addresses of 15 million people who have various diseases such as asthma, diabetes, and cancer. Other lists contain the names and addresses of every school principal in America, or even a list of people who are members of the American Society of Civil Engineers.

Personalization   Direct mail, more than any other controlled or mass medium, is highly personalized. It comes in an envelope addressed to the recipient (there is no such thing anymore as "occupant"), and the letter often begins with a personalized greeting such as "Dear Jennifer." In addition, through computer software, the name of the person can be inserted throughout the letter. Specialized paragraphs can also be inserted in the direct mail letter to acknowledge past charitable contributions, or make reference to localized information or contacts. The technology, which will be discussed shortly, also allows handwritten signatures and notes to make the basic "form" letter as personable as possible.

Cost   Direct mail, according to Media Distribution Services, is relatively inexpensive when compared to the cost of magazine ads and broadcast commercials. Typically, a rented list costs about $300 for 1,000 names. You can get these names and addresses on labels or, more commonly, have a software program print them directly on mailing envelopes.

Direct mail is cost efficient from a production standpoint. In many cases, it is produced in one color (black), with perhaps a second color for emphasis of key points. Graphics are not elaborate, and the whole emphasis is on economical printing. Postage is a consideration. First class is the most expensive, but it is more reliable and timely than the cheaper third class (often called "standard mail"). First class also ensures that mail is forwarded or returned without additional cost to the sender. Nonprofit postage rates, available to qualified organizations, is the cheapest. You can cut postage costs by presorting letters by zip code and mailing at least 200 pieces at one time.

Disadvantages of Direct Mail

The major disadvantage of direct mail is its image as "junk mail." All such mail, whether it is a first-class letter or a flyer from the local pizza parlor, is put into the same category of "useless" information that just clutters up a person's mailbox.

Indeed, *U.S. News & World Report* estimates that nearly half of it goes directly to the garbage without even being opened. Even if it is opened, it is estimated that only 1 or 2 percent of the recipients will act on the message. Despite such odds, however, U.S. consumers purchased $244 billion worth of merchandise in a recent year by responding to direct mail sales pitches. Studies show that, on average, every dollar spent on direct mail advertising brings in $10 in sales—a return more than twice that generated by a television ad. Nonprofit agencies that rely on direct mail for much of their fund-raising efforts also say the ROI (return on investment) makes direct mail a major component of their communication strategy.

Information Overload   It has already been noted that the average person receives more than 550 pieces of direct mail annually. Although it is argued that a person reads direct mail in isolation from other messages and distractions, there is the problem of clutter and the inability of people to cope with so many messages on a daily basis. Consequently, it is important to know how to write and format a direct mail piece that gets opened, read, and acted upon.

CREATING A DIRECT MAIL PACKAGE

The direct mail package has five basic components: (1) mailing envelope, (2) letter, (3) basic brochure, (4) reply card, and (5) return envelope. On occasion, a sixth component is added—"gifts" such as address labels, greeting cards, and even calendars that are designed to entice a person to open the envelope and at least read the message.

Mailing Envelope

The envelope is the headline of a direct mail package because it is the first thing the recipient sees. If this doesn't attract the reader's interest, a person will not "read on" by opening the envelope.

According to Media Distribution Services, there are several ways to make an envelope attractive and appealing. It can be visually enhanced through the creative use of paper stocks, windows, tabs, teasers, and other design options. Heavy, glossy paper can give the envelope the appearance of value and importance. Windows can provide teasers and other information that cater to the question, "Why should I open this?"

Sometimes, envelopes carry a preview of what's inside. UNICEF, in one of its fund-raising letters, used the envelope teaser, "Enclosed: The Life or Death Seed Catalog." The Sierra Club, on the other hand, simply marks its envelopes "Urgent," in big, red letters. Amnesty International also signals the content of the envelope. One such envelope used the term, "Emergency Alert on Kosovo."

On the other hand, some envelopes provide little or no information. They don't even give the name of the organization in the return address. The idea is to arouse the curiosity of the reader so he or she will open the envelope. Other organizations resort to trickery. They make the envelope look like it is an official letter from a government agency, or there is the misleading teaser that you are the winner of a large prize. Publisher's Clearing House, for example, once made such teasers standard practice, until the attorneys general in several states hauled them into court for misleading and false advertising.

In general, public relations writers should avoid misleading teasers and envelope designs that mislead readers or cause mistaken impressions. This causes credibility problems, and it often borders on the unethical. Your direct mail envelope should always have the name of the organization and the return address in the upper-left corner. Teasers should provide honest information. According to *Communication Briefings*, there is an ethical difference between saying "Free

PR Casebook

A Creative Direct Mail Package

How do you generate interest among potential tenants for a renovated office building in Chicago? The answer is a creative direct mail package that allowed the recipients to design their own office space.

Tishman Speyer Properties engaged the services of Words & Pictures, Inc., a design firm, to come up with a package that would attract interest. Remembering the peel-and-place sticker sets from childhood (sometimes called "Colorforms"), W&P created a direct mail kit that featured an office scene on a "board" and stickers that allowed the recipients to design their ideal office space, just as they could in real life if they chose to lease space at the renovated office building on Michigan Avenue. Recipients could also fill out a card and fax it back to request more details about the building and receive a free T-shirt or beach towel emblazoned with the 233 North Michigan logo.

The piece, shown here, generated an incredible 25 percent response rate. In fact, Tishman got the first response the day after they mailed the piece. The building experienced great success in its leasing program, with nine tenants signing leases subsequent to the mailing.

Figure 15.1 Selling Office Space
Shown are the components of the direct mail piece that was designed to attract tenants to a renovated office building in downtown Chicago. The colorful, bold graphics got attention, and the piece provided an opportunity for readers to interact with the material by moving stickers around to design their ideal office space.
(Courtesy of Tishman Speyer Properties and its design firm, Words & Pictures, Inc.)

Computer Map of Your City" and "How to Get a Free Computer Software Map of Your City."

Research has also found that a regular stamp is better than metered postage, and a commemorative stamp is the most effective. Such stamps are attention-getting, and it makes the direct mail envelope look more important. Of course, a name and address printed on the envelope is better than an adhesive label.

If you have the time and staff, the personal touch of a hand-addressed envelope tends to pay even larger dividends. According to *PR Reporter*, one business in upper New York state hand-addressed 1,000 pieces to customers, and a follow-up telephone survey showed everyone opened the envelope. In addition, the business got a 14 percent return on sales instead of the usual 1 or 2 percent response rate.

The Letter

For maximum effectiveness, the cover letter should be addressed to one person and start with a personal greeting, "Dear Ms. Smith." Some letters skip the personal salutation and just use a headline that will grab the reader's attention. A headline or a first paragraph is the most-read part of a letter, so it must be crafted to arouse the reader's interest. Some studies show that it takes a reader about one to three seconds to decide whether to read on or pitch the letter in the trash.

Headines and First Paragraphs

A sales pitch for a product or service often has a headline that emphasizes a free gift or the promise of saving money. Nonprofit groups and public action groups, on the other hand, often state the need in a headline. Planned Parenthood, for example, used the headline "Stop Clinic Violence" in an appeal to enlist support for legislation protecting health clinics from pro-life activists.

You can use a straight lead for the beginning paragraph, or a human-interest angle. The straight lead is to the point. The Sierra Club began one letter from the executive director with the following: "I am writing to ask for your immediate help to ensure victory for the most ambitious government plan to protect endangered wilderness in our nation's history—the Wild Forest Protection Plan."

Help the Children uses the human-interest angle. The organization's president, in a fund-raising letter during the Christmas season, began: "I love this time of year. I have so many special memories of children like Erica. Christmas used to be a sad time for Erica. When Christmas day would come to her home—there were no gifts, no trees, no Christmas dinner, and little joy." The letter then went on to describe how Help the Children helped restore Christmas joy in Erica's life, and ended with an appeal for funds to help ". . . children like Erica." The human-interest angle, telling a story, also is used in the fund-raising letter of ELCA shown in Figure 15.2.

Typeface and Length

Most direct mail letters are written on the organization's letter-size stationery. There is no rule about length, but experts recommend a maximum of two to four pages. A typewriter-style font for the text makes the letter appear more personal than a fancier typeface. Several devices are used to make

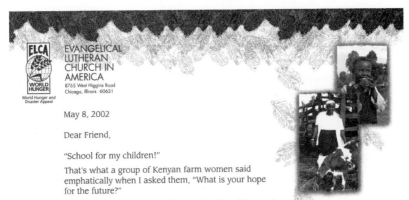

May 8, 2002

Dear Friend,

"School for my children!"

That's what a group of Kenyan farm women said emphatically when I asked them, "What is your hope for the future?"

These are strong women, with hands callused from using simple tools to grow beans and maize on small plots of land. Their hardened hands and their child-focused hopes remind me of my own immigrant grandparents, who worked so hard and whose dreams were realized in the lives of their children.

Life is hard for small farmers throughout the world, who often don't have enough food for their children, let alone money to pay their school fees. But hope comes on four feet – the feet of cows, goats and pigs. And hope comes on two feet – the feet of our Lutheran World Relief partners who provide quality animals and teach earth-friendly ways to raise them. Add small start-up loans plus training in marketing, and hard-working farm families can move beyond subsistence to stability – and to schooling!

Hope comes both on four feet and on two feet because you care – and because you give generously to the ELCA World Hunger Appeal.

Hope – in the form of a cow – made all the difference for Wambui Muigai and her family. The cow our Kenyan partners provided was bred to be a high-yielder; it produces abundant milk. Wambui's children now have the added protein and nutrients they need to grow up healthy and strong. Manure provides the fertilizer Wambui could otherwise not afford, so she is able to raise more food. And she has also become a shrewd businesswoman, selling both the excess milk and the cow's offspring. The extra cash has enabled Wambui's dream to come true: her children are now in school.

(over, please)

Figure 15.2 Human Interest Attracts Readers
This direct mail letter, by the Evangelical Lutheran Church in America (ELCA), engages the reader's interest by telling a story. The letter uses insert photos and bold-faced sentences to create an effective appeal for funds to carry out the work of the World Hunger Appeal program.
(Courtesy of ELCA, Chicago.)

the letter easy to use. One is short sentences and paragraphs. Another is putting key words and phrases in boldface or even larger type. Some organizations emphasize key messages with a yellow highlighter or underline them. Other tips for planning a direct mail package are given in the box on page 439. How to write a fund-raising letter is found on page 441.

Postscript   The most effective direct mail letters always end with a postscript, or P.S. Many experts say this is the second most-read part of a letter, after the beginning paragraph. It gives the writer an opportunity to restate the benefits of an offer or to underscore the urgency of a need.

The ECLA letter, shown in Figure 15.2, ended with this P.S.:

> Thanks again for responding to the many crises of the past year: from the September 11 terrrorist attacks . . . to the Afghan refugee crisis . . . to the current famine in Malawi . . . to the ongoing fighting in the Middle East. Your gifts to the ECLA World Hunger and Disaster Appeal make a world of difference in the lives of people in need! For more information, visit our Web site at www.elca.org/hunger.

Brochure

Chapter 12 discussed the writing and production of brochures, and one popular use is their insertion into direct mail packages. Typically, the brochure describes a product, service, organization, or company. It supports the mailing's offer, adding credibility to the overall message. An effective brochure must be brief but, at the same time, answer most of the reader's questions.

Professional Tips

How to Plan a Direct Mail Package

Here are several techniques that have proved effective over the years.

- **Define the audience.** Know exactly who you want to reach and why they should respond. The more you know about the demographics of the members of your audience and their motivations, the better you can tailor a letter to them. Don't waste time and money sending your material to people who can't or won't respond.

- **Get the envelope opened.** There is so much junk mail nowadays that many letters go directly into the trash without ever being opened. Put a teaser headline on the outside of the envelope that makes the recipient want to know what's inside. The opposite approach, which also raises curiosity, is to use a sender's address but not the name of the organization. Using stamps instead of a postal permit number also increases envelope opening.

- **Keep the idea clear and pertinent.** State the offer or request in the first two or three sentences. Tell what the advantages or benefits are—and repeat them throughout the letter. At the end of the letter, summarize the message. You cannot be too clear.

- **Make it easy for people to respond.** Tell the recipient exactly what to do and how to do it. Include a postage-paid reply card or envelope. Design forms that require only a checkmark to place an order or make a pledge.

- **Pretest the campaign.** Conduct a pilot campaign on a limited basis. Prepare two or three different appeals and send them to a sampling of the target audience. By doing this, you can find out what appeal generates the greatest response before doing an entire mailing.

Media Distribution Services (MDS) gives these elements that can increase a brochure's interest:

- **Testimonials.** List them in one place or sprinkle them throughout the text.
- **Questions and answers.** A good format. Your questions should address motivations, not just product features. They should seem natural, not contrived.
- **List of benefits.** Lists, when highlighted by large numerals or bullet points, make attractive visual reference.
- **Guarantee.** A guarantee seems even stronger when printed in more elaborate type or framed in a box.
- **Models, colors, options.** Customer product choices can be pictured or described with words.
- **Benefit tables, comparisons.** These help readers identify your offer's advantages quickly.
- **Call-outs.** These are free-floating captions arranged around a picture or text. Short sentences emphasize key points.

Most brochures used in direct mail are designed to fit into a standard #10 business envelope. This means that it should be about 4 by 9 inches in overall dimension. It may be two or three panels. See Figure 12.6 on page 362.

Reply Card

If you want a response from the reader, the best way to get it is to provide a reply card. The card, printed on index-card stock so it is more rigid, should contain all the information you and the reader require to process an acceptance to attend an event, a pledge to the organization, or to order merchandise.

Additional care should be used to prepare the reply form. Exactly what information do you need to process it? Typical reply cards give a space for the respondent to give his or her name, address, city, and zip code. In addition, you may want the person's telephone number, e-mail address, and fax number. This information is valuable for updating lists in future mailings to the same people.

If the person is making a charitable donation or buying a product, you need to provide categories for payment by either check or credit card. The credit card information you need is (1) name of credit card, (2) name of person listed on the credit card, (3) the card number, and (4) expiration date.

It is important to ensure that the space allowed for writing information is large enough to accommodate information. A short line may not be sufficient for a person to write his or her complete address clearly. In general, reply cards should be at least 4 by 6 inches, and many of them are 4 by 8 inches.

Return Envelope

Although reply cards can offer a self-addressed return address on the reverse side, an envelope with a return address is usually provided. This ensures privacy, and an envelope is definitely needed if you are requesting a check or credit card information. Commercial operations often provide a postage-paid envelope, but nonprofits generally ask respondents to provide their own postage. This reduces the cost, and more money can be spent on the cause itself.

Gifts

Many nonprofit and charitable organizations use direct mail packages that include a gift of some kind. Most common are address labels, greeting cards, and calendars. The theory is that the inclusion of such material cuts through all the competing solicitations and gives the person a "reward" for opening the envelope.

The inclusion of such items, however, considerably raises the cost of direct mail, and it's no guarantee that people will make a contribution out of "guilt" or even "gratitude." Indeed, there is some evidence that such "gifts" can increase the ire of individuals because they don't like charitable causes spending so much money on direct mail—money that could go to the cause itself.

Oxfam, the humanitarian aid agency, took this tact on one mailing. The envelope announced in big, bold letters the following: "Enclosed: No address labels to use, No calendars to look at, No petitions to sign, and No pictures of starving children." It followed through in the beginning of the fund-raising letter with the following statement:

Dear Friend,
    Here's what you won't find accompanying this letter.

- Address labels aimed at 'guilt tripping' you into giving
- An expensive calendar that you don't need (and we can't afford)
- A vague-sounding petition addressed to somebody in Washington
- Or heart-rending photos calculated to play on your emotions

Professional Tips

How to Write a Fund-Raising Letter

A large percentage of fund raising for charitable institutions is conducted through direct mail. The purpose of the letter, of course, is to elicit a response—a donation. Writers of fund-raising letters have learned to use these approaches.

- Make use of an attention-getting headline.
- Follow this with an inspirational lead-in on why and how a donation will be of benefit.
- Give a clear definition of the charitable agency's purpose and objectives.
- Humanize the cause by giving an example of a child or family that benefited.
- Include testimonials and endorsements from credible individuals.
- Ask for specific action and provide an easy way for the recipient to respond. Postage-paid envelopes and pledge cards are often included.
- Close with a postscript that gives the strongest reason for the reader to respond.

What you will find is a straightforward case for one of the most effective humanitarian aid agencies anywhere in the world.

In sum, it's best to avoid the extra cost of "gifts" in direct mail packages.

THE BASICS OF PUBLIC RELATIONS ADVERTISING

The American Marketing Association defines advertising as "any paid form of non-personal presentation of ideas, goods, or services by an identified sponsor." Melvin DeFleur and Everett Dennis, authors of *Understanding Mass Media*, go even further and state, "Advertising tries to inform consumers about a *particular* product and to persuade them to make a *particular decision*—usually the decision to buy the product."

They are describing the most common forms of advertising—national consumer advertising (the ad in *Time* magazine about a new car model) and retail advertising (the ad in the local paper telling you where to buy it).

However, advertising can serve other purposes besides just persuading people to buy a product or service. Todd Hunt and Brent Ruben, authors of *Mass Communication: Producers and Consumers,* say other purposes of advertising might be to build consumer trust in an organization **(institutional advertising),** create favorable opinions and attitudes **(goodwill or public service advertising)** and motivate people to support a cause or a political candidate **(issue or political advertising).**

These kinds of advertising can be placed under the umbrella of public relations advertising. In fact, the American National Advertisers and Publishers Information Bureau suggests several characteristics that distinguish public relations advertising. The following list uses the word "company," but the concept is applicable to any organization, including nonprofits, trade groups, and special-interest groups.

- It must educate or inform the public regarding the company's policies, functions, facilities, objectives, ideals, and standards.

- It must create a climate of favorable opinion about the company by stressing the competence of the company's management, accumulated scientific knowledge, manufacturing skills, technological progress, and contribution to social advancement and public welfare.

- It must build up the investment qualities of the company's securities or improve the financial structure of the company.

- It must sell the company as a good place in which to work, often in a way designed to appeal to recent college graduates or people with certain skills.

In other words, public relations advertising does not sell goods or services directly. Instead, its primary purpose is to inform, educate, and create a favorable climate of public support that allows an organization to succeed in its organizational objectives. Of course, an indirect by-product of this may be the selling of goods and services.

Advantages of Advertising

Advertising, like direct mail, is paid and controlled mass communication. This means that the organization completely bypasses the newsroom gatekeepers and places its messages, exactly as written and formatted, with the medium's advertising department. Thus a primary reason for advertising as a communications tool is that control of the message remains with the sender.

Some other advantages of advertising are its selectivity and the advertiser's control of the impact and timing.

Audience Selection Specific audiences can be reached with advertising messages on the basis of such variables as location, age, income, and lifestyle. This is done by closely studying the audience demographics of newspapers, magazines, and broadcast shows. BMW, for example, advertises in magazines such as the *New Yorker* and *National Geographic,* which have highly educated and affluent readers. The neighborhood deli, on the other hand, may advertise only in the local weekly that serves the immediate area.

Message Control Gatekeepers frequently alter or truncate the news or features they receive. Sometimes the changes do little harm, but occasionally the changes ruin an idea or eliminate an important point. Your communications plan may involve informing the public about subject A before you say anything about subject B, but if a gatekeeper changes the order or eliminates one story, the sequence is destroyed. With advertising, however, you can be sure that your message is reproduced in the exact words you choose and in the sequence you have planned.

Impact With advertising, you can make your messages as big, frequent, and powerful as you choose. The gatekeeper may think your message is worth a 4-inch space on page 9, but if you think it deserves major treatment, you can buy a whole page. And if you want the idea repeated, you can buy as many ads as the budget permits. The broadcast media present similar problems and opportunities. Your news item or feature idea may or may not be used—or, if used, may be cut to a few words—but your advertisement *will* be used without alteration.

Timing If timing is an important factor, advertising can guarantee that your message will be timely. Prompt response to a public issue, a fixed sequence of messages, continuity of communication—all can be maintained through advertising. To the gatekeeper, your message may be just as usable on Tuesday as on Friday; but for your purpose, Tuesday may be a day too early and Friday is too late. You can't be sure about the timing unless you pay for it.

Disadvantages of Advertising

Although institutional advertising can be effective in getting key messages to specific audiences, there are some disadvantages.

Cost   Paid space is expensive. Ads in multiple media, which are necessary for message penetration, can cost thousands of dollars in the trade press and millions in the consumer press. The most extreme example is the annual Super Bowl football game, during which a 30-second television commercial can cost $2.1 million. A national publication such as *The Wall Street Journal* charges about $125,000 for a one-page ad and $50,000 for a six-month banner ad on its interactive edition.

The high cost of buying space for advertising has led many companies to shift more of their marketing communications budgets to product publicity, direct mail, and e-marketing.

Credibility   Public relations executives are fond of saying, "Advertising raises awareness, but publicity published as news stories creates credibility."

Because they are controlled messages, advertisements are generally less believable than publicity that appears in the news columns or on broadcast news shows. The public perceives that news reports have more credibility because journalists, who are independent of the organization, have evaluated the information on the basis of truth and accuracy.

Indeed, a widely perceived value of publicity is the concept that a third party, the medium, has endorsed the information by printing or broadcasting it. Advertisements have no such third-party endorsement, because anyone with enough money can place an advertisement, provided it meets the acceptance standards of the medium.

Poor Defense Strategy   "Let's run an ad in the newspaper" is a frequent reaction to a crisis. This approach has one major fault: It is usually too late.

This is particularly true when the crisis has already been reported by the media, and the public has already developed strong opinions on the subject. For example, an organization accused of wrongdoing rarely does a good job of defending itself by spending a lot of money on advertisements denying responsibility.

After the *Exxon Valdez* oil spill in Alaska, Exxon placed several ads defending itself against charges of doing too little to contain the oil spill, but the public perceived the ads as self-serving and insincere.

Firestone, facing charges of making unsafe tires, and Sears, accused by state regulatory agencies of defrauding auto repair customers, also made the mistake of thinking that a large advertising campaign would change public perceptions.

TYPES OF PUBLIC RELATIONS ADVERTISING

The largest percentage of public relations advertising is done in magazines, with television and newspapers in second and third place, respectively. The advantage of magazines is a highly defined readership in terms of income, education, occupation, and specific interests.

There are several types of public relations advertising. At times, the distinctions between categories can become blurred; however, for the purposes of this discussion, we will deal with five basic types: image building, investor and financial relations programs, public service messages, advocacy, and announcements.

Image Building

The purpose of image-building advertising is to strengthen an organization's reputation, change or reinforce public perceptions, and create a favorable climate for selling the organization's goods and services.

A good example of an image-building campaign is one by Shell, a global oil company. The company's image, in recent years, has been somewhat tarnished by charges that it causes environmental damage in its drilling operations and it deals with repressive governments that violate human rights. Environmentalists and human rights advocates have conducted massive publicity campaigns via the Internet and have also occupied the London headquarters of Shell on more than one occasion.

Shell, in response, has tried to improve its image by running a series of ads in leading magazines that explains the company philosophy and social commitment. The series, titled "Profits and principles. Is there a choice?" tries to answer the critics. In one two-page ad showing people from a variety of ethnic backgrounds, the company talked about human rights:

> At Shell, we are committed to support fundamental human rights and have made this commitment in our published Statement of General Business Principles. It begins with our own people, respecting their rights as employees wherever they work in the world. We invest in the communities around us to create new opportunities and growth. And we've also spoken out on the rights of individuals—even if the situation has been beyond our control. It's part of our commitment to sustainable development, balancing economic progress with environmental care and social responsibility. In today's business environment, we don't pretend there are any easy answers, but we continue to stay involved. Because making a living begins with respecting life.

Another example of corporate image advertising is Maytag, the appliance company. Figure 15.3 show an advertisement that was part of the company's celebration of Ol' Lonely as the corporate symbol for 35 years. The advertising copy reinforces the company's image of producing reliable products.

Trade groups, whose membership consists of companies in a particular industry, also use image-building advertising to create awareness or to combat negative public perceptions. For example, the American Plastics Council spent $18 million on a campaign urging consumers to "take another look at plastic" when research showed that consumers had a negative image of plastics as a major contributor to environmental pollution and the problems of waste disposal.

One ad for the plastics council showed a blurred picture (to show motion) of a mother and son in the front seat of a car as air bags inflated to cushion the impact of an accident. Here are the headline and copy:

Some Benefits of Plastic Last for Only Half a Second.

A very important half-second, though. But while the lifesaving benefits of automotive air bags are well-known, what isn't well-known is that many components, including the bag itself, are all made of plastic.

Of course, plastic makes a lot of things safe. Like packaging that keeps medical equipment sterile. And harmful medicines out of the hands of children.

Figure 15.3 Image and Brand Reinforcement
Maytag Company conducted an integrated campaign that included an extensive media kit, a satellite media tour, and several advertisements to celebrate the 35th anniversary of its advertising icon Ol' Lonely. See previous references to this campaign in chapters 4, 6, and 8. *(Courtesy of Maytag Company and its public relations firm, Carmichael Lynch Spong.)*

Plastic wraps and trays that keep food fresh and safe. And shatter-resistant plastic bottles.

To learn more about how plastic can make a world of difference in our lives, just call 1-800-777-9500 Ext. 42, and the American Plastics Council will gladly send you a free booklet.

Because even though some benefits of plastic, like the air bag, may last a mere split second, it may be one your family will remember for a long time.

Take Another Look at Plastic.

The National Fluid Milk Processor Promotion Board spends about $30 million annually on a national campaign to promote the drinking of milk. The campaign has featured a number of celebrities over the years, such as Vanna White, Christie Brinkley, and Steve Young with milk moustaches, giving endorsements. In fact, singer Britney Spears was the 100th celebrity to appear in a "Got Milk" campaign. In addition to the ad, the milk board's public relations firm, BMSG in Los

PR Casebook

Muslim Group Works on Education and Image

Surveys show a serious lack of information about Islam in America, which has been compounded by the terrorist attack on the World Trade Center and the War on Terrorism. A Knight-Ridder poll found that a quarter of Americans say they have unfavorable feelings toward Muslim Americans, and a majority even want to limit the immigration of foreign Muslims into the United States.

The Council on American-Islamic Relations (CAIR), based in Washington, D.C., is working toward better understanding by conducting a multifaceted information campaign to educate Americans about Islam. One initiative is a series of advertisements (see Figure 15.4) that profiles the work and lives of American Muslims and how Islamic values have shaped their lives.

Another project is an extensive effort to provide libraries with a collection of books, videotapes, and DVDs on Islam that it hopes to place in 16,000 libraries nationwide. Included in the collection is one book, "Real Bad Arabs: How Hollywood Vilifies a People," which examines how the media portrays the Islamic faith.

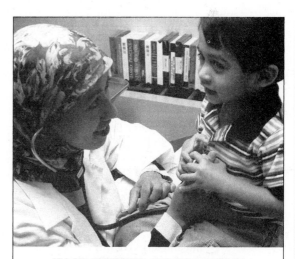

I'M AN AMERICAN AND I'M A MUSLIM

MY NAME IS DR. J. AISHA SIMON. I attended the Medical College of Virginia, completed my residency at Georgetown University and I'll be attending Harvard University to earn a master's degree in public health. I'm a family physician, a wife and a mother. I'm also involved in international relief work, traveling to places like Bosnia and Africa, and coordinating medical volunteers to serve in Guatemala. I was previously a regional coordinator for an anti-tobacco education campaign for elementary school children and I've served as an advocate for domestic violence survivors.

I'm an American Muslim woman and I believe in the importance of charity and service to my community.

The values I learned from my family and my religion while growing up in America have led me to a life of service. Islam calls upon us to strive with one another in hastening to good deeds, and to care for the less fortunate as we care for ourselves. The Prophet Muhammad taught us that when we serve our brother or sister, we are serving God.

I'M AN AMERICAN MUSLIM

CAIR
COUNCIL ON AMERICAN-ISLAMIC RELATIONS

Number six of fifty-two in the *Islam in America* series.
To learn more about the series, visit www.americanmuslims.info

Figure 15.4 Muslims Improve Their Image
This ad, part of a series on Islam in America, attempts to educate the public about the Islamic religion and improve the image of American Muslims.
(Courtesy of the Council on American-Islamic Relations (CAIR), Washington, D.C.)

Angeles, was able to generate considerable publicity about Britney posing for the ad. Many newspapers even ran a photo of the ad in their news columns.

Investor and Financial Relations

A different type of public relations advertising is targeted to the financial community—individual and institutional investors, stock analysts, investment bankers, and stockholders. Such advertising often has the objective of informing and reassuring investors that the company is well managed, worthy of investment, and has bright prospects for the future.

Such advertising is used extensively during proxy fights for control of companies, when a company is undergoing some major reorganization, or when a company believes it is being unfairly attacked by consumer groups or regulatory agencies. A variety of these ads appear in financial publications, notably *The Wall Street Journal*.

In one instance, Honeywell placed a full-page ad in *The Wall Street Journal* to announce that it had won a major lawsuit against the Minolta Camera Company for infringing on its patents. The winning of the suit and the protection of its patents assured the financial community that Honeywell would continue to make profits on its technology. Apple Computer, to cite another example, also took out several ads to bolster investor confidence when the company reported a quarterly loss of $68 million and the price of stock plunged to a new low.

Putnam Investments also had to reassure the financial community and individual investors after its top management was found to have overcharged individual investors and engaged in manipulation of mutual fund administrative fees. In a full-page *New York Times* ad, Putnam announced that it had replaced its top executives and was doing everything possible to cooperate with the SEC and other state regulatory agencies in its investigations.

The advertisement, signed by the new CEO and the vice chairman and chairman of the board, said in part:

> Integrity exists only if every employee is accountable and every system is reliable throughout the organization. To that end, Putnam's new management team will immediately evaluate and correct, where necessary, all systems related to controls and compliance. The hard work and dedication of more than 5,300 people have been called into question because of the unfortunate acts of a small number of individuals. We will do whatever is necessary to make sure Putnam's integrity is never again compromised.

Other forms of financial advertising are more routine. You can use an ad to announce a new corporate name, the acquisition of another company, or a new stock offering. Such ads help fulfill SEC requirements, discussed in Chapter 3, for full and timely disclosure. Releasing news to the media may be adequate, but many corporations also use advertising to ensure wide distribution.

Public Service

Public service advertisements provide information, raise awareness about social issues, and give how-to suggestions. A number of nonprofit and charitable organizations, as well as governmental agencies, use such advertising for public education:

- The American Cancer Society gives information about vegetables and fruits that can reduce the risk of cancer.
- The American Heart Association informs people about the warning signs of a heart attack.
- The American Red Cross gives information about limiting the spread of AIDS.
- The American Lung Association warns people about the dangers of smoking.
- The Partnership for a Drug-Free America, a consortium of nonprofit and governmental agencies, informs youth about the dangers of drug abuse. See Figure 15.5.
- Women in Communications raises awareness about sexual harassment in the workplace.

Figure 15.5 Public Service/Advocacy
The Partnership for a Drug-Free America, a consortium of nonprofit and governmental agencies, has an extensive advertising campaign in television, radio, and print. This print ad, as well as others, are available for downloading from the organization's Web site (www.drugfreeamerica.org).

Let them be who they are. But KNOW what they're into.

Keeping an eye on your kids is not taking away their freedom it's actually the best way to keep them away from drugs.

Talk > Know > Ask > Keep an eye on them. PARENTS. THE ANTI-DRUG.

For information contact us at 1-800-788-2800 or www.theantidrug.com

- The Network for a Hate-Free Community uses ads to educate the public about hate crimes and incidents (see Figure 15.7).

In many instances, the Ad Council prepares public service ads for national nonprofit groups. The Council, an association of advertising agencies, does this as a public service.

Corporations also do public service kinds of advertising to generate goodwill. In most cases, it is related to their products and services. For example:

- The Pacific Gas & Electric Company provides helpful hints on how to reduce energy costs during the winter months.
- The Shell Oil Company gives motorists hints on how to get better gasoline mileage.

Advocacy/Issues

Although it can be argued that advocacy is an element in all public relations advertising—whether it's the American Cancer Society telling you to stop smoking or a company telling you it's all right to buy its stock—the term "advocacy advertising" has a more exact meaning.

It usually means advertising to motivate voters, to influence government policy, or to put pressure on elected officials. A good example is the campaign by the Humane Society of the United States (see Figure 15.6) to put pressure on the Canadian government to stop the killing of baby seals for their fur.

Another example is numerous advertisements placed by business and special-interest groups during the national debate on health-care reform. The parmaceutical industry, one such group, ran a series of ads countering the public's perception that prescriptions cost too much. The American College of Surgeons also warned the public about "retaining the right of patient choice," and even Delta Dental made the case that any change in dental insurance plans would seriously reverse the progress made in dental care.

Other public issues subject to legislation have also spawned massive advertising campaigns. A good example is a campaign by the American Association of Railroads. Millions of Americans watched one of its commercials in which a woman and her two children are almost run off the road by the impatient driver of a triple-trailer truck.

What the viewers may not have known is that the American Association of Railroads was waging a campaign to discredit the trucking industry. The objective was to generate public opposition to congressional legislation that would allow the trucking industry to use larger and heavier vehicles on the nation's highways. Such legislation would, of course, make the trucking industry more competitive with the railroad industry.

Citizen and public policy groups often use advertising to reach opinion leaders about public issues. The Alliance for Better Campaigns, for example, is concerned about the high cost of political campaigns. In an open letter to America's broadcasters, former Presidents Jimmy Carter and Gerald Ford suggested that the high cost of campaigning could be drastically cut if broadcasters gave candidates

Figure 15.6 Advocacy
Advocacy groups often use advertising to give their cause high visibility and emotional impact. This full-page ad, with the headline in red, appeared in *The New York Times* and other major newspapers to protest a Canadian government policy that permits the harvesting of baby seals for their fur. It also asks Americans to boycott Canada until the policy is changed.
(Courtesy of the Humane Society of the United States, Washington, D.C.)

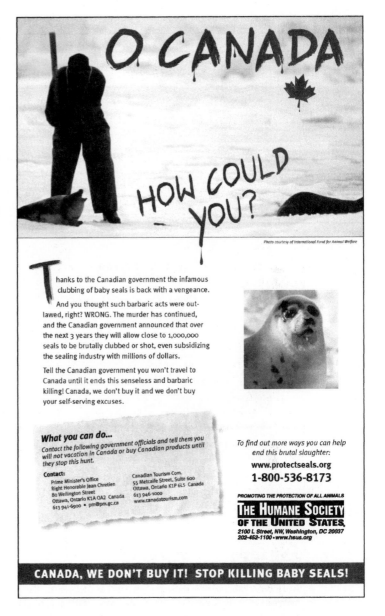

five minutes a night during the month preceding primary and general elections. The ad, which appeared in *The New York Times*, said, in part:

> . . . Broadcasters have been given licenses, valued at tens of billions of dollars, free of charge, to operate the public's airwaves. In return, you have pledged to serve the public interest.
>
> We can think of no greater public service at the start of a new millennium than to provide citizens with the information they need to choose their future, in

**WE DON'T STAND FOR HATE.
WE STAND TOGETHER.**

Stand tough against hate crimes and hate incidents. Don't tolerate insults or slurs based on race, religion, disability, gender

or sexual orientation. Speak out. To report a hate crime or to receive services, call the Santa Clara County Network for a

Hate-Free Community. 408-792-2304. **HATE IS THE ENEMY — YOU ARE ON THE FRONT LINE.**

hateistheenemy.com

SANTA CLARA COUNTY
NETWORK FOR A
HATE-FREE COMMUNITY

Figure 15.7 Advocacy/Public Service
This ad is short on words but has a highly visual element that reinforces the message. This campaign also used a radio PSA, which is shown on page 242 in Chapter 9. This is an example of a national campaign implemented at the local level. The national group, for example, provided the artwork but the copy at the bottom of the page gives a local organization and telephone number.
(Courtesy of the Santa Clara County Network for a Hate-Free Community, Santa Clara, CA.)

regularly nightly forums that can help break the chokehold that money and ads have on our political campaigns.

Mobil Oil, now ExxonMobil, is the classic example of a corporation using advocacy advertising. For many years, it ran **advertorials** expressing its views on a variety of issues. The ads, in the format of editorials, appeared on a regular basis in magazines that had high readership among opinion leaders and people interested in public policy.

An example of the Mobil approach is how it countered criticisms about the "high cost" of gasoline. Mobil, in its ad, pointed out that taxes averaged 40 cents on a gallon of gasoline, so the industry shouldn't take all the heat for gasoline prices. The ad, in part, said, "So, occasionally, we point out that we are not the only ones profiting from what motorists pay at the pump. In fact, a constantly larger chunk of what motorists pay at the pump goes directly to the tax collectors—federal, state, and local."

A number of consumer, environmental, and human rights groups also use advocacy advertisements to persuade the public and motivate citizens to take action. One such group, the Asian Immigrant Women Advocates, took out full-page ads in several major metropolitan dailies to urge a consumer boycott of Jessica McClintock, a manufacturer of expensive women's clothes. The group charged that the clothes were being made in sweatshops where Asian women were exploited and poorly paid.

Another group, Stop Teenage Addiction to Tobacco (STAT) placed an ad that featured mug shots of prosperous media CEOs and accused them of taking "blood money" for helping promote a harmful and addictive product. In this case, the ad got plenty of news coverage when it was disclosed that *The New York Times* and *The Los Angeles Times* refused to run the ad.

Indeed, one side benefit of advocacy ads is that they often create controversy and additional news coverage. The health-care debate ads, for example, generated news coverage worth many times the cost of the ad placements themselves.

In the case of the McClintock advertisement, *The Wall Street Journal* ran a full story on the manufacturing practices of Jessica McClintock and other apparel manufacturers. Other media, in turn, picked up the story. This is a good illustration of an activist group, with few resources, being able to place an issue on the public agenda for discussion and perhaps, ultimately, government regulation.

Charitable groups also do a form of advocacy when they use advertising to solicit contributions. The National Alliance to End Homelessness, for example, took out full-page ads in various daily newspapers to ask for money. The ad, which included a boxed donation form, had a large picture of a child's pensive face with this copy block:

> **This child will never be told to:**
> Clean his room,
> Take out the garbage,
> Turn off the TV,
> Sweep the garage,
> Bring in the mail,
> Mow the lawn,
> Help with the dishes,
> Weed the garden,
> Stop tying up the phone.
> It's not a perfect childhood, it's a homeless one.
> Some one million American kids are growing up homeless.

The National Alliance to End Homelessness is a coalition of individual, corporations, and government agencies working to stop this epidemic in its tracks. You'll help end childhoods that are living nightmares. Because more than mere shelter, kids and their families need homes. So please contribute what you can.

Announcements

Announcements can be used for any number of situations. The primary purpose is to inform the public promptly about something that might interest them. This might be the recalling of a product, apologizing for a failure of service, announcing a community event, or even expressing sympathy to the families who lost loved ones in a plane crash. Here are some other examples of announcement ads:

- Jack-In-The-Box reassures customers that it is taking precautions to make sure its restaurants meet new health standards after an outbreak of food poisoning at several locations in the Seattle area.
- State Farm Insurance tells residents of a disaster area how to file claims.
- Santa Clara Valley Transit Authority sets a series of community meetings to get public feedback on new transit proposals.
- PriceWaterhouseCoopers, an accounting and financial consulting firm, explains its reorganization.
- Children's Hospital of New York-Presbyterian announces the opening of a new center of excellence for children's health, the Morgan-Stanley Children's Hospital, which "will enable some of the world's leading health-care experts to provide the best care possible."
- Rolex announces the completion of the inaugural year of the Rolex Mentor and Protégé Arts Initiative, which will be held at New York State Theatre.

CREATING A PRINT AD

There are several key elements in a print advertisement. They are headline, text, artwork, and layout. Although broadcast advertising is not covered here, the basic format follows guidelines that were given for VNRs and PSAs in Chapter 9. You have to write copy for the ear, keep it short, and adopt a conversational style. For television, you need strong graphic elements.

Headline

Advertising expert John Caples says, "The headline is the most important element in most ads—and the best headlines appeal to the reader's self-interest or give news."

Headlines should be specific about a benefit, or they can be teasers that arouse interest. Here is a headline about a specific program: "The Phoenix Mutual Insurance Retirement Income Plan." Caples thought this was all right, but he created a headline that sold much more successfully: "To Men Who Want to Quit Work Some Day." This was accompanied by an illustration of a smiling senior citizen fishing in a mountain stream.

Caples gives these suggestions for writing an advertising headline:

- Include the interests of the audience.
- Use words such as "introducing," "announcing," "new," or "now" to give the headline a newsworthy appeal.
- Avoid witty or cute headlines unless they include reader interest and appear newsy.
- Present the headline positively. Don't say "Our competitors can't match our service" when you can say, "Our service surpasses that of our competitors."

Text

The headline is followed by one or several copy blocks. These are sentences and short paragraphs that inform and persuade. In general, copy should be limited to one or two major points. Sentences should be short and punchy and use active voice. A declarative sentence is much better than one that includes a dependent or an independent clause.

The copy should evoke emotion, provide information of value to the reader, and suggest a way that the reader can act on the information. You might include

Professional Tips

Effective Ad Elements

The following six elements of an effective ad are provided by the Newspaper Association of America in its annual planbook:

- **Visuals draw readers.** Visuals that occupy about half the total ad space are almost 30 percent more likely to attract readers. When a visual makes up nearly 75 percent of the ad space, readers are 48 percent more likely to take note than if the ad has no illustrations or visuals. Photos and illustrations of models are 20 to 25 percent more likely to get noticed than using simple line art. Show your product in use by a consumer, and 26 percent are more likely to notice than if the product is shown by itself.
- **Reverse type and white space.** Reversed copy or type is all right as long as it is legible. The extensive use of white space, as part of the design in proportion to type elements, increases readability.
- **Size does matter.** Full-page ads get noticed 39 percent more often than quarter-page ads. In fact, larger ads result in greater in-depth reading.
- **Color attracts reader attention.** Color ads get significantly more readership than black-and-white ads. Full color is better than two-color in terms of audience readership.
- **Know your place.** The position of an ad on a newspaper page doesn't seem to affect readership. However, if your ad is the first large ad in a section—or the back page of a section—it gets more readership.
- **Price information.** Readers respond more favorably and pay more attention to the ad if prices are given.

a toll-free telephone number, an address to write for more information, or give the organization's Web site. A review of the ads featured in this chapter will give you some idea about copywriting.

Artwork

An ad can consist of just a headline and copy, but the most effective ones usually have a strong graphic element. This may be a striking photo, a line drawing, or a computer-generated design. Visual elements attract the reader to the ad and break up large blocks of type.

Artwork and graphics are doubly important if the ad is on the Internet. In this case, text is secondary and graphics are primary. Web sites were discussed in Chapter 13, but the guidelines also apply to advertising. The graphics can't be too complex because of possible downloading problems, but the ad does need to be interactive, with buttons to click that allow the viewer to "self-tailor" the message.

Layout

The headline, copy, and graphic elements need to be integrated into an attractive, easy-to-read advertisement. A layout can be a mock-up of the planned ad, or it can be a detailed comprehensive that includes the actual type and artwork that will be used.

A number of tips about layout were given Chapter 12. Many of them are also applicable to preparing an advertisement. In general, avoid all-capital letters or large blocks of copy. Use serif type for body copy, avoid large blocks of reverse type (white on dark color), and use plenty of white space. See the boxes on pages 455 and 457 for more tips on creating an effective ad.

WORKING WITH AN AD AGENCY

Most public relations advertising is prepared with the assistance of an advertising agency. The agency has employees who are experts in all phases of creating the ads and purchasing space in the selected media.

In an integrated marketing communications campaign, personnel from a public relations firm and an advertising agency often work together on a campaign. Fleishman-Hillard public relations, for example, works with BBDO on anti-tobacco campaigns for the New Jersey Department of Health and Senior Services. In addition, BBDO has also worked on integrated campaigns with Golin/Harris (for Visa), Edelman Worldwide (for KFC), and Porter Novelli (for Gillette and M&Ms).

The key to a successful relationship is keeping the communication channels as open as possible. Kate Childress, SVP of Fleishman-Hillard, told *PRWeek*: "If there is mutual respect and everyone has the same end goals in mind, the two complement each other."

Maytag Appliances, for example, conducted an integrated campaign for the 35th anniversary of the Ol' Lonely. In addition to having a media kit and a satellite media tour, several ads were also prepared to reinforce the brand and focus on Ol' Lonely as the Maytag repairman with nothing to do. See Figure 15.3 for an example of this image advertisement.

Professional Tips

Getting the Most from Your Ads

A successful advertisement grabs the reader's attention. *Communication Briefings* offers these suggestions provided by Direct Response in Torrance, California:

- **Busy layouts often pull better than neat ones.** One split-run test showed busy layouts out-pulling neat ones by 14 percent.
- **Vary shapes, sizes, and colors.** People will get bored, and turn the page, if there is no variety.
- **Color will attract attention.** But it may not be cost-effective. Consider using color when the product itself demands it.
- **Putting something odd into a picture will attract attention.** David Ogilvy's Hathaway Shirts campaign used a model with an eyepatch. That odd little detail made the campaign a classic.
- **Too many extraneous props divert attention.** A curtain material company ran an ad with a cute teddy bear in it. The company got more calls asking about the bear than it did about its product.
- **Photographs are more convincing than drawn illustrations.** Photos can increase responses by over 50 percent.
- **Before-and-after pictures are very persuasive.** The technique is a great way to show the benefit of your product.

Sara Calabro, a writer for *PRWeek*, gives some pointers for working with an ad agency:

- Do clarify the respective responsibilities of each agency from the outset and communicate openly and frequently throughout the campaign.
- Do always view an integrated account from the perspective of how PR can complement advertising and vice versa.
- Do consider the compatibility of team member's personalities when selecting a partner agency.

OTHER ADVERTISING CHANNELS

Other forms of advertising that can be used as a tactic in a public relations program are (1) billboards, (2) transit panels, (3) buttons and bumper stickers, (4) posters, (5) sponsored books, (6) T-shirts, (7) promotional items, and (8) product placements.

Billboards

Most outdoor advertising consists of paper sheets pasted on a wooden or metal background. The 24-sheet poster is standard, but there are also painted billboards, which use no paper. Outdoor advertising reaches large audiences in brief exposures. Accordingly, advertising for this medium must be eye-catching and use few words. Ten words is a rule-of-thumb limit for outdoor copy. When design and copy are approved, the individual sheets of paper that will make up the whole advertisement are printed and then pasted to the background.

Location is vital in this medium—and prices are based on the traffic that is exposed to the site. Occasionally, nonprofit organizations can obtain free or heavily discounted usage of outdoor space that is temporarily unsold. Displays are usually scheduled in monthly units, and occasionally there are gaps in the schedules, so it may pay to keep in touch with local outdoor companies.

Transit Panels

This category includes both the small posters placed in subway and commuter rail stations and the cards used in buses and rail cars. Both types of transit advertising require eye-catching graphics, but the copy can be longer than for outdoor posters. The person waiting for a train or holding a strap or a bar on a bus or rail car has some time to absorb a message. Cards in transit vehicles often carry coupons or tear-off notes allowing readers to ask for more information or respond to some sort of offer.

Buttons and Bumper Stickers

Akin to T-shirts are buttons. They are widely used in political campaigns and at special events. They are also useful in fund raising, when they are distributed to people who make donations. In San Francisco one year, money was raised for the ballet by selling "SOB" ("Save Our Ballet") buttons to pedestrians in the downtown area.

In general, buttons have a short life span. They are worn by convention delegates for or by sales representatives during a trade show. Outside of these areas, people don't generally wear buttons unless they are highly committed to a particular cause.

Bumper stickers are another specialty item. They are often used to support political candidates and various political causes, but they can also be used to promote a special event or a scenic attraction or membership in an organization. In recent years, the use of bumper stickers has declined, but window decals are still popular.

Posters

Posters are used in a variety of settings to create awareness and remind people of something. Many companies use posters on bulletin boards to remind employees about basic company policies, benefits, and safety precautions.

A good example is the Nissan Motor Company's poster campaign to remind employees at various U.S. offices to buckle up when driving. Nissan used a series of posters with a lighthearted touch, using famous artworks and personalities. One poster draped a seat belt over a stock movie photo of Sherlock Holmes with the caption, "It's Elementary, Buckle Up Now."

Government agencies often use posters as part of public information campaigns about preventing AIDS, getting flu shots, or having pets neutered. Figure 15.8, for example, shows a poster from the California Department of Health Services.

The government of New Zealand used an extensive poster campaign to warn returning citizens from abroad about the dangers of bringing fruit and other banned products into the island nation. The large poster, in full color, carried the

Figure 15.8 Posters Must Be Colorful
This poster, in Spanish, is in multiple bright colors to ensure that it will be noticed on a bulletin board or a store window. It is targeted to Hispanics over age 50 and encourages them to get flu shots. The same information was conveyed in a 30-second television commercial on Spanish-speaking television stations reaching 45 counties in California.
(Courtesy of the California Department of Health Services, Sacramento, CA.)

headline "Lethal Weapon" and showed a collage of banned food products in the shape of a machine gun.

Museum exhibits and art shows lend themselves to poster treatments. The poster, often a piece of art itself, can promote attendance and can also be sold as a souvenir of the show.

To be effective, a poster must be attractively designed and have strong visual elements. It should be relatively large, convey only one basic idea, and use only a few words to relate basic information. A poster is a small billboard.

Posters, if done properly, can be expensive to design and produce. Therefore, you need to assess how the posters will be used and displayed. Costs can be controlled, often by buying ready-to-use posters from printers and having the organization's name or logo printed on them. Local chapters of national organizations, such as the American Cancer Society, also get posters from the national organization that can easily be localized.

Sponsored Books

Sponsored books may be written by anyone on your organization's staff. They may also be put together by freelance writers. If you should become involved in engaging such a writer, be sure that you read some of his or her work first. One large national corporation once hired a famous writer to put together a biography of the founder. It was so bad that extensive rewriting had to be done by a member of the company's staff.

A sponsored book can be published by the organization. In fact, most such books are produced in this way. It is simply a matter of hiring a printer to print and bind the necessary number of copies.

If the book is important enough to be produced by an established book publisher, the usual procedure is to guarantee the purchase of a sufficient number of books to give the publisher a profit. After the sponsor buys the guaranteed number, the publisher is free to market the book through its regular channels.

The New Arabians is a book that was underwritten by the Bechtel Corporation. It is no coincidence that the company has extensive engineering contracts in the Middle East. *From Three Cents a Week* is the official history of the Prudential Life Insurance Company.

Books that relate directly to a company's product are also often underwritten by the company. General Mills has long been producing Betty Crocker cookbooks for Random House. *Creative Cooking with Aluminum Foil* was published for Reynolds Aluminum, and *Protect Yourself* is from Master Lock and Dell Publishing. Of course, one can also purchase *How to Get Lost and Found in New Zealand*, which was underwritten by Air New Zealand.

T-Shirts

T-shirts have been described as "walking billboards," and some people, including sociologists, lament the fact that people are so materialistic that they willingly become walking ads for products, services, and social or political issues. Why people do this remains unresolved, but the fact is that they do spend their own money to advertise things with which they may or may not have any direct connection.

Because so many people are willing to serve as billboards, you may find an opportunity to use this medium, which is particularly convenient for causes such as environmental protection. Often such groups make sizable incomes from the sale of T-shirts.

Corporations don't usually sell T-shirts, but they do distribute them to attendees at conferences, sales meetings, picnics, and other events. In these situations, the T-shirts contribute to a feeling of belonging to a team.

Almost every town and city in America has at least one shop where you can order T-shirts. You can specify just about anything you can imagine—slogans, corporate logos, symbols, and so on. The process is simple and fast, and the costs are low. At some time, almost any organization may find T-shirts useful.

Promotional Items

An inexpensive item, with the organization's logo or name on it, often accompanies public relations events. Angela West, public relations manager for the Promotional Products Association International, writes in *PR Tactics,* "Whether you're conducting a media relations program, staging a press conference, or hosting a special event, promotional products are a valuable public relations tool."

Promotional items such as pens, coffee mugs, key chains, paperweights, mouse pads, vinyl briefcases, plaques, and even T-shirts constitute a billion-dollar industry in what some people call "trash and trinkets." An organization may include such an item in a media kit, although most reporters complain they have enough pens and coffee mugs to last a lifetime. At other times, they are made available at press parties and trade shows.

The main consideration, says West, is choosing products that bear a natural relationship to the product, service, or message being promoted. Sybase, for example, included a bright yellow tennis ball with its invitation to a press conference about its sponsorship of a tennis tournament. Donor Network of Arizona promoted its National Organ and Tissue Donor Awareness Week with the theme "Get in the game" and sent a golf putting cup to members of the media.

Product Placements

Do you ever wonder why the good guy in a TV show drove a Ford Explorer instead of a Jeep Wrangler? Or why the characters in a movie have lunch at McDonalds instead of Burger King? Or why the Hilton Hotel was the setting of a movie sequence instead of the Sheraton? The reason, of course, is something called a **product tie-in**, which was also discussed in Chapter 9.

Ford, McDonalds, and the Hilton are featured because they have negotiated a product placement with the producer of the TV show or the movie. Modern-day placements started back in 1982, when the Steven Spielberg film *E.T.* featured Reese's Pieces and sales of the then-obscure candy skyrocketed. Since then, companies have eagerly courted the entertainment industry to get exposure for their products and services.

Elaborate product tie-ins with a show such as *Dawson's Creek* can be more effective than traditional ad campaigns in paid media, experts say. American Eagle Outfitters, for example, signed a deal to provide the wardrobe for all the characters on the show. In addition to each weekly episode being a virtual fashion show for its clothes, the deal also allows American Eagle to feature the actors, wearing its clothes, in its catalogs, in-store ads, and Web site. Michael Leedy, American Eagle's vice president of creative services, told *The Wall Street Journal,* "It's like *Dawson's Creek* putting their stamp of approval on us."

Heineken Beer, prominently featured in *Austin Powers: The Spy Who Shagged Me,* also paid no money, but did agree to make the movie the centerpiece of an advertising and public relations campaign for the beer. New Line Cinema, a public relations firm, handled the movie publicity and worked with Heineken to get even more exposure. It, for example, organized a series of Austin Powers theme nights at bars and nightclubs around the country. Virgin Atlantic also was in the movie, and the airline agreed to paint a full-sized Austin Powers on the side of a 747.

Another type of "placement" involves social issues and diseases. A soap opera, for example, may have a story line in which one of the main characters has cancer, diabetes, or even AIDs. In many cases, the "disease" may have been written into the script because the American Cancer Society or a similar organization persuaded a TV or film producer that it would be a good way to educate and inform the public about a particular disease. Public relations people often pitch such ideas to producers in much the same way they pitch story ideas to reporters.

SUMMARY

- Direct mail, used primarily in marketing to sell goods and services, also can be an effective public relations tool to inform, educate, and motivate individuals.

- The three major advantages of direct mail are (1) ability to reach specific audiences, (2) personalization of message, and (3) cost.

- A major disadvantage of direct mail is the perception that it is "junk mail," which reduces its acceptance as a credible tool of communication.

- The direct mail package has five components: (1) envelope, (2) letter, (3) brochure, (4) reply card, and (5) return envelope.

- Advances in technology and market research allow you to rent or buy a mailing list that is compiled with scientific precision.

- Nonprofit and advocacy groups often use a compelling human-interest angle to start direct mail letters.

- Direct mail envelopes, experts say, attract more attention if they use commemorative stamps instead of metered postage.

- The headline and first paragraph, as well as the postscript, get the most readership in a direct mail letter.

- Advertising, the purchase of paid space and time in a mass medium, can be a useful tool in a public relations program.

- Public relations advertising does not sell products directly, but it can create a supportive environment for the selling of products and services by enhancing public perception of an organization.

- The major advantages of advertising are (1) ability to reach specified audiences, (2) control of the message, (3) frequency of the message, and (4) control of the timing and context.

- Advertising has the disadvantages of (1) high cost and (2) lower credibility than publicity that appears in news columns.

- There are five kinds of public relations advertising: (1) image building, (2) financial, (3) public service, (4) advocacy/issues, and (5) announcements.

- When you plan advertising, you must make sure that it fits into the public relations plan. Within that plan, you must determine the objective, the target audience, the appropriate media, and the message.

- Writing an effective ad requires considerable skill and imagination. You must think about the headline, text, artwork, and layout, and how they all relate to each other.

- Effective advertising copy is short and punchy. Copy must be oriented to the self-interest of the reader, viewer, or listener.

- Other channels of public relations advertising include (1) billboards, (2) transit panels, (3) buttons and bumper stickers, (4) posters, (5) sponsored books, (6) T-shirts, (7) promotional items, and (8) product placements.

ADDITIONAL RESOURCES

Burton, Philip Ward. *Advertising Copywriting,* 7th edition. Lincolnwood, IL: NTC Contemporary Publishing, 2001.

Calabro, Sara. "Firm Relationships: Working with an Ad Agency." *PRWeek,* June 23, 2003, p. 18.

Demetriou, Greg. "The Mailing List Maze: How to Find Your Way Out." *PR Tactics,* October 2002, p. 8.

Jewler, Jerome, and Drewniany, Bonnie L. *Creative Strategy in Advertising,* 7th edition. Belmont, CA: Wadsworth, 2001.

Fitzgerald, Suzanne Sparks. "Tips for Using Advertising in Public Relations." *Public Relations Quarterly,* Fall 2001, pp. 43–45.

Ries, Al and Laura. *The Fall of Advertising and the Rise of PR.* New York: Harper Business, 2002.

Vranica, Suzanne, and O'Connell, Vanessa. "For Immediate Release! Super Bowl Advertisers Use PR Firms to Generate News About Their TV Commercials." *The Wall Street Journal,* January 21, 2003, pp. B1, B5.

Whitman, Janet. "Translated Ads Can Miss the Point." *The Wall Street Journal,* September 18, 2003, p. B8A.

Chapter 16

Speeches and Presentations

S peakers and audiences are a fundamental part of human communication around the world. An executive of Ruder Finn, a public relations firm, once estimated that—in the United States alone—companies, organizations, and clubs convene more than a million meetings on a daily basis, all of them focusing on speakers in endless succession.

Speech writing and presentations are important tools in public relations, and they are being given more emphasis than ever before by corporations who need to convey a commitment to candid disclosure and corporate responsibility. Indeed, Michael Witkoski, writing in *PR Tactics,* says, "It's easy to understand the demand for good speechwriting. More than ever, we recognize the importance of giving large organizations a human face, desirably a fact that is trustworthy, competent, friendly, and coherent." See Figure 16.1 for an example of using a credible, third party.

During your career, you will be asked to write speeches for executives, prepare visual aids such as PowerPoint presentations, do speaker training, get executives on the agenda of important conferences, organize speaker bureaus, publicize speeches, and even give a few speeches and presentations yourself.

This chapter will give you the basics on performing all of these activities.

Figure 16.1 A Speech for Every Occasion
Speeches are important tools of public relations because they give organizations a human face. Here, American Idol II runner-up Clay Aiken announces the start of his Bubel-Aiken Foundation during a Wachovia financial center grand-opening press conference in Manhattan.
(Courtesy of Wachovia Corporation, Charlotte, NC. Distributed by PRNewswire and NewsCom.)

THE BASICS OF SPEECH WRITING

Public relations writers, as this book has shown, must be versatile writers in order to prepare material that meets the specific requirements of the many communications tools that are used in today's public relations practice. Speech writing is a specialized form of writing and, at some point in your career, you will be asked to write a speech for a client or an executive of your organization.

A good speechwriter has the ability to stand in the shoes of the person who must give the speech. Sociologists call this empathic ability—the ability to think and feel much as the person who will give the speech. In a sense, you become your client's alter ego.

Such understanding and empathic ability do not arise in a vacuum. They can develop only after a great deal of research and thorough discussion with the person for whom you are writing.

Researching Audience and Speaker

If you are given a speech-writing assignment, the first step is to find out everything possible about the audience. Who? Where? When? How many people? What time of day? Purpose of meeting? Length of speech? Purpose of talk? Other speakers on the program? To find answers to these questions, you should talk with the organizers of the event or meeting. Don't accept vague answers; keep asking follow-up questions until you have a complete picture.

A good example of defining the audience is when an EDS corporate executive was asked to give the keynote address for a meeting of the Association of American Chambers of Commerce of Latin America in Lima, Peru. Beth Pedison, executive speech writer of EDS, analyzed the intended audience the following way:

> Intended Audience: 400 top Latin American and Caribbean business executives, government leaders, and Chamber representatives. Because the audience came from diverse industries, countries, and company sizes, their familiarity with information technology varied widely. We didn't want to talk down to those who were technologically savvy, or talk over the heads of those who were not technologically proficient. English was the business language for the conference and the speech, although almost everyone in the audience spoke English as a second language. Therefore, we needed to keep sentence structures simple, and avoid the use of colloquialisms, contractions, or U.S.-centric language.

You also need to learn everything you can about the speaker. Listen to the speaker talk—to other groups, to subordinates, to you. See how his or her mind works, what word phrases are favored, and what kinds of opinions are expressed. In addition to listening, it is also a good idea to go over material that the client has written or, if written by others, that the client admires in terms of style and method of presentation.

Laying the Groundwork

Ideally, a writer should have lengthy conversations with the speaker before beginning to write a rough draft of the talk. In a conversational setting, you and the speaker should discuss the speech in terms of objective, approach, strategy, points to emphasize, scope, and facts or anecdotes the speaker would like to include.

This is how Marie L. Lerch, director of public relations and communication for Booz Allen & Hamilton, described her work with the company's chairman for a diversity awards speech to company employees:

> The central message, "Do the Right Thing," has been Mr. Stasior's core theme throughout his tenure as chairman. I worked with him to adapt that theme to the issue of diversity; researched quotes and other materials that would add color and emphasis to the message; and interviewed him to flesh out his ideas and words on the subject. With notes and research in hand, I developed a first draft of the speech, which Mr. Stasior and I revised together into its final form. . . .

Indeed, before you start writing a speech, you need to discuss with the client three things—objective, approach, and strategy.

Objective   First you must determine the objective. What is the speech supposed to accomplish? What attitude or opinion should the audience have when the speech is concluded?

Everything that goes into the speech should be pertinent to that objective. Material that does not help attain the objective should not be used. Whether the objective is to inform, persuade, activate, or commemorate, that particular objective must be uppermost in the speechwriter's mind.

Approach   The approach might be described as the tone of the speech. A friendly audience may appreciate a one-sided talk, with no attempt to present both sides of an issue. For example, a politician at a fund-raising dinner of supporters does not bother to give the opposition's views. An executive talking to the company's sales force does not need to praise the competitor's product.

Many speaking engagements, however, take place before neutral audiences (Rotary, Lions, Kiwanis, and any number of other civic or professional organizations) where the audience may have mixed views or even a lack of knowledge about the topic.

In such a case, it is wise to take a more objective approach and give an overview of the various viewpoints. The speech can still advocate a particular position, but the audience will appreciate the fact that you have included other points of view. From the standpoint of persuasion, you also have more control over how the opposition view is expressed if you say it, instead of waiting for an audience member to bring it up. When someone stands up and says, "What you say is fine, but you didn't consider the problem of . . . ," you have lost control. If you have included the "problem" in your talk—and perhaps have even admitted that this is a valid point—it takes the wind out of audience opposition.

Hostile or unfriendly audiences present the greatest challenge. They are already predisposed against what you say, and they tend to reject anything that does not square with their opinions. Remember the old saying, "Don't confuse me with the facts—my mind is already made up." The best approach is to find some common ground with the audience. This technique lets the audience know that the speaker shares or at least understands some of their concerns.

more powerful in the hands of an excellent speaker. Consequently, it is important to know the components of how to give an effective speech.

Know Your Objective

Knowing your objective, as previously noted, is the most important requirement of all. There is no point in making speeches unless they accomplish something. In preparing a speech, the first step is to determine what you want the audience to know or do. In other words, what attitude or opinion do you want the audience to have after listening to the speech?

A speech may inform, persuade, activate, or celebrate. It may also amuse or entertain. That particular kind of speech will not be considered here, but this does not rule out the use of *some* humor in the other kinds of speeches.

An informative speech is one that tells the audience something it does not know or does not understand. An informative speech might tell the audience about how the new local sewage system works, the results of the latest United Way campaign, the expansion plans of a major local corporation, or budget problems facing the state's system of higher education.

Professional Tips

How to Introduce a Speaker

You, on occasion, will be asked to be an emcee or introduce a speaker at a meeting or gathering. This is also a speech, which requires thought and preparation in order to be as brief as possible. A good introduction, for example, should be between 30 seconds and two minutes.

Introducing a speaker serves two primary purposes, according to Mitchell Friedman, a San Francisco public relations counselor and speech trainer. "First," he says, "it functions as a transition from one part of the program to another." "Second," he says, "your introduction offers valuable cues to the audience as far as what they should expect from the speaker and the topic."

In order to write an introduction, you should contact the speaker in advance and get a copy of his or her professional background. Second, you should ask the speaker about his or her objectives for the presentation, the value of the topic to the audience, and any other thoughts about the forthcoming talk.

Like any speech, the introduction should have an opening, a body, and a conclusion. Friedman says, "The opening should grab the attention of the audience by establishing the importance of the subject. . . ." The body needs to emphasize the importance of the topic, the relevance of the topic to the audience, and establish the credentials of the speaker to address the topic. The conclusion is a brief comment to make the speaker feel welcome and to lead the applause as the speaker steps up to the podium.

Friedman cautions that a good speech introduction does not summarize the speech and, even more important, it doesn't include every detail of the person's background. Indeed, the biggest mistake made in speech introductions is giving the speaker's background in agonizing detail. A final note from Friedman: "It is not typically an occasion to make a joke at the expense of the speaker or to embarrass him or her."

Again for emphasis: Keep your introduction short—30 seconds to two minutes—and everyone, including the speaker, will be grateful.

An activating speech is designed to get the listener to do something. Direct and specific action is suggested and urged. A basic principle of persuasion is that a speaker should provide an audience with a specific course of action to take: write to a congressional representative, vote for a candidate, purchase a product, take steps to conserve energy.

A celebratory speech is designed to honor some person or event. Such speeches are often trite and boring, but they don't have to be. If a person is being honored for lifetime professional achievement, why not start out with an anecdote that best exemplifies the feats being honored? This is much better than a chronological account of the person's life as if it were being read from an obituary.

Events such as grand openings, anniversaries, and retirements usually have friendly, receptive audiences. In such cases, you can be more emotional and get away with some platitudes, which will probably be warmly received. When you prepare such a speech, however, keep it brief. Five minutes should be ample.

Structure the Message for the Ear

The average speech has only one brief exposure—the few minutes during which the speaker is presenting it. There is no chance to go back, no time to let it slowly digest, no opportunity for clarification. The message must get across now or never.

You may be an accomplished writer, but you must realize that speaking is something else again. As Louis Nizer once said, "The words may be the same, but the grammar, rhetoric, and phrasing are different. It is a different mode of expression—a different language."

One major difference is that you have to build up to a major point and prepare the audience for what is coming. The lead of a written story attempts to say everything in about 15 to 25 words right at the beginning. If a speaker used the same form, most of the audience probably wouldn't hear it. When a speaker begins to talk, the audience is still settling down—so the first few words are often devoted to setting the stage: thanking the host, making a humorous comment, or saying how nice it is to be there. Here's the opening of the EDS speech for the Association of American Chambers of Commerce in Latin America:

> Hello. I am glad to be with you at this important event. I am enthusiastic about the event's theme, "The Transformation of the Americas," as well as the topic for this panel, "Opportunities Created by Advances in Information Technology." Because I truly believe we are in a major transformation, and tremendous opportunities abound.

You should also be aware that people's minds wander. As your speech progresses, you must restate basic points and also summarize your general message.

One platitude of the speaking circuit, but still a valid one, is to "tell them what you are going to tell them, tell it to them, and then tell them what you have told them." In this way, an audience is given a series of guideposts as they listen to the talk.

Some concepts used by writers are, of course, transferable to speaking. The words you use should be clear, concise, short, and definite. Use words that spec-

Professional Tips

How to Improve a Speech

Joan Detz, author of *How to Write & Give a Speech,* gives 10 tips on how to improve a speech. In an article for *Communication World,* she makes the following suggestions:

1. **Make it shorter.** A 15-minute speech gets higher ratings from an audience than a 30-minute speech.

2. **Make it sharper.** Give your speech a sharper edge. Use a clever statistic, create a shocking contrast, or articulate your point with vivid language.

3. **Use greater variety in your research.** Don't just use statistics and examples. Also consider customer comments, shareholder letters, witty quotations, professional endorsements, one-liners, surveys, news headlines, references to popular culture, and historical anecdotes. An EDS executive, speaking to a Latin American audience, used a quote from a novel by Vargas Llosa, a famous South American author.

4. **Start strong.** Skip the list of thank-yous and boring generalities. Get to the point with a strong statement.

5. **Use stylistic devices.** Put items in groups of three, use parallel structure, and repeat key phrases throughout the talk. An executive of Booz Allen & Hamilton, at a diversity awards program, constantly used the phrase "do the right thing" throughout his speech.

6. **Include rhetorical questions.** Such questions engage the audience because they instinctively start thinking about an answer. Before answering the question, you should pause briefly so the audience has some time to answer the question in their own minds.

7. **Avoid using audiovisual aids as a crutch.** A lot of slides or overheads with meaningless words distracts the audience.

8. **Use a light touch of humor.** Use humor to relax the audience and gain rapport, but don't overdo it.

9. **Respect wordsmithing.** Consonants articulate sound, while vowels express the musicality of the language.

10. **End strong.** If you say "in conclusion," you have 30 seconds to summarize the key message of your talk.

ify, explain, and paint pictures for the audience. In addition, avoid delivering a speech in a monotone voice. That puts audiences to sleep.

Tailor Remarks to the Audience

Because every speech is aimed at a specific audience, you must know as much as possible about yours. Who are they? Such factors as age, occupation, gender, religion, race, education, intelligence, vocabulary, residence, interests, attitudes, group memberships, knowledge, politics, and income may bear on what they will find interesting.

A talk before a professional group can also end up being more relevant if you prepare for it by doing some audience analysis and basic research. Talk to members of the profession. Get an idea of the issues or problems they face. If you don't know anyone in the profession, at least go to the local library and read five or six issues of the group's professional journal. This will give you some insight and perhaps even provide you with some quotations from leaders in the field.

In summary, most audiences have a core of common interests; this should help you to prepare a speech that will appeal to them. A talk to the stockholders of a corporation should be considerably different from one to employees or to a consumer group.

Give Specifics

People remember only a small part of what they hear. You must therefore make sure that they hear things they can remember. A vague generality has little or no chance of being understood, let alone remembered. The speech must be built around specific ideas phrased in clear and memorable language.

A vague statement—for example, "We ought to do something about gun control"—has no chance of being effective. If it were more specific—say, "We should ban all hand guns and make it an offense to be in possession of one"—it would offer the audience an idea that is definite and understandable.

In most cases, the person who is asked to speak is perceived as an expert on a given subject. Consequently, the audience wants the benefit of that person's thinking and analysis. They don't want platitudes or statements that are self-evident. An economist should offer more than the flat statement that the economy is in trouble; he or she should explain why it is in trouble and what the solution might be.

Professional Tips

Keep Your Audience in Mind

- **Know your listeners.** You can hardly know too much about the members of your audience: age, gender, occupation, education, socioeconomic status, and any other facts—and especially why they are listening to this speech.
- **Use their language.** Use terms and expressions that are familiar. Similes, metaphors, and anecdotes are valuable only if they are pertinent.
- **Use visuals.** Your audience will remember much more if you show *and* tell than if you only tell.
- **Use humor carefully.** Avoid side comments and jokes that may offend the opposite sex or various racial and ethnic groups.
- **Watch your facts.** Be absolutely certain that you are giving listeners information that is reliable. Check and double-check your information.
- **Focus on the benefit.** Any speech must tell listeners why they will gain from the ideas being expressed.

Keep It Short

Regardless of the nature and the objective of a speech, it must be interesting *now*. It must include up-to-date facts and information; it does no good to talk about a situation that is no longer current or has no present interest for the audience. If the topic is an old one, it is imperative that you talk about it in a new way. For example, everyone knows that dinosaurs are extinct, but their demise retains current interest as scientists argue over the reasons for it.

If the speech is one of several in a general program, it is wise to learn what others will be talking about. This will provide a context for your talk and add interest by reference to the other topics and speakers. It will also help you avoid saying the same thing as other speakers.

Another dimension of timeliness is the length of the speech. In general, shorter is better. For a meeting that has no other business, the talk should be about 20 minutes long. As previously mentioned, this is about 10 pages, double spaced.

It is a typical practice in many organizations to put the speaker on after a half-hour of organizational announcements and committee reports. In such a situation, since the audience will already be getting tired, the talk should last no more than 10 to 15 minutes. If it is one of several speeches, the limit should be 10 minutes.

The time of day is very important. A morning speech generally finds the audience most alert and receptive. At the end of the day, with the cocktail hour only minutes away, a speaker is at an extreme disadvantage. The latter situation calls for more skill on the part of the speaker; he or she must be more enthusiastic, more forceful, and more attention-getting than his or her morning counterpart.

Eye Contact and Gestures

Don't read a speech with your eyes glued to the lectern. It is important to constantly look up at the audience and establish eye contact. Experts recommend that you look at specific people in the audience to keep you from superficial gazing over the heads of the audience. Eye contact, according to research studies, is the major factor that establishes a speaker's rapport and credibility with an audience.

Gestures also play a major role in establishing credibility. Gestures should agree with the vocal message to be effective. If you are making a major point, you might raise your hand for emphasis. See Figure 16.2 for a speaker using her hands to make a point. Other experts say that you can "reach out" to an audience by extending your arms outward with the palms up.

Nervous gestures, however, are distracting to the audience. Don't play with your hair, fiddle with a pen, fondle your necklace or tie, or keep moving your leg or foot. Posture also is a gesture. Don't hunch over the podium; stand up straight. Remember your facial expression; smile at the audience, express interest and attention instead of boredom. Audiences pick up on nonverbal cues and assess the speaker accordingly.

VISUAL AIDS FOR PRESENTATIONS

The chapter so far has focused on the techniques of writing and giving a speech or presentation. We now turn our attention to the use of visual aids to enhance and improve the speaker's effectiveness.

Figure 16.2 Gestures Improve a Speech
Former Miss America Phyllis George uses her hands to make a point as she launches a national Alzheimer's disease campaign called "The Declaration of Independence" in Washington, D.C.
(Courtesy of Pfizer, Inc., New York. Distributed by PRNewswire and NewsCom.)

First, it is commonly recognized that visual aids can enhance learning, productivity, and message absorption. Consider the following findings:

- Sight accounts for 83 percent of what we learn.
- When a visual is combined with a voice, retention increases by 50 percent.
- Color increases a viewer's tendency to act on the information by 26 percent.
- Use of video increases retention by 50 percent and accelerates buying decisions by 72 percent.
- The time required to present a concept can be reduced by up to 40 percent with visuals.

This is not to say that every speech or presentation requires a visual aid. In many cases, such as a banquet or a formal meeting, the speaker uses no visual aids. Nor does the President of the United States need them when presenting the annual State of the Union Address to Congress. More often than not, however, most of us find ourselves giving presentations to a variety of audiences who need visual aids to keep their attention but to also increase their retention of the information.

It is important to understand the advantages and disadvantages of each visual aid technique to determine what will be the most effective in a given situation. Indeed, visual aids are planned for a specific situation and audience. If you are giving a workshop or seminar where the objective is to inform and educate an audience, a PowerPoint presentation may be the best approach. If, on the other hand, you are conducting a brainstorming session where audience interactivity is the objective, perhaps an easel with a blank pad of paper to record ideas is the only visual aid required.

A major speech for a large convention, on the other hand, may be more effective if one uses 35-mm slides and video clips. This was the case when Hector Ruiz, president of AMD, addressed the annual meeting of high-technology manufacturers at Comdex in Las Vegas. He used three short videos in his talk to illustrate how AMD partnered with other companies to solve their particular problems and, along the way, create new products.

PowerPoint

The leading presentation software is Microsoft's PowerPoint. *USA Today* business writer Kevin Maney said it best when he wrote several years ago, "PowerPoint users are inheriting the earth. The software's computer generated, graphic-artsy presentation slides are everywhere—meetings, speeches, sales pitches, Web sites. They're becoming an essential to getting through the business day as coffee and Post-it notes."

Professional Tips

Putting Together the Perfect Presentation

Claire Atkinson, in *PRWeek*, gives some guidelines for making presentations:

DO

- Check out the audience. What you say should depend on who's listening. If appropriate, do some research about what they want to hear and set your pitch accordingly.
- Try to project an image of confidence and charisma.
- Think about what you are wearing; suits used to be de rigueur, but now the dress code is becoming more relaxed. Call ahead of time and ask.
- Bring a backup presentation or make sure there's someone who can e-mail your speech if you forget it. Remember Murphy's Law: Technology breakdowns are a given—always bring a hard copy and transparencies just in case the computer projector doesn't work or isn't available.

DON'T

- Forget to figure out how the microphone works before you start. And don't forget to turn it off when you finish to avoid any gaffes.
- Get caught up with the flashy gizmos. The most important thing is what you say and making sure you have a coherent, well-organized message.
- Check the presentation with your luggage on a flight. Bags can be lost or delayed.

Source: PRWeek, August 14, 2000, p. 50.

Doug Lowe, author of *PowerPoint for Dummies,* succinctly explains the software program. He says:

> Essentially, PowerPoint is similar to a word processor like Word, except that it's geared toward creating presentations rather than documents. Just as a Word document consists of one or more pages, a PowerPoint presentation consists of one or more slides. Each slide can contain text, graphics, and other information. You can easily arrange the slides in a presentation, delete slides you don't need, add new slides, or modify the contents of existing slides.

PowerPoint is a program in Microsoft Office, but it can also be purchased separately. Most users like it because it allows you to make relatively attractive slides of information by simply following the directions and using any number of templates that are offered. By clicking on a variety of options, an individual can write the title and body text in a variety of fonts, select background and text colors, add photos and clip art, and even do multicolored charts and graphs. More sophisticated users also add sound clips, animation, and video files to their slide presentations through the increased use of such creative programs as *Photoshop, Illustrator,* and *Flash.*

PowerPoint is a very versatile software program from the standpoint of preparing information that can be used in a variety of ways. Here are some of the ways it can be used:

- **Use your computer monitor.** A desktop or laptop is ideal to show the presentation to one or two individuals. The laptop presentation is popular on media tours when you are talking one-on-one with an editor or a financial analyst.

- **Harness your laptop to a computer projector.** If you are reaching a larger audience, technology has now advanced so you can show a PowerPoint presentation on a large screen in a meeting hall.

- **Post the PowerPoint presentation on the Web.** You can post an entire slide presentation to the organization's Web site or the company intranet.

- **Make overhead transparencies.** Once you have created a PowerPoint presentation, you can print the slides on clear plastic sheets, called transparencies. Some speakers, for example, carry a set of transparencies just in case the computer projector doesn't work or—even more of a problem—the organization doesn't have a computer projector.

- **Print pages.** You can distribute copies of your entire presentation to the audience. The software also allows you to do thumbnails of each slide on the left column and give a place for individuals to take notes on the right side of the page.

- **Create 35-mm. slides.** Your presentation can be printed onto 35-mm slides and then shown using a carousel slide tray. This approach is also a good backup just in case the organization or the meeting room doesn't have a computer projector.

- **Create CDs and DVDs.** Many organizations put PowerPoint presentations on CDs or, increasingly, DVDs so they can be easily sent to media reporters, customers, and field personnel for their viewing and background. A low-tech version of this is to place a spiral-bound copy of a PowerPoint presentation in a media kit as a kind of extended fact sheet giving reporters key points about the organization or product.

Whatever the medium—be it transparencies, 35-mm. slides, or paper—there are some rules about the composition of a PowerPoint slide that you should keep in mind.

One key rule is don't make your slide too detailed or cluttered with too much clip art or the use of fancy borders. Another common mistake is to include too much copy. Peter Nolan, writing in *PR Tactics,* says, "The last thing any presenter wants is to have the audience reading a heavy text slide rather than paying attention to what is being said. Presentation slides should support the speaker with a few key words or easily understood graphics."

A good antidote to Nolan's concern is the four-by-four rule. Use no more than four bullets, and no more than four or five words for each bullet. Some experts advise that there should be no more than 10 lines of copy on a slide; others say no more than 20 words. This is not to say that every slide should look like the previous one; that gets boring. Transitional slides, from one topic or major point to another, may only consist of one or two words, or perhaps a photo or clip art. In general, remember the motto about text—less is better.

A standard rule is a minimum of 24 to 28 point type for all words. Anything smaller will be difficult to see from the back of the room. Also, be aware that you should have at least a 2-inch margin around any copy; this ensures that your copy will fit the configuration of a slide projector or a 35-mm. slide if you are using these mediums. PowerPoint has text boxes, which helps the amateur format the right amount of space around the text. An example of a basic layout, done with PowerPoint, is shown in Figure 16.3. One with a photo and sound byte is shown in Figure 16.4.

Color is also an important consideration. PowerPoint has hundreds of colors available in its palette, but that doesn't mean you have to use all of them. Multiple colors for the background and the text only distract the audience and give the impression of an incoherent presentation. It also leads to a common complaint about PowerPoint presentations. Manly, from *USA Today,* says, ". . . people spend too much time messing with the PowerPoint and not enough time messing with the message."

In other words, keep it simple. You should use clear, bold fonts for colors that contrast with the background. As for background, dark blues convey a corporate approach, green works well when feedback is desired, and reds motivate the audience to action. Yellows and purples are not recommended for most business presentations. In general, black is the best color for text, but remember the contrast rule. Black type on a dark blue or red background won't be readable. Other experts simply recommend that you use earth tones and middle-range colors for a slide's background so there is maximum contrast between the color of the text (black or another dark color) and the background.

Figure 16.3 Keep It Simple
PowerPoint slides should be an outline of the speaker's major points in three or four bullets. They can also illustrate key concepts.
(Courtesy of Sybase Corporation, Emeryville, CA.)

Business Challenge

Rapidly adapt to the e–Business landscape to:

- **Attract** new customers

- **Retain** existing relationships

- **Optimize** the experience

Sybase Enterprise Portal Briefing

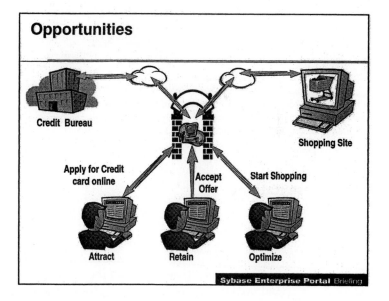

Opportunities

Credit Bureau

Shopping Site

Apply for Credit card online

Accept Offer

Start Shopping

Attract

Retain

Optimize

Sybase Enterprise Portal Briefing

Art Samansky, president of a public affairs consultancy, makes a final comment about the use of PowerPoint in presentations. His advice: "Slides, like a magician's wand, are only a prop. You are the act. If you are merely reciting the material on the slides, you might as well e-mail your audience a copy and save all precious time and travel expenses. Like your text, your slides should be simple and short." In other words, slides provide the headlines. You provide the details.

WHAT ARE OUR PARTNERS SAYING ABOUT STORAGE NETWORKING AND SEAGATE?

▶ **"Seagate brings to Compaq the financial strength and the ownership of the technology, which is key."**

- Michael Dodd
Director of Procurement, Corporate
Compaq Computer Corporation

PCHS100P6841010.PPT

Figure 16.4 Add Interest with Photos and Soundbites
An audio quote and an imported photo gives this PowerPoint slide another dimension.
(Courtesy of Seagate Corporation, Scotts Valley, CA.)

Slide Presentations

PowerPoint presentations, as previously mentioned, also can be converted to 35-mm. slides. This format is often used for presentations in school classrooms and at civic club meetings where a computer projector may not be readily available. The carousel projector may not be "high-tech," but it is still found in more meeting rooms and classrooms than the more expensive computer projector.

And even if there is a computer projector available, many speakers—through hard experience—have reservations about the reliability of the technology in general. The laptop runs out of battery power, the USB cable is a different standard, or the interface between the computer and projector just doesn't want to work. "Breakdowns are a given—always bring a hard copy and transparencies," advises Robert Baskin, director of corporate media relations and global communications, in a *PRWeek* interview.

Slides are also a good backup because they are compact and portable. Flexibility is another advantage. A person, without the aid of a computer or ad-

Professional Tips

Transparency Mistakes Are Apparent

Transparencies can be easily made from PowerPoint slides or a word processing program in two easy steps: (1) placing transparency film paper in your color printer and (2) clicking the "print" button on your computer.

Transparencies have several advantages. They are compact, inexpensive, and easily adapted at a moment's notice. The overhead projector is also a relatively "low-tech" piece of equipment that is found in almost every classroom or meeting room. In fact, overhead transparencies are still one of the most widely used visual aids.

If you are using an overhead projector for a presentation, remember these common mistakes:

- Transparencies with text or charts too small to be read at the back of the room. Keep the type size at a minimum of 24 to 28 point.
- Too much information crammed onto one transparency. Text should be four or five bullets and a maximum of 20 words.
- Speakers moving back and forth in front of the light projection, causing an "eclipse" of the information.
- Transparencies are crooked on the overhead projector glass.
- The speaker reads from the screen with his or her back to the audience. Speakers should read from the transparency on the projector.
- Too much clutter. Keep clip art and multiple type fonts to a minimum.

vanced knowledge of the PowerPoint software, can manually arrange and rearrange slides to fit the needs of the audience.

If you decide to use a 35-mm. slide show as your presentation, however, the first step is to conceptualize the outline and key messages. The second step is to think about what photos, graphs, and other artwork can be used to illustrate what the narrator is talking about. The third step is to write a script. One way of doing this is to use a two-column format. On the right side, write the narration that will be used, either through a prerecorded sound track or in your "live" narration. The left side is reserved for listing the slides by number and identifying subject matter that will illustrate the narration. See Figure 16.5 for an example of a slide script.

Every important point in the message should be illustrated. This means that the narration should be written before the slides are prepared or selected from an already existing stock. Keep in mind that what appears on the screen and what you are talking about have to be coordinated and smoothly integrated. In planning a slide presentation, keep the following points in mind:

- **Length.** Industry research has shown that 15 to 30 minutes is the optimum length for audience attention.
- **Sentence structure.** Keep the message short. Avoid complete sentences when possible, and use accepted abbreviations. It is better to have a slide

ID	VISUAL	AUDIO
1-4	UP TO BEAUTY SHOTS OF CALIFORNIA, SURF, SUN, ARGRICULTURAL SHOTS, THE WETLANDS	(Powerful, majestic, classical music up then under)
5 6 7 8	BEAUTY SHOTS OF BAY AREA PEOPLE PLAYING GOLF, SKIING, OCEAN, BICYCLING	NARRATOR: California... We're certainly lucky to live here. Great weather. Great scenery. Great resources.
9,10	AGRICULTURE (2 SHOTS)	One of those resources is water. It nourishes US and the food we eat. We could go weeks without food, but we'd only survive a matter of days without water.
11 12	SHOW SEMICONDUCTOR MANUFACTURING PROCESS PEOPLE BOATING	It's a vital ingredient in MOST manufacturing processes as well. We use it to produce products such as computers, clothing and cars. The bottom line is that water defines the quality of our life.
		(PAUSE FOR A MOMENT)
13	AERIALS DISSOLVE TO CREEKS, WETLANDS	Yes, water is one of our most precious resources. AND, it's limited.
		(PAUSE FOR A MOMENT)
14 15	SHOW PEOPLE WORKING AT HOME (Choose from old show #23, 40, 56, 57, 65, 75)	So, how do we protect this resource? Each of us <u>can</u> make a difference. Working together, residents and businesses can conserve water and prevent water pollution.
16 17	BEAUTY SHOT OF CREEKS AERIAL S.F. BAY	First we need to understand where our water comes from and where it goes. We also need to understand the uniqueness of the southern end of the San Francisco Bay, where our treated and untreated wastewater is discharged.
18	SKIERS	(MUSIC BECOMES MAJESTIC--INCLUDE AMBIENT AUDIO)

Figure 16.5 Slide Shows Need a Script
The text for a 35-mm slide presentation is concise and supports the visual image. The slides are numbered and described in the left column. Narrator copy appears in the right column.
(Courtesy of San Jose (CA) Convention and Visitor's Center.)

read "Houston Profits Up" than "Profits at Our Houston Facility Have Increased Substantially."

- **Word count.** Ten to twenty words per slide should be the maximum. Use only one point or idea per slide.
- **Big, bold lettering.** Use standard type fonts that are easy to read.
- **Statistics.** Use statistics judiciously. Use bar charts, pie charts, or graphs that give the "bottom line."

- **Variety.** Intersperse pictures with charts or words.
- **Human interest.** Show people doing things, not just buildings and equipment.

The length of a slide presentation depends on its purpose. It is possible to make a good presentation with only a few slides—provided that the story can be told briefly. Conversely, a presentation can use 100 slides if they are pertinent. One example is a presentation on the potential market for American food products in Japan. The presentation showed scores of scenes in food stores. The presentation was not too long because no one in the audience had ever been to Japan, and all were unfamiliar with the marketing procedures there.

Authorities differ radically on the rate of projection. Some say it should be about four slides per minute; others say it should be 10 or 12. Your guide should be to use enough time for each slide to permit the audience to see and understand it.

Some slides may stay on the screen for 10 or 20 seconds; others, especially in a related sequence, may be shown even more briefly. The pictures of the Japanese food stores were shown at the rate of about 10 per minute.

In preparing or selecting slides for use in a presentation, make sure that they are all visually clear and uniform. They should be in color. If graphs or diagrams are to be used, it is desirable to have the basic charts or diagrams prepared using computer graphics. See Figure 16.6 for an example of a basic graph that is easy to read.

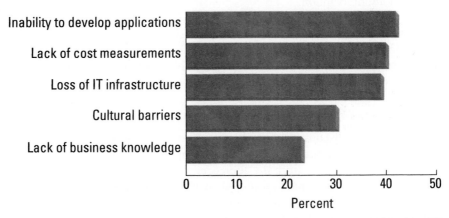

Figure 16.6 Simplify Charts and Graphs
Statistics and percentages should be formatted in easy-to-read format if they are being projected on a screen as part of a PowerPoint presentation.
(Courtesy of Unisys Corporation, Farmington, NY.)

Professional Tips

Some 35-mm Slide Mistakes to Avoid

- **The unrehearsed slide show.** Don't wait until you are up there at the podium to find the kinks in your slide presentation. Go through the entire presentation—with your slides—beforehand. Rehearse every move you are going to make. You don't want any surprises.
- **Relying on a slide operator.** Always check your slides yourself. Be sure to consider the projection format. Rear-screen projection requires that the slides be stacked differently than for front-screen projection.
- **The slide surprise.** An upside down or backwards slide does very little to help you look professional. Always check your slides yourself to make sure they are positioned correctly.
- **The awkward anecdote.** Keep your remarks concise and reflective of key points. Avoid unrelated remarks so as to keep your presentation moving along. If you feel that a particular part of your presentation will stimulate unrelated remarks, put in a blank slide so that the screen goes black.
- **Treating your slide like a script.** Don't read your slides verbatim off the screen. Try to use the same terminology, but speak in complete sentences and in a conversational tone.

OTHER SPEECH FORMATS

A speech is controlled by the speaker. He or she knows what is going to be said. The subject matter is complete and well organized. The speech has been well rehearsed, and the speaker has polished his or her remarks to give a solo performance without interruption.

The environment changes, however, when the speaker participates in activities such as panels, debates, and media interviews. Here someone else is directing the action, and a speaker's comments can't always be scripted in advance. Even so, these opportunities are valuable aids to public communication and should be used whenever possible.

Panels

A panel usually consists of a moderator and several people, each of whom makes a brief opening statement of five to seven minutes. The rest of the time is spent on answering questions from the audience.

The moderator may solicit audience questions in several ways. One common method, if the audience is relatively small, is simply to recognize people who stand up and ask a question. In larger audiences, a portable microphone is brought to the audience member, so everyone can hear the question. Another method is to have the audience submit questions on forms distributed to the audience. The moderator, in this case, goes through the written questions and tries to select questions that would be of most interest to the audience.

Individual panelists are asked to comment on questions, or the question may be addressed to the entire panel. In either case, it is your responsibility as a pan-

Professional Tips

Nonverbal Communication Speaks Volumes

A speaker doesn't communicate to an audience with voice alone. The audience also receives a great deal of nonverbal communication from the speaker. Veteran speaker Jack Pyle, writing in *PR Reporter,* offers this acronym method to help you appear confident and become a better communicator:

S=Smile. It's one of your best communication tools, always helps make a good first impression, and helps make others want to listen to you.

P=Posture. How you stand or sit makes a big difference. Your physical stance tells others how you feel about yourself. Confident people stand tall and sit straight.

E=Eye contact. A person who is believable and honest "looks you right in the eye." Don't stare, but look at a person's face for at least three seconds before moving on to look at another person. If you are talking to a group, give your message to one person at a time.

A=Animation. Show your interest in your subject with your energy and animation. Be enthusiastic. Animate your voice by speeding up and slowing down, talking louder and softer at times. Make your face animated. "A" is also for attitude. Make sure you feel good about yourself and what you are doing.

K=Kinetics (motion). Use your arms to make gestures that support your words. Use two-handed, symmetrical gestures, and hold your hands high when gesturing—at about chest level.

---

elist to give a short answer (one minute or less), so that other panelists will also have an opportunity to comment. It is unfair for any panelist to monopolize the forum by giving long-winded answers to any question.

Panels are good vehicles for getting audience involvement and participation, and they are a standard feature at most conventions. The key to a good panel, however, is an effective moderator. He or she must control the panel by policing the time that a person takes to give an opening statement, politely cutting off long-winded answers to a single question, and making sure all panelists have an equal opportunity to express their views.

Debates

In high schools and colleges, a debate has teams of several speakers. Most debates in the world of public relations are not team efforts. They pit two opponents against each other, and each carries the burden of making the case of his or her side and rebutting the statements of the opponent. The so-called debates of American political campaigns are not really debates; they are merely presentations during which the rivals offer their answers to the same questions.

The management of political debates is not within the purview of this book. That is best left to the political specialists. But any reader of this volume may at some time have to handle a debate on some public issue. Aside from the need to know something about debating, in general there is one special warning worth heeding. This involves the situation in which a moderator may try to split the debate into two parts, with each speaker being allowed a brief period for rebuttal. A toss of the coin determines who will be first.

It is advantageous to speak *last* in such a situation, because the last speaker may have 10 minutes or more in which to try to demolish the statements of the opponent. The rebuttal period may be only a minute or two, and this is hardly adequate to overcome the effect of a long windup statement. The audience is left with a much stronger impression of what the last speaker said. To avoid being caught at such a disadvantage, you should insist that the debate be in short segments—five minutes would be a good length. Then the debate would consist of several five-minute statements by each speaker and a short summary rebuttal.

SPEAKER TRAINING AND PLACEMENT

Giving talks and speeches is an important part of an organization's outreach to its key publics. A talk by an executive or an employee is a highly personal form of communication and adds a human dimension to any organization. It's a form of face-to-face communication, and it offers the chance for interaction between the speaker and the audience.

Speech giving should be an integral part of an organization's overall public relations program. Indeed, public relations personnel are often involved in training speakers and seeking appropriate forums where key publics can be reached.

Executive Training

Today, the public is demanding more open disclosure and accountability from organizations, which is forcing many executives to mount the speaker's platform. Ned Scharff, a longtime speech writer at Merrill Lynch & Co., says it best in an article for *The Strategist:* "If the . . . CEO is to excel as a leader, he or she cannot avoid giving speeches. People have a deep-seated need to see and hear their leaders actively expressing vision and conviction. The more trying the circumstances, the greater the need." *PR Reporter,* in one survey of executives, found that over half spend 10 hours or more each month meeting with outside groups. In addition, the majority average 20 speeches a year, about two-thirds spend time on press conferences, and another third appear on TV.

As a consequence, more executives are taking courses designed to improve their public speaking skills. Cincinnati Gas & Electric holds seminars of this kind for both managers and line employees. Levi Strauss & Company teaches "effective presentation skills" to middle managers. Other companies have also rushed into speech training for executives, creating a major boom for consultants who train employees at all levels to represent their firms in public forums or media interviews.

Because the costs of such training sessions often run into thousands of dollars, organizations with limited budgets may not be able to afford them. Therefore, the public relations department is often given the responsibility of training executives in media interview and speech skills.

Top executives who serve as spokespeople for the organization need media training, in particular. In most cases, executives don't know much about the techniques that reporters use to interview people. It is your responsibility, as a public relations professional, to train them.

First, you must get a commitment from the executive to spend some time learning how to give effective interviews. You can teach the person many of the basics that have been discussed in previous chapters and that will be discussed later in this chapter.

You can also play the role of the reporter and ask questions. Expected questions should be followed up by others, such as "trick-and-trap" questions. Charge the interviewee with ducking questions, and try in every way possible to make your student lose his or her temper.

Although your student may become somewhat irritated with you, such a session will build confidence in handling a real question-and-answer situation. If you feel uncomfortable in the role of reporter, another technique is to hire a local reporter or editor as a consultant to spend an hour or two in a simulated interview with your spokesperson. This will give your student a chance to meet a real reporter in a controlled situation.

The session should be videotaped so that the executive can actually see how he or she comes across in an interview. Witnessing oneself blushing, floundering, mumbling, getting defensive, or seeming incompetent is a powerful stimulus to do better next time.

Videotaping is also done to help an executive see how he or she comes across giving a speech. It's a powerful educational tool that almost always has more impact than telling a person how to give an effective speech.

Speech training can be divided in two parts: what to say and how to say it. Public relations personnel are most effective at helping executives crystallize what they want to say. Both of you should review the context of the speech from the standpoint of location, expected audience, and what information would be interesting to them.

Another consideration is what you want to say that will advance organizational objectives—to position the organization or industry as a leader, to plant the perception that the organization is successful or simply to show that the organization is environmentally conscious and a good community citizen. All speeches should have one to three key messages.

There are entire courses and many textbooks on how to give a speech. The ideal speaker is one who knows about the subject, whose voice and appearance will make a good impression, and who is comfortable standing in front of an audience. Steve Jobs of Apple is a good communicator because he comes across as an amiable personality with a deep commitment to his company's products.

Speaker's Bureaus

Top executives aren't the only ones who give speeches. Many organizations also effectively use technical experts, middle managers, and even rank-and-file employ-

ees on a systematic basic to extend the organization's outreach to potential customers, the industry, and the community.

Steve Markman, head of a conference and management firm, makes the case
in an article for *PR Tactics*. He writes:

> Companies need to expose their expertise and technologies to prospective cus-
> tomers and clients. What is a proven method of accomplishing this objective?
> Speaking at public forums produced by other organizations—at conferences,
> seminars, and forums held by independent event organizations, associations, pro-
> fessional and industry trade groups, and academic institutions and think tanks.
> There is much evidence that speaking at public forums often results in the at-
> tainment of business, by providing increased awareness of the company in gen-
> eral and specific subjects in particular, to an audience of potential customers or
> clients.

In every organization, there are individuals who are capable of giving speeches and
presentations. In many cases, it is part of their job description. Technical staff, for
example, are often asked by professional groups to share their research or talk
about the development of a particular product. In other situations, a community
group may want a general talk about how the company is dealing with a sluggish
economy.

One way of systematically organizing a company's outreach is to set up a
speaker's bureau. This is more than just a list of employees who are willing to
speak. It is also a training center that trains speakers, produces supporting audiovisual aids such as PowerPoint presentations and videos, and even develops key
messages about the organization, product, or service that should be included in
any presentation.

Ideally, a speaker's bureau will have a list of employees who are expert on a variety of subjects. A person in finance may be an expert on worker's compensation,
and an engineer in product development may have expertise with lasers. Markham
warns, however, that a speech or presentation to a group should avoid being a
"sales pitch." He says, "A presentation that turns out to be a sales pitch will ensure low evaluations by the audience and a one-way ticket home. . . ."

Placement of Speakers

Once executives and employees have been trained, your job is finding opportunities for them to speak.

An organization usually publicizes the existence of a speaker's bureau by
preparing a simple pamphlet or brochure and sending it to various clubs and organizations in the community that regularly use speakers. Another method is to
place advertisements about the speaker's bureau in local newspapers. Figure 16.7
shows such an advertisement for Southern California Edison.

The public relations department also encourages calls from various organizations who need speakers on various topics. At other times, you have to be more
proactive and contact the organization to offer the services of a speaker on a particular topic. One of the most difficult jobs in any club is that of program director, and they welcome any suggestions that make their lives easier.

Figure 16.7 Speaker Bureaus Must Be Promoted
Many organizations promote their speaker bureaus with posters, advertisements, and various mailings to civic and professional clubs. Southern California Edison has a multilingual speaker's bureau to reach out to the community and its customer base.
(Courtesy of Southern California Edison, Los Angeles.)

Once a speaker has been booked, the manager of a speaker's bureau usually handles all the logistical details. He or she briefs the speaker on (1) the size and composition of the audience, (2) the location, (3) availability of audiovisual equipment, (4) projected length of the presentation, (5) directions to the meeting, and (6) primary organizational contacts.

The placement of the organization's top executives, however, tends to be more strategic. Top executives often get more requests for speeches than they can ever fulfill, so the problem is selecting a few of the invitations that are extended.

The criteria, at this point, become somewhat pragmatic and cold-hearted. Public relations staff are charged with screening the invitations on the basis of such factors as the venue, the nature of the group, the size of the audience, and whether the audience is an important public to the organization. If most or all of these factors are positive, the executive will most likely consent to give a speech.

Media requests for interviews are treated in much the same way. Busy executives consent to media interviews only if the publication is influential, has high circulation, and reaches key audiences. A business executive, for example, rarely turns down an interview with a reporter from *The Wall Street Journal, Fortune,* or *Forbes.*

In other words, just because a reporter wants an interview with the chief executive doesn't necessarily mean that you automatically grant the request. One alternative is to ask the reporter if he or she would be willing to interview someone else in the organization.

At other times, public relations managers are proactive in seeking placement opportunities. If the chief executive officer wants to become a leader in the industry, for example, the public relations staff actively seeks out speech opportunities before prestigious audiences that can help establish the executive as the spokesperson for the industry.

A good example of how strategic executive speech placement works is what Ronald J. McCall, owner of his own executive communication firm, did for the chief executive of Duke Energy, a $15 billion gas and electric utility. He told *Speechwriter's Newsletter*:

> The company was perceived as a local utility, and we wanted more of a national presence, so I placed the chief executive on the *Business Week* symposium for chief executive officers. That was the first time he was able to tell the Duke Energy story, and he did it in front of a very influential audience of other chief executive officers from across the country. Every one of them needed some kind of energy, whether it be gas or electricity. Every one of them was a potential customer.

Another example of strategic thinking is United Parcel Service (UPS). Several years ago, the company organized an executive communications program that actively promoted its top executives as business leaders through speeches at national and regional business and trade events.

Matthew Arnold, writing in *PRWeek,* quotes Steve Soltis, head of the UPS executive communications unit: "The whole program was created for the express purpose of using senior management as a component of brand building. Using them as leaders, creating the platform for our values and strategies." He continued, "If business as a brand is blemished right now, good companies like us must be out there."

Publicity Opportunities

The number of people a speech or a presentation reaches can be substantially increased through publicity.

Before the Event Whenever anyone from your organization speaks in public, you should make sure that the appropriate media are notified in advance. This often takes the form of a media advisory, discussed in an earlier chapter.

An advisory is simply a short note that gives the speaker's name and title, the speech title, and details about time and place. In a brief sentence or two, describe why the speech is important and of interest to the publication's audience. If it is available and it is a major policy speech, you can also send an advance copy of the speech to selected reporters. Make sure they realize that they should not report the details of the speech until after it has been given. This request to the media is called an "embargo" and is often invoked in the case of an important speech being delivered at a specific time. See Chapter 11.

If the speech is a major event, you will also make arrangements with a vendor to do a Webcast of the speech so reporters and others not attending the event can also view it in "real time." See Chapter 9 for more details on how Webcasts are done. You may also make arrangements for the speech to be videotaped or for the audio to be transmitted in a telephone conference call.

Reporters attending the speech should be seated near the podium, and arrangements should be made for accommodating photographers and television camera technicians. Reporters should also be provided with a media kit that gives the background of the organization and the speaker. A copy of the speech is also enclosed.

After the Event   After a speech has been given, your work is just beginning. You must prepare audio and print news releases about what was said, so that the speech can be reported in appropriate publications or radio stations. Television stations should receive video clips that could be used on newscasts (see Chapter 9).

The speech also can be shortened and excerpted as a possible op-ed article in daily newspapers. (How to write and place op-ed articles is discussed in Chapter

Professional Tips

The Speech as News Release

The audience reach of a speech is multiplied many times when a news release is distributed that summarizes the speaker's key message. A speech news release follows many of the same structural guidelines outlined in Chapter 5, but there are some specific concepts that you should keep in mind.

"The key to writing stories about speeches is to summarize the speech or to present one or two key points in the lead sentence," says Douglas Starr, a professor of journalism and public relations at Texas A&M University.

In an article for *PR Tactics*, Starr says a speech news release should follow a particular format. He says, "Answers to the questions—Who, Said What, to Whom—must be in the lead of every speech story. Answers to the questions—Where, When, How, Why—may be placed in the second paragraph."

The most common mistake inexperienced writers make is to tell readers that a *speaker spoke about a topic* instead of saying what the *speaker said about the topic*. An example of the first approach is "Susan Jones, president of XYZ corporation, spoke about environmental regulations." A better approach would be, "Susan Jones, president of XYZ Corporation, says rigid environmental regulations are strangling the economy." See the difference?

The second sentence or paragraph of a speech news release usually describes the event where the speech was given, the location, the attendance, and the reason for the meeting. It is unnecessary, however, to give the title of a person's speech or even the theme of the convention or meeting. They are meaningless to the reader.

The third and subsequent paragraphs may contain speaker quotes, additional facts or figures, and other relevant information that helps provide context for the speech. When attributing quotes, "said" is the preferred verb. However, some writers vary this by using the terms "stated," or "added." Starr suggests you stay away from such attribution terms as "discussed," "addressed," and "spoke," because they don't say anything.

8.) Reprints, or excerpts of the speech, also can be posted on the organization's Web sites or sent through an organization's intranet to employees.

An example is AMD. Its president, Hector Ruiz, gave the keynote address at Comdex, a major trade show for the high-technology industry. This was a major platform for AMD and Ruiz to establish leadership in the industry, so the company spent considerable time and effort to ensure that the speech got wide coverage and distribution.

The company arranged for a Webcast at the time of the speech, but also placed it on the AMD Web site for later viewing. The Web page also included a photo of Ruiz giving the speech and a short summary of the key points. In addition, there was a link for "Read a transcript of the keynote address" and "Read what they're saying" in terms of press comments on the speech.

If a speech is particularly important, it can be printed as a brochure and mailed to selected opinion leaders. See Figure 16.8 for an example of a speech reprint.

Figure 16.8 Speech Reprints Expand the Audience
Packaging a speech in a brochure and sending it to current and prospective clients is a good way to get more publicity mileage out of a speech. Other techniques are to write a news release about the speech, convert it to an op-ed article, or post it on various Web sites as text or video clips.
(Courtesy of Ketchum, New York.)

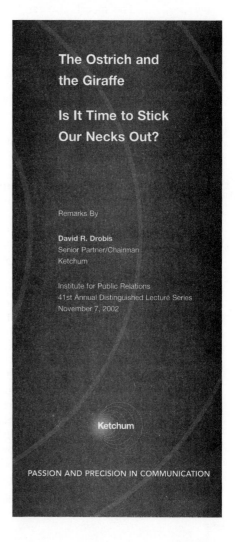

The Ostrich and
the Giraffe

Is It Time to Stick
Our Necks Out?

Remarks By

David R. Drobis
Senior Partner/Chairman
Ketchum

Institute for Public Relations
41st Annual Distinguished Lecture Series
November 7, 2002

Ketchum

PASSION AND PRECISION IN COMMUNICATION

Another outlet is *Vital Speeches,* which reprints selected speeches. You can also ask a member of the U.S. House of Representatives or the U.S. Senate to insert the speech in the *Congressional Record.*

SUMMARY

- Writing and giving speeches are outstanding public relations opportunities for organizations to increase their visibility and reach key publics.
- Speech writing requires clear objectives, effective organization of relevant key messages, knowledge of the audience, and a close working relationship with the person who will be giving the speech.
- A speech is a powerful communication tool. It must be prepared for listeners, not readers. It must fit the audience, be specific, get a reaction, have a definite objective, and be timely.
- Nonverbal communication is important in a speech. Speakers should be enthusiastic, make eye contact with the audience, and use gestures that support their words.
- The recommended length of a speech at a luncheon or dinner meeting is 20 minutes. Such a speech would be 10 pages, double-spaced.
- Speeches should have one to three key messages.
- Audiovisuals dramatically increase the ability of audiences to retain and understand information.
- PowerPoint software can create attractive slides that can be used in a variety of formats—paper copies, computer display, Web pages, overhead transparencies, 35-mm. slides, CDs, and DVDs.
- Computer projectors are becoming more common as prices go down; they are rapidly replacing overhead projectors.
- It is important to make backup hard copies, transparencies, or 35-mm. slides of your PowerPoint presentation just in case technology fails or the meeting site doesn't have a computer projector.
- The key to successful visual aids is brief copy and large type.
- It is important to write a script showing the narration and the visual elements for a 35-mm. slide presentation.
- Other presentations—panels, debates, and media interviews—follow the same basic principles as speeches. However, they also involve special preparation for dealing with opposition, interruptions, and hostile questions.
- Executive and staff speech training is often the responsibility of the public relations professional.
- A speaker's bureau is a good way to organize an effective program of community outreach.
- Top executives of an organization must be selective about what speech invitations they accept. Factors such as the sponsoring organization, the size of

the audience, and whether the venue advances organizational objectives must be considered.

- Speeches provide opportunities for additional publicity by (1) inviting the press to cover it, (2) preparing news releases, (3) distributing audio and visual clips, (4) converting the speech to an op-ed piece, (5) reprinting it in a brochure, and (6) posting excerpts on a Web site.

ADDITIONAL RESOURCES

Adams, William. "Ask the Professor: Points About PowerPoint." *PR Tactics,* February 2003, p. 2.

Arnold, Matthew. "Writing a Brand-building Speech." *PRWeek,* August 12, 2002, p. 32.

Atkinson, Claire. "Putting Together the Perfect Presentation—with Pizzazz!" *PRWeek,* August 14, 2000, p. 50.

Carillo, Frank, and Giuliano, Peter. "Writer's Notebook: Speeches" *Public Relations Quarterly,* Fall 2001, p. 48.

Lowe, Doug. *PowerPoint for Dummies.* New York: Hungry Minds, Inc., 2002.

Markman, Steve. "Speaking Engagements for Executives." *PR Tactics,* May 2002, p. 17.

Nolan, Peter. "Winning Techniques to Make Presentations More Compelling." *PR Tactics,* July 2001, p. 12.

Seitel, Fraser P. "Interview Your Own Speaker to Get It Right." *O'Dwyer's PR Services* Report, August 2003, p. 28.

Seitel, Fraser P. "Speeches Should Be Designed to Be Heard." *O'Dwyer's PR Services Report,* September 2001, pp. 40, 43.

Starr, Douglas P. "How to Cover Any Speech." *PR Tactics,* May 2002, p. 13.

Stewart, Joan. "Demystifying Speakers Bureaus." *PR Tactics,* April 2001, p. 10.

Struck, Kevin. "Workin' the Room: 112 Principles for Properly Lecturing Your Audiences." *Communication World,* February/March, 2002, pp. 27–29.

Witkoski, Michael. "Don't Let Eloquence Derail Your Speech Writing." *PR Tactics,* May 2002, p. 15.

Chapter 17

Meetings and Events

Meetings and events are vital public relations tools. Their greatest value is that they let the audience participate in real time. In this era of electronic communication, information overload, and voice mail, people have a need to gather, socialize, and be part of a group activity.

Effective meetings and events don't just happen. Detailed planning and logistics are essential to assure that defined objectives are achieved. This chapter discusses various types of meetings and events that require attention to detail and good communication skills.

You will learn how to conduct an effective staff or committee meeting, organize a monthly club meeting, put together a banquet, host a cocktail party, sponsor an open house, juggle all the logistics of a national convention, exhibit at a trade show, and do promotional events.

STAFF AND COMMITTEE MEETINGS

Staff and committee meetings are part of any organization, from the local garden club to the multinational corporation. Indeed, through such meetings, employees or group members have a chance to express their views and participate in decision making.

The two major complaints about meetings, however, is that they are time-consuming and they are often ineffective. The Wharton Center for Applied Research, for example, found that senior managers spend an average of 23 hours a week in meetings, while middle managers spend 11 hours. The study also concluded, however, that 20 to 30 percent of the meetings held could be handled better through one-on-one talks, by phone, or by memo. Another study concluded that executives spend an average of 288 hours a year—five full weeks—attending unnecessary meetings.

The productivity experts, given such statistics, also weigh in against excessive and, many times, unnecessary meetings. Steve Kaye, author of *Meetings in an Hour or Less: A Complete Guide to Fewer, Shorter, More Effective Meetings,* estimates that the waste equals 20 percent of payroll, which costs U.S. companies $420 billion a year.

This is not to say that meetings should be banned. It does say, however, that meetings should be held only if they are needed to accomplish specific objectives and other methods such as e-mail are not satisfactory. Kaye suggests asking what would happen if the meeting were not held. "If the answer is nothing, then cancel the meeting." Others simply ask the basic question, "Is this meeting really necessary?" If the answer is "yes," here are some guidelines for having an effective staff or committee meeting:

- **Limit attendance.** Only those who are directly involved should be invited.
- **Distribute the agenda in advance.** Let people know what will be discussed or decided, so they can think about the issues before the meeting. Experts recommend that you prioritize the agenda and plan to cover only two or three items.
- **Use a round table.** Everyone has equal positional status and equal access to each other. The next best alternative is a square table.
- **Set a time limit.** The agenda should clearly state the beginning and ending time of the meeting, so people can plan their day. A meeting should run a maximum of 60 to 90 minutes. The longer the meeting runs, the less effective it is.
- **Manage the meeting.** The chairperson must make sure the meeting stays on track. Do not allow an individual or the group to go off on tangents.
- **Budget time.** Set a time limit for discussion of a specific agenda item. Do not spend an excessive amount of time on an item that shortchanges other items on the agenda.
- **Know Robert's Rules of Order.** It may be unnecessary in an informal, friendly meeting, but knowledge of parliamentary procedure is helpful if the debate gets heated.

- **Close with a brief overview.** At the end of the meeting, summarize what has been accomplished, what will be done, and who will do it. Remember that meetings are held to make decisions, not just to discuss things.
- **Distribute a summary memo.** The chair or secretary should distribute a summary of the meeting within a day after the meeting. This helps remind people what was decided.

CLUB MEETINGS AND WORKSHOPS

Having meetings seems to be part of human nature. There are literally thousands of civic clubs, professional societies, trade associations, and hobby groups that have meetings that attract millions of people every year. In addition, many of these organizations sponsor workshops, seminars, and symposia on a regular basis.

Planning

The size and purpose of the meeting dictate the plan. Every plan must consider these questions: How many will attend? Who will attend? When and where will it be held? How long will it last? Who will speak? What topics will be covered? What facilities will be needed? Who will run it? What is its purpose? How do we get people to attend?

Location　If the meeting is to be held on the premises of the organization, the room can be reserved by contacting whoever is responsible for such arrangements.

Professional Tips

How Good Are Your Meetings?

Meetings are a way of life in all organizations, including all those committee meetings to brainstorm and plan a public relations campaign. Cliff Shaffran, writing in IABC's *Communication World*, suggests that the effectiveness of a meeting can be determined by asking yourself to rate the meeting from 1 (rarely) to 5 (always) on a number of criteria. How would you rate your last committee meeting on the following criteria?

- There is a clearly defined, results-focused theme and agenda.
- We make decisions and move forward; it isn't just a debating society.
- The meetings are friendly and don't generate conflict.
- Everyone contributes.
- No one dominates the discussion.
- Communication is open and positive.
- We generate many creative ideas.

- We challenge the status quo to explore alternative ideas and solutions.
- Everyone is energized and focused.
- We fully maximize the knowledge and expertise of all participants.
- We keep on time.
- We always achieve our desired results.
- We have good return on time invested.
- Everyone enjoys the process.

If the meeting is to be held at some outside location, you will have to talk to the person in charge. In a hotel or restaurant that person is the catering manager. In a school, it may be the principal; in a church, the minister or priest. Many firms have rooms that are made available to nonprofit groups, so consider this possibility if your organization is eligible.

The meeting room must be the right size for the expected audience. If it is too large, the audience will feel that the meeting has failed to draw the expected attendance. If it is too small, the audience will be uncomfortable. Most hotels have a number of meeting rooms ranging in size from small to very large.

Having selected a room, make sure that the audience can find it. The name of the meeting and the name of the room should be registered on the hotel or restaurant's schedule of events for a particular day.

Seating   A variety of seating arrangements can be used, depending on the purpose of the meeting. A monthly club meeting, for example, often features a luncheon or dinner. In this case, attendees are usually seated at round tables of six or eight, where they first have a meal and then listen to a speaker.

Seminars, designed primarily for listening, usually have what is called "theater" seating. Rows of seats are set up, all facing the speakers. Such meetings may be held in theaters or auditoriums.

A workshop or a small seminar, on the other hand, may use what is called "lunchroom" seating. This uses long tables with chairs on one side so that attendees can take notes or set up laptop computers.

Occasionally, large meetings are broken into discussion groups. Typically, the audience starts in one large room, where a speaker gives information and states a problem. The audience then moves into another room, or set of rooms, where round tables seating 8 or 10 people are available. A discussion leader is designated for each table. After the problem has been discussed, the leaders gather the opinions and the audience returns to the first room, where reports from each group are given to the entire assembly.

Facilities   A small meeting may not need much in the way of facilities, whereas a large and formal one may require a considerable amount of equipment and furnishings. Following are things that should be considered—and supplied if needed. You should check everything one or two hours before the meeting.

- **Meeting identification.** Is it posted on the bulletin board near the building entrance? Are directional signs needed?
- **Lighting.** Is it adequate? Can it be controlled? Where are the controls? Who will handle them?
- **Charts.** Are they readable? Is the easel adequate? Who will handle the charts?
- **Screen.** Is it visible to the entire audience? If some seats are badly located, how do you prevent people from using them? Who will refer people to better locations?

How to Plan a Club Meeting

Every meeting requires its own specialized checklist, but here is a general "to do" list for a local dinner meeting of a service club or a professional association.

In Advance

- What is the purpose of the meeting? Business? Social? Continuing education? Combination?

- What date and time are best for maximum attendance?

- What size audience do you realistically expect?

- Select restaurant facility at least four to six weeks in advance.

- Confirm in writing the following: date, time, menu, cocktails, seating plan, number of guaranteed reservations, and projected costs.

- Enlist speaker four to six weeks in advance. If speaker is in high demand, make arrangements several months in advance. Discuss nature of talk, projected length, and whether audiovisual aids will be used that require special equipment.

- Publicize the meeting to the membership and other interested parties. This should be done a minimum of three weeks in advance. Provide complete information on speaker, date, time, location, meal costs, and reservation procedure.

- Organize a phone committee to call members 72 hours before the event if reservations are lagging. A reminder phone call is often helpful in gaining last-minute reservations.

On the Meeting Day

- Get a final count on reservations, and make an educated guess as to how many people might arrive at the door without a reservation.

- Check speaker's travel plans and last-minute questions or requirements.

- Give catering manager revised final count for meal service. In many instances, this might have to be done 24 to 72 hours in advance of the meeting day.

- Check room arrangements one to two hours in advance of the meeting. Have enough tables been set up? Are tables arranged correctly for the meeting? Does the microphone system work?

- Prepare a timetable for the evening's events. For example, cocktails may be scheduled from 6:15 to 7 P.M., with registration going on at the same time. Dinner from 7 to 8 P.M., followed by 10 minutes of announcements. At 8:10 P.M., the speaker will have 20 minutes to talk, followed by an additional 10 minutes for questions. Your organizational leaders, as well as the serving staff, should be aware of this schedule.

- Set up a registration table just inside or outside the door. A typed list of reservations should be available, as well as name tags, meal tickets, and a cash box for making change. Personnel at the registration table should be briefed and in place at least 30 minutes before the announced time.

- Decide on a seating plan for the head table, organize place cards, and tell VIPs as they arrive where they will be sitting.

- Designate three or four members of the organization as a hospitality committee to meet and greet newcomers and guests.

After the Meeting

- Settle accounts with the restaurant, or indicate where an itemized bill should be mailed.

- Check the room to make sure no one forgot briefcases, handbags, eyeglasses, or other belongings.

- Send thank-you notes to the speaker and any committee members who helped plan or host the meeting.

- Prepare a summary of the speaker's comments for the organization's newsletter and, if appropriate, send a news release to local media.

- **Projectors and video equipment.** Are they hooked up? Focused? Is there a spare bulb? Are materials in the right order and properly loaded? Who will operate the equipment? Who do you contact at the facility if something is not working?

- **Seating and tables.** Are there enough seats for the audience you are expecting? Are they arranged properly?

- **Tape recorder.** Is it loaded? Set for the right speed? Hooked up? In the right position? Who will run it?

- **Telephone.** Where is it? If it is in the meeting room, who will answer?

- **Wiring.** For all electrical equipment, can wires be kicked loose or trip someone?

- **Speaker's podium.** Is it positioned properly? What about a reading light? Is there a PA system? Is it working?

- **Water and glasses.** For speakers? For audience?

- **Audience and speaker aids.** Are there programs or agendas? Will there be notepaper, pencils, handout materials?

- **Name tags.** For speakers? For all attendees?

Invitations   For clubs, an announcement in the newsletter of the meeting—time, place, purpose, and who is to attend—should be adequate. For external groups—people who are not required to attend but whose presence is desired—invitations are necessary. They should go out early enough for people to fit the meeting into their schedules—three to six weeks is a common lead time. See Figure 17.5 for an example of an invitation reply card.

The invitation should tell the time, day, date, place (including the name of the room), purpose, highlights of the program (including names of speakers), and a way for the person to RSVP. This may be a telephone number, an e-mail address, a reply card mailed back to the event's organizers, or even an online registration service that handles everything from making the reservation to processing the credit card information to pay for the event. A map showing the location and parking facilities is advisable if the facility is not widely known. See Figure 17.1 for an example of a basic invitation for the shrimp-eating contest that was mentioned in Chapter 4.

Registration

If everyone knows everyone else, registration and identification are highly informal, but if the group is large, it is customary to have a registration desk or table at the entrance. Here the names of arrivals are checked against lists of individuals who said they would attend. If there is no invitation list and the presence or absence of any of the people who were invited is not important (as at a regular meeting of a club or association), the arrivals generally sign in on a plain sheet of paper, and no one checks the membership roster.

Greeting   A representative of the sponsoring organization should be at the entrance of the room. If the number attending is not too large, a personal welcome

Figure 17.1 Invitations Should Give the 5Ws
Invitations can be relatively simple, like this one, or very elaborate. Whatever the format, you should give the basic information: Who, What, Where, When, and Why. The Old Bay Seasoning contest, also featured in Chapter 4, generated about 1,600 entries and was covered by television stations across the United States. *(Courtesy of Old Bay Seasoning and its public relations firm, Hunter Public Relations.)*

You are cordially invited to attend the first-ever Old Bay® Peel & Eat Shrimp Classic. Come witness seafood lovers from across the country competing in a timed shrimp eating contest for a chance to win $10,000.

Special guest emcee, Tory McPhail
Executive chef, Commander's Palace
New Orleans

Friday, August 30, 2002
Harborplace
200 East Pratt Street
Baltimore, MD
11:30 a.m. - 12:30 p.m.

To RSVP or for more information, please call Amanda Hirschhorn at Hunter Public Relations. Phone: 212.679.6600 x239 or call Laurie Harrsen at Old Bay. Phone: 410-527-8753

See reverse for directions.

is in order. Where hundreds of people are expected, this isn't possible, but the chairperson should greet the audience in his or her opening remarks.

Name Tags Name tags are a good idea at almost any meeting. You should use label-making software to prepare name tags for everyone with advance reservations. Names should be printed in bold, large block letters so that they can be read easily from a distance of 4 feet. If the person's affiliation is used, this can be in smaller bold letters.

For people showing up without advance registration, you can have felt-tip pens available for on-the-spot name tags. However, a nice touch is to designate one person at the registration desk to make these tags so that they look neat and consistent. Most name tags are self-adhesive. Plastic badges can also be used, but some people object to sticking pins through their clothes.

Program

At any meeting, the word "program" has two meanings. It is what goes on at the meeting, and it is the printed listing of what goes on.

The meeting must have a purpose. To serve that purpose, it is necessary to have a chairperson who controls and directs the meeting, introduces the speakers, and keeps discussions from wandering. It is necessary to have speakers who will inform, persuade, or activate the listeners.

The printed program that is handed out to the audience in a workshop or seminar tells them what is going to happen, when, and where. It lists all the speakers, the time they will speak, coffee breaks, lunch breaks, and any other facts attendees should know about the meeting. Because speakers may have last-minute changes in their plans, the programs should not be printed until the last possible moment.

Speakers   Speakers should be selected early—several months in advance, if possible. They should be chosen because of their expertise, their crowd-drawing capacity, and their speaking ability. It is a good idea to listen to any prospective speaker before tendering an invitation, or at least to discuss your intention with someone who has heard the person speak before. Many prominent people are simply not effective speakers.

When a speaker has agreed to give a talk, it is essential to make sure that the speaker has all the information he or she needs to prepare remarks and get to the meeting. Barbara Nichols, owner of a hospitality management firm in New York City, gave this checklist to *Meeting News* regarding what speakers need to know about your meeting:

- Information about the meeting sponsor and attendees
- Meeting purpose and objectives
- Presentation location, including meeting room, date, and hour
- Topic and length of presentation
- Anticipated size of the audience
- Session format, including length of time allowed for audience questions
- Names of those sharing the platform, if any, and their topics
- Name of person who will make the introductions
- Remuneration policy, including when payment will be made
- Travel and housing arrangements
- Meeting room setup and staging information
- Audiovisual equipment needed
- Dress code (business attire, resort wear, black tie)
- Request for presentation outline, handout material
- Release to tape or videotape the remarks
- Arrangements for spouse, if invited

Meals   Club meetings and workshops often occur at a meal time. In fact, many meetings include breakfast, lunch, or dinner.

Early morning breakfast meetings have the advantage of attracting people who cannot take the time during the day to attend such functions. A full breakfast, served buffet style, is a popular choice because it allows everyone to select what they normally eat for breakfast. People attending a half-day or full-day workshop often partake of a self-served continental breakfast—rolls, juice, and coffee—during the registration period just prior to the start of the meeting.

Luncheons are either sit-down affairs with a fixed menu or a buffet. A 30- to 45-minute cocktail period can precede a luncheon, usually during registration as guests arrive. A good schedule for a typical luncheon is registration, 11:30; luncheon, noon; adjournment, 1:30. In rare instances, the adjournment can be as late as 2 P.M., but it should never be later than that.

Dinner meetings are handled in much the same way as luncheons. A typical schedule is registration and cocktails, 6 P.M.; dinner, 7 P.M.; speaker, 8 P.M.; adjournment, between 8:30 and 9 P.M. Speakers, as mentioned in Chapter 16, should talk about 20 minutes.

You will need to have an accurate count of people who will attend a meal function. The hotel or restaurant facility will need a count at least 24 hours in advance to prepare the food and set up table service. The standard practice is for the organization to guarantee a certain number of meals, plus or minus 10 percent. If fewer than what is guaranteed show up, you still pay for the meals.

BANQUETS

Banquets, by definition, are fairly large and formal functions. They are held to honor an individual, raise money for a charitable organization, or celebrate an event such as an organization's anniversary.

A banquet or even a reception may have 100 or 1,000 people in attendance, and staging a successful one takes a great deal of planning. The budget, in particular, needs close attention. A banquet coordinator has to consider such costs as (1) food, (2) room rental, (3) bartenders, (4) decorations and table centerpieces, (5) audiovisual requirements, (6) speaker fees, (7) entertainment, (8) photographers, (9) invitations, (10) tickets, and (11) marketing and promotion.

All these components, of course, must be factored into establishing the per-ticket cost of the event. You are not just paying $50 to $100 for the traditional rubber chicken dinner but for the total cost of staging the event. If the purpose is to raise money for a worthy charitable organization or a political candidate, tickets might go for $100 to $250. The actual price, of course, depends on how fancy the banquet is and how much you are paying for a speaker.

A well-known personality as a banquet speaker usually helps ticket sales, but it also is a major expense in your budget. Karen Kendig, president of the Speaker's Network, told *PR Tactics* that the going rate is $3,000 to $10,000 for "bread and butter" business-type talks, $15,000 and up for entertainment celebrities, and $50,000 to $60,000 for well-known politicians. A number of firms, such as the Washington Speaker's Bureau in Alexandria, Virginia and the Harry Walker Agency in New York, represent celebrity speakers.

Such fees cannot be fully absorbed in the cost of an individual ticket so, in addition to sending out individual invitations, there usually is a committee that personally asks corporations and other businesses to sponsor the event or buy a table for employees, clients, or friends. A corporate table of eight, for example,

Professional Tips

Making a Budget for a Special Event

All events have two sides of the ledger: costs and revenues. It is important to prepare a detailed budget so you know exactly how much an event will cost. This will enable you to also figure out how much you will need to charge so you at least break even. Here are some items that you need to consider:

Facilities

Rental of meeting or reception rooms.

Set up of podiums, microphones, audio-visual equipment

Food Service

Number of meals to be served

Cost per person

Gratuities

Refreshments for breaks

Bartenders for cocktail hours

Wine, liquor, soft drinks

Decorations

Table decorations

Direction signs

Design and Printing

Invitations

Programs

Tickets

Name tags

Promotional flyers

Postage

Postage for invitations

Mailing house charges

Recognition Items

Awards, plaques, trophies

Engraving

Framing

Calligraphy

Miscellaneous

VIP travel and expenses

Speaker fees

Security

Transportation

Buses

Vans

Parking

Entertainment

Fees

Publicity

Advertising

News releases

Banners

Postage

Office Expenses

Phones

Supplies

Complimentary tickets

Staff travel and expenses

Data processing

may go for $25,000 or more, depending on the prestige and purpose of the event.

Working with Banquet Managers

When organizing a banquet, you usually contact the catering or banquet manager of the restaurant or hotel at least three or four months before your event. He or she will discuss menus, room facilities, availability of space, and a host of other items with you to determine exactly what you need.

Hotels and restaurants have special menus for banquets, which are often subject to some negotiation. If you plan a banquet during the week, for example, the restaurant or hotel might be willing to give you more favorable rates because week nights aren't ordinarily booked. However, if you insist on having a banquet on Friday or Saturday night—which is the most popular time—you can expect to pay full rates.

A banquet usually has a fixed menu, but you must also make a vegetarian dish available to those who request it. In general, a popular choice for a meat entree is chicken or fish. Pork may be objectionable on religious grounds, and many people refrain from red meats such as beef. Offering two entrees requires the extra work of providing coded tickets for the waiters, and the hotel or restaurant may charge more for the meal. Get the catering manager's advice before ordering multiple entrees.

When figuring food costs, many amateur planners often forget about tax and gratuity, which can add 25 percent or more to any final bill. In addition, there are corkage fees if you provide your own liquor or wine. In many establishments, corkage fees are set rather high to discourage you from bringing your own refreshment. At one banquet, for example, the organizers thought it was a great coup to have the wine donated, only to find out that the hotel charged a corkage fee of $10 per bottle.

Logistics and Timing

Organizing a banquet requires considerable logistics, timing, and teamwork. First, you have to establish a time line for the entire process—from the contacting of catering managers to the sending out of invitations and lining up a speaker. Second, you need a detailed time line for the several days or day of the event to ensure that everything is in place. Third, you should have a time line for the event itself, so it begins and ends at a reasonable time. A good example of time lines is Chevron's Conservation Awards banquet. Figures 17.2 and 17.3 show the day of the event and the event itself.

In addition, you need to work out the logistics to ensure that registration lines are kept to a minimum and everyone can easily find their table. Table numbers must be highly visible. If the group is particularly large (1,000 or more), you should provide a seating chart just inside the hall so people can locate where they are sitting.

COCKTAIL PARTIES AND RECEPTIONS

A short cocktail party, as mentioned previously, can precede the start of a club's luncheon or dinner. It can also be an event in itself or part of a reception. The purpose is to have people socialize; it also is a cost-effective way to celebrate an organization's or individual's achievement, to introduce a new chief executive to the employees and the community, or simply to allow college alumni to get together.

CHEVRON CONSERVATION AWARDS PROGRAM BANQUET

	Event Schedule	Staff Member
9:00 a.m.	Meet with hotel catering manager/staff Confirm event arrangements	Bill/Lauren/Deb
	5:00-6:00 VIP reception & photos 6:30-7:30 general reception 7:30-8:30 dinner (see attached schedule) 8:30-10:00 program-speaker & award presentation	
12:00-3:00	Coordinate ballroom set up Staging & A/V equipment	Deb/Bob
12:00-3:00	Media interviews-award honorees	B.J.
1:00	Complete seating arrangements	Bill/Mary
2:00	Complete and organize nametags	Lauren/Gail
2:00-3:00	Rehearsal/AV run through	Bill/Deb/Bob/Clair
4:00	Award booklets/program each place setting	Gail
4:30	Lobby signs	Gail
5:00-6:00	VIP reception-coordinate honoree photos (see attached)	Lauren/Gail
6:00	Brief hotel staff re reception table staffing	Gail

Figure 17.2 Time Lines Are Important
Banquets require coordination of logistics on the day of the event. This is a list of activities that had to be completed before the actual banquet scheduled in the evening.
(Courtesy of Chevron Corporation, San Francisco.)

In any event, the focus is on interaction; not speeches. If there is a ceremony or speech, it should last a maximum of 5 to 10 minutes.

Cocktail parties can last for several hours, and the typical format is a large room where most people will stand instead of sit. This facilitates social interaction and allows people to move freely around the room. Such gatherings, like any other event, require advance planning and logistics.

It is important, for example, that food be served in the form of appetizers, sandwiches, cheese trays, nuts, and chips. People get hungry, and food helps offset some effects of drinking. The bar is the centerpiece of any cocktail party, but you should make sure there are plenty of nonalcoholic beverages available, too. Urns of coffee, punch, and tea should be readily available in other locations around the room.

Such precautions will limit your liability if someone does get drunk and has an accident on the way home. You can also limit your liability if you have a **no-host bar**, which means that guests buy their own drinks.

CHEVRON CONSERVATION AWARDS BANQUET
JW MARRIOTT HOTEL
WASHINGTON, DC
WEDNESDAY, MAY 13

Crew Agenda

3:30 – 5:00 p.m.	Program agenda review – participants and staff only. Live run-through of C. Ghylin's remarks. (Grand Ballroom)
5:00 – 6:00	Private pre-reception for honorees, judges, Chevron staff. Honoree photo session including E. Zern and J. Sullivan. (Suite 1231)
6:30 – 7:15	Greetings and reception, open bar. Photo opportunities available. (Grand Ballroom Foyer)
7:15 – 7:30	Close bar, enter Grand Ballroom.
7:30 – 7:35	C. Ghylin: Welcome and opening remarks.
7:30 – 8:20	Dinner served.
8:20 – 8:25	C. Ghylin: Introduces special guests at head table, introduces E. Zern.
8:25 – 8:30	E. Zern: Welcome, honoree toast, introduces judges, completes remarks.
8:30 – 8:35	C. Ghylin: Introduces J. Sullivan.
8:35 – 8:45	J. Sullivan: Remarks.
8:45 – 8:50	C. Ghylin: Introduces slide presentation.
8:50 – 9:25	Slide presentation. (C. Ghylin remains at podium) (a) Introduces/explains honoree category; (b) Comments on professionals. Introduces/explains honoree category. (c) Comments on citizens. Introduces/explains organizations' honoree category.
9:25 – 9:40	C. Ghylin: Comments on organizations. Invites J. Sullivan and E. Zern for plaque presentation. Plaque presentation.
9:40 – 9:45	C. Ghylin: Final remarks.
9:45 p.m.	America the Beautiful.

Figure 17.3 Keep on Schedule
The Time Line for Chevron's Conservation Awards Banquet. The compilation of a time line, and going over it with the master of ceremonies, helps keep the event on schedule.
(Courtesy of Chevron Corporation, San Francisco.)

Most cocktail parties, however, have a **hosted bar**, meaning that drinks are free. This is particularly true when a corporation is hosting the cocktail party or reception for journalists, customers, or community leaders. In every case, it is important that bartenders be trained to spot individuals who appear to be under the influence of alcohol and politely suggest a nonalcoholic alternative.

Figure 17.4 Flyer for a Community Open House
This flyer, in multiple colors, was distributed to various community groups to promote the grand opening of a new city/university library. It gives the basic 5Ws and also entices the public with a list of activities for the day. The reverse side of the flyer gave the basic information in Spanish and Vietnamese to reflect the multicultural nature of the city. The outstanding programs and materials received an American Library Association (ALA) award.
(Courtesy of the Dr. Martin Luther King, Jr. Library, San Jose, CA.)

Organizations also try to control the level of drinking by offering only beer or wine instead of hard liquor. Still others issue two or three free drink tickets to arriving guests, with the understanding that there will be a charge for any additional drinks.

Figure 17.5 A Reception Reply Card
Events that cost money, such as banquets and receptions, require a reply card that individuals can fill out and use to pay for the event. This reply card and envelope was used for a VIP reception on the evening before the public grand opening of the city/university library mentioned in Figure 17.4.
(Courtesy of the Dr. Martin Luther King, Jr. Library, San Jose, CA.)

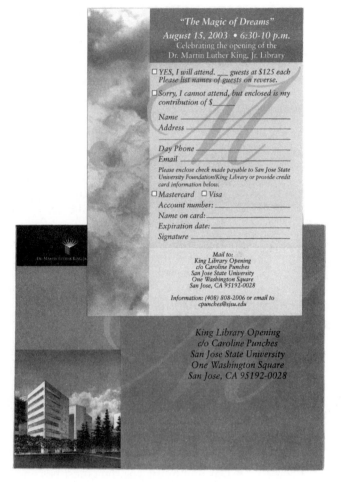

A cocktail party, like a meal function, requires you to talk with the catering manager to order food items and decide how many bartenders are needed. As a rule of thumb, there should be one bartender per 75 people. For large events, bars are situated in several locations around the room, to disperse the crowd and shorten lines.

It is also important to find out how the facility will bill you for beverages consumed. If the arrangement is by the bottle, this often leads to the problems of bartenders being very generous in pouring drinks because more empty bottles mean higher profits for the caterer.

Starting a cocktail party is easy—just open the bar at the announced time. Closing a party is not so easy. The only practical way is to close the bar. The invitation may indicate a definite time for closing, but don't rely on this. A vocal announcement will do the job. The smoothest way is to say, "The bar will close in 10 minutes." This gives guests a chance to get one more drink.

OPEN HOUSES AND PLANT TOURS

Open houses and plant tours are conducted primarily to develop favorable public opinion about an organization. Generally they are planned to show the facilities where the organization does its work and, in plant tours, how the work is done. A factory might have a plant tour to show how it turns raw materials into finished products. A hospital open house could show its emergency facilities, diagnostic equipment, operating rooms, and patient rooms.

Open houses are customarily one-day affairs. However, if large numbers of people are to attend, the event may be extended to more than one day. Attendance is usually by invitation, but in other instances, the event is announced in the general media, and anyone who chooses to attend may do so. See Figure 17.4 on page 510 for a flyer announcing a community open house. If you're having a community open house, you also have to think about entertainment and activities for the attendees.

Many plants offer tours daily and regularly while the plant is in operation. These tours are most common among producers of consumer goods such as beer, wine, food products, clothing, and small appliances. These daily tours are geared to handle only a few people at any one time, whereas open houses generally have a large number of guests and normal operations are not feasible during the tour.

Since the purpose of an open house or a plant tour is to create favorable opinion about the organization, it must be carefully planned, thoroughly explained, and smoothly conducted. The visitors must understand what they are seeing. This requires careful routing, control to prevent congestion, signs, and guides. All employees who will be present should understand the purpose of the event and be thoroughly coached in their duties. Rehearsal plus much checking and rechecking is imperative.

Among the principal things to include in the plans for an open house or a plant tour are these:

- **Day and hour.** The time must be convenient for both the organization and the guests.
- **Guests.** These may be families of employees, customers, representatives of the community, suppliers and competitors, reporters, or others whose goodwill is desirable.
- **Invitations.** These should be sent out well in advance. A month is common.

If a plant tour is a continuing daily event, the availability of the tour should be announced by signs near the plant and possibly by advertising or publicity. For any open house or plant tour, think of these points:

- **Vehicles.** Parking must be available, and there should be a map on the invitation showing how to get there and where to park.
- **Reception.** A representative of the organization should meet and greet all arriving guests. If guests are important people, they should meet the top officials of the organization.
- **Rest rooms.** If you are expecting a large crowd, arrange for portable toilets to supplement the regular facilities.

- **Safety.** Hazards should be conspicuously marked and well lighted. Dangerous equipment should be barricaded.

- **Routing.** Routes should be well marked and logical (in a factory, the route should go from raw materials through production steps to the finished product). A map should be given to each visitor if the route is long or complicated.

- **Guides.** Tours should be led by trained guides who have a thorough knowledge of the organization and can explain in detail what visitors are seeing on the tour.

- **Explanation.** Signs, charts, and diagrams may be necessary at any point to supplement the words of the guides. The guides must be coached to say exactly what the public should be told. Many experts can't explain what they do, so a prepared explanation is necessary.

- **Housekeeping and attire.** The premises should be as clean as possible. Attire should be clean and appropriate. A punch press operator doesn't wear a necktie, but his overalls need not be greasy.

- **Emergencies.** Accidents or illness may occur. All employees should know what to do and how to reach the first-aid personnel, who should be readily available.

CONVENTIONS

A convention is a series of meetings, usually spread over two or more days. The purpose is to gather and exchange information, meet other people with similar interests, discuss and act on common problems, and enjoy recreation and social interchange.

Most conventions are held by national membership groups and trade associations. Because the membership is widespread, a convention is nearly always "out of town" to many attendees, so convention arrangements must give consideration to this.

Planning

It is necessary to begin planning far in advance of the actual event. Planning for even the smallest convention should start months before the scheduled date; for large national conventions, it may begin several years ahead and require hundreds or thousands of hours of work. The main things involved in planning a convention are timing, location, facilities, exhibits, program, recreation, attendance, and administration.

Timing Timing must be convenient for the people who are expected to attend. Avoid peak work periods. Summer vacation is appropriate for educators, and after harvest is suitable for farmers. Preholiday periods are bad for retailers, and midwinter is probably a poor time in the northern states but may be very good in the South. Here, as in every area dealing with the public, it is imperative to know your audience and to plan for their convenience.

Professional Tips

How to Plan an Open House

Preplanning
Initial Planning

- Select and research the date.
- Set up your committees or areas of responsibility.
- Determine your budget.

Open House Announcement

- Notify employees and recruit their assistance.
- Invite staff and families, if appropriate.
- Develop your mailing list.
- Design and print invitations.
- Arrange advertising.
- Prepare and distribute press releases/posters.
- Create radio/TV spots.

Food and Beverages

- Decide on the menu.
- Arrange for catering or volunteer servers.
- Arrange for cleanup.

Equipment/Decorations

- Determine the equipment available from your organization.
- Arrange for necessary rentals, such as tables, chairs, or an outdoor tent.
- Arrange for table linens, plates, and silverware.
- Plan flowers in strategic locations.

Specialty Advertising

- Arrange for giveaways that increase your organization's visibility, such as balloons, T-shirts, and mugs.

Media Relations

- Invite the media personally and by mail.
- Develop and distribute press releases announcing the event.
- Arrange for media coverage on the day of the open house.

- Arrange for a photographer to cover the event (photos can be used for publicity or internal communications).

Day of Event
Reception

- Set up a staffed reception table with a sign-in book.
- Distribute information on your organization and giveaways.
- Have staff explain the activities to guests.

Tours
(Some preparation required in planning process)

- Develop a floor plan for tours to ensure consistency.
- Arrange a regular tour schedule, such as every 30 minutes.
- Offer an incentive (such as a T-shirt) to those who complete the tour.
- Brief tour guides on the key points to cover and how to field questions.
- Arrange for visuals such as a display or demonstrations during the tour.

Activities/Entertainment

This depends on the nature of your event but could include:

- Health education displays or screenings.
- A road race.
- Games, a magician, or a storyteller for the children.
- A local community band.
- A short questionnaire to evaluate community response to the event and issues related to your organization.

Ceremony

- Arrange a focal point for your open house, such as a ribbon cutting, awards ceremony, music/dance performance, or brief message from the company president.

Location   As real estate agents say, it's location, location, location. A national convention can be anywhere in the country, but one in Fairbanks, Alaska, is unlikely; yet one in Honolulu or New Orleans could be a great success because the glamor of the location would outweigh the cost and time of travel. Many organizations rotate their conventions from one part of the state, region, or country to another to equalize travel burdens.

Another factor in choosing a location is availability of accommodations. There must be enough rooms to house the attendees and enough meeting rooms of the right size. Timing enters into this, because many such accommodations are booked months or even years in advance. Large cities usually have large convention facilities and numerous hotels, but early reservations are necessary for such popular cities as San Francisco, New York, New Orleans, Las Vegas, and San Diego. Once a tentative location has been selected, you must find out if the convention can be handled at the time chosen. Early action on this can forestall later changes. Be sure to get a definite price on guest rooms as well as meeting rooms.

Small conventions are often held in resorts, but accessibility is a factor. If the visitors have to change airlines several times or if the location is hard to get to by automobile, the glamor may fail to compensate for the inconvenience.

Facilities   For every meeting of the convention it is necessary to have a room of the right size and the equipment needed for whatever is to go on in that room. The convention might start with a general meeting in a large ballroom, where seating is theater fashion and the equipment consists of a public address system and a speaker's platform with the necessary accessories. After opening remarks, the convention might break into smaller groups that meet in different rooms with widely varying facilities.

One room may require a computer projector; another may need a whiteboard or an easel for charts; still another may need a VCR and monitor. In one room the seating may be around conference tables; another may have theater seating. To get everything right, you must know exactly what is to happen, who is going to participate, and when.

Exhibits   The makers and sellers of supplies that are used by people attending conventions frequently want to show their wares. This means that the convention manager must provide space suitable for that purpose. Most large convention centers have display rooms that can accommodate anything from books to bulldozers. There is a charge for the use of these rooms, and the exhibitors pay for the space they use.

The exhibit hall may be in the hotel where the convention is being held, or in a separate building. For example, McCormick Place is an enormous building on the Chicago lakefront. It is an easy taxi trip from the Loop, where conventions are usually based and where the visitors sleep. Eating facilities ranging from hotdog stands to elaborate dining rooms are to be found in almost any such building. Exhibits are covered in more detail when trade shows are discussed.

Program

A convention program usually has a basic theme. Aside from transacting the necessary organizational business, most of the speeches and other sessions will be devoted to various aspects of the theme. Themes can range from the specific "New Developments in AIDS Research" to the more general "Quality Management and Productivity." Some groups use an even broader theme such as "Connections" or "At the Crossroads."

With a theme chosen, the developer of the program looks for prominent speakers who have something significant to say on the subject. In addition, there may be a need for discussions, workshops, and other sessions focusing on particular aspects of the general theme.

The printed program for the convention is a schedule. It tells exactly when every session will be, what room it will be in, and who will speak on what subject. Large conventions often schedule different sessions at the same time. Attendees then choose which session they prefer.

The program schedule should be small enough to fit in a pocket or a handbag. Large programs may look impressive, but they are cumbersome to carry and easy to misplace. Printing of the program should be delayed until the last possible moment. Last-minute changes and speaker defaults are common.

Recreation   Recreation is a feature of practically all conventions. This may range from informal get-togethers to formal dances. Cocktail parties, golf tournaments, sightseeing tours, and free time are among the possibilities. Sometimes recreational events are planned to coincide with regular program sessions. These are patronized by spouses and by delegates who would rather relax than listen to a speaker.

Attendance   Getting people to attend a convention requires two things: an appealing program and a concerted effort to persuade members to attend. Announcements and invitations should go out several months in advance, to allow attendees to make their individual arrangements. A second and even a third mailing often is done in the weeks preceding the convention. Reply cards should be provided, accompanied by hotel reservation forms. (Remember that hotels generally offer special lower rates for conventions.)

Administration   Managing a convention is a strenuous job. The organization staff is likely to see very little of the program and a great many delegates with problems. Among the things that must be done are arranging for buses to convey delegates from the airport to the convention (if it is in a remote location) and to carry them on tours. Meeting speakers and getting them to the right place at the right time is another task.

People arriving at the convention headquarters must be met, registered, and provided with all the essentials (name tags, programs, and any other needed materials). A message center should be set up so that people can be informed of phone calls or other messages. (This can be as simple as a bulletin board near the registration desk.) Special arrangements should be made for the media. A small convention may interest only a few people from trade publications, but larger conventions may draw attention from the major media. In this case, a newsroom should be set up with telephones, fax machines, tables, and other needed equipment.

TRADE SHOWS

Trade shows are the ultimate marketing event. According to *Tradeshow Week* magazine, about 6,000 trade shows are held annually in the United States. They range in size from more than 100,000 attendees to those in very specialized industries that attract only several thousand people. It is estimated that about 65 million people attend trade shows on an annual basis. Figure 17.6 shows a typical trade show for the computer industry.

Figure 17.6 The Ultimate Marketing Event
Trade shows attract millions of people annually. They provide an opportunity to see products from a number of companies, generate sales leads, and attract media coverage. *(Marcus/Sipa Press.)*

Comdex, once described by *The Wall Street Journal* as the "King Kong" of computer trade shows, attracted an estimated 230,000 attendees during the late 1990s. They occupied most of the 94,000 hotel rooms in Las Vegas, walked around various company exhibits that occupied about 30 football fields, and generated about $320 million for the city's economy. Today, Comdex is still a major trade show, but the dot.com implosion and the general economic downtown has significantly reduced its size to only about 50,000 attendees.

Trade shows are still popular, but companies are increasingly cutting back on the number they attend. According to *PRWeek*, the focus is on ". . . more focused shows with a better targeted and more qualified audience of attendees and journalists." Michael Busselen, chairman of Fleishman-Hillard's tech practice, told the publication, "The days of being at every single show are over. Budgets are just too finite, too tight. It's fundamental you show ROI. If all the trade show does is send hundreds of sales people to Las Vegas, you haven't advanced your agenda."

Exhibit Booths

Although food and entertainment costs are high, the major expense at a trade show is the exhibit booth. At national trade shows, it is not unusual for a basic booth to start at $50,000, including design, construction, transportation, and space rental fees. Larger, more elaborate booths can easily cost between $500,000 and $1 million.

Any booth or exhibit should be designed for maximum visibility. Experts say you have about 10 seconds to attract a visitor as he or she walks down an aisle of booths. Consequently, companies try to outdazzle each other in booth designs. Here is how Karen Chan of Dow Jones International News described one booth at the Telecoms trade show in Geneva that attracted 200,000 visitors:

> Hewlett-Packard Co.'s stand features a huge, upside-down glass pyramid with ever ascending pink neon lights rising from its tip. The 3-floor stand took 30 men three months to build and contains 56 tons of steel, 20 tons of glass, 7 truckloads of lumber, 1,000 meters of neon, and 5 miles of cable. Let's not forget the 5,000 bolts holding it all together.

Not every company has the resources of HP, but here are some points to keep in mind if you get involved in planning an exhibit booth.

- Make the display or booth visually attractive. Use bright colors, large signs, and working models of products.
- Think about putting action in your display. Have a video or slide presentation running all the time.
- Use involvement techniques. Have a contest or raffle in which visitors can win a prize. An exhibitor at one show even offered free foot massages.
- Give people an opportunity to operate equipment or do something.
- Have knowledgeable, personable representatives on duty to answer questions and collect visitor business cards for follow-up.

- Offer useful souvenirs. A key chain, a shopping bag, a luggage tag, or even a copy of a popular newspaper or magazine will attract traffic.

Most organizations feel that the large investment in a booth at a trade show is worthwhile for two reasons. First, a trade show facilitates one-on-one communication with potential customers and helps generate sales leads. It also attracts many journalists, so it is easier and more efficient to provide press materials, arrange one-on-one interviews, and demonstrate what makes the product worth a story. Second, a booth allows an exhibitor to demonstrate how its products differ from the competition. This is more effective than just sending prospects a color brochure. It also is more cost-effective than making individual sales calls.

Hospitality Suites   Hospitality suites are an adjunct to the exhibit booth. Organizations use them to entertain key prospects, give more in-depth presentations, and talk about business deals.

The idea is that serious customers will stay in a hospitality suite long enough to hear an entire presentation, whereas they are likely to stop at an exhibit hall booth for only a few minutes. Although goodwill can be gained from free concerts and cocktail parties, the primary purpose of a hospitality suite is to generate leads that ultimately result in product sales.

Indeed, if a company generates $200 million in sales from the expenditure of $500,000 at a trade show, this is a very favorable return on investment (ROI).

Press Rooms

Every trade show has a press room, where the various exhibitors distribute media kits and other information to journalists. Press rooms typically have phone, fax, and e-mail facilities for reporters to file stories back to their employers.

As a public relations writer, you are often responsible for preparing an organization's media kit. Remember the rules about media kits discussed in Chapter 8; keep them short and relevant, and offer newsworthy information. A common complaint of reporters at a trade show is that "media kits" are only a compilation of sales brochures.

Another important part of your job is to personally contact reporters attending a trade show and offer one-on-one interviews with key executives. The competition is intense, so you have to be creative in pitching your ideas and showing why your company should be singled out for coverage.

Sarah Skerik, director of trade show markets for *PR Newswire*, provides some additional tips for working with the media during a trade show:

- Plan major product announcements to coincide with the show.
- Include the name of the trade show in your news releases, so journalists searching databases can log on using the show as a keyword.
- Include your booth number in all releases and announcements.
- Make it easy for journalists to track down key spokespeople and experts connected with your product by including cell phone, pager, and e-mail addresses in your materials.

- Have your spokespeople trained to make brief presentations and equip them with answers to the most-likely-asked questions.
- Consider a looped videotape to run in the booth with copies available to the media.
- Provide photos that show the product in use, in production, or in development.
- Provide online corporate logos, product photos, executive profiles, media kits, and PowerPoint presentations to those journalists who cannot attend or who prefer to lighten their suitcase by having everything in digital format.
- Keep hard copies of news releases, fact sheets, and brochures at the booth and in the press room.

Planning Guidelines

A trade show requires extensive planning months in advance. Gary Allen, owner of Allen Communications in Roseville, California, offers these guidelines:

- **Start early.** You should start planning and developing your exhibit booth 6 to 12 months ahead of time. Exhibit designers and builders need plenty of time to develop a booth.
- **State your goal.** It may be one or more of the following: (a) to develop sales leads, (b) to test-market a new product, (c) to position your company as the leader in the industry, (d) to launch a public relations or publicity campaign, (e) to gather demographic data on potential buyers, or (f) to launch a new product.
- **Establish a way to measure success.** Establish goals for amount of press coverage, number of people who visit the booth, number of sales leads, and number of business cards collected or addresses added to your mailing list.
- **Select the right trade shows.** There are thousands of trade shows. You must research which ones will attract the key audiences that you want to reach.
- **Develop a compelling exhibit.** At a large trade show where there are many exhibitors, a general rule is that you have only 10 seconds to attract someone's attention. Consequently, you need large, colorful graphics and movement. Many companies use large-screen videos.
- **Train the exhibit staff.** Use the most personable and most knowledgeable people you can find in your organization. Conduct a briefing session before the show so that they thoroughly understand what key messages should be communicated.
- **Promote your attendance in advance.** Use direct mail announcements to your target customers, and take out ads in trade magazines. In addition, send media kits and background materials to selected reporters before the trade show. Another tactic is to telephone reporters and offer interviews with key executives who will be attending the trade show.

For more information on suppliers that build and design exhibit booths, as well as trade shows in general, see the following Web sites: www.tscentral.com; www.expoguide.com; and www.reedexpo.com.

PROMOTIONAL EVENTS

Promotional events are planned primarily to promote product sales, increase organizational visibility, make friends, and raise money for a charitable cause.

The one essential skill for organizing promotional events is creativity. There are multiple "ho hum" events that compete for media attention and even attendance in every city, so it behooves you to come up with something "different" that creates buzz and interest.

Grand openings of stores or hotels, for example, can be pretty dull and generate a collective yawn from almost every journalist in town, let alone all the chamber of commerce types that attend such functions. So how do you come up with something new and different for the same old thing? First, you throw out the old idea of having a ribbon cutting. Second, you start thinking about a theme or idea that fits the situation and is out of the ordinary.

The reopening of the Morgan Hotel in San Antonio is a good example. The hotel featured a new restaurant Oro (meaning gold in Spanish), so the theme for the opening night reception was gold—complete with gold flowers, gold curtains, and even bikini-clad women who were coated with gold paint and served as living mannequins.

You can also increase attendance at a promotional event by using a television or film personality. The creative part is figuring out what "personality" fits the particular product or situation. Hormel Foods, for example, used the "moms" from such television shows as "Leave It to Beaver" and "Happy Days" to open its SPAM (not the junk mail) museum in Austin, Minnesota. A small cosmetic boutique and day spa in a small New Jersey town, however, got plenty of local media publicity just by having a few *Playboy* Playmates of the Month attend the grand opening.

A celebrity, or "personality" as they are called in the trade, is not exactly the most creative solution to every situation, but it's a time-honored way to increase the odds that the media will cover your event, because "prominence" is considered a basic news value.

A personality, however, can be a major budget item. Stars such as Oprah Winfrey, Sharon Stone, and Jerry Seinfield typically charge $100,000 for an appearance. If you don't have that kind of budget, you'll have to make do with what the business calls the the "up and coming" or the "down and going."

Claire Atkinson, writing in *PRWeek*, explains:

> For $5,000 to $10,000, you'll get young TV stars. For $10,000, you can get Ivana Trump to open your restaurant. The cost of a personal appearance by Shirley Maclaine is $50,000. Members of the cast of Friends charge $25,000. Super models Claudia Shiffer and Naomi Campbell command between $10,000 and $15,000 per appearance. And soap opera stars tend to get between $5,000 and $10,000 as do lesser TV stars. . . .

PR Casebook

A Promotional Event Launches Vanilla Coke

A late-night Internet search was the creative seed for the launching of Coca-Cola's new Vanilla Coke.

Mark Martin, director of public and media relations for Coca-Cola North America, was surfing the Net and discovered the Vanilla Bean Café in Pomfret, Connecticut, a hamlet of 3,800. Such a location for a major product launch was certainly unusual, but the café had the right name and was situated at the bottom of a hill. This allowed Coke to set up a cinematic dawn arrival of the first Vanilla Coke delivery in the United States that was broadcast live by the media.

According to *PRWeek,* "The delivery truck was wrapped with the new product graphics. When it rolled up to the café, the crowd of 500 local citizens parted to greet its arrival." Martin added, "They erupted with excitement when the driver lifted the door to hand out the first bottles. It was dramatic. It was great TV."

Concurrent with the café event, Coke's public relations firm Weber Shandwick booked tastetest segments on the morning network shows and even gave out samples to the crowds outside the studios. The unusual event and the media coverage paid off. For the month following the launch, Vanilla Coke was the top selling 20-ounce soft drink in supermarkets and drugstores across the country.

On occasion, if the event is for a charity that the celebrity supports as a personal cause, he or she will reduce or waive an appearance fee. One source for finding celebrities for promotional events is Celebrity Access (www.celebrityaccess.com), which claims an online database of 20,000 performers and celebrities. Another major organization is Celebrity Source in Los Angeles, which matches requests with the 4,500 names in its database. If you are looking for a sports personality, you can contact Burns Sports Celebrity Service in Chicago. These services provide you information on how to contact a celebrity's manager and publicist and make suggestions about who might be available, at what fee, for your event.

Events that attract large crowds require the same planning as an open house. You should be concerned about traffic flow, adequate restroom facilities, signage, and security. Security should also be arranged to handle crowd control, protect celebrities or government officials from being hassled, and make sure no other disruptions occur that would mar the event.

Liability insurance is a necessity, too. Any public event sponsored by an organization should be insured, just in case there is an accident and a subsequent lawsuit charging negligence. If your organization doesn't already have a blanket liability policy, you should get one for the event.

Charitable organizations also need liability insurance if they are running an event to raise money. This is particularly relevant if your organization is sponsoring an event that requires physical exertion, such as a 10-K run, a bicycle race, or even a hot-air balloon race.

Participants should sign a release form that protects the organization if someone suffers a heart attack or another kind of accident. One organization, which was sponsoring a 5-K "fun run," had the participants sign a statement that read in part: "I know that a road race is a potentially hazardous activity. . . . I assume all risk associated with running in this event, including, but not limited to, falls, contact with other participants, the effects of the weather, including high heat/or humidity, traffic and the conditions of the road."

Promotional events that use public streets and parks also need permits from various city departments. If you are sponsoring a run, you need to get a permit from the police or public safety department to block off streets and you need to hire off-duty police to handle traffic control. See Figure 17.7 for an example of a run sponsored by a corporation.

A food event, such as a chili cook-off or a German fest, requires permits from the public health department and, if liquor is served, a permit from the state alco-

Figure 17.7 Corporate Sponsorships of Events
Participants celebrate their accomplishments as they walk along with several hundred others to complete the Avon Walk for Breast Cancer in Portland, Oregon. Avon sponsored walks in eight cities to raise money for finding a cure for breast cancer, which is a topic of high concern for its customer base. *(Courtesy of Avon and its distributor, Feature Photo Service.)*

Professional Tips

Corporate Sponsorships: Another Kind of Event

Many corporations, in order to cut through the media clutter and establish brand identity, sponsor any number of events that, in turn, are covered by the media.

Molson, the Canadian beer, sponsors a number of NHL activities and formula car racing events—where people drink a lot of beer. Volvo, seeking kinship with a higher-class audience, sponsors tennis tournaments. And General Electric, going for the gold, has paid about $200 million to become a worldwide Olympics sponsor through 2012.

On the other hand, some corporations are more adventure minded. Bertrand Piccard and Brian Jones were the first to circumvent the globe in a hot-air balloon that was named Breitling Orbiter 3, after the Swiss watch company that sponsored their endeavor. The result, of course, was terrific; the Breitling name emblazoned on the balloon was on practically every major magazine cover around the world.

In North America alone, about $10 billion is spent by corporations on sponsorship of various events. According to the *Economist*, about two-thirds of this total are sponsorship fees for sporting events. If your employer or client is thinking about sponsoring an event, here are some guidelines you should apply:

- Can the company afford to fulfill the obligation? The sponsorship fee is just the starting point. Count on doubling it to have an adequate marketing and public relations campaign to publicize the event and your particular event.
- Is the event or organization compatible with the company's values and mission statement?
- Does the event reach the organization's target audiences?
- Are the event organizers experienced and professional?
- Will the field representatives be able to use the event as a platform for increasing sales?
- Does the event give the organization a chance to develop new contracts and business opportunities?
- Can you make a multiple-year sponsorship contract that will reinforce brand identity on a regular, consistent basis?
- Is there an opportunity to get employee involvement and raise their morale?
- Is the event compatible with the personality of the organization or its products?
- Can you do trade-offs of products and in-kind services to help defray the costs?

Adapted from: Wilcox, Dennis L., Cameron, Glen, et.al. *Public Relations Strategies and Tactics*, 7th edition, 2003. Boston: Allyn & Bacon, p. 342.

hol board. If the event is held inside a building, a permit is often required from the fire inspector.

You must also deal with the logistics of arranging cleanup, providing basic services such as water and medical aid, registering craft and food vendors, and posting signs. Promotion of an event can often be accomplished by having a radio station or

PR Casebook

The World's Largest Ice Cream Cake

Creativity plays a major role in planning a promotional event. The challenge: how should Baskin-Robbins celebrate international ice cream month? The solution: garner worldwide publicity by building the world's largest ice cream cake in a highly unusual location.

The ice cream maker's public relations firm, Fleishman-Hillard in Los Angeles, suggested that media coverage could be enhanced if the event was held in one of the hottest places on earth—Dubai. Baskin-Robbins, for the occasion, created the ultimate summer dessert by creating a cake that contained 5.5 tons of ice cream. Figure 17.8 shows the cake and the children asked to sample it.

The photo of the cake, plus a caption, was picked up by the media in many countries. In addition, Baskin-Robbins achieved a bit of lasting fame because the cake made the *Guinness Book of World Records*.

Figure 17.8 Five Tons of Ice Cream
Baskin-Robbins made the world's largest ice cream cake as a promotional event for international ice cream month.
(Courtesy of Baskin-Robbins and its public relations firm, Fleishman-Hillard, Los Angeles.)

local newspaper co-sponsor the event. See Figure 17.8 for an example of a creative promotional event that generated worldwide coverage.

SUMMARY

- Events and meetings don't just happen. They must be planned with attention to every detail. Nothing must be left to chance.

- Before scheduling a staff or committee meeting, always ask, "Is this meeting really necessary?" You can make meetings more effective if you distribute an agenda in advance, adhere to a schedule, and keep people from going off on tangents.

- Club meetings and workshops require you to consider such factors as time, location, seating, facilities, invitations, name tags, menu, speakers, registration, and costs.

- Banquets are elaborate affairs that require extensive advance planning. In additional to the factors necessary for a club meeting, you have to consider decorations, entertainment, audiovisual facilities, speaker fees, and seating charts.

- Cocktail parties and receptions require precautions about the amount of alcohol consumed, and the availability of food and nonalcoholic drinks. Possible liability is an important consideration.

- Open houses and plant tours require meticulous planning and routing, careful handling of visitors, and thorough training of all personnel who will be in contact with the visitors.

- Conventions require the skills of professional managers who can juggle multiple events and meetings over a period of several days. A convention may include large meetings, cocktail parties, receptions, tours, and banquets.

- Trade shows are the ultimate marketing events and attract millions of attendees annually. Exhibit booths may cost from $50,000 to $1 million.

- A celebrity at your promotional event will attract crowds and media attention, but appearance fees can be very high.

- A promotional event may be a "grand opening" of a facility or a 10-K run sponsored by a charitable organization. It is important to consider such factors as city permits, security, and liability insurance.

ADDITIONAL RESOURCES

Achilles, Lisa. "Special Events: Check Your List and Check It Twice." *PR Tactics*, July 2002, p. 11.

Blumenfeld, Jeff. "Discover How Adventure Marketing Can Break Through the Clutter." *O'Dwyer's PR Services Report*, December 2001, pp. 32–33.

Gaschen, Dennis. "High Society: Generating Coverage for Special Events." *PR Tactics*, December 2002, p. 8.

Gordon, Andrew. "Must the Show Go On? Hi-tech Events Still Draw, but Bigger Is No Longer Always Better." *PRWeek*, January 27, 2003, p. 15.

Hall, James. "Advertisers Chase Rock Festivals." *The Wall Street Journal*, June 6, 2003, p. A6.

Kleinfield, N. R. "Times Square Countdown: 3-2-1, More Harrry Potter." *The New York Times*, June 21, 2003, p. A16.

Lovio-George, Christina. "Event Marketing for Building Brands." *PR Tactics*, July 2002, p. 10.

Shaffran, Cliff. "Mind Your Meetings." *Communication World*, February/March 2003, pp. 26-28.

Stewart, Joan. "Generating Local Event Publicity." *PR Tactics*, April 2003, p. 17.

Todorova, Aleksandra. "Out to Launch: Choosing the Right Venue." *PRWeek*, July 1, 2002, p. 18.

Walker, Jerry. "Ten Tips for Maximizing Trade Show Exposure." *O'Dwyer's PR Services Report*, April 2003, p. 38.

Ward, David. "Show and Tell: Making the Most of Trade Events." *PRWeek*, February 3, 2003, p. 18.

Wellnitz, Barbara. "Trade Show Exhibits: Fewer Attendees Means More Opportunities." *PR Tactics*, April 2003, p. 12.

Chapter 18

Program Planning

The primary focus of this book has been on the tactical aspects of public relations—news releases, feature placements, publicity photos, video news releases, satellite media tours, media relations, newsletters, speeches, etc.—that require considerable writing skill and creativity.

Now that you have mastered multiple "media techniques," it is important to devote a chapter to the key concepts of campaign management and public relations programming. Basically, we are now talking about the coordination of multiple "tactics" as part of an overall program to achieve some organizational objective.

A written plan is imperative for any public relations campaign. It improves effectiveness. By using multiple communication tools together, you ensure a greater overall impact. Put another way, a plan is a blueprint. It explains the situation, analyzes what can be done about it, outlines strategies and tactics, and tells how the results will be evaluated.

Laurie Wilson, author of *Strategic Program Planning for Effective Public Relations Campaigns,* gives some insight about the relationship of a program plan to the actual process of writing and distributing materials to key audiences. She says:

> Each communication tactic is planned before it is created. The copy outline requires for each communication tactic the identification of the key public, the desired action by the public to contribute to the accomplishment of the plan's objectives, and the message to be sent to that public to motivate its action. Each of these elements draws the information as it is specified in the strategic plan.

This chapter will give you a brief overview of how to write a comprehensive public relations program. With this skill, you will become much more than a public relations writer—you will also become public relations manager.

DEVELOPING A PLAN

The first step in developing a plan is to consult with the client or your management. There are two purposes in this. First, it gets these people involved. Second, it is likely to give you the basic information you need to start making a plan.

In talking with the people who will pay for the campaign, you strive to identify the problems and opportunities confronting the organization. In some cases, these will be apparent to all. At other times, one party will have ideas that have not occurred to the other. Out of this discussion should come an agreement as to the general nature of the problems or opportunities and a preliminary establishment of objectives. All of this, of course, is subject to change when more information is gathered.

A good example is the California Avocado Commission. It faced the problem of selling Haas avocados on the East Coast. Sales were not good, and with a bumper crop of 600 million avocados, the California growers realized that they had a problem. Some informal research found that New Yorkers were not acquainted with avocados that turned jet black when ripe; they thought the fruit was rotten. The objective, then, was to inform consumers that Haas avocados are supposed to have black skins and that they have excellent flavor. The campaign succeeded because it was based on sound information and analysis.

Gathering Information

You cannot know too much about the subject you intend to promote. Don't be satisfied with a cursory investigation—dig and keep on digging until you have the whole story. There are several sources from which you can get the facts and figures that will enable you to plan an effective campaign.

- **Organization.** Much basic information should be available within the organization. Ask for marketing research that has been conducted about the product or service. Talk to sale representatives who deal with customers. Get an overall picture of the organization's successes and failures. Find out why things have happened or have been done.

- **References.** Go through all the information in your files. Consult other files. Use libraries and online databases. Read Chapter 1; many sources of information are cited there.

- **Questions.** Ask colleagues for their ideas. Review the experiences of others in similar situations. Read any case histories you can find. The trade press is a good source.

- **Analysis of communications.** Field reports from representatives of the organization, inquiries on telephone hot lines, and consumer complaints should be checked and studied.

- **Brainstorming.** Get a group of 6 to 10 people together and ask for suggestions. Many of the suggestions will be irrelevant, but some may contain the kernel of a good idea or point out areas where more information is needed. See Figure 18.1.

Figure 18.1 Organizational Skills and Creativity Needed
Planning a public relations campaign or program requires the dynamics of group interaction, brainstorming, and delegation of responsibilities.

- **Focus group interviews.** Assemble a group of people who are representative of the audience you will want to reach. These interviews are not quantitative research, but they may point to a need for detailed research in a specific area.

- **Surveys.** In many situations, you will need to conduct a formal survey to ascertain the attitudes and perceptions of target audiences. Doing a survey takes a lot of time and money. If the organization does not have the relevant data on hand, you must either do the survey yourself or hire someone to do it for you.

- **Media directories.** To plan your tactics, you need to know which channels of communication will be most efficient. A number of media directories, including *Bacon's* and *Media Map*, provide profiles of various media outlets and their audiences.

- **Demographics.** The *Statistical Abstracts of the United States, American Demographics,* and the comprehensive *Simmons Index* provide insights into the characteristics of an audience. *Simmons,* in particular, will give you detailed information on consumer buying habits and their major sources of information. There are even lists that give you the demographics of people in various zip codes.

Analyzing the Information

Having gathered all pertinent information and conducted one or more surveys (if they are needed), your job is to analyze all the facts and ideas. You must consider the reliability of what you have found out. If there are contradictions, you must eliminate erroneous elements and confirm the credibility of what remains.

Now, with reliable information, you can start to draw conclusions. The situation, with its problems and opportunities, and the reason for the situation should be apparent. The objectives should be obvious and the strategy, after careful thought, should start to take form.

At this point, you should prepare an outline of your findings and discuss them with management or the client. You can say, "These are the facts that I have, this is the situation as I see it, these are the objectives I think we should select, and this is the strategy I suggest."

This discussion may result in an approval in principle. If it does, you can start writing a program or campaign plan that will outline the strategies and tactics required to address the problem or opportunity.

ELEMENTS OF A PLAN

There is some variation regarding the elements of a basic program or campaign plan. Organizations designate these elements in different ways, combining or dividing them as seems appropriate. Nevertheless, any good plan will cover eight elements: situation, objectives, audience, strategy, tactics, timing, budget, and evaluation.

Situation

An organization's situation can be determined by summarizing the organization's relations with its public or publics. This tells why the program is needed and points out the need or the opportunity. This may be the most important part of the plan. Unless a client or management is convinced that a campaign is necessary, it is not likely to approve spending money on it.

A need often is a remedial situation. For example:

- The beef industry experienced a decline in the per-capita consumption of beef because consumers perceived the product to be high in fat and not as healthy as chicken or fish.

- The state of Florida experienced a major decline in European tourism after considerable negative publicity about the murder of several foreign tourists in drive-by shootings or at rest stops on the interstate highway.

- Odwalla had to regain the confidence of its customers after a recall of its apple-based products because of *E. coli* bacteria contamination.

Most public relations situations, however, are not problems that must be solved in a hurry. Instead, they are opportunities for an organization to increase

Professional Tips

Components of a PR Plan

A basic public relations plan is a blueprint of what you want to do and how you will accomplish your task. Such a plan, be it a brief outline or a comprehensive document, will enable you and your client or employer to make sure that all elements have been properly considered, evaluated, and coordinated for maximum effectiveness.

- **Situation:** You cannot set valid objectives without understanding the problem. To understand the problem, (a) discuss it with the client to find out what he or she expects the publicity to accomplish, (b) do your own research, and (c) evaluate your ideas in the broader perspective of the client's long-term goals.

- **Objectives:** Once you understand the situation, it should be easy to define the objectives. To determine if your stated objectives are the right ones, ask yourself: (a) Does it really solve or help solve the problem? (b) Is it realistic and achievable? (c) Can success be measured in terms meaningful to the client?

- **Audience:** Identify, as precisely as possible, the group of people to whom you are going to direct your communications. Is this the right group to approach in order to solve the problem? If there are several groups, prioritize them according to which are most important for your particular objectives.

- **Strategies:** The strategy describes how, in concept, the objective is to be achieved. Strategy is a plan of action that provides guidelines for selecting the communications activity you will employ. There are usually one or more strategies for each target audience. Strategies may be broad or narrow, depending on the objective and the audience.

- **Tactics:** This is the body of the plan, which describes, in sequence, the specific communications activities proposed to achieve each objective. Discuss each activity as a separate thought, but relate each to the unifying strategy and theme. In selecting communication tools—news releases, brochures, radio announcements, and so on—ask yourself if the use of each will really reach your priority audiences and help you accomplish your stated objectives.

- **Calendar:** It is important to have a timetable, usually outlined in chart form, that shows the start and completion of each project within the framework of the total program. A calendar makes sure that you begin projects—such as brochures, slide presentations, newsletters, or special events—early enough that they are ready when they are needed. A program brochure that reaches its target two days after the event is not an effective publicity tool.

- **Budget:** How much will implementation of the plan cost? Outline in sequence the exact costs of all activities. Make sure that you include such things as postage, car mileage, and labor to stuff envelopes. In addition, about 10 percent of the total budget should be allocated for contingencies.

- **Evaluation:** Before you begin, you and the client or employer must agree on the criteria you will use to evaluate your success in achieving the objective. Evaluation criteria should be (a) realistic, (b) credible, (c) specific, and (d) appropriate to the client's expectations. Don't show stacks of press clippings if only sales results are important.

public awareness, advance its reputation, or attract new customers and clients. Here are some examples:

- Dole Food Company conducted a major public relations campaign to inform children and parents about the importance of fruit and vegetables in a balanced diet.
- Friskies PetCare Company increased brand awareness by sponsoring a national canine Frisbee competition.
- The New York State Canal System launched a campaign to make citizens more aware of the historic canal system as a first-class tourist destination.
- The County Hospital Council in Columbus, Ohio, conducted a campaign that significantly increased the number of fully vaccinated children.

Objectives

Neither employers nor clients are likely to approve a campaign without clear objectives. Furthermore, even if a campaign is approved, it will surely fail without objectives.

Within any campaign, there may be multiple objectives. Smaller campaigns may have only one target and one objective, but in any planning you must be sure that you thoroughly understand what you are trying to accomplish.

It is also important that you not confuse objectives with the "means" rather than the "end." Novices, for example, often set an objective such as "Generate publicity for the new product." Publicity, however, is not an end in itself. The real objective is to create awareness among consumers about the availability of the new product and to motivate them to purchase it.

There are basically two kinds of objectives: informational and motivational.

Informational Objectives   A large percentage of public relations plans are designed primarily to increase awareness of an issue, an event, or a product. Here are some informational objectives:

- To inform people about the kinds of food needed for good nutrition
- To tell people that cigarette smoking is a major cause of cancer
- To proclaim the virtues of raisins
- To alert people to the fact that aerosol sprays damage the ozone layer

Although informational objectives are legitimate and are used by virtually every public relations firm and department, it is extremely difficult to measure how much "awareness" was attained unless before-and-after surveys are done; these are expensive and time-consuming. In addition, awareness doesn't equal action. Consumers may have been made aware of your new product, but that doesn't necessarily mean that they will buy it.

Motivational Objectives   Motivational objectives are more ambitious and also more difficult to achieve. Basically, you want to change attitudes and opinions with the idea of modifying behavior.

Some motivational objectives might be:

- To get people to eat healthier foods
- To reduce cigarette smoking
- To increase the consumption of raisins
- To prevent the sale of aerosol sprays

Notice that motivational objectives are more "bottom line oriented." The effectiveness of the public relations plan is based on making something happen, whether it is increasing sales or changing public support for some issue.

By contrast, informational objectives merely inform or educate people. Take the informational objective of making people aware of cigarette smoking as a major cause of cancer. This might be achieved successfully enough, but people who are "informed" and "aware" often continue to smoke. A better gauge of the American Cancer Society's success in its efforts would be an actual increase in the number of people who stopped smoking.

In setting objectives, you must be sure that they are realistic and achievable. Furthermore, they must be within the power of the campaign alone to attain. Sometimes the unwary set objectives such as "to increase sales," without realizing that sales may be affected by such things as product quality, packaging, pricing, merchandising, advertising, sales promotion, display, and competitive activity.

In establishing objectives, you must state exactly what you want the audience to know (a new product is now on the market), to believe (it will cut utility bills), and to do (ask for a demonstration). Objectives must be measurable. At some point the people who pay for the campaign are likely to ask, "What did you accomplish?" Many practitioners rely on general feedback—random comments and isolated examples that indicate public reaction. True professionals give facts and figures.

Evaluation is covered in detail in Chapter 19; at this point, however, you must start thinking about setting objectives that can be measured with figures. In an informational campaign, it is easy to state an objective such as: "To increase the number of people who believe that carpooling is a good way to save energy."

A motivational objective in this situation could be "To increase the number of people who use carpooling." However, it would be far better to put it this way: "To increase carpooling by 50 percent."

As you think about these numerical goals, you should realize that there must be a base point for such measurements. To know how many people have been convinced by your campaign, you must know how many people believed in carpooling before you began your campaign. With this figure in hand, you can prove that your efforts have increased awareness. When you then get figures on current carpooling, you will be able to prove that the campaign has increased utilization and by how much. Finding these base points require research, which will be discussed later.

Audience

Public relations programs should be directed toward specific and defined audiences or publics. If you define the audience as the "general public," you are not doing your homework.

In most cases, you are looking for specific audiences within a "general public." Take, for example, the Ohio vaccination program for children under the age of two. The primary audience for the message is parents with young children. A secondary audience is pregnant women. This knowledge should provide guidance on the selection of strategies and tactics that would primarily reach these defined audiences.

Increasing the use of carpooling is another example of an objective for which you can define the audience more precisely than saying "the general public." The primary audience for the message on carpooling is people who drive to work. A secondary audience might be parents who drive their children to school.

A third example might be a company that wants to increase the sale of a CD-ROM program on home improvement for do-it-yourselfers. Again, the primary audience is not the "general public," but only those who actually have CD-ROM players and enjoy working around the house. Such criteria exclude a large percentage of the American population.

Another common mistake is defining the mass media as an audience. In 9 out of 10 cases, selected mass media serve as channels to reach the audiences that you want to inform, persuade, and motivate. On occasion, in programs that seek to change how mass media reports an organization or an issue, editors and reporters can become a primary "public" or audience.

Professional Tips

How PR Helps Fulfill Marketing Objectives

Public relations programs, particularly product publicity, can make a substantial contribution to fulfilling the marketing objectives of a business organization.

- It can develop new prospects for new markets, such as inquiries from people who saw or heard a product release in the news media.

- It can provide third-party endorsements—via newspapers, magazines, radio, and television—through news releases about a company's products or services, community involvement, inventions, and new plans.

- It can generate sales leads, usually through articles in the trade press about new products and services.

- It can pave the way for sales calls.

- It can stretch the organization's advertising and promotional dollars through timely and supportive releases about it and its products.

- It can provide inexpensive sales literature for the company, because articles about it and its products can be reprinted as informative pieces for prospective clients.

- It can establish the organization as an authoritative source of information on a given subject.

- It can help sell minor products. Some products are too minor for large advertising expenditures, so exposure to the market is more cost-effective if product publicity is utilized.

Gaining a thorough understanding of your primary and secondary audiences, which are directly related to accomplishing your objectives, is the only way that you can formulate successful strategies and tactics.

Strategy

Strategy is the broad concept on which the campaign will be based. Strategy must be keyed directly to the objective, and it must be formed with a thorough knowledge of what the primary audiences perceive as relevant and in their self-interest.

The vaccination program for children, for example, was based on the idea that parents love their children and want them to be healthy. Thus, the strategy was to tell parents how important vaccinations are in keeping their children out of danger. In fact, the theme of the campaign became "Project L.O.V.E." with the subhead "Love Our Kids Vaccination Project."

The program to increase carpooling was based on research showing that commuters were interested in saving time and money. Thus, the strategy was to show how people using designated carpool lanes could cut the time of their commute. A second strategy was to show how much money a carpooler would save annually in gasoline, insurance, and maintenance costs.

The strategy for the CD-ROM home improvement product was to let people know that multimedia visual instruction would help do-it-yourselfers complete their jobs more competently and with fewer hassles. The 2,200 full-color illustrations and 50 how-to narrated videos also appealed to those who wanted to do home improvements but didn't have much experience.

These examples illustrate two basic concepts about strategy. First, the strategy must reflect the audience's self-interests. Second, the strategy must be expressed in simple terms as a *key selling proposition*.

The key statement is the message of the communication process. It must be reiterated throughout the campaign in various ways, but the concept should remain clear and simple. Every campaign has what is called **key copy points,** which are expressed in every activity—whether it be in a news release, a feature article, a media interview, or even a VNR.

Indeed, one of the criteria for an effective public relations program is whether the audience was exposed to your key copy points and absorbed them. One way of determining this is a content analysis of media mentions, which will be discussed under evaluation and in the next chapter.

Tactics

This is the "how to do it" portion of the plan. In public relations, it often is called the "execution" part of the plan. Tactics are the actual materials that are produced in a public relations campaign by one or several public relations writers.

The children's vaccination project, for example, used a variety of tactics, including:

- Posters in child-care centers and doctors' offices
- PSAs on radio stations that had audiences of childbearing age

PR Casebook

The Anatomy of a Winning Campaign

There are thousands of public relations campaigns every year. Some fail, some are moderately successful, and some achieve outstanding success. And, each year, about 650 of these campaigns are submitted for PRSA's Silver Anvil award, which recognizes the very best in PR planning and implementation. Of this number, about 45 are chosen for excellence.

Catherine Ahles and Courtney Botsworth of Florida International University analyzed the campaigns that received Silver Anvil awards and found some common characteristics of outstanding public relations campaigns:

Budgets. There's no question that big budgets help a winning campaign, but it's more important to have a budget that is efficiently used. Most winning campaigns are in the $100,000 to $199,000 range and use innovative tactics to stretch dollars over large geographic regions.

Research. According to Jennifer Acord, regional manager for public relations for Avon Products, "The best campaigns use research to develop the objectives, create the strategy, and provide clear benchmarks for evaluation." In terms of Silver Anvil award entries, the most popular form of primary research was face-to-face personal interviews. Telephone surveys ranked second, focus groups ranked third, and impersonal mail surveys ranked fourth. Internet surveys were rarely used. In terms of secondary research, literature searches and competitive analysis were the most frequently used techniques. About half of the campaigns used demographic profiles of audiences. About 40 percent of the campaigns pre-tested messages on the target audience before launching a full campaign.

Benchmarking. A campaign's outcome must be measured against some benchmark so you know if the campaign "moved the needle" in terms of creating awareness, increasing sales, or even changing attitudes and perceptions. However, this seems to be a weakness in even award-winning campaigns. Less than half failed to establish a benchmark in terms of public attitudes about the product or service before launching the campaign.

Objectives. "The most important aspect of a campaign is the objective," says Gerard F. Corbett, vice president of Hitachi America Ltd. "You need to identify where you want to be at the end of the day and what needs to be accomplished when all is said and done." Four out of five Silver Anvil campaigns sought to change behavior in some way, and almost that percentage had awareness- and visibility-based objectives. There are four elements to writing a good objective, says Ahles. They are (1) a clear tie to the organization's mission and goals, (2) specifying the nature of the desired change, (3) the time frame for the change, and (4) specifying the amount of change sought.

Measuring results. It is important, in a winning campaign, to evaluate the impact of a program and the actions taken by the target audience. Too many Silver Anvil entries fail to do this. Instead, they emphasize press clips and the number of meetings held. There is nothing wrong with press clips as one index of success, but Silver Anvil judges say the winning campaigns also devote attention to documenting behavior change.

The X factor. There are many good, solid campaigns, but the X factor is that ounce of daring and creativity that lifts the campaign to the extraordinary level. According to Corbett, "It's the chemistry that makes the program gel. It could be an out-of-the-box idea; it could be the people involved or the manner in which the campaign was implemented. Or it could be many factors woven together like a resilient fabric."

> So what is successful campaign planning? Ahles, writing in *The Strategist*, concludes:
>
> The bottom line for campaign planning? Focus on those aspects of campaign planning that will help you achieve your goal. Do good, solid research that benchmarks your starting point; use that research to build your strategy; set complete objectives that specify type, amount and time frame for change; and document your outcomes. Sprinkle in a heavy dose of creativity, both in problem solving and tactical execution, and efficient use of funding, and you are well on your way to producing an outstanding PR campaign.
>
> *Source:* Ahles, Catherine B. "Campaign Excellence." *The Strategist*, Summer 2003, pp. 46–53.

- Articles in newspapers and magazines catering to parents
- Pamphlets sent to child-care service providers
- Booklets mailed to every new mother explaining vaccination and the schedule of shots
- Letters to doctors reminding them to ask about vaccinations when a child has a checkup
- Corporate and hospital sponsorship of two week-long "Shots for Tots" promotional events
- Endorsements by governmental leaders and child-care experts
- Information advertisements in community newspapers
- Stories about the L.O.V.E. Project on television and in the city's daily newspaper

The campaign on carpooling also used a variety of tactics. One tactic was to enlist the support of drive-time DJs on popular radio stations, who promoted carpooling as part of their early-morning and late-afternoon banter between songs. Billboards along major highways were also used. There was also a concentrated effort to distribute posters and pamphlets that businesses could post and distribute to employees. Editors of employee newsletters and magazines were given background information on carpooling for possible stories. Another successful tactic was the compilation of a kit for employers telling them how to organize car pools for their employees.

The CD-ROM program, because of budget, was primarily a media campaign. The public relations firm worked to place articles and product reviews in (1) publications that reached relatively affluent households that would most likely have a CD-ROM player, (2) publications that catered to home improvement do-it-yourselfers, and (3) publications that covered new titles on CD-ROM.

Calendar

Two aspects of timing must be considered: (1) when the campaign is conducted and (2) the sequence of activities.

A campaign must be timely; it must run when the key messages mean the most to the intended audience. Some subjects are seasonal; hence publicists release information on strawberries in May and June, when a crop comes to market. A software program on doing your own taxes attracts the most audience interest in February and March, just before the April 15th deadline.

At times, the environmental context is important. A campaign on carpooling might be more successful if it follows a price increase in gasoline or a government agency report that traffic congestion has reached gridlock proportions. A charitable campaign to provide for the homeless is more effective if the local newspaper has just run a five-part series on the human dimensions of the problem.

Other kinds of campaigns are less dependent on seasonal or environmental context. The L.O.V.E. vaccination program, a Red Cross drive for blood donations, and even the selling of a CD-ROM on home improvements could be done almost anytime during the year. The Christmas season, however, would be great for selling the CD-ROM but a bad time for running a vaccination project.

The second aspect of timing is the scheduling of activities during a campaign. A typical pattern is to have a concentrated effort at the beginning of a campaign where a number of activities are implemented. This is the launch phase of an idea or concept and, much like a rocket, takes a concentration of power just to break the awareness barrier. After the campaign has achieved orbit, however, it takes less energy and fewer activities are needed to maintain momentum. A good example of this is the product life cycle shown in Figure 18.2.

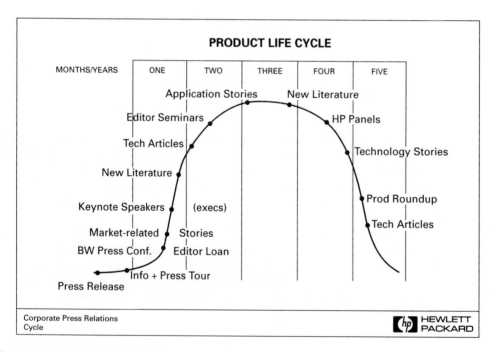

Figure 18.2 The Product Life Cycle
Planning requires strategies and tactics. This bell curve shows a product's life cycle and the kinds of public relations tools needed at each stage. Note that numerous tools are coordinated to launch a product.
(Courtesy of Hewlett-Packard Company, Palo Alto, CA.)

You must also think about advance planning. Monthly publications, for example, often need information at least six to eight weeks before an issue. If you want something in the August issue, you have to think about placing it in May or June. A popular talk show may work on a schedule that books guests three or four months in advance. The main idea is that you must constantly think ahead to make things happen in the appropriate sequence.

A brochure may be needed on March 29, but you must start the brochure long before that date. To determine the starting date, you must know every step in the production process and how long it will take.

This activity, as well as the scheduling of other public relations tactics, should not be trusted to your memory or to jottings on your desk calendar. It is important that the entire public relations team working on the program has a single source of information for the schedule of the entire campaign.

The easiest way to keep everything on schedule is to prepare a working calendar for detailed planning and internal use. The brochure example, cited above, might look like this:

Activity	Date Due	Responsibility
Outline brochure	January 11	J. Ross, G. Jones
Write copy	January 18	J. Ross
Photos and artwork	January 25	A. Peck and N. Lopez
Design and layout	February 8	A. Peck and N. Lopez
Final client approval	February 15	B. Boss
Printer prep and proofs	February 28	Ace Printers. G. Jones, supervising
Printing and binding	March 10	Ace Printers. G. Jones, supervising
Delivery	March 15	United Parcel Service. G. Jones, supervising

Other entries planned using this kind of format might be preparing news releases, drafting speeches, writing pitch letters, scheduling spokespeople on radio talk shows, arranging media tours, and commissioning a camera-ready feature article.

You can also map activities by listing the activities at the left of a chart, with days or weeks across the top. Lines or bars show graphically when various steps are being worked on. This is often called a *Gantt chart*. See Figure 18.3 for an example.

The main idea is that you should have a systematic means of tracking activities throughout the public relations program so everything stays on schedule. If a brochure or a media kit is delayed, it can delay other activities such as a media tour or a news conference that is dependent on having the materials available. All activities in a public relations program are interrelated for maximum effectiveness.

Budget

A budget can be divided into two categories: staff time and out-of-pocket (OOP) expenses. Staff and administrative time usually takes the lion's share of any public

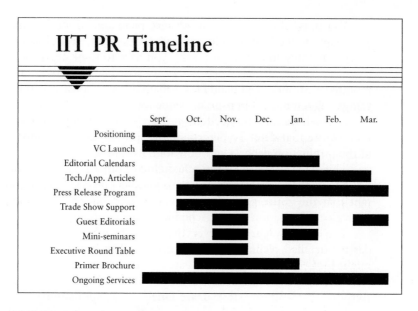

Figure 18.3 Timing Is Everything
Planning requires precision scheduling. This is a simplified time line showing the various activities and tactics in a public relations program. Some tactics, such as news releases, are ongoing; others are phased in during the campaign.
(Courtesy of Hoffman Agency, San Jose, CA.)

relations budget. In a $100,000 campaign done by a public relations firm, for example, 70 percent or more will go to salaries and administrative fees.

A public relations firm has different hourly rates for the level of personnel involved. The head of the agency, who would oversee the account, might bill at $200 per hour. The account supervisor might bill at $120 per hour, and the account executive at $100 per hour. Account coordinators, those who do a lot of the clerical work, might bill at $55 per hour.

A public relations firm, when submitting a plan, has usually constructed a budget based on the number of estimated staff hours it will take to implement a plan. Let's say that the plan calls for a media kit, the development of five news releases, the writing of a slide script, and a news conference. The public relations firm might estimate that all this work will take at least 150 hours of staff time, divided as follows:

President, 20 hours @ $200 = $4,000

Vice President, 40 hours @ $180 = $7,200

Account Executive, 50 hours @ $100 = $5,000

Account Coordinator, 40 hours @ $55 = $2,200

TOTAL STAFF COSTS: $18,400

The other part of the budget is out-of-pocket expenses, which includes payments to various vendors for such things as printing, postage, graphics, production of VNRs, travel, phone, fax, photocopying, and so on.

You can do a reasonable job of estimating out-of-pocket expenses by making a few phone calls. You would call a printer, for example, to get an estimate of how much 10,000 copies of a pamphlet would cost. If you are doing a media tour, you would decide what cities would be visited and then find out the cost of airline fares, hotels, meals, and ground transportation costs. The Internal Revenue Service even has a guide to daily living expenses in major cities around the world.

One method of doing a budget is to use two columns. The left column, for example, will give the staff cost for writing a pamphlet or compiling a media kit. The right column will give the actual OOP for having the pamphlet or the media kit designed, printed, and delivered. Internal public relations departments, where the staff is already on the payroll, often compile only the OOP expenses.

Budgets should also have a line item for contingencies, that is, unexpected expenses. In general, allow about 10 percent of the budget for contingencies.

Evaluation

Evaluation refers directly back to your stated objectives: it is the process by which you determine whether you have met your objectives.

If you have an informational objective, such as increasing awareness, a common procedure is to show placements in key publications and broadcast stations that reached the intended audience. Related to this is a content analysis of whether the news coverage included your key messages. A more scientific approach is to do a benchmark study of audience knowledge and perceptions before and after the campaign. In many cases, "before" activity has already been documented through marketing studies, so all you have to do is a postcampaign survey.

Motivational objectives, such as increased market share or sales, are much easier to determine. The Ohio campaign had the objective of increasing vaccinations—and it succeeded by raising the vaccination rates by 117 percent in public clinics over a two-year period. A campaign by Ketchum Public Relations on behalf of prune producers caused a 4 percent increase in sales after several years of decline.

Increased sales, however, may be the result of other factors, such as the economy, the additional use of advertising, or a reduction in prices. Because of this, it is often wise to limit your objectives to something that can be related directly to your activities. For example, you might get feature placements in various magazines that also give an address for a free brochure. Success could then be declared when there have been 10,000 requests for the brochure.

Chapter 19 expands on methods of evaluation in public relations.

REVIEWING THE FINAL DRAFT

Before you submit your written plan to a client or management for final approval, you should review it with a critical eye. You might even ask some knowledgeable person whose opinion you respect to read the plan and then discuss it with you. Check these points:

- Is the situation clearly stated?
- Is the audience the right one? Is it clearly defined?

PR Casebook

Maytag's Campaign Plan for Ol' Lonely's 35 Years

An excellent example of a well-planned public relations program is one conducted by Carmichael Lynch Spong for its client, Maytag Appliances. The various tactics of this campaign have been highlighted throughout the book. Here, in outline form, is the plan to reinforce brand identity by celebrating 35 years of its advertising icon, Ol' Lonely, the Maytag repairman.

Situation: Maytag Appliances, consistently voted one of America's most trusted brands, has personalized its dependability in the form of Ol' Lonely, the Maytag repairman who never has to make a service call. His series of television commercials and print ads (see Figure 15.3) have practically made him a household name. The year 2002 marked the 35th anniversary of Ol' Lonely in a Maytag commercial on the *Today* show in 1967, and the company saw an opportunity to build a campaign around a 35th anniversary celebration.

Objectives: There were two program objectives: (1) increase Maytag brand awareness and reinforce positioning of Ol' Lonely and (2) stimulate preference for the Maytag brand.

Audience analysis: Consumer profile: all-American mom, age 25–54, married, college educated, with a family income of 50,000 or more. Media profile: home, lifestyle, and feature newspaper and magazine editors; online media; television and radio producers and assignment desks.

Research: Key findings of qualitative research: (1) consumers' perception of Ol' Lonely reinforces the brand's dependability and image; (2) consumers regard Ol' Lonely as "part of the family" and portraying the "human side" of Maytag; and (3) the combined presence of two Maytag men has helped evolve the brand while maintaining its equity.

Budget: $75,000 fees and expenses.

Strategy: Reinforce the Maytag brand by celebrating the 35th anniversary of the Maytag Man through an equity-building media relations campaign.

Tactics:

- Created 900 commemorative "Ol' Lonely tool box" media kits. The kit was packaged as a repairman's tool kit and included media materials, a CD of historical advertisements, a commemorative Ol' Lonely bobble head, and B-roll. See Figure 8.11 in Chapter 8 for a photo of the media kit.

- Created a commemorative 35th anniversary logo for use on all celebration materials, including media materials, Web site, and dealer materials. See Figure 18.4.

Figure 18.4 Ol' Lonely Celebrates 35 Years
This logo was used by Maytag Appliances to increase brand awareness and increase consumer loyalty.
(Courtesy of Maytag Corporation, Newton, IA, and its public relations firm, Carmichael Lynch Spong.)

- Prepared a news feature giving tips and ideas from Ol' Lonely on how to deal with loneliness. See Figure 6.6 in Chapter 6 for this feature story.
- Staged an anniversary celebration at the "repair shop" with Ol' Lonely and the Apprentice and produced a B-roll video for distribution to television stations. The tape also included historical footage, evolution of the icon, and soundbites from marketing experts.
- Booked a 25-city satellite media tour from New York City with Ol' Lonely, the Apprentice, the Maytag brand manager, and a marketing professor from Northwestern University to discuss how brand icons impact consumers.
- Provided dealers with video highlights and bobble heads for in-store promotions.

Evaluation:

Objective 1: Increase brand awareness and reinforce positioning of Ol' Lonely

- Print and online placements resulted in 43.4 million gross impressions, including the *Arizona Republic*, *Des Moines Register*, and *Fresno Bee*.
- Television coverage resulted in 507 placements in 92 markets, including 9 of the top 10 markets. Nearly 90 percent of the stations featured footage from the B-roll and the bobble heads on the news desk during the satellite media tour.

Objective 2: Stimulate preference for the Maytag brand

- Media coverage generated nearly 40,000 inquiries on the company's Web site, Maytag.com.
- More than 10,000 bobble heads were ordered by Maytag dealers.

- Are the objectives attainable and measurable?
- Is the strategy logical and effective?
- Is the message persuasive and memorable?
- Are the tactics sound and effective?
- Is the timing right?
- Are the costs reasonable and justified?
- Will the proposed evaluation really measure the results?
- Is the plan practical, and appropriate?
- Is the plan logical, strong, and clearly written?
- Should any additions or deletions be made?

Your responsibility is to make the proposed plan as sound as you can make it, based on your professional expertise. You should remember, however, that any plan is a work in progress, and your client or management may suggest changes. They may not think a particular idea is very good, or they may decide to reduce the cost by eliminating a component.

In many cases, such feedback from the client or management sharpens and improves the plan. At other times, if you think the proposed changes would seriously impact the effectiveness of the plan, you have to express your rationale in a diplomatic manner and persuade them that your initial idea is the better one.

SUMMARY

- Most public relations activities occur within the framework of a program or program plan.
- A program plan has the elements of situation (problem statement), objectives, audience, strategies, tactics, calendar, budget, and evaluation.
- Objectives can be informational or motivational, depending on the kind of results expected.
- Creating publicity is not a valid objective; it is a means to an end.
- For public relations purposes, audiences must be clearly defined. In most cases, a specific audience is defined by income, interest, geography, lifestyle, and a host of other variables.
- A strategy is a broad conceptualization that gives direction to a public relations program. A good strategy is based on research and reflects audience self-interests. It can also be expressed as the program's key selling proposition.
- Tactics are the "how to do it" part of the program plan. They list the communication tools and activities that will be used to support the strategy.
- Timing of activities and messages is important. They must occur within a broader context of public interests and must be scheduled in advance.
- A detailed budget is an integral part of a public relations plan. Staff and administrative expenses usually consume more of the budget than out-of-pocket expenses.
- Working a plan means that you must have a detailed calendar of activities and who is responsible for carrying them out.
- A program is evaluated as a success if it meets the set objectives of the campaign. Objectives must be measurable for evaluation methods to be effective.

ADDITIONAL RESOURCES

Ahles, Catherine B. "Campaign Excellence: A Survey of Silver Anvil Award Winners Compares Current PR Practice with Planning, Campaign Theory." *The Strategist*, Summer 2003, pp. 46–53.

Austin, Erica W., and Pinkleton, Bruce E. *Strategic Public Relations Management*. Mahwah, NJ: Lawrence Erlbaum Associates, 2001.

Lukaszewski, James E. "How to Develop the Mind of a Strategist." *Communication World,* August/September 2001, pp. 9–11.

Matera, Fran R. , and Artigue, Ray J. *Public Relations Campaigns and Techniques.* Boston: Allyn & Bacon, 2000.

Smith, Ronald D. *Strategic Planning for Public Relations.* Mahwah, NJ: Lawrence Erlbaum Associates, 2002.

Wilcox, Dennis L., Cameron, Glen T., Ault, Phillip H., and Agee, Warren K. *Public Relations: Strategies and Tactics,* 7th edition. Boston: Allyn & Bacon, 2003, Chapters 4–7.

Wilson, Laurie J. *Strategic Program Planning for Effective Public Relations Campaigns.* Dubuque: Kendall-Hunt, 2000.

Chapter 19

Measurement & Evaluation

The final step in any campaign or program is measurement and evaluation. Was the program effective? Did it meet its objectives? It is important to ask these questions for two reasons.

First, you must show your client or employer that the money, time, and effort devoted to the program were well spent and actually contributed to fulfilling organizational goals. Second, you need to assess what worked and didn't work, so you can do a better job next time.

This chapter will give you a variety of tools for measuring public relations programs on at least five levels: (1) production/distribution, (2) message exposure, (3) audience awareness, (4) audience attitudes, and (5) audience action. The first two methods are categorized as measuring "outputs" because the focus is on the distribution of media materials and finding out if the media used the material (press clips). To a large degree, these methods are the most frequently used by public relations practitioners. Indeed, one survey indicated that practitioners spend almost 30 percent of their workweek analyzing media coverage.

The remaining three methods are known as "outcomes" because there is an effort to find out how public relations efforts affected attitudes, behavior, or even sales. This often requires more sophisticated and complex research methodologies involving before-and-after surveys (benchmark studies) or, at the very minimum, some baseline information. Although surveys indicate that this kind of measurement is the most important, many practitioners say they don't have the budget, the expertise, or the time to do such measurement.

This chapter will acquaint you with the various measurement methods and give you the tools necessary to do each one of them. In addition, you will learn the techniques for evaluating events and organizational publications such as newsletters and brochures.

THE IMPORTANCE OF EVALUATION

The final step in any public relations program or campaign, as the last chapter indicated, is measurement and evaluation.

Bill Margaritis, senior vice president of worldwide communications for FedEx, told *PRWeek,* "Measurement helps us prioritize and execute our programs; it's a road map to our activities. It also helps build alignment with business objectives, and gives executive management a sense of confidence that we are using a quantifiable process in which to invest our money and time."

You Mon Tsang, CEO of Biz360, a measurement firm, is more blunt about the need for evaluation. He is quoted in *PRWeek,* saying, "It's almost inconceivable to invest money in a significant program like communications without understanding the results. How would any other department justify its investments without understanding what they are getting out of it."

Andy Beaupre of Delahaye/MediaLink, a media measurement firm, says public relations efforts should be measured to:

- Document that PR efforts actually achieved prespecified objectives
- Apply lessons learned to future PR efforts
- Erase a frequent premise that PR is magic and too intangible to measure
- Prove that practitioners are doing their jobs
- Illustrate concern for PR quality and its impact on the organization

Another important reason for conducting measurement and evaluation, and perhaps the most compelling argument, is that clients and management are demanding more accountability. Today's public relations programs are highly sophisticated and expensive, so organizations want to be sure that they are getting good value for their money. In addition, PR personnel often compete with advertising and marketing for budget, so it is important to document how public relations activity is the most cost-effective use of funds.

Consequently, here are some general questions that you should honestly ask yourself upon completion of a public relations program:

- Was the program or activity adequately planned?
- Did recipients of the message understand it?
- How could the program strategy have been more effective?
- Were all primary and secondary audiences reached?
- Was the desired organizational objective achieved?
- What unforeseen circumstances affected the success of the program or activity?
- Did the program or activity stay within the budget?
- What steps can be taken to improve the success of similar future activities?

Answering these questions requires a mix of evaluative methods, many borrowed from advertising and marketing, to provide complete evaluations. To evaluate a public relations program fully, you must use formal and more systematic research methods to document message exposure, accurate dissemination of the message, acceptance of the message, attitude change, and change in overt behavior.

Message exposure and accurate dissemination of the message are fairly easy to evaluate by keeping track of the messages sent, compiling the resulting news clips and broadcast mentions, and performing a content analysis to determine if key messages were included. Indeed, measuring the delivery of key messages is the most common technique for showing the effectiveness of public relations, according to a *PRWeek* survey among public relations firms and departments. Collecting press clippings was the second most commonly used method of measurement.

These methods, however, emphasize the output of pubic relations staffs instead of the outcomes as a result of their work. Tudor Williams, writing in the online newsletter *NetGain,* explains: "For many years, organizations were content to measure the outputs of communication, how many newsletters were published, how many 'impressions' or column inches were created, or the size of the audience reached. But in a world where accountability matters, it is the outcomes that are important, the extent to which we were successful in achieving our goal. The output is but the means to achieve successful outcomes, not success itself."

Williams, when he discusses outcomes, is talking about a higher level of measurement that focuses on the effects of all our news releases, brochures, newsletters, and other materials. Changes in audience awareness and understanding, as well as changes in attitudes and preferences and even behavior, are all "outcomes" that are more difficult to measure, but are more meaningful to the "bottom line."

Increasingly, public relations departments and firms are using various research tools to measure outcomes. Indeed, in the *PRWeek* survey, more than half of the respondents said they used this type of measurement. Interestingly, they also rated change in attitudes, behavior as the most important form of measurement, but still used press clippings more frequently as a measurement method.

The following pages discuss the measurement and evaluation of "outputs" as well as "outcomes." The first step, however, is how you determine and write your program objectives.

Start with Objectives

Before any public relations program can be properly evaluated, however, it is important to have a clearly established set of measurable objectives. These should be part of the program plan, discussed in the last chapter, but some points need reviewing.

First, public relations personnel and management should agree on the criteria that will be used to evaluate success in attaining objectives. Does the client or management want to evaluate the program on the number of press clippings, or do they want you to show that you actually increased sales or market share? A frank discussion about objectives and client or management expectations, before a program is launched, can make a big difference in how you structure your campaign to achieve specific outcomes.

Second, don't wait until the end of a public relations program to determine how it will be evaluated. Albert L. Schweitzer, of Fleishman-Hillard public relations in St. Louis, makes the point: "Evaluating impact/results starts in the planning stage. You break down the problems into measurable goals and objectives, then after implementing the program, you measure the results against goals."

In other words, it is not wise to have vague, nonspecific objectives that you will be unable to measure at the end of your program. If the objective is to inform or make people aware of a product or service, you must use measurement techniques that show how successfully information was communicated to target audiences. Such techniques fall under the rubric of "audience exposure," which will be discussed shortly.

In an example of measurement reflecting program objectives, the Illinois Department of Public Health conducted a campaign among teenagers with two objectives: (1) increase adolescents' personal perception of risk for HIV/AIDS, STDs, and unintended pregnancy resulting from unprotected sex and substance abuse, and (2) generate adolescent calls to the Department hotline as an information source and place for HIV referral information.

Golin/Harris International, which conducted the program, reported the following results:

- One million Illinois residents were informed about the campaign through stories in print and broadcast media, plus radio public service announcements.
- Adolescent calls to the hotline increased by nearly 50 percent during the three-month campaign.
- A survey of Illinois teenagers found that 91 percent enjoyed the radio PSAs; 90 percent thought the situations presented in the PSAs could happen in real life; and 69 percent said the ads taught them ways to handle risky situations.

Professional Tips

Factors in Program Evaluation

What factors are important in judging the effectiveness of a public relations program? A survey of corporate communicators and marketers conducted by CDB Research & Consulting and Thomas L. Harris & Associates found that 99 percent of the respondents rated "increase in awareness" as the most important factor. Other findings:

- Delivery of message points (95%)
- Enhancement of company image (88%)
- Placement in key publications (87%)
- Increase in awareness of company or issue (85%)
- Change in attitudes (84%)
- Response to program (83%)
- Overall audience reach (72%)
- Increase in reported purchasing (59%)
- Bottom-line sales increase (58%)
- Number of placements (47%)
- Number of gross impressions (40%)
- Advertising equivalents (24%)

MEASUREMENT OF PRODUCTION/DISTRIBUTION

One elementary form of evaluation is simply to give your client or employer a count of how many news releases, feature stories, photos, and such were produced in a given time period.

This kind of evaluation is supposed to give management an idea of your productivity. However, this approach is not very meaningful, because it emphasizes quantity instead of quality. It also encourages the public relations writer to send out more news releases than necessary, many worthless as news, in an attempt to meet some arbitrary quota.

It may be more cost-effective to write fewer news releases and spend more time preparing truly newsworthy stories tailored to specific publications. Is it better to do 15 routine news releases in a week, or to spend the same amount of time pitching one story to the prestigious *Wall Street Journal*?

Closely aligned to the production of materials is their dissemination. Thus it may be reported that a news release was sent to "977 daily newspapers, 700 weekly newspapers, and 111 trade publications." Such figures are useful in terms of evaluating how widely a news release or feature is distributed, but sending out vast quantities of news releases just to impress management with big numbers is futile. For example, a large media mailing may be a waste of time and money if the news release in question has news value only to the 50 daily newspapers in a region or if the release is so technical that only five trade publications would be interested in it.

Large mailings are not necessarily the fault of publicists. Often management has a skewed view of what is newsworthy and wants everyone in the world to know that the company has a new vice president of research and development. In addition, many organizations figure that sending a news release is a relatively cheap proposition involving only postage or a group e-mail, so why not do a blanket mailing to increase the press clipping file and impress management?

Public relations firms often are not much help in stemming the tide of news releases that engulf the media. There are two reasons for this: (1) the philosophy that the client is always right, and (2) multiple news releases mean more fee income for the public relations firm.

As a professional public relations practitioner, you should document distribution but not succumb to sending out reams of news releases just to impress the boss. A better approach is to use targeted mailings that generate a high percentage of media placements.

MEASUREMENT OF MESSAGE EXPOSURE

The most common way of evaluating public relations programs is the compilation of press clippings and broadcast mentions. In fact, *PRWeek* surveyed public relations firms and found that 81 percent of them primarily used press clippings as their major tool to evaluate program success.

There are regional, national, and even global news clipping services that can be hired to review large numbers of print and online publications and clip all the articles about your client or employer. The three largest companies are Bacon's, Luce Press Clippings, and Burrelle's Information Services. Each has an extensive staff that reads every daily newspaper and virtually every weekly newspaper and magazine published in the United States. In addition, you can also order clips from newspapers and magazines around the world. Burrelle's, for example, can obtain clips from 70 countries, plus any others a client specifically requests.

All three services offer customers any number of ways to slice, dice, and compile press clippings according to their needs and budget. They can provide clients with clips giving the name of the publication, date, frequency, and circulation. Clients can also have the clipping service evaluate clips on such variables as article size, advertising cost equivalent, audience, editorial slant of the article, subject, number of keyword mentions, type of article, and byline. This aspect of media analysis will be discussed shortly.

Increasingly, online clipping services are offered instead of the traditional cut-and-paste approach. Bacon's, Luce, and Burrelle's monitor online publications (including the editions of the traditional print media) and clip the article for you electronically. One major advantage is that a client gets clips almost immediately, instead of waiting several weeks for a bundle of clips to arrive. The major disadvantage, however, is that not all print publications are available online. In fact, one expert estimates that only about 20 percent of the 20,000+ publications are available in electronic format. Also, online clips don't offer the headlines, photos, and graphics as they actually appeared on a newspaper or magazine page.

The main purpose of compiling press clippings is to find out if your news releases have been used by the media. By doing this, an organization can determine if the public was exposed to its message. The success of a campaign by ESAB Welding Products, for example, was evaluated by its public relations firm, Sawyer Riley Compton, as follows:

- . . . unprecedented consumer coverage for ESAB in 532 newspaper outlets in 26 states representing a total readership of more than 54 million.
- . . . trade media relations efforts resulted in 167 clips, including by-lined article and feature stories, which represents an increase of 26 percent over last year's figures.

Another purpose of press clippings is to monitor trends and the competition. AT&T may ask its clipping service to clip any articles pertaining to keywords such as "telephone," "fiber optics," and "information technology," to keep track of industry trends and developments. It may also have the clipping service send clips on MCI and Sprint, just to see what the competition is doing and saying.

Broadcast mentions can also be tabulated, but less reliably because this has to be done exactly at the time of the broadcast. Here, too, there are national companies that provide monitoring services.

One of the largest is Video Monitoring Services (VMS), which records all news and public affairs programs on local television stations in more than 130 markets, local radio stations in 14 markets, and all national broadcast and cable news and talk shows. VMS logs the shows on computer and, like the clipping services, will send you a summary of news or talk show segments on the subjects you have specified. Other major services include Medialink, Nielsen, and Lexis-Nexis.

Medialink, for example, has a Web-based TV news monitoring service called News IQ. The service automatically scans TV news broadcasts and reports back to subscribers any mention of clients, competitors, or other relevant information, based on keywords that the user has selected. According to John Morgan, vice president of Medialink, newscasts are fully searchable within the first five minutes of airing. In addition, a client can even arrange to have an e-mail sent almost instantly that tells about a mention on a news show.

Press clipping volume is still popular among public relations firms and clients, but the weight and number of press clips as something worth knowing is fast declining. Increasingly, senior management does not view the number of press clippings as a key measure of success. Mark Weiner, president of Medialink, says "if you think about the real intent of media relations, the media isn't the end game."

Matthew Creamer, a reporter for *PRWeek*, adds, "The clipbook, that old symbol of PR measurement, has been replaced by the more sophisticated evaluations of the quantity and quality of media placements which in more ambitious PR operations have been links to bottom-line results that resonate outside the corporate communications silo to those doling out the money." We will get to "bottom-line" outcomes shortly, but let's first discuss some up-to-date variations on the "old" clipbook.

Media Impressions

Another popular way of measuring output is to compile the circulation of the publications where your news release, feature story, interview, or product mention appeared. In the case of a broadcast mention on a radio program or television show, you use the audited average of listeners or viewers for that particular show.

This is known as compiling **gross impressions**, **media impressions**, or just **impressions**. Geri Mazur, director of research for Porter Novelli International, told *PRWeek*, "At a most basic level, clients expected to know how many impressions or how many bodies their message touched."

For example, if a story about an organization appears in a local daily with a circulation of 130,000, the number of media impressions is 130,000. If the story appears in a number of publications, you simply add up the circulation of all the publications to get the total impressions.

A story appearing in 15 or 20 publications can easily generate several million media impressions. Korbel Champagne Cellars, for example, generated a lot of media coverage with its "perfect marriage proposal" contest. In fact, Edelman Worldwide had set a goal of 70 million media impressions. The final result, after a year was almost 90 million media impressions as a result of about 1,000 media placements. The breakdown was as follows:

National print	11, 037,244
Daily and weekly print	37,906,106
National broadcast	9,872,620
Local TV broadcast	1,320,279
Local radio broadcast	6,941,050
Online	22,539,597
Total impressions:	**89,616,896**

Total media impressions are used in advertising and publicity to illustrate the penetration of a particular message. However, high numbers of media impressions only report total circulation and potential audience size, not how many people actually read, heard, or viewed that particular story.

Advertising Value Equivalency

The numbers game is also played by converting stories in the news columns or on broadcast news and talk shows into the equivalent of advertising costs. For example, the public relations department of a major corporation might give top management the following report: "When print inches are calculated as advertising space, the company received exposure worth $158,644 this year—a 27.5 percent increase over last year."

Some practitioners like the concept of advertising value equivalency (AVE) because it is a form of ROI. It shows management that the public relations staff is earning its salary by generating much more "income" (even if it is virtual) than it costs to pay the salaries of the public relations staff.

Mark Scott of HomeBanc Mortgage Company told *PRWeek*, for example, that AVE helps him "justify his PR budget to the CEO and head of marketing." The ad equivalency of HomeBanc's news coverage one year was $810,000, using a metric supplied by Burrelle's Information Services. According to Scott, "When you consider that I make considerably less than that, it's OK. For what they paid me and the expenses incurred, I don't think it exceeded $150,000 to $200,000. In other words, the ROI is about four times the expense—and that's looks pretty good to the corporate beancounters."

Some public relations practitioners even multiply the AVE figures by factoring in the idea that publicity is worth more than advertising because it is more credible and influential. Bacon's clipping service, for example, even has a clip calculator that allows for a flexible multiplier scale. This means that the software will compute the publicity value of a clip in terms of cost per inch multiplied by a value between 1 and 10 that is arbitrarily assigned by the account executive. In general, three is the most common multiplier. If such a multiple was applied to HomeBanc's $810,000, that means the news coverage was worth about $2.4 million.

Such exercises in multiplication are criticized by the Institute for Public Relations Research, headquartered in Gainesville, Florida. In a white paper on measuring and evaluating public relations effectiveness, the Institute called the use of multipliers "unethical, dishonest, and not at all supported by the research literature."

Indeed, the whole idea of advertising equivalency is highly suspect, because you are comparing apples and oranges. First of all, in advertising, you control the exact wording, graphics, and placement of your message. By contrast, news releases and features are subject to the whims of media gatekeepers who decide what is published and in what context. There is no guarantee, as there is in advertising, that your message will be communicated in the way you wish.

Second, a mystery remains as to what is actually being counted. If a 10-inch article in the local daily mentions your company along with several competitors, is this equivalent to 10 inches of advertising space? Does the university football team reap "millions of dollars of comparable advertising" if its losing season gets extensive media coverage?

Third, the practice of equating news stories and publicity with advertising is not particularly beneficial for promoting effective media relations. Editors often suspect that all that publicists seek is "free advertising," and this impression is reinforced when public relations people themselves take great pains to convert story placements to comparable advertising costs.

Although many public relations departments and public relations firms still measure print and broadcast clips by converting them to advertising rates, the practice is fading among professionals. *PRWeek*, in a 2002 survey, found that calculating advertising value was in next to last place in "type of measurement used." In addition, AVE was rated last in terms of "perceived importance of different types of measurement" and "satisfaction with different types of measurement." It is also telling that winning campaigns in the Silver Anvil awards competition sponsored by the Public Relations Society of America (PRSA) rarely use AVE to demonstrate the success of their programs. Instead, they use outcomes such as increased sales, awareness, change in attitudes or behavior, and contributions to overall organizational objectives. These measurements will be discussed shortly.

Systematic Tracking

Press clippings are still measured by the pound and the inch, but a more systematic content analysis can now be done thanks to the computer and various software programs.

In addition to getting the traditional information about a publication's name, date, frequency, and circulation, it is now possible to do a more complete analysis of news coverage. Burrelle's, for example, offers clip analysis that includes (1) article size compared to available space in the publication, (2) the editorial slant of the article, (3) mention of key messages, products, brands, and competitors, (4) the number of key word mentions, (5) the type of article, (6) the byline of the article's author, (7) degree of coverage in top markets, and (8) coverage by region. Other services, such as Factiva, Vocus, Biz360, Delehaye/Medialink, and CARMA, offer similar media analysis capabilities.

Such detailed analysis is a good diagnostic tool to tabulate details about the coverage and what audiences were exposed to it. You might find out, for example, that your new product or policy is getting a lot of negative news coverage. See Figure 19.1 for a chart summarizing editorial slant. Or you may find out that only newspapers in the West are using the information, leaving other key markets without any penetration.

Such an analysis may also show that 45 percent of your company's news releases are management and personnel stories, but that these releases account for only 5 percent of the stories published about the company. By contrast, stories about new product developments may constitute only 10 percent of the news releases but account for 90 percent of the press coverage. Given these data, a logical step might be to send out fewer personnel stories and more product

Total Circulation by Editorial Slant

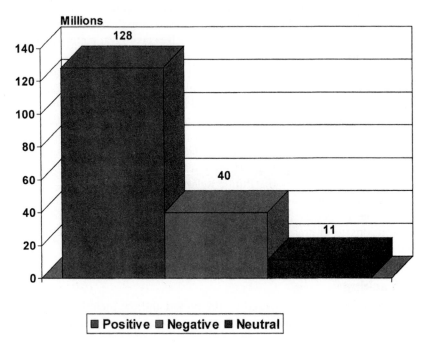

Figure 19.1 Media Analysis

Thanks to the computer, press clippings can be analyzed on multiple levels—by region, page, mention of key messages, type of article, etc. This chart, originally in color, summarizes the editorial slant of all your coverage by the total circulation of the publications where stories appeared. As the chart shows, a large percentage of the stories were positive. *(Courtesy of Burrelle's Newsclip Analysis Service, Livingston, NJ.)*

development articles.

A systematic tracking system also identifies which publications receiving the news releases are using them. Your mailing list may include 500 different periodicals, but by the end of a 12-month period, you may find that only half of these used your releases in any way. Given this information, you would be wise to prune your mailing list.

Computer analysis of press clippings also is a valuable way to make sure that key copy points are being included in the published stories. For example, a company may wish to emphasize in all its press coverage that it is a manufacturer of high-quality professional audio and video recording systems or that it is a well-managed company. Analysis may show that 87 percent of the stories mention the high-quality products but that only 35 percent mention or imply that the company is well managed. Such feedback can help you structure your news releases so that

PR Casebook

Media Analysis by the Numbers

Systematic content analysis of media stories is now possible through computer software and online access to services such as Lexis/Nexis. There are also vendors that provide monitoring services and sophisticated data analysis.

Burrelle's, for example, now has a "paperless" clipping service that delivers clips about clients and employers electronically, directly to your PC. Other firms, such as Vocus, specialize in computer analysis of clippings to give a statistical picture of whether the coverage was positive or negative and whether it carried key messages, and even a box score on the stories written by individual reporters.

As Katharine Delahaye, one of the pioneers in public relations measurement, says, "The world doesn't need more data. What it needs is analyzed data." Listed below is a sample of the kind of data that a measurement firm generates for clients:

Total Coverage	Total
Total impressions	89,641,378
Percent of positive impressions	26.98%
Percent of negative impressions	19.85%
Total articles	1,049
Percent of positive articles	35.65%
Percent of negative articles	16.02%
Percent of articles containing one or more positive messages	52.43%
Percent of articles containing one or more negative messages	18.78%

the more important points receive greater emphasis.

Monitoring the Internet

Measuring the reach and effectiveness of your messages on the Internet seems like an impossible task, but it can be done.

An organization's Web site is the easiest to monitor. Determining the circulation, or impressions, that a news release or piece of information receives is measured by the number of people who log on to a particular page (see Chapter 13).

You can get additional information about users by asking them to answer some demographic questions before they use the site or as they leave it. For best results, offer free software or something similar that must be mailed to users; this entices people to give their names and addresses. Marketers, for example, use this technique to compile databases of potential customers.

Chat groups, forums, and bulletin boards, and e-publications on the Internet should also be monitored to determine what people are saying about your products or organization. There are literally thousands of chat groups, so you have to determine what groups are most important to you. If you have a widely recognized product, consumer chat groups may be worth monitoring.

Gripe groups should also be monitored. For example, there is one chat group called *McSpotlight* that is anti-McDonald's and antimultinational corporations. Another chat group is more explicit about its purpose; it's called *The Mart Sucks Page* (anti-K-mart).

Monitoring chat groups is increasingly important in issues management. It gives you direct feedback about what people are thinking, and what rumors are circulating about the organization. While the people expressing their views may not represent the majority public opinion, their comments often give organizations a "wake-up call" about potential problems and issues.

A number of companies provide Internet monitoring services. One well-established firm is eWatch, which reminds organizations, "one customer tells their bad experience to 20 other people." According to eWatch, "Today, an estimated 75 percent of large corporations actively monitor the Internet's public discussion bulletin boards and 44 percent routinely monitor Web sites." eWatch not only monitors discussion groups, it also monitors and clips articles from more than 1,000 Web publications. Such a service supplements the traditional clipping services that still concentrate on print media and their electronic editions.

Requests and 800 Numbers

Another measure of media exposure is to compile the number of requests for more information. A story in a newspaper or an appearance of a spokesperson on a broadcast show often provides the impetus for requesting a brochure or even ordering the product.

In many cases, a toll-free 800 number is provided. The American Association of Clinical Endocinologists, through Fleischman-Hillard public relations, conducted a public information campaign about thyroid disorders and got 10,000 requests for its "Thyroid Neck Check" brochures. In addition, the organization's Web site increased its "hits" from 4,000 to 12,000 immediately after the launch of the information campaign.

The Washington Hospital Center, with the help of Crofton Communications, also did a public information campaign to make women aware of heart disease risks. Nearly 10,000 women called to request a Women's Heart Health Kit.

The readership of product publicity features is often monitored by offering readers an opportunity to write for a brochure or for more information. In this way, for example, Air New Zealand has measured the value of sending travel features to daily newspapers throughout the United States. Inquiries through toll-free telephone numbers are also monitored to find out where a person first heard about a particular product. Such monitoring often shows top management that product publicity generates more sales leads than straight advertising.

Cost per Person

The cost of reaching each person in the audience often is calculated as part of the evaluation process.

The technique is commonly used in advertising in order to place costs in perspective. Although a 30-second commercial during the Super Bowl telecasts costs about $2.1 million ($70,000 per second), most advertisers believe it is worth the price because an audience of more than 140 million is reached for less than a half-cent each. This is a relatively good bargain even if several million viewers probably visited the bathroom while the commercial played.

Cost effectiveness, as this technique is known, also is used in public relations. Cost per thousand (CPM) is calculated by taking the total of media impressions (discussed earlier) and dividing it by the cost of the publicity program. Skytel, for example, spent $400,000 to publicize its new two-way paging and messaging system, and obtained 52 million impressions, about seven-tenths of a cent per impression. You can do the same thing for events, brochures, and newsletters. Nike produced a sports video for $50,000 but reached 150,000 high school students for a per-person cost of 33 cents.

On the other hand, per-person costs often let you know that a program might not be worth the expense. One company spent $4.5 million participating in Comdex, a large electronics trade show. When this cost was divided by the number of good sales leads that were generated, the cost was $13,500 per lead. The company decided not to participate in Comdex the following year.

Event Attendance

Speeches, meetings, presentations, tours, grand openings, and other such activities have one important thing in common: they all involve audiences who are exposed to a message.

A first step in evaluating these activities is to count the number of people who come to an event. Port Discovery, a new children's museum in Baltimore, conducted a public relations program to let citizens know about its grand opening. Thanks to the efforts of its public relations firm, Trahan, Burden & Charles, Inc., almost 9,000 visited the museum in its first week—double the number expected.

Although numbers are impressive, you also can measure audience attitudes by observation and surveys. A standing ovation at the end of a speech, spontaneous applause, complimentary remarks as people leave, even the "feel" of the audience as expressed in smiles and the intangible air of satisfaction that can permeate a group of people, will give you an idea as to the success of an event.

A more scientific method is the survey. People leaving an event can be asked what they think in a 30-second interview. Another way, for a meeting, is to have attendees fill out a short questionnaire. A simple form might look like this:

Your Evaluation of This Meeting (Please check each item)

	Excellent	Good	Average	Could Be Better
1. Location				
2. Costs				
3. Facilities				
4. Program				
5. Speakers (These should be listed by name.)				

Why did you attend?

How did you learn about it?

Suggestions for future events:

MEASUREMENT OF AUDIENCE AWARENESS

The meeting survey, listed above, is one form of determining whether the audience actually became aware of the message and understood it. As you recall, the problem with audience exposure is primarily whether the media distributed the message with some degree of accuracy. This really does not answer the question, "How many people actually read or heard the message?"

The tools of survey research are needed to answer such a question. Members of the target audience must be asked about the message and what they remember about it. Such research, for example, found that Microsoft achieved a phenomenal 99 percent public awareness that Windows 2000 was coming and available for purchase. There was about the same level of awareness that Furby dolls were on the market and a "hot" item.

A good case study of measuring audience awareness is a public relations program conducted by Washington Mutual, a Seattle-based financial services institution. It had become one of the largest banks in California through acquisitions, but was entering the market with virtually no name recognition. It hired Rogers & Associates, a public relations firm, to conduct a program using the introduction of the newly designed $20 bill as the centerpiece. The idea was to give 20 consumers in seven major markets a chance to enter a wind cube filled with the new $20 bills and have 20 seconds to grab as many of the swirling bills as they could.

Shortly after this event, which was called "WaMoola Madness," a survey was conducted that showed that 80 percent of consumers surveyed in new markets were familiar with the Washington Mutual name. This percentage was up from virtually zero name recognition a month before the promotional event.

Another way of measuring audience awareness and comprehension is the day-after recall. Under this method, participants are asked to view a specific television program or read a particular news story; then they are interviewed to learn what messages they remembered.

Ketchum Public Relations, on behalf of the California Prune Board, used this technique to determine if a 15-city media tour was conveying the key message that prunes are a high-fiber food source. Forty women in Detroit were asked to watch a program on which a prune board spokesperson would appear. The next day, they were asked what they remembered about the program. Ninety-three percent remembered the spokesperson and 65 percent, on an unaided basis, named prunes as a source of high fiber.

MEASUREMENT OF AUDIENCE ATTITUDES

Closely related to audience awareness and understanding of a message is whether the audience actually changes its attitudes and opinions about the product, service, or idea.

One way to measure changes in attitude is to sample the opinions of the target audience before and after the campaign. This means conducting **benchmark studies**—studies that graphically show percentage differences in attitudes as a result of increased information and persuasion. Of course, a number of possible intervening variables may also account for changes in attitudes, but a statistical analysis of variance can help pinpoint to what degree the attitude change is attributable to your efforts.

Sears, for example, used a benchmark study to prove that its efforts at getting a positive story about the company on *The Oprah Winfrey Show* actually increased sales and influenced consumer attitudes. With the help of Delahaye/Medialink, Sears gauged the attitudes of consumers before and after they saw Oprah Winfrey announce the retailer's donation of $20,000 worth of Christmas gifts to families in need.

Following the show, according to a monograph published by Lawrence Ragan Communications, "a measurement survey showed a fivefold increase in perceptions that Sears does good things for the community and the environment. The respondents who said they agreed with the statement, 'Sears is a quality company' increased from 58 to 65 percent." In addition, consumers expressing an intent to shop at Sears increased from 59 percent to 70 percent, and estimated spending levels rose 39 percent per shopper, or about $13 million in incremental sales.

ExxonMobil, General Electric, and AT&T regularly use benchmark surveys to measure their reputation on a continuing basis. Surveys showed, for example, that Microsoft's corporate reputation dropped after the U.S. Justice Department filed an antitrust suit against the company. As a result, Microsoft considerably beefed up its public relations efforts and Bill Gates announced the formation of the Gates Foundation, now the largest foundation in the world. Benchmarking showed that the image of Microsoft improved among the public despite the antitrust case against it.

Other Forms of Feedback

Benchmark surveys are only one way to measure attitudes and opinions. You can also do evaluations on a less sophisticated level by keeping complete and thorough tabs on telephone calls logged and letters received and by conducting focus group interviews with cross sections of the publics being reached. Analysis of telephone calls and letters is very important in the area of consumer affairs. If a pattern can be ascertained, it often tells the company that a particular product or service is not up to standard.

MEASUREMENT OF AUDIENCE ACTION

The ultimate objective of any public relations effort, as has been pointed out, is to accomplish organizational objectives. David Dozier, of San Diego State University, says it succinctly: "The outcome of a successful public relations program is not a hefty stack of news stories. . . . Communication is important only in the effects it achieves among publics."

In other words, you should never say that the objective is to generate publicity. This is simply a tactic to achieve a specific outcome. The objective of Greenpeace, for example, is not to get publicity, but to motivate the public to (1) become aware of environmental problems, (2) understand the consequences of not doing anything about it, (3) form attitude and opinions favorable to conservation, and (4) take some action such as writing elected officials or even sending a donation to Greenpeace.

A change in audience behavior or motivating them to purchase a product or service is difficult to accomplish through public relations efforts because people are complex and make decisions on the basis of many factors. At the same time, however, measurement of audience action is relatively easy to measure. All you have to do is look at sales figures or increase in market share.

MCI WorldCom measured its public relations efforts promoting teleconferencing in such a way. In addition to showing the level of audience awareness and understanding achieved, the company also found that its campaign generated a 55 percent increase in call volume, versus only a 35 percent growth in the year before the campaign. It also found that the company's market share increased to 28 percent, compared to 21 percent before the campaign was launched.

Another campaign that measured audience action was one for Hungry Jack instant potatoes, pancake mixes, and syrups. The objective of the public relations firm, Carmichael Lynch Spong, was to increase the brand equity of Hungry Jack by sponsoring a national contest, "Who is Your Hungry Jack," to find hardworking, dependable and adventurous "Hungry Jacks."

The program, mostly through radio promotions, had a goal of 10,000 entries and received 22,000 entries. In addition, the contest promotion helped increase market share between 10 and 20 points in targeted markets. Following the campaign launch, there was a 23 percent sales increase in instant potatoes and a 9 percent sales increase for pancake mixes. The campaign received a Bronze Anvil award from PRSA.

In the case of Korbel Champagne Cellars, which was mentioned on page 555 in terms of media coverage, its "perfect marriage proposal" contest generated more than 500 entries, and champagne sales increased six percent.

The ballot box also can provide convincing proof. Beaufort County in South Carolina had a bond referendum providing for a 1 percent sales tax to raise $40 million over two years to improve a local highway. There was strong opposition to the sales tax, so the local citizens committee supporting the measure hired Chernoff/Silver and Associates public relations to conduct a campaign to persuade the voters. The theme "Vote Yes, Highway 170, The Wait is Killing Us," was used and a series of activities were organized. This included a grass-roots coalition with speaker events and letter writing, recruiting third-party endorsements, and getting media support. The result: the bond issue passed with 58 percent of the vote.

EVALUATION OF NEWSLETTERS AND BROCHURES

If you are an editor of a newsletter or an employee magazine, it is wise to evaluate its readership on an annual basis. This will help you ascertain reader perceptions of layout and design, the balance of stories, kinds of stories that have high reader interest, additional topics that could be covered, the publication's credibility, and whether the publication is actually meeting organizational objectives.

Systematic evaluation, it should be emphasized, is not based on whether all the copies are distributed or picked up. This is much like saying that the news release was published in the newspaper. Neither observation tells you anything about what the audience actually read, retained or acted on. If all newsletters or printed materials disappear from the racks in a few days, it may simply mean that the janitorial staff is efficient.

The following discussion focuses on periodical publications, but the same methods can be used to evaluate leaflets, booklets, and brochures. Since many of these may be used externally, you also need to study the reactions and opinions of people who are not employees. Informal questioning of readers, monitoring of mail, and requests for additional information can all show whether the material is being read and whether it is doing its job or needs improvement.

There are a number of ways in which a newsletter, newspaper, or magazine can be audited. These include content analysis, readership interest surveys, readership recall of articles actually read, application of readability formulas, and use of advisory boards or focus interview groups. An informal appraisal can be made by simply walking around the office or plant and learning whether employees are talking about items in the publication.

Content Analysis

Select a representative sample of past issues and categorize the stories under general headings. You may wish to cover such subjects as management announcements, new product developments, new personnel and retirements, employee hobbies and interests, corporate finances, news of departments and divisions, and job-related information.

A systematic analysis will quickly tell you if you are devoting too much space, perhaps unintentionally, to management or even to news of a particular division, at the expense of other organizational aspects. For example, you may think that you have a lot of articles about employee personnel policies and job advancement opportunities, only to find, on analysis, that less than 10 percent of the publication is devoted to such information.

By analyzing organizational objectives and coupling the results of a content analysis with a survey of reader interests, you may come to the conclusion that the publication's content requires some revision.

Readership Surveys

The purpose of readership surveys is to obtain employee feedback on the types of stories they read, and what they think of the publication. Figure 19.2, for example, shows a sample "feedback" form.

These are relatively simple surveys. You can provide a list of topics or statements and have employees mark each one as "very important," "somewhat important," or "not important." Another way is to have them circle numbers 1

FAX YOUR FEEDBACK!

Please take a few moments to fill out this questionnaire, and fax it to us by Oct. 9. Your answers will help guide Corporate Communications efforts to continually improve the usefulness to you of the company's varied communications publications and other media. Results will be published in an upcoming issue of Praxair News. Thanks for your time, and we look forward to hearing from you!

1. My primary sources of information about Praxair's business and strategies are (check 3):

_____Praxair News	_____"The Grapevine"
_____Electronic Bulletins	_____Telephone Conferences
_____Immediate Supervisor	_____Bulletin Board Postings
_____Group Meetings	_____Local Publications
_____Other (specify)_____	

2. Please indicate how strongly you agree or disagree with the following statements:

	Strongly Disagree	Disagree	No Opinion	Agree	Strongly Agree
Praxair communicates clear company goals.	___	___	___	___	___
Praxair communicates clear strategies to achieve its goals.	___	___	___	___	___
Praxair communications are believable.	___	___	___	___	___
The information I receive helps me do my job better.	___	___	___	___	___
My supervisor does a good job of communicating useful information.	___	___	___	___	___

3. Please circle the number for each phrase that best describes your opinion of *Praxair News*. You may circle any number from 1 to 5:

It's all old news to me	1	2	3	4	5	I learn a lot
The articles are boring	1	2	3	4	5	It has interesting articles
The stories are trivial	1	2	3	4	5	The stories have substance
The design is unappealing	1	2	3	4	5	The design is attractive
It is poorly written	1	2	3	4	5	It is well-written
It's too management-oriented	1	2	3	4	5	There's something for everyone

Additional comments:_____

Figure 19.2 Get Feedback from Employees
Employees publications need reader feedback to evaluate effectiveness. This is part of a questionnaire that was included as an insert in an issue of a company newspaper.
(Courtesy of Praxair, Inc., Danbury, CT.)

through 5 to show the degree of agreement with a statement. In such a survey, you may be surprised to find employees expressing limited interest in personals (anniversaries and birthdays), but great interest in the organization's future plans.

A readership interest survey becomes even more valuable if you can compare it to the content analysis of what your publication has been covering. If there are substantial differences, it is a signal to change the editorial content of your publication.

Article Recall

The best kind of readership survey is done when you or other interviewers sit down with a sampling of employees to find out what they have actually read in the latest issue of the publication.

Employees are shown the publication page by page and asked to indicate the articles they have read. As a check on the tendency for employees to tell you that they have read the publication from cover to cover (often called a "courtesy bias"), you also ask them how much of the article they read and what the article was about. The resulting marked copies of the publication are then content-analyzed to determine what kinds of articles have the most readership.

The method just described is much more accurate than a questionnaire asking employees to tell you how much of the publication they read. You do not get accurate data when you ask questions such as "What percentage of the newsletter do you read? All of it? Most of it? Some of it?" In this case, employees know that the company expects them to read the publication, so you get a preponderance of answers at the high end of the scale. Very few people will want to admit that they don't read it at all.

It is also somewhat fruitless to ask rank-and-file employees to evaluate the graphic design or the quality of the photographs. Most employees don't have the expertise to make such judgments. It would be much wiser to ask these questions of individuals who are versed in graphic design and printing quality.

A variation of the readership recall technique is individual evaluation of selected articles for accuracy and writing quality. For example, an article on a new manufacturing technique might be sent (before or after publication) to the head of plant engineering for evaluation.

On a form with a rating scale (excellent, good, fair, deficient), the person may be asked to evaluate the article on the basis of factors such as:

- Technical data provided
- Organization
- Length
- Clarity of technical points
- Quality of illustrations

Such a systematic evaluation enables you, as an editor, to make sure that the articles are accurate and informative.

Readability

Every publication should be evaluated for readability at least once a year. This can be done in several ways. An informal method is to ask people during a reader recall survey if they think the articles are clear and understandable. Comments such as "I don't know what they're talking about" and "I don't get anything out of some articles" might indicate that there is a readability problem.

Also available are various readability formulas that quantify reading level. Rudolf Flesch was one of the first educational researchers to develop a formula, now commonly called the Flesch formula. There are also the Gunning formula, the Dale-Chall formula, the Fry formula, and the Cloze procedure.

Basically, all these formulas allow you to determine how difficult a given piece of writing might be to read. They depend on measuring mean sentence length and counting the average number of multisyllabic words. Some also include the number of personal pronouns used. In general, writing is easier to read (is accessible to readers at a lower educational level) if the sentences are simple and short and there are many one- and two-syllable words.

If a randomly selected sample of 100 words contains 4.2 sentences and 142 syllables, it is ranked at about the ninth-grade level. This is the level that most daily newspapers strive for.

If you are writing for an employee publication, ninth-grade level is usually a good starting point. However, if a large percentage of the employees are recent immigrants and English is their second language, you might want to strive for six or seven sentences and 120 syllables per 100 words.

For news releases to the general media and publications geared to all employees, you should write at a ninth-grade level. News releases to trade publications with a primary audience of scientists and engineers as well as publications geared to managers can be written at a higher level. For example, readability formulas show that a college-educated audience can readily cope with 3.8 sentences and 166 syllables per 100 words.

Advisory Boards and Focus Groups

Periodic feedback and evaluation can be provided by organizing an employee advisory board that meets several times a year to discuss the direction and content of your publication. Between meetings, members of the advisory board would also be able to relay employee comments and concerns to the editor. This is a useful technique in that it expands the editor's network of feedback and solicits comments that employees may be hesitant to offer the editor face to face.

A variation of the advisory board is to periodically invite a sampling of employees to participate in a general discussion of the publication and its contents. It is important that all segments of the organization's employees be represented and that these sessions not become forums for charges and countercharges. The purpose is to share information, generate new ideas, and work mutually to make the publication more valuable as an instrument for obtaining organizational objectives.

WRITING AN EVALUATION REPORT

When you have finished evaluating a campaign, you must report the results to the people who paid for it. In some cases, it may be necessary to report on individual events or activities immediately after they have occurred. Even if an immediate report is unnecessary, an overall report on the entire program must be made—usually annually. Budgets and programs are generally reviewed at least once a year, and this is the time when you must convince management or the client that what you have done is worthwhile and that the program should be continued and improved.

To prepare the report, you should refer to the original plan and state what you accomplished under each heading. Answer the following questions:

- **Situation.** Was the situation properly appraised? While the program was underway, did you learn anything that forced changes? What happened, and what did you do?

- **Audience.** Was it properly identified? Did you reach it? How effectively did you reach it (numbers reached, response, feedback)?

- **Objectives.** Did you achieve what you planned to achieve? Provide figures. You should have set numerical goals; now tell how well you did in reaching them.
- **Strategy.** Did it work? Did you have to modify it? Should it be continued or changed?
- **Tactics.** Did all the tools accomplish what they were supposed to accomplish? Were changes made? Why? Here again you can give numbers: news items published, feature stories published, printed items distributed, response of readers or viewers, TV and radio appearances, and so on.
- **Timing.** Was everything done at the right time? Should changes be made next year?
- **Costs.** Did you stay within the budget? If not, why not? This is the point at which you set the stage for the next budget and perhaps explain why more money would have permitted greater accomplishment.

SUMMARY

- Evaluation is absolutely essential. You must tell what was done, how well it was done, and what good it did. Quantify your results.
- Evaluation and measurement starts with having a set of program objectives that are realistic, credible, and measurable.
- Public relations staff and the client or employer should mutually agree on objectives and how they will be measured at the end of the program.
- Measuring the production and distribution of news releases and features puts an emphasis on quantify instead of quality.
- The most common form of measurement in public relations is the compilation of press clippings. It is an indication that an audience was exposed to the message.
- Clipping services can be hired to monitor print, online, and broadcast mentions of your client or employer's name, products, and services.
- Impressions are the total circulation of a publication or the audience of a broadcast outlet. It does not tell you how many people actually read or heard your story.
- Advertising equivalency, the idea of converting publicity in the news columns to comparative advertising rates, is highly suspect as a legitimate form of measurement.
- It is important to monitor the Internet to find out what e-publications, chat groups, and public discussion groups are saying about your organization, products, and services.
- Requests for brochures and calls to 800 numbers give you an indication of people's exposure to a message.
- Cost per person is a way to analyze the cost of reaching your audience. Does it cost pennies or dollars?

- Attendance at an event is a form of measurement because it shows audience exposure to the message. You, through surveys at a meeting, can also ascertain attitudes and opinions about the meeting.

- Surveys are needed to tell whether an audience actually got the message and understood it.

- Benchmark surveys, done before and after a campaign, help you ascertain whether audience attitudes and opinions have changed.

- Measurement of action, although difficult to accomplish, is relatively easy to measure. You can use sales figures, market share, or even voting results.

- Newsletters and brochures should be evaluated on a frequent basis. Some techniques include content analysis, readership surveys, article recall, and readability formulas.

- After a campaign is over, it is important to write up the results for the client or employer. This report becomes a record of accomplishment, and a source of ideas for future programs.

ADDITIONAL RESOURCES

Calabro, Sara. "Measurement Not High Priority, Survey Shows." *PRWeek*, March 24, 2003, p. 11.

Creamer, Matthew. "Life Beyond the Clip Book." *PRWeek*, October 6, 2003, p. 17.

Creamer, Matthew. "Firms Put Emphasis on ROI Amid Competitive Climate." *PRWeek*, October 6, 2003, p. 11.

Hood, Julia. "The Value of Measurement: What's the ROI on Measurement, and Who Should Foot the Bill? *PRWeek*, February 3, 2003, p. 15.

Hood, Julia. "Measuring Up: Measurement and Evaluation Have Never Been so Important to PR. And That's Where Industry Consensus Ends." *PRWeek*, April 1, 2002, pp. 14–15.

Hood, Julia. "Evaluating the Landscape or PR Measurement Tools." *PRWeek*, February 18, 2002, p. 7.

Pratt, Cornelius B., and Lennon, George. "What's Wrong With Outcomes Evaluation?" *Public Relations Quarterly*, Winter 2001, pp. 40–44.

Schmitt, Kelly. "Don't Get Clipped By Clipping Services." *PR Tactics*, May 2001, p. 10.

"Still Counting Clips? More Companies Employ Metrics to Measure Their PR and Compare Themselves to the Competition." *PR Reporter*, October 14, 2003, pp. 2–3.

"The Great Debate: Like It or Not, PR Pros Still Rely on Ad Value Equivalency." *PR Reporter (Tips & Tactics)*, November 4, 2002, p. 2.

Glossary

Actuality A recorded statement by an identified person used in a radio newscast. See *Soundbite*.

Advertising Equivalency Converting news articles to how much it would cost to advertise in the same space.

Advertorial A paid advertisement expressing an organization's views on issues of public concern. Also, surveying public opinion on a periodic basis.

ANR (Audio News Release) Distributed to radio stations via cassette tape or telephone.

Application Story In feature writing, a story that tells how to use a new product or how to use a familiar product in a new way. Similar to a case study.

Backgrounder A compilation of information about an organization, a problem, a situation, an event, or a major development. It is given to media to provide a factual basis for news to be published or broadcast.

Benchmark Studies Surveying public attitudes and opinions before and after a public relations campaign.

Bio Biography. A brief summary of someone's background, often supplied in a media kit or as part of a printed program or event.

Boilerplate Standard news release copy, usually in paragraph form, that provides basic information about a company, including stock symbols and URLs.

Booker The contact person for a broadcast talk show who is responsible for arranging guests.

Brainstorming Sessions designed to generate creative ideas in which the participants are encouraged to express any idea that comes to mind, regardless of how impractical.

Branding The use of symbols to market organizations or products.

B-Roll Only the video portion of a tape, without an announcer. It may include additional soundbites that broadcast editors may include in a newscast.

Browsers Software programs that allow users to navigate the Internet, access URLs, and employ Web resources. Popular examples include Netscape and Microsoft's Internet Explorer.

Bulk Fax The faxing of materials to multiple receivers simultaneously.

Bureau of Alcohol, Tobacco, and Firearms (BATF) A federal regulatory agency that oversees advertising and promotion of alcohol, tobacco, and guns.

Camera-Ready News releases and features formatted in column format on glossy paper. Editors paste the material into the layout and prepare the page for offset printing. Camera-ready copy also is called a *repro proof*.

Caption The brief text under a photo that informs the reader about the picture and its source.

Case Study In feature writing, a story that demonstrates the value of a product or service by detailing how it works and by providing specific examples that are often supported with statistics or customer testimonials.

Channeling The use of a group's attitudes and values in order to create a meaningful message.

Clip Art Line art and other graphic designs that can be used in public relations materials. Clip art is available on diskette and CD-ROM.

Corporate Profile(s) A fact sheet that focuses exclusively on an organization's identity, particularly its nature and objectives, main business activity, size, market position, revenues, products, and key executives.

Cropping The editing of photographs by cutting off portions of the original.

Cyber Media Tour A media event that involves interviewing a spokesperson via the Internet or videoconferencing.

Editorial Calendar A listing of topics and special issues that a periodical will feature throughout the year.

E-Mail Electronic mail. Personal messages to individual receivers transmitted on the Internet.

EPKs (Electronic Press Kits) Press kits designed for electronic media.

Evergreen A news release or feature that has no particular time element. The subject matter can be used by media outlets at almost any time.

E-Zines Electronic newsletters distributed via the Internet or organizational intranets. Sometimes called *E-pubs*.

Fact Sheet A brief outline of who, what, when, where, why, and how. Sent to journalists so they have a quick review of basic information.

Fair Comment Privilege A legal concept derived from the First Amendment right to freedom of speech that allows for the public airing of opinion. To protect against libel, however, experts suggest that (1) opinion statements be accompanied by the facts on which the opinions are based; (2) opinion statements be clearly labeled as such; and (3) the context of the language surrounding the expressions of opinion be reviewed for possible libel implications.

Fam Trip Familiarization trip. Refers to journalists who go on a trip at the invitation of an organization to become acquainted with a situation, product, or service.

FAQ (Frequently Asked Questions) A variation on the traditional fact sheet in which information is presented in a question question-and-answer format. Often used on the Internet.

Fax on Demand Individuals can order specific materials via the telephone or e-mail, and a fax with including the information is automatically sent automatically.

Federal Trade Commission (FTC) A federal regulatory agency that scrutinizes advertising and publicity for fairness and accuracy.

Filler Video materials from an organization that are used to fill gaps in programming on a television station or a cable outlet.

Food and Drug Administration (FDA) A federal regulatory agency that oversees the advertising and promotion of prescription drugs, over-the-counter medicines, and cosmetics.

Historical Piece In feature writing, a story that stresses the continuity between past and present to garner reader interest.

Hits A term used in relationship to the number of people that click on a particular page on the World Wide Web.

Hometowners Stories custom tailored to a particular newspaper or broadcast station by focusing on the local angle in the first paragraph of the news release.

Hype Exaggerated publicity about a product, service, or a celebrity. Often characterized by flowery adjectives and inflated claims.

Implied Consent The unwritten and unstated consent employees give their employers to use their photographs in such items as the employee newsmagazine and newsletters. Implied consent does not extend to advertising or promotion, which requires *written* consent.

Impressions Relates to the circulation of a publication or the audience size of a particular radio or television program. If a story or ad appears in a newspaper with 100,000 circulation, this constitutes 100,000 impressions

Infographics Computer Computer-generated artwork used to display statistics in the form of tables and charts.

Intranet A private network within an organization for the exclusive use of employees. Intranets are based on the same principles as the Internet.

Letters-to-the-Editor (LTE) A concise letter designed intended to rebut an editorial, clarify information mentioned in a news story or column, or add information that might not have been included in an original story.

Listserv An Internet site that automatically e-mails messages to individuals who subscribe to the service.

Magapaper An organizational publication that has a newspaper-type layout but incorporates the design elements of a magazine.

Mailing House A commercial firm that prepares and mails materials on behalf of its clients.

M-A-O model A model developed by Kirk Hallahan to show various communication strategies for enhancing *Motivation, Ability,* and *Opportunity* among the inactive public.

Masthead The place on the layout of a newsletter, newspaper, or magazine where the name of the publication appears. This is usually at the top of the first page.

Mechanical Type, photos, line art, and copy assembled on a single board used for offset printing.

Media Alert A notification to assignment editors informing them of a newsworthy event that could lend itself to photo or video coverage.

Media Gatekeepers The people within media who decide what information is newsworthy and what is not. Factors that influence the final decisions of media gatekeepers include timeliness, prominence, proximity, significance, unusualness, human interest, conflict, and newness.

Misappropriation of Personality The use of a person's image, particularly a popular personality, without permission.

Mug Shot A slang term for a head-and-shoulders photo of an individual.

No-Host Bar Guests buy their own drinks. A hosted bar means that the drinks are free to guests.

Op-Ed Opposite the editorial page. A page that contains the views and opinions of individuals who are not on the staff of the newspaper.

Page Impression The number of times a Web page is pulled up by individuals. The term is used in relation to tracking "traffic" on the Internet.

Periodical Indexes Printed catalogs and electronic databases, organized by topic, listing newspaper, magazine, and journal articles.

Personality Profile In feature writing, a story that focuses on a person of public interest to stimulate reader awareness of that person and/or the organization, product, or service the person represents.

Photo News Release (PNR) A photograph with a long caption beneath it that tells an entire story.

Pica A printer's term for measuring the length of typeset lines. There are 6 picas to the inch.

Plagiarism A form of theft in which an author appropriates the writing or ideas of an another author and claims them as his own.

Plugs Refers to mentions of organizations, products, and services in movies and broadcast entertainment shows.

Product Positioning The contextual background used to market a product to the public.

Product Tie-in The appearance of a branded product or service in a movie or TV series as part of a contracted agreement between the organization and the producers. Such a contract may call for the organization to actively promote the movie or TV series in its product advertising.

PSA (Public Service Announcement) These short messages, usually by a nonprofit agency or governmental agency, are used on radio and television stations as a public service at no charge.

Pseudoevent A term coined by historian Daniel Boorstin to describe events and situations staged primarily for the sake of generating press coverage and media interest.

Public Service Announcement See *PSA*.

Publics The potential or actual audiences for any given public relations message. Often defined by income, age, gender, race, geography, or psychographic characteristics.

Research Study In feature writing, a story that uses information derived from surveys, polls, or scientific studies to garner reader interest and to demonstrate the value of a product or service.

Retouching The alteration of a photograph by the traditional means of airbrushing or, more frequently now, by the electronic manipulation of a digital image.

RFP (Request for Proposal) Organizations seeking public relations assistance often issue a RFP requesting public relations firms to prepare a proposal outlining their recommendations and capabilities.

RMT (Radio Media Tour) A spokesperson conducting a series of interviews with various broadcast outlets from a central location.

ROI (Return on Investment) A comparison of total costs to reach an audience divided by the amount of business that is generated.

Saddle-Stitched Refers to the binding of a magazine, where the pages are stapled together at the centerfold.

Satellite Media Tour See *SMT*.

Search Engines Software programs that allow users to search for topically identified resources and information on the Internet. Popular examples include Yahoo, Lycos, Excite, and Alta Vista.

Securities and Trade Commission (SEC) A federal regulatory agency that requires that any information affecting the value of a security be made known to the owners and to themselves.

Service Journalism The practice of publishing "news you can use," for example, stories featuring consumer tips, professional advice, etc.

SMT (Satellite Media Tour) A media event that involves arranging for news anchors around the country to interview a spokesperson in a television studio via satellite.

Snail Mail First-class mail delivered by the U.S. Postal Service.

Soundbite A statement or quote from an individual, which is inserted into audio and video news releases.

Speaker's Bureau An organization's effort to provide spokespersons to civic clubs and other organizations at no cost. Commercial speaker's bureaus serve as agents to book celebrity speakers who charge for an appearance.

Spin Doctor A pejorative term for a public relations person or political consultant who presents ("puts spin on") negative or potentially damaging information in such a way as to minimize or completely dispel its effect.

Sponsored Communication Refers to newsletters, magazines, brochures, and other materials that are prepared and distributed by organizations without the intervention of gatekeepers in traditional mass media.

Stakeholders The groups impacted by an organization's decisions. These potentially include employees, consumers, neighbors, suppliers, environmental groups, and investors.

Stock Footage Standard video shots of an organization's production line, headquarters, and activities that a television station can store until the company is in the news.

Storyboard A written outline of an audio or video news release. For video, a description of scenes, plus dialogue, is prepared.

Talking Head Refers to a television broadcast or a video news release in which the screen is dominated by a person who is talking.

Template The standardized format of a newsletter or magazine, so each issue has the same look and feel.

Usenet A network of Internet-based *newsgroups* that uses a bulletin board system to post and read messages. CompuServe's public relations and marketing forum *(www.Prsig.com)* is one of the oldest and largest Usenet groups.

VNR (Video News Release) A short publicity piece formatted for immediate use by a television station.

Webcasting The delivery of a broadcast (live or delayed) over the Internet. When it is done in real time, it is also called *streaming*.

White Paper An organization's analysis of a particular issue or the potential of a market for a specific product or service. Other terms used are *briefing paper* and *position statement*.

World Wide Web The location on the Internet where thousands of organizations display their own pages.

Index